Building the Nineteenth Century

Building the Nineteenth Century

Tom F. Peters

The MIT Press
Cambridge, Massachusetts
London, England

This book was set in Galliard by Graphic Composition, Inc.
Printed on recycled paper and bound in the United States of America.

Library of Congress Cataloging-in-Publication Data

Peters, Tom F. (Tom Frank), 1941–
    Building the nineteenth century / Tom F. Peters.
        p.   cm.
    Includes bibliographical references and index.
    ISBN 0-262-16160-5 (hc : alk. paper)
    1. Civil engineering—History—19th century.   2. Architecture, Modern—19th century.   3. Infrastructure (Economics)—History—19th century.   4. Building—History—19th century.   I. Title.
TA19.P47   1996
624′.09′034—dc20   96-6078
                                                                                                  CIP

Contents

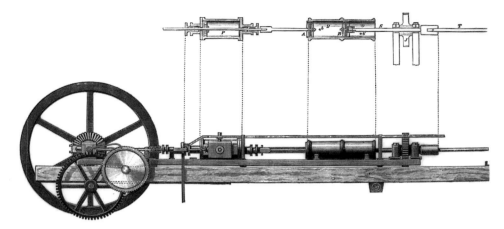

Acknowledgments

I've been lucky to have many people to discuss my thoughts with over the years. Essy Baniassad, Ted Cavanagh, André Corboz, Gregory Dreicer, Hans Hauri, Herbert Kramel, Chris Luebkeman, Christian Menn, Bernard Peters, Stephen Ressler, Steven Roethke, Felix Rosenthal, and Randy Swanson all helped me clarify how I think about building. Edward Tenner gave me the push I needed to rework this thinking into the present book. It turned out very differently from its German predecessor that Bernard Peters had helped me translate. Steven Roethke prepared the special illustrations of the Crystal Palace and the Kew Palm House, Zarli Sein those of the Sayn Foundry, and Carl Knutson and John Woynicki, Jr., that of the Ferris Wheel of 1893. Thomas Zieman and James Linsley analyzed the structural behavior of the Crystal Palace. Gregory Dreicer, David Landes, Chris Luebkeman, Hannah and Bernard Peters, and Randy Swanson reviewed the manuscript. Clotilde Peters helped clarify ideas and thoughts with formal critique. William Jelen photographed the illustrations. Lehigh University supplied a grant, supplies and the laboratory for photography, and permission to publish the following figures from their collection: 18, 19, 31, 121, 122, 123, and that part of 165 taken from Fairbairn. I am grateful to them all.

Preface: Building a Tectonic Culture in the Nineteenth Century

Building represents a significant percentage of the gross national product in most modern nations. Economists use it as an indicator of the condition of an economy, and in many countries the building industry forms the largest single industrial group. The building professions are obviously important to our civilization, but are they equally important to our culture? Is there a culture of construction?

I think so, and that's why I wrote this book: to find out how builders think and how that influences construction. The two are linked, because design thinking led to changes in building methods in the nineteenth century and to the understanding that building is a process in its own right. This preface explains what technological thinking is, the stages in which modern building process developed, and the method I used to examine them.

Technological Thought in Engineering and Architecture

Builders use a comprehensive or "soft" form of technology, which deals with making objects, not analyzing them mathematically. It crosses the boundaries between the high- and the lowbrow, the abstract and the practical, the ideal and the pragmatic, and it balances between *theories* of form and perception, *methods* of science and mathematics, and the practical *processes* of dealing with humans and materials. The form of thinking that corresponds to this wide range is the one that deals primarily with "how to make." I call it "technological thought." Scientists and humanists try to discover knowledge or gain insight into nature, and artists create objects that fulfill nonphysical needs. Technologists create objects for human use. Technological thought is an independent thought form, although it uses both a "matrix" or contextual form of intuitive thought and scientific, analytical thinking when it serves the purpose of making.[1] It is our culture's chief way of developing new directions.

Builders use two main types of technological thought, the engineering and the architectural. The "world of making" sets builders apart from scientists or humanists, who even use language differently. For instance, the word "detail" means "small-scale problem" in technology rather than "hierarchically subordinate part" as it does to a scientist or humanist. The details of the Crystal Palace or Eiffel Tower were as important to their builders as the whole. The very word "system" changes its meaning from the scientist's "ordering principle" to the technologists's "functioning object" or "building set."

A technical method's correctness lies in the functioning of the object, not in its logic. Builders do not care about the method of knowledge called epistemology. That is why unschooled inventors continually try to invent the *perpetuum mobile* in spite of its proven impossibility. We will see how appropriate this kind of technological thinking can be in Henri Maus's vision for the Mont Cenis Tunnel.

The Building Process

I found three stages of development in the modern building process. They weren't precise historical periods, since the development progressed at different rates in different building projects and environments. Western Europe, North Africa, and North America all had specific conditions that influenced the speed and, in part, the direction of development. However, the Suez Canal functioned as a catalyst for building activity both in Europe and in its Asian and African colonies and became a watershed in the development of modern building.

The first stage was a preindustrial one. Builders did not yet recognize the act of constructing as a process. The railways built by British firms between 1830 and about 1880 belong to this phase. It also included the Thames Tunnel (1824–1843), the first construction phase of the Suez Canal (1859–1862), and many smaller projects that were built manually even though their builders may have used some machinery.

The second stage was a transitional period, and it included some specialized railway structures, like the Britannia and Conway bridges (1846–1850), or parts of projects, like the second phase of the Suez Canal (1863–1868), that were initially planned for manual labor but were mechanized in execution. The transition depended on local site conditions. This phase was characterized by struggles to develop specialized forms of technological thought in building.

The third stage is represented by projects like the Mont Cenis Tunnel (1857–1871), the Langwies Viaduct (1912–1914), and the Panama Canal (1881–1914). Their builders planned and organized this group with mechanized and industrialized means in mind. Projects in this category opened new options and illustrated the breakthrough of mechanization and a mature form of technological thinking. Engineers trained in France, Germany, and America, rather than the British, led this phase; the reasons were different in each group. In contrast to earlier phases of industrialization, it seemed to be social organization that hindered change in Britain. The French created a culture of rationalization and organization through the quasi-military organization of the Corps des Ponts et Chaussées. In Germany it was the close contact between theory and practice that made its engineers so advanced, and in the United States it was the lack of highly trained labor coupled with the American workman's social and professional mobility.

Method

It is easier to trace building thought in structures than in a builder's writings. If builders wrote anything at all, they usually wrote to further a project or justify what they had done,[2] but what they built was what they meant. I examine a number of representative projects in depth. There were many influential ones, like the Eiffel Tower and high-rise framing, that I only mention briefly. My idea has been to restrict myself to those projects that would show the points I wanted most clearly. The discussion focuses around icons of nineteenth-century structure and deals with many lesser-known projects as well. Many of these lesser-known ones, especially the Sayn Foundry, the Kew Palm House, the Munich "Glaspalast," the "Brompton Boilers," the Galerie des Machines, and the Kehl and Langwies bridges, deserve to become more prominent.

I sometimes bring in areas outside my own, like economics and finance, services, energy control, and installation technologies. They were crucial to the decision-making process and played an increasingly important role in nineteenth-century building. I draw on them wherever they can clarify or qualify my main topics, but lack of space and expertise prevents me from describing their own development.

Some historians of technology stress a dialectic between evolutionary theory and invention. This does not work for building. Gregory Dreicer has pointed out that "evolution" is part of the web of mid-nineteenth-century cultural parameters.[3] This means that it was a cultural phenomenon and a symbol for nineteenth-century builders, but it cannot serve as a model for this analysis. The idea of evolution certainly influenced the ideology of "progress," and that is where I use it. On the other hand, I find "invention" too complex a process to be paraphrased in model form.

The distinction between "internalist" and "generalist" views of technology has helped me define different scales of approach to the issues. But no matter at what scale I work, my focus remains fixed on the technological material itself. Some will consider this "internalist," although I don't, because the argument doesn't exclusively use technology to explain developments. The social and economic "constructions" of technology are other popular and valid approaches. I believe that they need to be balanced by work that traces the opposite influence of technological thinking on society. So, at the risk of being called unfocused, I adopt shifting standpoints in order to examine the material closely, feeling a little like a film director using several cameras to understand the multidimensionality of the problem. I have made every attempt to verify facts and analyze sources critically, but hearsay, and with it error, have surely crept in now and again. This is regrettable but human.

Creating the Modern World through Communication, Commerce, and Progress

The Western world industrialized in the eighteenth and nineteenth centuries. Manufacturers needed new means of distributing products, and they built transportation and telegraph networks. In doing so, they transformed the European infrastructures and created new ones in the colonies and North America. These new communication networks changed the way people experienced time and place; they shifted cultural barriers and diminished topographical obstacles. Information transfer became instantaneous and travelers started measuring physical distance in hours or days, so that the world seemed to expand in scope and its subjective size to shrink correspondingly. Intellectually, the powerful new concept of progress — of continuous technological improvement leading to general improvement of society as a whole — inspired industrialists, inventors, builders, and social reformers alike.

Scientists propagated a faith in quantitative output, and people began to measure production. "Bigger" and "newer" were admirable qualities worth striving for. Progress appeared synonymous with mechanization and speed.[1] But speed was not the original reason for mechanizing production. Mining and the textile industry were the first to mechanize: the first used steam power to pump and lift and the second to drive the production process.[2] Both of them were trying to save or replace labor. Early steam engines were unreliable; they broke down frequently, and machines could only produce goods faster when engineers learned to build better ones. Expanding urban markets and a shrinking rural labor pool, not speed, started the shift from manual and animal labor to the machine-driven.

Speed was always important to information disseminators, and it entered the industrial world, appropriately, through newspaper publication. Charles Babbage discussed the mechanization of the fledgling newspaper industry in his 1832 book *On the Economy of Machinery and Manufactures*. He was a mathematician and an inventor, an intellectual border-crosser and sensitized to both the burgeoning systematization of science and the pragmatism of technology.[3] He based his observations on the London *Times*'s use of Augustus Applegarth's steam press.[4] *The Penny Magazine* reproduced his thoughts verbatim in a book review on 30 June 1832:

1.
The newspaper industry was the first manufacturing industry to feel the pressure of deadlines. This double-sided steam press helped meet those deadlines. (Paul Poirel, 1880, p. 679.)

Another instance of the just application of machinery, even at an increased expense, arises where the shortness of time in which the article can be produced, has an important influence on its value. In the publication of our daily newspapers, it frequently happens that the debates in the Houses of Parliament are carried on to three and four o'clock in the morning, that is, to within a very few hours of the time for the publication of the newspaper. The speeches must be taken down by reporters, conveyed by them to the establishment of the newspaper, perhaps at the distance of one or two miles, transcribed by them in the office, set up by the compositor, the press corrected, and the papers printed off and distributed before the public can read them. Some of these journals have a circulation of from five to ten thousand daily. Supposing four thousand to be wanted, and that they could be printed only at the rate of five hundred per hour upon one side of the paper (which was the greatest number two journeymen and a boy could take off by the old hand-presses), sixteen hours would be required for printing the complete edition; and the news conveyed to the purchasers of the latest portion of the impression, would be out of date before they could receive it. To

to the railways.[9] Open river traffic also improved through controlled water-release engineering, and most American canals regressed to portage loops. The situation was different in France, where the government continued to finance canals long after others had abandoned them; the Rhine-Marne Canal opened in 1853 when rail had long won out elsewhere. Government-controlled building programs can be larger, better organized, and less wasteful of resources than private enterprise, but they are invariably less adaptable.[10]

The ocean-connected canal was the only form that continued to prosper. It allowed steamships to cross narrow necks of land and penetrate to inland harbors. The Suez Canal, (1854–1869) was the first major one, and the development culminated with the Panama Canal (1904–1914), with the single later exception of the St. Lawrence Seaway, finished in 1959.

Road building paralleled canal construction. In France, Colbert initiated turnpike planning in 1661 in the service of Cardinal Mazarin's and later Richelieu's political centralization plans.[11] Napoleon's imperial ambitions led to the improvement of several western alpine passes at the beginning of the nineteenth century. The Mont Cenis Road (1803–1810) and Simplon Road (1806–1812) opened transalpine traffic to wheeled vehicles and followed the gentler Brenner Pass to the east, which vehicles had traversed since 1772.[12] While France, followed by Poland and Prussia, actively developed road networks, the British government remained reactive. Scottish rebellions in 1715

3.
The Erie Canal was the most successful American inland waterway. It was widened several times during a period in which other canals succumbed to railway competition. (Malézieux, 1873, plate 44.)

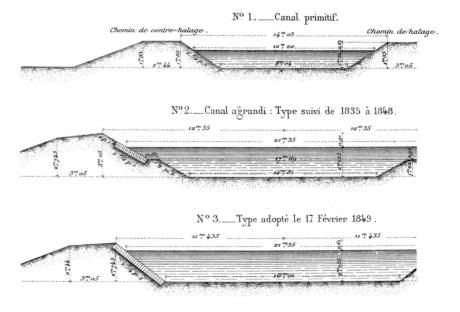

and 1745 did force the government to sponsor some roadbuilding, but in a far less organized way than continental governments did. Semiprivate turnpike trusts replaced the cumbersome British system of municipal financing around 1760 and began roadbuilding for civilian purposes. Britain became a technological leader when professional engineers replaced amateurs.[13]

Based on Pierre Trésaguet's work in France and John Metcalf's in England a generation before, Thomas Telford and his assistant John Benjamin MacNeil used large stones as a roadbed with crushed layers of graded gravel above. John Loudon McAdam successfully omitted the bed and introduced "macadam," a self-sealing compacted surface of graded, crushed gravel. Both systems provided a relatively smooth, weather-secure means of land transport. By 1821 England and Scotland boasted extended networks of "metalled" or "macadamized" roads.[14] A horse could pull only half a ton on the new roads compared with the twenty to fifty tons it could drag along a canal, but they moved faster and goods no longer had to be off-loaded from wagons to boats and back again in order to reach their destination. Wagons no longer mired fast when rain turned dusty roads into bogs. Traffic moved more safely at night and usually in straighter lines, too. The Comte de Sassenay developed a smooth and more weather-resistant gravel-asphalt paving in France around 1832, which A. Merian modified for the Travers-Pontarlier road in Switzerland in 1854.[15] It became our modern form of road surfacing.

Better roads benefited passenger traffic too. Carriages replaced sedan chairs after 1580 in England, and by 1625 London had hackney coaches for hire. Paris had a horse-drawn omnibus service in 1662 and there was a regular intercity service between London and Oxford four years later. It still took thirteen days to travel from London to Edinburgh at the beginning of the eighteenth century; by the century's end, the mail coach took only three. It ran at 11–13 kilometers per hour, and on Telford's Great Northern Road coaches soon sped giddily at 15–18 kilometers per hour, reducing travel time to forty-two hours between the two cities.[16]

America opened its first major turnpike between Philadelphia and Lancaster in 1794, and the first federal one was the Cumberland Road or National Pike. It started from Cumberland, Maryland, in 1811, reached Wheeling, West Virginia, on the Ohio in 1818, and Vandalia, Illinois, twenty years later. Both were macadamized between 1802 and 1818, but American roadbuilding was cut off in mid-development by the expanding railway.

Railways Widen the Scope

According to popular history, the railway was invented in England. This is imprecise. The first track locomotives were English, but engineers from all over contributed inventions that were universally adopted.[17] Austrian, British, French, and American engineers all built horse-drawn railways between 1825 and 1829.[18] The French began in 1827 and mechanized the St. Etienne-Andrézieux line in 1832. But for decades French railways expanded slowly, partly because of political upheavals, but also because they were private enterprises in a government-driven system that had chosen to support roads and canals.[19] Franz Joseph von Gerstner compared the advantages and limitations of roads, canals, and horse-drawn railways in 1813 and prepared the way in German-speaking Europe. Slowly but surely after 1830, the locomotive-powered railway replaced both road and canal traffic. It had a disruptive psychological, social, and economic impact on rural life.[20] Where canal traffic moved sluggishly and road traffic at a maximum of 18 kilometers per hour, the first commercially successful steam railway rocketed through the countryside from Manchester to Liverpool at 40 kilometers per hour. The horse restricted speed on both canals and roads, but "mechanical horses" seemed to know no limitations.

America and Canada welcomed any form of transportation. Canals connected existing cities, but railways became a medium of westward expansion, so the American railroad tripled in size between 1840 and 1850, while canals grew only ten percent.[21] In densely populated Britain the two forms of transportation competed for business from the outset, and the railway crushed the canal network.

By 1846, trains were running regularly at 65–80 kilometers per hour and had even reached speeds of 95.[22] Transportation prices were initially high, but dropped rapidly as volume and efficiency grew.[23] The combination of falling prices and increasing speed proved irresistible,[24] and a brief period of uncontrolled development swept Britain in the "railway mania" of 1845–1849, fueled by the speculator George Hudson. In 1845, parliamentary committees discussed about six hundred proposals for expansion totaling ten times the existing network, and the next year there were as many again.[25] Most of them, however, never made it beyond the permit-granting stage.[26]

The North American development accelerated while the British slowed after midcentury.[27] There were 25 kilometers of horse-drawn railway in Pennsylvania in 1829. This number doubled the following year, and tripled again the next.[28] Only the economic depression that followed the Civil War in the early 1870s briefly interrupted the pace. American railways were primarily long-distance, single-track carriers. They cost half as much to build as the German lines and a fifth to a quarter as much as the French or British, which were all double track.[29] But there was at first little coordination between lines of varying gauge, and no real network at all.[30] Rails crossed the Mississippi in the 1850s and became national when the unified-gauge, transcontinental line was finished in 1869.[31]

The first transcontinental railway was not American, however, but Indian. The Great Indian Peninsular Railway (1843–1854) was built from Calcutta in the east and Bombay in the west.[32] Canada began building railways in 1835 and chartered its transcontinental Grand Trunk Line a decade before the Americans in 1849.[33] However, both the Indian and the Canadian projects were really British, so it is inexact to compare railway expansion in Britain and the United States without taking events in the British colonies into account. British contractors also designed and built many continental European, early South American, and Asian lines, usually using British material, whereas American contractors worked almost exclusively in the United States and its continental territories at the time.[34]

Transporting Information

The railway industry of the 1840s experienced the same pressure as the newspaper industry had twenty-five years before. A new communication technology called telegraphy allowed the railway to spread and be coordinated. Before telegraphs, letters were the only way to communicate clearly with people out of sight and hearing. Empires were managed by means of courier networks that were only surpassed by French semaphore technology at the end of the eighteenth century.[35] Visual telegraphs or semaphores made information transfer quicker, but electrical telegraphy made the first real difference when it started to serve civilian commerce.

Information access governs our concepts of space, distance, and time and our modern ways of thinking. Today, facsimile and electronic mail are widely available. Our reliance on mass media, in which even the most inane gossip intrudes effortlessly into every household, makes it increasingly difficult to envision an era in which the private character of information conferred power. It used to be difficult and take a long time to send messages. This is no longer evident to us except in rare cases when the nerve centers of transmission are temporarily disabled. But at the beginning of the nineteenth century, depending on the urgency, weather conditions, sight lines, and the available means of transportation, fifty kilometers could mean a delay in the reception of information of three to ten hours or even more, and whoever received information first obtained real political, military, and commercial power.

Creating the Modern World

4.
Claude Chappe's semaphore was the first mechanical device to extend instantaneous communication beyond shouting distance. (Figuier, *Merveilles de la Science*, 1868–1870, vol. 1, p. 53.)

Telegraphy began as electrical laboratory experiments and found its first application in connection with the spread of the railway. Researchers tested several electrostatic systems in the second half of the eighteenth century in Scotland, the German states, Spain, and Geneva, but the Bavarian physician Samuel Thomas von Sömmering is generally credited with building the first successful galvanic telegraph in 1809.[36] The primitive invention he presented to the Munich scientific society had one cell for each letter. It was impractical and its importance lay solely in the notoriety it achieved. Sömmering's work inspired focused experimentation. Twenty-eight years later, it led to Sir Charles Wheatstone's and William Cooke's British patent. They tested it first on the London and Birmingham Railway between Euston Station and Camden Town in September 1837.[37] This bit of machinery can truly be termed "revolutionary," since it inadvertently altered the traditional relationships between space, distance, time, and communication, and turned information into a commodity.[38]

5.
Sömmering's 1809 galvanic telegraph had a wire for each letter. Cooke and Wheatstone's more successful pointer system was immediately adopted by the railways in 1837. (*Das Neue Buch der Erfindungen*, 1872–1875, vol. 2, pp. 350, 356.)

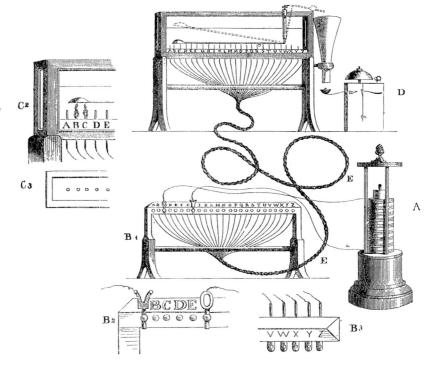

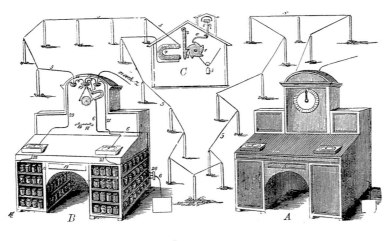

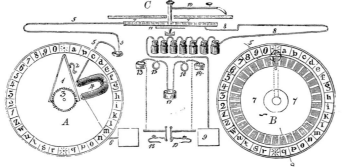

It was typical of Britain that the idea neither remained in the laboratory nor was preempted by government. Industrialists recognized its potential and George Bidder, Robert Stephenson, Isambard Brunel, and others immediately installed telegraph lines along their railway tracks.[39] The technology spread quickly to the European continent. By 1843 it was used on the inclined plane in Aachen, and two years later the Belgian and the Paris-Versailles lines all had it.[40]

Telegraphy dramatically increased the capacity of existing railways. Trains could be safely dispatched closer together. Better scheduling and management improved rolling-stock usage as much as 20 percent. Bottlenecks were reported quickly and empty wagons traced and dispatched by wire. When the British North Western Railway reached capacity in the late 1840s, it installed a telegraph line. As a result, the company coped elegantly with shortfalls and bottlenecks caused by a workers' strike. Ordinary traffic on the line doubled between 1840 and 1856 without additional track, and there was capacity to spare, so that an extra rush of 750,000 people was effortlessly transported to and from the London exhibition in 1851 on specially scheduled excursion trains.[41]

6.
A typical railway telegraph office furnished with 1837 and 1839 Cooke-Wheatstone models. (Figuier, *Grandes Inventions Modernes,* 1886, p. 372.)

Telegraphy served the dissemination of commercial and political information too. From 1848 to 1856 a group of New York newspapers successfully shared a telegraph service and became known as the New York Associated Press. Baron Julius von Reuter followed their lead in London 1858. Charles Havas's French agency quickly jumped on the bandwagon, and the three became the largest nineteenth-century news agencies.[42] Cooke's Electric Telegraph Company, founded in 1848, saw its revenues jump from £160 to £400 in its first year. Eight years later prices were down to a third of their original level, but revenues and volume had grown by several orders of magnitude.[43] By then there were 11,520 kilometers of lines and 3,000 employees in Britain who sent a million messages annually. The network grew even more rapidly than the railway. Samuel Morse's first line between Baltimore and Washington was laid in 1844, and American railroads were entirely managed by telegraph from 1851 on.[44] One year later the United States had a total of 24,000 kilometers of telegraph lines.[45]

Telegraphy Changes Our Perception of the World

The telegraph spread in the nineteenth century as computer technology has in our age. It became indispensable. Just two decades after the invention was first practically applied, the educated public of America and Europe eagerly followed the laying of a transatlantic telegraph cable.[46] It failed, but a second attempt succeeded in 1866, three years before the opening of the Suez Canal and the completion of Union Pacific's transcontinental railway.

The closing of the trans-American railway link was celebrated in a formal ceremony on the northeastern shore of the Great Salt Lake in a little valley in Promontory, Utah, on 10 May 1869 by hammering home a last, golden rail spike. The spike was connected to a telegraph transmitter and the first blow of the hammer was supposed to send a signal across the continent. Newspapers everywhere reported the melodramatic event in appropriate terms. The official apparently missed the spike, upon which the site operator sent out the agreed three-dot signal.[47] Finally, one of the dignitaries did at least hit the rail, which registered on the system. Whatever the mechanics of the event itself, the public perceived a simultaneity of hammer blow and reception thousands of kilometers away. The event marked the initiation of live news reporting, the now habitual, vicarious participation in an event occurring elsewhere on the globe. The experiential world had been pushed beyond the confines of human sight and hearing. The sensation of distance shrank and our awareness of the world expanded.

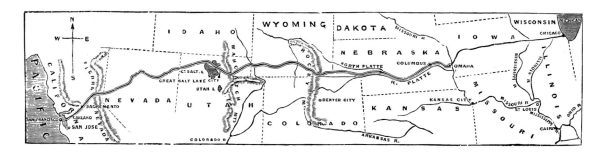

7.
The western and eastern segments of the first North American transcontinental railway met near the Great Salt Lake crossing in Utah in 1869. (Routledge, 1901, p. 117.)

Thoughtful individuals had already noted the collapse of space into time that this implied. The British toolmaker and Fellow of the Royal Society Sir Joseph Whitworth remarked in 1852, "Distances are now to be measured by intervals, not of space, but of time."[48] Train schedulers certainly knew this; telegraphy transformed a safe distance between trains into a block of time.[49] Two telegraph operators had collapsed distance when they played a game of chess by "wire" in England in 1845.[50] Greenwich began transmitting time signals by telegraph in 1852.[51] The Crimean War (1854–1856) depended on telegraphy, with information pouring into London and Paris from the front and orders ricocheting back, and Cleveland Abbe used information provided by a telegraphic network to predict weather from the Cincinnati observatory in the 1860s.[52] But the general public only began to suspect the consequences that telegraphy had for our concepts of time and space through the drama at Promontory, Utah.[53] Telegraphy changed the world irrevocably in large and small ways, and it was only finally displaced by the telephone when the first geostationary telecommunications satellites became operational after 1960.

Time Zones and Nationalism: The Telegraph Helps Organize the Globe

Railways eventually had to be coordinated into networks. To do that, railway companies had to standardize track gauges and railway time.[54] There were many reasons to adopt standard time. It was certainly less confusing for travelers and shippers than a plethora of local times. The problem of coordinating nonstandard local times first surfaced in 1834 on what was then the world's longest railway, the 219-kilometer Charleston-Hamburg line in South Carolina.[55] Isambard Brunel's Great Western Railroad was the first to standardize in 1840, the year after it got its first telegraph line. Two years later, passengers and freight were being booked throughout the British Isles by a Railway Clearing House that prepared the way for Greenwich Mean Time. It was popularly called "Railway Time" and applied de facto to the whole of Britain from 1848 on.[56] By the time the Atlantic cable was ready and the first North American transcontinental railway and its telegraph opened, there was an urgent need for coordinated timekeeping in North America, too.[57]

It was conceptually difficult to move from sun time to a modularized timekeeping system. For a while the Institution of Civil Engineers debated the best design for clocks that displayed both standard and local time.[58] People became time-conscious, and standardization caused emotional upheaval that mirrored contemporary political unrest. The 1840s saw bourgeois revolutions explode across the European continent, helping to consolidate the idea of the nation-state. Even stable Britain had its share of turmoil in the Chartist Riots of 1838 and the general strike four years later.

National standards became involved with politics and local pride, so coordinated timekeeping spread slowly and haphazardly over the North American continent. Fourteen years after the Union Pacific link, the United States adopted a five-zone Railway Mean Time. Local resistance persisted for a few years in isolated pockets until national legislation passed in 1918.[59] In many other countries capitals competed with provincial seats and larger towns with smaller ones to set the standard for time. National and regional institutions pitted their influence against one another to have "their" local time become the standard. France took years to settle the question. It was only laid to rest in 1889:

> The telegraph ministry and the railway companies have entirely discarded local time and keep the clocks of their stations and offices to the mean established by the Paris Observatory and received by the telegraph offices every morning. Station clocks show exact time, whereas the non-public, internal clocks used to regulate train departures run five minutes late. Thus railway time is not exact Paris time. And the clocks on public buildings generally display local time. . . . The telegraph and railways were the first to make a move to coordinate French time, and Colonel Laussedat, Director of the National School of Arts and Crafts, now proposes to take the final step. He asks that all clocks in public buildings and stations adopt Paris time starting on May 1, 1889, that is from the opening date of the Exhibition, thereby making it a true national time.[60]

The year marked the centennial of the storming of the Bastille that began the French Revolution. It appealed to national unity and pride. But France was not the only nation to have such a complicated system; modern

Creating the Modern World

8.
The first transatlantic telegraph cable broke several times and had to be grappled from the ocean floor in 1858. The thicker, successful cable of 1866–1867 ended in an instrument room at Valentia, Ireland. (Figuier, *Merveilles de la Science*, 1868–1870, vol. 1, p. 241; Routledge, 1901, pp. 578, 579, 580.)

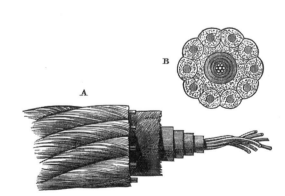

life had confused everyone, and convoluted systems had to be disentangled as far afield as Madras.[61] The industrializing countries recognized that standardization was essential for meteorology and navigation, too. They all gradually adopted national time zones, and Germany, the rising European industrial power at the end of the century, decreed a transnational, Central European Time on 1 April 1893.[62]

National time zones grew out of a need to communicate. Nascent nationalist movements defined their boundaries by time zone and used a national time as a tool to foster political or cultural identity. Britain, whose telegraph-linked, world-spanning colonial system it served best, lobbied successfully for international timekeeping. In 1884, an international congress established a worldwide system based on the meridian running through Greenwich Observatory outside London.[63]

International measurement coordination followed, based on the French metric system.[64] In 1875, the year the French Constitutional Congress ended, an "International Meter Convention" was held in Paris. In spite of the fact that the Anglo-Saxon countries did not participate, the international community agreed to adopt the metric system for scientific research by 1889. The French had originally defined the meter independently of time, but this changed in 1983 when it was redefined as the distance light travels in a vacuum in the time it takes heated cesium to oscillate a fixed number of times.[65] This completed the reduction of distance and space to time. But today the absolute nature of time itself is being questioned by the school of thought founded by the historian Fernand Braudel. He and others recognize that the space-time continuum is entirely dependent on awareness.[66]

The American television network Cable News Network gave the telescoping of space into time and time into awareness a new immediacy in 1991. During the Persian Gulf War CNN reported events to the world as they occurred. An unintended flow of allied information to the Iraqi High Command began to influence the course of the conflict. Precise, electronically guided weaponry allowed CNN to announce not only targets but hits as soon as the decision was taken to fire and before missiles were actually launched. The news channel made the Iraqis aware of an initiated causal chain, and this gave them a few minutes to react before impact occurred. The philosophical paradox of the "time machine" that can manipulate the sequence of time and influence past events had become, in a sense, reality. The Allied High Command even began to quote CNN for facts, and found itself obliged to break the "feedforward" loop by censoring and even falsifying information to counter the impact that that knowledge had on the outcome of the decision-making process. All of this started so innocently in a small valley in Utah in 1869. What it developed into illustrates how genuinely revolutionary the work of the telegraph pioneers was. It changed how we see our world, and that changed how we think and how we build it.

Insurance and Profit: The Criteria Behind the Suez Canal

Businessmen used telegraphy at a more prosaic level, to transmit orders and move money as credit information rather than as cash. This helped international trade, while the quick physical transfer of goods increased turnover so that industry could realize profits and reinvest them faster than before. Trade was also the impetus behind the investment in canal building.

When the French planned the Suez Canal in the 1850s, it was clear that British interests would benefit too. The new Crown Colony at Hong Kong and Assam's new shipping port at Calcutta would lie closer to London via Suez than around the Cape of Good Hope. The Great Indian Peninsular Railway and new ports at Karachi and Bombay would be even better utilized, but French dominance in Egypt posed political problems.[67] Several decades later, Panama Canal proposals attracted France, Britain, and the United States, and there the United States would profit most, since the sea voyage between New York and San Francisco would be halved.[68] Both canals would change the delicate international balance of commerce and power. This made the decision-making process technologically, politically, and financially complex.

No development runs rigidly in a single direction. The great projects of the age were more risky than we now perceive them to have been. An example is the interdependence between profit, insurance, and iron construction in shipbuilding, which shows how complex the considerations were that faced the Suez Canal's promoters and potential users. The quicker transportation was, the shorter trips would be. This made insurance risks lower, because the less time a ship spent at sea, the smaller the danger of shipwreck, piracy, or fire. One of the main arguments in support of the canal was therefore that it would save about 2 percent of a standard insurance premium on traffic to the Orient.[69] Since profit margins lay around 12 percent at the time, even slight savings on insurance premiums made a difference, especially since a shorter trip also meant that the merchant could reinvest profits more promptly. Insurance considerations also led merchants to choose iron as an incombustible structural material.[70]

Sailing ships depended on seasonal monsoon winds in the Indian Ocean and could not maneuver in canals.[71] However, advances in sailing ship construction and sea charts put the new clipper companies in a much better position to challenge steamers and the canal in 1869 than they had been ten years earlier.[72] The orient clippers' chief commodity was tea, a product that loses aroma and weight in storage. The problem had always plagued importers, so tea was an ideal product to test the relative efficacy of sailing a clipper around the Cape of Good Hope or steaming its iron competitor through the canal.[73]

Iron steamships had problems of their own. Wind was free, but coal cost money. Steamships had larger crews, machine rooms, and storage space for coal, so their operating costs were higher. They also needed organized maintenance facilities and coal depots at distances of about eight days' travel, which had to be colonized or secured through treaty, and it was expensive to transport coal to them. Moreover, marine engines were still unreliable and, in spite of being less combustible, they were more prone to explode than sailing ships.

Suez tipped the balance in favor of the steamship. Isambard Brunel had already proved that screw propulsion was more powerful and economical than side paddlers, even though the latter were more stable.[74] It also turned out that screws damaged canal banks less than any other form of mechanical propulsion. From the mid-1840s on, British screw-propelled iron steamers had already dominated inland canal trade, and with the opening of the Suez Canal, British shipbuilding expanded rapidly in the Forth and Clyde rivers.

Steamship and railway lines had been intimately associated from the very beginning. The Peninsular and Orient's Liverpool-Alexandria and Suez-Karachi lines, which opened in 1837, were linked by Robert Stephenson's Alexandria-Cairo-Suez Railway (1852–1858). Brunel built and named the steamship *Great Western* (1836–1837) as a westward extension of his Great Western Railway (1836–1841) from Bristol to New York, and his *Great Eastern* (1859) was designed as its analog for the Orient and Australia trade. Oceanic canals would eliminate the need for loading and unloading goods several times, and this too increased profitability.

Our world is unimaginable without the communication services that grew with the telegraphs, railways, and shipping lines that girdled the globe. These media spread the concept of speed into every facet of life and changed all aspects of our built environment. The Mediterranean, Indian Ocean, and transatlantic cables connected continents. The continent-spanning Indian and American railways were joined by the Canadian railway in 1885 and the trans-Siberian railway in 1916, and the Suez Canal was joined by the Panama Canal in 1914. These were the grandest projects, but there were many smaller, equally important ones linking them in a tight network. Commerce built a foundation for the new means of communication, and it blossomed in return.

Structural Changes in the Built Environment

The pioneers settled the original North American colonies on a European model, but settlement patterns to the west depended on the new means of communication. Almost all towns west of the Appalachians began as water stations, railheads, or transshipping nodes. There were no cultural or political boundaries to hinder the spread; preexisting native or rival French and Spanish political entities were swept away by the force of the Anglo-dominated railway and telegraph. New settlement patterns proliferated freely across the continent and dominated planning, structural form, and building methods. The only way to jeopardize colonization was to destroy the railway and telegraph lines, and this its enemies attempted to do with only indifferent and temporary success. The telegraph signal that informed the world of the completion of the transcontinental railway line in 1869 was the victory cry of a new transportation culture.

Railways changed the existing environment in the densely settled countries of Europe. Wherever they ran, they spawned new structures to service the system: larger and more complex harbors, bridges, exhibition halls for fairs, stock exchanges and banks for finance, and more and more varied and interdependent building types. The investor's goal, profitability, had previously driven inland canal construction in the eighteenth century. Railway construction now established a connection between the speed with which new structures were built and profitability. This forced builders to focus on the process of what they did and to rationalize their methods. Railway construction was the primary stimulus to industrial growth in Europe.[75]

Supporters of British railways were no longer the gentry and aristocracy of the early nineteenth century through whose lands the noisy, dirty trains would pass, frightening cattle, purportedly curdling their milk, and disrupting bucolic vistas. The landed upper classes had previously acted as amateur promoters of engineering "improvements" out of a feeling of civic obligation. They may have made a great deal of money out of their enterprises, as the Duke of Bridgwater did with his canals or as he and the dukes of Cornwall and Devonshire did with their mines, but the money they received from them was considered revenue, not interest on invested capital. These patrons saw no direct relationship between the amount of money an improvement cost and the revenue it brought, and their primary motive was "progress," not profit.

Railway financiers were different. Their money was not a periodically recurring revenue from land, to be consumed like any other product. It came from ingenuity, from competitive thinking and commerce, and it was a means of investment called capital. These new clients actively supported and even forced railway construction against all landed opposition. The railway investor wanted to maximize profit from a given amount of capital, not to assuage a feeling of social responsibility. Railways were not *ouvrages d'art,* or "works of artifice," as traditional French engineering called them, but "facilities." They were built to facilitate commerce as a means to an end. Investments had to produce interest as quickly as possible.

The rush to build parallel lines just before midcentury in Britain led to intense competition between designers, promoters, financiers, and legislators. The railway industry grossed £20 million in 1850, a sum that corresponded to half the revenue of the entire government.[76] By 1856 the system employed 90,000 men directly, while another 50,000 served it by manufacturing iron and timber, transporting materials, and making parts, buildings, and other facilities. This meant that about half a million people, or 2 percent of the British population, lived on wages generated by the railways.

Europe's rural landscape had hardly changed since the waves of bubonic plague had decimated its population between the fourteenth and the seventeenth centuries. The canals and metalled roads of the eighteenth and early nineteenth centuries brought the first real changes in rural life, but for several decades the population continued to live more or less independently of the cities, and the two parallel societies, urban-merchant and agricultural-rural, were frequently politically antagonistic, especially on the European continent.

Britain's farming population declined with the eighteenth-century agricultural reforms that improved yields. Mechanization continued the trend in the nineteenth century. Industrial production moved to the cities with the population and made the countryside increasingly dependent on the city, which in turn aggravated the demographic shift. Steam engines had made production independent of waterways and of traditionally powerful water rights, so that industry was free to develop wherever it wished. Industrialists were freed from feudal traditions and their social obligations, and many exploited the displaced labor force. Railways transported materials to feed the cities and their industries more and more cheaply. Soon cities no longer manufactured goods only for urban consumption but served the countryside, too. Rural artisans, merchants, and service providers lost their livelihood to their mechanized and centralized urban competitors. In swift internal colonization, the countryside degenerated to a producer of raw materials, provider of water, and consumer of manufactured goods. On the other hand, the same railroads transported fish inland from the coast and produce and livestock to the growing urban centers from ever farther afield, which increased the value of far-flung industries and agricultural land.[77] These changes occurred earlier in Britain than elsewhere; but wherever economic power changed hands, it called forth an equally forceful transformation of the built environment.

The urbanized population became mobile. The rise of service industries like news agencies was paralleled by that of travel agents. Thomas Cook and Sons was founded in 1844 and prospered from the patronage of the middle and upper classes. Excursion and vacation spots proliferated. Mass tourism was invented in Britain and spread from there to the European continent. Spas and resorts had formerly been the privilege of the wealthy, but new ones began to cater to the growing professional, commercial, clerical, and even working classes. Statistics of third- and fourth-class railway tickets show that salaries benefited from the rush to build railways even in rural areas: the newly affluent workers could now travel too.[78] Small harbors lost their importance as centers of distribution and degenerated or became resorts, while others regenerated or were created. The railways captured most of the transportation volume from the fifty-year-old canal system and, temporarily at least, from the newly winterized roads as well.

Communication Structures

Napoleon embarked on his military roadbuilding program over the alpine passes at the beginning of the century. After his defeat in 1815 and the subsequent publishing of the first civilian survey maps, his pass roads served commerce. The railways and especially the Suez Canal supported the integration of European traffic and accelerated the turn toward civilian commerce and transportation.

Structures like the Conway and Britannia bridges demonstrated how commercial pressure influenced design and construction. There were other causes of pressure, too: the Crystal Palace was built in record time because the exhibition was jeopardized by the failure of the international design competition and Britain's prestige as the world's leading industrial power hung in the balance. Its builders labored under political pressure to meet the opening date. Shortly thereafter the new eastern exit to the Mediterranean provided by the Suez Canal catalyzed the development of trade so strongly that building under stress became the norm, and the canal gave rise to a second generation of projects that reoriented the entire continental European distribution system. New networks had to be built quickly and old ones adapted to new conditions. A feverish building activity spread through Europe and its Asian colonies.

Warehouses, factories, and market sheds followed the bridges, stations, and exhibition halls. The large-scale public projects among them were almost invariably built by committee, in contrast to the great projects of previous centuries that were commonly financed by private patrons. At best committees work through consensus or synthesis and at worst through compromise. But however they function, they usually represent a common denominator of opinion and not individual preference. Procedural thinking was therefore usually clearer in the public projects funded by government or quasi-public corporations and less obvious in privately funded ones, which often catered to the idiosyncrasies of individual clients. In any case, such projects were not considered architecture. Stations, exhibition halls, and the like were pejoratively counted among works of engineering. They were "facilities."

Truly representational buildings were only gradually caught up in this trend. The Cairo Opera House was one of the earliest. Its construction went virtually unnoticed in the haste to ready the canal for the gala opening. It was built of wood and was planned and finished in six months for the canal's opening ceremonies. Avocani and Rossi, its architects, were undistinguished and have remained unknown. The building's one salient feature, that it was rushed to completion under the press of a relentless deadline, went unrecorded.[79] Deadline pressure presumably influenced the choice of timber, which was neither a local material nor a usual one for theaters in the nineteenth century in view of the many accidents caused by open footlights and flammable costumes and scenery. We can only guess at other changes, compromises, inventions, and shortcuts today. The building survived almost a century and succumbed to fire in the early 1950s.

Most major European public transportation works that were designed in the two decades following 1855 stood in some relationship to the Suez Canal.[80] The Mediterranean harbors had declined steadily since the Renaissance, when the newly discovered sea routes to India and the Americas began to favor the Atlantic harbors.[81] Now they began to retool for their new role. Genoa and Venice renewed their ancient competition by establishing railway links over the Alps. The route from Port Said to Genoa took half a day longer than to Venice, but coal, which came from Marseilles or Newcastle, was half-a-day's voyage cheaper in Genoa, so both harbors had approximately the same chances. Genoa had to force the cutting of the Mont Cenis Tunnel, as Venice already had her railway connection north via Kufstein. The Gotthard Tunnel would serve both harbors. But it was only finished in 1883, while Genoa's Mont Cenis connection via Savoy in 1871 was almost as good. Both tunnels had been dreamt of before midcentury and examined in the context of a possible canal and Italy's railroad potential.[82] The north-south rail connection became so imperative for Genoa's commercial survival as the canal neared completion that a speculator built a temporary railway line over the pass. It opened in 1868 and earned a handsome profit in the three years it took to finish the tunnel.

The French government hoped that the canal would divert some oriental trade from London to Marseilles and actively developed a national railway network after decades of neglect. Comprehensive planning soon made the French system the third largest in Europe and the most profitable. Marseilles's advantage lay in its industrialized hinterland and large coal deposits. The Rhone Valley runs straight north, and the rail link to Marseilles had no alpine barrier to contend with as the lines to the Italian harbors did. These advantages helped Marseilles retain its semiautonomous position in rigorously centralized France, and its wealth and facilities helped keep Genoa at bay, too. Just south of the Pyrenees, Barcelona also awakened from its long economic slumber, rebuilt its harbor, and expanded its city. Piraeus, Istanbul, and Odessa prepared too.

As harbors jockeyed for position, European upheavals changed the flow of continental trade.[83] One casualty of the disturbances was the plan to run the British-Indian mail overland from London to Brindisi.[84] But political instability, the many transfers from rail in Britain to ship across the Channel to rail again and then to ship in Brindisi, and the rapid improvement in steamships put an end to this idea. Brindisi wanted to improve its harbor to meet the demand, but the lack of a developed hinterland of its own caused it to dwindle again into insignificance as soon as its main client evaporated. There were many such projects, and aggressive speculators were always ready to pursue them.[85] The proverbs of the time bear witness to the general attitude: "You cannot make an omelet without breaking eggs" or "It's no use crying over spilt milk."

Commerce and Manufacture

In the early days of industrialization, production kept pace with demand by quantitative means like adding more machines or increasing the labor force.[86] Labor was still relatively inexpensive in most advanced European economies, thanks to the uprooted rural population. But in the mid-nineteenth century producers and their support industries came under pressure to manufacture faster.[87] The United States forced Japan and Britain forced China to open to foreign trade. Industrialists hoped this market expansion would bring millions of new customers.[88] Changes in customer demand also supported increased production. For instance, the quicker textiles were brought to the customer and sold, the shorter fashion cycles seemed to become. There were physical limits to factory growth, especially in the cities, where labor was available but space was congested. Manufacturing industries reached their limits quickly, and qualitative change was called for. Manufacturers had to increase their output with better planning and improved machinery.

As productive capacity increased, supply rather than demand began to drive development. When market expansion reached the limits imposed by the political and social conditions of the time, an internal colonization process began. The first wave was geopolitical and involved rural areas; the second was psychological and involved the creation of new needs. The automobile grew from a luxury to a necessity of life, first in North America, then in western Europe, and this trend is now spreading beyond. Henry Ford stated as much, saying that the role of industry was to create needs, not to satisfy them. Thus consumer society had one of its roots in the nineteenth-century spread of communication networks.

The Concept of Progress

As the century advanced and society became more complex, progress came to mean different things to different people. Living languages constantly deform and alter the definition of words; the meaning of the word *progress* as we use it today obscures our understanding of what it meant in the past. Progress is now a tarnished concept, but it was a powerful ideological tool in the hands of politicians, social reformers, and industrialists for over half the nineteenth century.[89] Allegorical sculptures depicting some aspect of "Progress Triumphant," "Science," "Industry," or "Art" still crown older fountains and buildings and testify to the emotive power the concept held right through the end of the century. Progress even outranked religion as a system of belief. Marx may have declared religion to be "the opium of the people," but he never qualified his faith in progress in the same way. It was the unquestioned driving force of the age. Until the last quarter of the century, progress was popularly equated with the new and the good, with the higher and the better.

We need to know how the positivist ideology of "progress" changed in order to understand technological development.[90] People undertook projects simply because they were novel, especially, it appears, in Anglo-Saxon countries. The words "never before" exercised a magnetic appeal and possessed an intrinsic ethical and social value. Progress met profit at the great

9.
The monumental fountain
named "Progrès" at the
Paris Exposition of 1889.
(*Exposition de Paris 1889*,
plate following p. 156.)

international exhibitions. The first "Great Exhibition of the Works of all Nations" was housed in the Crystal Palace, which became the radiant symbol of an epoch. The year 1851 also marked the apogee of the uncritical faith in progress. After the exhibition, astute observers noticed how this faith began to decay. The greed that spread in the uncontrolled early phases of capitalism was partly to blame for this, and so was the use of industry to serve war.

Original thinkers either anticipated what would later become generally received wisdom or sketched possibilities. Their more conventional contemporaries reflected established opinion. By looking at them both we can trace the concept of progress as it supported technology and industry through the century.

The term *progress* went through several stages. Originally it meant something unquestionably ordained by Providence and free from human intervention. Later it seemed that progress arose from a will to victory over the powerful and conservative forces of nature, and that human involvement could actively influence the future. This dynamic attitude was typical of the early Industrial Revolution and the North American and French Revolutions. Then some began to see progress as a natural process akin to the evolution of life; this outlook was similar to the first stage, with the important distinction that it involved human effort. Toward the end of the nineteenth century came doubt, rejection, and brave attempts at redefinition.

Progress as Fate Ordained by Providence

Comments about progress became frequent enough in the eighteenth century to form a decipherable pattern. Until around the French Revolution, progress was regarded as a directed form of fate. Europe was at war, and blind fate was a reality of everyday life. In the eyes of the devout, "progress" was an act of God, while to believers in science it was "purposeful nature." In both cases, however, it acted independently of human will and strove for perfection. Anne-Robert Turgot, who would briefly be finance minister under Louis XVI, exemplified this attitude in a 1750 essay on universal history: "The human species [remains] invariable through its upheavals, like the waters of the sea through its tempests, and constantly advancing toward perfection."[91]

Rousseau agreed that there was a drive toward perfection, but he claimed that social organization was the root evil, and that perfection lay in a "return to nature." The media by which this would occur were education, liberty, equality, and fraternity. In spite of Rousseau's intellectual attractiveness and his influence on the French Revolution, the positivist attitude proved more powerful than the regressionist. This was evident not only in French culture but also in British and German; appropriate sentiments can be found in Gibbon, Browning, and von Ranke.[92] They all considered progress to be independent of human effort, fatalistically fulfilling the spirit of the age.

While philosophers in Germany and elsewhere discussed the concept, it did not remain solely couched in philosophical abstraction.[93] Condorcet, Turgot's friend and biographer, whose writings influenced nineteenth-century thought, was quick to make the connection between progress and production. He presented progress as a fateful, mechanistic law, closely linked to industrial production and an inescapable consequence of earlier stages of technology: "In proportion as excellent productions shall multiply, every successive generation of men will direct its attention to those which are most perfect; and the rest will insensibly fall into oblivion. But the more simple and palpable traits which were seized by those who first entered the field of invention, will not the less exist for posterity, though found only in the latest productions."[94] There were dissenters, of course, Malthus prominent among them, who pointed out the naiveté of an unmitigated belief in limitless advance.[95]

Promethean Pathos

Under pressure from thinkers like Malthus and Rousseau, progress began to take on new overtones. From the French Revolution up to the middle of the nineteenth century, it came to be equated with human struggle. Shelley's 1819 poem "Prometheus Unbound" exemplified this view. Instead of nature and fate as abstract and implacable forces, progress was now seen as the result of endeavor, of incessant struggle against internal and external obstacles and conservative forces. Revolutionary experience showed that human intervention could and did alter the course of events. The image was not that of despairing Sisyphus; thanks to the enlightening influence of science and industry, mankind was indeed winning the battle. Economic liberals in the 1830s added their conviction that work could alter events in that sphere, too, and technocrats like the Saint Simonians in France joined the discussion.

Progress became personalized: it was brought down from the level of philosophical discourse to the human sphere. Man-made barriers replaced Turgot's fatalistic "waters of the sea." The sociopolitical upheavals of the period demonstrated to everyone that progress could be made, but they also showed that it was difficult and fraught with desperate pain. Wendell Phillips flatly contradicted the positivist ethos of the "Exhibition of the Works of all Nations" being held in London when he declaimed in 1851: "You may trace every step of progress the world has made, from scaffold to scaffold, and from stake to stake."[96] The miserable hardship was felt in Germany by the poet Heinrich Heine and expressed in France in Proudhon's letters of 1851.[97] Poets, historians, and philosophers felt the change; many, like Tennyson and Browning, changed their views over the course of their lives.[98] Politicians of both the left and the right laid claim to progress. In 1861, Wilhelm I of Prussia invoked the idea of progress in an attempt to discredit the revolutionary tendencies of the age: "Salutary progress can only be envisioned, after reflective and calm consideration of the tenor of the times, if one understands how to satisfy true needs and utilize the viable elements of the existing order."[99] From the other end of the political spectrum, Edouard René Lefèbvre de Laboulaye, an influential member of the Paris Constitutional Congress (1873–1875) and the spiritual father of the Statue of Liberty, declared eight years later that "Progress is nothing other than freedom in action."[100]

An Inescapable, Natural Process

A new wind began to blow after midcentury. People began to work at the process of betterment, stressing the road rather than the goal. This is the atmosphere in which Samuel Smiles wrote *Self Help* in 1859, a work that described how the working classes could "pull themselves up by their bootstraps." It became a best-seller for decades. This was also a time in which many activist temperance societies sprouted and flourished, of which the Salvation Army is a surviving example. These societies were originally formed to help the downtrodden and outcast, especially the "navvies," as socially disenfranchised, itinerant construction workers were called in Britain. This underclass of laborers had provided the workforce for building the canals and then the railways. They were the model for Friedrich Engels's *Lumpenproletariat.* Workmen's educational societies were founded to better the laborer's lot; John Ruskin and Robert Willis were only two of the many prominent thinkers to donate regular evening lectures to their cause. An early English-language weekly magazine, *The Penny Magazine of the Society for the Diffusion of Useful Knowledge,* began publication for a somewhat more educated public in 1832.[101] It carried the positivist techno-industrialist ethic "upward" into the British middle classes. Among "practical men," as British engineers defensively and self-consciously called themselves, the atmosphere was predominantly positivistic.[102]

In 1859 Darwin formulated his ideas on biological change by means of deterministic natural selection in *On the Origin of Species.* He was not the first to grapple with the concept; the idea of evolution was in the

Creating the Modern World

air.[103] The Irish rationalist historian William Lecky, for instance, interpreted the concept of evolution very differently from Darwin. He saw it manifested in the inventiveness of the Industrial Revolution: "The causes which most disturbed or accelerated the normal progress of society in antiquity were the appearance of great men; in modern times they have been the appearance of great inventions."[104] To many Victorians Darwin's term evolution implied an exalted guiding force, and evolutionists invoked the action of a mechanistic "law" that was independent of human agency. So in a sense they were a throwback to earlier times. But there was a new twist: they stressed the evolutionary *process*. Debates raged for and against the theory of evolution, and about thirty years later the link between evolution and progress had entered popular philosophy in all but the most obtuse intellectual backwaters.

Like so many other professionals, engineers were quick to adopt the evolutionary model, replacing "nature" with "technology."[105] Their espousal of evolution cluttered official oration in engineering societies, where pomp and philosophy congealed into hyperbole.[106] Progress had messianic overtones, and engineers had high hopes for a better, more peaceful and unified mankind, an exalted state of being to be ushered in by civil engineering.[107]

Many evolutionist arguments sheltered a hidden seed of fear, however, and gradually shadows of doubt began to spill over the axiomatic supposition that progress was invariably good. In the last decades of the century the hubris began to wear thin: "It is an error to imagine that evolution signifies a constant tendency to increased perfection. That process undoubtedly involves a constant remodeling of the organism in adaptation to new conditions; but it depends on the nature of those conditions whether the direction of the modifications effected shall be upward or downward."[108] The biologist Thomas Huxley, who wrote these lines, was concerned with progression and regression. He could no longer see life simplistically as continuous improvement, and he stressed change rather than development.

Of course, if we begin to regard progress as a process, we need to know how it begins and ends. Not only that, but the process cycle must be closed by introducing the principle of feedback, for which there was as yet no term.[109] Edison apparently claimed that perplexity and dissatisfaction were the preconditions for progress, which implies feedback in a roundabout way, while the Swiss painter and aviation pioneer Arnold Böcklin is said to have remarked that progress results from self-criticism.[110] This made thoughtful people question how valuable progress really was as a basis for human development. Misuse and exaggeration provoked reaction, and progress-euphoria dissipated.[111] World War I made the very idea anathema to many and associated the negative aspects of progress with standardization. Count Hermann

10.
A gradual disenchantment
with the concept of prog-
ress after midcentury led to
illustrations like this German one. (*Das Neue Buch
der Erfindungen*, 1872–
1875, vol. 6, p. 1.)

Creating the Modern World

Keyserling wrote: "The world worsens daily. America illustrates that this is the real meaning of progress with frightening clarity as it is here that the white man is most strongly type-cast as a creature of expedience."[112] Small wonder: industrial progress had made the mass killing possible.

Standardization, manufacture, and the belief in progress turned out to be closely linked phenomena.[113] A subtle consequence of doubt was the shift in emphasis from qualitative issues like "development," "evolution," and "process" to quantitative ones like "growth."[114] Progress descended from the ethical highroad to the bathos of profit. Along with this shift came another nuance, that of a gigantic, uncontrollable menace. Technology and its thought forms soon became imbued with sinister determinism. Again, it was the destructive power of war that was to blame.[115] Progress was no longer a shining lodestar but a massing of darkly conformist systems.[116] Many thinkers attempted to invest the term with a less apocalyptic and more constructive meaning, but progress had lost its place as an independent ideology and now served the insidious political-ideological conflicts that overshadowed most of the twentieth century.[117] But a century earlier, while the concept was still growing and expanding, technical thinking evolved along with it. The belief in progress manifested itself in building.

2

Structural Materials, Methods, and Systems:
The Prerequisites of Change

Nineteenth-century builders developed new structural types that needed new materials. As the population shifted from rural to urban in the industrializing countries and childbed and infant mortality decreased through better hygiene, nourishment, and medicine, nations had to build more working and living space. The only way they could do this was to mass-produce buildings and infrastructure, and this meant that building methods had to change.

Builders created new materials like reinforced concrete or altered and enhanced the properties of traditional ones like wood. As industrial production techniques improved their output and prices dropped, materials like iron that had formerly been too expensive for structural use became competitive in cost. Builders began to think, design, and build differently. Repetitive structure, modular elements, system thinking, monolithic structure, and modern statics and material science all made their debut in this period. A new breed of builder explored the potential of technological thought by combining design and analysis.

Iron had never been used on a large scale before engineers applied it to the machine industry. Then they began to use it in building, where it revolutionized construction and structure. Iron machinery also transformed the building material industry from small-scale cottage manufacture to large-scale production. Brick, lumber, and component manufacturers began to produce controllable products in bulk. Researcher-industrialists continually improved iron production and made products with better properties. Marc Brunel and others in England discovered that iron bonded with artificial stone, and James Barrett described its monolithic behavior. Their thinking combined observation, analysis, and practical experience. It led to the development of reinforced concrete, a new material with expanded structural and formal possibilities. The concept of monolithic structure—two or more materials combined so as to behave as one—grew out of their work with concrete as well as other engineers' need to create fixed connections in high-rise steel frames.

At first, industrially produced materials were often more expensive than manually produced ones. Production plants represented major investments, and they consumed expensive energy. Transporting large and often bulky components added another cost, which was reflected in the final price. But higher quality or a guaranteed deadline were sometimes worth the higher cost, and materials gradually became cheaper as production volume increased, plants amortized their capital investment, and competition between manufacturers or transportation firms grew. When steel rails were first introduced in the United States in 1837, they cost $115 a ton. By 1880 the price had dropped to $49.25, and by 1908 to $18.25.[1] Rising labor costs and recessions could only delay the trend, not reverse it. Rail traffic became more reliable as it steadily declined in price. Similarly, between 1858 and 1862 French railway tonnage costs fell by 4.25%.[2]

In the United States raw material was abundant, while capital and skilled labor tended to be scarce and more expensive than in other industrializing nations. However, those industries that required skilled labor also had access to capital.[3] This allowed the highly skilled iron industry to mechanize and rationalize, but not, for instance, the lower-skilled cement industry.

Iron: A Material with Expanded Uses

Whenever a new material is introduced into building, its enthusiastic supporters immediately claim that it can solve all the problems that have ever plagued construction. Over time, practical experience brings a more realistic evaluation. Builders initially regarded iron as a panacea for all fire hazards and only began to distinguish between incombustible materials and fireproof construction after using it for about half a century.[4] William Fairbairn pointed out in 1837 that iron need not reach its melting point before it failed structurally, and his collaborator Eaton Hodgkinson discussed the phenomenon in 1846.[5]

Protecting iron structures from fire was similar to the known problem of protecting wood. In 1778, Charles, Viscount Mahon (later Earl Stanhope) read a paper to the Royal Society on protecting wood in which he described the results of burning two identical houses, one of them protected by lime stucco containing chopped hay or hair.[6] Mahon was not a builder but a "natural philosopher," or what we would call a physicist. Natural philosophy was in the process of developing scientific methods of inquiry and analysis, and Mahon crossed the border between building technology and scientific analysis by applying experimental methods to the problem of fire protection. His work differed from that of the early theoreticians of building construction like the Jesuits Thomas Le Seur, François Jacquier, Ruggiero Boscovich, and Giovanni Poleni, or Charles Augustin Coulomb and Leonhard Euler, who applied preexisting theories to building problems. The Jesuit scholars' analysis of the cracking of the Vatican cathedral dome (1742), Poleni's work on catenary thrust lines (1748), Euler's letter on the buckling of columns (1774), and Coulomb's 1776 theory of foundations were all framed in mathematical language and were therefore beyond the grasp of practitioners, but Mahon's work took a concrete form that made it accessible to builders.[7]

Mahon's solution became standard practice for protecting wooden buildings, but iron structures required more. In 1849 Sir Charles Pasley explained to the Institution of Civil Engineers his discovery that a thin brick cladding sufficed to protect iron effectively.[8] His results corresponded to empirical observations in other areas of fire protection, and the ensuing discussion in the Institution of Civil Engineers showed how technological thinking could be advanced by a combination of "vertical" thinking, as practiced in science, and "matrix" or associative thinking, which we usually link to design or art. Robert May pointed out that sheathing iron columns in brick was analogous to coating cupolas for smelting iron with fire clay, and William Hosking referred to his own 1848 publication on the Parisian practice of "pugging" wooden and iron ceilings with protective coatings of plaster and lath.[9] Safe manufacturers also used sandwich construction, in which an insulating material like pumice, fire clay, or gypsum filled the void between two layers of wrought-iron plate.[10]

These examples had been known to British and perhaps French civil engineers, but they hadn't been "translated" from one material or type of construction to another. The process of translation takes time and an associative leap that shifts the thinker's focus from one object or method to another. This leap is typical of technological thought, and the time lag in the process of translation is characteristic of technology transfer from one culture to another. For example, only after the Chicago fire of 1871 did architect John van Osdel claim to "discover" the fireproofing nature of clay cladding for iron frames. Similarly, although it was well known that clay products are brittle, it took another disaster, the San Francisco earthquake and fire of 1906, to make it clear to builders that brick and terra-cotta would fail in an earthquake and that nonbrittle materials were better. Translating limiting criteria is even more difficult than translating potential advantages. Aside from the leap in thinking, it requires the technological translator to postulate hypothetical extreme situations. This is one area in which technological thinking has not yet followed science.[11]

Having recognized the distinction between incombustible and fireproof construction at midcentury, engineers had to deal with the fact that cast iron, wrought iron, and steel all expand at various rates.[12] They recognized that unless they somehow provided for expansion, changing temperatures would cause changes in structural geometry, and the distorted frames would destroy themselves or break through masonry bearings or restraints. No amount of theoretical knowledge could teach builders how to solve each detail problem; only experience, and sometimes analogy, could do it. Even though bridge engineers had been building expansion joints for a decade, they learned how to detail girders fixed in masonry walls only after the "fireproof" First National Bank and Tribune buildings collapsed in the Chicago fire of 1871.[13]

The textile industry was important for building technology, as Sir John Rennie was one of the first to point out in 1846.[14] Mill construction lay halfway between machine and building design, an ideal vehicle for translating the new technology from one engineering field to another. Iron frames, heating systems, lighting, ventilation, firefighting technology, insulation, and vertical transportation were all tested and developed in textile mills before builders installed them in other building types.[15] One night in 1791, the English mill owner William Strutt watched John Rennie's Albion Flour Mill (1784–1785) burn to the ground in London. It had been the first steam-powered mill, filled with James Watt's expensive machinery, and the insurance loss was enormous.

Iron output had tripled since 1740, and prices were beginning to drop within reach of normal construction. Strutt believed that fire-resistant construction could save insurance premiums and compensate for its somewhat higher cost. He had heard of Victor Louis's new roof over the Théâtre Royal in Paris and tried unsuccessfully to obtain plans of it, but Britain and France were at war and the continental blockade worked both ways. So Strutt depended on hearsay and his own logic when he decided to use cast iron for the loadbearing structure of his new mill in Derby (1792–1793).

At first, builders like Strutt imitated heavy timber connections.[16] But it did not take them long to discover how inappropriate wedged, pegged, and mortised cast-iron connections were, because they introduced tension and shear stresses into a material that couldn't accommodate them easily and were also complicated and expensive to cast.[17] They soon found that it was better to cast lugs and flanges on the components, as boilermakers did, and join them with wrought-iron bolts and rivets. It was a stepped translation process: first a simple step from traditional wood to a new material and then a more complex one from boilermaking to another field and scale.

Structural Materials, Methods, and Systems

12.
The simple exterior of the 1785 Albion Flour Mill in London hid a collection of innovative and expensive Boulton and Watt machinery. William Strutt watched the building burn in 1791 and devised a more fire-resistant construction for his own mill in Derby the following year. (Smiles, *Lives of the Engineers*, 1861, vol. 2, p. 138.)

Iron bridges show how the stepped modification of connection technology caused changes in design and form. Abraham Darby III's 1779 Iron-bridge over the Severn at Coalbrookdale in England was the first successful large-scale iron structure in the Western world.[18] Darby assembled it in half-spandrels to form five parallel arches, and it resembled a timber bridge made of stick members. The Coalport Bridge, a few miles downstream, was begun a few years later and designed in much the same way. But a few of its wood-type connectors had changed to the bolted flanges and lugs more typical of machine construction. Thomas Wilson's Wear Bridge at Sunderland (1796), John Rennie's Thames Bridge at Southwark (1819), and Telford's Mythe Bridge at Tewkesbury (1826) all exemplify a more advanced stage of transformation. They were designed with more modern connections and their builders organized them in a new way: as systems. Instead of designing them traditionally by first determining the bridge form and then subdividing it into parts for prefabrication, they used a bottom-up design process, standardizing the members and connections as they went and arranging them into an assembly. Their "kit of parts" determined the final form as much as the form influenced the parts—a form of matrix thinking.

13.
The mechanism Thomas Telford used to adjust the chains of the Menai suspension bridge in 1826. Keys, wedges, links, and mortised connections were common in the earliest iron structures. It was only later that builders adopted more appropriate techniques from boilermaking. (Tomlinson, 1852, vol. 1, p. 228.)

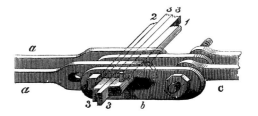

14.
The Ironbridge over the
Severn at Coalbrookdale,
built in 1779, was the first
successful European iron
structure. Its components
and connections were mod-
eled on timber framing.
(Taylor, 1829, plate 4.)

15.
Thomas Wilson built the
Wear Bridge at Sunderland
in 1796. The American revolutionary Thomas Paine
was responsible for its advanced structural concept
with cast-iron components
that could be preassembled
into a voussoir-shaped element using simple bars and
bolts. (Charles Taylor,
1829, plate 4; Cresy, 1847,
p. 497.)

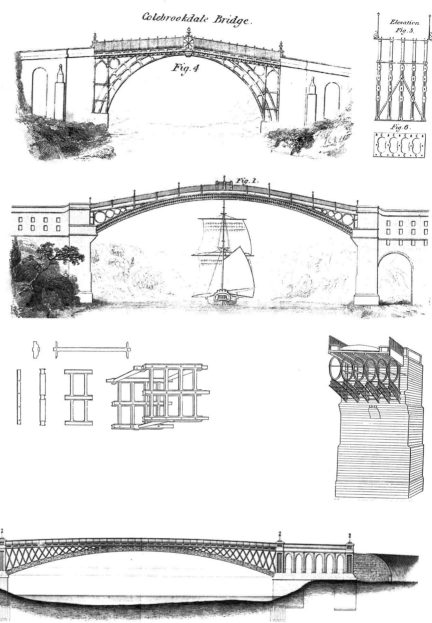

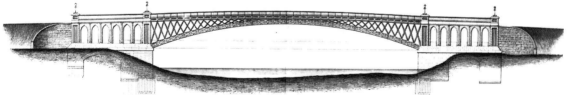

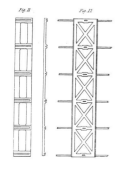

16.
Telford's Mythe Bridge at
Tewkesbury used a more advanced form of connecting
technology in 1826. (*Transactions of the Institution of
Civil Engineers*, vol. 2,
1838, plates 1, 3.)

The primacy of connection technology in iron changed the way designers thought about construction. Iron has to be produced in a factory; it cannot be rationally manufactured on a construction job or easily worked into parts on site. Iron construction is therefore the process of *assembling* prefabricated components with prefabricated connectors. Manufacturers and builders had to use their expensive molds more than once for economy. They designed structures with repetitive elements and took full advantage of the fact that parts were cast rather than individually fabricated. Repetitive elements and standardized connections characterize a system approach to design that implies *organizing* component hierarchies rather than *composing* forms.[19] In this way the material, iron, brought forth a new concept, the construction system. Its characteristics are repetitive prefabrication, standardization, and site assembly rather than site manufacture and manipulation of raw materials.

This change took several decades to work itself out in practice. Darby made a multitude of parts for the Ironbridge, each different and with individually solved connections. Wilson built his Severn Bridge from identical components, which he assembled into voussoir-shaped elements and connected together to make the arch.[20] Cast-iron buildings followed the same development. The 1811 Halle aux Blés dome in Paris by architect François Bélanger, engineer J. Brunet, and the innovative contractor Roussel is a transitional example.[21] A slightly more mature one is the iron shed for storing wine and rum that John Rennie built in the West India Docks in London in 1814.[22]

The trend was even more pronounced in wrought-iron construction. Wrought-iron components are manufactured by hot-rolling bars through grooved rollers. They are prismatic shapes that are easy to use in many types of construction, including combined forms with concrete.[23] Henry Hawes Fox and James Barrett used combinations of rolled or built-up iron girders in composite concrete floor construction from the mid-1840s on.[24] Unlike cast iron, wrought iron is as good in tension as it is in compression, so there was no need to differentiate between the size or shape of the top and bottom flanges of **I** and the legs of **H** profiles. Equal flanges made connection technology much simpler to standardize.[25] Richard Turner used them in the Kew Palm House (1846–1848) and for the roof of Lime Street Station in Liverpool in 1850.[26] William Fairbairn sent several composite wrought- and cast-iron buildings to Turkey between 1838 and 1840, including a foundry, textile mills, a corn mill, and a house. He later sent a floating flour mill to the Crimea and built his brother's "fire-proof" house at Leeds.[27]

As they grew more familiar with the new materials, engineers discovered the phenomenon of fatigue fracture in heavily used iron machine parts

17.
Early rolling mills produced wrought-iron rails and deck beams. The first structural I-beams were rolled around 1845 in France. (Paul Poirel, 1880, pp. 107, 109.)

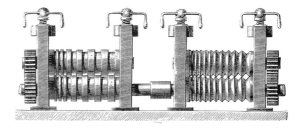

and in mill and bridge structures that were subjected to machine and locomotive vibration. They noted changes in material structure, from what they called the typical fibrous character of rolled wrought iron to a brittle, crystalline form, as early as 1854.[28] The observation was imprecise (iron is always crystalline), but it did lead to the development of a new field called material science and promoted experimentation with cast-iron components in which engineers would locally increase the cross section of highly stressed areas, giving them highly attractive, sculptural qualities.[29] Analogously, in rolled wrought-iron construction they layered riveted plates and angles to build up endangered cross sections.

Builders moved from cast to wrought iron and then to steel in a search for enhanced loadbearing capacity but also as a result of a series of accidents that illustrated the shortcomings of the more brittle cast iron. Chief among these in Britain were the collapse of Robert Stephenson's Dee Bridge in 1846, which led to the 1849 *Report of the Commissioners* on the use of iron in railway structures, and the collapse of Sir Thomas Bouch's Tay Bridge in 1879.[30] In the United States, too, the 1876 failure of the Ashtabula Viaduct in Ohio and the collapse of the thirteen-story frame of the Darlington Building in New York in 1904 undermined confidence in cast iron.

18.
The grain mill that Fairbairn shipped to Istanbul for Seraskier Halil Pasha in 1842 was entirely prefabricated in iron. (Fairbairn, *Treatise on Mills and Millwork,* **1871, pp. 119, 121.)**

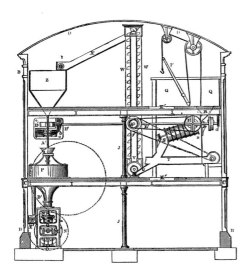
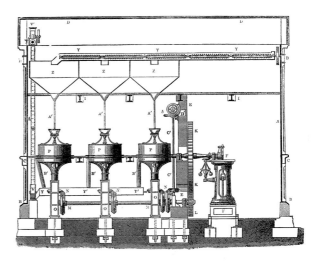

19.
Fairbairn shipped a large wool mill to Izmet for the Turkish sultan in the early 1840s. (Fairbairn, *Treatise on Mills and Millwork,* 1871, plates following p. 190.)

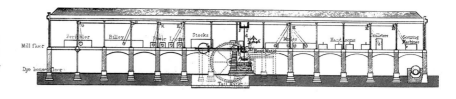

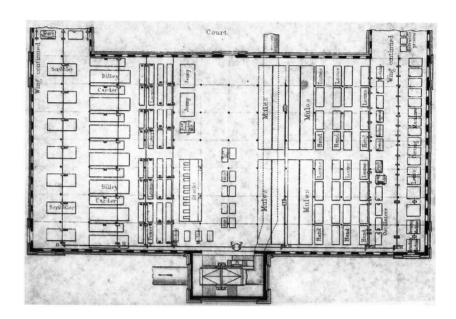

20.
When Sir Thomas Bouch's bridge collapsed into the Firth of Tay on 23 December 1879, the inquiry cited foundation and casting problems as well as underestimated wind loads. The accident led to widespread changes in design and construction practice. (Figuier, *Nouvelles Conquêtes de la Science,* 1883–1885, vol. 3, p. 633.)

Wood: Changing a Traditional Material

When the British toolmaker Sir Joseph Whitworth visited the New York exhibition in 1854, he was impressed with the ingenuity of American labor-saving woodworking machinery.[31] In contrast to craftsmen in the countries of continental Europe, neither British nor American carpenters were strongly bound to conservative professional guilds, and this freed them to develop nontraditional forms of woodworking technology. They were able to rationalize their use of material and their workforce, which led to a high level of mechanization in component production. This was especially true for American builders, who had to economize on their use of labor. Many sawmills and machine tool industries were founded in the 1830s and 1840s.[32]

Rationalization moved in the same direction in continental Europe and in North America, but for different reasons. European engineers designed simpler timber bridge forms than their predecessors with a minimum of members and connection points in order to clarify stress transfer and make calculation easier. They also introduced iron connectors to take full advantage of cross sections at the connections and avoid cutting into the members where shear stresses were greatest. Those who were trained in the French academic system were especially likely to design bridges to fit the theoretical models their professors had developed for their statics courses.

North American bridge builders also simplified their wooden bridges and used iron connectors. But their need for standardized connections was driven by the desire to simplify assembly methods for amateur carpenters. They had no need to economize on the number of connections. On the contrary, they tended to prefer large numbers of them as a strategy to increase structural redundancy: if a connection were improperly assembled or disintegrated through lack of maintenance, the surrounding ones held, and damage became apparent long before a structure collapsed. For example, in 1820 and 1835 the architect Ithiel Town patented wooden lattice bridges with multiple members and many connections that used this iterative approach to structural integrity. European engineers adopted Town's bridges, not for easy assembly or redundancy as much as for reasons that would eventually lead to the definition of monolithic structural behavior.[33]

It is an American cultural trait to make structures safe through a *quantitative* proliferation of parts rather than by guaranteeing the *quality* of individual connections.[34] American builders had no trouble accepting the idea that a new kind of quality can come from an increase in quantity. They intuitively understood that new structural characteristics can emerge from repetitive construction,[35] an understanding that would later influence the replacement of quality by quantity in consumer society. No labor may have been saved by trading quality for quantity, but there were major savings in skilled labor, maintenance, and the prevention of collapse through construction errors. This was advantageous to a society that was expanding and that was always overextending its professional capacity. America had immigrants to provide unskilled labor, but it lacked professionals to supervise sites and check structures. Perceptive mid-nineteenth-century Europeans noted the potential advantages of the tradeoff between quality and quantity:

> It is, however, in the United States of America, that the railway system has been most rapidly developed. Feeling the necessity of traversing their almost boundless plains, and piercing their dense forests, the Americans did not wait for the perfecting of the system, but adapting their wants to their means, began by laying down squared logs, on which were spiked flat bars of iron for rails; the viaducts were timber piles, carrying these primitive and inexpensive

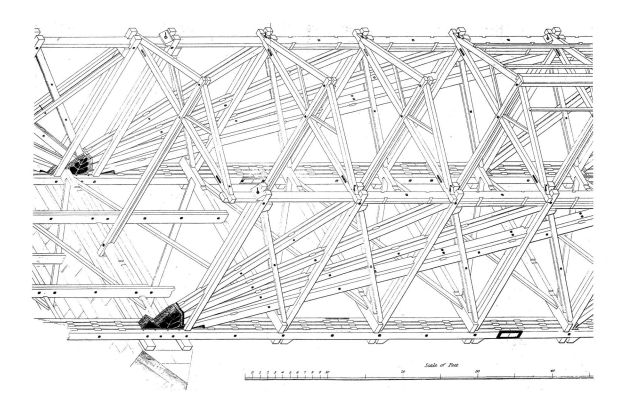

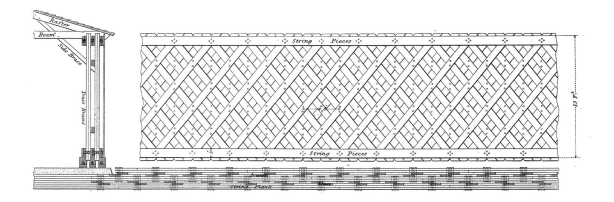

Structural Materials, Methods, and Systems

rails; the engines were so constructed as to traverse sharp curves, and ascend steep inclines; whilst their cars were made to convey the largest number of passengers, in one vehicle, and on one set of wheels; now, however, whilst their old pioneering system still, to some extent, continues, what a change has been effected on the main bulk of the railways; substantial works have been constructed, permanent rails have been laid, efficient engines and most complete cars have been provided.[36]

Since American builders tended to use many simple connections, their systems were preferably open-ended and flexible kits of parts rather than wholly prefabricated buildings. Standardized lengths, cross sections, and connectors created assembly conditions that were elementary to follow, and as long as the systems were standardized and simple, builders could even cope with complicated components, elements, and subassemblies and could build complex structural forms. Nowhere were the implications of this attitude clearer than in American light-wood frame construction.[37] British wooden and iron house construction was also standardized and simple, but these structures were generally manufactured as complete buildings or "closed" systems. British manufacturers exported large numbers of prefabricated buildings to Australia and the Caribbean Islands in the latter part of the eighteenth century and perhaps to the United States as well in the early years of the nineteenth.[38] Most such systems were mixed and depended on iron tension members or at least on iron connectors.

Builders and suppliers had to shift from a craft-based to an industrial viewpoint in order to rationalize lumber production and woodworking.[39] They were helped by a new professional group, the material scientists, who raised issues of chemical composition and the physics of microstructure rather than characterizing materials by hardness, color, grain, or surface pattern. Some builders used what the scientists discovered to modify the chemical and physical properties of materials, developing, for instance, means to make wood impervious to rot and insects.[40] This allowed them to use wood in direct contact with the ground or in other nontraditional ways.

Other builders improved the structural characteristics of timber. For example, vaulted roofs and wooden ships needed bent timbers. Naturally bent ones were the strongest, since their fibers followed the curve of the members. But naturally curved logs are rare, and as Europe's hardwood stands diminished through overuse, builders tried to bend wood artificially. Philibert Delorme had used overlapping layers of short boards strapped and doweled together to make plank arches for the roofs of the Tuileries stables

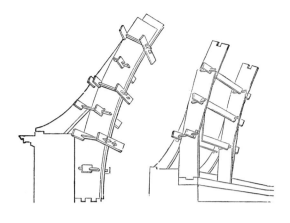 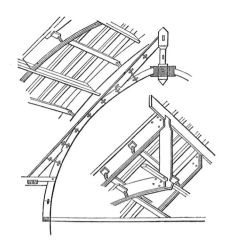

23.
The sixteenth-century builder Philibert Delorme pegged short, straight boards together to form wooden arches. They became models for later laminated timber systems. (Cresy, 1847, p. 1338.)

in sixteenth-century Paris.[41] The disadvantage of Delorme's arches and similar ones built in early nineteenth-century France and Prussia was that the clamping force prestressed the wood fibers.

One way of doing away with this stress was what shipbuilders and wheelwrights had traditionally done, namely, steam the wood until it became pliable and then bend and clamp it until it dried.[42] In 1820, a French boilermaker named Sargent took the first step in industrializing this method by bending series of identical elements in steel forms. Naval competition with Britain had depleted stands of mature oak in France, and Holland had a large merchant navy but little structural wood of any size, so the French and Dutch were the first to industrialize bentwood techniques, building ships with a third of the wood they had previously required.[43] François-Jonas Eustache apparently didn't know that the French navy was using Dutch wood-bending furnaces when he erected bentwood support arches under the damaged Pont aux Fruits in Melun in 1819.[44] But when he built the centering for the new Pont d'Ivry over the Seine in Paris seven years later, he used Sargent furnaces to bend sixteen-centimeter beams in nine hours with only three days in clamps. His first test beams cracked, but the next came out perfectly when he dried them in Sargent's patent steel forms.

Bentwood lent itself to experiments in structural form. In 1849 William King, the first Earl Lovelace (Byron's son-in-law) built a pointed-arch roof on his estate at East Horsley Park. It was a cruck frame with curved members running from the ridge to the vertical and was bolted low to the inside of the walls.[45] Lovelace wanted to divert the load gradually from the slope of the pitched roof to the vertical walls; he was trying to reduce the outward thrust and avoid using a hammer beam, external buttresses, or a tie rod spanning the hall.

Structural Materials, Methods, and Systems

The potential for new forms and structural types was attractive, but bentwood could not compete with the steady fall in iron prices, and it was only a matter of time until iron forced it out of the building market. Abandoned by the building world, bentwood reappeared in furniture. Michael Thonet, a cabinetmaker in Boppard near Koblenz, began experimenting in the early 1830s and patented bending techniques similar to Sargent's in 1841.[46] His most prominent client, Prince Metternich, invited him to relocate his business to Vienna, where Thonet built bentwood furniture in increasing volume and variety. He exhibited at the Crystal Palace, and soon his coffeehouse chair number 14 became an icon of Austrian elegance. Over 14,000,000 of these were eventually produced; even Emperor Franz Joseph's study was furnished with a bentwood desk chair.

Others tried to make wood more homogeneous. The inert surfacing material plywood initially appeared in piano construction at midcentury.[47] When the plies were glued with parallel instead of cross-grained fibers, it became what is now known as "gluelam" or "microlam," with yet other structural advantages.[48] (Today wood products with preprogrammed characteristics geared to appropriately specialized uses are also manufactured from chips or sawdust.)

The industrialization of the material brought forth woodworking machines, which helped distance the use of the material even further from its craft-based roots. Sir Samuel Bentham's mechanical planes were probably the

24.
Michael Thonet first exhibited bentwood furniture at the Crystal Palace Exhibition in 1851. (*Art Journal Illustrated Catalogue*, 1851, p. 296.)

first woodworking tools to be widely admired and copied.[49] His first, patented in 1791, was a slow reciprocating plane, while the second in 1793 and third two years later combined several functions and were forerunners of the later "universal" milling machines. Joseph Bramah improved them for Bentham at the Woolwich naval arsenal around 1797.[50] Bramah's 1802 patent covered all three basic types still common today: the flat plane with horizontally rotating disk and blades embedded on the underside, the milling machine with vertically rotating blades, and a reciprocating type with blades fixed in a frame.[51]

Most early planes in America, like Eli Whitney's in 1818, were reciprocating machines that copied manual planing as in Bentham's first patent. Thomas Blanchard's gunstock-milling lathe of 1820 was an exception. He built it for the Springfield Armory, and it led to manufacturing lines of linked machinery similar to the British one Marc Brunel had installed at Portsmouth arsenal (1805–1807), his shoe-manufacturing machinery for the army (1810), and the sawmill he built at Chatham (1812–1815).[52] The American development advanced quickly, especially with the development of complex jigs.[53] By 1820 wooden windows and doors were being industrially produced, but the industry stagnated again after 1828, when William Woodward patented his milling machine with so comprehensive a description that it hampered innovation until 1856.[54]

French manufacturers also initially preferred reciprocating planes.[55] The more precise ones inverted the manual process and moved the piece rather than the tool. However, machines with heavy moving tables take up much more floor space than ones with traveling heads; the French argued that moving tables were appropriate for small machines, but that the heavy heads of large planes had enough mass to guarantee a high degree of precision.[56] They preferred to avoid having to accelerate the return of the table on large machines, which was a problem that plagued British machine tool manufacturers. François Cavé patented a two-way plane with a head that changed direction on the return and saved time by cutting in both directions; Whitworth built one in Britain in 1842.[57] It was only useful for planing metal, however, since wood fibers cannot be worked against the grain.[58]

Wood and metal planes developed in parallel. Georg von Reichenbach from Brunswick, Matthew Murray in Leeds, James Fox in Derby, and Richard Roberts in Manchester all built metal planes between 1804 and 1818.[59] These may all have been independent developments, or they could equally well have influenced each other; for instance, Reichenbach had visited England in 1792. Industrial espionage played an important role in the spread of industrial technology in the eighteenth and nineteenth centuries,

Structural Materials, Methods, and Systems

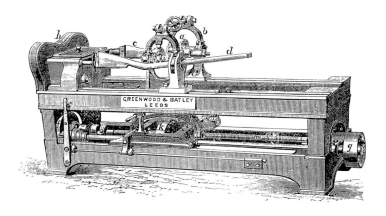

25.
Jigs guided the Blanchard-type lathe more precisely than even the best crafts-man. Inertia made planes with fixed heads and heavy, moving tables very precise, but they took up twice the floor space of planes with light, moving heads. (Routledge, 1901, pp. 93, 96; *Crystal Palace and Its Contents*, 1852, p. 407.)

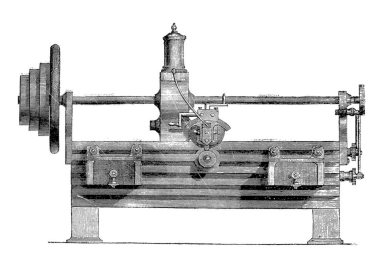

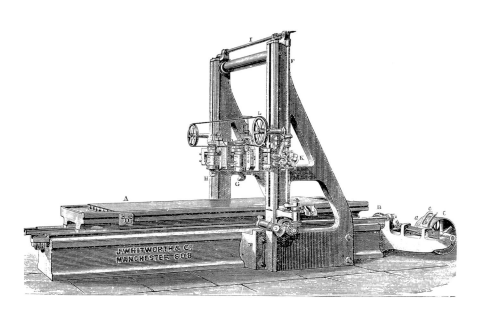

and it can only occasionally be traced reliably. Mechanics, engineers, industrialists, and businessmen all participated. According to their memoirs they made a sport out of memorizing what they had seen during the day and recording it at night in sketchbooks by candlelight in their inn rooms. These sketchbooks are often the only remaining record of many pioneering machines and processes and of the methods by which information was pirated and transmitted.

In 1828, while still gardener and estate manager at Chatsworth, Joseph Paxton experimented with machinery for making wooden mullions for conservatories. He first used circular saws, but soon abandoned them for the more precise revolving cutters.[60] By the end of the 1830s the price of labor had risen even in rural areas while machine tools had become reliable, and Paxton cut miles of mullions cheaply for the "Great Stove" conservatory at Chatsworth. Rising labor costs and the removal of manufacture from the construction site to the factory made machine tools increasingly important. When machines reached an acceptable degree of precision, inventors concentrated on speeding up the process. Fox and Henderson used a Bramah-type rotating disk to prepare timbers for a gutter-cutting machine for the Crystal Palace in 1850, and an advanced milling machine to rout them with consecutive banks of cutters that finished the workpiece in a single pass.

Machines were rapidly amortized as production speed and volume increased. Prices fell and wooden trim began to be used on the interiors and exteriors of building types that had never before been considered worthy of such treatment. The simplest sheds began to sprout elaborate fascia boards, beaded and dentiled cornices, and intricate window and door surrounds. Encrustation fulfilled mid-Victorian decorative ideals. Banks, offices, schools, museums, railway stations, warehouses, factories, jails: all had highly articulated surfaces, the more expensive in machine-cut stone and the more modest in wood.

High patronage spread the ideals of utopian and proto-socialist movements, of self-help and temperance societies, which mushroomed at midcentury. Building was one of the chief ways in which these patrons expressed their social concern. Prince Albert sponsored a hollow-masonry-block laborer's cottage at the 1851 exhibition.[61] Critics praised it, and agricultural and industrial patrons built copies all over Europe. Projects like this expanded the architect's domain to encompass every type of building, from traditional representational edifices to public lavatories. Professionals felt the need to treat everything to a proper style and decorate it accordingly. Machine-made moldings, fretwork, and carvings in wood made it economical to do so.

26.
In 1851, the Society of Arts exhibited a model cottage in hollow-block construction that Prince Albert had sponsored. (*Crystal Palace and Its Contents*, 1852, pp. 81, 82; *Official Descriptive and Illustrated Catalogue*, 1851, vol. 2, pp. 774, 775.)

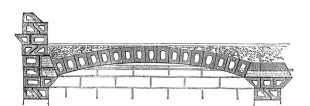

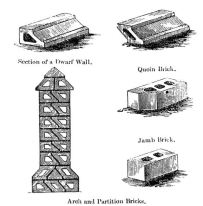

Section of a Dwarf Wall.

Quoin Brick.

Jamb Brick.

Arch and Partition Bricks.

Small workshops in Britain and the United States relied on "universal" woodworking machinery, which could plane, cut, drill, and turn large orders in a short time. One such machine built by Allan Ransome & Company of Newark-on-Trent could cut 300 pairs of tenoned glazing bars in twenty-four working hours or a hundred finished door frames in ten. A specialized form of universal machine was used for carving. William Irving patented a carving machine in 1843 and developed it in subsequent years.[62] John Tomes demonstrated one that Charles Holtzapffel had built for him to the Institution of Civil Engineers. It carved false teeth in ivory and copied casts of palates for fitting them.[63] The President of the Society of Arts, Prince Albert, awarded the Golden Isis Medal for 1845 to a carving machine by Thomas Brown Jordan, and it received the Prize Medal at the 1851 Exhibition too.[64] Jordan's machine was an adaptation of traditional jig-controlled machinery. It could carve low relief in boards at an incredible rate, cutting what a parallel-mounted pointer traced on a model.[65]

The carving machine contained the germ of the robotic manufacturing process, and it was used for almost everything made of wood. It cut industrial parts as well as the most trivial decoration.[66] Jordan's machine was one of the most admired exhibits in the Crystal Palace.

> One of the most important branches of ornamental manufacture in the Exhibition is that of carving and inlaying in wood. This branch of industry, as more generally accessible and applicable, and accordingly in far more extensive demand, than manufactures in the precious metals ever can be. . . . The specimens of Jordan's machine-carving are another promise of the unexampled facilities of the coming age in all mechanical resources.[67]

It vulgarized and spread "Gothick" over every imaginable item of manufactured trivia, contradicting John Ruskin's demand that design and manufacturing method form a stylistic unity.[68] What the mechanical plane had done for architectural moldings and the pantograph did for the Swiss lace industry the carving machine did for the industrial arts. Cheap decoration spread into the simplest households. Jordan's machine made everything possible, from the loftiest and most influential examples of furniture in Augustus Pugin's Gothic Court at the exhibition of 1851 to the simplest articles of daily use.

Structural Materials, Methods, and Systems

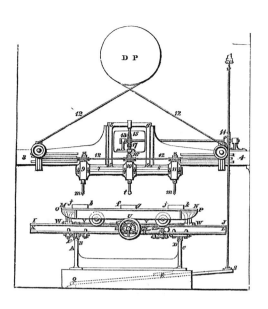

27.
Thomas Jordan's carving machine received awards from the Society of Arts in 1845 and the Exhibition in 1851. It spread high-Victorian encrustation from Pugin's fashionable "Gothic Court" to cheap articles of everyday use. (Tomlinson, 1852, vol. 1 ; *Art Journal Illustrated Catalogue*, 1851, p. xxiv.)

Reinforced Concrete: A New Material with Novel Possibilities

By midcentury iron was firmly established in construction and the wood industry was holding its own in innovative ways, but a third material promised even more radical changes. Reinforced concrete is a composite material that behaves monolithically. It expanded the methodological, structural, and aesthetic avenues opened by the other materials. Daring cantilevers, gossamer bridges, and frames more delicate than any Gothic cathedral are the stock in trade of the building industry today, yet they are still objects of architectural and engineering wonder. Reinforced concrete has been variously attacked as the destroyer of our environment and praised as its savior. Our world is unthinkable without it.

The material for casting walls was hydraulic cement, clay, or, in China, loess, with or without additives, which was tamped between boards in layers one to twenty centimeters thick.[69] Builders still use the technique in rural China, North Africa, the dryer regions of the Middle East, and the American Southwest, while Devonshire *cob,* French *pisé,* and Spanish *tapia* disappeared in the last century. Pliny the Elder described its pre-Roman use in the Mediterranean region, and many ruins throughout the former empire testify to the high quality of Roman concrete.[70] It was used as fill behind walls, as foundations, or as free-standing vaulting cast on timber centering. The Romans improved the material and used a natural hydraulic binder for underwater work called pozzolana, a volcanic tuff that undergoes complex chemical and physical reactions with water. The material is still quarried at Puteoli (now Pozzuoli) on the bay of Naples.[71] Puteoli probably could not supply the entire empire, however, and Roman engineers may have found other sources of natural cement, like "Dutch" trass that is still mined in Andernach on the Rhine.[72]

Western concrete did not disappear with the Roman Empire, and examples abound in medieval Christian and Arab construction.[73] It was considered inferior to stone and inappropriate for representative architecture, but several treatises did at least mention pozzolana, and it survived in vernacular construction.[74] Spanish and southern French traditions survived until modern concrete technology took over in the nineteenth century.

François Cointereaux, an architect and contractor in Lyons, discovered the pisé method in a building he was remodeling and became the first modern to publish a description of it in 1791, but it was Jean-Baptiste Rondelet who spread the knowledge of pisé beyond a restricted readership. His *Traité de l'art de bâtir* appeared in 1802 and had gone through seven editions

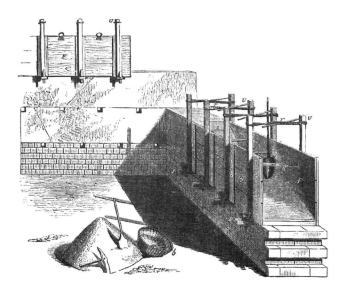

28.
François Cointreaux discovered an ancient form of cast concrete in southern French vernacular construction. Jean-Baptiste Rondelet's description of this in 1802 provided the basis for the development of modern concrete construction. (Tomlinson, 1852, vol. 2, p. 419.)

by 1867.[75] Books began to appear on the subject of pisé with increasing frequency. A variant construction method that had survived on the Amalfi coast was reinvented in 1828 and patented in Sweden, and by midcentury there was no dearth of information on the material.[76]

An Example of Technological Thinking

In 1756 the English engineer John Smeaton was the first to have hydraulic cement analyzed. He knew Bélidor's report on mortar as well as the chapters on cements in Vitruvius and in Christopher Wren's *Parentalia*.[77] With the help of the potter and chemist William Cookworthy, Smeaton analyzed several natural cements and found to his surprise that it was not the purest or hardest limestone that gave the best hydraulic characteristics, as Vitruvius and everyone since him had believed. The limestone needed an admixture of clay — in other words, silicates — to make it hydraulic.

Neither the ideals of theological thinking — "purity" and "faith" — nor the logic of "natural philosophy" that had begun to replace them could explain hydraulic mortar at the time, but the empiricism of chemistry could demonstrate it. Chemistry, and especially chemical engineering, have always had the strong hybrid tradition of analytical insight and synthesis that we now associate with technological thinking. We do not know how the discovery influenced Smeaton's engineering, but it did astonish him, and his insight influenced subsequent research on hydraulic mortars and the development of synthetic materials.

Cookworthy was an artist and a technologist, while the physicist, instrument-maker, and builder Smeaton was both scientist and technologist.[78] Both men were intellectual border-crossers in a period when modern scientific method was being formed.[79] They would have been acutely aware of the distinction between faith and empirical evidence, but not of the difference between scientific and technological thought, nor would it have meant anything to them. Their as yet unnamed form of thinking was a sign of things to come, an analytical construct we project *a posteriori* into their world in order to highlight the first stirrings of a development that still lay a century in the future.

Between the middle and the end of the eighteenth century men like Smeaton and Lord Mahon were forming a physics-based approach to understanding structure and materials that would gradually permeate building in the form of civil engineering. Smeaton was the first man to call himself a "civil," as opposed to a military, engineer. Many of his contemporaries, especially Jesuit mathematicians, were beginning to analyze structural problems using mathematics and physics, the newly developed tools of "natural philosophy."[80] A few of them, like Ritter Franz Joseph von Gerstner and Charles Augustin Coulomb, were also practicing builders, and they too crossed the borders between empiricism and science, inadvertently initiating the hybrid mode of thought we now know as technological thinking.

A Contrast between Empirical and Scientific Experimentation

Smeaton and Cookworthy did their research at midcentury but only published the results in Smeaton's *Edystone Lighthouse* monograph in 1791, by which time others had come to similar conclusions.[81] Smeaton's report was influential nevertheless, and researchers throughout Europe were inspired to discover natural hydraulic cements everywhere. Based on Smeaton's and the other reports, French researchers began controlled experimentation. Louis-Joseph Vicat, the most influential among them, published a first set of results in 1818.[82] English engineers translated his early writings, but largely ignored his later papers and other French and German work.[83] Anglo-Saxon researchers initially seemed reluctant to examine the scientific principles behind the physical properties of materials. Even Portland cement, the British-developed predecessor of our modern product of the same name, was first analyzed in 1849 by the German Max Joseph von Pettenkofer.

British concrete research began in the military engineering establishments. The Duke of Wellington, Master of the Ordnance, introduced construction into the curriculum of the Royal Engineering Establishment at Chatham in 1826. He ordered the school's director, Pasley, to develop the course, and Pasley grasped the opportunity to begin experimenting with hydraulic cement. He consulted the physicist Michael Faraday and Major Reid, who had some experience with the material. Pasley's report appeared in 1830 and was expanded in 1838.

Experimenters in France and Germany concentrated on the physical characteristics and the chemical composition of the material from the outset, while the earliest British research tended to focus on the strength of concrete structures in use. Where Vicat and Clément-Louis Treussart carefully measured the penetration of weighted needles and blades into fresh and cured mortar and drew analytical conclusions from their observations, Pasley shelled concrete vaults built by the contractor William Ranger to see how they withstood impact and tested the tensile strength of cement by seeing how far a row of mortared bricks could be laterally cantilevered out from a wall before collapsing. As bizarre as this empirical approach may seem to us, it did permit useful conclusions to be drawn. It led to what at first appeared

29.
Between 1812 and 1818,
Louis-Joseph Vicat con-
ducted mortar tests to determine how deeply a
needle penetrated into the
material as it cured. Clément-Louis Treussart de-
signed similar tests in 1829
to examine the material's
adhesive and cohesive characteristics. (Michaelis,
1869, pp. 230, 231, 232.)

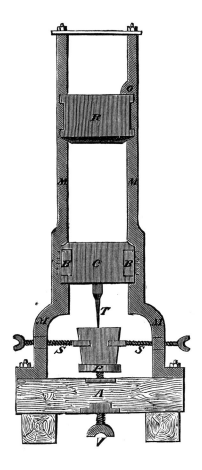

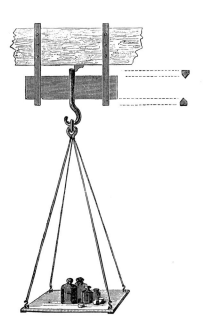

to be illogical hybrid structures, as researchers introduced first wood and then iron reinforcement to enhance the tensile and bending strength of mortar. This is another instance where fuzzy or hybrid thinking advanced building technology and influenced its mode of thought. However, since the British research thrust generally neglected to analyze the composition of the material itself, uncontrolled cement, water, and aggregate ratios introduced a substantial element of uncertainty into the results. Thus Pasley could write that concrete was useful in foundations and as fill in stone walls but, based on Ranger's negative experience in Chatham and Woolwich, not for exposed seawalls.[84]

It took years to develop acceptable standards for testing and manufacturing cement and to provide engineers with tools to make reliable comparisons and reasonable predictions. Wilhelm Michaelis of the Königliche Prüfungsstation für Baumaterialien (Royal Building Materials Testing Station) at Charlottenburg in Prussia designed the first codes for cement weight, fineness, curing time, and strength in 1878. He based them on research that John Grant, Chief Engineer of the London Metropolitan Board of Water Works, had done twenty years before while building the London sewer system.[85]

Natural and Artificial Cements

In the early years of the nineteenth century, builders discovered, refined, and packaged naturally hydraulic products. The two most popular in Britain were James Parker's "Roman Cement" and James Frost's "British Cement," but there were many others in France and elsewhere.[86] Artificial products based on research results gradually appeared on the market, and producers began to manipulate natural materials to improve their characteristics as well; for example, the quicker-setting cements had higher clay contents.[87] Conservative builders mistrusted the artificial material at first and preferred the more expensive natural pozzolana.[88] But as artificial hydraulic cements became cheaper and more common they replaced even traditional lime mortars.[89]

Joseph Aspdin's "Portland Cement" came on the market in 1824.[90] It had less clay than most and cured very slowly. This was an advantage in foundation work, where shifting subsoil conditions could crack concrete if it set too quickly. Quick-curing products had advantages of their own. John Marriot Blashfield, Parker's business successor, supplied a fast-curing Roman cement for the temporary Houses of Parliament in London after the fire of 1834. The buildings were ready to be moved into almost as soon as they were finished. Marc Brunel also chose Blashfield's cement mortar for the brick walls of the Thames Tunnel.

Manufacturers, always trying to get an edge on the market, continued to improve their products. William Aspdin published tests in 1848 that showed a much higher crushing strength than his father's original Portland Cement.[91] But our modern portland cement came neither from a scientific laboratory nor from experiments but from industrial espionage and a fortuitous discovery in an industrial kiln. In 1850 Isaac Charles Johnson, John Bagley White and Sons's production manager for fifteen years, tested an accidentally sintered and discarded kiln load of cement.[92] Johnson's hunch and experiment probably resulted from the same type of empirical, border-crossing thinking that had driven Smeaton to examine the hydraulic characteristics of his cements a century before. The result surpassed both the curing speed and the ultimate strength of previous products and approximated the characteristics of our modern cement. Johnson later admitted that he had tried to spy out William Aspdin's improved method, which his firm had not succeeded in licensing in 1845. Aspdin's product certainly led Johnson to search, but his discovery was even better than what he had been trying to copy.

White manufactured the new product alongside his others and Vicat wrote on cements made from vitrified clay, but it was Johnson who exploited the material commercially.[93] He left White's firm in 1850 and bought the Aspdin Ord and Company plant.[94] His stronger, quick-setting cement quickly replaced all older products in Europe, but an abundance of inexpensive American natural cements delayed industrial development there, and high-quality cement had to be imported for many years.[95]

Meanwhile, many builders experimented with the material. John Rennie found that an accidentally tipped load of mortar stabilized the Thames bed while he excavated the foundations for Waterloo Bridge in London in 1812. He told Sir Robert Smirke, who used concrete to save the sinking foundations of the Millbank Penitentiary in 1817. It worked so well that Smirke used it for the foundations of all his later buildings, including the British Museum (1823–1847).[96]

Prefabrication was another area in which builders could use the material. Artificial stone had been popular for garden sculpture, balustrades, and fountains in the baroque period.[97] In 1832 and 1834 Ranger cast structural blocks and used them in several buildings.[98] The product was not reliable, and the seawalls he built at Chatham and Woolwich had to be refaced in granite after a very short time.[99] Harbor engineers were therefore understandably prejudiced against the blocks. Their dislike only dissipated as familiarity with the material grew and allowed better control.

Concrete blocks, unlike bricks, can be made in any size. Léopold-Victor Poirel built his first quay in Algiers in 1833 using large blocks that he towed into position in specially built barges.[100] Poirel had better luck than Ranger and built quays all over France; from there his industrialized method spread to Germany, Britain, and the United States.[101] Modular panels were more complex to produce and use. They had to be connected together to form a system, which required a different kind of design thinking than simple blocks did. But by 1860 the French firm Lippmann, Schneckenburger et Compagnie was exporting prefabricated houses using a surprisingly sophisticated composite reinforced hollow-slab system.[102] As a contemporary described it,

> The inventors used their artificial stone to make decorated and portable hollow slabs for house construction. The hollow slabs have internal, iron, sheet metal, brick, or hollow-tile frames which make them light as well as strong. The slab edges are rabbeted and have internal means to facilitate erection and sealing. Since these houses are mobile, they can be exported.
>
> J. Henriques Moron, a wealthy Indian businessman and Brazilian Consul General on St. Thomas, suggested manufacturing the first Similipierre and Similimarbre structures for export. Alfred Bing Jr. first assembled and exported them. This clever exporter chartered the French steamer "*Elizabeth*" in April 1860 and sent the *first portable* houses completely manufactured in France to distant lands.
>
> Since then, several Similipierre and Similimarbre houses have been shipped to other colonies.[103]

From Monolithic Appearance to Monolithic Structure

Component systems were soon overshadowed by monolithic construction, however. Iron-reinforced stone, a truly monolithic material with controllable physical characteristics, turned out to be one of the most far-reaching developments in nineteenth-century building materials. It encouraged builders to develop new structural forms like three-dimensional frames, cantilevers, or membranes that could resist tension, compression, torsion, shear, and even bending.

The idea for improving the structural behavior of concrete by combining it with other materials is ancient. Vitruvius described bath ceilings suspended from embedded iron or bronze bars, and German baroque architects cast plaster vaults on iron bars suspended from roof trusses. Builders also cast concrete floors on timber beams, as in the two-millennia-old, second-story balconies still to be seen in the lower Via dell'Abbondanza in Pompei or the later, flexible terrazzo floors of Venetian *piani nobili*.[104] From the late Roman period to the baroque, masons also embedded horizontal and vertical logs in walls for tensile and shear strength. Sometimes they fixed iron bars to the logs and anchored them through to the outside of the building to tie perpendicular walls firmly together. Several logs could be cross-tied together or braced to make elaborate mortised frames that stiffened domes and arches or whole buildings against seismic forces.[105] Many medieval churches could not have stood without timber reinforcement in their arcades, vaults, and towers before the twelfth century, when iron tension members began to replace them.[106] Medieval European flat vaulting techniques also used timber members. One form, called *antuada* in the Italian alpine province of Sondrio and *volta plana* in the adjacent Swiss Poschiavo Valley, is made by wedging stones tightly between parallel, closely spaced joists of inverted voussoir-shaped cross section.[107] The wedging transforms most of the bending stress along the beams into thrust on the walls parallel to them. All of these highly developed masonry systems were composite, but none of them behaved monolithically.

Marc Brunel therefore followed a long tradition when he used iron post-tensioning rods to reinforce the brick and mortar cylinder of his open caisson for sinking the first shaft of the Thames Tunnel in 1824.[108] Brunel was an accomplished technological thinker who translated solutions from one technical field to another, as we shall have occasion to see later on.[109] He set up a series of experiments in which he embedded various materials including iron in a mix of two parts Roman Cement and one part sand. He then built a testing machine to pull them out while his assistant Richard Beamish tabulated the results.[110] The cement adhered to the iron as well as to the brick and bonded everything solidly together.[111] Brunel, who was searching for an inexpensive way to line the Thames Tunnel at the time, then asked the firm of Francis and White to build two opposing, iron-reinforced brick cantilevers with arched soffits.[112] He wanted to compare the tensile strength of Francis and White's Roman Cement with Blashfield's. Brunel first built the structure symmetrically, with two c. twelve-meter arms. He then extended one arm by half as much again and counterbalanced it with a load on the other. The test structure stood in a cellar at Nine Elms, south of the Thames, from 1832 until 1834. According to Henry Law, who was a ten-year-old apprentice on the tunnel, excavation near the support caused the structure to crack so badly that he could see light through the fissure, and only the reinforcement held it up. According to some, it failed when the roof collapsed on it, though Law wrote that water froze in the fissures and finally broke off the

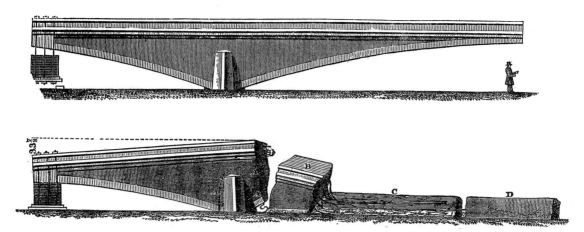

30.
Marc Brunel's double brick cantilever had iron bands mortared into its bedding joints. He may have intended to use the system in the Thames Tunnel, but there is no record that he did so. (*Rudiments of Civil Engineering,* 1862, part 2, chap. 4, pp. 134–135.)

longer arm.[113] The following year, Brunel used iron bands again to build a reinforced brick beam using Francis and White's cement. He cured it for eighteen months and tested it to destruction.[114]

Not only did Brunel use iron to enhance mortar's tensile strength, he also used iron bands in another original way to reinforce the tunnel face when he replaced the original tunneling shield with a second one in 1835–1836. He embedded hoop iron bands in earth to stabilize the soil in front of the shield. He surely knew that the iron would not bond with the clay, sand, and gravel mix as it did with cement. But he still tried the idea, refusing to accept that it was conceptually illogical. Just as he had done previously in his mortar tests, he tested the efficacy of the bands by pulling them out.[115] He translated the reinforcing technique from one situation and material to another, and it worked. The technique, now called "soil nailing," was one of Brunel's ingenious associative leaps of matrix thinking, which allowed him to translate technology from one field to another.

In these experiments Brunel was looking for a way to reinforce earth or brickwork, not cement, so the implications of his experiments for monolithic stone construction were not immediately apparent.[116] Nevertheless, they probably served as inspiration for Pasley and Frost's experimental brick beams at Chatham in 1837.[117] Pasley placed two iron bands in the top and bottom bedding joints and one in the middle. Another reinforced hollow-brick beam, built by J. B. White and Sons, was the most attractive of all the concrete exhibits at the Crystal Palace in 1851. It was ten bricks high, made with Aspdin's patent cement, and was otherwise similar to Brunel's and Pasley's. Originally, White's beam was supposed to have fifteen iron bands

31.
Like Pasley before him,
Marc Brunel tested brick
beams in bending, but he reinforced his with iron. (*Allgemeine Bauzeitung*, vol. 3,
1838, plate 201.)

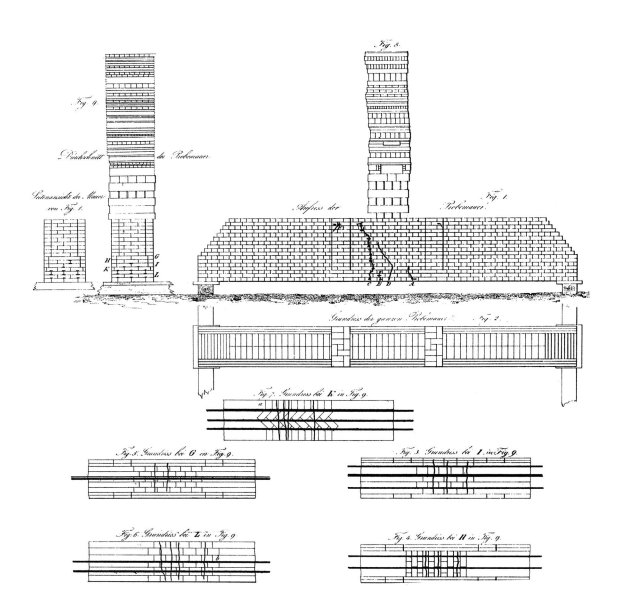

Structural Materials, Methods, and Systems

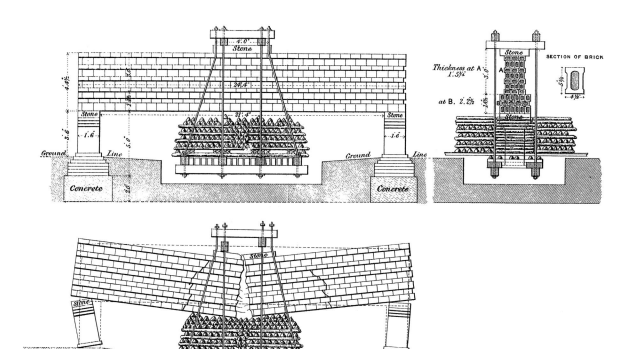

32.
Inspired by Marc Brunel's experiments, J. B. White and Sons exhibited a reinforced hollow-brick beam at the Crystal Palace and tested it to destruction at the end of the exhibition. (*Min. Proc. ICE*, vol. 11, 1852, plate 5.)

placed in the bedding joints of its tension zone, but workmen erroneously placed several of the bands above the neutral axis.[118] Nevertheless, when the beam was tested to destruction in the presence of the jury at the end of the exhibition it still withstood almost four times the 7.5-tonne load it had supported for several months.[119]

True reinforced concrete finally grew out of the search for monolithic floor construction. But builders had to resolve four issues before they could accept a conglomerate of iron rods and concrete as monolithic. The first issue was resolved when they applied the theoretical model of bending in beams and placed the iron rods in the tension zone of concrete cross sections. The second was taken care of when they recognized that hydraulic cement protects iron from rusting, which guaranteed the permanence of the rods embedded in concrete. They resolved the third when they realized that iron and hydraulic cement bond well enough to prevent the two materials from shearing apart when a beam or slab is loaded, and the fourth when experiments showed identical coefficients of thermal expansion for the two materials.

In 1826, C. M. L. Henri Navier popularized the interpretation of bending in a beam as the result of the moment created by a longitudinal, eccentric pair of tensile and compressive stresses.[120] The previous year he had written a report on a proposal for an underspanned suspension bridge at Fribourg, Switzerland. In it he suggested reinforcing the bridge piers vertically with iron so that their entire cross section could resist buckling stresses.[121] His suggestion showed a clear understanding that bending or buckling can be seen as the result of a pair of tension and compression forces, and he allocated each type of stress to a material ideally suited to counteract it. It took many years, however, before this conclusion permeated building practice.

In 1831 Vicat proved the second fact, that hydraulic mortar protects iron from rust.[122] He noted that the chemical action of the cement even reduced light rust. True as this was, it nevertheless proved disastrous for French wire cable suspension bridges. Vicat recommended that engineers grout their bridge cables directly into the ground rather than attach them to wrought-iron anchor bars. Although individual wires embedded in cement do not rust under laboratory conditions, the grout surrounding large cables shrinks, and cables vibrate in use; both phenomena cause cracking, which traps water between the wires.[123] This caused the cables to rust and fail.

Vicat was a practicing engineer, but as a researcher he focused on gaining new knowledge of materials and insight into concrete's behavior. When studying cement, he did not focus on making a functioning object as a technologist would. That is why he ignored the important issue of scale and

Structural Materials, Methods, and Systems

neglected to translate his laboratory model into a full-scale structure under field conditions. Issues of scale are questions that technological thinkers must routinely deal with. The uneasy relationship between the scientific mode of thought and practical technological thought patterns that led Vicat to misinterpret the practical application of his laboratory results has characterized civil engineering research from that day to this.

Eight years later the Institution of Civil Engineers also recognized the rust-protective qualities of hydraulic cement when they examined some cement-covered iron hoops that had successfully resisted corrosion since 1811.[124] Nevertheless, practitioners and building officials alike remained skeptical until the rust-reducing characteristics of portland cement were finally proved at the turn of the century.[125]

All this was of no practical use without the possibility of a bond between concrete and iron. This third issue was resolved by chance observations rather than formal experiments. When Pasley carried out his tensile experiments, he observed that cement adhered to polished granite as well as it did to roughened, soaked limestone, and when Marc Brunel experimented with mortars for lining the Thames Tunnel, he discovered that cement and iron bonded solidly.[126] His son Isambard, the resident engineer on the tunnel, also observed that the shovels used for mixing cement were almost impossible to cleanse after they had been left coated overnight.[127] An American working in London, Thaddeus Hyatt, showed the strength of the bond experimentally between 1855 and 1878, and he also demonstrated the fourth criterion, that iron and concrete have equal coefficients of expansion.[128] When the warehouse of an alderman named Humphrey near London Bridge burned down in 1851, observant members of the Institution of Civil Engineers already realized that reinforced concrete resisted fire—which, in essence, meant the same thing.[129] But the evidence was circumstantial, and building officials still needed the security of controlled tests corroborated by the careful examination of the debris of fires in reinforced concrete buildings. Only then could they recognize the fact in construction practice.

While this quintessentially technological combination of empirical discovery and scientific research was taking place, practitioners slowly gathered experience in combining iron and concrete in structures. Marc Seguin used iron to fix Vicat's concrete to the stone base and fascias of suspension bridge piers.[130] Edgar Dobbs patented a system for combining iron and concrete, Ralph Dodd designed concrete floors on cast-iron tubes similar to Venetian terrazzo systems, James Frost proposed a similar arrangement using beams instead of tubes, and John Claudius Loudon reinforced a concrete floor with iron laid crosswise in two directions.[131] But no one exploited these ideas.

Henry Hawes Fox, a Bristol physician, may have been the first actually to build an iron and concrete floor system, which he installed in his private sanitarium near Bristol in 1834.[132] Fox laid boards, slate, or other material between cast-iron joists and cast a layer of coarse mortar and a deep floor of concrete over them. He then finished the floors with traditional flooring and the soffits with a plaster ceiling. Fox wanted fireproof construction, not monolithic structure.[133] He only patented the system in 1844, probably at the urging of engineer and contractor James Barrett, who subsequently bought the rights. The Fox system was less expensive to build than iron joists with tile arches. Barrett knew that concrete had proved fire resistant in the 1851 Humphrey fire and claimed that its use would therefore also lower fire insurance premiums. He also correctly predicted that his system would spread.[134] Sixty years later, in 1909, the Barrett Manufacturing Company was still advertising "Barrett Specification Roofs" in eleven American cities and in London.[135]

Barrett initially presented the system in a brief comment to the Institution of Civil Engineers in 1849 and read a lengthy paper on improvements he had made since then in 1853.[136] He used cast- or wrought-iron beams, joists, and girders. Sometimes the girders lay half embedded in the concrete and half exposed below, sometimes they were fully incorporated. He reported that the fully embedded type reduced floor vibrations in the Royal Porcelain Works in Worcester and wind-induced vibration in the New Hotel in Carlisle.[137] Others had already observed the sound- and waterproof characteristics of concrete construction, and the acknowledged bond between the materials was claimed to resist the expansion of iron, an oblique acknowledgment of the equal coefficients of thermal expansion.[138] Barrett used wrought-iron plate girders and I-beams with cast-iron joists in his addition to Guy's Hospital, London in 1852. The top two thirds of the girders were embedded in the concrete floor.[139] Barrett observed that the loadbearing capacity increased when he poured the concrete around the ironwork:

> The strips, or pipes, form the ground-work of a continuous strut, which is completed by the subsequent application of the mortar and concrete: the latter completely imbedding the whole of the iron work. . . . Thus it will be seen, that the force of compression acts upon the joists, only through the medium of the concrete, and this material is well known to be one of the best for resisting that force. The extent of addition, to the original strength of the joists, by firmly fixing the ends, and then by the perfect union and combination, obtained in the process of construction, has not been ascertained . . .

Structural Materials, Methods, and Systems

In assuming 25 per cent., as the gain in strength, a low estimate is taken, for an increase of twice this, or 50 per cent., is commonly reckoned as due to the firmly fixing of a beam alone, while
the great principle of this system is the gradual development of
strength and firmness; the effect of the load being transferred,
through the medium of the concrete, to the walls, or other vertical
supports; the entire floor becoming, in effect, one solid slab, or
beam, with iron ribs.[140]

These remarks were of import for the future, since they marked the
earliest known observation of the loadbearing capabilities and the monolithic
behavior of the composite material. In recognition of what they perceived to
be the importance of his work, the Institution awarded him the 1853 Telford
Prize for his paper. But it was to be years before Barrett's observations were
confirmed by official experiments. Most builders conservatively calculated as
though the load lay entirely on the beams and regarded the concrete as fill.
Nevertheless, the Fox-Barrett floor really behaved as a composite structure in
which the two components worked together.

Building thought did not develop in a linear fashion. Barrett failed
to pursue the consequences of his observation that his composite reinforced concrete floors carried more load than the iron alone. So when late
nineteenth-century professionals began to shift from monolithic form to monolithic structural behavior, few of them continued to develop composite systems, which were conceptually ambiguous and harder to grasp analytically
than monolithic ones. This is one instance where analysts and researchers
with their scientific methods and thought forms won out against the hybrid
technological thinkers in building and retarded a development that the analysts could not model adequately. It is only in recent years that composite systems have begun to resurface, especially in high-rise building construction.

Among the first to take a real step toward monolithic structure was
William Boutland Wilkinson, a British plasterer and manufacturer of artificial
stone in Newcastle. He began producing prefabricated window mullions,
coffered permanent shuttering for concrete ceilings, and other components
around midcentury. Wilkinson was the first known builder to utilize the full
potential of the combination of cast-in-place and prefabricated construction
and to bridge the gap between the two approaches.

In 1854 he patented the use of wire rope reinforcement in coffered
ceilings.[141] Wilkinson's technique and materials were technologically avant-
garde: even the wire ropes he used were a new industrial product.[142] He
draped them in the ribs of prefabricated, 23-centimeter coffered shuttering so

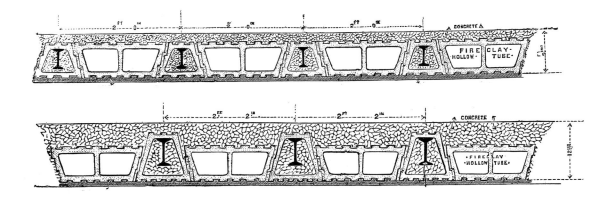

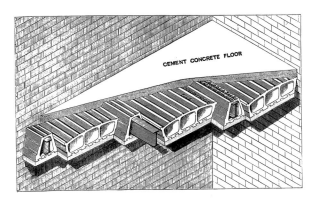

33.
An inventor named Hornblower made Fox and Barrett's floor system even lighter by using hollow block as permanent formwork. The Chicago Tribune Building had this type of flooring. It failed in the 1871 fire. (Henry Reid, 1879, pp. 278, 282, 285.)

Structural Materials, Methods, and Systems

that they corresponded precisely to the tension trajectories in the ribs. They lay near the bottom of the forms at midspan, gradually moving to the top where the coffered ceiling passed over walls. Wilkinson called the ropes "tension rods" in his patent, showing that he intuitively understood how reinforcement works many years before other builders did.[143] He cast truly monolithic floors only a sixteenth of a span thick. The firm still existed in Newcastle at the beginning of the twentieth century, with a branch office in London. But since Wilkinson was a contractor who did not read papers or publish, his achievement never attained the renown of the less sophisticated Fox-Barrett floor.

Several proprietary systems began to appear in Britain and France in the 1850s.[144] Like Wilkinson, François Coignet developed a comprehensive system with its own construction method in the space of a very few years. By 1855 he was ready to patent a fully developed reinforced concrete system in France and Britain using a mixer that made bulk concrete production easier for large sites.[145] Coignet periodically read progress reports to the Société des Ingénieurs Civils from 1855 on, wrote a brochure on his system in 1861, and exhibited models at the London Exhibition of 1862.[146] George Godwin, editor of *The Builder,* publicized Coignet's system in Britain and did much for its spread in that country. So, although his system was less refined than Wilkinson's, it became far better known, and Coignet received more important commissions. He built the lighthouse at Port Said in the late 1860s as well as many sewage and other conduits reinforced with wire mesh. He also proposed using reinforced concrete for large-span halls, but does not seem to have built any himself.[147] Several of his structures still stand, and one of his buildings was tested half a century later to validate Vicat's alleged rust protection.[148]

Hyatt began to coordinate his individual ideas into a system around the same time.[149] He published a report privately in London in 1877, but this small edition was poorly distributed and was ignored by the profession. Hyatt solved several basic problems of reinforced concrete construction, and many of his inventions predated what were to be later recognized as seminal improvements.[150]

Shuttering systems and mixers appeared in increasing profusion during the second half of the century. Patents were licensed willy-nilly, and clever entrepreneurs profited from the boom. One of them, Joseph Monier, licensed his primitive patents in Austria and Germany in 1880 and 1881 and then sold the rights to several firms.[151] Many of his inventions had been presaged by Joseph-Louis Lambot's alleged planters (1845), and some had even been patented, like Coignet's conduits (in the 1860s) or Matthew Allen's stairs (1862). The fact that Monier could patent them at all was a sign of the confused state of the field.[152]

34.
François Coignet's reinforced concrete lighthouse at Port Said (1868). (Figuier, *Nouvelles Conquêtes de la Science*, 1883–1885, vol. 4, frontis.)

G.FRAIPONT

Structural Materials, Methods, and Systems

Gustav Adolf Wayss, who had founded a contracting firm in Germany in 1879, saw Monier's work at an Antwerp exhibition and took out a license on his German patents. Wayss soon angered Monier by placing his reinforcement in the tension zone instead of in the centroid of the cross section as described in the patent specifications.[153] Nevertheless, Wayss continued to advertise Monier as the "inventor" of reinforced concrete to enhance his firm's image and secure a public relations advantage over the many other systems that were beginning to appear on the market. Wayss's claim was spurious, and many of Monier's patents were quickly challenged and revoked. But the ploy worked, and Wayss was able to build a large firm that still exists under the name of Wayss & Freytag.

As contractor for some of the floors in the new Berlin Reichstag in the mid-1880s, Wayss met the client's representative, Mathias Koenen. Koenen joined Wayss & Freytag as technical director and wrote in 1886 the earliest known mathematical analysis of reinforced concrete, in which he developed tentative methods to dimension reinforced concrete structures.[154] Wayss republished this treatise in book form a year later. It was followed in 1902 by the more comprehensive *Der Betoneisenbau,* written by another employee of the firm, Emil Mörsch.[155] In France Paul Christophe published his book in 1899, followed by M.-A. Morel in 1902, while Albert Wells Buel and Charles Shattuck Hill published theirs in the United States two years later in 1904.

It was fireproofing, and not primarily its monolithic characteristics, that helped the new material spread. Eighteenth-century constructors had been disappointed in their hopes that iron would be fireproof. Toward the end of the nineteenth century builders had the same high hopes for reinforced concrete. Theaters, with their long record of destructive fires, began to use reinforced concrete around 1860 in France, and the fire at the Ringtheater in Vienna in 1881 promoted its use in the German-speaking world. Other places of public congregation followed.[156] Engineers prized reinforced concrete for its economy in large-scale building, where its monolithic qualities helped save weight. It found acceptance in "facilities" such as water reservoirs or factories, but slower recognition in representative structures. Everything of representational character continued to hide the novel monolithic structure behind traditional stone cladding.[157]

The French contractor François Hennebique was especially successful in promoting reinforced concrete. He built a world-spanning industry by licensing a conglomerate of patents that he melded into a coherent system between 1880 and 1890. Hennebique collected the results of several years of experimental work in a comprehensive patent in 1887. Although much of his work can be traced to earlier inventors, it was the system and the method he developed for licensing it and controlling his intercontinental corporation that made him so influential. He was able to repatent two of Hyatt's seminal inventions, the T-beam and the hoop for making framing cages, under his own name and develop the reinforced concrete cantilever that would influence architectural and engineering form so strongly. Hennebique built his first concrete-frame factory in Lille in 1893. His many licensees modified and propagated the type and developed it into the prototype of the modern reinforced concrete frame.[158]

Although small contractors were most often the inventors and pioneers, large contractors promoted the spread of reinforced concrete.[159] Even before methods were developed to analyze the material, the large firms had the advertising and public relations potential to be able to convince manufacturers and conservative public officials to build structures in reinforced concrete. But it was only with the acceptance of new theories of monolithic structural behavior, their methods of analysis and dimensioning, and the codes provoked by the 1901 collapse of a Hennebique structure, the Hotel zum Goldenen Bären in Basel, that the profession really began to appreciate and use with confidence the material-, weight-, and labor-saving advantages of contiguous structure.[160] New forms gradually emerged based on this confidence, appearing first in the work of contractors, engineers, and architects with a special interest in structure.[161]

Following Hennebique's example were other system builders like Ernest Ransome, who patented formwork, floors, and details and developed his own reinforced concrete system, supported by six patents, in 1902.[162] Ransome's system influenced the spread of reinforced concrete in the United States more than the many European systems that were introduced over the years.[163] By 1904 eleven companies were using it.[164] However, a strong indigenous steel industry and the lack of high-quality cement until 1895 hampered the spread of reinforced concrete in the United States. A group of engineers and contractors did build concrete grain elevators across the northern United States and Canada, and a group of architects designed several reinforced concrete buildings in the cities of Ohio, including the sixteen-story Ingalls Building (1902–1903) using Ransome's system, but concrete remained a secondary structural material in the United States until recently.[165]

3

The Human Element: Manual Work, Mechanization, Progress, and Technological Thought

Forms and methods changed as mechanization and rationalization progressed in nineteenth-century building. There was no deterministic mechanism or simplistic causal relationship that made these changes happen; it was not a linear process.[1] Human thought, action, reaction, and prejudice, based on personal experience or vicariously transmitted through education, drove these developments. The decision-making process depends on value judgments, and evaluation is basically culturally conditioned, although it is refined through professional experience.[2] Builders had to categorize and assign relative value to the different aspects of what they did and what they intended to do. But when they applied rational, industrial principles to human labor and attitudes, they also raised a tangle of political and social issues that went beyond rational argument.

Machinery fascinated nineteenth-century people. They valued the self-acting prime mover as an icon of their age independently of the material advantages it could provide. Movement, noise, steam, and power were expressions of progress to them. The English writer Samuel Smiles idealized technological invention, lauding its values in his morally loaded engineering biographies and in his book *Self Help,* which went through edition after edition. Architectural theoreticians like Gottfried Semper or William Vose Pickett and journalists like Lothar Bucher praised the "new" materials iron and glass and hoped for a renewal of architectural form based on their use. In their enthusiasm they chose to see only the advantages the mechanized world would bring.

There was also a countercurrent that developed in reaction to their exaggeration and that celebrated only hallowed cultural traditions. Its proponents refused to recognize technology as an emerging thought form and as the benchmark of modern culture. They relegated the new and brash world of "civilization" to the realm of low-class, social-climbing vulgarity and saw only the loss of inherited values. Though they realized that they were losing the battle, they fought to stem the barbaric tide and hoped for a better day.

Strangely enough, these conservatives continued to influence educational curricula and accepted social values despite excluding technology. Pockets of admiration for technology did develop among conservatives, especially among industrialists and engineers. They became visible in minor ways, above all in the young United States, which was home to periodicals like *Scientific American* and, later, *Popular Mechanics*.[3] But even *Scientific American,* which was the more highbrow of the two, retrogressed into popular science at the beginning of the twentieth century and ceased to pursue its original technological bent quite so vigorously.

John Ruskin, one of the most influential cultural theoreticians in the nineteenth century, typified the reactionary forces. He fought vehemently against love of the machine and all the evils it symbolized to him. One of his biographers preserved an eloquent and graphic image of his protest:

> Mr. Ruskin was expatiating, as was his wont, on the vandalism of the modern world. On an easel beside him was a water-colour drawing by Turner of (I think) Leicester. "The old stone bridge is picturesque," he said, "isn't it? But of course you want something more 'imposing' nowadays. So you shall have it." And taking his paint-box and brush, Mr. Ruskin rapidly sketched in on the glass what is known in modern specifications as a 'handsome iron structure'. "Then," he continued, "you will want, of course, some tall factory chimneys, and I will give them to you galore." Which he proceeded to, in like fashion. "The blue sky of heaven was pretty, but you cannot have everything, you know." And Mr. Ruskin painted clouds of black smoke over the Turner sky. "Your 'improvements'," he went on, "are marvelous 'triumphs of modern industry', I know; but somehow they do not seem to produce nobler men and women, and no modern town is complete, you will admit, without a gaol and a lunatic asylum to crown it. So here they are for you." By which time not an inch of the Turner drawing was left visible under the "improvements" painted upon the glass. "But for my part," said Mr. Ruskin, taking his sponge, and with one pass of the hand wiping away those modern improvements against which he has inveighed in vain in so many printed volumes — "for my part, I prefer the old."[4]

The ultimate symbol of progress was the smoking factory chimney, and Ruskin understood how to dramatize his viewpoint by contrasting an idyll with Dickensian horrors. He expressed his fears for the future of cul-

The Human Element

ture; flying as they did in the face of accepted thinking, they shocked his audience. Ruskin used a Turner watercolor to dramatize his picture of "paradise lost," but Turner's own industrial vision had contrasted with his champion's disgust.[5] In 1846, a good thirty years before Ruskin's lecture, he produced one of his most famous canvases, *Rain, Steam and Speed*, a hymn to progress and the railway. Regarding this painting Sir Kenneth Clark noted, "I suppose that everybody today would accept it as one of the cardinal pictures of the nineteenth century, on account of its subject as well as its treatment. One must think back to a time when most sensitive men, Ruskin above all, felt that railways were an abomination."[6]

Smoke, steam, and speed: Ruskin's abhorrence of these symbols was emotional and intuitive. Technology destroyed much that he treasured, and Ruskin feared a progress gone rampant. His protest lay in the period in which the concept of progress began to be doubted, whereas Turner's painting lay earlier and under the influence of progress felt as pathos.

35.
A late nineteenth-century engraving of William Turner's celebrated 1845 oil painting *Rain, Steam and Speed*. (Routledge, 1901, p. 1.)

Mechanization and Progress

An eighteenth-century steam engine was a slow and clumsy mover built of
traditional materials. It was anchored solidly in the earth, and its pulse and
sighing sound resembled animal or human respiration. By the beginning of
the new century Richard Trevithick's high-pressure engine had transformed
the steam engine into a formidable iron-bound, quick, precise, and hectic
monster.[7] Its many moving parts graphically demonstrated the transformation of caloric into kinetic energy.[8]

Mechanization was identical with progress to a nineteenth-century
way of thinking. As long as an industry used manual or animal labor, mechanization remained an untapped potential.[9] The cost of labor, plant, and transportation and the lack of education and organization in the workforce usually
tipped the balance in favor of manual methods. But as soon as an engineer
chose to mechanize a process for whatever reason, the tangled structure of
financing the change and the need for plant amortization, specialized labor,
and energy manufacture prevented any return to manual technology. It was a
one-way street, a process that could not be easily reversed.

There were many reasons that could make an engineer prefer a
mechanized method. Strikes, for instance, were a problem for American contractors because labor was always in short supply. American industrialists
therefore exploited every opportunity to mechanize, even where capital was
scarce. This forced development influenced the way technologists thought
about manufacturing and building processes and quickly brought the poor
and newly independent nation to the forefront of industrial development.
In a few decades it even surpassed in some areas rich and industrialized England, which was reduced to trying to catch up to its former colony, with
only mixed success.

Early nineteenth-century workers formed clandestine unions to try
to protect their interests. Social conditions were miserable, though responsible employers tried to do what they could. Their philanthropy worked to
mitigate the lack of system in ways that are foreign to us. Considering the social environment in which he lived, Marc Brunel was progressive in 1812
when he advocated child labor as a major advantage of a sawmill he built:

> To these important economic advantages to the public was added
> the high gratification to Brunel himself of being able to employ chil-
> dren in the manufactory. The love of the young was a distinguishing
> and abiding feature in Brunel's character; and now, after a few

36.
An eighteenth-century
steam engine was fixed to
its site and built of traditional materials. Its pulse
was slow and it sounded
like a sighing animal. Its
nineteenth-century counterpart was quick, light, portable, and noisy. (Tomlinson,
1852, vol. 1, facing p. 391;
Illustrated Exhibitor, 1851,
p. 370.)

hours' instruction and one day's practice, he had the happiness to reflect, that for a large number of these special objects of his sympathy
he had provided the means of earning an honest and sufficient
livelihood.[10]

This form of philanthropy had, of course, a delaying effect on the full mechanization or automation of industrial processes, and it influenced inventors
and responsible manufacturers when they thought about technology and
how to use it in relation to human labor.

While they may have tried to help the workers on their own terms,
industrialists fought worker organization, because they felt that it hindered
them in the free exercise of their options. Most European labor unions were
illegal in the 1830s.[11] The Chartist riots and strikes (1838–1842) gave British laborers their first real bid for power. The Manchester liberals inadvertently supported them by opposing the Corn Laws and striving to abolish
the economic advantages landed farmers held over industry and commerce.
The Corn Laws were repealed in 1846. Revolutions broke out all over continental Europe in 1848 and 1849. But any advantages workers may have
gained were temporarily obliterated by the triumph of the merchant and industrialist class, Karl Marx's bourgeoisie.[12] Workers had little political influence and could not protect their interests. Their only recourse was to destroy
the machines that threatened to make them redundant, and the ensuing anti-
machine riots gave labor movements a bad name.

Violence was an old problem in European labor relations, and fear
was not confined to any one country. From the seventeenth century on riots
occurred wherever mechanization threatened traditional labor environments.
The best-known examples are British: the protest against a Dutch entrepreneur who tried to introduce a sawmill around 1663; the riot against John
Kay, inventor of the flying shuttle, who had to flee from a group of angry
weavers in 1753; the destruction of John Houghton's sawmill at Limehouse
in 1768; and the colliery laborers' riot against John Curr when he introduced
cast-iron rails in mines in 1776.[13] The Luddite riots of 1811–1812 in northern England were followed by the agricultural riots of 1830, in which agricultural steam engines were destroyed. But there were instances of machine
smashing in other countries, too, for instance when a group of sailors, fearful
of losing their jobs, destroyed Denis Papin's steamship in 1707, and when
workers resisted mechanical printing in Turkey, the ribbon loom in the Papal
States, or the erection of a crane in Strassbourg.[14]

Resistance to mechanical innovation was usually far less dramatic
and individual acts of sabotage rarely made the press, but this type of resis-

37.
Fearing for their jobs,
angry sailors demolished
Denis Papin's steamship at
Münden, Germany, in
1707. (Figuier, *Merveilles
de la Science,* 1868–1870,
vol. 1, p. 57.)

tance was more pervasive. The mobile, disenfranchised railway navvies, as the
itinerant British construction workers were called, were a cohesive group.
Any suspicion of an attack on their livelihood made them stop the mechanization of large British building sites for decades. Around the middle of the century, they repeatedly broke the mechanical winches that the contractors had
tried to install to reduce accidents.[15] Railway builders were unable to introduce American steam shovels for the same reason. William S. Otis's twenty-
horsepower steam shovels appeared in America in 1839 and quickly became
popular there, but British contractors used very few until 1875, when Sir
Alexander Rendel's Albert Docks in London finally became the first British
building site to rely extensively on mechanized means.[16] Coleman suggests
that contractors remained conservative as long as they did not suffer financially and were able to find sources of cheap labor,[17] but it was sociological
more than technological or financial reasons that prevented British builders
from taking advantage of site mechanization. British railway companies were
well organized and highly capitalized in the early part of the century. They
were lucrative and expanding businesses.[18] Paying £1,500, or one to three
percent of a typical contract, for a steam shovel would surely have been a
worthwhile risk if it promised quicker completion. The price would have
presented even less of a risk on larger jobs like Sir Samuel Peto's £900,000
contract with the Southampton-Dorchester Line, which employed several
thousand navvies.

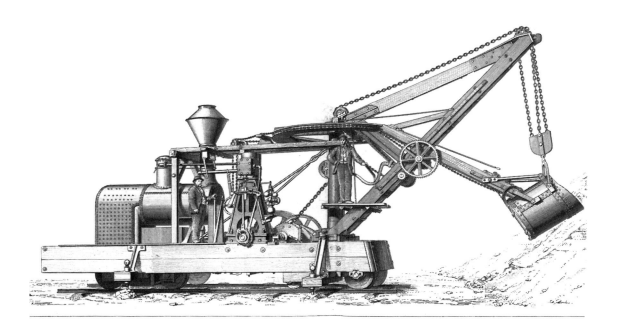

38.
American contractors and laborers both welcomed mechanization. The "steam-shovel" was simply a tool to them. The British called it a "steam-navvy" and used it to replace itinerant building workers, which explains why British workers resisted it. (Malézieux, 1873, plate 37.)

It took decades for builders to introduce steam-powered construction machines into Britain on a large scale, although it wasn't for lack of trying. John Weale wrote about the steam shovel in 1843 and Joshua Barrows Hyde in 1845; both insisted it would save time. The "excavator," as it was first innocuously called, was tried with success on the Eastern Counties Railway, but as Sir John Rennie admitted, it was "not as yet much employed."[19] His father, John Rennie, had used steam-powered pile drivers to advantage as early as 1801 in the coffer dam for the London Docks and again at Sunderland.[20] Peto Brassey and Betts's employees used steam shovels on the Grand Trunk Railroad in Canada, and Thomas Brassey had used steam-powered cranes for lifting earth directly into carts on the Northern Mid-Level Sewer in London.[21] The technology was known and admittedly successful. But the contrasting terms "steam shovel," used in the United States, and "steam navvy," as it came to be called in Britain, well characterized the sociological differences between the two countries and the problem. The one expression described a tool and the other the replacement of a workman.[22]

Well before midcentury, Britain began to slip behind the United States in construction technology and metalworking machinery. David Stevenson's 1838 report on technology in the United States was a somewhat bemused but admiring paean to the Rube Goldberg–like technological wonders he encountered there.[23] When an imported British traveling steam crane didn't work on the Victoria Bridge site in Montreal in 1854, the engineers installed a North American one that did. How could it be that a higher standard of mechanization existed in the struggling, former renegade colony than in the wealthy center of world industry? Sir Arthur Helps speculated in 1872 that border crossing seemed to have fostered the ingenuity of English mechanics when they emigrated to the new continent.[24]

Border crossing, literal and figurative, is typical of creative thinking in many fields, including technology. Many English workmen found themselves sociologically and psychologically liberated when they emigrated to North America, and that freed their innovative drive. American contractors and workmen immediately embraced any form of mechanization, whereas British and most other European contractors chose to avoid the issue because workers resisted it. It was a vicious cycle: wherever builders could accelerate the building process without curtailing profits by increasing their workforce, they did. Labor was relatively abundant in Britain before midcentury. Artisans and navvies alike were financially and socially inhibited from changing their status. American workers were less class-bound and intellectually freer in the nineteenth century; they could move on to colonize new land or change profession and find work anywhere. Those in Britain who did break out of the ancestral mold frequently came from border regions like the counties of Shropshire or Durham, or from Scotland, Wales, Ireland, or from abroad, where border crossing liberated them from their traditional social bonds. Most of these changed their social class too. Rarely in the Industrial Revolution did a British inventor or industrialist spring from an upper-class milieu or come from the English heartland, whereas the equally new "class" of scientists, especially physicists, seemed mainly to come from the leisured classes of the eighteenth and nineteenth centuries.

The traditional British mistrust of mechanization and innovation came from a feeling that these were instigated by management to the disadvantage of labor, a feeling that continued to characterize labor relations in railways, newspaper industries, and dockyards until the middle of the twentieth century. American industrialists, on the other hand, sought to supplement scarce labor with machines, and American workmen and laborers never developed an antagonistic relationship toward industrialization or mechanization.[25] Even during the quickly suppressed workers' movements that arose between the late 1870s and the first years of the twentieth century, American workers never saw the machine as belonging to "them," meaning the boss or the capitalist, before World War II. On the contrary, it was seen as a harbinger of democracy, as having facilitated independence from colonial tyranny. Mechanically produced weapons certainly had strengthened the young republic, and the inventor is considered an American folk hero to this day. American working-class attitudes toward mechanization, so different from those of British machine smashers, influenced the development of new construction methods.

Industrial Production and Construction

Americans had to rely on their own skills in colonizing new territories and wresting them from what the immigrants saw as wilderness or from an indigenous population. A do-it-yourself mentality was imperative for the colonists' survival. It was the antithesis of reliance on expert craftsmanship; Americans preferred simple construction technology because it needed little in the way of specialized knowledge. Highly refined solutions became the purview of the prefabrication industry, and American machine culture came to rely on interchangeable parts early in its development. It was an easy step from there to the concept of planned obsolescence, in which industry expanded the principle of interchangeability to encompass whole machines. As long as materials were abundant and cheap, it was considered more rational to exchange even a relatively simple part than to acquire the skill and knowledge to repair it. This principle applied not only to production machinery and vehicles but also to building. The American light-wood frame, with its standardized members, connectors, and nails, was one consequence of this mentality. The result of this outlook has been that the industrial replication of parts and their assembly into additive, repetitive forms still underlie American building design.

It is easier to enhance mechanical work than manual labor. Minor changes could make noticeable improvements: the replacement of a weak bolt in a steam shovel accelerated excavation at the Suez Canal, and the Panama Railway's spoil train dumped its load faster when the site engineer strengthened the link between the clearing plow and the dragline.[26] Mechanical improvement is only limited by human ingenuity, which represents an entirely different category of limitation than human or animal power. As nineteenth-century builders shifted their focus from the building as an object to the process of its creation, they used mechanical means to increase productivity and developed organizational structures to control and manipulate construction. Clients forced them to be inventive by demanding deadlines and enforcing these with fines and premiums.

Production quality was more important than speed in preindustrialized building. Commercial pressure made the sequence change and put the focus on speed. This had radical consequences in new areas like railway construction. Traditional building methods are not easy to accelerate or change.

Wherever they could, British contractors made it simple for themselves and increased their labor force. They put pressure on the workers and treated them as consumable machines.

> Whereas the long list of canal and road works for which Thomas Telford was responsible had been completed without a single serious accident, the railways were built at a terrible cost in human life. The reason for this was the rapid growth of commercialism which brought increasingly heavy pressure to bear on all ranks . . . forcing them to take risks in order to speed the day when a new line would begin to earn revenue. . . . What we now refer to as the commercial rat-race had already begun in early Victorian England, but because it had not yet produced ingenious machines to replace men, it took its toll in flesh and blood.[27]

This sad state of affairs was not always caused by a lack of appropriate machinery. Sometimes, as noted above in the case of the steam shovel, the machines were available but for psychological or social reasons were not used.

The limits of social tolerance were exceeded in one extreme case on the Woodhead railway tunnel (1839–1845). Site engineer Wellington A. Purdon was called to defend himself before a parliamentary Select Commons Committee against an accusation of irresponsible site management.[28] Purdon had neglected to adopt the simplest of safety measures to protect his workers during blasting. This was the most stressful period in Britain's railway development. The times were hectic and politically unsettled, engineers worked under pressure, and workmen felt they had been exploited long enough. The Chartist riots and their aftermath in northern England had split Parliament's sympathies. Purdon tried to convince the committee of why it was so important to save time in railway construction:

> In great railway works, the interest [upon the money borrowed] is so great when it is spread over a number of years, and the company sacrifice that interest until the line comes unto operation, and they bind their contractors to knock off the work quickly to save the enormous amount of interest; this requires them to man the works in a very masterly style.[29]

Like most of his contemporaries, Purdon used quantitative means to increase construction speed: increasing the number of man-hours. He also tried to increase efficiency by disregarding safety measures, replacing the copper stemmers by cheaper iron ones and omitting safety caps. Soft copper makes no sparks, but it takes a little longer to ram the powder charge home and place the caps. Purdon saved money but wasted thirty-two lives. The safer technology was usual at the time and the committee believed that there was no excuse for not using it.[30] When confronted with what he had done, and asked whether the safety caps would not have been less dangerous, Purdon callously replied: "Perhaps it is; but it is attended with such a loss of time, and the difference is so very small, I would not recommend the loss of time for the sake of all the extra lives it would save."[31]

Traditional forms of feudal responsibility had long since degenerated. They disappeared altogether with the population drift to urban centers, and that led to the de facto enslavement of the laborer. A workman no longer owed allegiance, and an employer was no longer answerable to anyone. There were notable exceptions, of course—people who felt obligated to take responsibility for their employees—but there was no social contract to underpin and enforce mutual responsibility, and the British engineer's lowly social standing did not encourage high ethical standards either.[32] Writers as diverse as Dickens and Engels tried to awaken the public's social conscience. Reformers saw an answer to the problem in Smiles's self-help and in the form of adult education that Ruskin and Robert Willis advocated. But even those who were not activists in those harsh times found Purdon's naive brutality scandalous.

The Purdon affair dramatized the need for a transition from quantitative to qualitative methods of improving the building process. Wherever builders lacked the organizational or technological means to improve their output they faced a grotesque equation between speed and human life. There had to be another way to satisfy the demands of commerce, and Robert Stephenson struggled to find one when he built the Conway and Britannia bridges a few years later. He faced the same financial criteria as Purdon, but what he did was revolutionary for the building industry. Stephenson solved the critical bottleneck in his building process by making the construction of the piers independent of the final design of the deck, and he separated the two into parallel construction sequences.[33] This was a qualitative way of manipulating the timeline, and it allowed him to produce an acceptable level of work and still meet his deadlines.

The Human Element

Gilbreth's Motion Studies

Early American builders like Ithiel Town also applied organizational principles to construction. They did this by standardizing simple connections and repeating them over and over again to create new structural types with desirable characteristics like redundancy. Builders were free to choose either organizational or mechanical means to enhance their building processes qualitatively. But once they chose machines to do the job, the die was cast and the investment they had made in plant, energy, and skilled labor made it impossible to revert to manual methods. Mechanization and organization are coupled, however, and the unstable equilibrium shifted toward mechanized solutions wherever special conditions or difficult sites increased the cost of feeding and housing laborers or where the press of a deadline made mechanization an attractive option. A site engineer could mechanize some parts of a process and leave others as before. The builders of the Crystal Palace used machines for component manufacture in 1850 and left their assembly to hordes of navvies. It was only when a bottleneck developed in the erection process that Charles Fox invented a method to speed erection.[34]

Today site managers have methods like teamwork, division of labor, piecework, and time-and-motion studies to help them decide between quantitative or organizational methods. These means can help them raise output within the parameters of the human "machine" and the human psyche. Such methods have their roots in the beginning of the twentieth century, when a new professional group called management consultants began to include the human being in the rationalization process. Their approach was the consequence of a search for economical working methods that had been gaining impetus for over fifty years in the writings of the Prussian military theoretician Carl von Clausewitz, the French engineering theoretician Charles Dupin, and the English mathematician and mechanical inventor Charles Babbage.[35] They took the final step by treating the laborer as a machine. Henri Fayol apparently invented the time-and-motion study in France in 1886, but since he only made it public in 1916, Frank Bunker Gilbreth could hardly have used it to develop his own form of motion study in the last years of the nineteenth century.[36] Gilbreth had just established himself as a building contractor when the other American pioneer in the field, Frederick Winslow Taylor, presented his paper "A Piece Rate System" based on his work in the steel industry in 1895.[37] Taylor went on to work with Sanford Thompson in concrete construction sometime before 1905 and met Gilbreth in December 1907.[38]

While Taylor concentrated on improving the time needed for a specific task, Gilbreth streamlined motion.[39] He modified Étienne-Jules Marey and Eadweard Muybridge's photographic methods.[40] He attached lights to laborers' limbs, traced their movements on film, and translated the diagrams into three-dimensional wire models for further study.[41] Taylor and Gilbreth's efforts culminated in time-and-motion studies, a new basis for objectively evaluating human labor. These men differed from earlier rationalizers only in their belief in an absolute configuration of criteria that they called "scientific" and that they were convinced would provide the "one best way."[42] Like Mahon a century and a half before, both of them used analytical methods to examine technological processes. Our unease with their work stems from the blindly positivist ethos it exuded and the callous, Purdon-like equivalence of machines and human beings. But Gilbreth was only being logical when he recognized that speed was essential to the economics of work.[43] Rationalization was the principle that took precedence over everything else, and the building process was a matter of rational management. Two factors made this form of manipulation possible: a lack of solidarity in immigrant American labor and the fiction of equal social standing. The very real social mobility in America dangled the promise of equal opportunity in front of everyone. Every worker dreamed of climbing to the position of his boss, and the "American dream" encouraged the laborer to look upon his social and economic condition as temporary. It was far easier to convince an American worker to identify with the goals of his firm and the aspirations of its owners than was possible in the more rigid frameworks of European society.

Gilbreth coined the term "speed work" to denote the quickest a laborer could accomplish work of the highest attainable quality. Machinery had become so reliable that the weakest link in any building process was now the human factor. Gilbreth recognized that workers are controlled not only by rational and measurable reactions but by psychological factors as well, and he built these into his speed work system.

His firm prospered as a result of his radical approach to manual work, and Gilbreth built factories, dams, canals, houses, and industrial complexes throughout the United States and in Britain. He carried out several turnkey projects, delivering factories to his clients complete with installations. Gilbreth pioneered advertising as well, and created the slogan "Gilbreth's Towns to Order."[44] He experimented with novel forms of corporate organization, attempting to define them on the lines of his rationalization studies.[45]

An industrialist acquaintance convinced him around 1906 that a system had to be written down to be really clear. Gilbreth had already used written and photographed building reports as a means to control his wide-ranging business, and from then on he supplemented them with written guidelines, both to standardize the building process and to gain quantifiable feedback from the site.[46] At first he kept the guidelines confidential as a company manual, but in 1908 he published them as *Field System*. Two further books followed: *Concrete System,* also in 1908, and *Bricklaying System* in 1909. He then left construction and expanded into general management consulting.

Gilbreth's were by no means the first building guidelines, but his books were among the first to specify each step of a method right down to individual hand movements. How much did Keyserling's ominous remarks on American expedience owe to the writings of people like Taylor and Gilbreth? Fritz Lang's film *Metropolis* (1926) and Charlie Chaplin's frightening image of individual impotence in *Modern Times* (1936) also reflect the general fear and disquiet that the mechanization of human labor evoked in many people—but not in Gilbreth himself. He was far less complicated and felt the need to accompany each dictum with an explanation and measurements. His standards were rigid, regulating the behavior of management and workmen alike. Along with Taylor and Ford, Gilbreth shaped the development of American manufacturing. The "how" entirely replaced the "what." His viewpoint dominated the building site and consolidated the changes that had been evolving for a century.

Gilbreth's *Field System* advocated a "suggestion system." "Members of the organization"—no one was called an employee—were encouraged to propose improvements and to identify themselves with the success of the firm. Gilbreth rewarded useful ideas and published them in the firm's newspaper. Participatory fictions like the one Gilbreth used remained rare in other societies, but they spread quickly through American industry and became a standard management tool.

"Speed building" expanded to include the whole firm hierarchy from management to labor and influenced the organization of Gilbreth's "field system."[47] Laborers unloaded bricks twice as fast as normal when he advertised an extra hour's wages for the quickest crew. In one case a team drove piles twenty percent faster simply because Gilbreth allowed them to fly their national flag from their rig for a day. Almost all construction workers were recent immigrants: all were proud of their ancestry, while paradoxically striving to lose their identity in the American melting pot. The paradox caused tension, and Gilbreth discovered that crews worked better when segregated in national groups.

The second book *Concrete System* was more focused and better grounded in practical experience than his first. Gilbreth dealt more with the rationalization of concreting methods than with the material or structural issues discussed in other early concrete treatises. He discussed designing building sites with the shortest paths for materials and workmen, provided information on where to expect procedural bottlenecks, and devised recipes for avoiding them.[48] He always looked at problems in the context of the whole process.

Gilbreth strove for complete control of the building process under all conditions and in all its aspects. He and his wife, Lillian Moller Gilbreth, examined resistance to sustained or repeated physical effort and fatigue. They examined stress and frustration caused by delays and particularly by the fear of temporary unemployment, for which there was no insurance at the time. They used these factors as arguments in support of rationalization, cleverly aligning the needs and demands of labor and management. The Gilbreths and Taylor carried forward the banner of "progress" and their belief in an abstract "scientific method" almost as a religion in a time in which many had skeptically abandoned them.

By 1909, in his book on bricklaying, Gilbreth was writing on professional training. He demanded simultaneous training for speed and economy of movement, which he claimed led most quickly to good professional work.[49] In the central chapter of this book, called "Motion Study," he brought his control of every movement to its peak. He described in detail how to hold a trowel, step rationally, and move the arm and the eye, and supported the learning process by an almost pavlovian system of competitions and rewards. The medieval guilds' rigid ways of training every aspect of a craft were nothing compared to Gilbreth's. The guilds had had neither the mechanistic nor the mechanical model to build upon, and they didn't have the concepts of progress and rationalization to dehumanize the learning process either. Gilbreth tried to extract the last ounce of systematization from his workers. Although he didn't put his workmen's lives in jeopardy like Purdon, men and machines were equivalent entities for him too.

We have now looked at the criteria of commerce, the élan of progress, the industrialization of material production, and the adaptation of the human participants in building. These were the factors that changed the building world and the way builders thought, and their development went through many steps. The following series of examples documents the major stages of this development and illustrates the complex interrelationship between thinking and building.

39.
Gilbreth choreographed his bricklayers down to their hand and foot movements. He wanted to optimize manual work as thoroughly as industrial production had been. (Gilbreth, *Bricklaying System*, 1909, p. 154.)

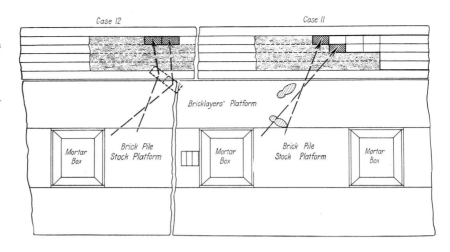

Part II   The Genesis of the Building Process

4

Worlds Apart: From the Thames to the Mont Cenis Tunnel

Building processes changed radically between the beginning and the end of the nineteenth century. In some cases we can narrow the window in which the changes occurred down to a small time period at midcentury, although the impact of innovation often took decades to spread. Tunnel engineering, for instance, changed radically in the few years that lay between the completion of the Thames Tunnel in 1843 and the start of the Mont Cenis Tunnel in 1857. The first project belonged socially, financially, and technologically very much to the *ancien régime* of building. It appears to us as though it were a haphazard affair. And yet its builder, Marc Brunel, was a capable professional. But in the decade between the two projects, new building technologies and new organizational thinking emerged. Intelligence and inventiveness hadn't changed, but the conceptual, financial, and social conditions in which they acted had.

Tunneling and mining are closely related fields. The irrigation and well tunnels of Babylon, Greece, and Palestine and the many different types of tunnels built by Roman engineers remain high achievements of manual excavation and subterranean surveying.[1] All of them, like the later Renaissance tunnels, were laboriously dug by hand.[2] The techniques engineers used didn't change much until François Andréossy used gunpowder to blast through soft limestone in the Languedoc Canal Tunnel at Malapas (1679–1681).[3]

Tunnels proliferated as canal construction began in the eighteenth century and traffic increased in the nineteenth. When barge traffic became so heavy in James Brindley's Harecastle Hill Tunnel on the Grand Trunk (Trent-and-Mersey) Canal that it turned into a bottleneck, the owners hired Telford in 1824 to drive a second tube next to the first.[4] It was the same year that Brunel began digging the Thames Tunnel. The proposed Liverpool and Midland railway put pressure on the board of directors, and they urged Telford to finish the work quickly. He manned the site day and night and finished it in three years. The sixty-nine-year-old Telford was unused to working under that kind of pressure, and also complained bitterly about another of his ongoing projects, the Saint Catherine Docks: "As a practical engineer, responsible for the success of difficult operations, I must be allowed to protest against such haste, pregnant as it was, and ever will be, with risks, which in more instances than one severally tasked all my experience and skill, involving dangerously the reputation of the directors and their engineer."[5] Telford's peaceful world had clashed with a new one, although neither he nor anyone else could recognize it then. The connection between time and money is so deeply ingrained today that we can hardly imagine that speed ever played a subordinate role in building. But it once did, and the shift in thinking that accompanied the change catapulted the West into world dominance in the nineteenth century. It created a gulf between cultures that participated and ones that didn't, and it distanced modern builders more effectively from traditional building than any previous event.

The Thames Tunnel (1824–1843) and the first great Alpine tunnel, the Mont Cenis under the Mont Thabor mountain chain (1857–1871), lay on opposite sides of this divide. Both of them were important in their day. Both were widely admired and quickly overshadowed by even more impressive feats. Both tunnels were long in the planning and completed far later than originally intended. But they differed not only in the methods their builders used, but in the criteria that drove them to build in the first place.

The Thames Tunnel in London was touted as the first subaqueous tunnel in the world. In fact, there had been several earlier ones. The Babylonian Euphrates and Roman Marseilles harbor tunnels were perhaps the most spectacular, but there were also a number of mines tunneled under the sea along the British coast in the eighteenth century, notably in Cumberland. But all, save perhaps the Babylonian, were through rock, not silt, and an attempt to tunnel the Severn at Newnham had failed for lack of funds.[6]

The Thames Tunnel was unique among traffic tunnels in that it was planned and built without being part of an existing transportation network. The exhilarating idea of joining the banks of the Thames under water and the supposition that tolls would match the high ferry prices were considered justification enough.[7] The attraction of walking in the dry under a river outweighed considerations of larger purpose, and the reason for building a tunnel remained nebulous. As chief engineer Marc Brunel wrote in an early manifesto: "We may soon anticipate a speedy and total change in the face of the maps of this great metropolis — in that portion of it which has hitherto presented nothing but swampy desert — namely the parish of Rotherhithe. . . . This parish will soon display a scene of activity that is not to be witnessed anywhere else."[8]

Brunel and everyone else assumed that the tunnel's very existence would instigate economic development. No one planned or organized the building process in a modern sense. The tunnel commission neither purchased nor even budgeted for a site for the Wapping entrance until the tunnel had suffered two major break-ins and the company was practically bankrupt.[9] At that time a journalist could still admiringly write that the tunnel was not "an ordinary speculation in which the capitalist advances his money in the expectation of its yielding a profitable return, neither has it a political character, nor one in which the religionists can take part. It is, if we may use the term, at present purely monumental — a stupendous work of art — evincing the daring genius of its author and showing what human skill and enterprise can accomplish when the convenience of civilized man directs their operations."[10]

It also seemed a matter of indifference that the tunnel opened several decades later than everyone originally thought it would. The enterprise was open-ended, and the delay did not hinder any other development. Indeed, the finished tunnel lay fallow for over twenty years without provoking further planning. And yet it was one of the most celebrated and frequently published and discussed building projects of the age!

Tunneling under Mont Cenis was quite another matter. That tunnel was planned and executed as a link in a projected railway network with the clear goal of accelerating the transportation of goods and passengers between what were originally the northern Savoyard and the southern Piedmontese portions of the Kingdom of Sardinia (later regions of France and Italy). Its purpose was to obviate the slow and costly unloading, portage, and reloading of goods necessary for traversing the Alps and to make the crossing independent of weather. Initially the plan was fueled by the desire to unify the kingdom against possible Austrian aggression; later it was the development of European commerce and the imminent opening of the Suez Canal that carried the project forward. The tunnel was designed from the outset to replace a weak link in an existing communication network as quickly as possible. Its completion stimulated a flurry of transalpine projects, two of which, the Gotthard and Simplon tunnels, became reality.

The tunnels under the Thames and through the Alps were not contemporary, but were close enough to be considered together and to provide a striking contrast. They raised problems of comparable difficulty and novelty, but the histories of their genesis were entirely different. The first was characterized by a dilettante approach and the second was conditioned by the criteria of commerce.

The Thames Project

The canal engineer Ralph Dodd presented the original idea for the Thames project in an 1798 pamphlet proposing to dig from Gravesend to Tilbury Fort, now part of London.[11] Dodd's tunnel would have lain too far east of the City for commercial traffic and would only have been convenient for pleasure travel between Kent and Essex. He began work and sank a shaft. Water continually entered the shaft, and Dodd dropped the project when a fire destroyed the engine house in 1803.

William Chapman renewed interest in the enterprise when he proposed connecting Rotherhithe in the south with Limehouse to the north, a route that would have served commerce better.[12] It was the passenger route the Thames watermen used, ferrying up to 3,700 people a day across the river while goods took a cheaper, circuitous route via London Bridge.[13] The Cornish mining engineer Robert Vazie, nicknamed "the Mole" for his tunneling expertise, made a few trial borings on both sides of the river, and was convinced that he could dig a tunnel for less than had been estimated.[14] Surveys were made, plans drawn up, and the Thames Archway Company chartered in 1804. Parliament issued a construction permit the following year, and in 1807 Vazie began excavating a 3.35-meter vertical shaft a hundred meters from the south bank at Rotherhithe.

The company raised the money they needed by subscription. The people who contributed were more interested in the idea than in an investment, considering their donations in the same way as they would regard money they gave to a philanthropic foundation and not as though it were capital intended to earn interest. This made the project very different from a business venture. The directors were subscribers rather than businessmen or engineers, and they supervised the company in an honorary capacity.

The unfamiliar project began with no experimentation other than a few test cores. Vazie sank his shaft 12.8 meters deep. He repeatedly encountered quicksand and quickly exhausted the company's capital.[15] Additional borings seemed to indicate favorable substrata, and support from a major subscriber permitted a shaft of smaller diameter to be sunk another 10.4 meters, at which point Vazie judged it dangerous to continue and digging stopped in August 1807. The directors consulted John Rennie and Chapman, who were unable to agree on how to continue. They finally decided to consult Richard Trevithick, one of the best-known mining engineers of the time. He worked with Vazie for three months and had succeeded in driving a small pilot tunnel 120 meters under the river when Vazie was suddenly dismissed and Trevithick continued on his own.

Excavation progressed for several months until only about sixty meters remained to reach the north bank. Trevithick's crew worked under hazardous conditions. The shaft was confined, and the miners pushed through soft silt for all but the last forty-two meters. Water broke into the confined tube several times, and once the workmen even broke through into a cavity. Then, on January 26, 1808, the pilot tunnel collapsed during a high spring flood that destroyed bridges up and down the river. Trevithick immediately cleared the wreckage and continued until February, when the tunnel flooded again and was abandoned a matter of two weeks before it was scheduled to reach the north bank.[16]

Trevithick knew that it would be even more hazardous to expand the pilot tunnel to full size, and he proposed to save the project by digging a "trench tunnel." He wanted to excavate a bed in the dry behind an open caisson made of sheet piling and bury prefabricated, interconnected brick or cast-iron tunnel segments laid end-to-end in it.[17] But the directors did not even consider this intelligently industrialized variant of the method the Babylonians had used to dig the Euphrates tunnel.[18] After rejecting Trevithick's proposal, the directors announced a competition for the completion of the project. About fifty proposals were submitted and were evaluated by the mathematician Charles Hutton and William Jessop, chief engineer of the Grand Junction Canal and the East India Docks.[19] Hutton and Jessop recommended six of the projects and finally settled on another build-and-sink proposal. The proposer, Charles Wyatt, experimentally sank two brick tubes and successfully linked them underwater.[20] But the method proved exorbitantly expensive. The company was bankrupt, and the directors and consultants concluded that no underwater tunnel could be dug at reasonable cost.[21] They abandoned the project in 1809.

The works lay fallow until Marc Brunel invented the tunneling shield. Brunel was a physical as well as an intellectual border crosser. He had escaped the French Revolution while a young naval cadet and emigrated to New York, where he worked on the mapping of New York State, helped Robert Fulton with the experiments that culminated in the first commercial steamboat, and became a United States citizen and briefly chief engineer of New York City. In 1799 he moved to Britain, where he developed a mechanized method for manufacturing tackle blocks for the Royal Navy. By the end of his career he had been knighted and was vice-president of the Royal Society and the Institution of Civil Engineers.

In the early years of the century, Tsar Alexander I had commissioned Brunel to design a bridge across the Neva at St. Petersburg. Brunel asked himself how he could dig a tunnel instead, which would be unaffected

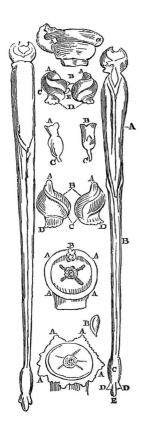

40.
A worm-shaped mollusk
gave Marc Brunel the idea
for his tunneling shield.
The middle diagrams show
the hinged shell at its head,
which drilled through ship
timbers. (Cresy, 1847, p.
1291.)

by driving ice floes in the spring melt. In 1818, while he was pondering how to tunnel through the river silt, a mollusk called pipeworm or *Teredo navalis* caught his attention in Chatham Dockyard. The destruction these shellfish caused by drilling through ship timbers had always been a major maintenance problem.[22] Like many other inventors of genius before and since, Brunel turned his observation into the solution of a different question in another field, crossing the intellectual boundaries between timber technology and tunneling, between animal behavior and machine construction. He examined how the pipeworm drilled, and transformed what he found into two mechanical proposals for a tunneling shield, which he patented the same year.[23]

Brunel translated the information he gleaned from the pipeworm from a zoomorphic into a mechanical format. A great deal has been written about the transformation of reciprocating to rotary motion in steam engines, but little on the concept of translation. Information is *transformed* when it is altered or remolded while remaining within the borders of a field and applied to the same object; it is *translated* by applying it across a border, moving it from one field or object to another. In the process of translation the train of developmental thought continues while the focus shifts to a new object. We currently lack information on the steps Brunel's thinking went through when he developed the idea for his tunneling shield, but translation procedures like the one he must have followed are characteristic of associative or matrix technological thinking. Translation figures prominently in several of the industrial projects for which Brunel became celebrated, as well as in his previously described use of iron to reinforce mortar and "nail" earth.

Five years after Brunel patented the tunneling shield, one of the directors of the Thames Archway Company approached him to reopen the project.[24] Another subscription drive began in February 1824, and Parliament issued a new construction permit.[25] Brunel chose a site between Rotherhithe and Wapping, about 2.4 kilometers downstream from London Bridge. He had a great deal of geological data from the Vazie-Trevithick pilot tunnel 1.1 kilometers away, and "the Committee of Subscribers employed competent persons, unconnected with the Engineer, to take borings across the River in that part, in three parallel lines; and on the 4th of April, 1824, they reported that there was upon each line a stratum of strong blue clay of sufficient density and tenacity to insure the safety of the intended Tunnel."[26]

Francis Giles took preliminary soundings, and then Sir Edward Banks of Jolyffe and Banks, previously masonry contractor on several of John Rennie's bridges and at Sheerness Dockyard, made over forty corings in two parallel lines along the 400-meter-long underwater portion of the proposed tunnel. Although the number of cores was probably sufficient, Banks was unable to judge the geological composition of the river bed correctly.[27] He was

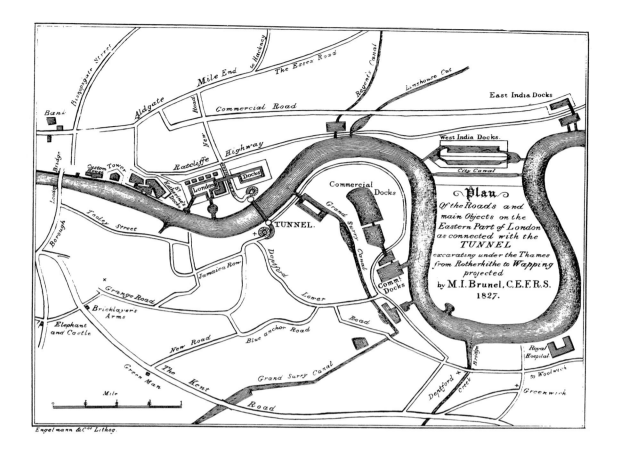

Of the Roads and
main Objects on the
Eastern Part of London
as connected with the
TUNNEL
excavating under the Thames
from Rotherhithe to Wapping
projected
by M.I.Brunel, C.E.F.R.S.
1827.

Engelmann & Co. Lithog.

41.
In 1799, Ralph Dodd located his Thames Tunnel proposal too far east of the City of London for commercial traffic. Marc Brunel's proposed site in 1823 lay right in the dock area, where it would be most useful. (*Sketches for the Works, 1828.*)

obviously not as thorough as he should have been, since he concluded that a nine-meter clay ceiling would protect the tunnel and that at least 8.7 meters of good ground lay below.[28] In reality the clay cover and base were variable and fissured. It must be admitted in the subcontractors' defense, however, that it was very difficult to take reliable soundings.[29] Brunel and various members of the board did have further tests made and Brunel declared himself satisfied.[30] Later, in 1826, when it became clear that the earlier ones had not provided reliable results, the younger Brunel made more soundings, and the directors had Giles make still more after the first "blow" in 1827.[31]

Like Vazie before him, and in contrast to earlier and later epochs, Brunel was expected to promote his own project. Engineers had to be their own public relations managers, lobbyists, and promoters in those days. He was also very much involved with the fundraising subscription, which yielded £179,000.[32] The Duke of Wellington, hero of Waterloo and a Brunel patron, was among the subscribers.[33] Wellington discussed Brunel's project

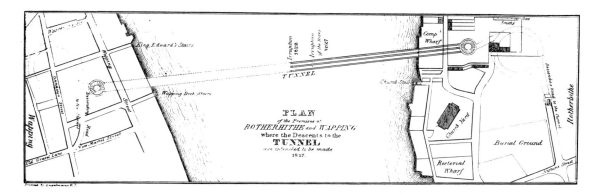

42.
Plan of the tunnel showing the circular stairwells at either end and vehicular ramps that were never built. The sites of the two major "blows" of 1827 and 1828 are also marked. (*Sketches for the Works*, 1828.)

with various engineers and with William Hyde Wollaston, vice-president and commissioner of the Royal Society, whose responsibility it was to foster contact between the Society and government. Wollaston recruited his brother George, who became involved in the organization of the subscription and brought in several other prominent people as subscribers including the statesman Sir Robert Peel. It was characteristic of the subscription system that the names of socially prominent supporters were published to advertise a project and legitimize its intentions.

The subscribers founded the Thames Tunnel Company to take over from the older organization and began work in March 1825. For the first three years William Smith, a member of Parliament and political promoter of the project, sat as chairman of the board, which grandly called itself "the Court." George Hyde Wollaston became deputy chairman and his brother a board member. The politician Benjamin (later Sir Benjamin) Hawes, a boyhood friend and future brother-in-law of Brunel's son Isambard, was another member. In 1836, Hawes, who supported the engineers where Smith did not, became chairman. The board also included several mechanical engineers, Thomas Brunton, Timothy Bramah, and Bryan Donkin, which was unusual for the time. Donkin and Bramah bid unsuccessfully on the shield contract. Donkin was the low bidder, but Brunel considered him too inexperienced, perhaps because his construction experience had hitherto been restricted to paper-making machines.[34] Donkin's failed bid may have made him antagonistic to Brunel, and he and Smith were in constant opposition to the engineers. Brunel biographers tend to consider Smith a villain; this is probably an exaggeration, as his objections often made sense, but the fact remains that the two board members did cause Brunel no end of trouble.

Brunel built a 15.25-meter open caisson to sink the vertical shaft. It was almost 13 meters high and 90 centimeters thick and was designed to sink with the excavation and shield the walls as it progressed downward.[35]

43.
Brunel dug the vertical access shaft using a brick caisson post-tensioned with iron rods. It sank as the workmen excavated the soil beneath it. A steam-driven ladder dredge evacuated the spoil. (Beamish, 1862, plate opposite p. 212.)

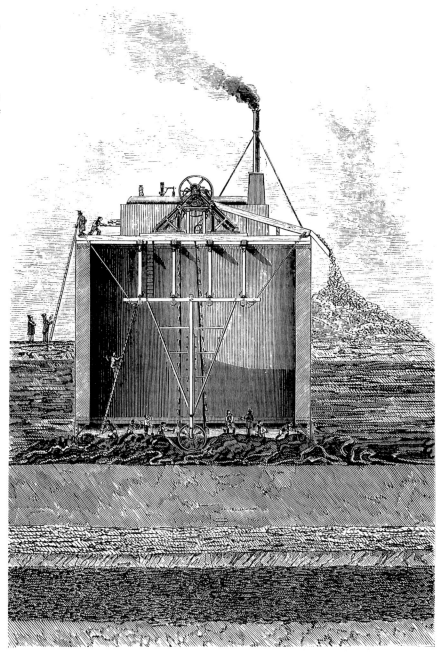

The technique had been used earlier in India, but apparently only for small wells.[36] Brunel rendered the caisson wall's outer and inner brick faces with James Parker's hydraulic cement and filled the cavity between with rubble set in the same cement. Timber hoops girdled the caisson and clamped vertical wooden posts tightly against the cylinder. The whole was vertically post-tensioned with threaded wrought-iron rods that spanned between a sill fixed to the sharp cast-iron curb at the bottom and a timber crown at the top. It was this post-tensioning mechanism that reportedly gave Marc Brunel the idea of reinforcing his experimental brick cantilever at Nine Elms with iron bands in 1832, yet another instance of the translation of a technique from one field to another.

Brunel made sure that he avoided Vazie's problems. He sank a well next to the shaft to depress the water table and mounted a steam engine on top of the caisson to pump water and drive a ladder dredge for spoil removal. The "sinking tower" was a social attraction. Brunel's patron Wellington came to view the works and his interest drew many other prominent people to the site. Vazie's work had led Brunel to expect quicksand, so he stopped the caisson at twenty meters and sank a smaller sump another 4.4 meters, sheathing the excavation at the bottom of the shaft with piling and propping the caisson walls from beneath with masonry, until quicksand began to well up.[37] This forced him to stop a little higher than he had originally planned, and he began to slope the tunnel downward at 2.25 percent, trying to keep as close as possible to the bed of the river and between the two presumed loadbearing layers of clay.[38]

From this beginning, it would take eighteen years to dig the 459-meter tunnel, eighty percent of which lay under the river. The London *Times* soon nicknamed the project "The Great Bore," but it never lost its popular appeal. Technical details were periodically published in broadsides and souvenir brochures, and professionals and the lay public avidly followed the tunnel's progress.[39] Visits to the site remained fashionable even when the works closed down for seven long years.

Marc Brunel's primary gifts lay in mechanical engineering and in the organization of manufacturing processes. He was what we would today call an industrial engineer rather than a builder, and he was unfamiliar with the specific problems and conditions of building processes. He had also just returned from debtor's prison when the project began and was obliged to delegate much of the work since he was swamped by financial problems and a variety of other projects. He did move to Blackfriars in order to be near the site, but his poor health frequently kept him away from the works. He had no mining or tunneling experience, nor did he have any building site experience. He could have used expert advice, but he apparently neglected to consult professionals. The shield form, the geology of the site, and the lack of depth hampered the work critically. A group of directors headed by Chairman Smith and the disgruntled Donkin continually interfered and compounded the problems. At one point they demanded that Brunel double the advance at the face; they also prevented him from cutting a culvert to drain the leakage and obliged him to introduce piecework to speed the digging.

The inventive Brunels were supported by capable assistants. William Lindley later built German railways and Hamburg's innovative water supply system. William (later Sir William) Armstrong became a successful inventor and contractor, and Richard Beamish became a Fellow of the Royal Society and Marc Brunel's biographer. Lewis D. B. Gordon became one of Britain's first engineering professors and George Thomas Page a well-known dock builder.[40] The sometimes naive enthusiasm and haphazard preparatory exploration, the lack of site organization and process management, were more characteristic of the times than they were specific to the Brunels, who labored under crippling opposition and often reacted by abandoning caution. This was also typical of the period, as we saw in Purdon's case. The Brunels were unable to translate the demand for speed imposed upon them into novel building procedures, as Marc Brunel had done so well in his translation of animal drilling into mechanical or in his technical response to the needs of industrial production.[41]

Brunel's interest really lay in the design and functioning of the shield, possibly the largest single piece of machinery of its time.[42] It was certainly the most complex and by far the largest machine that had ever been developed for a building site, and was also the consummate manifestation of Brunel's impressive mechanical talent. The shield was flexible, adaptable, and mobile. Brunel's colleagues appropriately called it "an ambulating coffer-dam, traveling horizontally," and it influenced all later tunneling projects.[43]

The original 1818 patent described two forms of circular shield and cast-iron tubbing for the tunnel wall, but in practice Brunel deviated from his own recommendations.[44] Maudslay, with whom Brunel had worked closely for two decades, built the shield as a recumbent rectangular frame 11.6 meters wide and 6.9 meters high. It was divided into twelve vertical segments that abutted each other like books on a shelf. Each of them was separately jacked top and bottom against the brick lining that followed the excavation and could be moved forward on large articulated cast-iron "feet." Similar "feet" pressed against the earth above. The mobile segments were divided vertically into three "boxes" with a miner working in each. The faces of these thirty-six chambers were walls made of horizontal "poling boards" jacked sep-

44.
Twelve of these three-story shield frames stood together side by side. They balanced on cast-iron feet and were jacked forward individually as the excavation advanced. (Beamish, 1862, p. 220.)

arately against the frame to hold back the earth face. The miner in the "box" dug behind and advanced each poling board individually, working down the face of the chamber in eleven-centimeter steps, so as not to expose too big a gap between the boards. When this had been done twice in each of the chambers, the workmen advanced the whole segment twenty-two centimeters and repeated the process.

Under pressure from the directors, Brunel once reluctantly doubled the advance, but he quickly countermanded the order when the frames began to crack and the segments deviated from the axis. Even without doubling the pace, the segmented shield often shifted or slipped, and the continual realignment was a masterpiece of site management. After the stoppage of the works from 1828 to 1835, Brunel had Rennie build a heavier shield with coupled segments to help alleviate the problem and with iron tails to support the exposed neck of the cutting as the original patent had proposed.[45]

The tunnel cross section was massive brick pierced by two tubes 4.3 meters wide and 5 meters high with an arcade cut through the separating wall between them. A traveling stage carried an ingenious jack that supported the roof centering and the masons who built the brick lining. The space was confined, and light and air were poor. Material consistency was a problem. Brunel had trouble finding high-quality bricks, and he tested each barrel of cement for porosity and for tensile strength by mortaring unreinforced brick cantilevers out from a wall on the Pasley method as well as crushing cement cubes in the manner of Vicat and Treussart. He also built his iron-reinforced double cantilever in the cellar at Nine Elms as a long-term test. Did this lead Brunel to reinforce the tunnel lining? No mention was ever made of any iron reinforcement, and yet the massive brick tube has not fractured or settled unevenly in the soft subsoil to this day, even under the vibrating loads of the heavy subway trains it now carries.[46]

A recumbent rectangular cross section was the worst possible choice for the loads the tube had to withstand. The cylindrical shape Brunel described in his patent would have been safer, but instead of building smaller, circular shields for each tube, he chose the unstable cross section to minimize height and stay where he believed safety lay within the narrow band of impervious material.[47] In fact, the top of the frames lay only ten to twenty feet under the soft, shifting, tidal river bed. The basic problem was the often precariously thin, heterogeneous layer of clay and silt sandwiched between two weaker, porous layers. It was difficult to protect the exposed cutting. Brunel had originally designed the frames with cast-iron tail plates to overlap the brick cladding as it followed the excavation, but he incautiously omitted the plates as a result of Banks's report. The face often leaked so badly that the

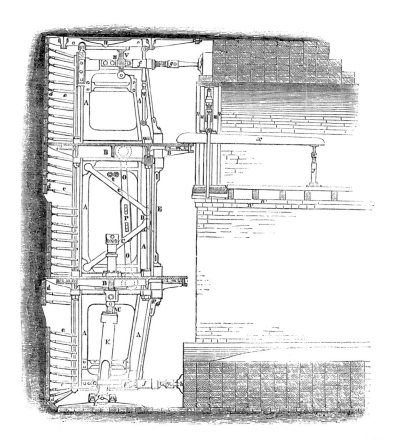

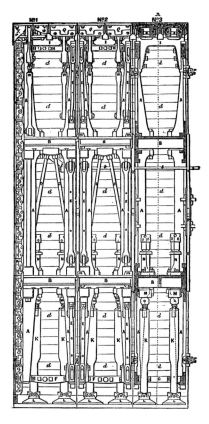

45.

The second shield of 1835 had several improvements over the first. It was heavier, the frames were linked to prevent them from deviating from their alignment, and tail plates shielded the sides of the excavation. (*Rudiments of Civil Engineering*, 1862, part 3, p. 28; Tomlinson, 1852, vol. 2, p. 371.)

46.

Small jacks braced the boarded face against the frames. The workmen loosened each board, excavated, and rebraced it against the neighboring frame. When they had "worked down" all boards, the frame was free to advance. After moving it, they repositioned the jacks on their own frame and worked down the adjacent frames. The second shield introduced rockers, called "quadrants." They fitted in sockets mounted on every second frame and rotated against their neighbors, forcing them to keep their distance while tie rods held them together. (*Rudiments of Civil Engineering*, 1862, part 3, p. 33.)

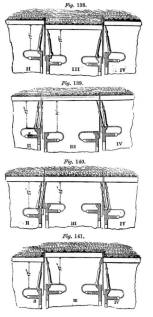

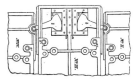

47.
A miner worked in each of the thirty-six shield cells. Other workmen jacked the frames forward and masons followed to brick up the cross section. (Sketches for the Works 1828, and 1836; *Rudiments of Civil Engineering*, 1862, part 3, p. 25.)

48.
The top of Brunel's recumbent rectangular brick structure lay dangerously close to the shifting Thames bed. (Beamish, 1862, plate opposite p. 302; *Rudiments of Civil Engineering*, 1862, part 3, p. 24.)

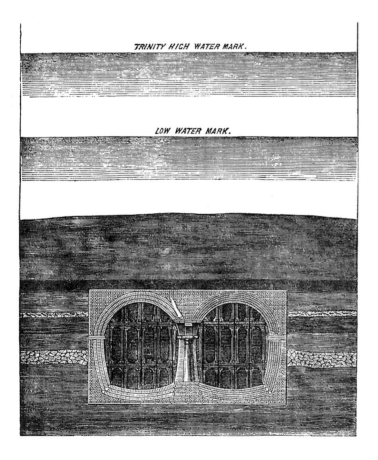

TRINITY HIGH WATER MARK.

LOW WATER MARK.

workers had to caulk the gaps in the poling boards during the "working down" of the face. The laborers were plagued by seepage and groundwater throughout the excavation process.

After only three and a half weeks of excavation, the shield stepped forward into a bank of quicksand that took almost two months of slow work to clear. "Normal" excavation resumed in March, and by the end of June the shield had advanced to the river bank. Surprisingly enough the river did not break into the excavation right then, although there had been some sinking in the ground above the works. As the tunnel continued out under the water, Brunel observed some sinking in the river bed, too. He borrowed a diving bell from Sir John Rennie to continue observing the site from above. Rennie's father had earlier observed that a load of hydraulic cement dumped on the Thames bed not far from the future tunnel site had had a stabilizing effect on the river bed. That may be the reason why Brunel tried to close a depression in the river bed with concrete before the big blow occurred, but apparently it didn't work.[48]

When the tunnel roof did collapse in May 1827, the tunnel was 167 meters long and about a third done. It took two months to repair the damage. Brunel had the six-meter breach stuffed with 2,500 tons of clay and gravel-filled sacks reinforced with hazel rods, similar to what Trevithick had used at the same spot two decades before, and he covered the site with three large tarpaulins weighted down with clay and iron.[49] The fifty-eight-year-old engineer fell ill from stress. The antagonistic editor of *Mechanics' Magazine* claimed that he knew two far more effective ways to stop the hole, one of which an engineer named Peter Keir had already proposed to Brunel.[50] Since various engineering professionals either emotionally endorsed or opposed the project, publicly and within the company itself, it is difficult to distinguish between professional critique and chicanery even in the professional press. The company had hired a professional engineer with unrivaled expertise in industrial mechanization and large-scale machinery, but one who was no expert in building. Industrial processes and building processes follow a different logic, and when it came to building, Brunel's lack of experience and overconfidence served him ill. In this respect too, he was a child of his time.[51]

The repair cost the company £12,000, and the directors hoped for financial aid from the government. *Mechanics' Magazine* suggested that someone review the budget to determine why 85 percent of the funds had been exhausted after only a third of the work had been completed (although the tunnel had so far cost only 39 to 48 percent of what it had cost Trevithick to dig the far smaller pilot tunnel).[52] But no one was responsible for auditing

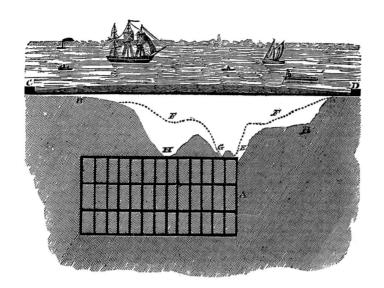

49.
The first "blow" or break-in occurred on 18 May, 1827. Brunel had to plug the cavity with bags of clay from above before he could crawl to the workface and assess the damage. (*Mechanics' Magazine*, vol. 8, 1828, p. 201; Beamish, 1862, plate opposite p. 252.)

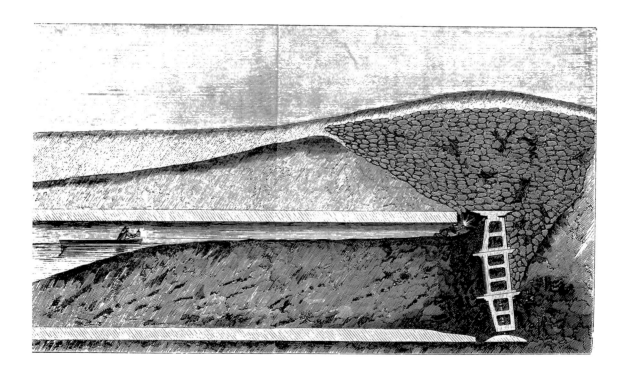

From the Thames to the Mont Cenis Tunnel

the company. And, the editor wanted to know, what would guarantee that other costly accidents would not occur? Only when the case had been fully examined, he wrote, should the government be approached.

The ailing elder Brunel tried to talk himself out of the affair: "When Mr. Brunel had been blamed for the present irruption to the works, as establishing a failure in his calculations, his constant answer has been that 'there was nothing in it, for that it was what he had from the first anticipated.'"[53] To which the relentless editor of *Mechanics' Magazine* responded: "If, therefore, it was anticipated from the first, it can have had but a small share in occasioning this great difference between the estimates and actual expenditure."[54] Then, at the general meeting of the subscribers on June 19, Brunel claimed "that the bricks which had been used, were, he feared, *too green,* and had not presented sufficient resistance to the water."[55] The whole point in using Roman cement for the mortar had been the fact that it set more rapidly than similar products, and we know that Brunel paid careful attention to the curing of the bricks, since there had been ongoing problems with their quality.[56] Again, the editor stated flatly that this had nothing whatever to do with the accident, since the "blow" had occurred at the face and not in the wall.

The Thames Tunnel Company was not alone in having trouble fundraising at the time. The moneyed public was skeptical of harebrained projects.[57] Nevertheless, the *Times* trumpeted public support.[58] The feeling among subscribers was that "to abandon the tunnel would be to disgrace the nation."[59]

Keenly in need of funds, the directors published a *Sketchbook* in 1827 and sold it at the site for £0.13.[60] The Brunels had an aggressive appreciation of the uses of publicity, and the company regularly republished and distributed the charmingly illustrated brochure in several languages at least until 1862, long after the tunnel was completed, which indicates the site's popularity as a tourist attraction. The directors also encouraged site visits and charged visitors £0.05 a head for the thrill of seeing the technological marvel. Sir Samuel Bentham made an appointment with Marc Brunel to see the works with a party of friends, and he was followed by "society" in general.[61] As desirable as these visitors were financially, their presence in the tunnel was dangerous and caused the site engineers no end of additional headaches.

After the blow the directors had Giles reexamine how thick the clay layer actually was above the shield. He found that it was more than the twelve feet he had originally claimed. Since the shield would soon pass the middle of the river, Brunel incautiously did not consider securing the excavation any more than he had already done.

The blow of 1827 gave rise to an unsolicited flood of proposals (sources speak variously of 400 to 600) from European and North American engineers, inventors, and laymen. Several would have merited closer study. The twenty-five-year-old Genevan physicist and engineer Jean-Daniel Colladon sent one at the suggestion of banker Benjamin de Delessert, who was the most prominent French subscriber to the tunnel.[62] Colladon's lifelong interest lay in the propagation and transportability of energy, and he proposed putting the whole tunnel under compressed air, an idea that later came to dominate underwater tunneling. Apparently Brunel considered both Colladon's idea and Sir Thomas Cochrane's slightly later air lock patent seriously.[63] But he did not act on them since pneumatic technology was still in its infancy and the method they proposed was untried. The only available valve sealant at the time was oiled leather.[64] The directors dismissed all of the proposals as utopian, and, in spite of the skepticism of all concerned, Giles was briefly credited with a workable solution. He may have been a mediocre engineer, as some described him, but he was championed by Brunel's detractors.[65]

Wellington and Brunel's friends won out, however, and he was allowed to continue. But long stretches of tunnel wall were still exposed even after the works flooded again in January 1828. The second blow killed six workmen. More voices now claimed that this had been as predictable as the previous accident. The directors briefly considered hiring Vignoles to finish the job. This time it took 4,000 tons of material to close the hole, and the work stopped for seven years for lack of funds. The whole Western world still followed the project and further proposals poured in. As an addendum to his earlier and less informed proposal, Thomas Deakin suggested that Brunel should temporarily clad the tunnel so as not to expose the wall and that he dig it sequentially as two parallel, round tubes. Deakin was right that a round tube would be more stable. Donkin had already proposed excavating one tube at a time, but he had either been outvoted by the board or the Brunels had simply disregarded his advice.[66]

Two weeks after the second accident, the *Mechanics' Magazine* again attacked the engineers:

> Mr. Brunel is now busily endeavoring to stop up the new hole by means of bags of clay, which he hopes to find as effectual on the present as on the former occasion; and he is said to 'express himself in the most sanguine manner as to the completion of the undertaking, if capital can only be obtained.' Shall we tell Mr. Brunel the surest way to get the capital which is still wanted? Let him satisfy the public that he has taken such measures (which he may do) as will

effectually prevent the river from again bursting in; let him only do this, and capitalists will be found in abundance to advance the money requisite to complete the undertaking (on the security, of course, of the *first returns*). There is a talk, we observe, of raising, by *subscription,* the necessary funds. Nothing but absolute despair could suggest any dependence on such a resource. A few *decoy ducks* may make a display of the fifties and hundreds which they are ready to give in aid of the concern, but the public at large must have sense enough to perceive that it is none of their business to find money to save individuals from the consequences of their own miscalculations and errors. He must be simple indeed, who supposes, for a moment, that it can reflect any reproach on us, as a nation, that a speculative engineer (of no experience in mining), and a few other speculators, of more wealth than wisdom, have attempted more than they may be able to accomplish.[67]

It had never been as clearly stated before that the shareholders were really subscribers: the two terms were interchangeable. But they were in fact donors, not investors. Railways were being established in 1828 and they would be modern shareholding companies.[68] The new, commercial form of financing quickly expanded into building, and the Thames Tunnel was one of the last great public works to be funded and directed by amateurs for their personal pleasure and to fulfill what they perceived as their civic obligations. It was built on the verge of a new age, and the editor was feeling a new wind blow when he questioned the appropriateness of the subscription system.[69]

The directors tried to raise funds by promising the payment of interest to be drawn from the money visitors paid to see the site, and this indicates a changing approach from "sinking" funds into a project of this type to "investing" them.[70] Wellington's fundraising speech brought in only £9,660, or less than ten percent of the budgeted £100,000. Finally the British exchequer came through with a treasury loan in 1835, in spite of the rising railway fever that predisposed Parliament to concentrate all available public funding in railways.

The *Mechanics' Magazine* did give some space to defenders of the Brunels, but only to underscore its own points. "S. Y., a young engineer," penned an impassioned letter accusing the journal of unjustly attacking the engineers. The whole undertaking was so novel, he wrote, that mistakes were bound to occur, and it was undoubtedly easier to be wise in retrospect. The main error, he continued, "seems to be, not having had the bed of the river *properly* examined. It was, doubtless, examined in such a manner as was

50.
After the first "blow," Brunel borrowed John Rennie's diving bell to examine the river bed and then used it to monitor the site. Thomas Deakin suggested sloping the tunnel downward and draining it from the middle, but Brunel had to avoid digging into unstable lower layers. (*Mechanics' Magazine,* vol. 8, 1828, p. 204; Fowler, *Practical Treatise,* 1914, p. 19.)

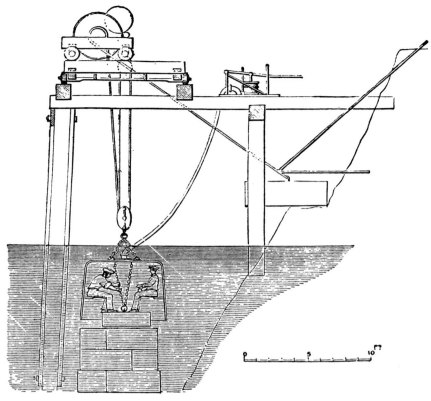

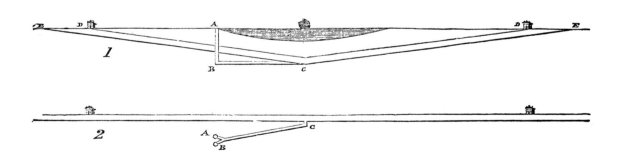

deemed sufficient."[71] The editor attacked this point and implied that it was astonishing that nothing had been undertaken to rectify this after the first accident.[72] This was not strictly true; both Isambard Brunel and Francis Giles
did undertake further borings. But the fact that Marc Brunel had neither really foreseen the need nor reacted to the information he did get with healthy
skepticism or at least caution was indeed a measure of his inexperience in
building.

Brunel finally did constantly sound and pave the river bed with bags
of clay over the workface. Progress became more regular, also helped by an
increasing thickness of clay over the top of the shield. Brunel piled up to ten
percent of the excavated material over the shield to compensate for subsidence, although that couldn't prevent three further major blows, none of
which, however, was as disastrous as the first two had been. The shield repeatedly encountered groundwater and drainage mixed with noxious gases that
seeped both from the filthy river and from the approaching river bank.[73] Fifteen years wiser by then, Brunel saw a solution to the groundwater seepage,
but the stipulations that bound the use of the government loan prevented
him from sinking a well at the Wapping terminus to depress the watertable
and divert effluvia and gases. Brunel could only try to ventilate the site by
running a forty-centimeter pipe from under the fire of the steam engine at
Rotherhithe to the workface.[74]

In its final years, the project profited from the experience engineers
were gaining from the many railway tunnels being built in England (and, of
course, these tunnels benefited from the Thames Tunnel too).[75] Marc Brunel
had been hampered by the limiting criteria of the era and the understanding
of progress as a Promethean struggle, but he did finish the tunnel. Queen
Victoria knighted him in 1841 when it became clear that the project would
succeed after all. Marc Brunel walked through a small pilot tunnel from the
new shaft at Wapping to the shield and from there into the tunnel on 13 August, and the shield finally broke through in November, after which subcontractors built the stairs and cleaned up the site.[76]

The inauguration took place on Saturday, 25 March 1843. Fifty
thousand people paid a penny to cross the Thames underground in the first
twenty-seven hours. Fifteen weeks later the millionth visitor passed
through.[77] Queen Victoria visited it in July and was duly impressed. But the
structure never served the purpose for which it was built. The rosy development of Rotherhithe never materialized. By day the tunnel was a covered
street market, and by night it served as a refuge for London's homeless. The
spiraling vehicular access ramps remained unbuilt and the twin tubes served
only pedestrians. Brunel suggested elevators as an inexpensive solution and
proposed ventilators, to no avail. The directors had tired of the affair.[78]

51.
View through a finished tunnel tube. (Beamish, 1862, p. 267.)

Today, this strikes us as the strangest part of the story. We cannot understand why the government and subscribers were not anxious to finish the project and recover at least some of their investment by levying tolls on passage. The exchequer had advanced £250,000 and the private sector about £190,000. The tunnel was open to the public for a total of nine months and was visited by 1,817,336 paying visitors, grossing £7,572.19. The sole income the "Great Bore" seems to have generated was these visitors' pennies. Even though the access ramps had almost doubled in price since Brunel's original estimate due to wage inflation during the railway boom, the cost could not have been a serious concern after the immense sums spent on the tunnel itself.[79] It is even unlikely that the tunnel turned a profit when it was finally sold to the East London Railway in 1865. The only conceivable explanation for this apparent fiscal irresponsibility is that the structure was not seen as an investment or part of a traffic system at all, but as a technical curiosity, a tour de force, more akin to the "follies" and conservatories in the grand parks of England than what we today call a "facility."

Generations of laudatory biographies have celebrated Brunel's strengths while successfully obscuring his weaknesses.[80] It is understandable that the unpleasant aspects of the building process would be downplayed, since the tunnel was so novel and ultimately successful. The problems he had to deal with certainly contributed to Brunel's illness. And the career of his son Isambard, whom the father closely associated with the tunnel from 1826 on, definitely had its shadows too. The arrogant audacity that characterized Isambard's impressive abilities and weaknesses and the personal conflicts it engendered certainly helped embitter him and accelerate his death in 1859, only ten years after that of his father. Criticism was harshly expressed in the nineteenth century, certainly more harshly than in our day, where libel laws tend to temper unruly comment. For our purposes, however, the disputes surrounding the building of the tunnel reveal more about the development of the building process and about technological thought than does the praise the finished structure rightly harvested.

Social and Commercial Stress in Engineering

The gradual emergence of civil engineering as an accepted profession had a great deal to do with changing attitudes toward building. The alumni of the French engineering *Écoles d'application* enjoyed the elevated status of a profession, whereas their British counterparts, issuing as they did from an apprenticeship, suffered the social stigma of a trade.[81] "Trade" is still a social stigma in Britain, whereas its American counterpart, "business," is an admired quality. The very term "engineer" was derogatory when it applied to a British builder. Engineers were not considered to be gentlemen in British society. As a former French naval cadet and American self-made engineer, a breed that combined practicality and social standing, Marc Brunel was especially sensitive to this form of discrimination. His son Isambard had applied to the École Polytechnique in Paris, only to be turned down as "foreign born."

It is curious that a nation that built its colonial and financial empire on engineering and international commerce would socially undervalue the basis of its power. British engineers were aware of their lowly status and envied their French colleagues. Too many of them spoke or read French not to know the difference, as the deliberations of the Institution of Civil Engineers demonstrate. The stigma cracked very slowly, and as it did the newly won professional confidence expressed itself in new ways of thinking. Engineers like Marc Brunel were knighted for invention, Charles Fox, Joseph Paxton, and William Cubitt for building the Crystal Palace, and others followed. The Marquis of Northampton was an honorary member of the Institution of Civil Engineers and worked to make the profession socially acceptable. The Earls Stanhope, who researched fireproof construction, and Lovelace, who experimented with structural bentwood, were supporters.[82]

The change dawned first in British railway construction. Where French engineers worked as state functionaries or independent consultants, the British were mostly employees hired to do their clients' bidding. They struggled to meet the deadlines imposed on them. Deadlines for governmental permits and for planning, building, and opening new lines kept everyone from parliamentarians and financiers to draftsmen in a state of stress. Engineering offices were overloaded in 1845.[83] Competition was keen and seductive profits enticed the quickest. Social and political contacts were crucial for processing petitions quickly in the labyrinths of loquacious parliamentary committees. The railway engineers most in demand in those years didn't age well. The "Great Triumvirate" certainly did not live long: Robert Stephenson died at fifty-six, Joseph Locke at fifty-five, and Isambard Brunel, the youngest, at fifty-three, all within a year of each other (1859–1860). The pioneers had died at an intermediate age—Richard Trevithick at sixty-two and George Stephenson at sixty-seven—while a secondary group lived to a riper age: George Parker Bidder to seventy-two, Sir William Cubitt to seventy-six, Charles Blacker Vignoles to eighty-two, and William Henry Barlow to ninety. An Englishman of forty could expect to live to the age of sixty-nine in the years 1838–1854, and that included the disadvantaged lower classes.[84] If we take the 1849–1852 obituary lists of the Institution of Civil Engineers as representative of the profession, the average life expectancy of the British engineer over forty was only 61.9.[85] As far as can be ascertained none of the recorded deaths was due to professional accidents, which makes the numbers even more indicative of the stress engineers suffered. Engineering was clearly a hazardous profession.

A contemporary account has a familiar ring a century and a half later: "Throughout the month of November there are constant notices in Vignoles's diary of the terrible race against time which had become the normal condition of the engineering world in 1845; and he particularly observes on the tremendous pressure of work in his own office at Trafalgar Square to get all the plans for the reorganized North Kent line (together with about twelve or thirteen other railways) ready for deposit in the Parliamentary offices by the night of November 30. He remarks that up to that date for a week previously 'some of us were engaged incessantly on the various plans and sections for twenty-four hours at a time'."[86]

The pressure had long been building, in fact ever since the first commercial railways were planned, as Vignoles recounted: "You have no idea how we were driven to get our plans ready for lodging at Preston before November 30 (1829). The hurry and anxiety were five times greater than with the Liverpool and Manchester line. For three nights none of us went to bed, and when all was finished every one was completely knocked up. I have, however, accomplished my task; but it has left me full of nervousness, and I am reduced to a skeleton. The worst is that I can see no end to it, for the public estimation and enthusiasm for new railways and locomotive machines is daily augmenting; and I find that my opinion and service are in constant requisition."[87]

European architects and engineers who participate in public competitions will recognize the condition now so commonplace in modern professional life. The goal was to get the contract and build as quickly as possible, even if it cost more. In 1837, a segment of the Great Western Railway between Hanwell and Acton cost £50,000 more to build because the builders did not wait for the appropriate act of Parliament, but the line was operational six months earlier.[88] No one yet knew how to organize for speed. Commerce alone drove the development, and commerce is not particularly process-oriented; instead, deadlines play a central role. The concentration on deadlines rather than on the means to attain them could have pernicious effects, as the Purdon affair demonstrated.

A New Technology

Railway networks needed tunnels, and new techniques like pneumatic technology were developed to help build them.[89] Compressed air solved hitherto impossible problems. It came to be used in several ways: as a new form of energy to drive machines and drills, to ventilate enclosed sites, and to keep underwater work sites dry.

Traditionally, piles and raft foundations were the only means builders could use to found bridge piers under water. Both techniques were Roman in origin, as were open caissons and heavy-timber coffer dams. By the eighteenth century open caissons were commonly used in India, followed by Britain, France, and the United States.[90] Marc Brunel and others adapted well-drilling technology for foundation caissons.[91]

Open caissons have severe limitations, however; they are difficult to keep dry and tight and cannot be used in rivers that are too deep or in water that moves too fast. Pneumatic caissons that trap air like inverted cups burrowing into the riverbed are better. Brunel's caisson and shield or Sir Thomas Cochrane's air lock patent may have influenced Charles-Jean Triger to attempt an underwater machine of comparable complexity in 1839. Triger had to build an access shaft to a coal mine that penetrated the water table on an island in the Loire at Chalonnes near Angers.[92] He turned Brunel's "ambulating coffer-dam, traveling horizontally" to the vertical, used compressed air as Colladon had proposed, added compressors and valves for passing men and machinery into and spoil out of the chamber, and lined his shaft with cast-iron tubbing. It earned him the grand prize of the Institut de France for mechanical invention in 1853.[93] Triger used the method for founding bridges in 1845, E. Mougel subsequently applied it on a dam in Egypt, and François Cavé used it for the harbor walls at Toulon.[94]

Successful pneumatic and vacuum technology needs good pumps and valve sealants. Oiled leather was the only sealant available for valves until about 1850, and it worked indifferently at best.[95] But this did not deter engineers from trying to use compressed air and vacuum as a motor force. On a visit to Istanbul in 1838, Fairbairn was surprised to find a powder factory powered exclusively by compressed air, and he recommended that British engineers try it.[96] Several nations became so interested in French and British proposals for "atmospheric" railways that they commissioned a rash of governmental reports.[97] However, the real breakthrough in pneumatic technology only occurred after 1839, when the rubber industry gradually introduced vulcanization.[98]

In the early 1840s, the English physician and engineer Laurence Holker Potts inverted Triger's method and used it to build foundations in mud.[99] Potts used a double-cylinder hand pump to evacuate large iron tubes, which sucked themselves down into the ground, filling with earth as they sank.[100] Potts used the method to drive vacuum piles under one of Robert Stephenson's viaducts on the Chester and Holyhead Railway in 1847 and

52.

Charles-Jean Triger developed a pressurized caisson for coal mining in 1839. A pump forced air into the caisson, but the spoil had to be laboriously raised through the air lock. (Maigne, 1873, p. 348.)

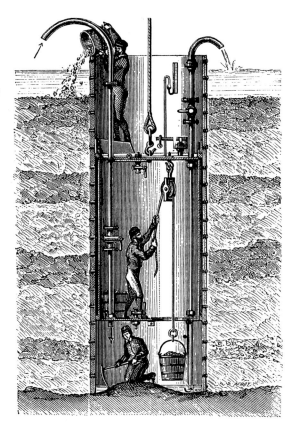

then sold his patent to the contractors Fox and Henderson. They made the method more effective by adding a rotor to agitate and loosen the earth at the tip of the pile and a vacuum cleaner–like arrangement to suck it up.[101]

The Potts method worked for piles in soft ground, but men still had to excavate rock at the bottom of larger foundations manually. William Cubbitt's 1851 Rochester-Strood Bridge over the Medway in Kent spanned a site where ancient foundation debris obstructed vacuum piling. While the cast-iron abutment piles were driven as tubes, site engineer John Hughes suggested that Fox and Henderson use Triger pneumatic caissons for the larger intermediate piers.[102] The solution cost almost twice as much as piling, but it was a little faster, and soon variants of the Triger-Fox-Henderson method were used on many bridges, including Isambard Brunel's Saltash Bridge over the Tamar (1854–1859) and Eiffel's Garonne Bridge at Bordeaux (1858–1860).[103] Pneumatic caissons were soon used for bridge piers, underwater abutments, and quays all over Europe, and they were introduced to the United States in 1852.[104]

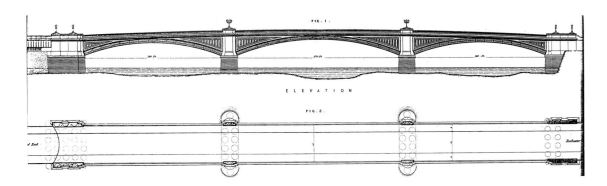

53.
William Cubitt's Medway
Bridge at Rochester, Kent
(1844–1851). (Humber,
Complete Treatise, 1861,
vol. 2, plate 1.)

54.
Site engineer John Hughes
and the contractors Fox
and Henderson built the intermediate piers on tubular
pneumatic caissons.
(Humber, *Complete Trea-
tise,* 1861, vol. 1, plate E
facing p. 164.)

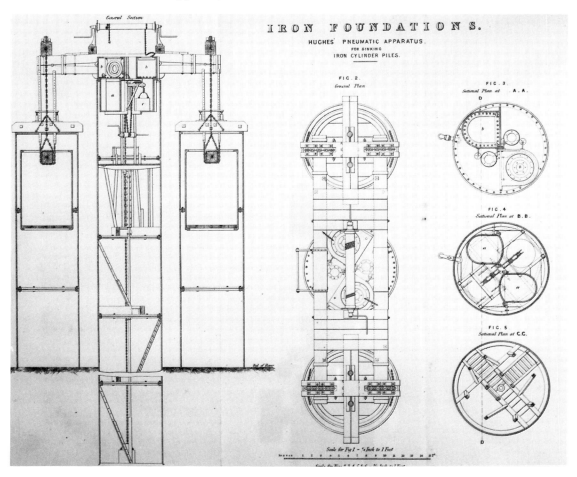

The pneumatic caisson method came of age with the underwater foundations for Edouard Fleur Saint-Denis and Emile Vugnier's Kehl-Strasbourg Bridge over the Rhine (1857–1861).[105] Fleur Saint-Denis and Baron von Weber, chief engineer of the grand duchy of Baden, both proposed the idea, and their contractor Castor built, installed, and managed the caissons.[106] The large, rectangular wrought-iron caissons had access tubes surmounted by valves for workmen and materials and others filled with water in which ladder dredges were installed to remove the spoil. The caissons were weighted with cut stone and a concrete backfill to keep them submerged, and as they sank Castor added masonry above the waterline to form the finished piers.

The river bed was unstable, and Fleur Saint-Denis and Castor had a problem to solve analogous to Marc Brunel's in London. The volume of spoil they lifted out of the caissons exceeded the foundation size by far, which serves as an indicator of the degree of difficulty the engineers had to deal with. Three-quarters of the cost of the bridge, or seven million francs, went for preparatory and foundation work, even though the superstructure was unusually expensive.[107] Nevertheless, and in contrast to the Thames tunnel, the foundations were finished on schedule.

The method had its drawbacks, however. Triger observed the mysterious "bends" or "caisson disease" as early as 1839. The cause was discovered around 1861, but workmen continued to suffer from the effects of dissolved gasses "boiling" in the bloodstream until the end of the 1870s.[108] Air lock blowouts were rarer and killed fewer workmen, but they provided more sensational press copy, and whenever one occurred it delayed a project more than the less spectacular caisson disease.

The Mont Cenis Tunnel

By the time Colladon proposed pneumatic technology for the Mont Cenis Tunnel in 1852, it was well established in foundation work, and its problems and hazards were known. The building of the twelve-kilometer Mont Cenis Tunnel illustrates the concept of progress as a law of nature. The feat itself was quickly eclipsed by the fifteen-kilometer Gotthard Tunnel and later by the twenty-kilometer Simplon, but the techniques that made these more spectacular works possible were developed at Mont Cenis.

It is difficult for us to realize what a hindrance the Alps posed to traffic at the beginning of the last century and how the imagination of central Europeans could be fired by the idea of tunneling through the Mont Thabor chain to link the valleys of French Savoy with upper Italy. The Alps blocked

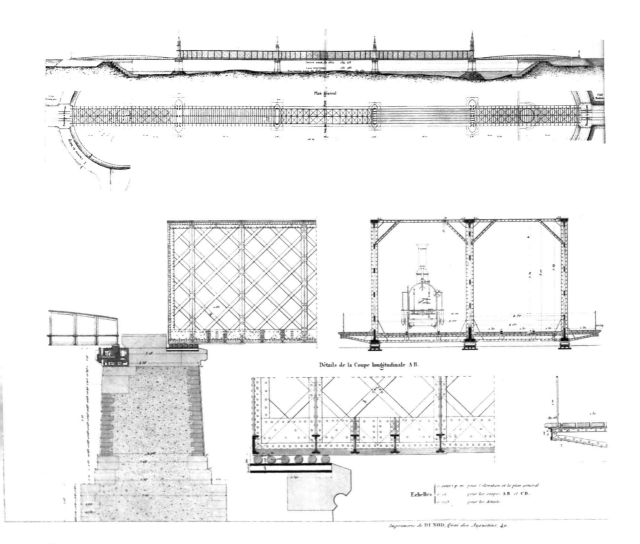

55.
Edouard Fleur Saint-Denis
and the contractor Castor
designed and built the first
fully developed pneumatic
caisson for the Rhine
Bridge at Kehl (1857–
1861). (Vugnier and Fleur
Saint-Denis, 1861, plate
19.)

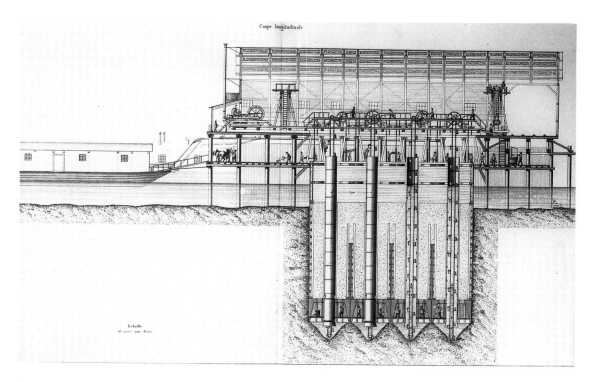

Coupe longitudinale

Echelle
de mm par Mètre

56.
A steam-powered ladder
dredge drew spoil up
through water-filled tubes
in the caissons at Kehl. Carbon arc lamps lit the site at
night, while oil lamps flick-
ered below. When the foundations were deep enough,
the workmen withdrew
through the airlocks and
filled the caissons with
concrete. (Vugnier and
Fleur Saint-Denis, 1861,
plate 19.)

Worlds Apart

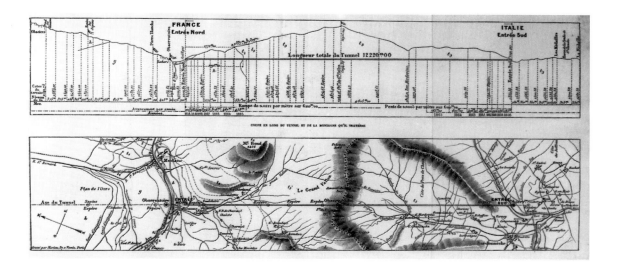

57.

The twelve-kilometer Mont Cenis Tunnel was the first major alpine tunnel. Its builders needed new drilling techniques to dig and ventilate headings six kilometers deep in rock. (Figuier, *Nouvelles Conquêtes de la Science*, 1883–1885, vol. 2, p. 148.)

cultural, political, and commercial expansion as rigorously as the Himalayas and the Andes still do. Mule and foot traffic were originally the only way to cross the great European divide, and the crossing was entirely dependent on weather conditions. This changed in 1772 when the gentle Brenner Pass in Austria was crossed by a carriageable road and when Napoleon built the western alpine Mont Cenis (1803–1810) and Simplon Pass (1806–1812) roads to consolidate his conquest of Italy.[109] The roads survived Napoleon's empire, and the Gotthard trail was also widened to serve civilian wheeled vehicles in 1832.

The European nations were just planning their first railways in the 1830s and 1840s, and political and engineering groups naturally discussed possible transalpine connections.[110] These connections would need tunnels, because the pass roads were too steep for locomotives and their curves were too tight. Two small road tunnels had been built, and the Austrian engineer Karl von Ghega dug the first alpine railway tunnel through the Semmering between 1848 and 1854,[111] but the twelve-kilometer base tunnel under Mont Cenis was still a utopian idea when it was first proposed in 1841.[112] There was certainly no technology yet available to dig it.

Large-scale utopian projects invariably have political origins. An English Channel tunnel was first proposed by Napoleon in 1804, and digging began several times from both the English and the French coasts, but it was only the formation of the European Common Market that finally guaranteed its success in 1994. The great sweetwater lake across southern Algeria and Tunisia, proposed in 1869, was intended to secure the French African empire.

It would have provided an evaporation surface to raise clouds and precipitate rain on the Atlas mountains to the north, making the region arable, and created a barrier to protect the colonies' southern boundary at the same time. Ferdinand de Lesseps supported it, but the government finally abandoned it in favor of a far cheaper proposal to water the eastern Sahara by artesian wells.[113] The French also regarded the Suez and Panama canals as instruments of empire, while the base tunnel through the Mont Cenis, or the Monte Cenisio as it is called in Italian, was originally a bid by King Carlo Alberto of Sardinia to unify his transalpine kingdom by connecting Piedmont in the south with Savoy in the north. He needed a power base to push Austria-Hungary out of northern Italy. This was why the far-fetched idea received any official attention at all.

The proposal was submitted to the Sardinian government by Joseph Médail, a former customs official turned building contractor. Médail had roamed the area from 1814 on, determined to find the best line for a tunnel. He finally settled on the narrowest point in the alpine chain, two roughly parallel valleys 1,100 and 1,350 meters high and thirteen kilometers apart. The Savoyan Arc Valley sloped from east to west, and the Doria Valley to the south sloped the other way. Both lay below the heaviest snow zone. In 1839 Médail sent a memorandum to engineer General Rachia, who forwarded it to the king.[114] Médail's route was about twelve kilometers long and penetrated deep under Mont Fréjus between Modane and Bardonnechia, where

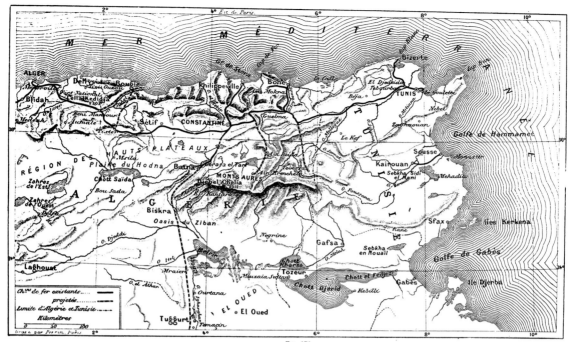

Fig. 170.

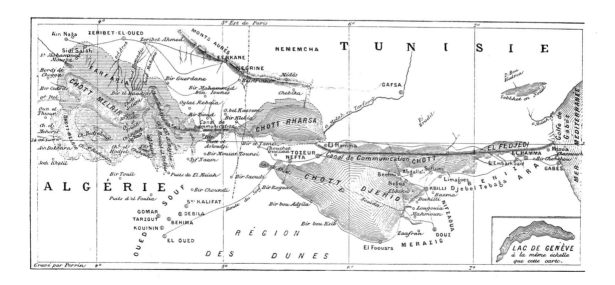

From the Thames to the Mont Cenis Tunnel

no ventilation or secondary work shafts were possible. He optimistically estimated excavation at five to six years, although the project would have taken more like thirty-six using available mining technology.[115] Médail later tried to make his idea more attractive by siting the tunnel higher up and reducing its length.[116] Traditional tunnels were built with vents every several hundred meters to provide air and multiple headings, so Médail's idea raised two major questions: the first was how to ventilate the six-kilometer-deep working faces that lay up to 1,000 meters under the surface, and the second was how long it would take to complete the excavation working from only two headings.

The political, commercial, and strategic implications of the tunnel fascinated the king, engineer Pietro Paleocapa, who was on the verge of retirement as Minister of the Interior, and statesman Marchese Michele Benso di Cavour. The Sardinian government was planning the country's first railway between its main port at Genoa and the capital, Turin. They recognized that the two projects would form a strategic chain. Isambard Brunel was invited to design the railway in 1843. Like all early railway builders, he was convinced that locomotives could not climb well and that they needed elaborate cuttings, viaducts, tunnels, and "inclined planes" in which stationary winding engines winched trains up unavoidable inclines. The Genoa-Turin line had a 450-meter-high pass to cross between Turin and the sea. So the government called in a Belgian specialist in inclined planes, Jean-Marie Henri Maus, who had just completed two large ones for the railway in Liège.[117] Maus was awarded the contract to build the whole line, and Médail's related project naturally came up in discussion.

Maus examined the tunnel idea and restored Médail's proposal to its original length.[118] According to the final project of February 1849, the tunnel was to run 12,290 meters under Fréjus Pass between Modane and Bardonecchia, twenty-two kilometers to the west of Mont Cenis. Maus estimated it would take thirty-five to forty years to dig using traditional methods. Even the longest tunnels of the time had been worked from multiple headings: the 4.1-kilometer Blaisy Tunnel on the Paris-Dijon Railway from twenty-two headings less than two hundred meters deep and the 4.6-kilometer Nerthe Tunnel from twenty-four shafts and fifty faces. Experienced engineers agreed that three hundred meters was the maximum practicable depth for access and ventilation shafts.[119] Mont Cenis could therefore only have two headings, one at either end, and no ventilation shafts. This did not deter Maus, who began experimenting with a water-powered mechanical drill in 1846.[120]

Maus designed a battery of 116 drills arranged in five lines. They would split the face into horizontal layers that could then be broken out using wedges. He wanted to place waterwheels in the cascades at either end to

60.
Engineer Agudio designed
an inclined plane on the
Genoa-Turin Railway. Its
wire rope drive gave Henri
Maus the idea for powering
his Mont Cenis drills. (Figuier, *Nouvelles Conquêtes
de la Science,* 1883–1885,
vol. 3, p. 53.)

pump water to the face to cool the bits that hammered the rock 150 times a
minute.[121] Maus designed a system of thick wire ropes over 2,400 rollers
spaced at ten-meter intervals to deliver the driving force to the headings. He
was familiar with wire ropes because he had used them on his inclined planes
in Liège, but transmissions of that length running at speeds of up to 12
meters per second were as yet unheard of.[122] It was doubtful whether they
would work, especially since Maus had himself calculated that 71 percent
of the energy would be lost in friction, elasticity, and slippage. They would
also be expensive to build and maintain.[123] Unknown to either Maus or the
Sardinian government, an Alsatian industrialist in Colmar named Gustave
Adolphe Hirn had begun to distribute energy in factories in 1850 using wire
ropes. Hirn's transmission was more efficient than any before. By 1858 he
claimed that he could transport energy three or four kilometers without major losses, and at the Paris exhibition of 1867 he suspended a wire rope
transmission over a quarter of the site.[124] But even Hirn, working under controlled factory conditions, never considered one six kilometers long installed
in a messy tunnel site.

61.
Gustave Adolphe Hirn's cable transmission could transport energy over long distances in 1850. He demonstrated it at the 1867 Paris Exhibition, where it spanned a quarter of the site. It was more efficient than Maus's system, but it still couldn't have driven the Mont Cenis drills and ventilation fans. (Ducuing, 1867, p. 337.)

Another open question was how to ventilate the workface. The tunnel simply could not be built if that problem were not solved. Dust and noxious explosion gases would pollute any air that managed to reach the heading and make it unbreatheable. Maus envisaged huge fans in an exhaust pipe driven by the same wire rope that ran the drills, and he planned to abandon blackpowder altogether in order not to foul the air more than absolutely necessary. Even if the transmissions would have run before, this would surely have overloaded them. But in spite of all this, Maus claimed optimistically that he could advance five meters a day on each side without explosives. The pilot tunnel would be open in six years and the tunnel finished in ten.

Maus's enthusiasm in the face of overwhelming evidence to the contrary is typical of technological thinking before physics influenced it. It is similar to the many attempts by inventors throughout history to make gold or build the *perpetuum mobile*. The empiricist refuses to recognize the validity of scientific proof, which is based on an exclusive, scientific method of reasoning. This exclusivity is foreign to technological thought, which uses many modes of thinking and recognizes that they all have their shortcomings.

Since scientists have been proven wrong before, the technologist argues, they may very well be proven wrong again. This is indeed true, as subsequent developments have often showed, when a slight change in the parameters of a project or a technology modified the logic and the basis of the whole argument. And so Maus, the technologist, could persist in a project that other forms of logic had abandoned as hopeless.

As it stood, Maus's proposal was very shaky, but the king was determined to pursue it. A royal commission, first under the chairmanship of Minister Galvagno, and then under Paleocapa, finally supported Maus.[125] However, the king was prevented from foolishly pursuing this unrealizable project by the failure of his campaign against the Austrians in 1849, which emptied the state coffers and led to his abdication. His successor Vittorio Emanuele was more skeptical, and since the government had no money anyway, the proposal was published and shelved.[126] But the need for a transalpine crossing was so pressing that Prussia, Piedmont, and Switzerland set up another commission in 1851 to determine the best possible route. They found that all of them would need long tunnels.[127]

Jean-Daniel Colladon was a border-crossing physicist and engineer who had already proposed compressed air for the Thames project.[128] In 1828, at the age of twenty-five, he made a name for himself with experiments on the underwater propagation of sound waves, and he was familiar with general problems of energy.[129] In 1850 Colladon contacted the Sardinian councilor of state, Theodor de Santa Rosa, obtained a copy of Maus's report, and developed a pneumatic method to transmit energy and solve the ventilation problem. His jury work at the Crystal Palace Exhibition delayed the start of his experiments until 1852. He probably did not know of the system Fairbairn had discovered in Istanbul in 1838 and which had since been implemented in a British powder mill at Waltham Abbey, but he showed that careful manufacture of cast-iron conduits could reduce energy loss due to friction even more than some were willing to believe.[130] This instantly brought the tunnel within the realm of the possible — vindicating Maus's faith — and by the end of the year his results were ready to present and patent.[131] Federico Luigi Menabrea, a member of the royal commission, was impressed, and wrote: "He has perfected Mr. Maus's machine, or rather invented a new mechanism and proposed new and powerful means which will considerably shorten the work and make it far less expensive. . . . The commission recognizes above all how important Mr. Colladon's inventions could be for speeding up the construction of railways crossing the Alps."[132]

The issues covered in the patent were: energy transmission and storage when the pumps were inactive; ventilation; temperature control of the compressors, the workface, and the tunnel; flushing and drying the drill holes; machinery to remove spoil; and communication from the entrance to the work face—all using compressed air. The only aspect he did not patent was the drill itself. Menabrea had advised him to leave that out, probably so as not to antagonize Maus, who had begun working on his own drill and who was then at the height of his influence as technical inspector and director of the Genoa-Turin Railway. Menabrea had introduced Colladon to Maus in 1852, and Maus had refused even to consider anything but his own system.[133]

Maus had no success with his drill, but Thomas Bartlett, a contractor's superintendent on the Savoyan Vittorio Emanuele Railway, tested one in 1854 that he patented in Turin the following year.[134] Bartlett's drill had a small steam engine attached to it, and the piston was cushioned by trapped air, which directed the whole force toward the bit rather than the housing. The drill worked well in open-air tests near Chambéry in 1855. It hammered the rock face 250 to 300 times a minute and took only ten minutes to drill thirty-three centimeters into solid granite and fifty centimeters into limestone.[135] But Bartlett's drill was difficult to maneuver inside a narrow gallery deep within a mountain. Steam from the pistons and combustion gasses from the fire also prevented its use. It could only work if it were adapted for compressed air, as Colladon suggested.[136]

As soon as Colladon applied for his patent, three Sardinian engineers named Germain Sommeiller, Sebastiano Grandis, and Severino Grattoni developed their own primitive compressor that used a waterfall to compress air and force it into a storage reservoir.[137] They originally intended it to replace the wire rope winch on the Giovi inclined plane at Busalla after

62.
The Bartlett steam drill's pneumatic cylinder cushioned the force and directed the thrust forward. It worked well in open air, but would have been unwieldy in the tunnel. (Figuier, *Nouvelles Conquêtes de la Science*, 1883–1885, vol. 2, p. 99.)

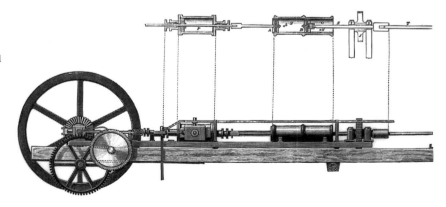

Maus left the Turin-Genoa Railway. Convinced of the value of their compressor, and thanks to the fact that Sommeiller had just been elected to a seat in the Turin parliament, the three engineers were able to enlist the patronage of Conte Camillo Benso di Cavour, the marquis's son, in exchange for political support. It cost the government 90,000 French francs, which Cavour thought fair exchange, particularly if the project should prove even moderately successful. However, the money was exhausted in building a prototype, and it was clear that Cavour's support of the project had become a political liability for the government. So when the compressor then failed on the inclined plane, something had to be found to show for the government's investment. Cavour grasped at the abandoned tunnel idea to justify exceeding the budget, and the Cenis project was reintroduced through the back door.

Based on this situation and his disenchantment with steam-engine-producing Britain, which had hindered his plans to declare war on Austria, the farsighted Cavour began to renew interest in water power as an energy source that could literally empower Italy: "If this invention is successful it could produce important results. . . . A waterfall provides everything we demand from coal. We have more motor power in waterfalls than England has in all its coal mines."[138]

This argument turned the political embarrassment into an opportunity, and the government ordered a series of experiments to compare the Sardinian and Colladon compressors using a modified Bartlett drill. The tests took place in March and April 1857 in the presence of the commission and Cavour. They had to prefer the Sardinian compressor for political reasons, even though the giant, almost 100-centimeter cylinders needed a twenty-six-meter head of water to produce a mere five or six atmospheres of pressure at two to five revolutions per minute, while Colladon's compressed thirty percent more air with sixty percent of the effort at sixteen revolutions per minute.

Cavour and Paleocapa staked their reputations on the project's success. The state coffers were impoverished by Carlo Alberto's losses, and money was tight. But the profits to be gained through railway trade were attractive. Figuier noted a fall in French rail transportation prices from 100 to 95.78 French francs per kilometer in the period 1858–1862, parallel to the completion of the national railway network. At the same time, he noted a rise in profitability. The French system was the third largest in the world at the time and the most profitable in Europe.[139] Although profits subsequently declined with the further extension of the international network, the economic argument for deciding to undertake the risky tunnel project was forceful, especially for Italy, which hoped to capture much of the continental Suez trade.

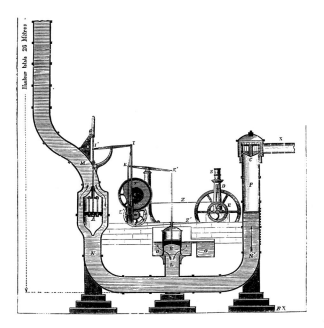

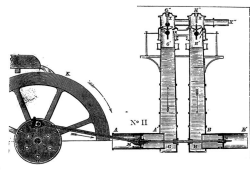

63.
The clumsy compressor
Sommeiller used until 1863
and the more efficient one
Colladon built for the
Gotthard Tunnel in 1873.
(Figuier, *Nouvelles Con-
quêtes de la Science*, 1883–
1885, vol. 2, p. 137.)

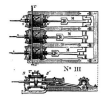

With the decision about energy production out of the way, the Turin parliament voted 98 for and 28 against the tunnel on 29 June 1857. Digging began by hand in the first week of September. Political support for the project broadened as the unification of Italy progressed between 1859 and 1861. At this time Austria still controlled the Adriatic ports Venice and Trieste. Karl von Ghega's Semmering Railway had established a rail connection to the Austrian hinterland in 1854, and Karl von Etzel's line over the Brenner Pass (1864–1867) was in the planning stage. The Mont Cenis line and the coastal railway between Genoa and Toulon were essential to balance the powerful presence of Austria to the east.[140]

France, Switzerland, Italy, and Germany were interested in the north-south connection across the Alps because of the impending Suez Canal project, and the advantages of a winter-secure crossing under Mont Fréjus were clear. Paulin Talabot, intimately involved in the Suez Canal project, submitted a Lukmanier Pass railway proposal to the Italian government.[141] Eugène Flachat paid four visits to the Gotthard Pass and two to the Simplon before 1859.[142] From his own visits and from information sent to him by Gottlieb Koller, who was studying the alpine railway question for several Swiss cantons and railway companies, Flachat looked at ten possible routes, each of which would benefit different regions. Seven of them led over Swiss territory, which Flachat judged politically and militarily advantageous to both France and Piedmont, and which, according to him, also offered advantages in "economy, regularity and speed."[143] He changed his mind when Swiss and French claims on Savoy led to tensions between the two countries, and shifted his support to the Mont Cenis route.[144]

Building the Mont Cenis Tunnel was an adventure with too many open variables. Almost everything depended on untried technologies, and the project could only work with public support. Government involvement kept funds flowing to the risky project, but it also made progress ponderously bureaucratic. Private interests, which would otherwise have shied away from the whole affair, chafed at the bit because of the slow-moving bureaucracy. British coal sold for 55–65 French francs per ton in Milan in 1861, and Flachat estimated that Saint-Etienne coal would cost ten to thirty percent less via the Cenis Tunnel.[145]

The Sardinian railway lines were government projects, and the Mont Cenis was planned slowly, albeit thoroughly.[146] Angelo de Sismonda, professor of geology in Turin, surveyed the route, and Jean-Baptiste Élie de Beaumont of France verified it. The line was designed by two young engineers, Capello and Borelli, who adopted the Blaisy Tunnel's thirty-meter cross section. Borelli was put in charge of the south side of the works, and a

64.
Germain Sommeiller used
the French Blaisy Tunnel
cross section as a model for
his Mont Cenis Tunnel. (Figuier, *Nouvelles Conquêtes
de la Science*, 1883–1885,
vol. 2, p. 156.)

young engineer named Henry Mella organized the plant and site installation. He began by building housing for the laborers, channeling and damming streams for water power, and installing a battery of ten Sommeiller compressors at Bardonecchia.

The government ordered another round of tests on the compressor together with a modified Bartlett drill and a lighter model designed by Sommeiller.[147] Menabrea reported the results to the Sardinian Academy of Sciences on 29 June 1858. The compressor worked, and he thought that the waterfalls at either end would provide enough air to run the drills and ventilate the site even if the drills worked at top speed, a concern that suggests mounting political and commercial pressure. The commission members recommended driving a pilot shaft two hundred meters ahead of the main gallery for safety and to facilitate spoil removal. They requested yet another round of system tests before the contract documents were drawn up. The report estimated completion in six or seven years, but the contract conservatively more than doubled that to fifteen years. The caution was justified: painstaking on-site system adjustments eventually stretched the completion time to almost thirteen years.

Under the 1860 treaty that ended the Italian war of liberation, the government of the former Kingdom of Sardinia, now Italy, ceded Nice and Savoy to France as payment for Napoleon III's support of the war against Austria. Thus the northern end of the tunnel would now be on French territory. Italy reserved the right to finish the tunnel and the two countries agreed to split the construction costs. France also agreed to pay Italy 600,000 francs for every year gained on the conservatively projected deadline.[148] The engineers were to receive half that bonus, or about 1,000 francs per working day, if the tunnel were finished in the course of 1871, and they were to be fined the same amount for every day that work continued after January 1, 1872.[149]

The engineers began digging even though they had only transported pneumatic energy through a ten-centimeter 389-meter-long conduit. But their experimental results were promising and indicated that enough energy would reach the workface to drive the drills, cool them, and ventilate everything at a depth of 6,500 meters, even with an estimated drop in pressure from 6 to 1.3 atmospheres.[150] Years later, Louis Figuier's poetic description showed how successful the ventilation really was: "No sooner is the powder ignited than a black, thick cloud spreads through the gallery. Soon, however, the smoke cloud twists, begins little by little to tear apart, and vanishes like a stage set revealing the end of the tunnel."[151] In fact, the workmen breathed a purer air than their factory-bound contemporaries in the cities.

The ventilation was so successful that there was no need to replace the black-powder with the cleaner but far more dangerous nitroglycerine that was then being used in the Hoosac Tunnel.[152]

Work started by hand while the drills, compressors, and conduits were still being manufactured and tested. By 1859 only 160 meters had been excavated on either side. A year later the total was 750 meters at Bardonecchia and 520 at Modane, where progress was slower because most of the gallery had to be clad in brick. Early visitors to the site described the drama:

> I took the smoking lamp in my hand. . . . We went down the dark tunnel . . . along the walkways that accompanied the finished double track.
>
> Wagons filled with debris passed us. The farther we advanced the more feeble and hazier the lamps appeared to gleam in the thick smoke. The growl of thunder seemed to reach us from the end of the tunnel; that was either a mine that had just been fired or the compressed-air valve that opened to renew the air.
>
> We reached the end of the tunnel in the midst of the workmen laying track, chipping away at the vault, and chiseling new blast holes in the face with hammers, and in the glow of the lamps that poured forth more smoke than light. The eyes, ears, and lungs finally accustomed themselves to the heavy darkness, to the intense sound, and even to the air that grew rarefied and heavy with vapor. The worst sensation one feels in this atmosphere, deprived of moving air, is the heat.
>
> But, all of a sudden the valve opens, filling the tunnel with waves of compressed air. In this instantly refreshed and purified atmosphere we breathe completely easily and a palpable comfort fills us. We were 870 meters into the heart of the mountain and isolated from all external air.[153]

Hopes rose for quicker progress when the large cast-iron drill frames began arriving toward the end of 1861. Mella set up the machines at the Bardonecchia end in January using first one, then two, then four drills.[154] Eventually up to 2,000 men were employed on that side of the mountain, working round the clock in three eight-hour shifts. International attention focused on the new technology and adapted it to many uses. In 1861 a windmill compressed air on a factory roof at Gennevilliers near Paris and stored it in containers. Pneumatic drills appeared that year in the Swedish Perseberg coal mines and were soon copied all over.[155]

A Viennese professor named Hans Kraft designed the drill mounts on two mobile half-frames, each of which carried a maximum of eight drills. The Société John Cockerill of Seraing in Belgium manufactured the assembly at a cost of 1,300,000 francs apiece. The number of drills must have varied, as different sources speak variously of ten toward the end of the project and sixteen or seventeen earlier on. They were mounted in meter-high layers and acted in three ways: hammering steel chisels against the face, advancing them as the blast hole deepened, and rotating them to prevent jamming.[156] Water jets constantly cooled and rinsed the holes to keep them free of debris. The water was fed directly into the pneumatic duct to save an extra pump, as Colladon had proposed. Workmen could retract the bits individually for replacement, and four drills were kept in reserve for each one in use.[157]

A single miner tended each half-frame with its long, unwieldy drills. The frames advanced one behind the other on tracks pulling tenders carrying water and containers of compressed air for pumping the tunnel floor dry. It took six hours to drill a battery of forty-millimeter holes and a larger central one that provided space for blowing the debris loose. As soon as the holes were eighty to ninety centimeters deep, two miners cleaned and dried them by closing the water valves and flushing them with the air flow before packing them with explosives. The logistics of setting the frames up, drilling, cleaning, packing, and withdrawing the apparatus had to be carefully choreographed if it were really to save time.[158]

When the face was ready, the teams withdrew their frames thirty meters along the tracks and secured them behind heavy oak barriers. The blasters then mined the holes with preassembled charges, leaving some empty to create lines of weakness, and set them off in groups of eight, working from the center outward. The pneumatic duct remained open to dissipate the gasses as quickly as possible. Then the spoil was loaded on hand carts small enough to pass the retracted frames, reloaded beyond on larger carts, and removed by horsepower along the track.

The pneumatic machines worked twelve times as fast as hand drilling. They took so little space that eighteen holes could be drilled simultaneously instead of three by the manual method. That promised substantial savings, since drilling typically represented about seventy-five percent of the work. But it didn't solve the whole problem of building the tunnel. Tunneling involved three categories of work: breaking the rock, removing the spoil, and smoothing, cleaning, and sometimes cladding the tunnel surface. The degree of difficulty in each category depended on the type of rock, the ease with which the site could be ventilated, and the size and shape of the tunnel cross section. Explosives speeded the mining process, but they stressed the ventilation system and slowed spoil removal.

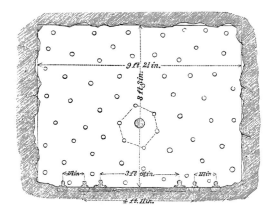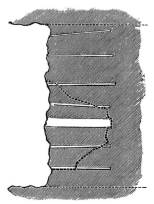

65.
Although the artist posed a whole crew at the face, only one man worked each half-frame. He drilled a concentric pattern, with a larger hole in the center to give the rock room to crack when the charges were fired in series from the center outward. The small tracks carried the drilling frames and the larger one carried spoil trains. (Figuier, *Nouvelles Conquêtes de la Science*, 1883–1885, vol. 2, p. 151; *Harper's Monthly*, vol. 43, no. 154, July 1871, p. 175.)

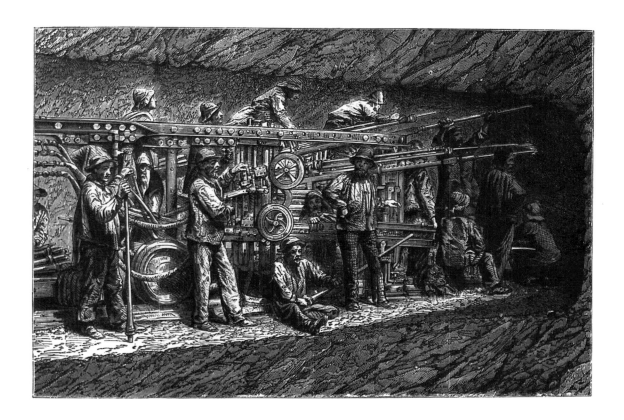

The various functions could progress simultaneously in manual excavation, but the mechanical process was sequential, so drilling was initially slower than anticipated. A third of the holes still had to be drilled by hand because the fixed bits often hit fissures or other weak spots. It also took time to withdraw the frames, cover them, and clear the air, and the frames could only be redeployed after cleaning up, which took about four hours. The cleanup phase included spoil removal; evening out the floor, walls, and work face; and manually breaking out loose rock. In the latter years of the project, small hand-held pneumatic drills were brought in to accelerate this work. Finally, the heavy and brittle cast-iron pressure conduits had to be rehooked, cushioned carefully against the uneven floor, and protected from falling rock.[159]

The rock at Bardonecchia proved soft, which made it difficult to drill effectively. Underground streams hampered progress, and the machinery slowed blasting and rock removal. Flachat doubted whether mechanization could speed the process at all. One idea was to drill by hand, reserving the pumps for ventilation and running them on steam power. Unlike Brunel, however, Sommeiller and his site engineers kept in close contact with experts all over Europe and slowly worked their way through the logistics of the process. Work picked up speed as they streamlined their methods. By 1862 the frames advanced in ten-hour cycles and drilled 180 centimeters a day. In January 1863 mechanical drilling began from Modane.[160] There was harder rock on that side and this meant quicker progress, since the holes only had to be drilled half as deep.[161] Sommeiller and Mella hoped to advance 360 centimeters per day or 1,296 meters per year, and they reduced the projected deadline from fifteen to ten years in anticipation. They couldn't yet know that quartzite on the French side would blunt the drills faster and slow the process down.

66.
The longest cast-iron conduit ever built carried compressed air to the workfaces. Toward the end of the project it was flanked by a telegraph cable that allowed instantaneous communication between the site offices and the heading. (*Harper's Monthly,* vol. 43, no. 154, July 1871, p. 171.)

The French side was late in starting because the Arc River fell only 5.6 meters, compared to a 26-meter drop at Bardonecchia, and thus did not supply enough water power for compressing air. Neither a waterwheel nor a pump would help, so Sommeiller built a piston-driven, Colladon-type compressor like the ones the commission had used in its tests. He patented it in 1860 and installed it at the site in 1862.[162] Work proceeded smoothly after Colladon's compressor and all his other improvements had been pirated with the tacit approval of Cavour and the Sardinian government. Three times as much air was compressed at seven atmospheres. Drilling accelerated, the ventilation improved, and the completion date was pushed forward again. The first six years of work had brought only 2.2 kilometers of excavation, while at the end of the second six years Sommeiller and Mella almost reached their ambitious goal of three cycles a day, totaling 1,512 meters in 1867 alone.[163] Excavation increased from 70 to 500 centimeters a day and surpassed the most optimistic original estimates. The telegraph line Mella installed between the site office at the entrance and the work face, and the exhaust pipe with its own pump that he laid next to the original pneumatic conduit, greatly improved efficiency.[164] The site had been mechanized for eight of the total eleven years when the shaft broke through on Christmas Day 1870.[165] By the end of the following summer the tunnel was clad, the lateral sidewalks installed, and the track laid. Gottschalk, chief engineer of the Southern Austrian Railway, visited the site in the last construction phase and noted that a strong wind swept the tunnel from north to south, proving those wrong who had feared asphyxiation. Mella retained the fans that had been used during excavation just to be sure, and Gottschalk suggested using Thierry locomotives on that part of the line because they produced less smoke than others.[166] The client finally took possession of the tunnel on 15 September 1871 and inaugurated it two days later. Sommeiller was dead by then, and Italy was united under the House of Savoy. Vittorio Emanuele had triumphed where his predecessor had failed, and he reaped the advantages of what the unlucky Carlo Alberto had sowed, even though transalpine Savoy was now French. The tunnel was justly celebrated as a triumph of technology.

Fell's Temporary Railway over the Pass

Flachat had originally forecast a monumental wastage of funds and almost insurmountable difficulties in digging the tunnel, and claimed that a pass railway would entail laying only thirty-five to seventy-five kilometers more of

67.
It was difficult to produce energy on the French side of the tunnel at Modane, where there was little water and a small drop. So Sommeiller installed a water tank to increase the pressure. (Figuier, *Nouvelles Conquêtes de la Science,* 1883–1885, vol. 2, p. 129.)

68.
Henry Mella built the Bardonecchia compressor building to house Sommeiller's huge machines. (Figuier, *Nouvelles Conquêtes de la Science*, 1883–1885, vol. 2, p. 121, 145, 165.)

69.
The first train arrived in Modane with a load of Italian dignitaries on September 17, 1871. (Figuier, *Nouvelles Conquêtes de la Science*, 1883–1885, vol. 2, p. 489.)

track.[167] In spite of steep inclines and curves, and the danger of rock falls, avalanches, snow, low temperatures, and floods, he considered pass railways to be generally worthwhile because they reduced the length of tunnel needed at the pass to two or three kilometers. He also claimed that they would cost less. He cited Talabot's Lukmanier plan in support of his views, and proposed another pass railway for the Simplon in 1861, fully realizing that the Italian government was probably too conservative to adopt it.[168] Except for very short stretches, the gradients of the existing Simplon and Gotthard pass roads were less than those of several temporary American lines.[169] So Flachat proposed importing the most advanced American-built locomotives and using improved Swiss rolling stock as well. Both countries had material that was suited to extreme rail conditions. The articulated American locomotive bogies, Flachat claimed, could use curves of 100-meter radius instead of 300-meter ones like most of the European rolling stock.[170] Where winding curves would be smaller than the minimum, his partner Jules Petiet proposed running track in circles, in tunnels, on viaducts, or in lateral valleys to gain height gradually.[171] Impatient engineers and businessmen were even willing to consider building a temporary zigzagging American switchback system with its slow speeds and reduced loads.[172] They preferred it to the costly missing links in the European railway lines that remained while the question was being endlessly debated and the long Mont Cenis Tunnel was being dug. "Let us agree," wrote Flachat, "that the alpine crossings should not be left to the tedious execution and haphazard progress of projects already begun, that we need an immediate solution, albeit perhaps temporary, and that consequently we should not hesitate to cross the passes in the open air. We shouldn't have to assemble, as we have already done, so many new methods for solving the problem, and it seems to us that we can reach the goal using currently available methods."[173]

From 1868 until the tunnel opened in 1871, a seventy-seven-kilometer-long railway did run alongside the pass road between Saint-Michel and Susa. Although it was projected for five years and only ran for three, the link was a financial success. It probably grossed more than 2 million francs a year in spite of a serious derailment on 2 December 1869 and snow that reduced the ability of the locomotives to pull more than two or three cars in winter.[174] Toll revenues had grown ten percent per year between 1861 and 1864. Projections for 1865 estimated three trains in each direction a day, transporting 132 passengers and 88 tonnes of goods and cutting the travel time from London and Paris to Genoa, Turin, and beyond to Egypt, India, and China.[175]

In 1843 Baron Armand Séguier had conceived the idea for a traction railway with horizontal wheels that pressed against a central rail and could take curves of only forty-meter radius.[176] John Barraclough Fell built the first one on the Cromford and High-Peak Railway in Derbyshire in 1864 and demonstrated the system to an Italian commission the following year on a two-kilometer stretch with a gradient of 7.5 percent on the French side of Mont Cenis.[177] The commission was satisfied, and Italy issued a building permit contingent upon the French granting one for the other side.[178] Fell approached Thomas Brassey, who had just finished the railways on both sides of the pass and eastward to the former Austrian border at Buffalora on the Ticino River. Brassey was willing to fund the project himself as a speculative venture, and they formed Brassey Fell et Compagnie to build the line. Their railway had the unheard-of maximum grade of 8.3 percent, and the third rail was only installed where the gradient exceeded 4 percent. Fifteen kilometers, or about a fifth, had to be covered to protect the tracks from snow and avalanches. The line cost one-third the cost of a traditional railway with heavier locomotives, heavier substructure, and curves of larger radius.[179]

70.
The pass railway was only open three years, but it turned a handsome profit. It climbed gradients of 8.3 percent using a third rail to increase traction. (*Das Neue Buch der Erfindungen,* 1872–1875, vol. 1, p. 284; Figuier, *Nouvelles Conquêtes de la Science,* 1883–1885, vol. 2, p. 33.)

The railway served its purpose. It disappeared when the tunnel opened and the Alps could be crossed under Mont Fréjus in a few minutes. The long, winding railway over the pass and the necessity for up to ten hours' loading and reloading time for merchandise had become history. Louis Figuier had used all three modes of transport: his first crossing over Napoleon's road in winter had taken fifteen hours under extremely harsh conditions, the second used Fell's temporary pass railway, which was far more comfortable and lasted only five hours, and the third time he rode through the tunnel in comfort in a matter of minutes.[180]

By 1871 the Suez Canal had been open three years, and the tunnel saw heavy use. Transportation prices fell to 20 francs per tonne from the 50 francs per tonne it had cost over the pass, and Genoa thrived. Italy, Switzerland, and Germany negotiated further lines and began planning the Gotthard and Simplon tunnels in 1871. The *Mémoires et Compte-Rendu* announced the formation of the Gotthard tunnel company with Louis Favre as chief engineer and Colladon as consultant in 1872.[181] Milan supported the Gotthard crossing, and digging began in 1873. Savoy promoted the Simplon Tunnel, which began twenty years later, and Venice, already well served by the Brenner railway, supported routes via Splügen or the Lukmanier that failed to materialize as the Austro-Hungarian empire declined.

5

The Transition and the Catalyst: The Conway and Britannia Bridges and the Suez Canal

The new building process grew from a host of factors acting in concert: the ideology of progress, the industrialization of materials, human support and resistance, the changing engineering profession, and new technologies. The Mont Cenis Tunnel was a modern process in some aspects. The Britannia and Conway bridges were in others—for example, when Fairbairn, their design team's industrialist, decided to trade time for money, saving construction time by spending more on the structures. No one recognized it then, but the seed of a novel "aesthetic of process" lay in his decision. A few years later, the contractors working on the Suez Canal had their hands full warding off the British government's attempts to hinder the project. They mechanized the site without finding the time to rethink its organization. But mechanization changed them too, and the canal served as a catalyst for establishing the new building process.

The Conway and Britannia Bridges

When clients pressed their engineers for speed and economy in building, they did not usually call for new technology. Businessmen were interested in results, not methods. Builders improved technology to respond to specific project conditions and to pursue speed. But neither clients nor builders regarded construction as a process that had to be organized. They saw the act of building as a simple concatenation of steps toward a goal, and no one yet searched for solutions to methodological problems. The first building research institutes were only formed in the last quarter of the nineteenth century. Slowly, however, around midcentury the accumulation of fortuitous technological advances in the accelerating number of large-scale projects forced designers to react more consciously to the changes that were taking place.

This was the climate in the mid-1840s that made building the Conway and Britannia railway bridges more of a process than the just completed

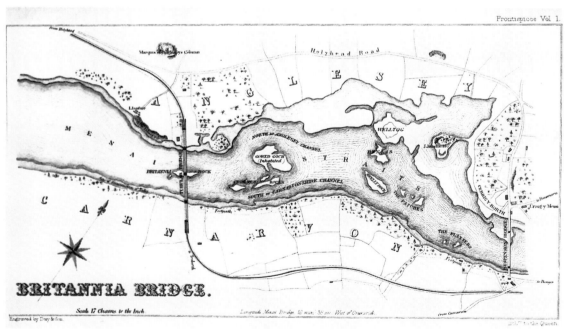

The Transition and the Catalyst

71.
The Britannia railway
bridge crossed the Menai
Straits over Britannia Rock,
close to Telford's 1826 suspended road bridge. Both
carried connections from
London to the Dublin
Ferry at Holyhead. (Edwin
Clark, 1850, vol. 1, frontis.; Tomlinson, 1852, vol.
1, frontis.)

Thames Tunnel. The bridges were to be integral elements of the Chester-and-Holyhead line that connected London via north Wales and the island of Anglesey to the Dublin ferry dock at Holyhead. In a major step toward understanding building as a process, Robert Stephenson, the engineer of the line, designed the two bridges so that he could treat their manufacture and erection as part of the same problem. The Britannia Bridge was to be the longest beam span ever and the first major bridge in wrought iron; Stephenson decided to build the smaller one at Conway first so that he could use it as a full-scale test for the larger one. The plate girder and the box beam featured in their designs were useful new bridge types, and Fairbairn, William Cubitt, and others used them in several small structures while the larger ones were under construction.[1] The new forms spread quickly, and "hollow box-girders of sheet iron" were soon recommended for buildings, too.[2] The Britannia and Conway bridges featured novel cellular honeycomb slabs for the top and bottom members that presaged modern hollow-core panels and orthotropic decks. Deadline pressure to complete the bridges determined the pier shape, the site organization, and the erection method. A team of specialists organized, manufactured, tested, and built the structures, and this made the project an early, partially successful example of teamwork in building. And yet, although we can detect the first glimmer of a critical-path method in their work, the designers were still not quite able to mold the diverse elements into a comprehensive building process.

Only seven years separated the Thames Tunnel opening and the inauguration of the Britannia Bridge. Yet their backgrounds were radically different: unlike the tunnel, the two bridges were links in a traffic network, built to satisfy a preexisting need. The design team pretested their structure and erection method and anticipated every conceivable contingency. Stephenson left very little to ad hoc decision making. As in all other railway companies, the directors and shareholders of the Chester Holyhead Railway Company were no longer subscribers but businessmen, and they had a financial stake in the success of their investment. Although their company did not have to compete with parallel lines, as many other railways did at the time, the directors were still keen to have the line operating and earning revenue as soon as possible. Stephenson, the experienced and dynamic chief engineer of the whole line, did not have to promote his project as Marc Brunel had done. He was a professional builder hired solely to get the job done.

As soon as he began working on the two bridges in 1845, Stephenson enlisted the help of Fairbairn, the locomotive and ship builder and a close friend of his father's. Fairbairn had two decades of experience in wrought-iron construction; the hollow-box beams for the bridges were similar to the wrought-iron ships he had built in his Manchester factory since

72.
Stephenson assembled the Conway tubes on staging along the river bank and used the smaller bridge as a test structure for the larger Britannia Bridge. Then he built the Menai tubes using gantry cranes that moved back and forth over the assembly platform. (Smiles, *Life of George Stephenson*, 1868, p. 450.)

1816. Fairbairn approached naval construction in a new way, using the science of hydraulics to determine hull shapes and employing mathematics to dimension them. For years he had relied on an analytically inclined engineer named Eaton Hodgkinson to design experiments and provide reliable formulae for understanding the material characteristics and stresses in his ships and structures.[3] Hodgkinson had published several papers on the structural behavior of iron beams and had realized the potential of wrought iron as a structural material while editing and annotating the fourth edition of Thomas Tredgold's *Practical Essay on the Strength of Cast Iron* in 1842. So when Fairbairn agreed to collaborate with Stephenson on the bridges he naturally turned to Hodgkinson for help.

Hodgkinson's analytical approach to structural behavior was more common in France than it was in Britain at the time. The standard British method was trial and error, typified by Telford's preference in 1819 for suspending a full-sized chain to measure the sag in the chains he proposed for the Menai Bridge rather than calculating it with a simple catenary equation.[4] Olinthus Vignoles reported an anecdote that had supposedly occurred in 1839 and that would have been inconceivable in France:

> An amusing record of a conversation on a similar subject [structural collapse] heard by a living engineer of the highest eminence has been communicated to the writer. The letters A, B, C, must suffice to stand for the names of three engineers of the greatest repute in those times, some fifty years ago. [in 1839]
>
> Mr. A. related that, on reaching his London offices one day, he received a report that another bridge had fallen. The sub-engineers in the department, hearing of this, held a conference amongst themselves, and began to bet on "whose bridge it was." Heavy odds were laid on its being one superintendent's by a Mr. X., who had earned a grim notoriety in this respect. But Mr. X. confidently denied it, and declared he would accept odds to any amount; and as this cooled the ardour of his brother engineers, he quietly explained: "I knew right well it could *not* be mine, as my last fell in a couple of days ago!" In the course of the same conversation, Mr. A. acknowledged to ten bridges that had failed on his (a very important) line. Mr. B. owned to fifteen or more, on another equally important line. On Mr. C. being asked how he had fared in this respect, he being the engineer of a line as notable now as it was then, replied: "I really can't undertake to say how many bridges of mine have fallen down, but one has certainly failed *six times over.*"[5]

In 1839, A, B, and C would undoubtedly have been the "Great Triumvirate," Isambard Brunel, Joseph Locke, and Robert Stephenson. As Stephenson began work on the Britannia Bridge eight years after this conversation, his thirty-meter truss bridge over the Dee at Chester on the same line collapsed, killing five workmen.[6] This understandably shook his confidence in cast-iron beams, even though others like John Hawkshaw and John Errington continued to support their use.[7] In designing the Conway and Britannia bridges Stephenson must have been grateful to be able to rely on Fairbairn, who supplemented his intuition with experience, and when Fairbairn felt that his limits had been reached he could call on Hodgkinson to verify his empirical conclusions by means of series of controlled model experiments.

The lion's share of the structural development presumably fell on Fairbairn and Hodgkinson. It was they who had experience with long-span hollow beams in wrought iron, whereas Stephenson was responsible for the whole line and was moreover engaged in several other railway projects in Britain, Italy, and Switzerland and thus had little time to devote to the development of a new concept. Fairbairn did, however, credit Stephenson with the invention of the tubular idea, even though his ships were wrought-iron tubes and small ones had been used in arches since 1824.[8] The patent "Improvements in the construction of iron beams for the erection of bridges and other structures" was granted to Fairbairn, but in agreement with Stephenson, and they shared the profits.[9]

Stephenson was less than forthright when he later claimed that he had engaged Fairbairn and Hodgkinson independently of one another and only used their advice in the solution of certain detail questions. Teamwork was still an unfamiliar concept. Stephenson may have felt that sharing the credit would threaten his professional reputation as chief engineer, and he was known to be opinionated. There may also have been a question of interpretation. The term "detail" means "small-scale problem" in technological parlance, whereas to laymen like the directors and shareholders of the Holyhead Railway Company it clearly meant "minor, subordinate part."[10] Fairbairn may correctly have felt that the "details" he developed were crucial to the novel structure, while Stephenson was still right, if perhaps not quite aboveboard, in calling them "details" in a sense the nontechnological directors were sure to understand differently. Stephenson made another, analogous "simplification" to the same body when reporting the reasons for choosing a rectangular tube.[11]

While Fairbairn went on to build over a hundred plate girders and some box beam bridges, Stephenson designed only two minor and one major box beam of the Britannia type before renouncing his right to the patent.[12] The problem of attribution was further complicated by the fact that neither Stephenson nor Fairbairn had sufficient leisure to follow the project intimately through all its stages, and delegated its day-to-day management to subordinates. From 1846 Edwin Clark represented them on the Britannia Bridge and William Evans at Conway. Evans was also the masonry contractor for the Conway site and the builder of the tubes for both bridges.[13] Stephenson also hired an architect named Francis Thompson to design the masonry piers and abutments.

The group originally worked as a team, a new form of professional relationship that was beginning to appear as engineering specialties emerged.[14] Hodgkinson and Thompson were hired as what we today would term "consultants," and in spite of Stephenson's later statement to the contrary, Fairbairn and he were contractually jointly responsible to the company.[15] It is true that the four had roles of differing importance to play, but they were independent agents, and only the two site engineers were employees. The group experienced the problems still commonly associated with teamwork, and Stephenson and Fairbairn separated in conflict over their responsibilities in 1848. Each wrote a report stressing his standpoint and defending his role. Fairbairn, who felt he had been overridden, published his in 1849, a year before Clark published Stephenson's story. By washing their dirty linen in public they provided a complete and detailed account of the entire decision-making and building process.

Stephenson had originally revived Telford's 1810 idea for a cast-iron arch of daring cantilever construction over the Menai Strait. But the Admiralty posed the same conditions in 1845 that had defeated Telford's earlier proposal. The strait was shallow and would have been ideal for the placement of scaffolding, but the navy did not permit even a temporary structure to block the channel. Like Telford, Stephenson found that his arch spandrels cut into the proscribed 137 meter by 32.5 meter cross section, and the Admiralty also criticized the thickness of the proposed intermediate pier on Britannia Island for disturbing the wind flow.

73.
William Fairbairn and others developed various forms of riveted plate and box girders in wrought iron while the bridges were in the design phase. (Humber, *Complete Treatise*, 1861, vol. 1, plate A opposite p. 84.)

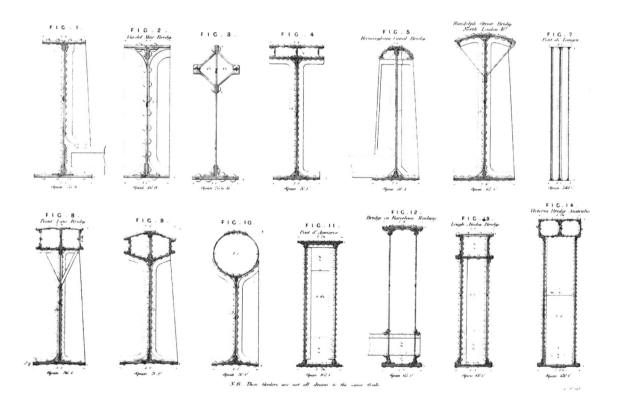

Telford had solved the problem by building a suspension bridge, which began the preeminence of that system for the world's longest spans. So Stephenson next considered a suspension bridge on the Telford model. The system performed well for road traffic, but he knew that it was too flexible for the larger dynamic loads of a moving train. Stephenson and his father George had built a small suspension bridge on their Stockton and Darlington railway near Durham in 1825, and their experience had been entirely negative. So he decided to add a stiffening truss to reduce deflection. Fairbairn and Hodgkinson initially thought that a round or oval stiffening tube would represent the best distribution of material in relation to strength. This is true for a tube's resistance to compression along its axis, but it is not as effective in resisting bending caused by forces perpendicular to the axis. The tube became larger and more exaggeratedly oval with each test, and ultimately turned into a rectangular box beam that was self-supporting and large enough for the train to run through it.

The question then arose whether the bridge needed the suspension chains at all.[16] The engineers pursued this question by examining failure under bending and the phenomenon of crippling or flaring in the walls, for which they designed appropriate stiffeners.

74.
The continuous box girders had stiffening ribs for the walls and cellular plates for the top and bottom. Gussets at each rib stiffened the connections between walls, roof, and floor. (Routledge, 1901, p. 281.)

The Transition and the Catalyst

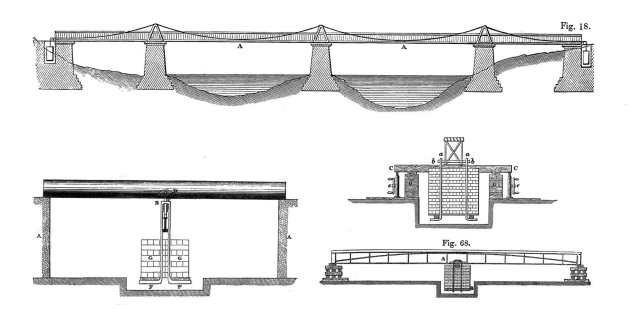

Fig. 18.

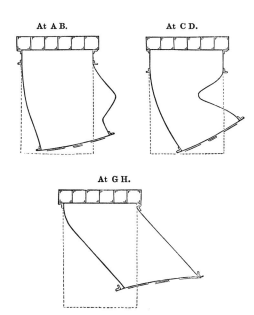

Fig. 68.

75.

As the project developed, the tubes Stephenson had originally designed as stiffening for a suspension bridge grew larger until they ended as huge box girders through which the train ran. Fairbairn and Hodgkinson set up tests to dimension the tubes and to determine whether chains were still needed or might help the erection process. (Fairbairn, *Account of the Construction*, 1849, pp. 49, 211, 251; Edwin Clark, 1850, vol. 1, p. 165.)

At A B.

At C D.

At G H.

Fairbairn set up a series of experiments at Millwall and Hodgkinson tried to derive the general laws of iron beam behavior from the test results. Hodgkinson correctly presumed that the number of experiments he wanted would meet with resistance from the directors, so he initially requested fewer and gradually stepped up his demands.[17] This form of subterfuge is still widely practiced in building to reduce the bid price on a construction job; clients are often presented with inflated bills for "unforeseeable extras" that are entirely predictable to an experienced builder or for items questionably listed as client demands. In this case Hodgkinson used the ruse to indulge his interest in a more general study than was necessary for building the bridges and to have the railway company pay for it.

The final rectangular cross section had double upper and bottom plates connected by honeycomb webbing, an idea that Stephenson claimed to have revived from a bridge he had proposed in 1841.[18] However, Fairbairn and Hodgkinson made a distinction that Stephenson did not and that was crucial to the development of the cellular structure of the top and bottom flanges: they differentiated between material failure and structural failure in their experiments, a distinction that would influence the future development of thin-walled structures.[19] But although they built the bridges as rigid box beams and called them "tubes," everyone still thought of them as plate girders and neglected their three-dimensional behavior. Also, while the beams were linked to form a continuous structure, the engineers calculated them as a series of independent simple beams for added safety, and thus overlooked the fact that the linkage caused a thermal expansion of ten centimeters on either end.[20]

The site organization, component manufacture, and bridge erection were avant-garde. The engineers carefully planned all phases of the operation, and their effort paid off. The slightly reinforced Conway Bridge still serves the railway, while the Britannia Bridge remained in use until it was critically damaged by fire in 1972. The only thing missing from the plan was a timetable, so that as the projects neared completion and the Britannia Bridge presented the last obstacle to opening the line the pressure to finish mounted.

Designing the tubes took the most time. Hodgkinson repeatedly asked for further models, and the theoretical evaluation of the experiments took longer than anticipated. Everything he and Fairbairn did was scrupulously checked by Clark on Stephenson's orders.[21] The team members had different priorities: Hodgkinson was interested in theory, Fairbairn in its applicability, and Stephenson in the results. Stephenson and Fairbairn gradually grew impatient with Hodgkinson, whose complex calculations promised

76.

The roof had more cells than the floor but used only single-plate thicknesses. The internal gussets ran over two cells in the roof but only one in the floor so as to leave enough room for the tracks. Plate splices were staggered, and vertical ribs ran the whole height both inside and out. (Fairbairn, *Account of the Construction*, 1849, p. 142; Dempsey, 1851, pp. 104, 107.)

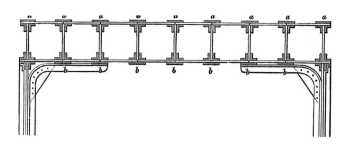

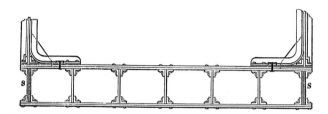

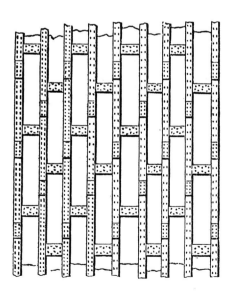

little if anything beyond what the experiments had already shown. Soon Fairbairn found himself in a dilemma: his sympathies lay both with the theoretical interests of his friend and with the practical needs of his partner. "The time had now arrived when it became absolutely necessary that we should proceed with the construction of the tubes. Six months had nearly elapsed, waiting for the results of Mr. Hodgkinson's investigations; but it appears that his labours were advancing unsatisfactorily to himself, and embarrassing to others. Mr. Stephenson was urgent, and the Directors were impatient in consequence of the delay."[22]

Finally, at the end of February 1846, Fairbairn took matters into his own hands and finished the experiments quickly without Hodgkinson, while Stephenson fumed with impatience. The excessive caution with which Hodgkinson proceeded, and which had impressed him so favorably at the outset, now seemed rank indecisiveness. Stephenson, the man of deeds, demanded results, and in July 1846 he wrote the researcher a peevish letter:

> I much regret the view you take of the matter, but in my position as engineer of the Holyhead Railway Company, and upon whom the responsibility of the Conway bridge being completed in time for opening that portion of the line [rests], you must perceive the difficulty I labour under. The Directors are pledged to the shareholders to have this portion of the line open by a certain period, and I am bound (even at the risk of not having arrived at the very best mode of distributing the material of the tube) to proceed; for what the consequence of delay, in a commercial point of view, after upwards of a million of money has been spent in finishing the works, not simply the interest, but the loss of income and these together, you will at once see, must become a very serious consideration both to the directors and shareholders.[23]

Hodgkinson ended his involvement with the bridge project after March 1846, and Fairbairn continued the experiments and construction without him.[24] How different this was from the atmosphere surrounding the digging of that "Great Bore," the Thames Tunnel! Stephenson's letter expressed with all possible clarity the urgency passed on to him by the directors.[25] Commercial criteria controlled his building site, and he meant to apply them to building research, too. It was a little more difficult for Fairbairn to press for speed uncritically. His own industry throve on research and development, and he tried to tread the middle ground. For quite a while he prepared as much material for Hodgkinson's experiments as far in advance as he could.

Fairbairn claimed to have designed innovative manufacturing and erection techniques to save time. Whether the ideas were his or not, they came from the same source as the structural idea itself: from boiler, machine, and shipbuilding. Fairbairn's industrial experience stood him in good stead, and Stephenson, son and partner of the first commercial locomotive builder, was also used to dealing with deadlines.[26] Machine builders expected stress and deadlines, and the analogy between ship construction and bridge building facilitated the translation of the construction phase into a process.

The same ease of transition characterized the erection method. Millions of rivets were placed by a machine invented during a boilermaker's strike at Fairbairn's suggestion and patented in 1837 by Robert Smith (although Smith seems to have patented one a year earlier).[27] Scaffolding was out of the question, and the alternatives were cantilever construction, floating the bridges in, or some form of launching. All of these methods were fraught with tricky technological problems. Fairbairn, possibly using an idea Clark had originally developed, wrote to Stephenson suggesting that they lift the entire spans with giant presses fixed to the piers. His comment was the earliest explicit statement I have yet discovered that consciously makes technological or organizational method responsible for saving construction time: "I would suggest that you give the subject your serious consideration; as, in case we can accomplish this, a saving of time and one-half of the cost of the bridge may be obtained."[28]

The method was related to ship launching, particularly to the resolution of an accident that had happened to H.M.S. *Prince of Wales,* which Clark alluded to in 1850 as a demonstration of the bending strength of tubular construction.[29] (During the launching, the ship stuck suspended in midair, only supported at stem and stern, yet the structure did not fail.) The bridges' huge box beams were floated in on barges and raised up the piers by hydraulic presses of unprecedented capacity for a building site; the longest beam weighed 1,400 tons. The reports do not clearly state who solved the details, that is, the small-scale technical problems. It was more than likely that the whole engineering wing of the team participated at some time or other. Clark and Evans must certainly have been intimately involved all along.

Stephenson had a scale model of the Menai Strait built to test the floating operation. The engineers had to coordinate their movements with the tide and the currents, and the site personnel practiced again and again to develop strategies that would cover all eventualities. When everything was ready, Fairbairn test-loaded the first Conway tube to make quite certain that the results corresponded to the latest Millwall model experiments. Then Evans and he floated it in and raised it in the first week of April 1848.[30] This was a simpler operation than they had tested on the model, since the Conway River had no tidal currents. When the first tube was securely in place, Fairbairn resigned on 16 May, and Evans went on to build and raise the second tube on 8 December.[31] The bridge opened eight days later. It took another eighteen months to complete the larger Britannia Bridge. The caution with which the team had practiced the floating method paid off in the tidal strait. They used their carefully studied emergency procedures twice before the last link in the London-Holyhead line was finally closed on 18 March 1850.

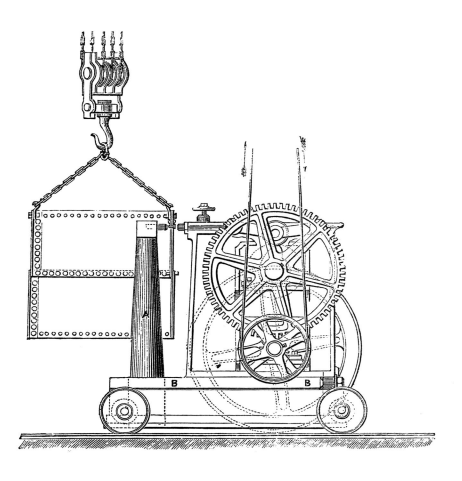

The Transition and the Catalyst

77.
Fairbairn had used his
1837 track-mounted, belt-
driven riveting machine for
boilermaking in Manches-
ter. His Conway and Britannia machines were steam-
driven and stood in the site
workshops, where they riveted components that teams
of workmen then assembled
manually on waterfront
staging. (*Official Descriptive
and Illustrated Catalogue,*
1851, p. 287; Humber,
Complete Treatise, 1861,
vol. 1, plate D opposite
p. 144.)

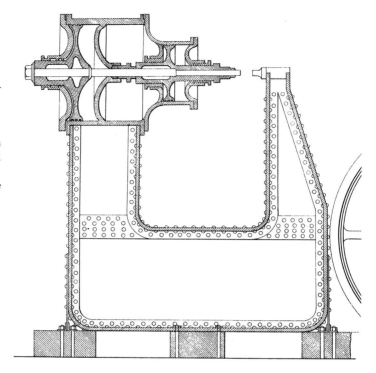

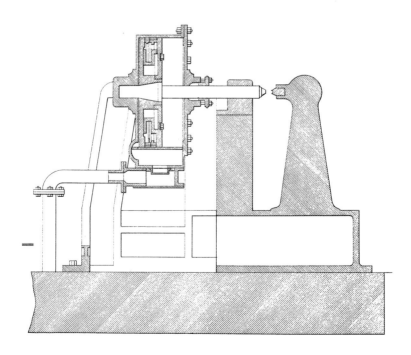

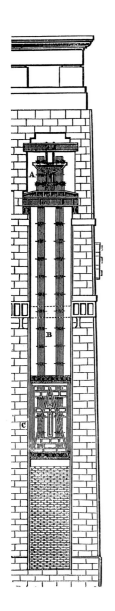

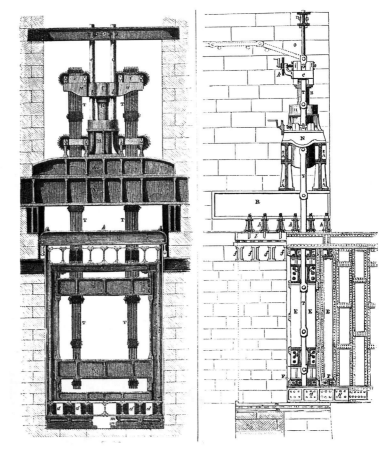

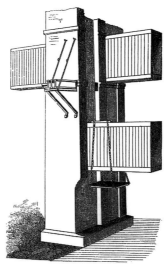

78.
The lifting beams for raising the main girders pierced
the masonry and braced
against the tower for additional stability. The masons
filled the space under the
rising tubes from scaffolding suspended from them.
Only the Britannia side
spans were built piecemeal
on centering. (Tomlinson,
1852, vol. 1, p. 249;
Routledge, 1901, p. 336;
Dempsey, 1851, p. 116.)

The Transition and the Catalyst

79.
One tower leg was cut back so that Evans could maneuver the girders into position. Then the workmen attached the lifting frames. The view from the tower on Britannia Rock toward Anglesea shows one girder in place, with side-span scaffolding visible in the background. (Edwin Clark, 1850, vol. 2, pp. 542, 689.)

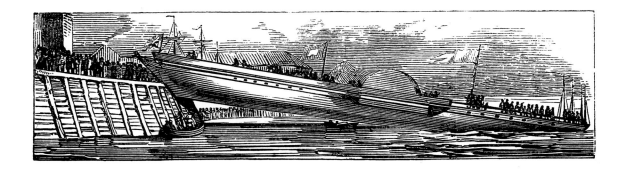

Fig. 37.

80.
A launching accident in Millwall Dockyard convinced the railway directors that the girders would hold without chains. Prefabrication depended on floating the girders in. At Britannia the girders floated off at high tide, while they were lowered mechanically onto pontoons (suggested by Fairbairn) in the nontidal Conway River. (Edwin Clark, 1850, vol. 1, p. 30; Fairbairn, *Account of the Construction*, 1849, pp. 92, 99; Dempsey, 1851, p. 115.)

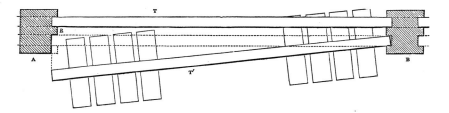

Process, a New Aesthetic Consideration

The question of the chains remained unresolved until quite late, and was one of the reasons that Hodgkinson's delays were tolerated so long in spite of opposition. Opinion differed as to whether chains would be useful; some thought they would be unnecessary or even dangerous to the box beams. Engineers were still unable to calculate statically indeterminate structures at the time, and they therefore regarded them with suspicion. Pasley, who was then one of three Chief Inspecting Officers of Railways, considered chains to be essential. Hodgkinson thought them at least useful, while Fairbairn had been confident all along that the tubes would be strong enough to dispense with them and thought that he could hoist the tubes with no intermediate support. Stephenson felt unsure when he reported to the shareholders in 1846:

> You will observe in Mr. Fairbairn's remarks, that he contemplates the feasibility of stripping the tube entirely of all the chains that may be required in the erection of the bridges; whereas, on the other hand, Mr. Hodgkinson thinks the chains will be an essential, or at all events a useful auxiliary, to give the tube the requisite strength and rigidity. This, however, will be determined by the proposed additional experiments, and does not interfere with the construction of the masonry, which is designed so as to admit of the tube, with or without the chains.[32]

Stephenson was referring to the fact that he had asked Thompson to design the bridge piers to accommodate both possibilities. Thompson crenelated the Conway pier tops to match the adjacent ruin of Conway Castle and designed those of the Britannia piers "in the Egyptian style," but in both instances their height was determined by the exigencies of the building process. Evans carried all masonry piers well above the beam supports and provided them with openings for possible suspension chains. This was done in advance so as not to prejudice the decision. Hodgkinson was late with his calculations, later than Stephenson could wait with construction, so Stephenson took the only route open to him and expended extra effort on the piers in order to save time later.

Saving time in one part of the construction process by increasing construction in another was a stroke of genius on Stephenson's part and a crucial step in the conceptualization of building as a process. As far as I have been able to trace, this is the earliest recorded example of parallel planning, in which a linear construction sequence is decoupled and different parts — in this case, the experimentation, the construction of the masonry piers, and the decision on the superstructure — run parallel in order to gain time. To do that, Stephenson must have used a primitive form of critical-path and matrix thinking. These would have allowed him to optimize his choices in context. The parallel process organization gave him the flexibility he sorely needed to trade more construction for speedier completion.

The often-repeated contemporary opinion that the Britannia Bridge was an aesthetic failure is quite unjustified from a procedural standpoint.[33] We cannot judge engineering structures solely by the standards we apply to works of architecture. Architectural critics and historians traditionally regard buildings as pristine and isolated objects. But engineering design and practice deal primarily with processes in their context rather than with products. If we accept the premise that engineering aesthetics should include issues that engineers consider important, we need an "aesthetics of process" to judge engineering works, and not a variant form of "aesthetics of product."[34] The decision Stephenson made to raise the Conway and Britannia piers above the level of the beam supports must be seen in its procedural context and recognized for the elegant invention it is. Like Smeaton's first attempts at technological thought, Stephenson's matrix thinking and the birth of a new perspective on the aesthetics of building signaled a change in Western culture. We are still exploring their repercussions.

The Suez Canal as a Catalyst

Planned processes like the Britannia and Conway bridges were still rare in the middle of the nineteenth century, and a catalyst was needed to strengthen the trend. The Suez Canal was the project that performed this function, and its influence made itself felt while it was still no more than a twinkle in Ferdinand de Lesseps's eye. Lesseps's efforts on its behalf prompted anticipatory structural changes throughout Europe's traffic network. The canal did not exemplify the new approach to building itself, but it mediated the breakthrough of procedural thinking by bridging the gap between old and new.

A canal had run from the Nile through the Bitter Lakes to Suez in ancient times until it was finally abandoned around A.D. 770. Ancient authors described various routes, but they all agreed that it was only used about two months a year, when it was fed by the Nile in spate.[35] The philosopher and mathematician Leibnitz, who was also director of the Hanoverian Port Authority, revived the idea in a memorandum he sent to Louis XIV in the middle of the seventeenth century, and for a hundred years French ambassadors vainly raised the issue with the sultan's government in Istanbul.[36] In

81.

The Suez Canal begins at Port Said on the Mediterranean, crosses brackish Lake Manzala to El Kantara, and passes through the depression that became Lake Ballah to the town of El Ferdan. Then it cuts through the heights of El Gisr to Ismailia, crosses the depression of Lake Timsah, and passes Serapeum and its ridge to the south before reaching the depression that became the Bitter Lakes. Finally it cuts through Shallufa Plateau to the town of that name and on to Suez on the Red Sea. (Figuier, *Nouvelles Conquêtes de la Science*, 1883–1885, vol. 4, p. 113.)

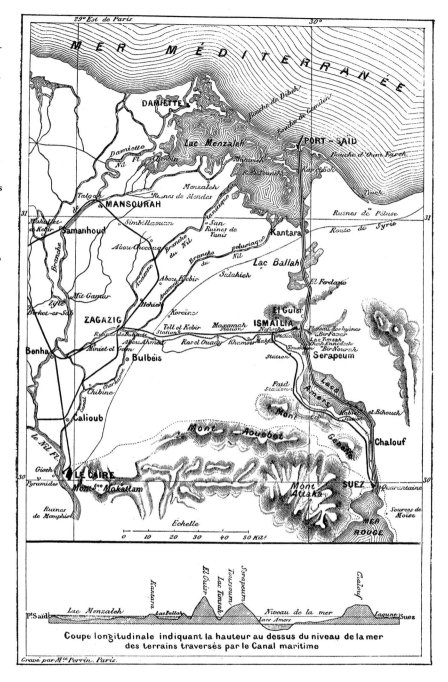

1798 Napoleon had Jacques-Marie Lepère, a member of his Commission des Sciences et des Arts d'Egypte, survey a direct canal route from south to north.[37] Lepère erroneously measured almost ten meters difference in level between the Red Sea and the Mediterranean, apparently confirming the opinions of the ancient canal builders.[38] In his report Lepère therefore proposed recutting the ancient canal with locks. French cartography was otherwise reliable, and Lepère's imprecision was likely due to war, hostile inhabitants, and the rigors of desert life. The route was reexamined in 1830, but it was only in the course of the following decade that a new survey team corrected the mistake.[39]

In the meanwhile, British entrepreneurs began to show interest in the Isthmus route to India and in 1837 organized the Peninsular and Orient steamship line from Suez to Bombay to supplement an existing service from Liverpool to Alexandria. It was so successful that passenger traffic increased almost elevenfold between 1844 and 1847, and a railway was proposed for the overland portion of the route.[40] British engineers built a segment from Alexandria to Cairo between 1852 and 1856 under Khedive (viceroy) Abbas I, and Robert Stephenson extended it to Suez in 1858 under Abbas's successor Mohammed Said. This reduced the London-Bombay voyage via Egypt to forty days, while the route around the Cape of Good Hope took three times as long.

82.
Robert Stephenson built the second leg of the Cairo-Suez Railway in 1858 using the same serf labor that the British government would later attack so vehemently to stop the canal project. (Figuier, *Nouvelles Conquêtes de la Science,* 1883–1885, vol. 4, p. 25.)

83.
A panoramic view of the canal from Suez. (Figuier, *Nouvelles Conquêtes de la Science*, 1883–1885, vol. 4, p. 109.)

Others pursued proposals for a canal. The Austrian government had expressed interest to Mohammed Ali, the first khedive to win effective independence from Istanbul, but he was suspicious of any foreign involvement and refused. L. Maurice Adolphe Linant de Bellefonts, head of Egypt's Department of Public Works, continued to press the matter under Mohammed Ali's grandson Abbas I.[41] Linant and E. Mougel, the same engineer who used pneumatic foundation technology on the Nile dam, studied a direct and an indirect route, making test cores of soil composition along both. They also consulted Ritter Alois von Negrelli, inspector general of Austrian Railways; Paulin F. Talabot, a Saint-Simonian refugee in Egypt; and, at Talabot's invitation, Robert Stephenson.[42] Talabot's engineers surveyed the Isthmus from September 1846 to January 1847 and determined unequivocally that Lepère's numbers were wrong: there was no appreciable difference between the levels of the Red Sea and the Mediterranean.[43]

While Talabot's men surveyed the line, Negrelli's looked at the Bay of Pelusium, and Stephenson examined maps of Suez harbor.[44] Stephenson had been convinced that the previously measured differences in sea level would serve to flush the cutting and keep the canal and a Mediterranean port free of silt.[45] Since this was not the case, Talabot decided that a port on Pelusium Bay would be impracticable, as Nile silt always drifted eastward from the Damietta branch, and Stephenson agreed after visiting the site in 1850.[46]

Khedive Abbas I soon lost interest in the project. Like his grandfather, Abbas was wary of European interference and particularly of the British *démarche* in Istanbul. When he was assassinated in 1854, one of his uncles—the ambitious Mohammed Said, Mohammed Ali's son—succeeded him. Mohammed Ali had been helped in his rebellion against Istanbul by the French diplomat Marquis Mathieu de Lesseps. The sons of the two were school friends in Paris. When Mohammed Said ascended the throne, he invited his friend Ferdinand, by then Marquis de Lesseps and cousin of the new French Empress Eugénie, to join him in Egypt. Lesseps had been an enthusiastic supporter of Napoleon's direct route ever since he had read Lepère's report *Sur la jonction des deux mers* in 1831. He convinced the khedive to grant him a charter with attractive conditions for himself and his investors. The European convention of 1841 had given the khedive administrative independence from the sultan, so ratification in Istanbul was a matter of form. Nevertheless, the British were able to obstruct it, so the khedive issued a second one in 1855 and left the original one to run its slow official course until 1866.[47]

Lesseps was an excellent promoter with useful social, diplomatic, and financial skills, and he inspired several of the engineers who had studied the isthmus to publish their projects. Talabot's was an unrealistically expensive version of Lepère's idea to reopen the ancient canal with an aqueduct over the Nile and a vast reservoir to water the four-hundred-kilometer-long route.[48] Alexis Barrault, a fellow Saint-Simonian, agreed with Talabot on the inappropriateness of Pelusium Bay and proposed another long route that ended west of the Nile delta at Alexandria.[49] Stephenson soon became involved in the second construction phase of the Egyptian railway and opposed a canal altogether. He claimed it would require constant and prohibitively expensive dredging to maintain and stated so in Parliament in June 1858.[50] Negrelli and Stephenson disputed the idea in an exchange of letters in the *Oesterreichische Gazette* in 1858, demonstrating how two competent professionals with differing agendas can reach diametrically opposing conclusions based on the same facts.[51] Lesseps visited Britain five times to promote his idea, but with little success, principally because of Stephenson's influence. Whether Stephenson's opposition was due to a conflict of interest or not has never been fully resolved, although his retainer of £55,000 from the railway company may have swayed his opinion. Stephenson apparently had a history of opposing innovative projects that were not railways.[52] He died in October

1859, six months after digging had commenced, having successfully inhibited British interests from participating until well after the canal was finished.

Faced with many conflicting opinions, all of which sounded logical, Lesseps urged Linant to submit the studies to an international blue-ribbon commission, which met in 1855 and 1856. It included Negrelli but not Stephenson. The committee members were among the most eminent engineers of their day. The president was Jan Frederick Willem Conrad, chief engineer of the Water-Staat of the Hague; the secretaries were Charles Manby, secretary of the Institution of Civil Engineers, and de Lieussoux, hydrographic engineer to the Imperial French navy. The other members were James Meadows Rendel, past president of the Institution of Civil Engineers; John Robinson MacClean; Captain Harris of the East India Company's navy; Alois von Negrelli, inspector-general of Austrian railways; Pietro Paleocapa, Sardinian minister of public works; Karl von Lentze from Prussia, chief engineer of the Vistula works; Cypriano Segundo Montesinos, director of the Spanish Puentes y Caminos; Captain Jaurès, member of the council of the French admiralty; Regault de Genouilly, French rear-admiral; and Rénaud, inspector general and member of the council of the French Ponts et Chaussées.[53]

The commission examined the project and recommended the direct route Lesseps had espoused. Since major work would have to be done to dredge a port at Pelusium, the commission suggested moving the Mediterranean port closer to the ruins at Sais, where there was no evidence of silting and a natural, eight-meter draft was to be found only three kilometers from the shore.[54] According to Lieussoux locks were unnecessary. Any difference in level between the two seas would be rendered harmless by flooding the basin of the Bitter Lakes, and the southern branch of the canal might develop a current of at most 116 centimeters per second. The Société des Ingénieurs Civils reacted skeptically: the current could still pose problems if sailing vessels were allowed to use the canal.[55]

Lesseps had organized his Compagnie Universelle du Canal Maritime de Suez as a traditional shareholding company in 1854. Like the early British railway companies, Lesseps's original plan was to split the capital into large blocks of shares and sell them to financially powerful investors. He planned to promote them in all the major western countries, but was disappointed when neither American nor British investors seemed interested.[56] So in 1858 he split the two hundred million franc issue into four hundred thousand unprecedentedly tiny units of five hundred francs each and offered them to the general public. Just over half (55.6 percent) of the shares were bought by 21,229 small investors in France, 44 percent was owned by the viceregal government of Egypt, and the remainder was purchased by Russian and "east-ern" capitalists. Only 188 of the French shareholders owned more than a few shares, and only one held as many as 1,000.[57]

The issue was really only successful because Lesseps persuaded the khedive to buy far more than the sixteen percent he had originally agreed to purchase. The company called on investors to pay up only 100 francs of the 500-franc face value, and Khedive Mohammed Said paid only a fraction of that and floated treasury bonds to cover the rest. Nevertheless, the broad financial base in France was novel, and the Suez Canal was an early example of anonymous public financing.[58] As Lesseps said when the canal was completed, "When the son of Mohammed-Ali called me to him and gave me the canal commission, engineering science and the new concept of the association of small investments made the project feasible however difficult or expensive it might prove to be. Today you know where this has landed us thanks to French participation, thanks to the participation, not of little people as Lord Palmerston said, because there are no little people in France today where everyone is part of the democracy, but of small savings."[59] Lesseps understood perfectly how to capitalize on the social goals and ideology of a bourgeoisie strengthened by the revolution of 1848–1849. As a result, the French middle class had a stake in the canal's success, and the project became a French national undertaking.

When the anglophile Khedive Ismail succeeded Mohammed Said in 1862, he consulted John Hawkshaw, who was on a visit to Egypt, without using Lesseps as intermediary. Hawkshaw, president of the Institution of Civil Engineers, reported positively on the project in March 1863, and British politicians suddenly awakened to the implications of the French influence in Egypt.[60] The government launched a frantic diplomatic maneuver to stop the project and forced the Egyptian government to end serf labor for its construction. The value of shares plummeted to 40 francs, or eight percent of their nominal value. The company had to mechanize to replace the serfs, and the directors called for investors to pay another 200 francs per share.[61] Khedive Ismail was unwilling or unable to pay, and the directors voted to widen the cutting. Although the two facts seem unconnected, it was a clever maneuver to sweeten a public appeal for more capital to finance the forced mechanization. Slowly and painfully another one hundred million francs were raised, this time by lottery.[62]

A project of this prominence raised major logistic and organizational problems. It should have become a testing ground for new ideas and a vehicle for technological innovation; we would expect lengthy deliberations with planning and experimental phases to precede the work. But the contractors only seriously attempted to mechanize the site after 1863, and the organization remained haphazard. The terrain was flat and easy to dig and there was originally an abundance of cheap labor. The site lay far from industrial centers and energy sources and this made capital-intensive mechanical installations prohibitively expensive to import. Mohammed Said had already imported a few steam dredges on his own to clear the derelict Mahmoudieh Canal from the Nile to Alexandria and repair and enlarge Suez harbor, and the company had, almost reluctantly, begun to use dredges at Suez in 1859 and had ordered twenty steam shovels in 1862.[63] But the only other mechanical installations in the early years were a few steam pumps and a large tank that provided fresh water to the northern work sites from a bluff overlooking Ismailia.[64]

The company's contract with the government stipulated that Khedive Mohammed Said was to provide 20,000 indentured laborers as a work force.[65] They were rotated each month and paid and housed at the company's expense, earning more than they would otherwise have in the Egyptian economy. Twenty-five thousand of them manned the site in 1862, and there were forty thousand in 1863, just before the hiatus that led to mechanization. The sudden change was a panic reaction to the British attempt to stop the project. The British ambassador to Turkey, Sir Henry Lytton Bulwer, had repeatedly tried in vain to convince the sultan's government in Istanbul to have the digging stopped.[66] Twice his efforts almost led to war. The new Khedive Ismail changed the political constellation: he was as anglophile and as subject to British domination as his predecessor had been influenced by the French. Prime Minister Lord Palmerston now saw an opportunity to cripple the project by protesting against the use of what he chose to see as "slave" labor.

Britain's reaction had complex causes. Between 1854 and 1856 the Crimean War had distracted the government's attention from the urgency of countering the French influence in Egypt. When Lesseps turned the first sod at what would become Port Said in April 1859, Palmerston, then foreign minister, wrote perceptively to the editor of the *Times* that the granting of a French canal concession amounted to "a French colony in the heart of Egypt."[67] Britain had no interest in helping France gain a colony and possibly endanger Britain's lifeline to India and China; it also had no intention of helping France or Russia gain a second exit from the Mediterranean that the British could not control as they could at Gibraltar. Britain considered the shorter trade routes it stood to gain by using the canal to be insufficient compensation for weakening the containment of its colonial and commercial competitors. Britain had just forced trade and diplomatic concessions from China in 1862 and wanted to exploit them alone. The Confederate States of America were also trying that year to force Britain to support their revolt by throttling the export of their cotton to British mills, even before the Union embargo against them became effective. The attempt backfired, but it did push Britain to seek alternative sources of cotton. Egypt was a prime candidate with its long-staple, clean material and new anglophile khedive.[68]

With these motives for reducing the French influence in Egypt, Palmerston appealed emotionally to British public opinion to stop the serf labor on the canal. He genuinely abhorred slavery and used his dislike to further British interests.[69] However, British indignation was selective. Labor conditions had not been an issue in the building of the Panama railway, the trans-Indian railway, or the Alexandria-Cairo-Suez railway. The last two were British projects and the last had used Egyptian labor, too, but all three had been built at grievous loss of human life. And when the jury at the London Exhibition of 1862 suggested giving the Suez Canal Company a medal for its humanitarian care of its workers — so clearly at odds with the conditions that had existed on the Panamanian, Indian, and Egyptian railways — the issue was avoided by arguing that the company was not an exhibitor.[70]

The mix of moral indignation and political opportunism succeeded where diplomacy had failed. The British government almost succeeded in killing the project by pressuring the khedive to forbid "slavery," or at least to reduce the number of his laborers working on the canal to six thousand, and also by forcing him to repatriate most of the land ceded to the company.[71] Mohammed Said had originally preferred Egyptian laborers in order to reduce the threat of a potentially dangerous group of foreigners in Egypt.[72] Ismail, on the other hand, wanted to regain authority over the territories his predecessor had deeded to the company and to reassign his work force to the cotton harvest.[73] The French government had every interest in strengthening the khedive's independence vis-à-vis Istanbul, and Emperor Napoleon III agreed to mediate. Various aspects of the resulting agreement pleased the governments of Egypt, Turkey, Britain, and France, all for different reasons. However, the company suffered, even though it received compensation for the land and workers. There were no other sources of cheap labor to be had, and the company appealed to industry for succor.

In 1863 seventy-five kilometers of canal had been dug and eighty-five remained untouched. A narrow primary channel ran from Port Said to Lake Timsah, and the ancient freshwater canal carried Nile water to Lake Timsah and south to Suez.[74] Chief contractor Hardon resigned in April and a Parisian public works contractor, Borel Lavalley et Compagnie, replaced him. The new firm contracted for two lots totaling 24.5 million cubic meters between El Gisr and the Red Sea. Part of their site lay in the dry and part had to be dredged. Abel Couvreux (père), a steam shovel manufacturer and builder of the Ardennes Railway, subcontracted to finish the fifteen kilometers through the heights of El Gisr, a total of nine million cubic meters, while William Aiton, a British contractor chosen for his experience in dredging the Clyde River, undertook to enlarge the primary cutting from Port Said through Lake Manzala and its continuation to El Gisr from the north (a total of 21.7 million cubic meters) using French dredges.[75] Dussaud Frères was hired to build the two jetties at Port Said.

Borel Lavalley et Compagnie took on the incredible task of reorganizing the shambles left by British and viceregal diplomacy into a dynamic building site. The firm's principals, Paul Borel and Alexandre Lavalley, were academic engineers trained in the paramilitary French engineering tradition and were excellent organizers. In his introductory words to Lavalley's September 1866 talk before the Société des Ingénieurs Civils in Paris, President Eugène Flachat reminded the members "that right up until the last report made to the Society on the cutting of the Isthmus of Suez, work was organized almost entirely on the basis of serf labor. England's influence, having caused an upheaval in the technical conditions of the execution of the contract by suddenly barring the Company from using manual resources, mechanized work remained the only option."[76] Only 3,500 to 6,000 paid workers remained after the army of serfs was disbanded. The site had to be mechanized immediately if the project were to be saved, and even then, as Flachat correctly estimated, at least 10,000 men would still be needed.[77]

Many ideas were put forth, such as a sluicing method used to mine gold in the Pyrenees. A quick, narrow cutting through the high Serapeum Ridge could generate the necessary water power by letting the Mediterranean waters flood the Bitter Lake basin that lay ten meters below sea level, or, as Lavalley pointed out, simply by using the existing freshwater canal, which lay another six or seven meters higher. And when they were full, the lakes would be deep enough to dredge.[78] Flachat and Léon Molinos had proposed flooding all the low-lying areas and dredging the canal from both ends as early as 1856.[79] They had not wanted to speed the process but merely to replace the uncertain cost of human labor by the calculable cost of mechanical work. In a way, their ideas presaged Taylor and Gilbreth's later concerns.

Plans were so far advanced that it first seemed impossible to reorient the building method. The contractors were new, but work progressed more or less according to the original plans. Lesseps was no engineer, and luckily for the project he concentrated on politics and finance, in which he was an expert, leaving the professional problems to his engineers and contractors. He

led the company's appeal to the machine industries of continental Europe and found a sufficient number able and ready to build the specialized machinery his contractors needed at short notice. It was astonishing that French industry was able to rally to his call and produce machines that could move fifty million cubic meters of earth in the thirty months that lay between 1866 and the opening of the canal in 1869. It was the largest amount ever dug in such a brief time.

Lavalley tried American bucket steam shovels, but they proved too unstable to mount on rafts or tracks, so Couvreux designed and built a ladder or bucket-chain excavator.[80] Cochaux, a Belgian firm, supplied about twenty small steam dredges, and E. Gouin et Compagnie built a few more small dredges and ten large ones as well.[81] The Forges et Chantiers de la Méditerranée provided another ten;[82] the first took up to eight months to assemble and become fully operational, while the last were ready in about a month.[83] The twenty large dredges were eventually fitted with articulated, suspended, and cantilevered troughs or with chain conveyors supported on pontoons in the water and on tracks that ran along the banks. These ancillary spoil disposal mechanisms were adapted from a twenty-meter-wide British

85.
Conditions were primitive. While the contractor assembled the first dredges at Port Said, teams of camels laboriously transported the parts of others overland through the desert. (Figuier, *Nouvelles Conquêtes de la Science*, 1883–1885, vol. 4, pp. 145, 147.)

86.
In the waterway the
dredges, conveyors, and
spoil barges had less room
to maneuver than in Lake
Timsah at the northern
foot of the Serapeum
Ridge. (Figuier, *Nouvelles
Conquêtes de la Science*,
1883–1885, vol. 4, pp.
181, 187.)

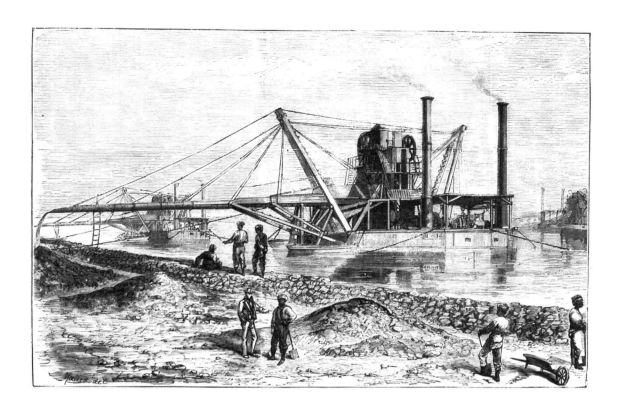

87.
Lavalley mounted spoil troughs on the dredges to deposit the sand directly on the low embankment. He lubricated them with water, and sometimes, where the soil was sticky, he mounted scrapers to prevent clogging. (Figuier, *Nouvelles Conquêtes de la Science,* 1883–1885, vol. 4, p. 177.)

dredge, which Lavalley also tried with some success.[84] After initial trials and adjustments, he deployed these systems sometime after 1864.[85] In their final form the conveyors had a vertical lift of 14.7 meters and were used wherever the banks lay more than eighty centimeters above water, while the troughs had a reach of seventy meters. The height of the conveyors and the reach of the troughs could not be exceeded without making the dredges unstable. Aiton used the troughs on the flat first sixty-one kilometers of canal through the Manzala and Ballah lakes up to El Ferdan, and Lavalley used them at the southern end.[86] The troughs sloped slightly and were lubricated by mixing water into the spoil. This enhanced the flow and ejected the sand with sufficient force to cause it to flow to a great distance.[87] Eventually Lecointre, chief engineer of the Forges et Chantiers de la Méditerranée, fitted them with scrapers to help move soil with a high clay content.[88]

In 1866, Borel Lavalley et Compagnie bought out Aiton, purchased an interest in Couvreux, and took over the whole project. The new corporation alone built over eighty excavators, twenty cranes, and thirty conveyor arms, as well as tractors, entire railways, and boats and barges of various descriptions. The machine industry of continental Europe was still relatively young, although a few firms had been producing since the early years of the century. The sudden demand for building machinery came as a boon to a market that had been slow to develop in spite of steadily growing building activity. Foundries and machine shops must have had the capacity available to be able to accommodate the sudden large-volume request. The same was to occur later in the Ateliers Levallois Perret, Gustave Eiffel's company, when he was suddenly asked to build the locks for the Panama Canal in 1887.[89]

In contrast to the disaster the British government had hoped to create with their maneuver, the French machine and construction industries were strengthened by this crisis, but the transition from manual to mechanized work on site was not easy. The canal was the largest project ever attempted until that time, and thirty-five million francs were invested in material alone.[90] Problems were solved empirically as they arose, although both Flachat and Edmond Badois, the company's chief engineer, made attempts to approach the issues conceptually.

Badois examined the site with an eye to the building process when mechanized work began on a large scale in 1864. He divided the canal into three zones. The first stretched sixty-one kilometers from Port Said through the Manzala and Ballah lakes and El Kantara to El Ferdan. Badois proposed a three-tiered excavation plan for this section. The first stage involved finishing the eight-meter-wide service canal, partly manually and partly using small dredges. The second would widen the canal to the full breadth using the large dredges and short twenty-five-meter troughs, and the third would excavate the waterway to its full depth using inclined planes, conveyors, and barges.[91] Badois's second and third zones were cut by three ridges and required a more complex organization. The second began at El Ferdan and crossed the dunes and the nineteen-meter-high El Gisr Ridge to Ismailia on Lake Timsah, while the third ran from Ismailia to Suez and included Lake Timsah, the six-meter Serapeum Ridge, the Bitter Lake depression that lay ten meters below sea level, the fourteen-meter Shallufa Ridge, and the swamps at Suez.

Badois and Lavalley were articulate supporters of the organization and mechanization of the site. None of the other participants discussed concepts or logistics. The site presented complex problems, especially south of El Ferdan, and the urgent issue was to design, deliver, and set up the machinery; once the general stages of the work had been set, no one really had time to look much farther than that. Most engineers didn't seem to realize that mechanization was radically different from a quantitative increase in manual labor and that it demanded an organizational concept. Badois was an exception, but Lesseps was not aware of the difference and Lavalley was totally absorbed by pragmatic problems:

The Transition and the Catalyst

The transformation was difficult and long. Finding and preparing the apparatus was to take a great deal of time. Besides, the first channels which had sufficed for watering the manually driven sites, had to be transformed into a deep and wide waterway capable of carrying heavy apparatus. Whole towns had to be built at intervals along the canal with masonry houses which now provide quarters suitable for our engineers, our employees, and our European workmen, and where chapels, hospitals and shops sprung up.[92]

Interconnected chains of pragmatic problems simply smothered Lavalley's organizational efforts. Clearly he found it difficult to prioritize his problems. The advantage of technological thinking lies in its matrix approach to problem solving, which recognizes that details make the whole function, while the drawback is that the nonhierarchical matrix also makes it more difficult to prioritize and coordinate a large project. In Lavalley's time technological problem solving and site organization seemed to be two very different fields. They can be synchronized, however, by doing something Lavalley didn't do: attack the organizational problems as though they were technological ones and define the elements that make up the organizational system. Stephenson had begun doing this in a small way by inventing elements of the critical path method, and George Goethals would later refine it and run the world's largest building site by intelligently delineating and delegating responsibility when he built the Panama Canal.

A typical problem chain of the type that made it difficult for Lavalley to organize began with the difficulty he encountered in dredging the fine sand that made up the coastal areas.[93] The material clung to the dredge buckets and clogged the troughs. The only remedy was to slow the dredges, let gravity dislodge the muck, and add water to the troughs to increase the flow. But to do that, the contractor had to install water pumps on the dredges and find out by trial and error how much water he needed for each different type of soil. The spoil moved quicker when just the correct amount was added, and it caused less wear and tear on the machinery, too. Sand needed the most water, but when the dredge dumped the well-lubricated sand into the barges it remained in suspension and escaped through the trap doors at the bottom. So the barge manufacturer had to rebuild the trap door seals and redesign their operating mechanism.[94]

This was only one of many serial problems that required quick, pragmatic decision-making skills. No one had the time to make a survey of possible new technologies. Individual improvements seemed uncoordinated and unrelated to the whole. In 1863 the company was in disarray and did not

clearly define individual responsibilities. By 1866, when the canal was more than half finished, Borel Lavalley et Compagnie had grown into the role of general contractor and was, thanks to Badois's help, in a position to begin re-organizing the project. Until then, however, Lavalley had to make most of his decisions in reaction to problems rather than in anticipation of them.

Badois and Lavalley had determined that they needed to widen the freshwater canal and float in dredges in order to use their capacity to the fullest. That was an example of an organizational decision made to influence the development of the process. But every decision that followed from this one was reactive. Where the tops of the sandy slopes lay too high for the can-tilevered spoil troughs, Lavalley tried cranes. They proved useless because they sank into the sandy banks of the cutting, so he installed conveyors. Where the canal traversed the El Gisr Ridge, which was too high for con-veyors, he cut a narrow channel manually. While the bluffs were being stepped back by hand, dredges entered the narrow channel from the north and dug it wider and deeper. They moved fanlike from side to side and dumped their load in barges that pulled it northward to Lake Ballah and de-posited it to form banks.[95] These solutions were inventive and they worked, but they were single measures that were not coordinated to form a system.

With time the site grew more organized. At the November 1866 flood of the Nile Lavalley broached the freshwater canal and flooded the Serapeum heights, filling manually prepared channels and two natural depressions. Stripped, light dredges were towed southward from Port Said to Ismailia and raised six meters to the freshwater canal through two locks he had built. Then they floated down the higher canal to Serapeum, where they advanced fanlike as at El Gisr. When the Nile and the freshwater canal rose again the following summer, the engineers flooded a third depression in the Serapeum heights and dug the last three kilometers of the eight-kilometer segment.[96] By mid-1867, Lavalley could finally report that the works had been successfully mechanized.[97]

Lavalley's rationalization efforts saved time and labor, but they often prevented him from organizing the site systematically, and several levels of technology thus existed side by side throughout the digging.[98] The most highly mechanized form of earth moving used troughs, conveyors, or bottom-dumping barges in the flooded sections. Close by, on the Shallufa Plateau, the men used wheelbarrows where the stepped, cut-back slopes had lifts of less than four meters each.[99] And where the plateau was high, mules still hauled earth up inclined planes, and Lavalley couldn't even find the time to install a simple winch.[100] Finally, as the site began to wind down, he did find the time to install a few steam winches and inclined planes.[101]

As digging progressed southward, the engineers discovered a kilometer-long bank of hard rock at Suez, and the Red Sea entrance had to be moved eastward to what became Port Tewfik. Lavalley drained the Suez swamp, opened a narrow waterway manually, and then dredged it to full size as before.[102] There were delays because he still needed the dredges in the northern sectors and the rest of the freshwater canal had to be deepened to bring in the machinery.[103] Dredges, steam engines, and winches were still being delivered to the site right up to the end of the work.[104]

The Shallufa Plateau south of the Bitter Lakes is nineteen meters high and fourteen kilometers long. It is made of hard limestone and a mixture of gypsum and clay that is too hard for dredges or steam shovels and had to be dug by hand. Lavalley reserved that segment to take laborers as they were freed from other sites, even though that made the work slower and more costly than digging the other high sectors.[105] If he had used the pneumatic drills Mella had installed a few years before in the Mont Cenis Tunnel, he could have excavated the plateau easily and quickly. It was hardly possible that Lavalley and his engineers did not know of them, since the *Mémoire et Compte-Rendu* published articles on the progress of the Mont Cenis Tunnel alongside accounts of his own work. At Mont Cenis the drills cut much harder stone than the Shallufa Plateau offered. But Lavalley didn't even try them, despite the fact that he had unharnessed water power to hand and was already using steam power for railways, mobile conveyors, tractors, boats, and winches at various points along the canal. Compressed air seemed to be the prime mover of the future and there appeared to be no end to its potential uses. It was being used to drill tunnels and ventilate sites, and inventors were experimenting with compressed air for factories, railways, and postal services. But Lavalley never mentioned pneumatic technology at all. His site appeared to offer ideal conditions for trying the time- and money-saving medium, but he missed the opportunity.

Had he used pneumatic technology to cut the Serapeum Plateau quickly, Lavalley could have flooded the Bitter Lake depression from both ends. Without explaining why, he admitted that he had never considered doing that, but had only planned to flood the larger depression from the north and the smaller later from the south.[106] As the opening date neared, the company directors finally forced the contractor to dig faster so that the lakes would flood from both ends and take only five months to fill.[107] It was a simple organizational measure, and one that a modern builder would have foreseen. No one seems to have asked which would cost more: five months of delayed canal revenues or five months of expensive steam or pneumatic

89.
Mediterranean water began to flow into the Bitter Lake basin at a formal ceremony on 14 March, 1869, while the Red Sea was let in almost as an afterthought five months later. (Figuier, *Nouvelles Conquêtes de la Science*, 1883–1885, vol. 4, p. 209.)

The Transition and the Catalyst

power? Perhaps Lavalley could even have harnessed the six-meter drop from the freshwater canal to produce less expensive energy. It was obvious that he, like everyone else at the time, understood building as a linear concatenation of events, not as a matrix of parallel occurrences through which a builder had to weave a critical path.

As the opening date approached and the pressure grew unbearable, Lavalley finally took a few more organizational steps. Among the simplest were the creation of a spare parts depot and the anticipation of breakdowns by reinforcing machine parts that had proven susceptible to failure. Lavalley justified the cost of such anticipatory measures as a form of insurance.[108] Like the extra structure in the piers of the Britannia Bridge, they guaranteed the deadline.

Lavalley had thought about plant amortization in relation to mechanical breakdowns, but the amount of time the machines worked was apparently not part of his thinking at that time.[109] He did think about the relationship between amortization and construction cost while considering an alternate route through the Bitter Lakes: "The Company, being in possession of a huge, already amortized machine park, would only have to pay for the working of the dredges, and the work wouldn't be any more expensive than that of the dry cuttings even when done by the fellahs working under the terms of the former contract."[110] But he only used the steam shovels twelve hours a day and the small dredges sometimes two hours more, depending on how long they took to fill their allotted barges, while the large dredges worked up to fifteen hours.[111] It is hard to believe that he let the machinery lie idle for part of the day and failed to organize night shifts at the various sites. It is true that it would have been hazardous to run a night shift before he deployed the cantilevered conveyors in 1864, especially with the typical clutter of boats, wagons, materials, and rails lit only by flickering torches and the glow of lanterns. But with the conveyors, and especially with carbon arc lighting, which had been known since 1844 and widely available since 1853, night work would have been relatively simple.[112]

Lavalley was certainly aware of the proliferation of night-lit sites in France. Professional journals had reported on them in detail, and so had Louis Figuier, whom everyone read. But for some reason Lavalley reserved night shifts for "unforeseen problems."[113] However useful it may be to reserve time for unforeseen events in a planning process, it is senseless to neglect to use that time during the building phase. Perhaps he thought the lights too expensive or too difficult to install and maintain, or it may just have been another avenue he neglected to explore. If we compare Lavalley's report with Figuier's description of the Rhine bridge site at Kehl twelve years before, we can see how much cleaner and tighter Vugnier and Fleur Saint-Denis organized the latter. Kehl was electrically lit from 1857 on. It was a rationally run site, and the building process was clearly directed toward mechanization:

> The huge workshops suspended above the river presented a magnificent spectacle. The steam hammers which played so great a role in the sinking of the piles for the piers; the aspirating pumps that compressed the air inside the caissons; the steam sawmills; the wagons sliding along the rails which lined the site; the dredging machines casting the spoil taken from the riverbed: all moved at once filling the air with sharp cries, groans, with thudding and repeated noises. Nightfall did not interrupt the work; electric lighting then replaced the light of day and threw fantastic shadows on this immense antheap of workers engaged in one of the most beautiful enterprises which human industry has ever conceived and accomplished.[114]

Sometimes, labor-intensive and nonmechanized methods could be more appropriate. The contractor Dussaud Frères built the long harbor breakwaters at Port Said using Poirel's system. They had previously built similar quays at Algiers in 1833 and later at Cherbourg, Marseilles, and Toulon using the same method.[115] Dussaud cast twenty-five thousand twenty-five-tonne concrete blocks on the beach using a mixture of sand and hydraulic cement.[116] Ten-cubic-meter blocks were left to cure for two months before loading them three at a time onto specially built barges and dumping them in seven meters of water. The uppermost blocks lay only partly submerged and were placed with the help of winches. Poirel's method was low-tech but highly rationalized. It used little energy or skilled labor and there was almost nothing that could break down and cause delays.

Cheap labor, the distance from machine manufacturers and energy sources in France, and long supply lines originally made the engineers choose the simplest possible technology for the canal. But the situation was different in the second construction phase, where deadlines had become critical. We may wonder whether the site might have profited if Lavalley had tried modern harbor technology. After all, the two months it took the Poirel blocks to cure was a factor to be considered. Pneumatic caissons had replaced Poirel's method in France, and it might have made very little difference whether Lavalley added caissons to the cranes and locomotives he used for moving the concrete at the quay site. But mechanization and rationalization depend on a tangle of factors. The simple technology Dussaud Frères used required hardly

The Transition and the Catalyst

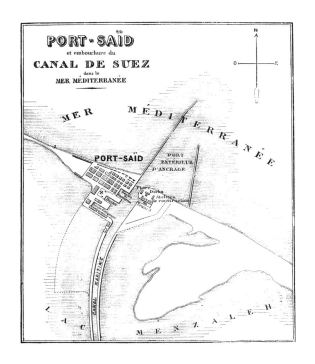

90.
The company built Port Said on a narrow spit of land that separated swampy Lake Menzaleh from the Mediterranean. It was named after Lesseps's friend and supporter, Khedive Mohammed Said. (Figuier, *Nouvelles Conquêtes de la Science*, 1883–1885, vol. 4, pp. 201, 248.)

The Transition and the Catalyst

any skilled labor, which would have had to be housed and paid to European standards, and the large volume of excavation that remained to complete the waterway was surely more critical to the project than finishing the jetties. This last fact especially made it unnecessary to introduce a higher level of organization, trained labor, or specialized machinery in this instance.

However, changes did occur wherever time was a factor. British rail-way companies set contractual deadlines and imposed fines for delay; the 1863 Suez contracts, like the contemporary Franco-Italian agreement on the Mont Cenis project, went a step further, stipulating fines for delay and offer-ing bonuses as incentives for early completion.[117] The premium and fine for Borel Lavalley et Compagnie were both set at 500,000 francs per month, and the deadline was 1 July 1868. But one year into the contract, Lavalley pro-posed doubling the width of the waterway wherever it was not constrained by hills.[118] Of course no report documented whether this was a ruse to avoid the fine when Lavalley realized he couldn't meet the deadline, or an attempt on the part of the directors to obscure unavoidable delays and cost overruns from the shareholders' scrutiny. In all probability both reasons contributed, as well as a legitimate desire to increase the capacity of the canal. In any case, the shareholders accepted Lavalley's proposal, and the contracts were re-newed without the incentive and penalty clauses.

Borel recognized that mechanization improved productivity. He was close to realizing that rationalized building was a matter of organization and that mechanization demanded a new concept of labor when he wrote, "One of the advantages of the type of work we do lies in its utter sameness. Cubic meters follow one another, always the same. This is not the case in railway construction which requires totally diverse cuttings, all sorts of masonry work, carpentry, track-laying, etc. For us, everything is reduced to a question of site installation."[119] Lavalley also understood the basic relationship be-tween mechanization, division of labor, and the principle of speed in build-ing, and after the startup phase he tried to apply it to the site, with moderate success:

> Each of our dredges has a certain number of thousands of cubic me-
> ters to excavate for the duration of the contract, and this specific
> number of thousands of cubic meters covers a certain length of ca-
> nal, 2, 3 or 4 kilometers depending on the natural height of the ter-
> rain. We assign one of these canal lots to each dredge and it will stay
> there until the end of the contract so that the men who put it up
> will remain under the same geological and topographical conditions
> with the same depth to dig, etc. Doing the same thing repeatedly
> they will do it better and better, in other words, more and more
> rapidly.[120]

As opening day approached, the 7,000 North African and 6,900 European workers used the growing pressure for speed to demand and receive higher wages.[121] Both the specialist and the unskilled were aware of their value and potential power. The site conditions had made management as dependent on labor as labor was on management. This was unusual in the nineteenth century, where laborers were commonly abundant and so desperate for work and disorganized that Purdon and others like him could callously risk lives. Lavalley recognized his unique dilemma, and remarked after a breakdown: "We are subject to different conditions: we cannot lay off and rehire our dredgemen. We only have a very limited time to do the work. Each day is encumbered with high machine amortization costs; on no account may our dredges ever stand still."[122] How familiar this sounds to a modern ear, and how different it was from the Thames Tunnel site, where building could stop after a disaster and the works be closed for years and then reopen as though nothing had transpired in the interim!

As the canal progressed in spite of their tactics, the British government recognized that it was impossible to hinder the project without starting a major war. Britain was forced to bide its time until an opportunity presented itself in 1874–1875 when Khedive Ismail finally bankrupted his government's finances. Prime Minister Benjamin Disraeli, Lord Beaconsfield, reacted quickly, purchasing the khedive's controlling interest of 176,602 shares for the government, and Britain came to control the canal by a simple method that Ambassador Bulwer had proposed more than a decade before.[123]

The canal took years to become financially successful. Sailing ships couldn't use it, and in 1869 they still comprised a large percentage of the world's maritime tonnage. Steam vessels of maximum draft only begin to use the waterway in 1880.[124] As traffic grew, the company straightened curves, increased the number of passing points, and gradually dredged the cutting deeper and wider. Eventually ships could pass each other over most of the length of the canal, and the time it took to cross the isthmus decreased from forty-nine hours to seventeen.[125]

6

Patterns of Technological Thought: Buildings from the Sayn
Foundry to the Galerie des Machines

The new concept we now call "system" changed both construction methods and built form. Builders had to mold the methodological consequences of the shift into procedural thinking. This was not easy, as Lavalley's case demonstrated, but it could be done. Designers had to grapple with the formal implications of open-ended or closed systems, of assembly line production and the interchangeability of parts, and this meant that they had to reinvent architectural meaning. Several examples show how this could be done. The builder of the Sayn Foundry of 1830 dealt with widely diverse issues ranging from the more traditional architectural concerns with religious symbolism and mythology to the unfamiliar new ones of industrial form, the relationship between building and machine, structural redundancy, and corporate advertising. The designer of the Kew Palm House of 1848 cleverly segregated conflicting construction requirements in order to address them individually and then reassembled the detail solutions into a system. The contractor of the Crystal Palace of 1851 reconciled modular planning and structural system with a linear erection process, and the builders of the Paris Exhibition of 1889 transformed the act of building into assembling.

Aggressive sales propaganda accompanied commercial expansion in Europe and beyond. All the industrialized nations vied for growing markets, and most of the customer wooing took place at expositions. These fairs had their origins in the medieval trade fair; they turned into competitions when the organizers began to award prizes at the London fair of 1756–1757. The French were particularly active, and dated the development of the modern exhibition from their own first national one, which publicized the industrial capability of the new republic in 1798.[1] Britain's Prince Albert raised the level of competition to the international sphere when he began promoting "The Great Exhibition of the Works of Industry of All Nations 1851." He timed it well—in the midst of the economic boom that followed the suppression of Chartism in England and workers' movements all over Europe—and he planned it to compete with the increasingly ambitious French productions.

92.
Hector Horeau took first place in the Crystal Palace design competition with a five-bay design that had a transept and a domed apse. The cross section was similar to his later market hall designs. Richard Turner placed second with a three-bay design that also had a transept and terminal apses. (*Illustrated Exhibitor*, 1851, pp. 65, 142.)

The 1851 exhibition building occupies a widely recognized position in the development of modern architecture. It has become the benchmark against which all other developments are measured, so much so that, unfair as it may be to some really innovative work, all glass and iron buildings are labeled as being pre- or post-Crystal Palace. The committee held an international design competition that resulted in several interesting proposals. The Hanovarian architect and engineer Georg Laves submitted a partly prefabricated design built mostly of railway rails. The French engineer Hector Horeau's first prize was a linear, cast-iron market hall of triangular cross section with five naves, a transept, and a half-domed apse. Glass, sheet iron, and porcelain covered the exterior. The Irishman Richard Turner's second prize featured a barrel-vaulted shed, completely made of wrought iron and partly covered in glass. The interior was subdivided into three "avenues" corresponding to the arched construction. It too had a transept, with a glass dome at the crossing. Both projects were buildable. Horeau hadn't built much, but Turner had demonstrated his mastery of wrought-iron construction in the Palm House at Kew Gardens (1848) and at Lime Street Station in Liverpool (1850). In his Presidential Report to the Institution of Civil Engineers, William Cubitt, a member of the exhibition committee, praised Turner's proposal: "Mr. Turner . . . brought forward his designs, of which, though they were not adopted, it is but fair to say that as examples of construction ability, and of tasteful combination of materials, they will bear a very favorable comparison with the actual building."[2]

But the jury rejected all the submissions. It seemed that political considerations dictated an English competition winner ruling out Horeau and Turner. Britain was committed to the exhibition and it would have compromised national prestige to delay or cancel it. The clock was ticking just as urgently as it had during the railway scramble five years before. The committee members tried but were not able to formulate an acceptable alternative. Their brick structure would have consumed more than the annual output of all British kilns. Even the quickest-setting contemporary mortar took longer to cure than the exhibition was to stand, and the humidity inside would have damaged the exhibits. The inexorable opening date became the chief criterion for the building's design. At the urging of committee member Henry Cole, the businessman Joseph Paxton submitted a sketch for a multistoried glass shed. His plan was simple and obviously buildable in the allotted time.

Britain stood at the height of its industrial power and commercial expansion, with a world-spanning network of colonies to protect her markets, trade routes, and sources of raw materials. Britain's political thinking was founded on commerce, and it was a commercial mentality that guided

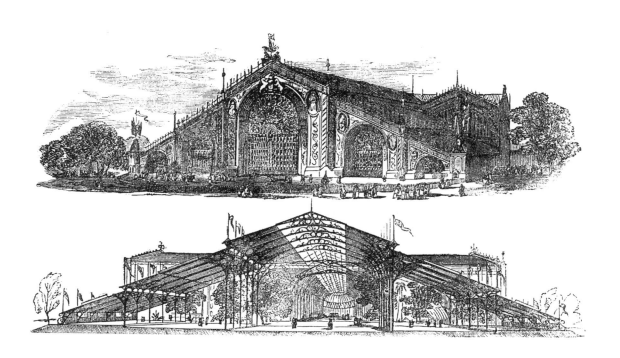

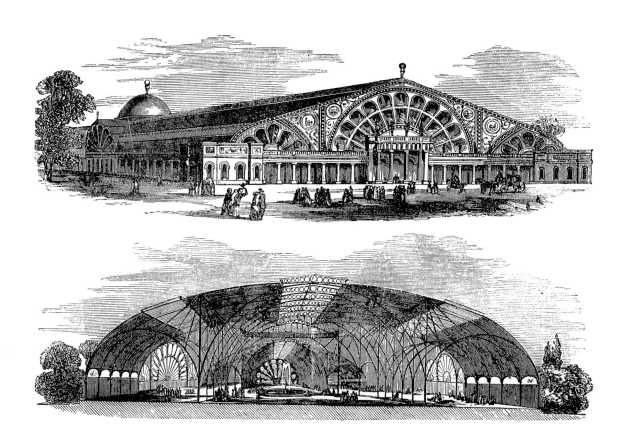

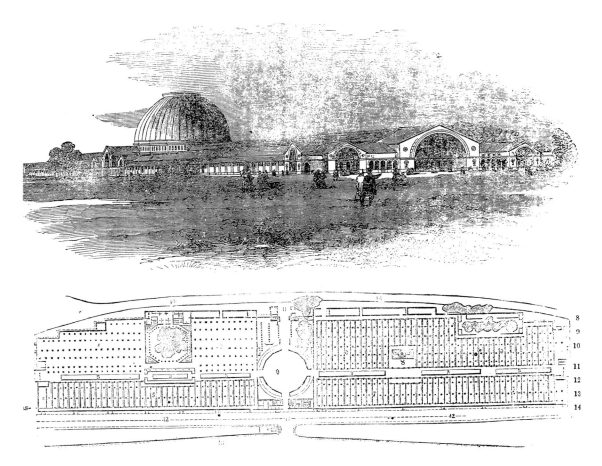

93.
After rejecting the first two
prizes, the Royal Commis-
sion's Building Committee
came up with an ungainly
and impractical design of
their own. (*Illustrated
Exhibitor*, 1851, p. 46.)

the Crystal Palace design, with a rigor that builders had hitherto only applied to transportation construction. Like most other early prefabricated systems, the Crystal Palace was a composite of cast and wrought iron, wood, and glass. It came directly from Paxton's greenhouse designs, and it was part of a fifty-year technological tradition of prefabricated iron-and-wood buildings.[3] Its catchy name was coined by a journalist in "Punch." It perfectly expressed the public fascination with the glass and the light that flooded the interior.

Some critics found the building an abomination. Ruskin was prominent among them, and he polemicized vehemently against its popularity by attacking one of its defenders in his book *The Stones of Venice*.[4] The object of Ruskin's ire was the architect Edward Lacy Garbett, who had just published a popular *Rudimentary Treatise on the Principles of Design in Architecture*.[5] Garbett had obviously intruded on what Ruskin considered to be his turf. Ruskin's dislike of the building is curious, but typical of his flamboyant illogic. He had earlier championed transparency, light, and atmospheric nebulosity in J. W. M. Turner's painting, yet he now decried it in the Crystal Palace. However, even Ruskin was powerless to turn public opinion against the building.

The Crystal Palace was really less transparent than many contemporary hothouses like Kew. Almost all ground-floor cladding panels were wood, as were the ventilation louvers on the upper two stories that took up about a quarter of the surface. Linen sheets were spread across the large glazed ridge-and-furrow roof to dampen glare and spread the light more evenly.[6] A watery light suffused the interior, banished shadows, and "dematerialized" the structure.

This light, the slenderness of the iron, and the decorative sparseness of the building were what made the Crystal Palace so striking. It was not the designers' aesthetic intent to eschew decoration; they left it out because there was no time to include it. Victorian architects decorated their buildings as a matter of course. Pugin had begun to think of decoration as the overlaying of form to give a building meaning beyond the structural; he tentatively separated it from the straightforward enhancement of visual reading or ornament.[7] Based on this distinction, the Crystal Palace's ornament was rich and varied, while its decoration was almost nonexistent. The ornamental aspect included masking differences in column gauge and detailing, color-coding all trusses and columns to suggest uniformity of material where there was none, and hiding the fact that two wooden mock-columns were set between each pair of structural iron ones along the perimeter to underscore the modular reading.

Engineers acclaimed the industrialized manufacture of the building, the rational erection process, and the speed of construction, while the use of glass and the filigree iron members astonished the public. Everyone recognized the building as an advertisement for British industry. One of its prominent icons, as popular then as it is forgotten today, was the iron-reinforced "Crystal Fountain" by the firm Osler & Company. It stood at the crossing of the nave and transept, and the ethereal material boundaries in the shimmering play of glass, water, and light provoked ecstatic descriptions.

94.
The play of light that so enchanted the public on the interior of the building culminated in the "Crystal Fountain" by Osler of Birmingham. It stood at the crossing of nave and transept. (*Crystal Palace and Its Contents,* 1852, p. 17.)

Patterns of Technological Thought

The Sayn Foundry and Associative Design Thinking

One of the Crystal Palace's more fascinating antecedents was the Sayn Foundry in Bendorf, a German town on the Rhine near the Dutch border. The building still stands and is an excellent example of the complex and high-quality technological and border-crossing thinking that went into designing early iron structures. It was built in 1830 by a Prussian engineer and iron founder named Karl Ludwig Althans.[8] The iron foundry is a cruciform basilica in plan, with the furnace replacing the altar and the nave serving as casting floor. In its structural detailing the foundry is typical of the time in which it was built. The frame elements were interconnected like a jigsaw puzzle; each piece was tailored to fit with the next, and no overarching connection system or typology regulated how the pieces were assembled. We find wedging, mortising, and bolting used opportunistically throughout the structure. However, in all other respects the Sayn Foundry was innovative. The ambiguity with which we can interpret the building makes it one of the more fascinating of its period. We can read it on four discrete levels: iconographically, industrially, structurally, and architecturally.

There are several complex cultural layers to the building's iconography that underscore the connection between metalworking, magic, and religion in Western culture. The myth of Vulcan, the smith of the gods, underlies the interpretation of the building as a religious structure, while the furnace as high altar reminds us of the biblical Moloch, Christian iconography depicting the heart of Christ flaming with love, and the long relationship between ironworking, alchemy, and magic. The plan form and neo-Gothic detailing defuse any heathen connections and make the nineteenth-century foundry a safe and appropriate place to worship the new, uplifting beliefs of the Enlightenment: science and progress. At the same time, the building confidently boasts the strident commercialism of the nineteenth century. It is readily readable as an industrial icon and an early example of a building as corporate symbol and advertisement.

The foundry incorporates a number of elements that suggest other industrial forms. The columns are 6.5-meter-long, 18-millimeter-thick cannon barrels, and the swiveling derrick cranes they carry (added by Althans in 1844 and 1845) turn on ball bearings made of cannonballs.[9] The lower chords of the fishbelly trusses supporting the gantry that lifted the molten iron from the furnace to the casting floor are oversized laminated-steel wagon springs.[10] These gunbarrel columns, cannonball ball bearings, and wagon spring truss chords suggest that Althans was a border crosser who solved his technological problems associatively, using the same form of matrix thinking that inspired Marc Brunel to observe the behavior of the pipeworm and invent the tunneling shield. Althans must have had a complex and

95.
Interior of a typical
nineteenth-century iron
foundry and an axonomet-
ric view of the Sayn
Foundry (1830). The
highly redundant cast-iron
frame is braced against the
surrounding masonry wall
and stabilized by the lateral
arches, the glass-filled
"Gothic" tracery of the
front, and the longitudinal
"clerestory" lattices.
(Routledge, 1901, p. 29; axonometric researched and
drafted by Zarli Sein.)

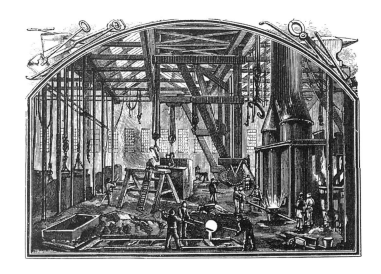

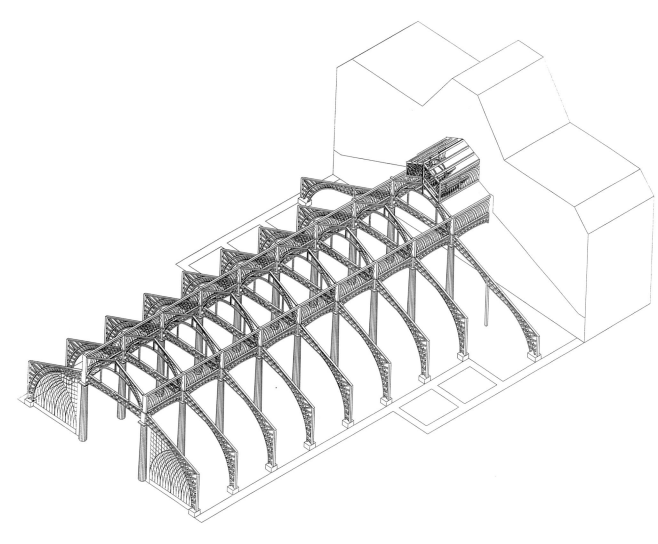

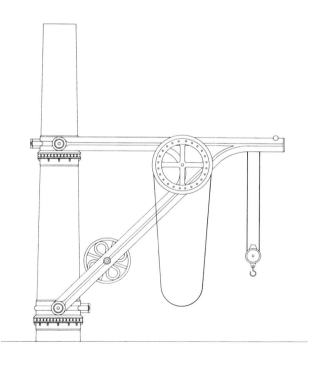

96.
The cross section shows a conjectural configuration of the traveling crane. The derrick cranes rotated around the cast-iron columns on ball bearings made of cannon balls, and the large, hollow columns advertised that the foundry could cast large-bore cannon. (Researched and drafted by Zarli Sein.)

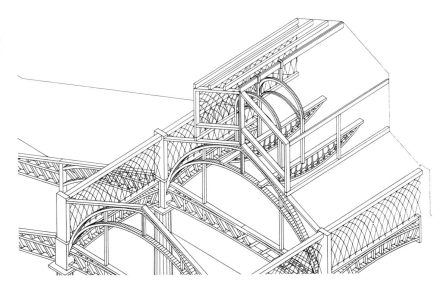

97.
The gantry hovered outside the furnace door to lift crucibles of molten iron to the casting floor. Like the tracery lattice trusses and the longitudinal trussed beams, the fishbelly trusses helped transfer some of the building's longitudinal load to the massive furnace block. (Researched and drafted by Zarli Sein.)

fascinating mind to include so many multilevel aspects in his design. As a nineteenth-century ironfounder he must have been aware of the cultural and industrial connotations, and the close, ambiguous relationship between building and machine would have been natural to him, too. The three types of cranes—the traveler that once hung from the nave framing, the swiveling derricks on the columns, and the gantry at the furnace mouth—are all integrated mechanical parts of the building, not separate industrial "furniture." The severe dynamic loads these cranes had to withstand explain the need for a high level of structural redundancy and the building's complex stiffening mechanism.

Structurally, the foundry's cross section combines a three-dimensional frame and several overlapping configurations of trussed arch that spread the live- and deadload paths to all members in a number of ways simultaneously. This gave the cross section the structural redundancy that helped the building survive so long. The front windows' intricate Gothic tracery not only strengthens the ecclesiastical connotation but also forms a lattice stiffener for lateral movement and, with its glass infill, a shear membrane as well. The continuous clerestory window bands have the same tracery configuration and also function as effective longitudinal stiffening trusses, remarkably similar to the wooden lattice bridge trusses that Ithiel Town had patented in the United States in 1820 and that German builders had begun to copy at that time. The window bands are attached to the tops of nave columns, and as these carried the large liveloads of the traveling and derrick

Patterns of Technological Thought

98.
The flow of forces in the structural bent can read as two superimposed, trussed arches or as a bowstring truss supported by arched struts. Its redundancy helped it survive the heavy moving loads it once carried. (Researched and drafted by Zarli Sein.)

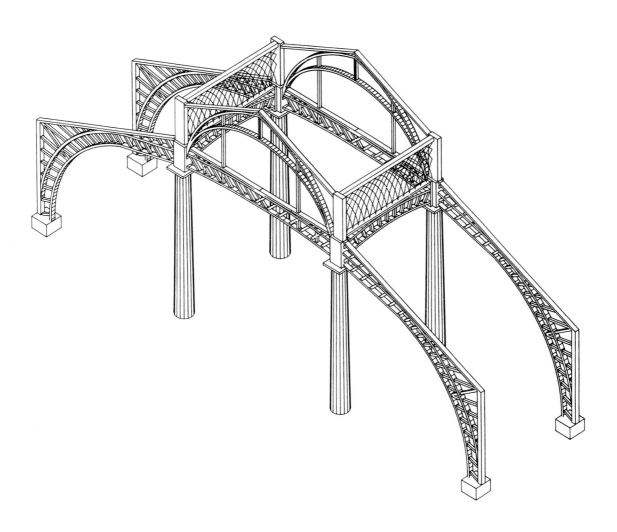

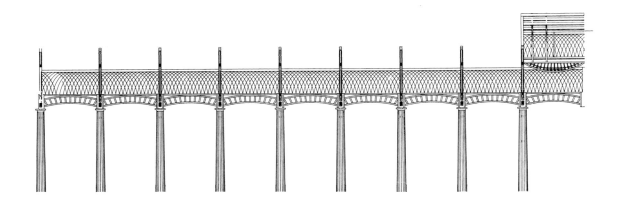

99.
Longitudinal section and facade. The nave crane and
the column derricks are not
shown, but the furnace gantry on its fishbelly truss is.
(Researched and drafted by
Zarli Sein.)

Patterns of Technological Thought

cranes, the tracery stabilized them in a very efficient manner. The complex structure is further braced against two lateral masonry walls and the furnace block at the back.

This structural redundancy is the one area in which hindsight provides us with more interpretive possibilities than were available to Althans, and even there it is difficult for us to imagine what a mind so fertile may have been capable of conceiving. After all, he did invent ball bearings over a decade before a French patent recognized their industrial value, and he developed the fishbelly truss out of Gothic tracery and a wagon spring equally prematurely.[11] It was difficult at the time to cast high-quality iron elements, and Althans was surely aware of the dangers of overoptimization. In contrast to the conceptual clarity that contemporary engineering theoreticians like Franz Joseph von Gerstner, Johann Albert Eytelwein, or C. L. M. Henri Navier were striving for in their simplified modeling of structural behavior, Althans's structural ambiguity and redundancy may well have been his clear-headed and successful way of introducing a safety factor into the structure.

All this found architectural form in the traditional plan of a Christian basilica. Iron originates in the earth, and so did the new field of archaeology that fueled the neo-Gothic movement in the treatises of antiquarian societies at the end of the eighteenth century. The romantic movement, with its concern for the "picturesque," the "sublime," and stylistic appropriateness, is manifest in the painterly setting of the foundry under the looming brow of the neo-Gothic reconstruction of Sayn Castle on its crag. The bitterly fought aesthetic debate, current in 1830, between the appropriateness of Gothic or classical form reverberates in the uneasy relationship between the Gothic tracery and arching and the elongated Tuscan columns. The front windows look remarkably like the gable end of Friedrich Gilly's unbuilt Berlin riding hall, and Karl Friedrich Schinkel, whose Public Works Department in Berlin granted the building permit, also recommended that Althans study his *Sammlung architektonischer Entwürfe*.[12] Nevertheless, Althans transformed all of the many architectural and engineering models he may have used and varied them to solve the many parts of his building. The result was a more sophisticated and complex design than any other iron building of its time.

Each of the many aspects of the building was dependent on all the others. Althans integrated the foundry's products, machinery, structure, form, and cultural meaning in a way that made them inseparable aspects of the whole. We can explain the structural elements as advertisements, as machine supports, as religious form, or as building parts, and we can read the Sayn Foundry's function either as a building that houses a production process or as a machine with space in it for humans to service the industrial process. This makes the foundry an even more complex organism than other

100.

Turner designed the building as a closed system, or one in which the building's structure is the form. The arches and the apses stabilized it against lateral forces. Three lines of purlins made up the horizontal parts of the system. A wedged tension rod, enclosed in a tubular spacer, post-tensioned the arches. A bar purlin supported the glazing mullions and a glazing bar stabilized and connected them to form a grid. By separating the purlin functions in this way, Turner solved each problem optimally. He then reassembled the three purlins in a system that was rigid enough to stabilize the system and yet flexible enough to accommodate lateral forces and expansion. (Researched and drafted by Steven Roethke.) The first purlin line is the tension rod inside the tubular spacer, the second is the bar purlin supported by the tubular spacer and supporting the glazing mullions, and the third is the glazing bar interconnecting the mullions to form a grid.

large machines and industrial buildings that preceded it, such as Brunel's tunneling shield, Triger's pneumatic caisson, or the mahogany storage shed John Rennie built at London's West India Docks in 1814.[13]

The subtle and complex Sayn Foundry is a successful statement of technological thinking in building and of the new concept of the building as facility. As an amalgam of iron building, cultural artifact, public relations statement, and machine it resembles the later Crystal Palace, which trumpeted the power of British industry and its capacity to produce large amounts of iron and glass quickly and efficiently.

Kew Palm House and the Pattern of Technological Method

Before the Crystal Palace there were few iron structures that didn't need masonry walls for stability. The first was probably the 1823 Camelia House in Wollaton Park, Nottinghamshire.[14] Richard Turner's Kew Palm House of 1846–1848 was another unsupported iron building, and it boasted an advanced structural and stiffening system.

The Palm House was entirely wrought iron except for the columns and their brackets. It was prefabricated in components, and compared to the generation of iron buildings that preceded it it shows a notable advance in the simplification and standardization of connections. For example, the frame is post-tensioned by an ingenious system of iron "tubular purlins." The tubes served as spacers between the structural arcs, and wedged tension rods running through the tubes and the webs of the arcs held the structure together. The arcs were rolled deck or bulb beams, precursors of our modern I-beams. Two half barrel vaults stiffened the frame laterally and two domed apses held it longitudinally. Turner had adopted the stiffening vaults and domes from previous schemes by Decimus Burton and John Smith, and they had been used in several previous free-standing hothouses, notably in Paxton's 1839 Chatsworth conservatory.[15]

Builders discovered early on that iron buildings had entirely different problems from stone or wooden structures, with contradictory structural requirements. A fixed beam-column connection, for instance, would stiffen a structure, but could not accommodate thermal expansion at the same time. Turner was one of the first to adopt what is now standard practice in technological design: he segregated technical problems and solved each aspect independently. His tubular purlins were only post-tensioning devices. Secondary purlins carried the glazing bars at the edges of the arcs. The only connections between them were intermediate supports for the thinner purlins at the third or quarter points of each bay. A third, even thinner bar ran parallel to the

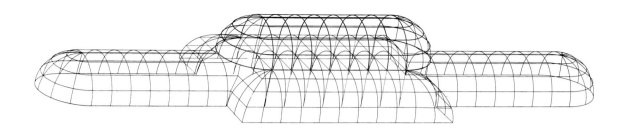

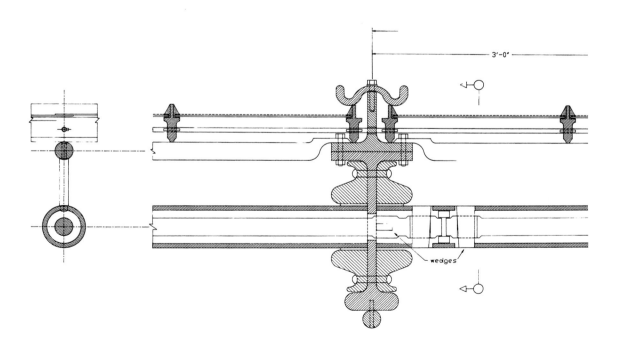

wedges

3'-0"

other two through holes drilled in the glazing bars, which it connected and stabilized. The triplication of the purlin seems needlessly complicated at first. However, it did separate the different construction problems into three distinct layers, and it also helped stabilize the frame in two ways. Each connection was at best semirigid and could adapt ever so slightly when it was loaded; even the welded bars between the primary purlin tube and the secondary purlins were somewhat flexible and acted as rocking beams. These flexible connections helped stabilize the frame by moving slightly and absorbing a little energy whenever lateral forces acted on the building. Likewise, each connection also absorbed a little of the building's thermal expansion, thereby avoiding stress concentrations that would have made single stiff connections fail.

Turner's clear hierarchy of structural members and their relationships advanced technological thought in building. He demonstrated that it was possible to fulfill contradictory criteria in a single detail by decoupling the problems, solving each on its own serially, and then reuniting the solutions to form a component subset in a construction system. In a way, he did for structural design precisely what Stephenson was to do a few years later for the building process.

Like Thomas Paine and Thomas Wilson in his work on the Sunderland bridge, Turner expanded the concept of system to include an intermediate level, the subassembly. This would have far-reaching consequences in construction, because the repetition of identical or similar components could be designed to produce a different technological result than a single larger component. Town's lattice bridges, with their many identical components repeated over and over again, had demonstrated the same approach to incremental problem solving through iteration and to the system dictum that "the whole is more than the sum of the parts." Turner's innovation was slow in spreading in iron construction, since it required a sophisticated level of reasoning on the part of a builder that was beyond most engineers and contractors at the time. But it did provide a rationale beyond the economics of reusing casting molds for the many modular, repetitive systems that were beginning to appear at the time.

New Approaches to Systems

In order to isolate and solve his technological problems incrementally, Turner probably had to think of his building as a complete shape and then dissect it into parts for prefabrication.[16] Most of the prefabricated structures that preceded the Crystal Palace were designed that way. British and French factories shipped prefabricated houses around Cape Horn to California's Gold Rush communities in 1849 and 1850. The Société des Comptoirs Français de Californie ordered a four-story iron apartment house for a hundred inhabitants with business premises on the ground floor.[17] British entrepreneurs exported modular buildings and standardized timbers to Australia during its gold rush two years later. All these structures — as well as bridges, lighthouses, the Sayn Foundry, the Kew Palm House, all machinery, and Fairbairn's, Cubitt's, and Brunel's prefabricated structures — were closed systems, in which form and structure are two aspects of a single design process.[18]

Closed systems are simple to understand, but they cannot easily adapt to different uses. Open systems are more flexible. They result from two levels of design: first the design of the structural system and then the design of the building form. Such structural systems can be put together in many ways to make different buildings. But this also makes them more complex to design, because the system has to accommodate many configurations that may not all have the same characteristics. Their connections have to satisfy criteria that are only completely known when the formal design is complete. Therefore, open-system elements are ideally designed to be stiff in themselves, so that they do not need secondary stabilizing mechanisms. Two factors supported the development of the open system: component manufacture and system logic.

Assembly Line Production

Open systems need large numbers of identical parts. Modular, prefabricated construction depends on serial component production, and that in turn depends on rationalized, assembly line manufacture. Manual assembly lines had been used in Renaissance shipbuilding in Venice and in the Birmingham sewing needle factories that Adam Smith examined in the late eighteenth century.[19] Smith recognized that goods could be produced quicker by dividing labor into linked series of repetitive, simple procedures, an understanding that would reach its apotheosis in Gilbreth and Taylor's studies at the turn of our century. A visitor to Fairbairn's boiler works in Manchester in 1839 also recognized the advantages of rationalized production: "In every direction of the works the utmost *system* prevails, and each mechanic appears to have his peculiar description of work assigned, with the utmost economical subdivision of labour. All is activity, yet without confusion. Smiths, strikers, moulders, millwrights, mechanics, boiler makers, pattern makers, appear to attend to their respective employments with as much regularity as the working of the machinery they assist to construct."[20]

Primitively mechanized assembly lines grew from the early manual methods. General Gribeauval introduced one in French ordnance before the Revolution. Oliver Evans may have developed another in the United States in 1783, and when Thomas Jefferson reported on the French system, Eli Whitney adopted it at the Springfield Armory in Massachusetts.[21] While eighteenth-century French and American systems relied on manual intervention and guidance, Marc Brunel was one of the first to use automation to control the manufacturing process. The principles of his block-making line at Portsmouth Naval Depot (1802–1807) spread quickly in all branches of ordnance. Brunel may have been influenced by the self-acting, and in part self-coordinating, textile machines the British built between 1767 and 1790 and by complex tools like Bramah's milling machine.[22] But since he had also worked in France and the United States, it is conceivable that he had at least heard of their ordnance systems.[23] The Springfield armory was certainly known among engineers when Brunel lived in New York.

In 1797, Bentham, who was then inspector general of naval works installed machinery developed by Bramah and Walter Taylor at Portsmouth.[24] Brunel replaced it all in 1805 with his automated production line, which he worked out in detail with Henry Maudslay. Brunel designed the saws and the block machinery that drilled, cut, and milled, and Bentham himself designed the winch for pulling timbers into the shop from the lumberyard outside.[25] A string of forty-five mostly self-acting machines produced the parts, but workmen still had to assemble the sheaves, pins, and pulleys manually.[26]

Brunel made sure that his client knew that his components were interchangeable: "The shivers with metal oaks made by these engines are executed with precision and celerity, and any number of a determined size being gauged most minutely, it will be found that one does not differ from another, either in diameter or thickness, so that any one of these shivers will suit equally well any shell of the size for which it was intended."[27] It wasn't easy to attain this high a degree of precision, which depended on the precise measuring instruments for which the British were famous.[28] Bentham recognized potential advantages in the ease with which a multimachined production line could be retooled and adapted to improve a product:

> As to the particular blocks which Mr. Brunel has sent as specimens
> for their Lordships' inspection, they appear from their form and the
> proportion of their parts, to be better suited to their intended pur-
> pose, than the blocks in general use; but although the particular
> form which Mr. Brunel has adopted in the first instance, should,

101.
Between 1802 and 1807,
Marc Brunel combined a
string of forty-seven semiautomated machines to
form an assembly line for
making tackle blocks at
Portsmouth Dockyard. The
three pictured here are the
mortising machine, the pin-
hole drill with its jig, and
the circular corner saw.
(Tomlinson, 1852, vol. 1,
pp. 140, 141, 143.)

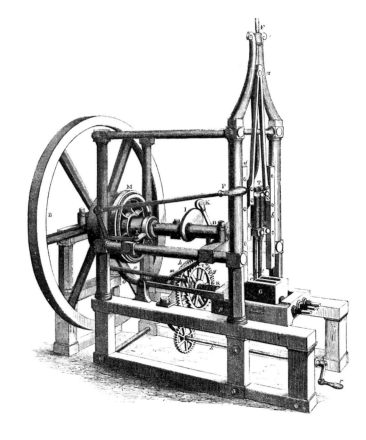

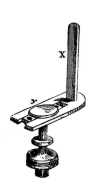

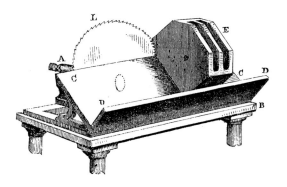

after farther consideration or experience, be deemed anywise objectionable, the engines could, on any day, be set to any other form or proportion, which may be decided on as preferable; and whatever that form or those proportions may be, there will be no doubt but that the blocks manufactured by these engines will, every one of them, be made in future of that exact form, until there be found reason to change it.[29]

Brunel installed automated production lines in several further navy and army depots. He designed and constructed them so well that three were still in use in 1967.[30] The Duke of Wellington was convinced that Brunel's 1810 shoe factory had contributed to his victory at Waterloo. Another successful installation was the automated sawmill at Chatham (1812–1815), in which he anticipated Henry Ford by moving the workpiece past the laborer.[31] The Chatham "disassembly" line transported logs entirely mechanically from the basin where they were floated in, through the sawing process, to the lumberyard for seasoning, and from there to covered storage. Other ordnance units, like the Biscuit Manufactory at Deptford, adopted Brunel's system, and automated manufacturing gradually spread to the private sector, for instance to the English locomotive factories (1868) and the meat-processing plants in Cincinnati (1862–1867), where Brunel's concept was elaborated on a large scale.[32]

Manufacturing processes are relatively simple to mechanize and even automate because factory conditions are stable and controlled. Foundries cast machine parts and were familiar with repetition and interchangeable parts; it was no problem for them to cast multiple structural elements. Fabricators assembled components into prefabricated elements in the same way as they built machines, ships, or firearms. Prefabrication in wood and iron gradually influenced the design of reinforced concrete systems like Lippmann's 1860 hollow-panel construction. But site assembly was a different matter. Construction machines have to work under unpredictable and constantly changing conditions. Spatial orientation, weather, climate, subsoil stability, and even material characteristics vary. Dirt and damage are unavoidable. This made the building process more difficult to mechanize than the building material industry, and it had to be done in a different way. The first step was to introduce the concept of building system, and to do this, designers had to think differently.

Patterns of Technological Thought

Logic and the Beginning of a Systems Approach

The leap into mathematical literacy between the middle of the eighteenth century and the beginning of the nineteenth began to change the way technologists thought. Mathematics was used to quantify and control technological design. It permitted designers to compare analogous objects and to form conceptual models.

The new method of computing liveload on a bridge deck exemplified the change. In 1825 the suspension bridge pioneer Guillaume-Henri Dufour designed an underspanned suspension bridge for the Swiss city of Fribourg. The proposal was sent to the French theoretician Navier, who suggested using a standardized liveload of 200 kilograms per square meter as a basis for dimensioning the bridge.[33] Dufour disagreed with the idea and wrote in rebuttal:

> As to the load, I am well aware that it is usual to count on a maximum overload of 200 kg per square meter. But this manner of calculation does not seem to be necessary except for those large bridges in very populous capital cities such as Paris, London &c. Everywhere else, probability should govern decisions so as not to succumb to exaggerated expense. And indeed it appears to me that on a toll bridge in one of our Swiss cities, one could not reasonably suppose that there would be more than one thousand persons congregated at any one time on each half of the bridge, as two thousand persons congregated on a bridge make a very large crowd and one could not have three per square meter unless they were to be placed side by side in closed ranks which would not be possible. Furthermore, police regulations can always prevent large crowds from gathering on bridges.[34]

There is no sense in overdesigning a bridge. The logic in Dufour's argument is incontestable given the size of Fribourg's population, which had been stable for several centuries at about four thousand. His argument applies to bridges of differing spans on a single road too: the longer will be uneconomical compared to the shorter if they are designed for the same per-unit load. But Dufour entirely misses the point of Navier's idea. Navier was concerned with the equivalence of load types and with the possibility of comparing similar bridge structures of different span. He was more interested in types and concepts than in the economy of any one structure. Dufour and

Navier differed only in the premise on which their logic was based. Their argument illustrates the shift from an approach to the solution of problems based on a single object to a more general system approach.[35]

As engineers developed models, architects strove for appropriate design, manufacturers created means of production, and builders devised strategies in construction, architectural theoreticians advocated new thinking as well. William Vose Pickett pleaded for a new architecture in 1845: "We possess in our own country, and in this very day, an abundance of available materials, sufficient for all the purposes, whether as regards effect of utility, of 'A FUNDAMENTALLY NEW ARCHITECTURE'. It need scarcely be added, that the materials referred to are *metals,* in almost every form and method of preparation, in which modern science and manufactures have presented them."[36] He went on, "England, and the world, are now in possession of the means, by which a new and entirely *dis*similar, and a more beautiful Architecture may be realized and established."[37]

Pickett expressed his reasons for advocating the use of iron in a prioritized list that was different from one a builder would find logical. To him, metals were incombustible, earthquake resistant, slender, healthy, and economical. The director of the Belgian Museum of Industry joined him three years later in a call for a new, "restrained" architecture in iron and glass.[38] Thus when the Crystal Palace finally appeared, many saw it as a harbinger of renewal.

The Crystal Palace

102.
The Crystal Palace was a giant, modular greenhouse built of cast and wrought iron, wood, and glass. Charles Fox masterminded the design and building processes. (Tomlinson, 1852, vol. 1, 2nd frontis.; exploded plan researched and drafted by Steven Roethke.)

This is the background against which Paxton, Charles Fox, and the Royal Commission members planned the Crystal Palace. Paxton, who had built several hothouses at Chatsworth as the Duke of Devonshire's estate manager, provided the initial sketches. The railway contractors Charles Fox and John Henderson provided the manufacturing and construction expertise. They had published a book on bowstring trusses in 1849, built numerous large-span railway sheds, and produced complete iron systems in their shop at Smethwick.[39] Fox and his firm's employees, among whom were future eminent engineers like Rowland Mason Ordish and Edward Alfred Cowper, transformed Paxton's ideas into a complete set of detailed working drawings in six weeks. Certain members of the Royal Commission were intimately involved with the project. Henry Cole was the driving force behind the exhibition as a whole. Owen Jones and Charles Barry, architect of the Houses of Parliament, reviewed the plans from an architectural standpoint, and Barry also designed the column. Charles Heard Wild designed the trusses and calculated the

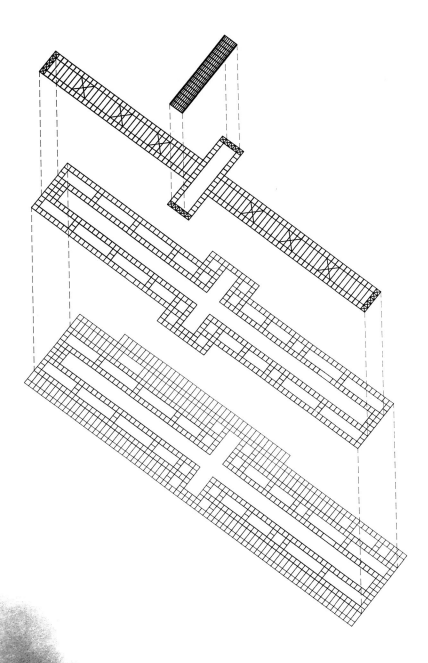

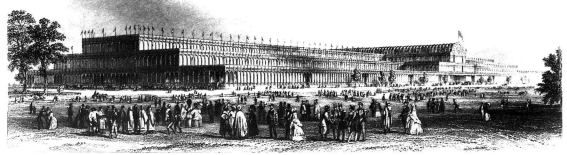

frame with Fox under William Cubitt's direction.[40] Matthew Digby Wyatt, Wild, and Jones represented the Royal Commission's building committee, while Cubitt was the committee's liaison to the building site. Cubitt exercised a greater influence on the Crystal Palace and the development of its system than has been hitherto acknowledged. He was president of the Institution of Civil Engineers in 1849 when Prime Minister Sir Robert Peel, who was an honorary member of the Institution, appointed him chairman of the management committee and supervisor of construction.

The group worked efficiently. The only way Fox and his staff could design the structure so quickly was to develop it as an incremental, open system. They produced all the plans and details while the building shape was still schematic.[41] The public understood how innovative this approach was, as this assessment by the *Art Journal* indicates: "The very nature of that idea which rendered a single section of the building completely explanatory of the whole, would seem to have rendered elaborate plans of the proposed edifice, in its entirety, less a work of mind than of mechanical dexterity. A single bay of 24 feet square would, if we except the transept and its semicircular roof, supply the means of making a correct drawing of the whole."[42] The *Art Journal*'s enthusiastic statement was correct in principle, though oversimplified; the nine variant girders and ten column types with their specialized connections all needed to be worked out.

Like other iron structures of its day, the building itself was part machine. Mobile steam engines turned driveshafts and leather belts transferred the energy to the machinery.[43] A mechanism regulated the thousands of ventilation louvers, and the roof drainage ran through the structural columns to a sewer system beneath the floor. Transmissions were common in workshops and factories, ventilation systems in glass conservatories, and drainage through structural columns in buildings like Turner's Lime Street Station— all "facilities," not "works of architecture."

Conflicts in Implementing the System

An industrially manufactured system should ideally be designed to combine a few types of generalized components into many specialized subassemblies. Adhering to this principle, the Crystal Palace frame was a modular assembly with standardized interfaces. The structural unit was based on a 732-by-732-centimeter (24-by-24-foot) grid and had columns, collar pieces, and trusses running in both directions. Most prefabricated iron systems, like those used at Sayn or Kew, spanned in one direction and expanded in the other. But the Crystal Palace unit was multidirectional: it spanned and expanded equally

Patterns of Technological Thought

103.
The exploded axonometric
and detail show the com-
plex spatial and volumetric
configuration. The struc-
tural module was stackable
and addable in both directions. It permitted any
number of building configurations. (Researched and
drafted by Steven Roethke.)

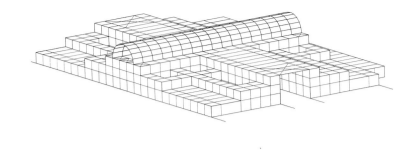

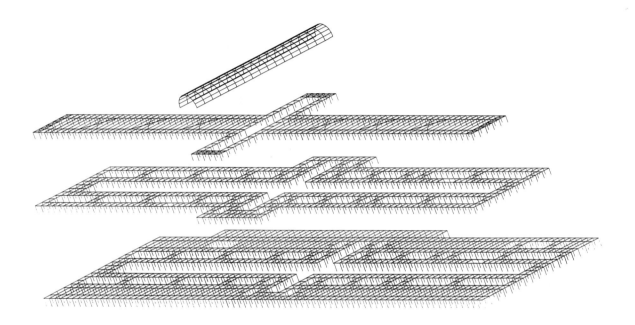

in both directions and was stackable in multistory heights. Double or triple spans could be made by exchanging a few components. Partitions and surfacing panels were fixed between the columns.

Fox and Paxton were aware of the implications of their incremental system: "It is only by minutely examining all the parts of a small section, and then observing how many hundred times such a portion is repeated, that the labour can be estimated. Those who will take the trouble thus to investigate the building will soon discover that, although vast in extent, in design it is exceedingly simple. . . . it will be seen, therefore, that the columns form the corners of a number of rectangular figures, which are either squares of 24 feet each way, or consist of two or more such squares; and thus the plan of the building may be said to be divided into its elements."[44] The original version of the building was simple and used the module throughout. But the committee insisted on a change that made it more complicated. The vaulted transept that became the building's hallmark was added in reaction to a protest over the planned removal of several large elms. It gave the building a façade and a formal entrance, but it also added construction problems.

One of the conditions for using the site in Hyde Park was the ease with which the structure could be removed. Builders were experimenting with demountable structures in those years, and several mobile field hospitals had been manufactured for army campaigns.[45] However, demountability exacerbated the problem of frame stiffness. Fox tried to solve the problem by designing simply bolted columns, wedged girders, and base pieces that were not attached to their foundation blocks. The Institution of Civil Engineers queried whether this would give the frame enough rigidity: Fox increased the number of diagonally braced frames to make sure.

Althans had used the Sayn Foundry's perimeter walls, the arc form laterally, and lattice girders longitudinally to solve the problem of stiffness. Turner had avoided a rigid beam-column connection at Kew by using the flexible yet strong triple purlin idea, combining it with curvilinear forms to solve the problem differently. Both of them used combinations of different element types that reinforced each other, but neither solved the problem systemically. Turner and Horeau had proposed designs for the 1850 exhibition that dealt similarly with the problem, using the formal elements of their closed systems to stabilize their frames. But Paxton and Fox had an open system to contend with and needed to turn the column-girder connection into a rigid frame corner, or at least solve the problem within the boundaries of the module.

Cast iron is a material that does not resist well the bending and shear stresses that frame corners must withstand, so the stiff frame only be-

104.
Diagonal rods stiffened the transept vault's surface longitudinally, and baywide, flanking "lead flats" helped brace it laterally. But no tie rods crossed the transept, so the vault fortuitously formed an expansion joint through the building. (*Official Descriptive and Illustrated Catalogue*, 1851, vol. 1, plate 1, p. 57.)

came a reality at the end of the century, when wrought iron and steel became inexpensive enough to replace cast-iron columns. Even then it took half a century of intense theoretical and practical work to do it, stretching roughly from the mid-1880s, when wrought iron became common, to the publication of Hardy Cross's moment distribution method in 1932. In 1850 there was really only one way to stiffen orthogonal frames: by triangulating the structural bay with iron rods. It was a reliable method when carried out properly, but it did block the space between columns with stiffening members. The Crystal Palace had to be as free of encumbrances as possible, so Paxton and Fox compromised, relying on the partial stiffness of the wedged beam-column connections and adding diagonal bracing wherever the consultants or the contractor felt that it was indispensable. This proved to be at either end of the building and in the bays adjacent to the transept; illustrations of the building concentrate almost exclusively on these parts and give the illusion that the whole structure was stiffened.

Astronomer Royal George Bidell Airy opposed the original design because he felt it had too few stiffening members; Turner agreed,[46] while John Scott Russell thought that the frame action of the connections alone would suffice.[47] Airy was right, and he suggested the tried-and-true British factory structure with an internal iron frame buttressed by a ring of solid stone walls. From the standpoint of contemporary construction knowledge, he had a point. As Robert Mallet later wrote: "The building was taken down, and has been reerected at Sydenham in a manner greatly to increase its stability, as regards the greater part of the structure at least; and from 1851 to the present day London has never been visited by one of those 'first-class' tornadoes that about twice in a century sweep over even our temperate regions. Yet, nevertheless, a very large wing of the Crystal Palace has been actually blown down in the interval—that portion of the whole, that probably more accurately represented the structure of the building as it stood in 1851, than any other part of it now does."[48]

The collapse escaped notice because it appeared in a report written eleven years after the exhibition. The public never realized how insecure the building was, but the engineers must have known even though they never openly voiced concern. Computer analysis of the structure has shown that the building was almost certainly unstable as originally designed and that it would have failed under a mild breeze of about a sixth of the wind load low-rise buildings are required to resist today. A last-minute addition of three large sets of diagonal cross braces in the nave roof on each side of the transept made the building work a little better, but still not well enough.[49] The contractor probably added the additional bracing after the Institution of Civil

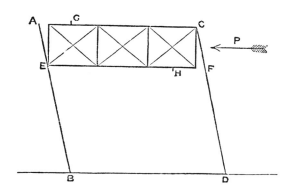

105.
John Scott Russell and
George Airy debated the
stability of the frame at a
meeting of the Institution
of Civil Engineers in 1850.
Airy's diagram demon-
strates the design's weak
points, and the interior
view shows how skimpy the
bracing system was. (*Record
of the International Exhibition*, 1862, p. 58; *Illustrated Exhibitor*, 1851,
p. 81.)

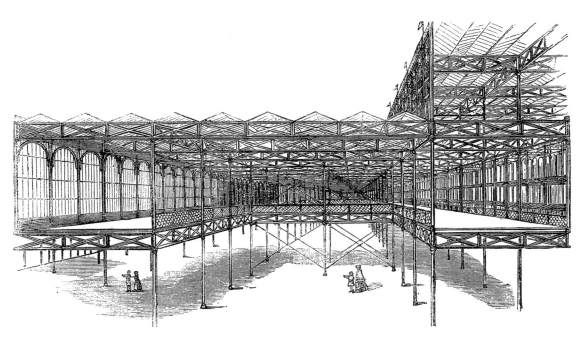

Buildings from the Sayn Foundry to the Galerie des Machines

Engineers criticized the project. There are only two known plan sets, one that predates the ICE's discussion and the other that postdates construction.[50] The frame's stability was probably enhanced by the stiffening effect of the building's skin, and to a lesser extent by that of the gallery floors, factors that were not included in the computer models. However, in the models two events occurred that relieved some of the stress on the rest of the frame: at a critical wind pressure individual columns lifted their base plates from the foundations, and some column lugs fractured in the cornice zone of the first floor.[51] When the building was dismantled after the exhibition closed, the contractors may have discovered such fractures. No one wrote about any defects, but the substantially larger building that was built in Sydenham in 1854 using the original parts was visibly stiffer than the original.[52]

As difficult as it was to solve the problem of corner stiffness, the building also needed expansion joints, and that compounded the issue. Most of the Crystal Palace detailing was highly sophisticated, but no one had ever attempted prefabrication on so large a scale before, and errors were bound to occur. Machine builders and watchmakers had grappled with similar issues and Fox might have learned from them, but border-crossing analogies are difficult to recognize, and Fox and Paxton thought differently from Brunel, Althans, or Turner. Fox was unable to devise a solution that could resist the distorting effect of thermal expansion, as Robert Mallet observed:

> We ourselves, however, had an opportunity, during the early afternoon of one of the hottest days of the summer of 1851, of examining with some accuracy the effects of expansion by solar heat upon the frame of the building; and we can testify to this as a fact, that at the extreme western end, and at the fronts of the nave galleries, where they had been here the longest and the most heated, the columns were actually about two inches out of plumb in the first range in height only. Unaided by instruments, we could not perceive that any change in the plumbness of the coupled columns at the corners of the intersection of the nave and transept had taken place. Their rigidity, and probably other causes, appeared to have resisted the whole thrust, and visited it upon the extreme outer ends of the frame of the building.
>
> As we gazed up at these west-end galleries densely crowded with people, and over the ample spread of the nave equally thronged, and thought of the prodigious cross-strains that were at that moment in unseen play in the brittle stilting of the cast-iron fabric, we certainly felt that 'ignorance was bliss'. From this expansion

Patterns of Technological Thought

producing distortion being confined in great part to the lower range of columns it has less serious effect in producing leakage in the roofing. The mere *fact,* that by expansion some of the columns were put out of plumb, is an effectual reply to the asserted sufficiency, in allowing for it, of the wood keys and wedges. . . . Either wood keys are so hard and forcibly driven as to act as keys, and in that case they will not compress further, but are rigid enough to propagate the pressure of expansion from bay to bay; or they are of soft wood, and not driven in tight; and in that case are useless as keys, conferring no structural security.[53]

Like Turner's, Robert Mallet's expertise in iron construction came from his involvement in a successful family foundry in Dublin, and he considered "the unbroken columnar and girder structure . . . neither safe nor durable." His view was shared by many knowledgeable contemporaries.[54]

Fox had designed the wedging intelligently, but it didn't work. The girders were raised and slid sideways onto flanges that jutted out from the intermediate column connectors. They were seated snugly and keyed in place with cast-iron wedges in the transverse direction to give the frames fixity and with oak ones longitudinally, except for the six bays from each end and from the transept, which were keyed in iron.[55] The building cross section was subdivided into roofs of different heights, the widest being four modules, or 29.3 meters, so that some of the movement could be taken up by the columns as they rocked a little out of plumb. This, of course, put stress on the cast-iron column flanges and the bolts.

Fox's idea was that the oak would compress a little when the iron trusses expanded with rising temperature. But wood is not particularly elastic and cannot be counted upon to expand again when pressure is removed, so we may presume that the detail did not work. What probably happened is that the workmen drove the wedges so firmly that they actually fixed the frame fairly tightly. So, instead of accommodating thermal expansion at each frame corner, the force simply pushed each module a little farther out of line, which led to the deflection in the longitudinal direction that Mallet observed.[56] Luckily the structure's length was cut by the transept vault, which lay two modules, or 14.65 meters, west of the center. The vault functioned as a large expansion joint, so that the longest continuous frame segment was the 278-meter-long eastern one. Since the one-story parts of the building had wooden trusses that expanded very little, only the columns in the two- and three-story segments were endangered, and these were a little more flexible since they were longer.

106.
Wedges at *S* and *T* fixed the girders to the collars. Fox used cast-iron wedges across the building, but he used oak in the longitudinal direction. The oak was supposed to do two incompatible things: compress to allow for thermal expansion, and fix the frame corner at the same time. (Downes, 1852, plate 8.)

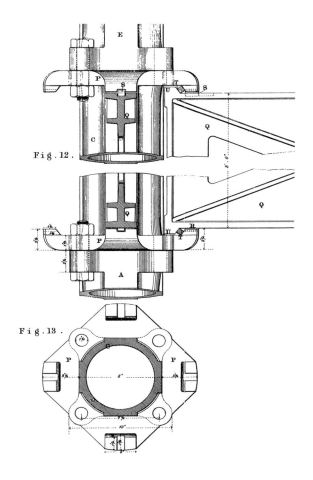

Fig. 12.

Fig. 13.

All of these mitigating circumstances helped diffuse the problem in the greater part of the building, but the conceptual issue remained: Fox conflated the need for erection tolerances, expansion joints, and stiffness. In this matter Turner, who separated the issues in order to solve them, was the more astute designer. But the Crystal Palace was an order of magnitude larger than the Palm House, and construction problems change with scale.

Engineers developed solutions for expansion joints over the next two decades, and they began to appear routinely in long-span iron bridges after midcentury. However, no development runs linearly, and there had been earlier examples. John Rennie, for instance, had included simple expansion joints in his 1814 wine storage shed in the West India Docks in London. As Charles Taylor put it in what may have been the first published description of an expansion joint:

107.
John Rennie's 1814 wine shed at the West India Docks featured an ingenious and simple expansion joint. (Charles Taylor, 1829, plates 17–18.)

To form an idea of the difficulty of constructing so vast a shed with solidity, it is sufficient to remember how the alternations of cold and heat affect iron, and expand or contract it, even where this metal is least exposed to the usual variations of temperature: this has been guarded against in a most ingenious manner; — the iron beams which run from one column to the next, and which are supported by small arches, do not join closely; but a small interval is left between their extreme points, which otherwise would be in contact, while at the same time, the other parts of the structure were so perfectly joined, that they prevent the latitudinal action which might result from the longitudinal play thus allowed to these beams.[57]

The mechanism of knowledge transfer from one project to another is a complex phenomenon. Sometimes knowledge can be lost for a time or it can be swamped by other concerns, and half a century later Robert Stephenson and Alexander Ross were still unable to detail expansion joints in the Victoria Bridge at Montreal (1858–1862) elegantly. The floors of the 2,006-meter tubular bridge were connected to form two continuous twenty-five-span iron plates with no other provision for expansion than the discontinuous tube walls. The engineers simply presumed that the heavy track ballast would suffice to counteract buckling in the rails.[58]

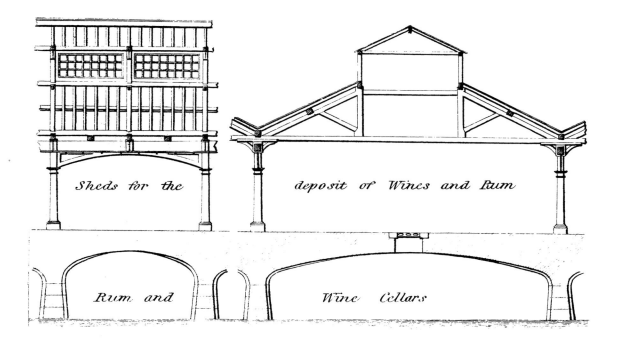

Sheds for the

deposit of Wines and Rum

Rum and

Wine Cellars

108.

There was no need for Robert Stephenson to keep all twenty-two spans of the Victoria Bridge at Montreal free for traffic at all times, so he assembled the girders in place. Construction progressed continuously, with the erection gantrys rolling on tracks from span to span. (Smiles, *Life of George Stephenson*, 1868, pp. 474, 478, 480, 483.)

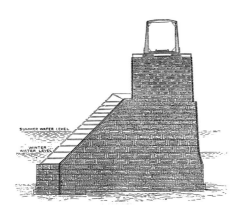

SUMMER WATER LEVEL

WINTER WATER LEVEL

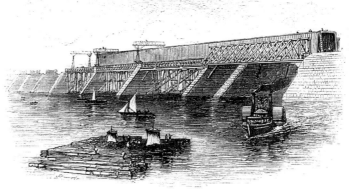

It took even longer to solve expansion joint design in enclosed buildings, because they had to incorporate weatherproofing and thermal insulation. Alexis Barrault, the engineer of the 1855 Paris exhibition building, was aware of this: "To meet the evil there is but one method—that pointed out and recommended by M. Barrault—namely, to subdivide all right-lined continuations in iron, cutting them up into separate short lengths, without abutting faces, though still connected by such ingenious management's as shall preserve at those points, staunchness or the other conditions required of the structure."[59] That may well be one of the reasons he conservatively enclosed the iron structure behind stone walls, and it may similarly have motivated Francis Fowke a few years later to erect a stone skin around the 1862 London exhibition building too.[60]

Another example that demonstrated Fox's lack of experience in large-scale mass production, was the design and placement of the column bases. Instead of casting the tops of the concrete foundation blocks to the same horizontal level and making the 1,074 prefabricated bases all the same length, Fox had the blocks poured to a constant height above the sloping site. His idea was to let the base pieces make up the difference between their tops and the baseline.[61] If he had made the baseline horizontal, there would have been about 250 centimeters difference in length between the base pieces at either end of the building. So Fox made the floor follow the site gradient but at a lesser angle, so that there were only about 120 centimeters to climb at the lower, eastern end of the building.[62] He set the base pieces plumb in the north-south direction and inclined them eastward and perpendicular to the floor along the length of the building.[63] This made the three-story columns 6.4 centimeters out of plumb at their tops and added eccentric forces to the already stressed cast-iron frame.

Industrial Prefabrication and Site Plant

From the earliest Chinese chain bridges to the intricate and sophisticated Kew, all iron structures were made of repetitive parts.[64] Cast and rolled iron lend themselves to mass production techniques, and iron and wooden building prefabrication was a well established industry by the time the Crystal Palace was built. All of the building's elements with very few exceptions were made in workshops.

Fox and Henderson coordinated the many subcontractors. Chance Brothers of Birmingham, which had glazed the Palm House two years before, won the glass contract over a rival firm that offered even larger panes of

109.

In the 1855 Paris Exhibition building, Alexis Barrault strengthened the beam-column connection by adding knee braces, but the glazed barrel roofs still had problems with thermal expansion and leaked. (*Record of the International Exhibition*, 1862, plate opposite p. 17, p. 25.)

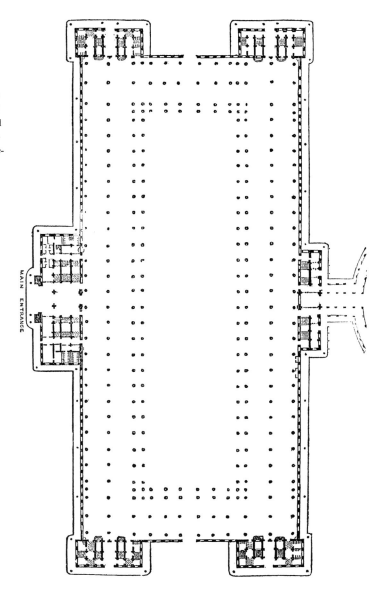

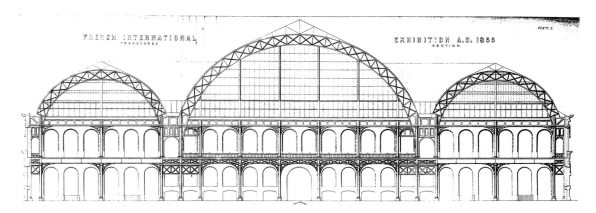

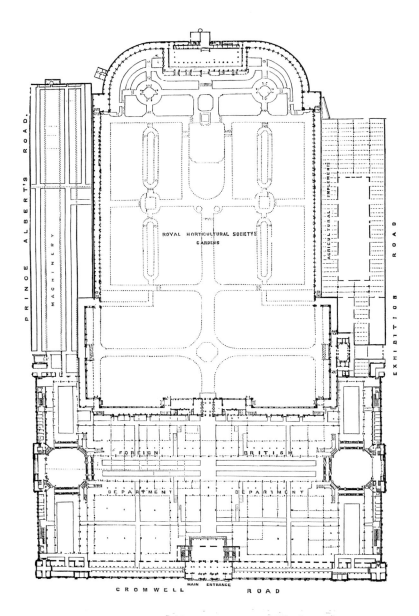

110.
Francis Fowke designed the
1862 London Exhibition
building as a permanent
structure. He hid the glass-
and-iron structure behind
an enclosing stone wall that
braced the frame and
helped solve the problem of
expansion joints. (*Masterpieces of the Centennial International Exhibition*, 1876,
vol. 3, p. xliii; *Record of the
International Exhibition*,
1862, plate 5 opposite
p. 33.)

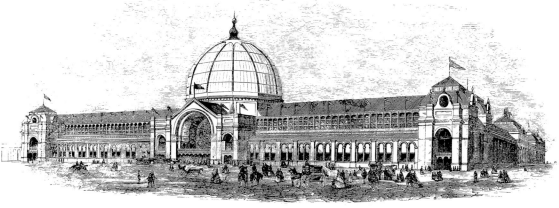

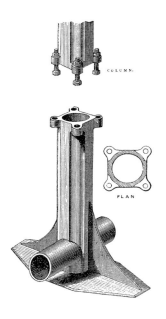

111.
The hollow column bases were sealed to the drains with lead castings. They were all of different lengths to compensate for the sloping site. (*Official Descriptive and Illustrated Catalogue,* 1851, vol. 1, p. 53; *Illustrated Exhibitor, 1851,* p. 80.)

112.
David Henderson's derrick crane stood in the machinery court of the Crystal Palace with one of the cast-iron girders suspended from its boom. (*Crystal Palace and Its Contents,* 1851, p. 28.)

cast glass that Fox thought too heavy.[65] Their contract for 300,000 panes represented a third of the entire national production of about 1,200 tons.[66] Alexander Cochrane of Woodside and Jobson of Holly-Hall, both near Dudley, cast most of the girders and columns, and Fothergill and Company supplied the wrought iron that was made into trusses on site. These three firms were hard pressed to deliver 4,000 to 5,000 tons of iron to the site at such short notice, and quality control was always a problem.[67] But the iron components represented only a fraction of Britain's annual production of 2.75 million tons.

Fox and Henderson manufactured the minor ironwork themselves in Birmingham, and John Henderson used his older brother David's patented swiveling derrick crane on the site.[68] The crane was more flexible than the one Althans had installed at Bendorf a few years before. It had a variable reach and was easily moved from place to place. Fox and Henderson also purchased the Chelsea Saw Mills in order to mill the boards and cut the 33.5 kilometers of Paxton gutters on a machine that their employee Edward Cowper built.[69] The gutters were preassembled with a wrought-iron pretensioning mechanism before shipping them to the site. The Phoenix Saw Mills in Camden Town contracted for the over 320 kilometers of sash bars, the ridges of the glass roof, and the mullions of the facade elements. The owner, Birch, improved the mullion machine developed by Paxton by replacing his

THE GREAT HYDRAULIC PRESS

Buildings from the Sayn Foundry to the Galerie des Machines   243

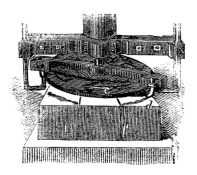

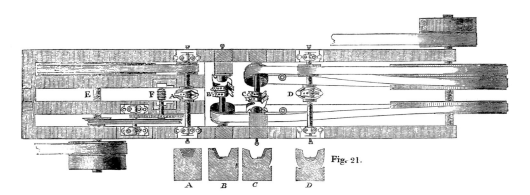

Fig. 21.

113.
Fox and Henderson manufactured the Paxton gutters in their Chelsea workshop. A circular plane prepared beams for the milling machine, a circular saw cut them to size, and finally workmen mounted wrought-iron post-tensioning rods on their undersides. They also made the ridge purlins. (*Official Descriptive and Illustrated Catalogue*, 1851, vol. 1, pp. 72, 73; *Illustrated Exhibitor*, 1851, p. 112.)

circular saws with rotating cutters.[70] Yet another firm, Dowson and Company, supplied the stair treads, railings, and other minor timber parts.[71] Cowper supervised the site plant: the punches and drills for the site-built wrought-iron trusses, David Henderson's crane, Wild's hydraulic girder testing machine, William Furness of Liverpool's sash bar mortising machine, the general assembly workshops, and the painting "machines."[72]

Observers of 1850 were intrigued by the fact that the building formed its own scaffolding and by the division of labor.[73] Fox was responsible for both. He made the site into an assembly line. "The building has been truly characterized as a gigantic specimen of our manufactures, and, as such, it is natural to expect an extensive use of machinery for the reproduction of the various parts. It was only in this manner that the erection of such a building in so short a time became a possibility at all."[74]

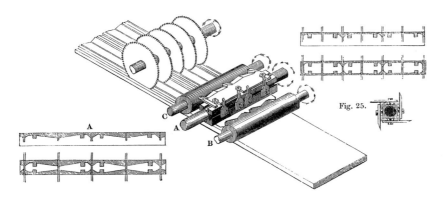

Fig. 25.

114.
The Phoenix Saw Mills milled the mullions and sash bars and predrilled the nail holes while a jig held the pieces at the right angle. Workmen dipped each piece in a paint trough and pushed it through ten fixed brushes to remove the excess. Drips were collected and recycled. (*Official Descriptive and Illustrated Catalogue*, 1851, vol. 1, pp. 74, 76; *Illustrated Exhibitor*, 1851, pp. 113, 114.)

115.
People came daily to watch the assembly in Hyde Park. They were astonished that the building formed its own scaffolding. (*Illustrated Exhibitor*, 1851, p. 185.)

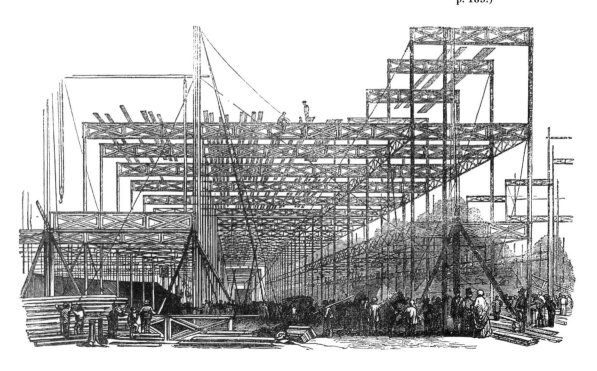

Fox's Spatial Pattern of Technological Thought

Fox displayed a peculiar brand of three-dimensional technological thinking in the Crystal Palace. Most structural designers think primarily in two dimensions, even today. They design a building in plan and cross section and create frames two-dimensionally, then stack them one behind the other to form a three-dimensional building. Both Althans's and Turner's buildings are in principle extrusions of two-dimensional frames. Paxton's sketch for the Crystal Palace is also a cross section, and the design he developed from it was an extrusion of that cross section. But Fox designed his structure differently, as a gridded module that was the same in both directions. A cross section of his module east-west is identical to its north-south cross section. He designed the module to be the same in both the x- and the y-axes so that it could be added to equally in both directions. This meant that it was structurally nondirectional, and the trusses on all four sides of the module were the same.

However, he had to carry the roof and a wooden floor on those trusses, and both of these subsystems were directional because the gutters and joists spanned in one direction only. In the case of the roof, Fox had one set of trusses carry spread loads, while the other carried the underspanned gutters, which lay 2.4 meters apart, as point loads. The floor was more of a problem: the joists had to be more closely spaced than the roof gutters because boards can only span 40 to 60 centimeters. The joists that lay over the trusses could transmit very little load to the one set of trusses, while the other trusses would have to carry far more. Either Fox had to raise the whole floor higher and put the joists on beams, which would have been wasteful, or he had to devise another system to spread the load equally over the trusses spanning in both directions. To solve this geometrical problem he used the same technique he had developed to post-tension the gutter, but rotated the wrought-iron tension rods at right angles. The rods held up two beams that could be weaker because they were supported at their third points. He notched the joists into the beams and leveled their tops with the girder, attaching them to the girders by means of primitive strap hangers. The tension rods ended at the third points of the other pair of cast-iron girders, which enabled him to distribute the floor loading equally to all four edges of each module and make the girder pair that ran parallel to the floor beams carry their full share of the load.[75] The point is not whether or not this was a good solution, but that the rotation was a simple modification of an underspanning technology that required a shift in geometry and a complex ability to think three-dimensionally.

116.
The directional floor and
roof rest on the nondirectional structural module.
The roof construction was
straightforward, but Fox
transferred the floor loads
by underspanning the
beams at right angles to
their axes. This distributed
their loads equally to the
third points of both sets of
girders. (Researched and
drafted by Steven Roethke.)

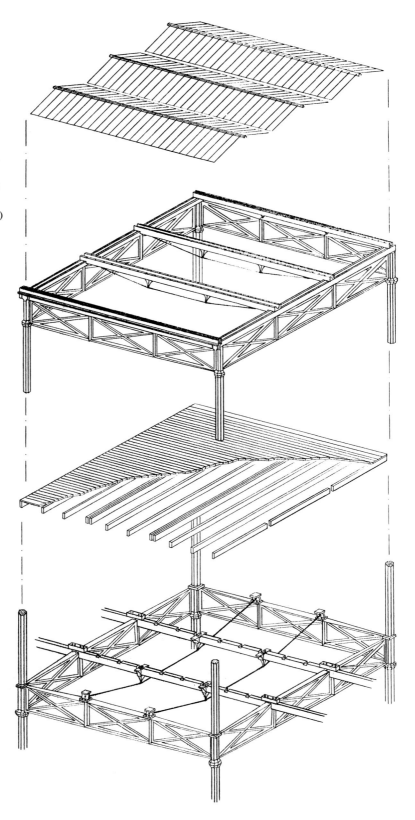

117.
The assembled module shows the transition from both directional subsystems to the nondirectional girder configuration. (Researched and drafted by Steven Roethke.)

118.
A view of one quarter of the ridge-and-furrow roof. Fox's rationalized glazing method was instrumental in delivering the building on time. Initially the roof was glazed by workmen on ladders, and each bay needed a scaffold and several men. This took too long. (*Illustrated Exhibitor*, 1851, pp. 8, 64; *Record of the International Exhibition*, 1862, p. 13.)

This was not an isolated instance, either. Another example of Fox's three-dimensional thinking was the glazing wagon he built to rationalize the construction of the hectares of flat roofs. This cart seems to have introduced the first real split between modularized construction and linear erection methods. When the roof glazing began, several men worked in each module. The men were served by a boy whose job it was to go up and down the ladder carrying glass panes, glazing bars, and putty to the laborers. The workmen set up scaffolding in each module separately, and the process was slow and wasteful. The roof became a critical bottleneck that threatened the whole process. There were 504 single, 267 double, and 69 triple roof modules to glaze, not counting the lead-covered areas adjacent to the transept and the vault itself. This made a total of 1,245 grid modules, or an area of 66,623 square meters. Fox realized that the work would never finish at the rate they were proceeding, and that he would have to increase the manpower beyond practical limits if he were to continue using that primitive system. There already were between two and three thousand workmen on site. So he decided to enhance productivity by rationalizing the movement of men and materials.

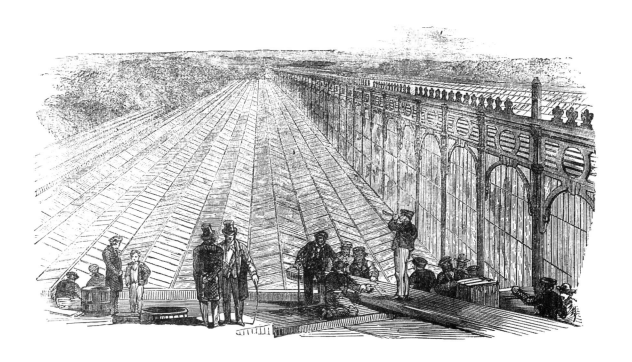

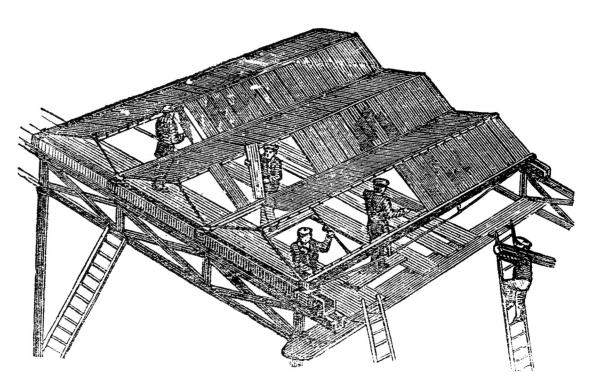

Buildings from the Sayn Foundry to the Galerie des Machines 251

119.
Fox's simple glazing cart, covered in rainy weather, used the gutters as tracks and rolled in a straight line over the modules. One man sat on either side of the ridge; they placed mullions, strings of putty, and panes in front of them, pushing themselves back as they worked. A boy passed materials forward from a stockpile. (*Record of the International Exhibition,* 1862, p. 14; Tomlinson, 1852, vol. 1, p. xliii.)

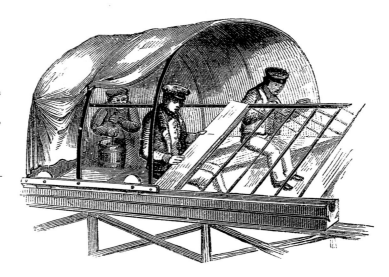

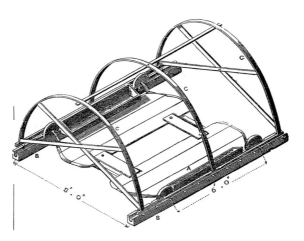

Fox designed a covered wheeled cart to hold the workmen and their materials and protect them from the weather. It used the gutters as tracks. Each cart carried two workmen, who placed glazing bars, strings of putty, and panes economically and rhythmically directly in front of them. One sat on each side of the ridge, and they pushed themselves backward as they worked. They moved along the gutters from module to module and from end to end of the building without having to leave their seats. A boy, seated behind them, fed them materials from a store on the cart. Each workman placed an average of 108 panes a day, traversing four modules and covering over twenty-eight meters.[76]

The keys to Fox's ingenious solution to the problem were the intermediate material depot on the mobile work site and the disassociation of the linear glazing process from the modular planning of the building. Reversing his previous transformation process, he translated a three-dimensional construction module into a linear process. He also inverted the assembly line principle and moved his workers past their work. This was a logical step to take when assembling something that was fixed to the ground. Gilbreth could not have analyzed the situation or rationalized the movement any better.[77]

It takes intellectual effort of a high caliber to develop and integrate complex systems. Paxton may have designed the overall form of the Crystal Palace and solved some of its manufacturing problems, but neither his previous construction work at Chatsworth and Kew nor his subsequent architectural practice give any clue to the genesis of the complex and sophisticated solutions needed to build it. Fox, on the other hand, was one of the most versatile building contractors in England. He built railway, bridge, and large-span iron sheds and was certainly the one who detailed the structure and designed the construction process. Fox's construction design and erection methods paralleled the equally sophisticated but very different models on which Althans and Turner based their thinking. Each designer had his particular way of thinking technologically, his specific areas of concentration, and his special problems to solve. Each of them solved some problems better than others. But because of the Crystal Palace's industrial and political importance, Fox's work became especially prominent and influential. Prime Minister Peel recognized Fox, Paxton, and Cubitt's contributions to the prestige of British industry, and Queen Victoria knighted them for their accomplishments.[78]

Others learned from Fox's experience with his open, modular system and its weaknesses, even though no one seems ever to have discussed these weaknesses in the professional press. Fox and Cubitt built better structures because of this experience. Paxton, however, lost interest and worked as a traditional Victorian architect in the years that followed. Only his small portable greenhouse design of 1838 was of interest as a system. Most of his glass and iron structures, like the "Crystal Sanitarium," used the ridge-and-furrow patent or the glazed barrel vault, but some, like his project for the New York fair in 1853, didn't even do that. Even his grandiose schemes for rebuilding the Crystal Palace at Sydenham in 1854 and for an exhibition palace for St.-Cloud, a suburb of Paris, in 1862 were only superficially system structures. Their many rounded shapes were inappropriate for his modular, open system and seem to indicate that he may not have fully grasped the implications of his own invention. All the many other "Crystal Palaces" that shot up out of the ground in the following years in Dublin, New York, and elsewhere aped the superficial forms of the original, but they all had oblique angles and curves, too. Victorian elaboration seemed to have won out against the clarity of the open system.

Only one building, the Munich Glaspalast built in 1854 by the architect August von Voit and Klett und Compagnie's chief engineer Ludwig Werder, manifested the same sparseness as the original and seemed to solve the problems of expansion and frame rigidity, too. The Glaspalast burned down in 1931 and no photographed or drawn details appear to have survived, but Werder clearly benefited from the lessons learned from the Crystal Palace. He designed the peripheral walls as Howe trusses on the upper levels and stiffened the structure horizontally with wire diagonals.[79] He also strengthened the truss-column connections with wrought-iron "brackets" that he twisted around the bolted flanges. Werder must have done this in the building phase since the brackets were evidently missing from the original plans.[80] Werder is repeatedly mentioned in connection with many of the most interesting iron structures of his day. Like Roussel two generations earlier, he was a system pioneer, innovative builder, and technological thinker of the caliber of Charles Fox.[81] Both their careers merit closer scrutiny.

Hybrid Types: The American Light-Wood Frame

Another kind of open system, this time in wood, was beginning to spread across the United States around 1850. American builders were pragmatic and used a construction method that they knew worked without troubling about conceptual issues. Their unusual light-wood frame grew out of specifically American conditions that were different from the parameters of traditional heavy-timber construction. Heavy construction used relatively few members, which therefore had to be of reliable quality. Each beam, strut, or post could also be different because it was laboriously hand-sawn. Mechanical sawing came early to the United States, however, so American mills could produce standardized cross sections in large quantities quicker and more cheaply than sawyers could.[82] This meant that they could isolate and discard flawed pieces and still produce good material from the bulk of almost any log. As framers began assembling buildings from larger numbers of smaller components, they discovered that their frames could tolerate some flawed members without compromising the finished product.

The more pieces of lumber builders used, the more connections they had to make between them. They nailed their frames together because the lumber sizes they used were too small and the pieces too numerous to mortise. At the end of the eighteenth century Yankee inventors developed machines to produce cut nails cheaply, and framers used them in increasingly large numbers. Prices dropped from an initial twenty-five cents a pound to eight cents in 1828 and three cents by 1842.[83] Frames had so many nails spread evenly throughout the whole structure that if any one of them failed the others that surrounded it would carry the load safely. Light-wood frames made of many thin sticks and many simple nails seemed to be flimsily built, but they were really more redundant and more resistant to failure than heavy frames, and they behaved astonishingly as though they were monolithic.[84] This meant that even amateur builders with no structural knowledge could alter or remove major parts with a freedom that would be unthinkable in any less redundant system.

James Bogardus tried to project this advantage of wooden framing systems onto cast iron in his brochure of 1849.[85] Bogardus was evidently trying to forge a relationship between the system everyone knew and his own, suggesting the open, light-wood frame system as the conceptual model for a development that would eventually lead to the high-rise steel frame. The light-wood frame and Bogardus's ideas developed parallel to the Crystal Palace's open system and began to influence iron construction in the following decade.[86]

In Chicago in the 1850s the American light-framing system finally matured into a kit of parts with assembly rules, called Chicago construction or balloon framing.[87] Its pragmatic form was similar to Althans's and Turner's contemporary approach to iron construction. But in contrast to these closed systems, the light-wood frame industry delivered lumber or easily modifiable units and prefabricated building sets all over the country.[88]

One characteristic that set it apart from iron systems was that it did not require precise tolerances. Stud, joist, sill, and plate cross sections, board widths, nail sizes, and connector hardware could vary without compromising either the strength or the redundancy of the end product. Builders cut lengths on site and made details with a handsaw and a standardized nailing template. The procedure was so simple that nonskilled laborers could easily erect and modify the light frame to suit any form. That, and the availability of cheap lumber, suited it ideally to American conditions.

American prefabrication developed in a different way than elsewhere. Americans were still an unusually migrant nation in the nineteenth century, and they thought of their buildings as independent of a specific site. No one disassembled and reassembled a balloon frame, but they were frequently picked up in one piece and transported to new locations. St. Mary's

120.
James Bogardus wanted to translate the concept of redundancy and the flexibility of light-wood framing into cast-iron construction. He demonstrated his idea graphically in his 1856 public relations pamphlet. (Bogardus, 1856, frontis. and plate 1.)

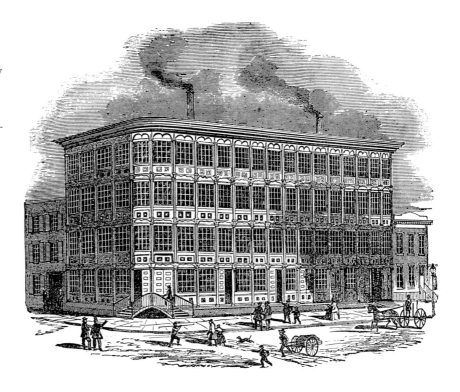

Patterns of Technological Thought

Catholic Church in Chicago, a predecessor of the balloon frame, was moved three times between 1833 and 1843.[89] The Viennese *Allgemeine Bauzeitung* published an article on moving a house in New York City in 1844.[90] George Pullman jacked up and raised parts of Chicago, house by inhabited house and street by street, out of the swamp it was built on between 1855 and 1859. As a result, Americans regarded their wooden houses as mobile, industrial objects. For example, to celebrate the completion of the short-lived first transatlantic telegraph cable, San Francisco held a parade on 27 September 1858 in which the principal Californian industries demonstrated their manufacturing processes on floats. The newspapers printed flyers, the cigar maker rolled his wares and distributed them to the public, and on one float a group of carpenters assembled a frame building.[91] Evidently they considered their building an industrially manufactured product like newspapers or cigars. This attitude touched every aspect of construction, and it influenced domestic forms and the country's social structure.[92]

There was an analogous development in Britain. Between 1815 and 1854, when his contracting firm was destroyed by fire, Thomas Cubitt, one of William Cubitt's brothers, mass-produced speculative row houses or "terraces" ranging from elegant Grosvenor Square to squalid Clapham.[93] The units were built of wood and brick between brick party walls and were standardized and identical within each economic bracket.[94] Construction methods and materials remained traditional, but material production was rationalized. Kilns improved brick firing and wood seasoning.[95] The idea was to make an economical product by standardizing planning, prefabrication, and mass production, and by speeding up the building process through rationalization. The terrace house sprang from the same industrial mindset as Eli Whitney's standardized weapons and Marc Brunel's industrialized tackle blocks and boots. Endless expanses of terrace housing came to be built in city after city. Street after dismal street of identical cheap houses, miserably lit until the window tax was repealed in 1851, covered flat and hilly ground alike with no respect for topography. Direct sunlight was not yet a criterion, and neither expensive nor cheap units varied with orientation.

Different cultures treat similar forms of standardization very differently. American light-wood framing is designed for individual interpretation and elaboration. From the nineteenth-century balloon frame to twentieth-century Levittown, houses were meant to be expanded and individualized.[96] In Britain, planned obsolescence was implicit in the concept of product amortization on the British leasehold system.[97] Terraces remained unchanged on the exterior and could at most be subdivided on the interior. In the more expensive ones materials and building methods were better and space and dimensions were ample. The simpler ones were unbelievably shoddy. Speculators made fortunes in cheap construction, and socially conscious writers railed against the deplorable conditions in these ready-made slums. Charles Dickens, Friedrich Engels, and Samuel Smiles all attacked the evils of the socioeconomic system that encouraged them, each in his own way.

The "Brompton Boilers"

J.-N. L. Durand developed his incremental and modular design method around 1800 in France to control architectural form and scale. Paxton and Fox transformed Durand's Beaux-Arts method by downplaying the primacy of form and giving it a manufacturing dimension it had never had before. In the decade that followed, many engineers and architects explored prefabricated systems and their advantages. Most of these systems were still closed, although they were often more flexible than they might have been before the Crystal Palace. Charles Denoon Young's corrugated iron-covered Kensington Art Museum of 1856 was a particularly interesting demountable one, especially since it was built by the Royal Commission of 1851.[98] According to his promotional catalog, the contractor had built a wide range of "Iron Structures for Home and Abroad."[99] The Commission erected the building just south of the former Crystal Palace site in Kensington on land purchased from the Gore family estate. Among other things, the structure was to house the "trade collection" made up of the objects that various exhibitors had donated to the Commission in 1851, Bennett Woodcroft's patent collection, and an educational museum. Once again Henry Cole was the driving force behind the project and Sir William Cubitt the Commission's supervisor. The structure was part of a complex that also housed red brick offices and an art and architecture school built by Francis Fowke.

The Commission could have used brick or parts of the original Crystal Palace for the museum had they wanted to, but they purposely chose something radically different. Nothing could have looked less like the Crystal Palace. Clearly the Royal Commission intended it to be an uncompromisingly industrial structure. The building looked a little like Barrault's 1855 Paris Exhibition building in miniature, but completely clad in corrugated iron.[100] It was 81 meters long, 38.7 meters wide, and covered by three identical barrel vaults with elevated bands of skylights at their crowns. The roof was covered in galvanized sheet iron, like most station and shed roofs at the time.[101] Cost and thermal expansion led builders to shy away from glass for roofs after the Crystal Palace, where both movement and vapor condensation had caused problems. Even where representation demanded glass, it was wise to use it sparingly, as Barrault discovered in 1855.

121.
Site plan of the "Brompton
Boilers," showing its rela-
tionship to Fowke's art
school and the original
Crystal Palace site.
(*Builder*, 27 June 1857,
p. 357.)

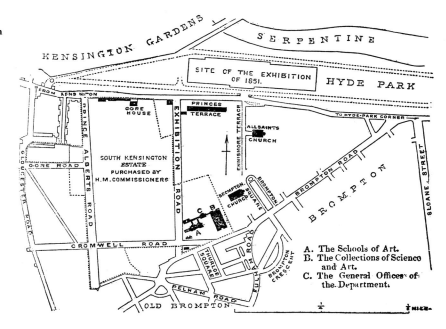

A. The Schools of Art.
B. The Collections of Science and Art.
C. The General Offices of the Department.

Young spaced his ten-centimeter-square cast-iron H-columns 2.14 meters apart along the periphery of the building. He used slender T-sections for the delicate wrought-iron roof trusses and rested them directly on the columns at the edges of the building. On the interior he bolted them to continuous wrought-iron girders that lay on round columns spaced at 4.28-meter intervals. The two side spans and the ends of the middle one were divided by intermediate gallery floors, while the rest of the central bay was open to the roof.[102]

The architectural community was outraged at the design and had nothing good to say about the building. However, it did avoid a few of the Crystal Palace's structural shortcomings, and it also resembled the American light-wood framing system in some ways.[103] The peripheral cast-iron columns were interconnected by a cast-iron pipe that ran through their feet like a balloon frame's sill. They were also fixed laterally to the gallery floor beam like a balloon frame's intermediate ribbon, but they were attached neither to their concrete footings nor to the wrought-iron roof vaults they carried. The building's corrugated-iron skin formed a continuous sheathing, interrupted only by the central skylight bands on the roofs and by small windows on the lower story. It acted like a stiffening membrane to the overly slender roof trusses and columns, similarly to the way diagonal boarding sheathed and stabilized a skimpy-seeming balloon frame. The light eighteen-gauge skin with

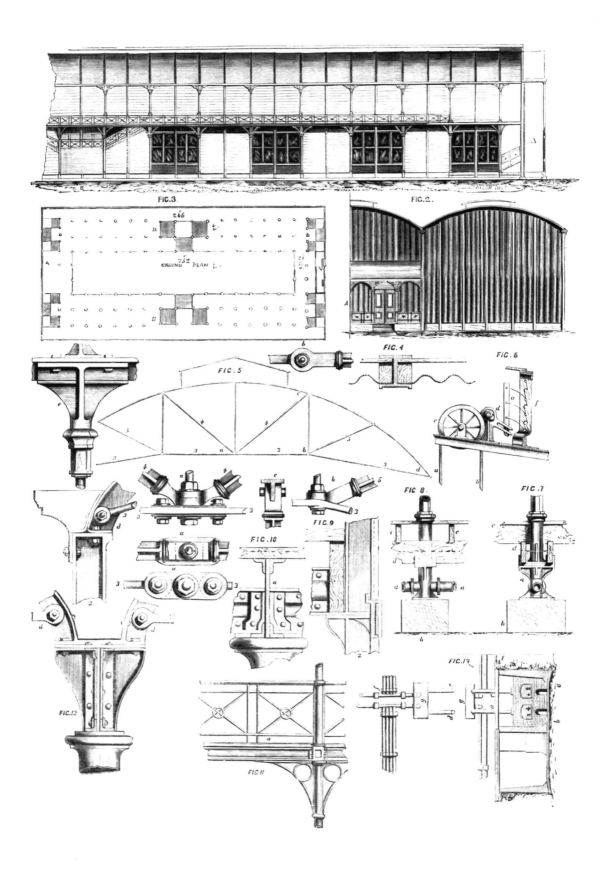

FIG.3

FIG.2.

266
GROUND PLAN

FIG.4

FIG.6

FIG.5

FIG.8.

FIG.7

FIG.9

FIG.10

FIG.12

FIG.11

122.
Plan, elevations, and details
of the "Brompton Boilers."
(*Engineer* [London], 2 May
1856, p. 44.)

its backing of tongue-and-grooved boarding and the wooden gallery flooring made the four-walled box into a stiff structure, and the twenty-gauge skin on the vaults did the same for the independent roofs. By concentrating his primary stiffening mechanisms in the roof, ceiling, and upper-story skin, Young followed a concept similar to the one Voit and Werder had used in the Munich Glaspalast two years before and kept his exhibition floor free of encumbrances.

Unlike the continuous exterior H-columns that ran unbroken from foundation to roofline, the tubular internal supports were cut by the floor girders at the gallery level. They appear to have been only semifixed, held in place by the iron railings, some diagonal cross bracing, and the gallery flooring. Young supported the girders with knee braces at midheight and at the roof line but without bolting them to the horizontal members. It is unclear whether or not he intended this to be some form of expansion joint.

The Royal Commission's choice of material was provocative for a museum, especially following the 1851 exhibition. Victorian aesthetic sensibilities clearly expected something else from a building of that type. Its nickname, the "Brompton Boilers," expressed the public's disappointment and contrasted sharply with the loving name it had bestowed on the Crystal Palace.[104] The Commission's design and technological statement were all the more astonishing as it counted arbiters of Victorian taste like Sir Charles Barry, Henry Cole, Sir Charles Lock Eastlake, Owen Jones, and Matthew Digby Wyatt among its members.[105] The brutally direct and yet modest "Brompton Boilers" contrasted with the flashy Dublin and New York "Crystal Palaces" that merely aped fashion and misunderstood the technological implications of the original. The "Boilers" were intended as a temporary structure, and they were soon demolished to make way for the Victoria and Albert Museum. The original structure was rebuilt in London's East End, where it still stands but slightly modified as the Bethnal Green Museum, clad with a modest brick exterior.[106]

Sir William Cubitt, whom the architectural critics tried to hold innocent of the aesthetic horror by virtue of the fact that he was an "excellent engineer," remained active in the pursuit of new construction systems.[107] He is another builder who has not been studied enough. Like Paxton and Isambard Brunel, he exported some very practical prefabricated structures to the Crimea in 1854.[108] But those were of course "facilities" and did not wound architectural sensibilities.

The Tallest Tower and the Biggest Shed

The conflict between cultural standards for facilities and for works of architecture grew sharper and came into the open a generation later with the Eiffel Tower and the Galerie des Machines. Eiffel's tower realized a fifty-year dream that had dogged builders and politicians alike. Competing for superlative height or span was a typically nineteenth-century preoccupation. The competition had begun with Richard Trevithick's 1832 design for a thousand-foot, gilt, cast-iron truncated cone surmounted by a statue of Winged Victory. Trevithick had planned to build it in London in anticipation of the Reform Bill. The idea was resurrected in 1852 by an architect named Charles Burton as a proposal for recycling the components from the demolished Crystal Palace, and it reappeared at the Philadelphia centennial exhibition of 1876 in the form of a segmented cast-iron tube designed by Clarke Reeves & Company.[109] The firm was one of America's most prolific and experienced bridge builders and their design was far more realistic than Trevithick's or Burton's had been. The tube was to be put under compression with a surrounding net of wire guy ropes post-tensioned from top to bottom, where it was attached to a concrete ring-shaped foundation. It would not rely entirely on the bolts and cast-iron lugs that had proven unreliable in the Crystal Palace and many times thereafter.[110] The exhibition organizers rejected the proposal, fearing a repetition of the embarrassment surrounding the Washington Monument. The world's tallest obelisk had been stuck at a height of thirty-nine meters since 1848 and would not be ready for the exhibition. It was bad enough that a stump should bear witness to national shame at a distance in Washington, and the organizers were understandably loath to risk a similar failure in Philadelphia.

Like towers, bridges and roofs are ideal for pushing the limits of materials, structure, and erection method. Many new ideas in iron construction were first tested in station roofs. Turner, who had built Liverpool's Lime Street Station in 1850, and Fox and Henderson were at the forefront of the profession in Britain. In 1854, Birmingham's New Street Station, built by Ordish of Fox and Henderson, succeeded Lime Street as the world's largest roof span.[111] There was a functional reason for the jump in size from 45.7 meters (just over twice the size of the Crystal Palace nave and transept) to 64.6 meters: train sheds had become complex buildings. The Birmingham span increased diagonal freedom of train movement across the many tracks it covered. By placing columns as far as possible from the tracks, designers could decrease the danger of a derailing train hitting a column and bringing the roof down.[112] Like the Menai and Britannia bridges, train sheds had to be

123.

Clarke Reeves & Company probably could have built their thousand-foot tower for the Philadelphia Centennial Exhibition. It was a segmented cast-iron tube constrained by four tension rings at various heights and guyed down to a concrete base with a braced network of wire ropes. The exhibition's organizers feared it would not work and abandoned the project. (*Scientific American*, vol. 30, 1874, pp. 48, 50.)

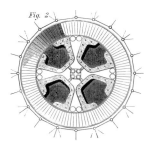

kept clear for moving traffic even during construction. Profiting from his boss's linear glazing idea, Edward Cowper designed the roof and the building method for mobile scaffolding. On level and clear ground, forty men could move the rolling staging from one 7.3-meter construction bay to the next in two and a half hours.

Eiffel's Thinking and the Galerie des Machines

All the many building types mentioned thus far—from the balloon frame and terrace housing to the Brompton Boilers, to the towers, open sheds, and halls—were hybrids of open and closed systems that profited from the model developed by Fox and Paxton. The open system concept came into its own thirty years after the Crystal Palace in Gustave Eiffel's work. Where Durand had used a hierarchy of axes and symmetries to organize form and space two generations before, the technologist Eiffel used a matrix of structural constants and variables to develop the idea of structural system. Where Turner had separated issues to reunite them in an individual component design, Eiffel recombined them to form an open system. It is doubtful whether he conceptualized his thinking in this way, but he clearly had some form of logically ordered thinking process that helped him develop a simple and yet sophisticated catalog of wrought-iron parts and connection rules. Eiffel kept member cross sections and connections constant in his system, and he varied component length to produce similar, rather than congruent, elements. This enabled him to build complex objects without using the special components his predecessors had needed. As Eiffel demonstrated in *La Tour de 300 Mètres,* his tower uses only nine basic connection gussets (shown on plates 9 and 10 of his book and especially clearly in Emile Monod's).[113] These are the generator of his construction system. They define the system geometry, together with the standardized cross sections he uses to make his subassemblies, while the configuration and length of the linear members are less critical. The Eiffel Tower has been well publicized ever since it broke ground, but less as a system than as a monumental tour de force and a building process.[114]

Wilhelm Nördling played an important role in developing Eiffel's approach to system in construction in the 1860s.[115] Nördling, E. Mathieu, Henri de Dion, Jean-Baptiste Krantz, the Compagnie de Fives-Lille, and the Cail companies were all experimenting with trussed wrought-iron construction at the time. As a young engineer Eiffel tested Dion's trusses for Krantz's Paris Exhibition building of 1867. Both Eiffel and Jean-François Cail worked as contractors on secondary buildings at that exhibition, and Eiffel was also the contractor who built the Neuvial and Sioule viaducts on Nördling's

Patterns of Technological Thought

124.
Even the largest building
sites still used a great deal
of manual labor at the end
of the nineteenth century.
The Eiffel Tower's sophisticated climbing cranes ex-
isted side by side with
primitive building methods.
(*Exposition de Paris 1889*,
vol. 1, p. 5.)

Eiffel built the Garabit Viaduct (1880–1884) in cantilever construction. His open construction system allowed him to use the same elements and connectors to erect structures as different as a bridge and the Eiffel Tower. (Eiffel, *Notice sur le viaduc de Garabit*, 1888, plate 3.)

Commentry-Gannat Line in 1869.[116] The design of these two bridges was almost certainly Nördling's, although Eiffel may have contributed to the small-scale solutions. Eiffel's rise to preeminence as an engineer is generally dated from these structures, but his system matured only later, especially in the 1884 Garabit Bridge and the 1889 tower, both of which reconcile a clear and simple rectilinear kit of parts with nonorthogonal form. Eiffel's structural ideas were also influenced by the clarity of Karl Culmann's "graphic statics." In 1879 he hired Maurice Koechlin, one of Culmann's students from the Swiss Polytechnikum in Zurich, to work on the Douro Viaduct, which was then under construction. Koechlin was instrumental in the design of the two later projects.

Like Turner before him, Eiffel segregated issues to solve detail problems. But where Turner reunited the detail solutions in a specific building, Eiffel designed an open system that he could use to build any iron structure. Along with the work of others such as Charles Strobel, who standardized rolled-steel cross sections and sizes for the Carnegie group in 1881, Eiffel's kit-of-parts approach to construction influenced and simplified steel bridge and high-rise construction. It was even adopted by Meccano, an open-ended British engineering construction toy for boys in 1904. Meccano (known as Erector Set in the United States) embedded the concept of open-ended, standardized assembly kits in the minds of generations of future engineers and manufacturers.[117] The toy both mirrored and reinforced the cultural implications of the open system.

The Eiffel Tower and the Galerie des Machines at the 1889 Paris exhibition celebrating the centennial of the French Revolution were shining examples of this approach to construction design. The thousand-foot tower became the new symbol of Paris, the clarion of French heavy industry, a Phoenix risen from the ashes of defeat in the 1870–1871 Franco-Prussian war, loudly crying "Progress." Though the Galerie des Machines has long stood in the shadow of the more famous structure, it was equally impressive technologically. Its 115-meter span broke the world record for an interior space, held since 1869 by William H. Barlow's St. Pancras Station shed in London, although it was far from being the largest span in the world.[118]

Like the Eiffel Tower, the three-hinged Galerie des Machines was built on heterogeneous fill.[119] The hall was 420 meters long with twenty 43-meter-high arches. Double-storied galleries ran along either side and stiffened the building longitudinally. The hinged structure allowed the hall to deform with temperature changes without expansion joints and without causing secondary stresses in the framing, the foundations, or the roof glazing. While

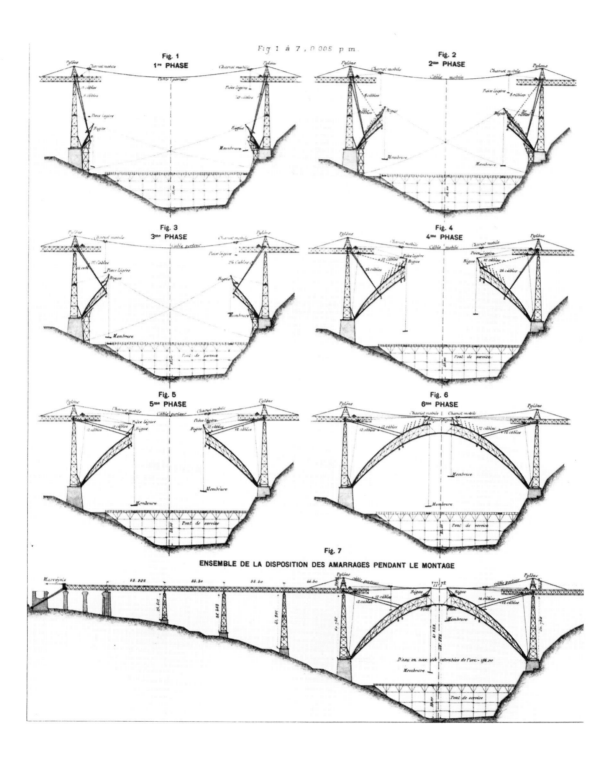

126.
William H. Barlow's
wrought-iron St. Pancras
Station was the largest hall
of its time. Warehouses,
port facilities, and stations
were more than single
buildings; they were integral parts of the expanding
railway infrastructure. (*Das
Neue Buch der Erfindungen,*
1872–1875, vol. 1, p. 219;
Figuier, *Nouvelles Conquêtes
de la Science,* 1883–1885,
vol. 3, p. 497.)

Patterns of Technological Thought

Eiffel chose pneumatic caissons burrowed beneath the water table for his rigid tower, the builders of the Galerie chose the three-hinged arch form because the subsoil was unstable. They placed the flexible Galerie on thick concrete blocks, some of them cast over wooden piles. The lower hinges transmitted no overturning moments to the foundations and did away with the need for eccentric foundation blocks or tension rods under the floor. This made them simple and cheaper to cast than would otherwise have been possible. The hall had eighty foundation points in contrast to the tower's sixteen, so any simplification underground meant a saving of construction time and money. The only complicated parts of the foundation were inverted underground arches that took the thrust of the side galleries.

The ram that drove the piles for fifteen of the main arch foundations moved along the axis on tracks and crossed the hall on a dolly to reach the feet of the main arcs and the side galleries. Even if it did take a whole day to move the pile driver from one bay to the next, it took relatively few men to do so, and the ram's two-dimensional mobility was an improvement over Henderson's derrick crane, Fox's glazing cart, and Cowper's linearly mobile Birmingham scaffolding.[120]

The Galerie's architect, Charles-Louis Ferdinand Dutert, worked closely with Victor Contamin, the exhibition's chief engineer. Most historians deny that Dutert had much if any input in the structural design, although he did work with Contamin to have the exhibition committee accept the unclad bottom hinges of the arches.[121] Dutert's interest was unusual, as engineering and architecture were separate fields by that time and a higher cultural value was placed on decoration than on construction.

The site organization and building process benefited from the decades of experience that the two contractors, the Compagnie de Fives-Lille and the Société des Anciens Établissements Cail, had in railway shed and hall construction. They began the arch erection in April 1888. It lasted only six months. There were eighteen three-hinged arches, spaced about twenty-four meters apart, and two double ones at each end. The end bays were slightly larger, as was a middle one where a short passage connected the hall to the Palais des Industries Diverses.[122]

The two contracting firms assembled the hall in competition with each other. They had both worked on the exhibition hall of 1867, and they were experienced in the quick erection of large iron structures. Fives-Lille began from the Avenue de la Bourdonnais, while Cail took the ten arches from the Avenue de Suffren. Cail guaranteed the same deadlines as Fives-Lille, which had begun a month earlier. Both worked in shifts around the clock and managed to finish at the same time, actually coming in under schedule.

127.
The 1889 Galerie des Machines almost doubled St. Pancras Station's span. Even the two-story, lateral galleries that stiffened the hall longitudinally were substantial buildings in their own right. (*Exposition de Paris 1889,* vol. 1, p. 53, plate following p. 36; Huard, 1889, vol. 1, p. 65.)

LE PALAIS DES MACHINES

ET SES CONSTRUCTIONS

Buildings from the Sayn Foundry to the Galerie des Machines 271

128.
Glass covered most of the
roof. The glazing process
could have been rational-
ized, but it was evidently
not a critical issue in this
building process. (Monod,
1889, vol. 1, p. 252.)

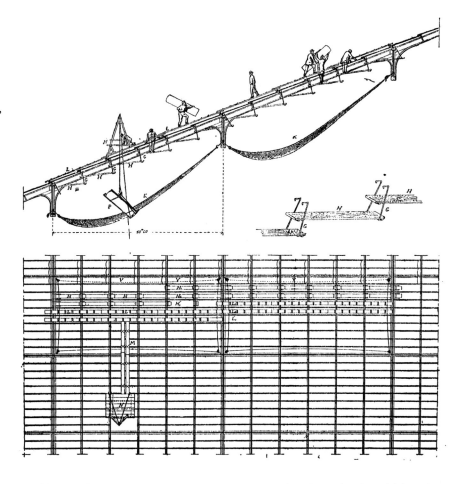

(This was the period in which Henri Fayol is said to have developed his early
time-and-motion studies in France.)

Each firm used a different method. Cail fit together preassembled
segments on a continuous scaffolding that supported the whole arch. A
three-tonne traveling crane ran along the top of the scaffold and lifted the
pieces into place. Fives-Lille used another method specifically designed for
the project. The assembly crew built three mobile wooden piers on tracks parallel to the hall axis. Then workmen preassembled the arch into four segments on the ground. The largest two were fixed to the base hinges, rotated
up into position, and rested on the tops of the outer scaffolding towers. The
difficult part was starting the rotation, because the forty-eight-tonne segments had a tendency to tip to the side. They became progressively more
stable the higher they rose. When they were safely in position, cranes lifted
the two remaining pieces to the center pylon where workmen riveted them
to the side sections and assembled the top hinge.

129.
The Eiffel Tower was built
on pneumatic caissons,
while the Galerie des Ma-
chines had eighty individual
foundations under the main
arches and the lateral galleries. Only a few of them
needed piles. (Monod,
1889, vol. 1, pp. 137, 231,
233.)

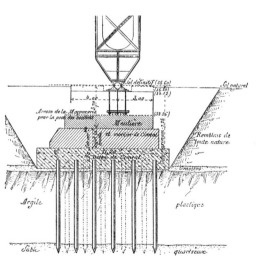

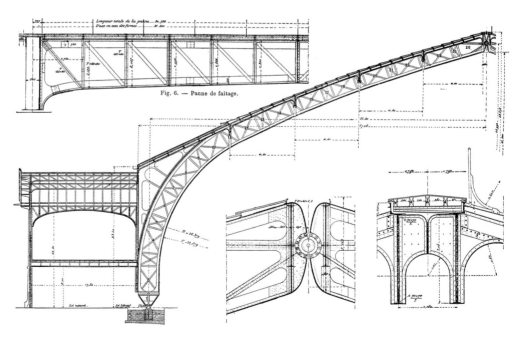

Fig. 6. — Panne de faitage.

130.
The Galerie des Machines
had overhead drive shafts
for the exhibits, a mobile
"bridge" that carried visitors back and forth along
the axis, and several types
of overhead electric lighting. (Monod, 1889, vol. 1,
p. 249.)

131.
Cross section and details of
the main arches and lateral
galleries. (Monod, 1889,
vol. 1, p. 235.)

If the building process was machinelike, so was the building itself.
The clatter and steam of machinery filled the huge hall. The overhead drive
shafts rumbled and drove slapping leather bands that turned the wheels of
hundreds of exhibits, while the moving bridge glided serenely overhead like a
train, a horizontal elevator, or a giant piston, carrying a platform-load of visitors effortlessly over the entire length of the hall. Like the Sayn Foundry, the
various glass houses, or Eiffel's 1884 observatory at Nice (with its mobile
iron dome floating in a ring of oil—a machine for viewing the heavens), the
Galerie des Machines was a hybrid building-machine.

Dutert was aware of this. It may have influenced him to limit the
decoration of the structure and concentrate on ornament.[123] Contemporary
critics considered this appropriate, given the mechanical contents and designa-
tion of the building—a refreshingly rational approach to structural form at a
time when architects were mostly interested in eclectic issues or were verging
on a shift to emotive abstractions like "organic" or "dynamic" that would
soon dominate design.[124] Architectural theoreticians like Ruskin, Pugin,
Cole, Semper, and Pickett had called for "honesty" in the use of materials
after the design excesses of the products shown in the Crystal Palace. But
each defined honesty differently, and public taste still expected exuberant
iconography. The decorative excesses of the halls that surrounded the Galerie
des Machines stood witness to this demand.[125] The public did not generally
consider structural frames beautiful; iron was "vulgar." "Honesty" and "de-
cency" seemed almost to be opposites. Even table and piano legs were
deemed indecent and had to be decorously draped in cloth or sheathed
modestly in wooden casing.

The Eiffel Tower was vilified by the celebrated protest of famous artists and vigorously defended by others, but the Galerie des Machines was not
controversial and could appropriately make its iron structure visible because
it was a machine hall, a "facility." Dutert stood with the few like Henry Cole
or the designer Christopher Dresser who followed functional rationalism and
the dictates of manufacturing processes.[126] Dutert's concern paralleled what
untutored builders were doing in bridge structure, in factories, and in grain
elevators in reinforced concrete. He was a Prix de Rome winner, part of the
aesthetic establishment, and could therefore get away with it. He allowed
technological logic to determine architectural form even more confidently
and directly than Robert Stephenson had in the Conway and Britannia
bridges.

Monod, writing in 1889, held the Galerie des Machines to be the
most appropriate use of iron in all the exhibition. Even the beautiful Eiffel
Tower was not, according to him, the result of design intention but of mere

132.
The Cail company's scaffolding took up the width of the building. It rolled on tracks along the hall and had two mobile tower cranes mounted on its top that lifted preassembled structural components to the top of the hall. (Monod, 1889, vol. 1, p. 243; *Exposition de Paris 1889*, vol. 1, p. 9; Huard, 1889, vol. 1, p. 69.)

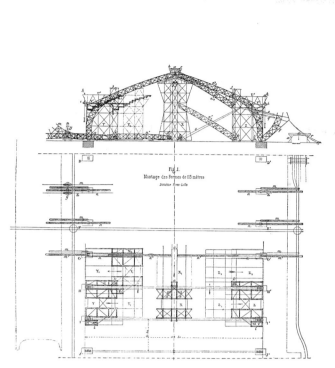

133.
The Fives-Lille company
used a smaller, three-part
scaffold, but they lifted
their components in much
heavier sections. The bottom segment was the largest
and had to be rotated up
into position; the top pin
was assembled on the scaffolding. (Monod, 1889,
vol. 1, pp. 239, 240; *Exposition de Paris 1889*, vol. 1, p.
4.)

computational logic, while the iron frames of the palaces of the Arts Liberaux, the Industries Diverses, and the Beaux-Arts were nothing but loadbearing elements smothered in stucco and swathed in stuff, with their formal potential ignored. The Galerie des Machines, on the other hand, synthesized Dutert's frame with Contamin and Chardon's calculations. The result reflected both the construction method and the material. Monod termed it the beginning of an "architecture of iron."[127]

The Galerie was certainly not the first iron frame in which structure determined formal expression. But it did mark the point at which the analytical engineering model, the material, and the manufacturing method became the form. In 1851 the Crystal Palace had expressed the open system by default because there had not been time to cover it appropriately. Thirty-eight years later, the Galerie des Machines expressed system and structure by choice.

135.
While it was under construction, the Palais des Industries Diverses dome had an airy and romantic aspect. When it was finished, it was so smothered in stucco, terra-cotta, and cast stone that no part of the frame remained visible. (*Exposition de Paris 1889*, vol. 1, pp. 20, 33; Monod, 1889, vol. 1, p. 204.)

7

The Result in Small and Large: The Langwies Viaduct and the Panama Canal

The construction field changed as builders gradually shifted their focus from composition to organization and from product to process. Their concerns varied with the scale of their projects. Eduard Züblin's Langwies Viaduct in Switzerland was a straightforward small-scale project, but he still had to organize it carefully to take advantage of the short alpine building season and the difficult terrain. At the other extreme, Lesseps failed to recognize that he had to approach the Panama Canal in a different way from Suez because the project was so large and complex. Others subsequently recognized the level of coordination it would take to do the job and created a railway distribution system, established a health organization, and designed new types of building processes. George Washington Goethals treated the project like a military problem: he orchestrated and controlled the hierarchy and interaction of all the parts.

All the building projects we have examined so far lay in large economies, primarily in Britain, France, Germany, Italy, and the United States. But small countries like Belgium, Holland, Denmark, and Switzerland also contributed actively to the development of processes and methods: a smaller scale of construction and minor capital investment could still foster innovation. In many cases the smaller scope and more intimate professional environment of such projects allowed builders to adapt more flexibly and imaginatively to changing criteria.

Citizens of smaller European countries have often been forced to look beyond their borders to fulfill personal ambitions, and yet they have often managed to accomplish much within their own economies, too. Belgians advanced steel production and metallurgical knowledge based on that country's iron and coal deposits both at home and in the Congo. Holland and Denmark had stable agrarian economies and a seafaring past with widespread commercial networks. Dutch hydraulic engineers had helped found the British engineering profession in the seventeenth century, while the Danes have been very actively developing their urban infrastructure and concrete construction in the past two centuries. Switzerland's topography and position at the crossroads of Europe's trade routes encouraged the Swiss to pursue all areas of transportation construction.[1] Holland and Denmark had no indigenous resources for wood or steel construction and were forced to look to brick and later concrete. Switzerland had poor clay for brickmaking, but it had the ingredients for concrete. All of these small countries relied on external contacts for trade, innovative impulses, industrial production, and education, particularly Belgium and Switzerland, which were heterogeneous cultures and newly federally organized at midcentury.

Building is economically important to many nations, but it is crucial to the existence of an alluvial country like Holland or a mountainous one like Switzerland, which must fight ceaselessly against the destructive powers of gravity and nature. The Swiss had to conquer their divisive topography and create and maintain elaborate communication networks in order to survive. Their contribution to building technology began with the first alpine crossings and it snowballed as modern commerce spread. The Langwies Viaduct illustrates the small scale at which Swiss industry has excelled, and at which Swiss industrialists have consciously operated.[2]

Eduard Züblin and the Langwies Viaduct

The Langwies Viaduct carries a narrow-gauge railway that connects Chur, the capital of the canton of Grisons, to the alpine resort Arosa. It was the last project designed by Eduard Züblin, one of François Hennebique's most prolific licensees. German Swiss by origin, Züblin was an internationalist by birth and upbringing and a professional border crosser by training and inclination.[3] He studied mechanical engineering in Switzerland and began his career as an architect in Naples. Like the nation, the Swiss building profession is border-crossing by tradition. Structural engineers and architects still share a single professional organization and journal, then called the *Schweizerische Bauzeitung*. In 1893 Züblin came across an article in this journal describing Hennebique's new reinforced concrete system.[4] He tried it out on a terrace addition to his own house, licensed the patent for Naples in 1895, and became a contractor. Concrete became highly successful in the European building boom at the end of the century. Züblin quickly established his firm and successfully bid for the Hennebique license for southern Germany in 1898. Hennebique valued the dynamic, polyglot contractor, who combined engineer, architect, and contractor in one person. He planned to rely on Züblin to build his international corporation.

The Result in Small and Large

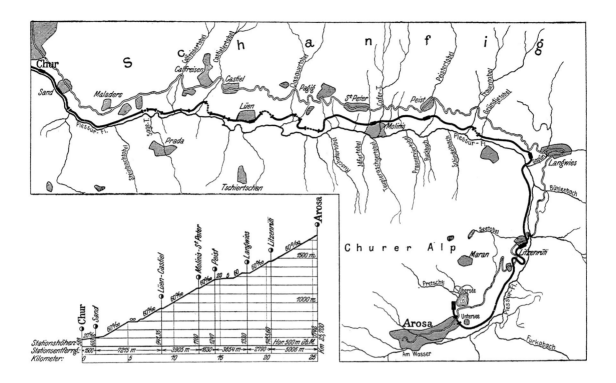

136.
Plan and profile of the
Chur-Arosa railway
through Schanfigg Valley.
(Schürch, 1914, p. 2.)

Strasbourg in Alsace straddles the border between German and French cultures. Züblin chose it as his international headquarters in 1899 and built on family contacts and on projects already started by Hennebique. He soon obtained the freedom to solicit and negotiate contracts himself, paying Hennebique a seven percent commission for the privilege. Over the years Züblin patented several improvements to the Hennebique system, especially in silo construction and concrete piling. By 1904 he was able to avoid paying licensing fees altogether while remaining in close professional contact with his former mentor.[5] He built the earliest known reinforced concrete swimming pool for the municipality of Guebwiler in Alsace as well as silos, factories, and other special structures in Germany, France, Italy, and Switzerland.[6] Thus the firm came well prepared and recommended for its most important Swiss commission, the building of the Langwies Railway Viaduct (1912–1914).

Hermann Schürch, Züblin's son-in-law, had been with the firm since 1903. He designed the hundred-meter span, but it was Züblin's daring that carried the project.[7] Porcheddu, Hennebique's licensee in Turin, had built the slightly longer Risorgimento road bridge over the Tiber in Rome in 1904, but the Langwies Viaduct was the highest arch of its time and a more highly stressed railroad bridge.[8] The site's inaccessibility conditioned the building process. Everything had to be brought up in horse-drawn wagons from Chur along tiny mountain roads. Large machine parts presented logistical problems, and Züblin exploited every available idea to solve them.

Swiss authorities hesitated to grant permits for reinforced concrete railway structures in the first years of the century. A few small-span bridges had been built, but some theoreticians still had doubts about the monolithic bond between steel reinforcement and concrete.[9] Building inspectors all over the country were aware of their colleagues' bad experience with the 1906 Rhone River bridge at Chippis in the canton of Valais. The skew bowstring arch had suspenders encased in concrete that had cracked, exposing them to the weather.[10] To make matters worse, the tracks were fixed to the substructure and locomotives shook them loose.[11] As a result it became virtually impossible to build a railway bridge in reinforced concrete. By 1912 it was evident that the building authorities had overreacted, and they waived their restrictions for the two bridges on the Chur-Arosa line.[12]

The remote alpine village of Arosa had only a few huts in 1890. Visitors arrived at the idyllic, wooded, and lake-dappled site after a six-hour dusty or muddy mail run up the deep and narrow Schanfigg Valley. The town's tax base grew ninety-three-fold between 1887 and 1912.[13] The influx was mainly due to the proliferation of sanatoria for the treatment of asthma and tuberculosis. Nineteenth-century cities with their fine acrid powder of desiccated horse droppings, gritty coal dust, and sulfurous fumes from heating, railways, and factories were far more polluted than most urban agglomerations of the late twentieth. Wealthy patients with pulmonary diseases spent time at the seashore or in alpine environments where air cures and then sunbathing became the rage. Resorts like Arosa flourished, and when winter sports followed in the first decade of the new century there was a push to build railways. Patients would accept a lengthy journey to a spa where they planned to stay several months, but tourists demanded quicker transportation for a vacation that would last a few weeks at most.

The municipality proposed a railway in 1902 and the federal government in Bern granted a concession four years later. Swiss democratic processes are complex, and five more years were needed to convince the taxpayers at the termini of the line, Arosa and Chur, to fund the project. The city of Chur owned developable land in Arosa and the complex intermunicipal negotiations also involved the cantonal government, which exercised its option to enforce the establishment of a zoning plan. The railway company incorporated in 1912 and the line opened in time for the start of the winter season two years later. The 25.7-kilometer line had a six percent gradient, thirty-two bridges, and nineteen tunnels, which made the railway comparable in complexity to many more spectacular projects.

The building process was rapid in contrast to the political process that preceded it. Züblin began building the bridge in August 1912. Builders had learned by then to estimate construction processes with a fair degree of accuracy. Their ability to control them had grown from none at all when the Thames Tunnel was built, to vague notions at the time of the Britannia Bridge and the Mont Cenis Tunnel, to an attempt to manipulate events with bonuses and penalties in the case of the Suez Canal. By the end of the century, contractors were generally so sure of their organizational abilities that deadlines became parameters of the building process on which they could base calculable business risks. External influences, called "acts of God," were still excluded, of course. One of the arts of formulating contracts and arbitrating disputes became the definition of what constituted an "internal" parameter and what an "external" variable. The expropriation of land for the Chur-Arosa railway, for instance, was an external variable. It had to go through a complex judicial process that delayed the project by three months, but the construction time remained the same as projected and the bridge was finished by May 1914.

Schanfigg Valley stone crushed too easily to be used for building, but there was plenty of good sand and water. The road to the site was too narrow and winding to transport large steel members, which would in any case have had to be imported at great expense from abroad. So the engineers used concrete for all bridges, tunnel linings, and retaining walls on the line so as to reduce material and transportation costs and avoid delay.[14] They built many of the minor bridges without reinforcement and clad them with stone for aesthetic reasons; the entire Grisons railway network was tied to the spread of alpine tourism, and aesthetics is a prime asset in the tourist industry.[15] Several small concrete bridges had been built in Switzerland in the early years, but there were not many firms that could undertake such a complex structure.[16] The railway chose Züblin without competitive bidding for the bridge at Langwies and the Zurich firm Zeerleder und Gobat for the other major bridge on the line at Gründjetobel.

Site geology and the canyon depth were major design determinants at Langwies. Schürch calculated that the most economical span would lie between 80 and 140 meters in length. But Züblin did not want to press the hesitant building authorities too hard, since they had to grant the permit variance he needed to build the bridge in concrete. So he cautiously settled on a span of one hundred meters, which he and Schürch also decided would look best.[17] Aesthetics contributed to the design of the Langwies Viaduct on an equal footing with economic and structural arguments. The explanation for the unusually strong influence of formal considerations probably lay both in the client's interest in the tourist trade and in Züblin's decade of experience as an architect.

Züblin wanted to stress the structural reading of his bridge.[18] As a former architect, he was more aware of the cultural implications of aesthetic issues than most engineers. He may not have followed Pugin's distinction between ornament and decoration consciously, but he intuitively adhered to the sensory reading rather than the intellectual meaning of form, and like others of his generation he designed shapes to express the concept of monolithic structure. Theorists of the modern movement in architecture later attributed this achievement solely to the unusually gifted Robert Maillart, but the interest was widespread among early builders in concrete.[19] Züblin must have influenced Schürch, who wrote in 1916: "It [the bridge] expresses the congruence of material and form. We may thus consider it a work of technological art which satisfies our aesthetic sensibilities, even though, due to the lack of precedent, the eye must first accustom itself to the purely statically determined reinforced concrete forms as a new material, stone that can withstand bending."[20] Schürch was evidently not totally comfortable with his own daring, however, because he couched his profound observation in an apologetic traditional "architectural" description of the bridge with reference to the secondary questions of the pier tops, the railings, and the placement of the overhead electric wire, and included an inane comment on how well it "fit into the landscape."

The geology of Langwies, the height of the arch, and the confidence practitioners had gained in dealing with statically indeterminate systems all supported the choice of a fixed arch. Züblin and Schürch framed their bridge

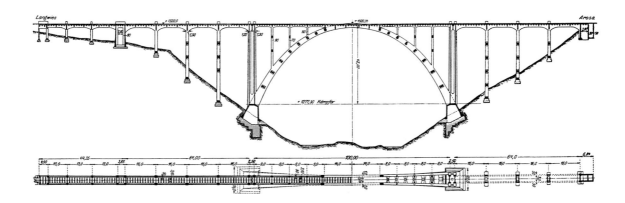

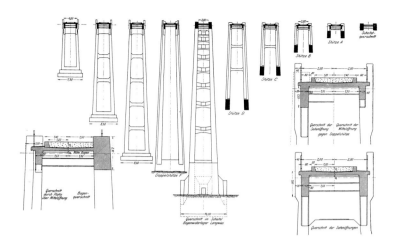

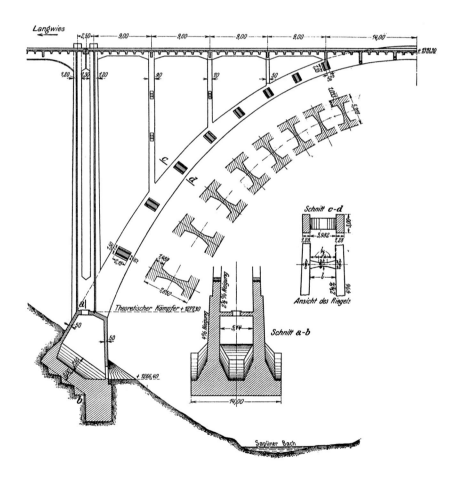

137.
The longitudinal section
and cross section of the
Langwies Viaduct's main
arch show how thin its
members were. (Schürch,
1916, pp. 18–20.)

The Langwies Viaduct and the Panama Canal

as two thin, parallel arches connected by correspondingly thin braces. By making no abrupt changes in cross section they avoided undesirable stress concentrations in the structure and reduced deadload and foundation size at the same time. Robert Maillart had adopted a similar strategy in his Zuoz and Tavanasa bridges in 1901 and 1905. He used shells, slabs, and shear membranes that were too thin to stand on their own, much less carry traffic. But they all helped support and carry each other. This load-sharing idea was new to engineering theory, although American light-wood framing and early cast-iron prefabrication had intuitively depended on it. Maillart and Schürch could build their centering lighter than traditional falsework, but it had to stay in position until the structure was complete and had gained its monolithic characteristics. Monolithic structures carried more load with less material, and lighter centering saved money. Soon others began to build integrated structures, too.

Economy was the all-important criterion. Saving time, money, material, and design effort drove builders to innovate. Every new form or process had to satisfy commercial as well as functional criteria, as Schürch noted: "Although a solution with smaller spans was rejected . . . due to the placement of intermediate piers in the rubble delta and the lack of character this would give the entire structure, we still studied one because it was of primary importance to find the most economical solution."[21] Quick erection and simple centering more than balanced the higher cost of formwork for a single arch and the longer permit-granting process. Züblin recognized that real savings lay in optimizing a matrix of interdependent variables. It was a typical problem for technological thinkers.

Züblin and Schürch also examined the approaches in the same way and decided to interconnect them to form a monolithic frame. The piers became slender and the load was spread evenly over the foundations. Since the approaches and the arch were of different scale, the builders decided not to integrate them. They separated them by doubling the piers where they met; this provided a visual separation and an expansion joint at the same time. Again Schürch used aesthetic arguments in support of their decision: "The double piers were not only introduced for structural but also for aesthetic reasons because they clearly demarcated the three different parts of the main structure, even in elevation. . . . The originally planned standard solution . . . which provided for a single pier with wide, massive elevation and shear walls articulated top and bottom like those of the Gmündertobel Bridge . . . couldn't have provided this effect satisfactorily in spite of a major waste of mass."[22]

Emil Mörsch's 1908 Gmündertobel Bridge in Appenzell was a little smaller and heavier. It looked superficially similar, but was designed on a completely different model. Mörsch, the first academic theoretician of reinforced concrete in the German-speaking world, did not even consider the monolithic implications of his design. He designed his arch to support the entire superstructure on its own, which made his erection process iterative: the heavy centering carried the arch and the arch carried the verticals and the deck. This was traditional masonry construction, not the integrative thinking and process that monolithic structure permits. Monolithic structure and matrix problem solving go hand in hand; both are integrative and multileveled. If one variable changes, the whole system changes with it. Good engineering design has always combined technological and formal thinking, and the Langwies Viaduct's smallest details were designed to underline structural behavior. For instance, Schürch initially proposed rounded haunches for the ribs that carry the deck slab. But they made the ribs look like flat arches, so Züblin and Schürch redesigned them with straight haunches that corresponded visually to the frame system on which they had based their structural design.[23]

Schürch set up a work yard on the future site of Langwies station. The construction site was remote. Everything had to be brought in on one side of the canyon. Teams of four horses hauled 2.5 tonnes a trip up from Chur; a team could only make two round trips in three days, and they made a thousand trips in the two years the site was in operation. At the height of construction the site consumed material twice as fast as it could be brought up. Schürch foresaw the problem and established large site depots in advance. He slung a cable crane across the canyon to connect the depot with the other side. This was common practice on deep bridge sites and it saved the expense of building a secondary scaffolding to carry a temporary roadway.[24] Skips, filled from mixers positioned on both sides of the gorge, crossed every three to five minutes while concreting was in progress. The municipal generating plant at Arosa supplied electricity to drive the crane. This too was an advantage Langwies had over the remote sites of the preceding century. At Mont Cenis and Suez in the 1860s energy generation and transportation had been a major problem. At Langwies fifty years later, the electric cable provided a clean, cheap, and simple solution.

The site was narrow but long and the crane operator stood on the Arosa side of the canyon across from the work yard and depots, so Schürch linked them by telephone. Langwies may have been one of the first European sites to use this new means of communication, which would soon revolutionize large building sites. For the first time building machines could safely have

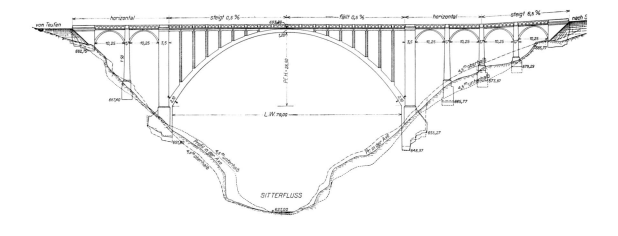

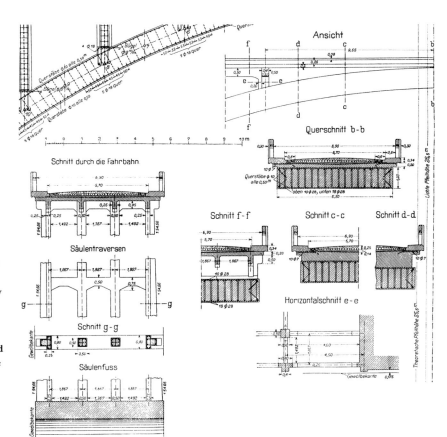

138.
Emil Mörsch built the
Gmündertobel Bridge four
years before the Langwies
Viaduct. It was superficially
similar in appearance, but
very different in concept.
Its arch was separate from
the rest of the structure and
designed to carry the entire
superstructure on its own.
The cross sections show
how much heavier it was.
(Mörsch, 1912, pp. 542,
544.)

a longer reach than the human voice. Telephones accelerated the building process and helped avoid mistakes and accidents. The Panama Canal could not have functioned so well without them, although there were none in 1884 when the French began digging, or when Eiffel's tower and the 1,700-meter-long Firth of Forth Bridge were under construction. All these projects had simply used messengers and progressed slowly. A few earlier projects like the Suez Canal and the Mont Cenis Tunnel had used telegraph lines, at least in their later stages of construction.

Another organizational technique was the bar graph. It was an eighteenth-century invention but relatively new in building. Züblin and Schürch used it to enhance their control of the building process.[25] Like the telephone, it went beyond Stephenson's and Eiffel's organizational methods. The bar graph coordinated contractors by showing graphically how far each was supposed to have progressed in relation to the others at any time. As inevitable delays occurred, Schürch made adjustments to identify and head off trouble further down the line. The very concept of the timeline enabled him to prepare his material depot against a shortfall well in advance, and he used the bar graph to control minor bottlenecks in material supply, too. In contrast to the Suez Canal's fortuitous organizational pattern, Langwies demonstrated how planning smoothed the way for complex building processes. Eiffel must have used similar means to organize his large projects, although he never explained his system. We know that he prefabricated, coded, and preassembled hundreds of thousands of components for the tower. It would have been impossible to manufacture, warehouse, and deliver each of them to meet its own specific deadline without some sophisticated form of coordination.

Züblin rationalized the concreting process, too, and used an early kind of slipform to cast the piers and the columns that held up the deck. He slung trussed working platforms between the columns to make it easier to erect the formwork and the intermediate cross ribs. The platforms rose with the forms and finally became the centering for the deck ribs and slab.

Schürch took core samples at the site and drove exploratory foundation shafts during the summer before construction started. He needed a clear picture of the subsoil configuration before Züblin committed them to large lateral arches or to series of small spans.[26] He drove the shafts deeper than the future foundations and discovered dense but plastic soil. What he found corresponded to what others had found elsewhere along the Rhaetian Railway, and he decided to drain the slope and put down deeper foundations than he had originally planned.[27] The approach rested on an unstable slope on the Arosa side, and Schürch decided to interconnect the frame supports

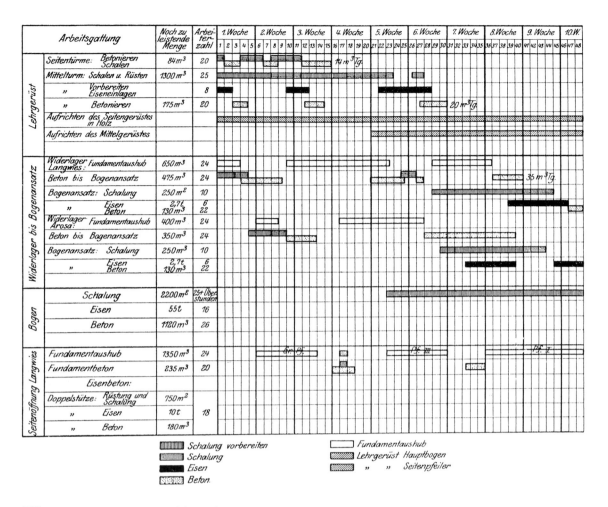

Arbeitsgattung		Noch zu leistende Menge	Arbeiterzahl	1.Woche	2.Woche	3. Woche	4. Woche	5. Woche	6. Woche	7. Woche	8.Woche	9. Woche	10.W.

(Lehrgerüst)
- Seitentürme: Betonieren / Schalen — 84 m³ — 20 — 14 m³/Tg.
- Mittelturm: Schalen u. Rüsten — 1300 m³ — 25
- " Vorbereiten Eiseneinlagen — 8
- " Betonieren — 175 m³ — 20 — 20 m³/Tg.
- Aufrichten des Seitengerüstes in Holz
- Aufrichten des Mittelgerüstes

(Widerlager bis Bogenansatz)
- Widerlager Langwies: Fundamentaushub — 650 m³ — 24
- Beton bis Bogenansatz — 475 m³ — 24 — 35 m³/Tg.
- Bogenansatz: Schalung — 250 m² — 10
- " Eisen / Beton — 2,7 t / 130 m³ — 6 / 22
- Widerlager Arosa: Fundamentaushub — 400 m³ — 24
- Beton bis Bogenansatz — 350 m³ — 24
- Bogenansatz: Schalung — 250 m³ — 10
- " Eisen / Beton — 2,7 t / 130 m³ — 6 / 22

(Bogen)
- Schalung — 2200 m² — 25 + Überstunden
- Eisen — 55 t — 16
- Beton — 1120 m³ — 26

(Seitenöffnung Langwies)
- Fundamentaushub — 1350 m³ — 24
- Fundamentbeton — 235 m³ — 20
- Eisenbeton:
- Doppelstütze: Rüstung und Schalung — 750 m² — 18
- " Eisen — 10 t
- " Beton — 180 m³

Legend:
- ▨ Schalung vorbereiten
- ▤ Schalung
- ▬ Eisen
- ▨ Beton
- ▭ Fundamentaushub
- ▨ Lehrgerüst Hauptbogen
- ▨ " " Seitenpfeiler

139.
One of the bar graphs Schürch used to coordinate the building process. (Schürch, 1916, p. 35.)

with a subterranean strut supported against the arch abutment. This instability was another factor that may have helped him decide to separate the arch and the approaches. His caution was well rewarded when the structure moved slightly because the railway company was a little slow in draining the site.

The workyard was fully stocked and ready in autumn 1912, and Schürch cast the arch abutments and concrete base for the centering before work stopped during the severe alpine winter. When spring arrived, he poured the remaining foundations, and by summer subcontractor Richard Coray had prepared the giant arch centering. Züblin had to keep the valley as clear of structure as possible because the two streams flooded frequently, so he couldn't build the centering in standard trestle form. Coray, who specialized in centering and built falsework for almost all of the best-known Swiss

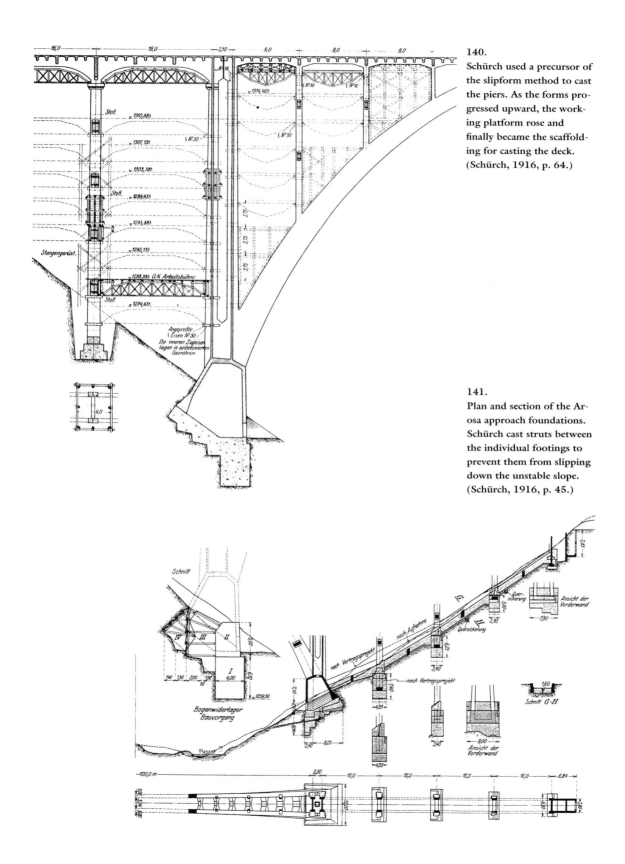

140.
Schürch used a precursor of the slipform method to cast the piers. As the forms progressed upward, the working platform rose and finally became the scaffolding for casting the deck. (Schürch, 1916, p. 64.)

141.
Plan and section of the Arosa approach foundations. Schürch cast struts between the individual footings to prevent them from slipping down the unstable slope. (Schürch, 1916, p. 45.)

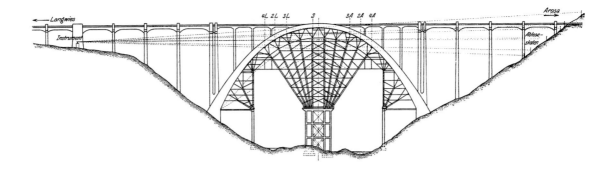

142.
Because the arch was so light, Coray's fan-shaped centering had to remain in place until the bridge was complete and all parts could work together mono-lithically. (Schürch, 1916, p. 61.)

bridges in the first forty years of the century, fanned the temporary structure forty meters out from three points.[28] He used raw logs for compression members and wood trusses or steel rope for tension members. Coray designed it as a splayed space frame so that only the edge timbers that carried the concreting trough were subjected to bending. His team laid it out on a floor at the foot of the site to make sure all butt joints in the spokes of the fan fit snugly. Here and there he used sheet metal to make the logs fit tighter. It took from mid-May to the beginning of September 1913 to finish the centering. Even though it was much lighter than usual for such a large arch, it still represented twenty-five percent of the total construction cost.

Coray raised the centering into position using the cable crane and winches. Concentrating the load at only three points meant that Züblin had to design the bases in concrete and ground them deep in the gravel moraine. The central base was a twenty-two-meter space frame with post-tensioned steel members. It resembled the bottom of a coal hopper of the type Züblin

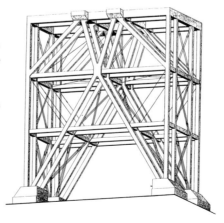

143.
Schürch built a reinforced concrete space frame under the main centering to carry the fanned scaffolding structure and protect it from being washed away in the spring melt. (Schürch, 1916, p. 56.)

had built earlier in his career. Concreting proceeded in segments, keeping the centering wet to prevent shrinkage. Schürch left open joints between the sections to allow for possible formwork deformation. He closed the last of them over the crossing points of the three fans after three or four weeks. There was very little deformation because of the care Coray had taken in butting the log ends. Schürch monitored the centering and tested the concrete on site. Probes were also regularly sent to the Eidgenössische Materialprüfungs-Anstalt (Swiss national testing laboratory) in Zurich. Casting the Langwies approach and the arch took a month and a half and was complete by the end of October, just before the first snows. Schürch left them to cure through the winter, and the following year he cast the Arosa side and the superstructure.

Coray struck the centering on 14 June 1914. His team first removed the wedges under the wind struts and then those under the turnbuckles, which were released a little at a time in sequence over an eight-hour period until the arch stood free. Schürch cleared the site before the larches turned that fall. He had to hurry, as there were only 395 construction days in the two-year building schedule. World War I broke out in the middle of July. It delayed load testing for four months and the formal opening until December 11. By that time traffic had been rolling over the bridge for a month.

Panama: A New Order of Magnitude Demands Novel Organization

Site organization, system configuration, component manufacture, and erection procedure define large projects even more stringently than smaller ones. As complex as the logistics of the Swiss site were, those at Panama were immeasurably more so. The extreme difference in scale coupled with site-specific conditions not only demanded more plant, men, and coordination, they called for entirely new strategies.

The Langwies Viaduct was a small project that fulfilled a local transportation need, while the Panama Canal was a large one built to solve an international problem. What had been minor concerns on the smaller site were transformed into crucial issues on the larger one, and the small-scale problem became as important as the overall design. Health concerns, housing, and related services like water and sewage grew more complex with increasing size. Transporting men, materials, energy, and machines became more important. The logistics of manufacture and placement had conditioned construction at Suez, while in the gigantic Panama project, health, housing, recruitment, and transportation were all magnified until they became the principal elements of the project, almost more important than the digging itself.

Commercial interests wanted a canal across Panama. The European powers wanted it for easy access to eastern Asia, and the United States needed it to consolidate its hold on the North American continent. It was dangerous to cross North America on insecure paths or make the longer and equally hazardous trip around Cape Horn. After 1855 the Panama Railway made the voyage quicker, and the unified transcontinental line inaugurated easy direct coast-to-coast shipment in 1869. But both lines were monopolies with high tariffs, and they still did not really simplify direct shipment from Asia to the east coast or from the west coast to Europe. The monopoly weakened in 1907, when shippers began lowering their costs by using a new rail line across the Mexican Isthmus of Tehuantepec from Coatzacoalcos on the Gulf coast to Salina Cruz on the Pacific, but it was expensive to transship from ship to rail and back again, and this kept interest in a publicly supported canal alive. The United States government was also interested, especially after the naval attack on Havana in 1898 made it clear that the United States had either to build two navies or somehow shorten travel between the east and west coasts. President William Taft learned in 1912 that ships sailing between New York and San Francisco would arrive 23 to 32 days earlier by canal than via the Cape.[29]

There was a long history of interest in the connection. Hernán Cortés proposed a canal via the Isthmus of Tehuantepec to Emperor Charles V in 1524.[30] Ten years later, Spanish adventurers discovered Lake Nicaragua and the partly navigable San Juan River. Philip III briefly encouraged a southern route via the Gulf of Darien (Golfo de Urabá) and the Atrato River, until British government-encouraged piracy all but destroyed Spanish power in the region.[31] A Nicaraguan route attracted British interest when Britain was losing its colonial hold on the northern continent in 1780, and in 1804 Graf Alexander Humboldt visited and suggested five candidates: the isthmuses of Tehuantepec, Nicaragua, and Panama, and two routes starting from the Gulf of Darien in Colombia. Nineteen possible variants were proposed in all.[32]

After the last Mesoamerican colony seceded from Spain in 1823, Antonio de la Cerda proposed a canal to the new legislative chamber of Nicaragua, and the Mexican government began to support the Tehuantepec route. The short-lived Federal Republic of the United Provinces of Central America adopted Cerda's idea in 1825 and called a conference. A contract with an American contractor failed for lack of financial backing, and in 1828 King Willem I of Holland decided to devote part of his private fortune to the project. The revolt of what was to become Belgium in 1830 put an end to that plan.

144.

Five of nineteen Central American canal projects were seriously considered. The northernmost lay across the Tehuantepec Isthmus in Mexico. The southernmost was the St. Blas route, one of two that started at the Gulf of Darien. It needed a long tunnel under the continental divide and was expensive. The Panama route originally had a tunnel too, but later variants planned a sea level cutting or an open, locked waterway. Two variants through Nicaragua appeared to be the simplest to build. The northern one passed through Lake Managua and was a little longer, but it avoided crossing the mountains. The southern version cut through the mountain range to San Juan del Sur on the Pacific coast. (Figuier, *Nouvelles Conquêtes de la Science*, 1883–1885, vol. 4, pp. 351, 371.)

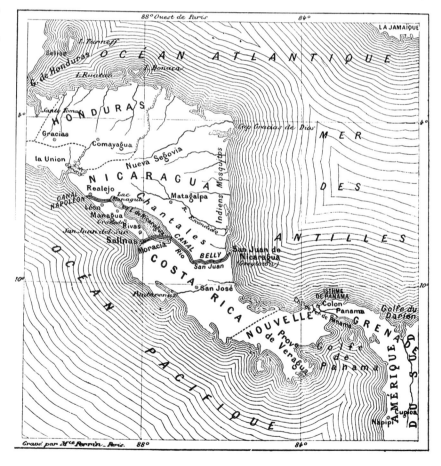

Meanwhile, Colombian President Simón Bolívar commissioned an initial survey of the Isthmus of Panama in 1826.[33] The successor Republic of New Granada granted a concession in 1838 to a French company, which sent Félix-Napoléon Garella to survey the site. Garella designed a 48 to 60-kilometer cutting through marshland with a 5-kilometer tunnel through Culebra Mountain, 44 meters above sea level. He planned eighteen locks on the Caribbean side and sixteen on the other, watered by the Chagres River.[34] The project would cost $25 million, and three million more if an open cutting were to replace the tunnel and the summit were raised another 46 meters. Like the earlier Nicaraguan proposal, Garella's idea failed for lack of support. But technologically it seemed no more utopian than the contemporary Saharan lake or Mont Cenis projects.

When Britain and the United States settled their northwest boundary dispute and the latter gained its first piece of Pacific coastline in Oregon in 1846, the American government began to show interest in a water link between the Atlantic and Pacific coasts. Above all, it was imperative to prevent the British, who still had designs on Nicaragua, from controlling it. Then the Mexican War added California to the union and gold was discovered. New Granada was persuaded to grant free passage to American citizens and goods via the Isthmus, and the newly formed, American-owned Panama Railroad Company acquired the lapsed French railroad concession in 1849.[35]

This company negotiated what would prove to be a clever clause that no other interoceanic communication could be built in the area without its consent, and it hired George M. Totten and John C. Trautwine, Sr., to build the railway.[36] They began in 1850, and the 77-kilometer line was already carrying gold rush emigrants part of the way across the isthmus the following year while its 170 bridges and culverts were still under construction.[37] The railway followed the approximate route of the later canal. It began at Colón on the Caribbean, crossed the low Mindi marshes for about thirteen kilometers to the Chagres River at Gatun, and climbed the river valley for thirty-two kilometers to Matachin where it crossed to the Obispo Valley. Another ten kilometers brought it to summit grade 78.6 meters above sea level at Culebra. From there it descended the Rio Grande Valley to Pedro Miguel and ran the last ten kilometers through marshes to Panamá on the Pacific. In spite of the exorbitant tariffs that the company charged, ostensibly to prevent traffic from swamping the line in the early years, it was as successful as the Mont Cenis Railway was to be in the following decade. The line carried virtually all transcontinental traffic until the Union Pacific Railway opened in 1869, and it earned more than five times its investment between 1855 and the end of the century.[38]

The Result in Small and Large

While American private interests were securing the railway in Panama, the government was pursuing Nicaragua. The two governments negotiated a canal treaty in 1849 and an American contractor made several test borings along the proposed line. When Congress refused to ratify the treaty in Washington, the United States and Britain signed the Clayton-Bulwer Treaty in 1850 under which both countries renounced all colonial and military influence in the region.[39]

The French became involved when Prince Louis-Napoléon became president in 1848. He published a brochure proposing to create an isthmian empire similar to Turkey on the Bosphorus. Napoleon preferred the Nicaraguan route and had engineers analyze it in detail. While Napoleon, who became emperor in 1852, was building his international power base, engineer Félix Belly negotiated a contract in 1858 between Costa Rica, Nicaragua, and himself, using the emperor's idea as modified by Aimé Thomé de Gamond for Panama as a point of departure. Belly proposed three variants, the most realistic of which had seven locks. Excavation was poised to start on the Suez Canal in 1859 when the Société des Ingénieurs Civils began examining the merits of Belly's proposals.[40]

The French Project

French influence culminated in the short-lived Mexican Empire (1862–1865), established while American external interest was at an ebb during the Civil War. French imperial aspirations dissipated when the Habsburg emperor Maximilian was executed and America refocused its interest on the region, but its commercial interests survived. Six years after the Suez Canal opened, the Société Civile Internationale du Canal Interocéanique grew out of a geographical congress in Paris with General Étienne Türr as president. Türr's brother-in-law, Lucien Napoléon Bonaparte Wyse, surveyed eleven possible routes and submitted a report.[41] Wyse returned to Colombia and negotiated a concession in 1878. The Société des Ingénieurs Civils joined the discussion in 1879 following another geographical congress in Antwerp, and Türr approached Ferdinand de Lesseps to take titular charge of the project and give it credibility. It was ten years after his triumph at Suez, and Lesseps was the internationally acknowledged expert in oceanic canals. He used his fame to foist his uninformed technical preconceptions on the enterprise and set his hubris and ill-advised opinions against the better judgment of thoughtful engineers like Eiffel.[42] He also let himself be manipulated financially and eventually led the enterprise into bankruptcy.

The Société debated three variants. The first was the 280-kilometer Tehuantepec route in Mexico with 120 locks climbing a 213-meter divide. The second route was the Nicaraguan, which was about half as long. It used the partly navigable San Juan River and the Nicaragua and Managua lakes at thirty-three meters height to feed the remaining twenty-five to thirty kilometers of cutting. A third possibility was a sea level or tunneled canal of about eighty-five kilometers at Panama, where the watershed lay 176 meters high. This variant needed an artificial lake fed by the Chagres at about the same height as the Nicaraguan, and was the most expensive.[43] The Société did not consider any of the other routes previously discussed by Humboldt or cataloged by Wyse. It was clear to the Société that the American canal would never become as profitable as the Egyptian, and that some form of governmental support would be essential. Lesseps consulted with the contractor Hildevert Hersent, whom he trusted implicitly, and asked Abel Couvreux fils, son of Hersent's partner who had worked at Suez, to examine the proposals.[44]

In spite of the difficult terrain of the Cordillera range, Lesseps preferred the sea level canal proposed by Wyse and Armand Reclus, who had joined Wyse on his second voyage. Their proposal featured a tunnel through the continental divide at Culebra and a slope toward the Pacific to account for the difference in tidal level. It was evident to engineers that very little could be extrapolated from the Egyptian experience. The only similarity between the two sites was the fact that both were narrow isthmuses. The low-lying, stable sand and rock desert in Suez and the seismically unstable and heterogeneous jungle terrain in Panama were very different. Suez had too little water and Panama too much. Everything from geology to human survival had to be reconsidered. Lesseps failed to understand what these differences would mean to the design and the organization of the work.

Lesseps convened a Congrès Internationale d'Etudes du Canal Interocéanique as soon as Wyse returned with the Colombian concession. He collected 135 lawyers, bankers, promoters, and scientists and 42 engineers to study the issue. Wyse had estimated construction time at twelve years and the cost at $240 million, twice as expensive as a locked canal along the same route and thirty percent more than one through Nicaragua.[45] Lesseps appointed a six-member blue-ribbon technical subcommittee, consisting of Inspecteur-Général des Ponts et Chaussées Lefébvre de Fourcy; Voisin-Bey, whom Lesseps had known in Egypt; the elder Abel Couvreux, a veteran of the Suez Canal; Chief-Engineer of the Water-Staat of the Hague Jan F. W. Conrad, who was a member of the Suez Canal commission; for a brief time Louis Favre, who was building the Gotthard Tunnel and who died in July

145.
Ferdinand de Lesseps finally chose a sea level project for Panama. Construction began in 1881. (Figuier, *Nouvelles Conquêtes de la Science,* 1883–1885, vol. 4, p. 389.)

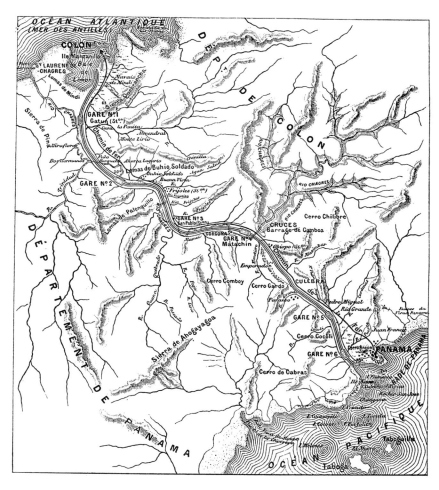

1879; and an engineer named Huyssen.[46] The subcommittee considered several Panama variants, among them one by Ingénieur-en-Chef des Ponts et Chaussées Adolphe Godin de Lépinay that was very similar to what would eventually be built. The members thought that Wyse had estimated the price too low and the construction time too short. Lesseps disagreed and considered the price too high. He estimated that the canal could be built in only eight years for $131.6 million.[47] The plenary session of the Congrès was well-larded with Lesseps's supporters, and it opted for the Wyse-Reclus version he preferred. Many delegates abstained or chose to absent themselves from the vote rather than oppose Lesseps.[48] Eiffel was one of the engineering delegates who contended from the outset that the apparent freedom a sea level canal would permit was illusory because the waterway would be too narrow to allow movement in both directions at once.[49]

Lesseps visited the site in early 1880, and the Compagnie Universelle du Canal Interocéanique de Panama was chartered in 1881. Lesseps became its president and his son Charles its vice-president. A public appeal for funds found no echo, and Lesseps approached bankers to organize the fund-raising. As Suez Canal shares had risen so rapidly, from 290 francs in 1869 to 1,250 in 1880, the banks immediately exceeded the original funding goal of $60 million and raised $262 million.[50] The company bought out the Türr group by purchasing the Wyse concession for $2 million. Wyse himself was retained long enough to negotiate the purchase of the Panama Railroad Company for another $18 million.[51] The railway owned all the rights in the area and was needed to validate the Wyse concession.

The company sent Reclus to Panama to finalize the project in January 1881.[52] He found soft ground on the Caribbean side and a negotiable summit seventy-five meters high. The most difficult section would be about fifteen kilometers long and forty meters deep, about the same total volume as the contemporary Corinth Canal excavation.[53] But whereas engineers at Corinth had to cut through a fissured but stable limestone, the only hard rock in the Panama site lay near Obispo Falls. Worse conditions were expected at Culebra in the upper Obispo Valley. Hersent recognized that the slopes were unstable and warned that the terrain would have to be examined carefully.[54] The engineers hoped that Lesseps would agree to a locked canal like the one that Adolphe Godin de Lépinay had suggested, with less than half the cutting.[55] They assured Lesseps that at least one lock would have to be built on the Pacific at Panamá, where the funnel-shaped bay raises a tidal bore over six meters high.[56]

Couvreux and Hersent agreed to serve as general contractors with Reclus as their agent. Like Marc Brunel, Lesseps didn't listen to experts.

Reclus resigned in 1882 and was followed in quick succession by two others named Louis Verbrugghe and Commodore Richier, after which the site engineer took over.[57] In Suez, Lesseps had enjoyed better relations with his contractors than with the engineers. Although both categories included academically trained engineers, Lesseps trusted only those who worked as contractors, like Lavalley, Hersent, and Couvreux. Perhaps his bias was based on the trouble men like Negrelli and Robert Stephenson had caused when they encroached on what he felt to be his diplomatic turf. Perhaps his reason was an aristocratic disdain for officious bureaucrats in the guildlike Corps des Ponts et Chaussées who refused to allow their members to work as contractors. Whatever the reason, Lesseps limited himself in his choice of consultants at Panama, and the project suffered in consequence. He chose a San Franciscan subcontractor for the Gatun-Colón lot of about six million cubic meters and a New York firm for the Panama side.[58] They moved twenty-five to thirty thousand cubic meters of earth the first year, mostly by machine on the Caribbean side, and denuded and prepared half the Chagres Valley.[59]

The company's first site engineer, Gaston Blanchet, died of yellow fever in 1883 and was replaced by Ingénieur-en-Chef des Ponts et Chaussées Jules Isidor Dingler. Dingler was a capable organizer who immediately got rid of Richier, the company's third agent in as many years. This simplified the chain of command and made his job easier because it weakened the coordination between the site and the contractor's head office in Paris.[60] Dingler stayed two years and developed the site plant. He left when he lost his whole family to yellow fever. His assistant Maurice Hutin took over but fell ill and left after a few weeks. Responsibility for the site passed temporarily to a young engineer named Philippe Bunau-Varilla until Léon Boyer, who had just worked with Eiffel as the government's representative on the Garabit Bridge, was sent out in 1886. Boyer succumbed to yellow fever the same year.[61] The heavy turnover of chief engineers and the lack of coordination between the many contractors and with the head office contributed to the failure of the company.[62]

Most machines and other materiel came from Belgium and France, and the company ordered some from Scotland, England, and the United States. Most designs were initially derived from the machinery used at Suez fifteen years before. About half of the forty-two kilometers of track, several hundred wagons, forty locomotives, six steam shovels, four small and one large ladder dredge, fifteen boats, and assorted cranes arrived at Colón in 1881, but few of them were assembled and put to use quickly.[63] Indiscriminate ordering and lack of coordination rapidly inflated the plant.[64] By autumn 1885 there were 150 locomotives of various types, 800 wagons, 4,400

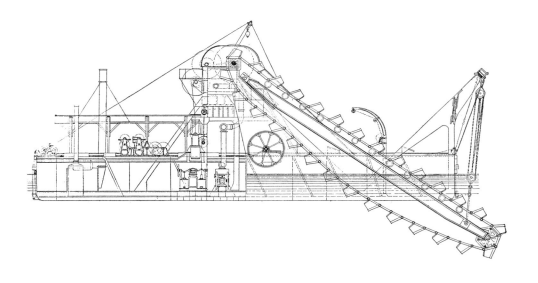

The Result in Small and Large

146.
The French bought their machinery from many countries. The large dredge had a spoil trough modeled on the one used at Suez. The ladder dredges came from Belgium, probably from Cochaux, who had provided similar machines to Suez fifteen years before. One of the contractors used American machinery like this Osgood steam shovel at Culebra. (Wyse, 1886, pp. 181, 185, 195, 313; Comber in *Transactions*, 1916, vol. 1, plate 2.)

large and 6,000 small dump cars, 600 kilometers of standard gauge rails, un-counted lengths of other track, 80 ladder excavators, 60 bucket steam shov-els, 800 cranes and sundry winches and other lifting gear, 20 seagoing dredges, 8 small and 4 large American dredges, 14 other dredges, 50 steam-boats, 15 steam barges, 100 scows, 200 tractors, 500 pumps, and uncounted prefabricated wooden houses and workshops.[65] A few French and Belgian lad-der dredges, the cantilevered, floating, Suez-type conveyors, and the French barges were later salvaged and reconditioned by the Americans and proved to be as economical and reliable as newer plant.[66] At least one piece of salvaged equipment, a forty-tonne floating crane, had been built by Lavalley.[67]

Each subcontractor worked differently, and there was little coordina-tion on site. Ferdinand and Charles de Lesseps visited the works in 1886. It was clear by then that the original estimated spoil volume, seventy to eighty million cubic meters, was far too low. They dismissed the general contractor and all subcontractors and redivided the work among large contracting firms. Twenty-six-year-old Philippe Bunau-Varilla, who had inherited the site engi-neer's job *ad interim* for the simple reason that he had not succumbed to yel-low fever, convinced Charles de Lesseps that the company itself should take the Culebra section in hand.[68] Charles de Lesseps asked Bunau-Varilla to form a contracting company, which he did with his brother Maurice, hiring two canal engineers who, curiously, gave their names to the firm: Artigue, Sonderegger et Compagnie.[69] Philippe Bunau-Varilla officially resigned from the Panama Canal Company and was granted a special leave of absence from the Corps des Ponts et Chaussées to serve as contractor. The transfer contract stipulated an indemnity to the original contractor for each cubic meter exca-vated, ostensibly in order to avoid a lengthy severance suit according to Co-lombian law. There were many strange deals of this type. This one resulted in an accusation of mismanagement and graft when the French project finally collapsed.[70]

Many factors contributed to the bankruptcy of the first canal proj-ect. A revolt broke out on the isthmus and American troops intervened in 1885. The company spent vast sums on public relations, secondary projects, and unnecessary site work.[71] When the money ran out, Lesseps suggested a $160 million bond lottery like the one he had organized for Suez. French officials visited the site in 1885 and 1886 and recommended that the govern-ment authorize the lottery on condition that the engineers redesign the proj-ect as a locked canal.[72] Lesseps grudgingly acquiesced while still insisting on a later, permanent sea level solution. The experienced Dingler had left and the young Bunau-Varilla convinced Lesseps to accept the condition by proposing an inexpensive method to dynamite rock underwater. This, he explained,

147.
This tree grew around an abandoned French dump truck between 1884 and 1914. The exuberant tropical growth helped prevent erosion in the cut areas. (*Panama and the Canal Zone*, 1914.)

would make it easy to dredge a locked canal to sea level.[73] Bunau-Varilla was a clever negotiator who knew how to gloss over inconvenient facts. His company had struggled to dig a twenty-meter-deep cutting in the unstable Culebra Saddle. He knew that he would have had to excavate a total of 110 meters and remove an unprecedented amount of material to reach sea level.[74] The canal would also have had to close while mining and dredging were going on. But he also knew that Lesseps would always hear what he wanted to hear.

What had started as a $114 million, 9-meter-wide, open waterway at sea level had now become a $351 million, 4.5-meter-wide, locked canal. Bunau-Varilla organized another contracting firm to excavate the lock chambers, and Eiffel's Ateliers Levallois Perret was brought in to provide the gates and other hardware.[75] Eiffel was building the tower, finishing the dome of the Nice observatory, and prefabricating mobile bridges for Indochina at the time, yet he managed to manufacture ninety percent of his contract and deliver sixty percent of that to the site before the project collapsed at the end of 1888.

By then it was clear that the company's public relations division had exaggerated every step of the work, sometimes even resorting to blatant falsehood. The lottery was mismanaged by the banks. Bankers, the minister of public works, and Charles de Lesseps and his father were implicated in accusations of graft and extortion, and Ferdinand de Lesseps himself became known as the "Great Undertaker."[76] The company went into bankruptcy in

1889, the year of the Exposition Universelle de Paris where the Eiffel Tower and the Galerie des Machines were proudly presented as symbols of French industry and engineering prowess. Suppliers and contractors like Eiffel were accused of trying to milk illicit profits from a project they knew to be doomed in advance, thereby cheating the shareholders. It took years to identify and punish some of the real culprits, and many innocent participants were ruined in the interim. No one proved graft against the directors Cottu, Fontane, and the two de Lesseps, or against Eiffel, whose name was cleared and who finally retained his officer's cross of the Légion d'Honneur.[77]

The funds had been grossly mismanaged. About one hundred million dollars had been used at Panama, eighty million for salaries and office expenses, thirty-two million to float the loans, and seventy-five million for general expenses in Paris, while thirty-one million had gone for bribes to the minister of public works, the banker, the man who proposed the lottery, politicians, and journalists and for unspecified "publicity" and "banking expenses."[78] In Panama, machinery and materials were ordered without coordination. The problem lay not so much on site—where French engineers carried out their work well, as Bunau-Varilla took great pains to prove—but in the supervision of contractors and suppliers in Paris.[79] The company had no auditing system, and many took the opportunity to enrich themselves. In spite of everything, the company had excavated fifty-four million cubic meters in seven and a half years, which was a respectable tally. The revised plan of 1887 projected another eighteen million cubic meters, which was estimated to take a further two and a half years. The French project finally failed for three reasons: lack of a coordinated fight against disease, financial mismanagement and corruption, and Lesseps's high-handed inflexibility.

Lesseps's financial and diplomatic gifts had declined as he aged, while his engineering hubris had increased proportionately. At the beginning of the project he had been invited to speak at many prominent gatherings and had even addressed the École Polytechnique.[80] But he soon became less popular, and from the end of 1882 to the collapse of 1889 the transactions of the Société des Ingénieurs Civils make no mention of the canal project at all. This contrasts with their intense preoccupation with both the Suez Canal and the Mont Cenis Tunnel twenty years before. Lesseps may have alienated them by not seeking their advice. But it is characteristic of professional skepticism about the project that the one professional society that should have been the most interested in the project removed itself entirely from the discussion.

A new group tried to renew the company's charter in 1893, and Wyse returned to negotiate a ten-year extension of the concession.[81] The new company's technical committee suggested in 1899 that a lack of preliminary studies had been the chief reason for its predecessor's failure.[82] There was a grain of truth in this, although the committee itself admitted that the engineers had done a great deal of preparatory work and that they were competent professionals who had promptly reported problems and proposed strategies.[83]

The technical committee retained Hersent as the only survivor of the first company. It sat from 1896 to 1898 and modified the planning committee's plan, cautiously pointing out that the estimated construction time of eight years was overly optimistic.[84] The new plan created two lakes in the Chagres Valley with dams at Bohio and Alhajuela. There were to be locks at Miraflores, Pedro Miguel, and Paraíso on the Pacific side and at Bohio and Obispo on the Caribbean. Summit level lay 5.25 meters lower than the later American version.[85] But the technical committee still underestimated Culebra. A small work force remained on site in those years, but the only ongoing work was some digging at Culebra and a little dredging in Panama Bay. Finally, late in 1898, the company offered to sell the concession to the United States.[86] Of the total of nineteen canal and seven railway proposals that had been made over the years, only the Panama Railway had been built, and the Panamá-Colón and Nicaragua canals had only been started.[87]

The American Government Takes Control

The 1880s and early 1890s saw a rash of canal proposals and construction worldwide, albeit none so large as the Panama Canal. James Eads, who had finished the Mississippi Bridge at St. Louis seven years before, designed a portage railway for Tehuantepec in 1881.[88] The Cronstadt-St. Petersburg Canal, the Manchester Ship Canal from Manchester to Liverpool, the Kaiser-Wilhelm Kanal or Kiel Canal linking the Baltic to the North Sea south of Denmark, the Corinth Canal, and the Chicago River Drainage Canal were built in those years.[89] The Saulte Ste. Marie and Suez canals were enlarged, the Amsterdam Canal was widened for the second time, and a second expansion was planned for the Erie Canal.

Speculation on the imminent failure of the French project raised a flurry of American interest in 1886. Professional and political opinion in the United States had always favored Nicaragua. When the first French company succumbed, an American firm called the Maritime Canal Company of Nicaragua began work, but after three years the company folded when Congress deadlocked on how to build the waterway in 1895.[90] The 127-kilometer San Juan River had to be deepened or paralleled by a canal. The thirty-seven-

148.
James Eads, builder of the
Mississippi Bridge at St.
Louis, proposed a ship portage system at Tehuantepec
in Mexico. He wanted to
haul oceangoing vessels on
gigantic flatbeds over
twelve sets of parallel tracks
across the 250-kilometer-
wide isthmus. (Figuier,
*Nouvelles Conquêtes de la Sci-
ence*, 1883–1885, vol. 4, p.
342.)

meter difference between low tide on the Caribbean and the lakes required fourteen locks, whether Congress chose the 306 kilometer route with a twenty-five kilometer cut through the watershed between Lake Nicaragua and the Pacific at San Juan del Sur or the route through Lake Managua, which was 160 kilometers longer.[91]

Even though this project was no longer an obstacle by 1898, French sympathy for America's opponents during the Spanish-American War did nothing to help the company sell its assets in America. Still, the three months the USS *Oregon* took to reach Cuba from California via Cape Horn highlighted the missing link in American naval security, and Congress created the Isthmian Canal Commission to supersede the deadlocked Nicaragua Canal Commission.[92] The new body voted for Nicaragua but recognized that the Panama route was both shorter and better researched. Meanwhile, Bunau-Varilla lobbied intensely for Panama throughout the United States in early 1901, converting commission member George S. Morison to his cause and meeting with President William McKinley.

Two months after McKinley's assassination and the transition to the Roosevelt administration, the commission again recommended Nicaragua in November 1901, with Morison's as the sole dissenting voice.[93] The commission did admit that it only supported Nicaragua because the price the French company quoted for its property and rights was so high. This forced the French company to abandon its asking price of $109 million and accept the American offer of $40 million, whereupon the commission reconvened and reversed its recommendation. The French had spent $300 million, about ten percent of which was for excavation and installations useful to the American project, so the price was realistic.

American pragmatism preferred Nicaragua and the French conceptual penchant Panama.[94] American politics kept both doors open. A Nicaragua bill still couldn't pass Congress, so the rival Spooner Act authorized the president to buy out the French company and acquire a canal zone from the government of Colombia, or, failing that, to get one from the governments of Costa Rica and Nicaragua and construct the other variant.

Mont Pelée erupted on Martinique in 1903 and made the American public aware that something similar could happen in Nicaragua. Bunau-Varilla cleverly used this fear and seismic activity in Nicaragua to help shift American sentiment in favor of Panama.[95] Colombia and the United States quickly negotiated the Hay-Herran Treaty, but the Colombian government used a revolt in Bogotá as an excuse to delay ratification. The renewed French concession was scheduled to lapse in three years and Colombia would then be able to sell the concession directly to the United States without having to reimburse the French company. The French, who stood to lose everything, were not averse to supporting insurrection in Panama. The agents of support were Bunau-Varilla, who allegedly owned stock in the new company, and William Nelson Cromwell, who was general counsel for the New Panama Canal Company.[96] Manuel Amador, former physician to the Panama Railroad Company, organized the insurrection. He was in New York ostensibly to visit a sick son.

The northernmost Colombian province resented centralized rule from the capital and had been semiautonomous from the 1840s to the 1880s. The inhabitants saw an opportunity in the growing American interest in their region and staged a first insurrection that failed because the American government withheld its support. President Roosevelt forbade the use of the railway by any faction and enforced his order by sending marines to Panamá and Colón. Bunau-Varilla, by then spokesman for the Panamanian malcontents, met with Roosevelt in October 1903 before organizing a second attempt.[97] He boldly guaranteed the financing and, according to him, engineered American support.[98] The rebels agreed to cede the canal zone and grant the canal concession and certain military rights, too. In return, the United States guaranteed to protect the new nation and pay it a lump sum and a percentage of the revenue from the canal. All interested parties—Colombia, the United States, Panama, the French company, Bunau-Varilla, and the revolutionaries—acted with deviousness and duplicity.

Seven of the forty million dollars the American government paid the French company were for the Colón-Panamá railroad and its Colón-New York steamship subsidiary. The railway's antiquated hardware was hardly worth thirty-nine percent of the price the French had paid two decades before, but the concession certainly was.[99] The railroad was scheduled to revert to Colombia in 1967, so the commission decided to separate it from the canal. This also ensured that the railroad and its steamships and hotels could operate as a commercial enterprise without running its finances through the treasury and government appropriations.[100] The government paid for using the railroad during construction by rebuilding the entire line between 1909 and 1912.[101]

The commission adopted the revised French project, but Congress reopened the debate when the government took control in early May 1904. The president appointed an international panel that included Inspecteur-Général des Ponts et Chaussées Adolphe Guérard, Consulting Engineer E. Quellenac of the Suez Canal, Chief Engineer Eugen Tincauzer of the Kiel Canal, Chief Engineer William H. Hunter of the Manchester Canal, Chief Engineer J. W. Welcker of the Dutch dike system, and Isham Randolph, builder of the Chicago Drainage Canal, to study the question of a sea level or locked canal again.[102] The majority argued that locks were vulnerable and voted for the sea level variant in February 1906. Some of the American engineers and the newly appointed chief engineer, John Frank Stevens, disagreed, and proposed locks watered by a single large lake dammed at Gatun, which corresponds to the version eventually built, without the small Miraflores Lake on the Pacific side.[103] They bolstered their opinion with the same arguments Godin de Lépinay had given the Paris congress in 1879: quicker passage and a larger volume of traffic than through a narrow sea level canal, greater safety through a wider and deeper channel that could not be as easily blocked by a sunken ship, and cheap, quick construction. The majority balked at the idea of building a single reservoir, and discussed possible foundation instability, construction methods, and the danger that the strong current might damage the locks.[104]

The panel thought that the most complex engineering problem was controlling the Chagres. They knew that the Culebra Cut required much flatter slopes than the rest of the canal, but they still judged it to be stable.[105] As it turned out, the 84 million cubic meters they estimated for a sea level cutting was about the amount removed from the Culebra Cut alone, where the bottom now lies twenty-six meters above sea level. Not only did the Culebra Cut push costs up, but the commission had to offer fifty percent higher salaries and benefits than in the United States in order to attract qualified workmen. Other factors increasing costs were the reduction of the ten-hour workday to eight and an economic boom in the United States that raised material prices.[106]

President Roosevelt disregarded the commission's decision in favor of the minority plan. Congress concurred with the president, tacitly acknowledging that the canal was part of America's defense system.[107] Although Congress was no longer directly involved, public discussion of the design details continued and forced the government to respond.[108] Public pressure is part of government planning procedures in British and American culture; the press can manipulate opinion and exert real influence on the development of a project. The detail design of the Panama Canal was influenced by public debate in much the same way that the London Crystal Palace had been sixty years before.[109]

The first chief engineer, John F. Wallace, inherited an abandoned site with little in the way of immediately useful plant, housing, or transportation. As a first step he demanded and got the reorganization of the Canal Commission and had the railway placed under its jurisdiction.[110] Disillusioned by bureaucratic red tape, he resigned in 1905 before work could really get under way. His successor, Stevens, arrived in July and immediately set about organizing the services and the all-important transportation system. The lengthy planning phase frustrated the uninformed public and therefore infuriated Congress, which wanted "to see dirt fly."[111] But the sheer volume of people and material to be organized and moved was daunting and required careful planning if Stevens wanted to avoid the chaos that had characterized the French attempt. The Panama Railroad Company had to buy all of the project's subsistence supplies and the Isthmian Canal Commission purchased unprecedented quantities of construction materials and machinery with appropriated funds under ponderous government procurement rules in Washington.[112] A joint resolution of Congress in 1906 made things even more cumbersome for Stevens by stipulating that all material should be of American manufacture.[113] Three years later President Roosevelt alleviated the problem with an executive order that allowed the purchase of some foreign material.[114] By that time Stevens had resigned; the government system and the frictions and overlapping responsibilities of the chief engineer, commission chairman, and civilian governor had frustrated him, too. However, during his brief tenure he had applied the results of Taylor's early studies to good effect and was able to lower his costs. When he left early in 1907, a reorganized railroad, housing, a commissary system, and a health organization were firmly in place.

Roosevelt next appointed George Washington Goethals, a military engineer with extensive experience in canal, lock, and railway construction, and explicitly charged him to place the project under the auspices of the army.[115] He wanted continuity and a chief engineer who could not resign without his permission.[116] This decision changed everything. The French had never considered Suez or Panama to be essential to their national defense, but the Americans did. Goethals knew that the engineering was not going to be the main problem at Panama.[117] He took an extreme step and put the site under martial law, which enabled him to plan and make decisions autocratically.[118] At the same time he simplified the chain of command by insisting that the chief engineer's and commission chair's positions be united in his office and that the governor be placed under him. Like Dingler twenty years before, Goethals could now make decisions by executive order without the lengthy negotiation and ratification procedure that had hampered his immediate predecessors. These two steps cleared his organizational path of its chief obstacles. As a military officer, Goethals knew the parameters of control and how to manipulate them to his advantage. His two civilian predecessors had been unprepared for the type of organism they commanded. Their civilian education lacked the historical case study approach of military training in strategy. They were used to having free rein over a project once their plans had been approved by a board of directors.

The Result in Small and Large

In military fashion, Goethals laid out strategy himself and kept the tactics of day-to-day decision making under tight control. His staff had to make continual tactical adjustments and balance their desire for cost effectiveness with the political imperative to show quick, visible progress. The key to Goethals's success was his West Point education. Military training traditionally follows Clausewitz's maxim, focusing on *how* to accomplish an objective and leaving the objective itself to be decided by politicians and designed by planners. Process development is a military skill. It concentrates on strategy, logistics, supply, and tactics, which are also the hallmarks of procedural thinking.[119] Analysis and feedback are standard procedures in military education and practice, and Goethals put them to good use at Panama.

The American project succeeded not because American engineering was superior to French but because the Americans prepared better, especially when Goethals organized the site on military lines. America had no monopoly on engineering or organizational ability: Eiffel had developed a sophisticated, systematic organization of design, manufacture, delivery, and erection, and Godin de Lépinay had first proposed the actual canal design. The Americans had the French experience to build on, and this led them to take a broader range of issues into account.

As soon as he took over the project, Goethals revised the projected earth-moving to 103 million cubic meters. Later this amount was more than doubled by the 91 hectares of slides that flowed into the Culebra Cut, by the additional Miraflores Lake between the Pedro Miguel and Miraflores locks, and by silting in the Chagres River and in the oceans at either end of the canal. The military tradition of applying analytical studies like Taylor's and Gilbreth's to practical problems explains how Goethals could steadily increase output and undercut his own projected deadline even though the volume of earth-moving increased so dramatically. In the project's final years, he moved as much material every fifteen months as Lavalley had excavated on the whole fifteen-year Suez Canal project.[120]

The sheer scale of the Panama Canal made non-construction issues of primary concern to the project. Health issues, for instance, had been negligible in Langwies, more important in the building of the Kehl-Strasbourg Bridge, and still more in Suez, but in Panama they became central to the success of the project. Solving the health problem was one of the most visible successes of the military organization. The region had long been known as the "pest hole of the world." The French had not eradicated the problem. Reclus and his successors had built two excellent hospitals, but they were inexpertly run. Water was a problem. Patients were charged more than a laborer earned a day, so very few applied for admission. No one knew the contagious media of malaria and yellow fever: hospital beds were placed with their legs in water to keep out ants; mosquitoes bred in the wards and transmitted disease from patient to patient.[121] The annual work force averaged about 13,000, and there were 16,500 to 22,000 deaths between 1881 and 1889. This meant that between sixteen and thirty percent of the work force had died in Panama![122]

One of the Commission's first actions in 1904 was to appoint William C. Gorgas of the army's medical corps to deal with the health problem. Gorgas had an international reputation for eradicating yellow fever from Cuba, where it had been endemic ever since the Spanish invaded in 1511. Malaria debilitated more than it killed, but yellow fever was a mortal disease. It attacked each new batch of immigrants in Panama and completely demoralized the work force. Gorgas knew that the primary system of yellow fever transmission occurred through certain types of mosquitoes discovered in 1881 by Carlos Finlay in Cuba, and that malaria was transmitted by another type discovered by Sir Ronald Ross in 1898 in India. Transmission, he realized, was the factor to be fought, not dirt, despite nineteenth-century health theory that stressed "general sanitation." He organized his preventive campaign accordingly and concentrated on eliminating potential breeding grounds. Gorgas divided his medical corps into three groups: quarantine, hospital, and sanitary, with health inspectors and an entomologist for each district.[123] He built new hospitals and a specially outfitted hospital car that crossed the isthmus at least once a day. In military fashion, he defined the goal and organized the process by which he would reach it.

Only the female *Aëdes aegypti* carries the type of yellow fever Gorgas fought.[124] The mosquito lives and breeds close to human habitation in stagnant water. In 1904 and early 1905, the arrival of a new labor force brought a dramatic increase in the number of yellow fever cases. Workmen panicked and fled. Gorgas fumigated infected houses and their surroundings and quarantined all suspected cases. Gorgas drafted municipal engineers into helping eradicate the carriers' breeding grounds. They built a piped water supply and a mixed sewer system to replace open cisterns and cesspools and screened all open water supplies and houses. They paved streets to eliminate standing puddles and channeled all surface runoff, even outside the settlements. As a result, the last case of yellow fever disappeared in December 1905.[125]

Gorgas found malaria more difficult to control, since all formerly infected persons remain reservoirs of the disease and can infect anopheles mosquitoes that ingest their blood. This mosquito breeds in marshes and along the banks of running streams in the countryside. It prefers to fly against the wind, so Gorgas's crew drained only those marshes and ponds that lay downwind from the settlements and cleared grass and brush in a 500-meter zone around rural and suburban areas. They also filled ponds, marshes, and puddles with spoil from the canal cutting, cleared river banks and stagnant pools by burning or construction, flooded low-lying areas with sea water, and introduced larvae-eating fish.[126] They sprayed up to a quarter of a million liters of oil monthly to destroy larvae on grass and in swamps, and mounted automatically dripping oil drums that were regularly checked and replenished at the head of streams.[127] Environmentally polluting measures of this magnitude would be unthinkable today; they had the desired effect, but surely wreaked havoc on the flora and fauna of the Canal Zone. Gorgas also forcibly segregated new immigrants from the indigenous population and gave prophylactic doses of quinine to as many of them as possible, distributing up to 1.5 tons yearly.[128] Gorgas also controlled a pneumonia epidemic among the laborers between 1906 and 1908 by moving the patients from barracks to housing, while he eradicated smallpox by compulsory vaccination.

Goethals budgeted sanitation separately from the special fund for disease control. It cost about $4 million, or one percent of the budget for the total project, and represented half the sum spent on municipal engineering.[129] The sanitary engineering was a feat of organization. Gorgas checked and purified the water supply and protected the catchment area from human contamination to reduce dysentery and typhoid fever. He collected and incinerated garbage and manure to reduce flies and rats and prevent plague. Gorgas's work expanded the focus of military medicine from cure to prevention and influenced the development of public health programs under civilian law in the United States and elsewhere.

It was more difficult to recruit workmen for Panama than it had been for the Suez Canal. The climate was inhospitable, and there was no indigenous pool of cheap or qualified labor. A few French officials and a thousand West Indian laborers remained on site in 1904, about 800 of them in construction.[130] Most of the abandoned 20,000 West Indian laborers had been repatriated by their own governments in 1888 and 1889.[131] Chief engineer Wallace personally recruited workers in the United States, but it took three years to organize an efficient recruitment system. The size of the work force did begin to grow slowly in mid-1904, but appreciable numbers of men only began to apply when wage levels were raised in 1905. Living conditions were so poor that many recruits immediately left again. When Chief Engineer Stevens arrived, he recognized the need for a major investment in infrastructure and preventive medicine. By 1906, his efforts began to show results.

The workers were divided into two main categories, called the "gold" and "silver" forces according to the coin in which they were first paid. Officials, staff, and skilled labor formed the first group and semi- and unskilled labor the second. They were organized like army officers and enlisted men.[132] The number of federal employees, including railroad workers but excluding the contractors' men, grew from about a thousand in May 1904 to a maximum of 39,962 in August 1913.[133] Of these the American group averaged about five thousand and never exceeded 12.5 percent of the total.[134] About forty percent of these had families with them. The total population, including Canal Zone government and public service employees, peaked at about 50,000 at the height of construction.[135] This was arguably the largest group ever assembled for a single construction project. Only the military was equipped to organize and care for such an army.

Most of the "gold" force came from railway construction in North and South America, while the unskilled labor originally came from the West Indies. As part of their legacy from the French, recruiters had difficulty convincing the island governments that good conditions awaited their citizens. Island planters also opposed recruitment and fought to retain their surplus of cheap labor. Most of the men that did finally come were from the severely

150.
Today, the canal is tranquil. The view from the upper Miraflores Locks gives no inkling of the effort that went into its construction. (*Panama and the Canal Zone*, 1914.)

overpopulated island of Barbados. Spaniards were considered better laborers and furnished an increasing percentage of the unskilled workforce as the project advanced.

The Panama Canal is now a tranquil, ninety-one-meter-wide ribbon of water flanked by gentle, grassy verges. Like all finished projects it tells us nothing about the work that went into making it. The Toro Point Breakwater stretches languidly 3.4 kilometers into the Pacific, protecting a seven kilometer waterway leading from Panamá to Miraflores, where a flight of two locks raises the level 16.7 meters to a small lake. Two and a half kilometers farther on, a single lock at Pedro Miguel raises the canal another 9.3 meters, where the Middle Division begins with the 14.5-kilometer Culebra Cut. Culebra leads to Gatun Lake at Gamboa, where both the canal and the Chagres River enter. The fifty-one-kilometer lake ends at Gatun, where the huge dam and a flight of three locks begin the twenty-six-meter descent to the Atlantic Division. Finally, a thirteen kilometer sea level section flows gently into the Caribbean at Colón.

The heart of the project was the twenty-nine-meter-high, 2,500-meter-long Gatun Dam built by William L. Sibert. The dam stores the irregular discharge of the Chagres, receives its silt, and waters the canal. Two earthen gravity dams flank "Spillway Hill" with its masonry overflow channel in the middle of the valley. Subsoil conditions were as varied as everywhere else in the region. Sibert began with extensive tests of loadbearing capacities, stability, and porosity before he finalized the design. His team studied several methods of pumping fill on two twelfth-scale cross-sectional models. As a result, they lowered the height of the crown, established cores of rock at either toe to contain the hydraulic fill, and reduced the slope and the foundation load.[136] They designed their models as thoughtfully as Stephenson had prepared his Britannia model sixty years before.

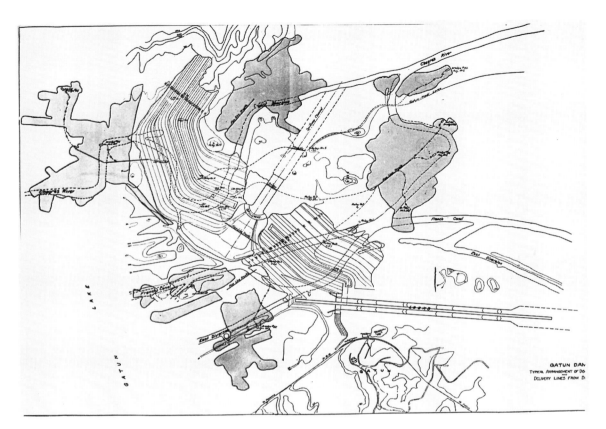

151.
The Gatun Dam lay on the
Caribbean side and col-
lected the waters of the Chagres River. (Sibert in
Transactions, 1916, vol. 1,
plate 11; Hilgard, c. 1915,
p. 36.)

The Result in Small and Large

The process was a complex exercise in logistics. Sibert carried out all preparatory work in the dry season, when the Chagres was low. His engineers dug temporary channels and built shoring, coffering, diversion dams, and spillways to tame the river. Pumping the hydraulic fill was repetitive and simple because it was carefully prepared, calculated, and mechanized. There were very few hitches. One major slide occurred because the ground subsided under the load of the fill; other slides happened while the slurry was unstable and before it had time to dry out.[137]

The four Miraflores Lake dams were small in comparison. At Pedro Miguel, one was a simple earth dam made from dumped spoil from the lock and the other had a concrete core to prevent seepage. At Miraflores, one was made of hydraulic fill, also taken from the locks, while the other was of concrete and contained the spillway.

The line between structure and machine is blurred in canal locks even more than in buildings that contain habitable space, like the Crystal Palace or the Sayn Foundry. Locks are composite structures in a different sense than we use the term today. Reinforced concrete in a modern composite structure takes compression and some of the shear, while the steel resists tension. In the locks, the reinforced concrete resists all the static forces, while the steel members take the dynamic loads. The 305-meter locks can be subdivided to accommodate small ships. They are as deep as a six-story building, and the culverts that empty and fill them are as large as train tunnels. The valve-operating mechanisms and the 300 to 600-ton gate leaves designed by Henry Goldmark were among the largest machinery of their time. The locks themselves were designed by Harry F. Hodges.[138] The hydraulic generating plant at Gatun and the auxiliary plant at Miraflores were built early to provide power for all the construction sites; they were in themselves major projects.

Goethals put Sibert in charge of the Gatun locks, which he excavated in the dry except for the bottom of the flight, which he dredged. Sibert had suction dredges floated in from Colón through eleven kilometers of the sea level segment, which he connected to the site by a narrow, two-kilometer cutting. The dredges could only dig 12.5 meters deep,[139] so Sibert closed the channel behind them and they burrowed their way down into the stagnant pool until they reached the canal bed at 16.7 meters below sea level.[140] Water for maneuvering and operating was pumped into the pit. While this was going on in the lower lock, concreting and steel installation were in full swing at the upper end.

Sibert's men poured just under half of the 1.53 million cubic meters of concrete between June 1910 and June 1911. At the height of construction, each twelve-hour shift averaged 2,300 cubic meters.[141] The culverts and

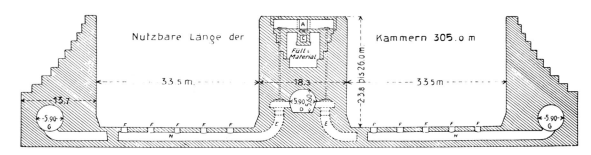

152.
Huge iron gates closed off the locks. The conduits for filling and emptying the chambers were embedded in the thick concrete walls and floor, and the culverts were cast using collapsible steel forms. (Hilgard, c. 1915, p. 41; *Panama and the Canal Zone*, 1914; Bennett, 1915, plate following p. 428.)

other repetitive parts used collapsible steel forms, and the nine solid side walls were cast in reusable braced-steel forms in eleven-meter-square sections. A centering team could dismantle and reerect a wall section in two days, and a complete casting cycle took about a week. While one segment was being cast, the last was freed and the next prepared. Each segment swallowed between 2,700 and 3,400 cubic meters, or just over a twelve-hour day's worth, of concrete.[142] The cold joints between sections became the expansion joints. No one had ever cast such large masses before, and Sibert carefully monitored the process. He discovered that the heat generated in the curing process took a full year to dissipate, but no cooling mechanism was required.

Sibert moved the materials in large clamshell buckets that traveled on double cableways, built by the Lidgerwood Manufacturing Company of New York. Lidgerwood probably modeled them on the system the French had previously used at Culebra. Nothing is known about Lidgerwood, but he appears to have been responsible for several of the most intelligent mechanical systems and methods at Panama. His cableways spanned the lock sites and a second set spanned the mixing plant and the storage area that lay some distance away. He suspended the ropes from twenty-six-meter-high towers that moved on tracks so that the mix could be dumped right where it was needed in the forms.

Barges brought materials to Gatun through the old French cutting and later through the finished Caribbean segment. Sibert used local sand and gravel, while most of the 6.5 million barrels of cement came from the Atlas Cement Company of New York.[143] The French canal lay at a distance from the lock site, which is why it was served by a second set of cableways. Lidgerwood's cableways lifted the materials from the barges to bins at the edge of the site. Electric carts on circular tracks ran under the bins and loaded calibrated amounts of sand, gravel, and cement.[144] From there they ran to batteries of continuous mixers. A second track with double carts ran on the off-loading side of the mixers. Each cart took the contents of two mixers over to the lock cableways, where two full kips were exchanged for two empties. Then the cableways lifted the concrete to the forms, where it was spread and tamped. Workmen cast the lateral approach walls on either end of the lock area traditionally, using more manual labor.

Sidney B. Williamson, a civilian engineer who had worked with Goethals in the 1890s in Tennessee, was put in charge of the Pacific Division.[145] There was no old French canal on the Pacific side, so Goethals's engineers built a railyard for site traffic right next to the lock site with several junctions to the main line. Williamson had to relocate the lower locks at Miraflores relatively late in the planning process, so he built the upper,

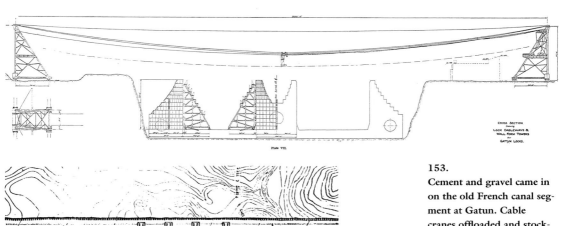

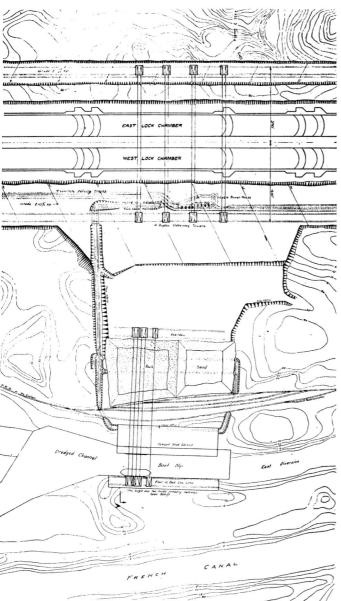

153.
Cement and gravel came in
on the old French canal segment at Gatun. Cable
cranes offloaded and stockpiled it, and railways carried it to the concreting
plant, which lay within
reach of other cable cranes
that spanned the locks.
Lidgerwood's cable cranes,
modeled on earlier French
ones, dumped concrete into
the eleven-meter-high steel
formwork. (Siebert in
Transactions, 1916, vol. 1,
plates 7, 9; Bennett, 1915,
plates following pp. 352,
356.)

154.
The Pedro Miguel site was differently organized. Outrigger "berm cranes" ran along the stockpiles at the end of the site and fed the batching and mixing plants. Small railways carried the concrete from there into the lock chambers, where chamber cranes picked it up and placed it in the formwork. (Williamson in *Transactions*, 1916, vol. 1, plates 6, 7; Bennett, 1915, plate following p. 164.)

single lock pair at Pedro Miguel first. First he set up a quarry and an electrically driven crushing plant at Ancón that was serviced by steam shovels and a rail spur. The plant was ready for use in October 1909, when a slide just below the crusher demolished part of the plant and its approaches.[146] The damage was repaired by early 1910 and the plant eventually supplied material to the locks, the buildings, and the Gatun Locks as well. The reserve power plant at Miraflores provided power to the crushing plant and the construction sites on the Pacific side. Sand came from a beach on the Pacific coast that was worked by a restored French ladder dredge. The foundations were simpler at Pedro Miguel than at Gatun because the subsoil was all rock. Steam shovels did most of the digging between 1909 and 1913, and only the final clean-up and the trenches for the lateral culverts had to be done manually with power drills and a little careful blasting, since concreting had already begun.[147]

Williamson devised a simpler delivery system for the lock construction on the Pacific side of the canal. He had no need for cable cranes because the railway brought everything in on one line directly to the locks and there was no secondary off-loading from barges or transportation from a separate plant and storage site as Sibert had at Gatun. Rail cars ran alongside long sand and gravel stockpiles on either side of the work site, and two "berm cranes" on each side of the lock unloaded the material. The sand and gravel moved along an outrigger from the rail cars to the stockpiles and from there to a batching tower under each crane. The cement had to be protected from the rain, and Williamson timed the shipments so that only half had to be stockpiled in sheds at the end of the site while the rest was delivered on a separate rail spur directly under the batchers.[148] The outriggers were balanced by

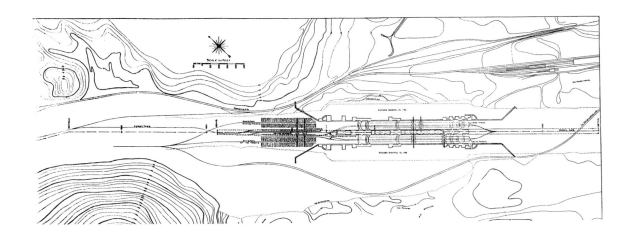

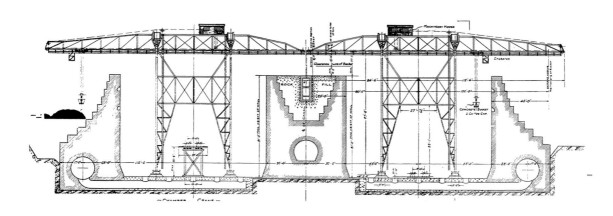

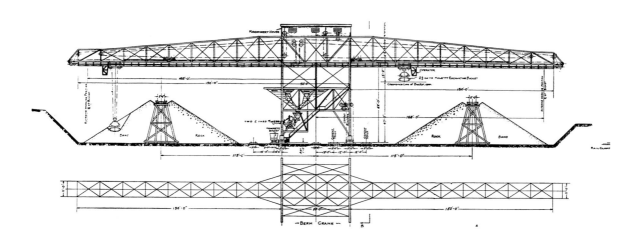

booms on the inside of the cranes. The dry-mix traveled along these booms from the batcher to the mixing plant, which lay within reach of the "chamber cranes." Two chamber cranes ran in each lock, covering one side wall and half the middle. The sides proved too soft for this system at Pedro Miguel, so Williamson rebuilt two berm cranes into symmetrical cantilever cranes running in the canal axis between the approach wing walls. These cranes lifted material from symmetrical stockpiles on either side to central batching and mixing plants in the canal axis. From there, small trains carried the concrete to the laterally displaced, parallel axes of the two sets of chamber cranes. This made the material flow a little more complicated, but it worked. When the cranes were relocated to the double flight at Miraflores, Williamson used the original configuration and carried the concrete directly to the locks without an intermediary.

Taylor and Thompson's book on concrete, with its large sections on plant, and Gilbreth's *Field System* and *Concrete System* had recently appeared. The canal's engineers knew of them, and they were familiar with the principles of semiautomated assembly line manufacture from ordnance. When Henry Ford subsequently introduced assembly line method into civilian industrial manufacture in 1913, he, like the entire nation, was aware of Sibert's and Williamson's building processes.

The huge canal project was far more complex than any previous building process had been. Panama's organizers went a step further than Stephenson, Eiffel, and Sir Benjamin Baker (the builder of the Firth of Forth railway bridge), who had planned carefully, developed strategies, and anticipated contingencies before they organized a process that would take everything they could think of into account. Unlike their military counterparts, the civil engineers were not trained in tactics; they were not used to problems with continually shifting, interlinked parameters and were not trained to learn from historical precedent. Even though their mode of thought and educational system were derived from military engineering, civil engineers would have needed a far more sophisticated education in process planning to deal with the unanticipated problems that occurred almost daily at Panama.

The president and the navy ordered changes in both the canal width and the lock design as late as 1908, after the plant was partly installed. This threw Williamson's scheduling into disarray and forced him to modify the plant and do some extra digging. He began concreting with temporary mixers at Pedro Miguel in March 1910, using wooden formwork for all but the culverts, which used the same collapsible forms as at Gatun. The wooden forms had to be built each time, which required pauses in the casting process. No explanation was given for not using steel forms. Because last-minute changes had disrupted the schedule, some of the concrete work had to wait until after the cranes had been moved to Miraflores, so Williamson reactivated the temporary plant to finish the job between January and May 1911.

Miraflores lay in a swampy flood plain thirteen kilometers inland from the Pacific. A hydraulic dredge was brought in along a temporary cutting, as at Gatun, and dug from 1909 to 1912, finishing just before the engineers at Pedro Miguel were ready to send their cranes down. The dredge pumped part of its spoil into one of the Miraflores dams as hydraulic fill and spread the rest to reclaim the surrounding swamp. Williamson used auxiliary concrete plant at Miraflores, too, both for inaccessible parts of the works and to compensate for the last-minute changes in lock design. The berm cranes backfilled the lateral walls while trains carried the last loads of concrete for the approach wing walls and into the chambers to finish the center wall. Concreting ended in the last days of June 1913.[149] Both the Caribbean and the Pacific construction methods and their improvisations worked so well that the locks came in four percent below estimate.[150]

The Culebra Cut in the Central Division was the most difficult part of the canal to estimate and dig. It stretches 14.5 kilometers from Gamboa on the Chagres southward to Pedro Miguel and crosses the continental divide. Both the French and the American engineers repeatedly underestimated the difficult terrain and ran over budget. The French managed to dig a third of the 40.5 million cubic meters they thought they had to remove for a twenty-two-meter-wide sea level cutting with conservative slopes of 1:4.[151] Of course they were nowhere near a third done when they quit. The final tally turned out to be double what the French had guessed for a canal over four times as wide that lay twenty-six meters higher.[152] The top width of the cutting was originally planned to be 204 meters, but at places it ended up being almost three times that.[153] The deepest point lay 150 meters under the original surface, and the maximum cost was $9.3 million per kilometer.[154] Contradicting Bunau-Varilla's claim that it would be cheap and easy to dredge to sea level, David D. Galliard, whom Goethals put in charge of the Central Division, excavated the cutting entirely in the dry because it was so unstable.[155] Just the opposite of Suez, he preferred dry excavation wherever he could rationally employ steam shovels, even between Gamboa and Gatun where the Chagres crossed the line of the canal twenty-three times and frequent flooding hindered work. Sibert and Williamson did the only major dredging in the sea level channels between the Miraflores Locks and the Pacific and between the Gatun Locks and the Caribbean.[156] Steam shovels did as much as possible, and where it was impractical to use them the material was either sluiced into the river or the engineers fell back on manual labor that they paid as piecework.[157]

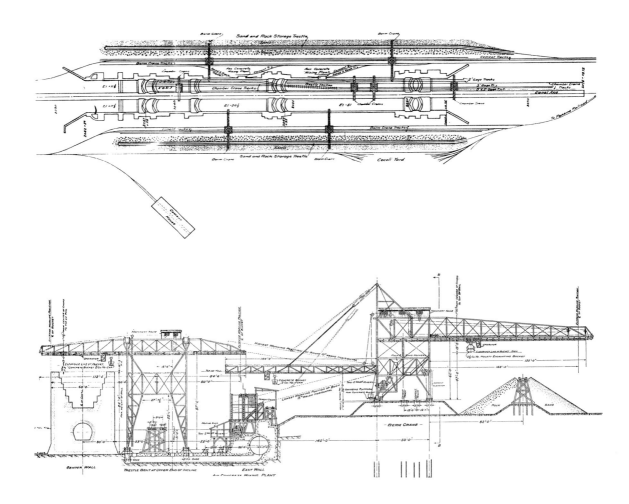

The Result in Small and Large

155.

The berm cranes flanked the entire site at Miraflores and transported the materials from stockpiles to the batching plants, from there to mixing, and inward to the chamber cranes for distribution to the forms. This superior arrangement did away with one railway loop. (Williamson in *Transactions*, 1916, vol. 1, plates 5, 10; *Panama and the Canal Zone*, 1914.)

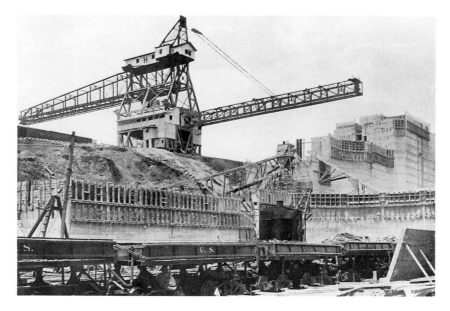

The second French company had used steam drills and ladder shovels on tracks, similar to those Lavalley had used twenty years before at Suez. The steam shovels deposited their spoil via chutes in railway cars that ran alongside. Galliard retained the French stepped excavation and imported heavier shovels when he saw that the site would become substantially larger than originally planned. He gradually replaced the steam drills with pneumatic ones except in inaccessible locations.

All details and large-scale problems were interconnected at Culebra. The engineers observed underground vibrations when deep holes were blasted. This led them to believe that blasting encouraged the slides that increased in number as the cut deepened. They couldn't prove this, but they cautiously chose surface blasting whenever possible. This meant that Galliard had to reduce the stepping of the excavation from 5 to 3.5 meters in order to reduce the amount of explosives, and this had implications for the whole site organization.[158]

In order to install and service the site, the Americans expanded the workshops the French had left behind and rebuilt the Panama Railroad with heavier rails and double track. The army coordinated the different engineering tasks better than the French civil system had been able to, but it still took about two years to get the Culebra sector fully operational. Experience

156.

The Culebra Cut lay on the continental divide and proved to be the most difficult segment. The cross section shows the original terrain, the depth of the projected French sea level cutting, the French excavation from 1881 to 1904, the American excavation from 1904 to 1912, and the amount left to remove in July 1912. (Siebert in *Transactions,* 1916, vol. 1, plate 1; Hilgard, c. 1915, plate following p. 52; Bennett, 1915, plate following p. 180.)

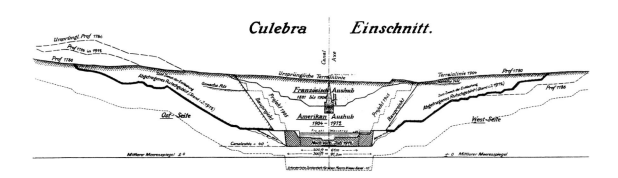

Culebra Einschnitt.

SECTIONAL ELEVATION
ON CENTER LINE OF CANAL

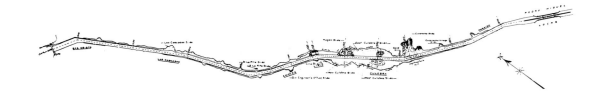

gradually improved productivity, and the ninety-six-ton Bucyrus shovels reached their maximum output late in 1911.[159] Between 1907 and 1914 the steam shovels doubled their output.[160] On average there were thirty-seven shovels on site, with a maximum of sixty-eight in 1909.[161] Competition between steam shovel operators was keen. The *Canal Record* published their performances weekly from 1907 on, a year before Gilbreth made similar recommendations for increasing productivity.[162] Galliard's staggered and stepped digging at Culebra was a coordinated series of parallel, linear processes on tracks, more complex in its organization than Fox's analogous glazing cart or Eiffel's and Baker's climbing cranes.

Galliard fully expected the shovels to break down because he worked them so hard. He had the site shops modify their design as problems appeared, much as Lavalley had done at Suez. But in contrast to Suez, he

157.
The largest steam shovels were the ninety-six-ton Bucyrus machines that worked the Culebra Cut. (Bennett, 1915, plate following p. 354.)

scheduled night crews in mobile workshops to carry out repairs and alterations in the field, using machine down time to the best advantage. The shops contained all the necessary tools, a forge, and a thirty-ton crane on a railway car. Roving coaling teams also supplied each shovel with forty to fifty tons of fuel during the night shift. Although no construction crews worked at night, nighttime servicing kept productivity practically as high as if they had been. Shovels were only actually taken out of service when they needed a complete overhaul.[163]

The same approach guided the design of the canal's safety features. The redundant Gatun Dam is designed to accommodate a river twice the capacity of the Chagres with leeway to spare.[164] Everything is controlled from a central console at the dam and at each lock flight. All switches are sequentially linked to reduce the likelihood of human error. The electric towing locomotives have friction couplings, an early form of automatic gear, and deadman switches automatically stop all machines if an operator is incapacitated. The engineers designed a giant chain with a shock-absorbing payout mechanism to stop runaway vessels. It was an improved version of the celebrated wrought-iron chain George Washington had spanned across the Hudson at West Point 130 years before. As a backup for the chain, each set of gates was doubled by a second pair. If these fail, an emergency barrier rotates across each of the six head locks and drops yet another gate that provides a fourth line of defense.[165]

Energy management in the Central Division was another major problem for which Goethals devised a system. He built compressor plants at three locations between 1905 and 1907 and upgraded them in 1909, while Galliard installed an elaborate system of pneumatic conduits for the machines and water mains and pumps for the generating plants.[166] He laid a complete ring around the site so that energy could be accessed from either side and kept flowing in spite of damage.[167] Frequent slides did rupture mains, and Galliard had to relocate and restore up to 122 kilometers of conduit monthly. Goethals had to cope with extreme site conditions and a high level of industrialization that made energy distribution more costly and elaborate than anything Sommeiller and Mella had dealt with at Mont Cenis.

Two meters of rain fall in the isthmus in each nine-month wet season, which also made drainage an issue of prime concern. Drains carried water away from the site, filled the lake that fed the system, and provided the Canal Zone's drinking water. Wherever possible Goethals combined disposal and storage. The French had worked uphill from either end of the Central Division. This made it easy to drain the works, and loaded spoil trains benefited from the slope too.[168] The Americans adopted the idea, but after the French

158.
Emergency dams formed a fourth line of defense against accidents. Normally they lay to the side, but they could be swung across the locks and dropped into position in minutes. Steel panels slid down the "fingers" to block the chambers. (*Panama and the Canal Zone*, 1914; Bennett, 1915, plate following p. 396.)

left they moved the canal axis, increased the cross section from twenty-two to sixty-one meters and then to ninety-one meters in 1908, and raised the canal bed from sea level to twenty-six meters. This meant that none of the French drainage ditches were useful and the Americans had to redesign the whole system.[169]

Transporting the spoil involved perhaps the most inventive new system of all. Galliard produced millions of cubic meters of earth at Culebra, which went to fill swamps and build dams or breakwaters. Steam shovels loaded the earth on flatbed cars, which Lidgerwood designed with the side that faced the shovel and both ends left open. The simple, open design was worthy of the genius of a Charles Fox. A closed loading side would have forced the shovels to lift their load higher and diminished the stepping cut by 120 centimeters on each level.[170] The closed side opposite the shovel stopped the dirt from spilling over and piled it up against the barrier. To compensate for the asymmetrical loading, the flatbeds extended an extra thirty centimeters over the open side. The open ends with their overlapping flaps from car to car provided a continuous articulated loading surface twenty cars long and increased the train's capacity by ten to fifteen percent. The continuous load also made dumping easier using Lidgerwood's plow, which was winched along the train from front to back on a dragline.[171] The lip on the open side helped throw the spoil well away from the track, and it took only ten minutes to clear a twenty-car train with a total capacity of 290.5 cubic meters.[172] Galliard loaded the incredible number of 230,000 trains in the Culebra Cut in the eight years he worked there, or upwards of 95 trains per working day![173] Traffic densities this high required flawless organization and management. Lidgerwood's spreaders ran on the same track as the trains and plowed the material down the edge of the embankment.[174] When the fill covered the trestle on which the track was built, railway-mounted track shifters moved the track to one edge of the berm and the plows and spreaders worked on.[175] The Lidgerwood system worked for curved or straight loading tracks and for straight unloading areas. Galliard used traditional dump cars for other unloading conditions.

The advantages of having an independent transportation system were proved over and over again. The railway laid special track and moved it wherever needed for bringing and removing material or dumping earth. Track moving was done manually at first. When it threatened to become a bottleneck, W. G. Bierd, superintendent and later general manager of the Panama Railway, mechanized the process by mounting a crane on a railway car. The crane could lift and displace whole sections at a time. In one instance the track shifter moved two kilometers of track three and a half meters in just under two hours.[176]

The Result in Small and Large

159.
The Lidgerwood spoil cars had only one side wall. They formed a continuous, flexible loading surface the length of the train. (Bennett, 1915, plates following p. 188; Hilgard, c. 1915, p. 71.)

160.
The Lidgerwood plow cleared the spoil trains and pushed the material into the Atlantic at the Point Toro breakwater. The Lidgerwood spreader pushed the spoil dumped by the plow away from the track and down the growing embankment. (Bennett, 1915, plates following pp. 316, 348; Hilgard, c. 1915, p. 74.)

The Result in Small and Large

161.
The whole project stood
and fell with its transportation system. Tracks had to
be moved continually to
serve changing site needs.
When manual track-shifting
threatened to become a bottleneck, W. G. Bierd de-
signed a crane that ran on
the very line it displaced. It
reestablished track in a fraction of the time a crew took
to do the job. (Bennett,
1915, plate following
p. 332.)

The Result in Small and Large

Seventy-five trains moved constantly along the 51.5-kilometer Central Division, and time-saving simplifications were always welcome. The engineers were constantly developing detail improvements. Where the plow scraped and damaged the side wall as it bumped from car to car, they added an iron edge that steered the plow away from the link.[177] They searched for and found better wire cables, designed backups for the car coupling, which broke frequently, strengthened the link between the plow and the dragline, and made fifty-one alterations on the spreaders.[178] Careful railway management, the Lidgerwood car, plow, and spreader, and Bierd's track shifter formed a mature, rationalized system. It was similar to Charles Fox's glazing cart in efficiency. Both made an incremental module—the structural bay or the railroad car—serve a linear method.

Once Stevens had set up the railway system, the chief obstacle to its smooth functioning was the many slides that destroyed track and cut energy and communication lines. Four types of slides plagued the engineers: structural breaks and deformations, gravity slides, fault zone slides, and surface erosion.[179] All in all there were twenty-two slide zones along the canal, ranging from a minor one at Pedro Miguel to the 6.88-million-cubic-meter East Culebra Slide. They flowed rather than fell into the cutting, sometimes bulging the bottom of the site. Over a quarter of the material removed from Culebra had been displaced by slides.[180]

The first type was typified by the notorious Cucaracha Slide. It was a tiny, 1.6-kilometer section of the cut near Culebra where the material was particularly weak, slippery, and permeated by groundwater.[181] The Caribbean-side drainage works lay close to Cucaracha and were partly responsible for the slides that repeatedly blocked excavation between 1884 and 1913. When the material was disturbed by excavation or shaken by blasting, a slide would start as a series of fissures parallel to the slope. The cracks could appear close to the work site or several hundred meters uphill. Then blocks would slowly tilt outward at the work face, crush, and flow into the excavation. Usually this was accompanied by an upswelling of the lower slope and bottom of the cutting.[182] The only remedy was to remove material from the upper slope and flatten the cutting.

In most cases the engineers chose to terrace back the hillsides on either side of the cut to relieve the pressure. Using gravity to let slides fill the cut and removing the material from the bottom would have saved labor initially but destabilized the hillside even further. Steep breaks twelve to twenty-five meters high invariably formed at a slide face and slid again. Each new slide crushed and weakened the underlying material and made even flatter slopes necessary.[183] At Cucaracha and Culebra the slope was too weak to

162.
Earthslides at Culebra caused no end of trouble, disrupting communications, burying materiel, and covering the excavation. Sometimes the only way to remove the most unstable material was to sluice it away with water jets. (Abbot, 1914, pp. 205, 218; Bennett, 1915, plate following p. 114.)

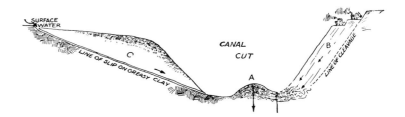

carry the load of track and machinery, so the engineers washed the slope into the cutting, using the sluicing method that had worked so well at the Pacific locks.[184] Toward the end of work, when dredges were brought in to remove slides from the finished canal, fissures sometimes opened up beyond the crest of the hills. The sluicing apparatus was used again to wash the material into the adjacent valleys.[185]

The second type, the gravity slide, was a classical slip that did not crush material below the plane of slip or weaken the remaining slope. These were most economically removed as they occurred, and the only remedy was sufficient drainage.[186] The third type, the fault zone slide, occurred only twice, on the east bank between Empire and Las Cascadas. Aided by water seepage, the first slide at La Pita sent 15,290 cubic meters into the cut, while the second, slightly later and to the north of the first, broke off 229,350 cubic meters. The only way to avoid this type was to flatten the slope and drain, although the reinforced concrete technology then available would theoretically have permitted shoring work.[187] The final type of slide, erosion, occurred all over the Culebra Cut, where an estimated total of 50,000 cubic meters washed into the works. The quick-growing tropical vegetation quickly counteracted erosion and stabilized the exposed surface against further washing.

In spite of the enormous size of the project, suppliers did occasionally band together in trusts to control prices. This happened in the case of dynamite suppliers, but Goethals was able to find an alternative product.[188] Great care was taken with the storage and use of explosives. The workmen handled about 2,700 tons of dynamite yearly, with an average of eight hundred detonations each day. In the three years in which 2,870 tons of explosives were used at Culebra, only eight fatalities were recorded.[189] Goethals studied each accident and had the cause remedied. His concern was not lessened by the fact that most of the laborers who handled explosives directly were not American citizens. Aside from the fact that American society placed great value on the individual, the times—and with them, working conditions—had changed from Wellington Purdon's day. Goethals and Gorgas carefully planned and supervised the safety, health, and welfare of all workers.

An efficient accounting system made it easier to run the gigantic project. Everything was reduced to unit cost and compared to equivalent costs elsewhere. This system owed more to ordnance practice than it did to Taylor or Gilbreth, and it was a logical adaptation of the comparative model assumptions that Navier had used to organize his system of statics and to render differing structural scales comparable.[190] Costs diminished from year to year in actual dollar amounts under this system, helped by the influence of

Taylor and Gilbreth's ideas.[191] The cost-comparative procedure appeared so self-evident to the military engineers who organized and built Panama that they did not waste a single sentence on it in the papers they presented at the international engineering congress in 1915. It was the popularizer Frederic J. Haskin who described its influence on the project.[192]

A large amount of work went into the military and civilian installations too. Harry H. Rousseau built forts and terminals at either end, together with the harbors and breakwaters. The main naval and service facilities lay on the Caribbean, including storehouses, a bakery, and a laundry that accepted a ship's washing on one end of the canal and delivered it fresh as the ship emerged at the other end.[193] Rousseau built a dry dock the size of one of the canal locks and a large coaling station in which half the storage was under water for security reasons. There were similar but smaller facilities on the Pacific. Military field installations were set up for 6,000–20,000 mobile troops at the lock and dam sites and permanent army quarters built at Miraflores. Much of the structural work was founded on concrete pneumatic caissons that were lubricated hydraulically by pumping water alongside them into the ground.[194] Urban and transportation infrastructures had to be built too. The Canal Zone ran on hydroelectric power, which provided the energy for the cities and the locks and gates as well lighting for military searchlights and the nocturnal operation of the canal. Two cities and the administrative center were built on the Pacific side. One city served the Americans and the other sheltered all others. All of this work was also organized by the Isthmus Commission under Goethals, and it all proceeded expediently and to schedule.

In May 1913, two shovels steamed from opposite directions to meet in the middle of the cutting, an average of 36.5 meters below the original terrain.[195] Their tracks finally lay on the future canal bed. Galliard was dying and had left by the time the machinery was removed in September. Water began to flow gently into the canal on October 1 through pipes laid in the dike at Gamboa. Goethals had closed the sluice gates at Gatun in June, and the lake level had gradually risen since then. On October 10, President Woodrow Wilson symbolically opened the waterway by blasting part of the dike electrically from Washington. The Cucaracha Slide still blocked the waterway, but the canal was ready for traffic around December 15.[196]

Half a century earlier at Suez, the most innovative thinking had gone into the design and manufacture of machinery. At Panama, Goethals and his team emphasized the design of integrated systems and processes. The canal was militarily important to the United States, and the government wanted no aspect of its function left to chance. Goethals's two first steps—

his simplification of the chain of command and the decree of martial law —
prepared his success. His single-minded concentration on organization, transportation, and supply guaranteed it. His approach and training came from
the military, an organization interested only in process, not product, and his
leadership at Panama concluded the transformation of the building process
from an unplanned interlude between design and inauguration to a mature
and necessary profession of its own. Whether he knew it or not, the way he
worked was based on a century of development. The previous step, the
French effort to which he reacted, had incorporated all that had gone before.
Modern building owes a great deal to Goethals and his team, as do many
other processes our world depends on, from modern oil prospecting to space
programs.

Conclusion: The Building Process and
Technological Thinking

All of the many examples in this book led step by step to the definition of building as a process and to our modern building culture. People like Navier introduced scientific thinking into building analysis, as Mahon did into research. Vicat inadvertently exposed the limitations of scientific thinking, and Smeaton intuitively linked analysis and design. Maus's skepticism of scientific "proof" highlighted the independence and advantages of the hybrid thought form. Althans, Pasley, and Marc Brunel demonstrated the subtle complexities of matrix thinking and border-crossing translation. Charles Fox and Robert Stephenson introduced critical-path considerations, while Richard Turner and Fox decoupled assembly from construction and thereby recognized building as a process. Town, Paine, Thomas Wilson, John Rennie, Telford, and Eiffel developed system thinking in construction, and Marc Brunel and Lidgerwood did the same in building machinery. Gilbreth tried, with only partial success, to take the ultimate step in mechanization and rationalize human work, too, and Goethals carried the building process to its logical consequence through military thinking.

The thought form that drove this development is a hybrid of scientific method and an empirical, associative form of matrix thinking.[1] Designers are matrix thinkers. They use personal and cultural values to define relationships between design elements and relate them to their context. The associative quality of matrix thinking led Isaac Johnson to discover a better hydraulic cement in a kilnload of sintered waste, Karl Althans to *transform* cannonballs into ball bearings or a wagon spring into a truss chord, and Marc Brunel to *translate* information from a zoomorphic to a mechanical format. A transformation remolds information within the boundaries of a field, while a translation process crosses borders and moves it from one field to another. We will never know the precise mechanics of how Brunel hit upon the idea for his tunneling shield, but processes of translation like his are characteristic of the associative or matrix aspect of technological thinking. Translation figures prominently in all the industrial projects for which he became known:

his assembly lines for boot manufacture, sawing lumber, and block making. Cultural border crossing can evidently foster the translation process; according to Helps, British mechanics seemed to build better machinery when they emigrated to North America.

The scientific side of technological thought stays within clearly delineated boundaries and is independent of the thinker's personal value system. Science uses methods that anyone can replicate to provide unambiguous answers to questions. Technologists need it to analyze designs and help control the process of design synthesis. Navier introduced scientific method into building when he developed analytical structural models that were independent of scale and material. As an example, his new understanding of bridge loading (as opposed to Dufour's traditional view) allowed engineers to compare different spans and loading conditions objectively. This enabled them to recognize abstract and quantifiable characteristics that were common to a range of specific cases. Half a century earlier, Mahon and Smeaton had introduced scientific method to design by using it to resolve detail questions. Although he was a physicist, Mahon treated a detail question like a true technologist, as a problem in its own right rather than a minor part of a system. His intentions were technological: to build a better object, not merely to provide new insight or knowledge. Mahon's work pointed in a direction that would eventually distinguish the technological thought mode from other forms.

Scientific thinking helped builders understand technological behavior, but it did not help them design. Builders needed associative thinking, the other half of technological thought, to create structures or processes. Smeaton was a builder who went a step further than Mahon when he used his chemical analysis of hydraulic cement as a decision-making tool in building the Eddystone Lighthouse. This delicate relationship between analysis and synthesis characterizes a mature design process. It was another step in the development of technological thought.

Pasley followed Mahon in fireproofing research. When the Institution of Civil Engineers discussed his paper at a meeting in 1849, they discovered similar ideas in iron smelters, wooden ceiling construction, and safe manufacture, indicating how building technology advanced through a combination of scientific analysis and matrix thinking.[2] This type of associative leap typically shifts the designer's thinking into its technological context.

Pasley and Marc Brunel brought a designer's approach to research on concrete, choosing to examine structures rather than the material samples Vicat and Treussart preferred in France. They built tensile structures and embedded all sorts of materials in the mortar to improve its tensile strength. Although they weren't looking for it, Brunel observed that iron, alone of all the materials they tried, bonded with the cement. This observation was a fortuitous discovery and not the result of logical, step-by-step searching as in the vertical problem-solving mode of physical or chemical analysis. But that did not make the discovery any less valuable, since it eventually led to the development of reinforced concrete and to the concept of monolithic structure.[3] Brunel's invention of "soil nailing" was another case in which an apparently illogical leap in matrix thinking permitted a translation to take place. Apparent illogic has never daunted technologists, as shown by Henri Maus's unflagging enthusiasm for digging the Mont Cenis Tunnel in the face of overwhelming "proof" of its impossibility.

Science and technology live in an uneasy relationship because they follow different goals. One of their chief differences lies in the concept of scale, which plays entirely different roles in either field. Vicat inadvertantly crossed the limits of what scientific analysis can do for building because he neglected the all-important issue of scale. He was an engineer, but when he studied the rust-reducing characteristics of cement he did not focus on making a functioning object, as a technologist would. Bridge cables failed when they were grouted in mortar, whereas individual wires did not. Vicat had neglected to translate his laboratory model into a full-scale structure under field conditions. The small-scale problem or detail needs different treatment from the large-scale problem. The success of Eiffel's component assembly system hinged on issues of scale. Sculptors and architects intuitively know that a change in scale alters all proportions and all relationships between parts, and ever since Galileo Galilei, engineers have also developed model laws that define such relationships.[4] The Marly pumping station, the Thames shield, Triger's and Castor's pneumatic caissons, and the Panama lock gates all could not have been built without a working knowledge of these laws.

Organizational Thought

Iron bridge builders began to use an early form of system thinking in Britain. They did not design hierarchically from the whole to the part, but rather developed standardized members and connections while they worked on the overall form. It was a dialectic approach to design, and it made the part as important as the whole. It followed that these builders began to understand design and parts manufacture as processes. Their system thinking standardized the relationships between structural members, and this advanced organizational thinking in building generally. American builders applied similar organizational principles to wooden bridges and house frames, and they made use of characteristics like redundancy. Labor conditions in the United States forced American builders to increase the number of parts they used and to stress a statistical approach to structural safety, while European engineers were more interested in the monolithic characteristics of their systems.

At Kew, Richard Turner separated a design problem with conflicting requirements into its constituent parts and solved it serially. When he had done that, he reunited the results into an overall solution. It was a new technique that expanded system design, and it provided a rationale for modular, repetitive construction beyond the economics of reusing casting molds.

While he was building the Crystal Palace, Charles Fox began to regard the hiatus between the design and the finished building as a separate phase worthy of study and organization. He manufactured the components quickly and efficiently by machine, but at first he still assembled everything manually. It was only when a bottleneck threatened to disrupt the erection process that he devised a method to accelerate assembly. He decoupled the erection sequence from the structural geometry and made the building phase independent.

Turner's method had implications for the erection process, too. Fox was not the only one who had to decouple building methods from construction because of deadline pressure. Robert Stephenson and William Fairbairn encountered similar conditions on the Conway and Britannia bridges. They made their bridge piers taller than the beam supports in order to postpone deciding what structural system to choose and still allow construction work to progress. They saved time by organizing the experimentation and construction in parallel sequences and using a primitive form of critical-path thinking to coordinate the whole. Stephenson did for the building process exactly what Turner had done in design: separate a problem into its parts and reunite them after solving each on its own. It was yet another step in conceptualizing the act of building as a process.

Gustave Eiffel developed a decision matrix of structural constants and variables to complete this development and carry the idea of building system to maturity. He left no statement to show that he conceptualized building thought in this way, but he clearly did use some form of logically ordered thinking process. As a result, he developed a simple yet sophisticated catalog of wrought-iron parts and connection rules that he used to build the complex, nonorthogonal Garabit Bridge and his tower. Like Turner, Eiffel dissected issues to solve detail problems. But where Turner reunited his detail solutions in a specific building element, Eiffel formed them into an open system that he could use to build any iron structure. His kit-of-parts approach to construction simplified the job for steel bridge and high-rise builders.

Even though their mode of thought and educational system originated in military engineering, civil engineers were not trained in quite the same way. Civil engineering curricula did not include the military historical case study format for training strategy, so civil engineers had no tools to solve problems with continually shifting, interlinked parameters and unanticipated occurrences like the ones that characterized the Panamanian site. Goethals's military training allowed him to progress a step further than Stephenson and Eiffel and treat the construction process like a military campaign.

Structures and Machines, Building Method and War, Process and Life

There are many aspects to building culture, but three of them seem dominant: the relationship between structures and machines, the relationship between military thinking and the building process, and the conceptual connection between building and the principle of life. When cast and wrought iron were introduced as structural materials, they blurred the distinction between buildings and machines. The only real difference between the two was that machines performed work.[5] Nineteenth-century engineers had to build machinery to manufacture and assemble their buildings, and as a result they began to look at what they did from a production and procedural point of view. They integrated manufacturing plant and site installations into many of their building designs, and this changed the nature of construction irrespective of the material they used. At first manufacturers only made repetitive parts in iron, but machines could and did produce iron, wood, and even concrete parts for the building industry. The way we now *assemble* buildings as systems rather than *construct* them on site is a direct result of the factory methods that the machine and building material industries used to produce repetitive and interchangeable parts. This has influenced design, organization, and the erection process even more profoundly than it has changed building aesthetics.

Machine and building structure drew even closer in their goals and methods as engineers gradually incorporated complex heating, ventilating, plumbing, gas, or electrical installations and vertical or horizontal transportation machinery into buildings. John Rennie's mechanized shed for mahogany storage was designed around its crane system, and elevators and cranes were mobile parts of Brunel's sawmills. The relationship was still clearer in buildings like the Sayn Foundry that were entirely determined by their mechanical

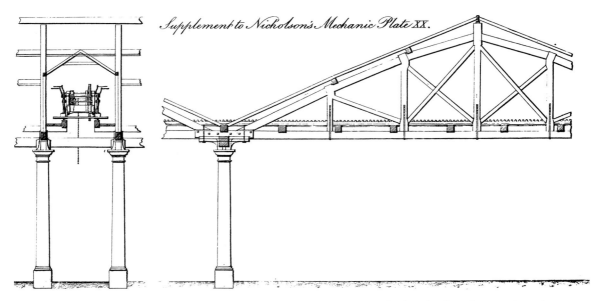

Supplement to Nicholson's Mechanic Plate XX.

163.
John Rennie's warehouse for mahogany logs in the West India Docks (c. 1814) was an early example of a hybrid structure, part building and part machine. Its traveling crane ran on a track laid between the roof trusses. (Charles Taylor, 1829, plate 20.)

parts. From a traditional architectural standpoint the foundry may have been a neo-Gothic, cast-iron basilica with an alienated function, but for a manufacturer it was a gigantic machine for casting iron with space for humans to participate in the process. Paxton built the Chatsworth Conservatory largely of wood, but its nickname, the "Great Stove," indicates how much it, too, was considered a machine. Similarly, the Kew Palm House, the Crystal Palace, and the Munich Glaspalast were all climate-controlled showcases, not palaces of culture. Eiffel's tower was the product of the steam cranes that climbed the track they built. The tower's feet were embedded in hydraulic presses that could be activated to adjust the level of each leg as the tower grew. Eiffel's Nice observatory was a mechanism for viewing the heavens, while Dutert's Galerie des Machines was an exhibit hall designed as the interior of a machine.

As train stations, hospitals, banks, and even elaborate and gaudy opera houses incorporated machinery, they became true "facilities" — which is what we now call these machine-buildings — rather than works of architecture in a traditional sense. It was the safety elevator and the water pump as much as the stiff iron frame that made the skyscraper a new building type. Our cities and their services and structures became as much complex machines as they were built environments. Charles Garnier illustrated the crossover between the building as art and the building as machine in the plates of his monograph on the Paris Opera in 1880, as did Eiffel in his book on his tower.[6] Large ships are both machines and floating structures. Fairbairn's expertise in iron shipbuilding stood him in good stead when his team designed

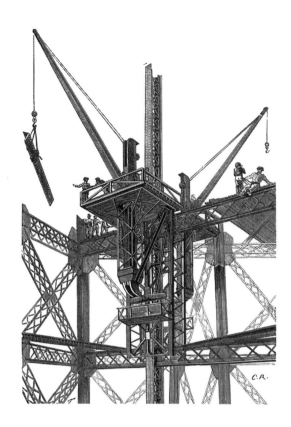

164.
The Eiffel Tower's steam cranes climbed the structure they built. They were as much a part of the structure as the later passenger elevators. Like the hydraulic presses under the tower's feet, they blurred the distinction between machine and building. (*Exposition de Paris 1889*, vol. 1, pp. 32, 68.)

The Building Process and Technological Thinking

and built the Britannia Bridge and its lifting mechanism.[7] Other hybrid structures, like the floating grain mill Fairbairn built for the Crimea in 1854 or George Ferris's giant wheel at the Chicago Columbian Exhibition in 1893, reflected developments in iron and steel framing techniques as much as they did advances in transportation technology.

Transportation networks were strictly speaking neither structures nor machines, but the Thames Tunnel was successful because of the machine that built it. The machine was the primary technological invention, and the tunnel was simply its casting. So in a way, it was more machine than structure. Canals are even more fully integrated structure-machines: their operable mechanical lock parts are just as important as their static masonry. The nineteenth-century structure-machine tradition continued well into the twentieth with Le Corbusier's *machine à habiter* and the *Frankfurter Küche* of the 1920s. The unfortunate contortions that architectural historians from James Fergusson to Peter Collins went through to draw the distinction between architecture and machine design missed an important point. They aimed at the definition of beauty in the traditional *object,* rather than in the dynamic aesthetic *processes* of problem-solving or design.

The men who changed the course of building construction by introducing procedural issues either were military officers or belonged to a field that had arisen out of military training. Strategy and its branches, tactics and logistics, the rationale of supply lines, and critical-path thinking all formed part of the way they thought, and the more clearly they followed the military model, the better and more rationally organized was their work.[8] There was little procedural thinking in the projects that empirically trained men built, while process was the main theme in those that professionally educated engineers organized. Where military engineers were in charge of a work, they guided it by reasoned strategies. As engineering academies grew out of military schools and proliferated in the course of the nineteenth century, their influence became more pervasive. So did the procedural bias in building. Quite often, too, builders described their work as a "battle" against nature or the elements, so consciously or subliminally they accepted the connection. The concept of industrial production and assembly also emerged from military ordnance, and the machine production of elements and whole systems influenced how we conceive of building as process.

The key issue in both the machine-structure and the war-building method relationship is process, a term that implies life and change. Our modern term "life cycle" indicates how intimately the processes of design, building, use, decay, and renewal or demolition are related to the principle of life. Process implies *organization,* a vital function that goes deeper than the formal, *compositional* anthropomorphism of European architectural tradition.[9]

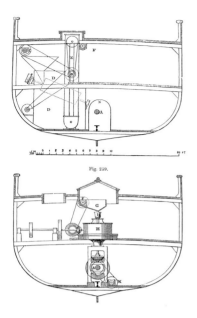

Fig. 259.

165.
Fairbairn's floating grain mill for the Crimean War (1854–1856) was a hybrid machine, ship, and building. Structurally it was a hollow box like the Britannia Bridge. George Ferris's wheel, built for the Chicago World Fair in 1893, combined the steel frame of contemporary Chicago and New York skyscrapers with a revolving, tensile "bicycle wheel." It was the ultimate machine-building. (Fairbairn, *Treatise on Mills and Millwork*, 1871, p. 136. Ferris Wheel researched and drafted by Carl Knutson and John Woynicki, Jr.)

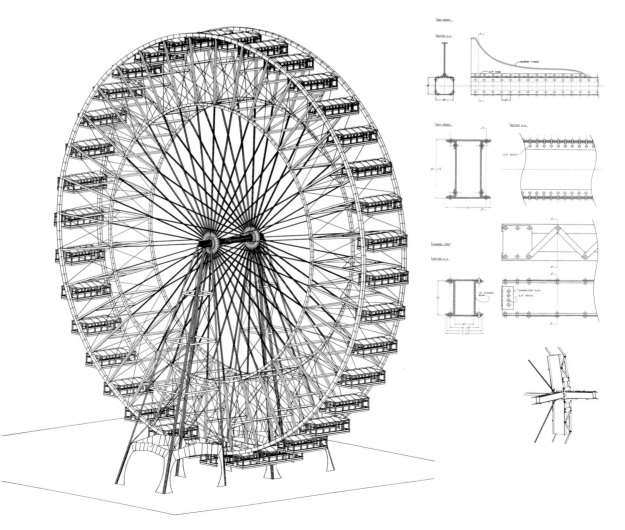

While principles of composition are supported by an "organic" theory of architecture that aims at beauty, organizational concepts come from "functionalist" theory that has viability as its goal.[10] Strangely enough, it is the "organic" theory that is generally equated with growth and life, at least at the semantic and formal levels, while it is really the second that translates and conceptualizes the principles of life beyond the issues of form in builders' terms. More than "beauty," which is traditionally concerned with pristine and isolated objects, organization and functionality connect an object with its context. The broad view of an object in its spatial, functional, or organizational context is characteristic of matrix thinking, on which so much of our technological thinking and design work depends. The very word *matrix* implies an environment or context. Matrix or contextual thinking characterizes the "aesthetics of process" and distinguishes it from the traditional "aesthetics of object," and contextualism itself is a principle that architectural theory borrowed from the concept of the biotope.[11]

Most architectural theoreticians, including Peter Collins, who perhaps thought the deepest along these lines, were interested in the aesthetic import of the biological metaphor. But going a step further than aesthetics, we find that the principle of life, with its connection to process, functionality, organization, context, and the act of building, reveals something about the most fascinating aspect of our technological culture: the conflation of space, time, and awareness. As we have seen, the reduction of space into time that occurred with the proliferation of the telegraph and the reduction of time into awareness that occurred more recently through live coverage of news illustrate this intimate relationship.

The machine, war, and life are concepts we can trace *a posteriori* in older building processes. But their conscious application to construction dates from the period in which machine-making, war, and biology themselves evolved from arts to technologies. In this way building has helped form, and not merely followed, our cultural development. Although building trades may often be among the last to adopt new techniques, building itself is conceptually very much a part of its time. The implications that this has had for built form and for the concept of space-time awareness in our built environment curiously did not take root in our engineering and architectural education until quite recently, when the emphasis began to shift from built objects to their life cycles in the environment and consequently to the processes of designing, building, maintenance, regeneration or demolition, and recycling. Building as an activity is an archetypal preoccupation. It mirrors human development on both a personal and a cultural level. Where will we go from here?

Notes

References that are relevant to the general history of construction can be found fully described in the bibliography; in the notes these are abbreviated under the author's name. All others, and those that were used only once to confirm or establish a fact, are listed fully in the notes. The illustrations, with the exception of those noted in the acknowledgments, are from the author's collection. I use the term "tonne" to refer to metric as opposed to British "tons." Dates of patents are abbreviated as day.month.year.

Preface: Building a Tectonic Culture in the Nineteenth Century

1. I prefer to use the term "matrix" thinking instead of Edward de Bono's "lateral" as the complementary form to "vertical" or scientific thinking, because it better describes the multidimensionality of that thought form in contrast to "vertical" thought's linear nature.

2. There are a few exceptions to this, demonstrated for instance by Marc Brunel's and Guillaume-Henri Dufour's papers.

3. Dreicer first expressed these ideas in a paper called "Technology, Biology, and History" at the conference "Technological Development and Science in the 19th and 20th Centuries," Eindhoven, Netherlands, 8 November 1990.

1 Creating the Modern World through Communication, Commerce, and Progress

1. Nef, p. 151.

2. John Smeaton's improvements in wind- and water mills spurred the development of the textile industry in another way, independently of the coal industry (*An Experimental Enquiry,* 1760), but this was temporarily overshadowed by steam power. Camillo de Cavour was to reintroduce the issue of hydraulic power in the 1860s (see chapter 4).

3. Peters, "Architectural and Engineering Design."

4. Applegarth modified König and Bauer's press in 1828 (Frederick Koenig, GB patents 3321, 29.03.1810; 3496, 30.10.1811; 3725, 23.07.1813; and 3868, 24.12.1814). The London *Times* installed the original König and Bauer machine on 24 November or 29 November 1814 (Stanley Morison, *The English Newspaper* [Cambridge, 1932], pp. 205, 211). Marc Brunel's improvement was neither implemented

nor patented (Beamish, pp. 148–151), but Edward Cowper's (GB patent 4194, 07.01.1818) and Augustus Applegarth's (GB patent 5613, 26.01.1828) were. Applegarth quadrupled König's output from 1,100 to 4,000 sheets an hour. Later he introduced rotary movement and more than doubled the output again between 1830 and 1851. By the late 1850s improvements in presses brought the number of sheets printed in an hour to 40,000 (Beamish, pp. 151–154).

5. Babbage, pp. 269–272 in the 3rd ed.; *Penny Magazine,* 1832, p. 131.

6. John S. McNown, "Canals in America," *Scientific American,* July 1976, p. 117.

7. Ibid., p. 118.

8. 22 British tons at 2.5 mph (*Min. Proc. ICE,* vol. 5, 1846, p. 25); McNown, "Canals in America," p. 117.

9. Rennie, p. 25; Grenier, p. 109. See *Min. Proc. ICE,* vol. 13, 1854, p. 211, for discussion of railway superiority by Rawlinson and Hawkshaw; see also Robert Stephenson's later opposition to the Suez Canal and not altogether altruistic support of the Egyptian Railway.

10. Beamish, pp. 157–158, 163–164.

11. The paramilitary Corps des Ponts et Chaussées was formed in 1716 to support the program and opened its own training school, the later École des Ponts et Chaussées, in 1747.

12. Flachat, "Mémoire no. VII," pp. 357–358, 392–396.

13. Smeaton's Markham-Newark road of 1768 was an early example (Rennie, pp. 64 ff). Sir Henry Parnell (later Lord Congleton) sponsored national turnpikes between 1800 and 1834. Telford built the Great Northern Road between London and Edinburgh and the Holyhead Road to Liverpool and the Anglesea coast that consummated the union with Ireland in 1800, earning his jocular nickname "Colossus of Roads." After 1816, the Earl of Lonsdale funded McAdam's road expansion in the Bristol area.

14. England had 39,330 km and Scotland 12,800 (Rennie, p. 67).

15. British engineers adopted Sasseney's invention for footpaths in 1836 (ibid., p. 68).

16. Ibid., pp. 66–67.

17. Marc Seguin built the first tubular boiler in France in 1828. The Austrian von Gerstners, father and son, began Russia's system. It grew from the 27-kilometer Zarskoe Zeloe–St. Petersburg line (1836–1843) to 1,093 kilometers by 1851 (Elton, *Railways,* no. 46; Petitti, p. 611). They also built 60 kilometers in Poland, which were operational by 1843 (Petitti, p. 611). The son, Franz Anton von Gerstner, began work on the St. Petersburg–Warsaw continuation to the west. The Gerstners died early: the father, Franz Joseph, in 1832, and the son in 1840. Bavaria's development began in 1835, also without British help; by midcentury the German states had built over

6,400 kilometers (Siemens, in Window, pp. 362–366). Still, the British built much on the European continent, too. Vignoles built the Moscow–St. Petersburg line and began Belgium's first railway in 1834. It was virtually complete in 1843 at 559 kilometers (Petitti, pp. 606–607) and grew only slightly over the next decade, to 621 kilometers in 1853 (*Mém. et Compte-Rendu,* 1857, pp. 190–191). Robert Stephenson and Isambard Brunel constructed Sardinia and Piedmont's.

18. Austria and Britain in 1825, France in 1828, and the United States in 1829. Regular steam traction began in 1830 in Austria, Britain, and the United States, with France (1832), Ireland (1834), Bavaria (1835), Canada and Russia (1836), Italy (1839), Poland (1843), Switzerland (1847), and Spain (1848) joining before midcentury. The first international line ran from Strasbourg to Basel in 1841, but Basel only connected to it in 1845 (*Handbuch der Schweizer Geschichte,* 2 vols. [Zurich: Buchverlag Berichthaus, 1980], vol. 2, p. 1030). The first transalpine connection was Karl von Ghega's Semmering Railway (1851–1860) on the Vienna-Trieste line. John Stevens and Jonathan Knight were among the earliest American railway engineers, and Marc Seguin, Antoine-Rémy Polonceau, Eugène Flachat, and Jules Petiet among the French.

19. 967 kilometers total length by 1843 (Petitti, p. 610). By 1853, France still had only 5,876 kilometers (*Mém. et Compte-Rendu,* 1857, pp. 190–191).

20. For a personal view of the role of railway development in the spread of London, see Smiles, *Lives of the Engineers,* vol. 3, p. xvii. Smiles also mentions the influence of railway construction and maintenance on rural laborers' wages (pp. xxviii–xxix).

21. From 1840 to 1850 the railways grew from 4,800 to 14,500 kilometers and the canals from 5,300 to 5,750 kilometers.

22. Rennie, pp. 75–76.

23. In 1830 a ton of goods took four to five weeks to ship from Liverpool to Manchester and cost £ 2.0; by 1846 it arrived in three to four hours and cost £ 0.15 (ibid, p. 67).

24. Ibid., p. 78.

25. In 1845 proposals totaled 594 lines, 33,100 kilometers; in 1846, 556 lines (Elton, *Railways,* nos. 111, 112). Smiles, *Lives of the Engineers,* vol. 3, footnote p. 408, has 620 projects in 1845. Britain had 3,500 kilometers of broad and narrow gauge track in 1846 and another 28 percent or 982 kilometers under construction. Rennie gives 5,717 kilometers (p. 77).

26. Between 1846 and 1851, the British system grew "only" threefold to 11,200 kilometers (Rennie, in *Min. Proc. ICE,* vol. 11, 1851–52, pp. 146–161).

27. From about 70 kilometers at the introduction of steam traction between Charleston and Hamburg, South Carolina, by Knight in 1830, the American system reached its apogee at slightly over 192,000 kilometers about sixty years later in 1884 (Hadley, pp. 154, 198; Jones, maps opposite pp. 52, 54). Between 1851 and 1853 British railways expanded 9 percent while the American lines increased by 69 percent to 12,055 kilometers (*Mém. et Compte-Rendu,* 1857, pp. 190–191).

28. In 1830 25.5 kilometers were added to the B&O by Knight (McNown, "Canals in America," p. 122).

29. *Mém. et Compte-Rendu,* 1849, p. 209.

30. In 1843 the US had 178 lines and Great Britain had 74 (Petitti, pp. 592–605). By 1851, the small state of Massachusetts alone had 26 lines (Grenier, p. 115). Two years later Massachusetts had 2,444 kilometers and New York had 3,572 (*Mém. et Compte-Rendu,* 1857, pp. 190–191; J. M. Rendel, pp. 148–161).

31. The transcontinental line was proposed along with several others in the first period of railroad speculation, 1840–1850. The construction bill passed Congress in 1862, and the line was the amalgam of two competing companies, the Union Pacific and the Central Pacific (Hadley, p. 3). Fifteen years later, several lines crisscrossed the continent (Emory R. Johnson in *Transactions,* vol. 1, p. 52).

32. Buchanan writes that the railway was completed in 1853 (p. 153). The line was planned simultaneously with the American and was 2,400 kilometers long. Robert Stephenson, Isambard Brunel, William Cubitt, and George Turnbull were all involved, and James Rendel was engineer-in-chief. The eastern segment from Calcutta to Raniganj, built by R. Macdonald, and the western segment from Bombay to Thana, by chief-engineer James J. Berkley, opened in 1853 (*Min. Proc. ICE,* vol. 11, 1851–52, p. 153). The Pakistan Eastern and Western railways followed in 1861 and 1862 (Elton, *Railways,* no. 89).

33. Thomas Brassey built the Montreal-Toronto segment and Robert Stephenson furnished many of the bridges. The Scottish-Canadian Sir Sandford Fleming built the Intercolonial Line (Montreal-Halifax) from 1867 to 1876 and did the Canadian Pacific survey. The firm of Peto Brassey and Betts was one of the chief contractors. For Fleming, see Hugh Maclean, *Man of Steel: The Story of Sir Sandford Fleming* (Toronto: Ryerson Press, 1969); an unpublished doctoral dissertation c. 1972 at the University of Alberta by David Randall Richardson, "The Pacific Cable: 1879–1928" (information from A. A. den Otter, Newfoundland, in a letter to the author, 29 November 1989); John W. Abrams, in *Transactions of the Newcomen Society,* 1977–1978, pp. 133–137.

34. The list is endless. Burton tried to catalog the most prominent examples. The Panamanian line (1850–1855) by the Americans George M. Totten and John C. Trautwine, Sr., and Henry Meigs's work in Chile 1858 were exceptions. Meigs's work in Bolivia and Peru was slightly later.

35. Maximilian I organized a courier network in 1490, three years before he became Holy Roman Emperor. China had an even better system of imperial roads, caravansaries, and mounted messengers (Alain Peyreffite, *L'Empire Immobile* [Paris: Fayard, 1989], pp. 289–291). Guillaume Amontons's optical telegraph was designed in 1690, but France had to wait a century until Claude Chappe installed it (Adley, pp. 300–301). Prussia quickly followed suit (Herbarth, pp. 13–18).

36. Maury Klein traces the invention back to Ørsted's and Ampère's work in the 1820s ("What hath God wrought?" p. 37; also Adley, pp. 303–304, and Window). See G. R. M. Garratt in Singer et al. for Francisco Salvá's work in Barcelona.

37. Joseph Henry in the US and Karl Friedrich Gauss in Prussia made significant developments that influenced the British patents (Maury Klein, "What hath God wrought?" pp. 38–39). Wheatstone held GB patents 7390 12.6.1837, 7614 18.04.1838, 8345 21.01.1840, 9022 07.07.1841, and 10655 06.05.1845. Patents 7390, 8345, and 10655 were also registered under Cooke's name. The tests are mentioned by Window, p. 333.

38. See discussion of "revolution" in Paulinyi, "Revolution and Technology," esp. p. 261.

39. Bidder installed it on the London-Blackwall Railway in 1838 to increase the efficiency of the stationary engine between Fenchurch Street and the Minorities. Stephenson extended an improved, 1839 version to the whole line in 1840. One was installed on the Norfolk Railway. Brunel put up a permanent line between Paddington and West Drayton on the Great Western Railway, extending it to Hanwell in 1839 (Rolt, *Victorian Engineering,* pp. 213–214).

40. Aachen: *Min. Proc. ICE,* vol. 2, 1843, pp. 181–183; Paris-Versailles: Vinchent, p. 257; Window, p. 339, footnote 1. Twenty years later, they were everywhere; R. Stephenson put one up on the Alexandria-Cairo line in 1854 (Landes, *Bankers,* p. 82). By the mid 1860s Belgium, the smallest of the big six in Europe, had 252 offices and a 2,647-kilometer aerial network. Mirroring the confusion in other countries, ninety-seven Belgian stations worked with Morse, while the others used Siemens, the Belgian Lippens system, and the French railways' Bréguet system (Vinchent, pp. 166, 255–257)

41. R. Stephenson, "Presidential Address," pp. 145–146.

42. Ritzaus in Denmark in 1866, Mosse in Berlin, and many others followed the three major agencies. Havas, founded before telegraphy in 1835, became Agence France-Presse in 1945.

43. Revenues in 1856 were £ 3,000 (a 750% increase) and volume was 2,250% larger (R. Stephenson, "Presidential Address," p. 147).

44. The line was built with money appropriated from Congress, an unusual situation in the United States. Morse used the system he had patented the previous year and Ezra Cornell's plow for laying underground cable (Maury Klein, "What hath God wrought?" p. 42).

45. Like the European, the American lines initially used several systems (Bartky, "Adoption of Standard Time," p. 31).

46. See the histories by William Russell and Henry Field.

47. Maury Klein, *Union Pacific,* p. 225. According to another source, the current failed and the final hammer blows were mimicked and passed on by the chief officer of the telegraph office on the Missouri River (Spearman, p. 261).

48. *Min. Proc. ICE,* vol. 11, 1851–52, p. 384. Time and space were coupled by Christiaan Huygens in Holland and Robert Hooke in seventeenth-century Britain when

they used chronometers to compute longitude at sea. The problem of determining longitude had plagued seafaring nations for centuries. Landes describes the long genesis of the problem (*Revolution in Time,* pp. 112, 124–128).

49. Bartky, pp. 31–32. Etienne-Jules Marey's graphic railway timetables of the 1880s were based on Charles Ybry's 1846 patents (GB patent 11,368) (Edward Tufte, *The Visual Display of Quantitative Information* [Cheshire, CT: Graphics Press, 1983], p. 31, and *Envisioning Information* [Cheshire, CT: Graphics Press, 1990], p. 108). Ybry's work, in turn, stemmed from the French graphic tradition of René Descartes and Gaspard Monge.

50. The chess game is mentioned in Monika Wagner, "Wirklichkeitserfahrung und Bilderfahrung. William Turner," in Wagner et al., eds., *Moderne Kunst* (Reinbek, 1991), p. 126, citing the *London Illustrated News,* 12 April 1845, p. 233.

51. The United States Naval Observatory began sending time signals in 1877.

52. Herbert, p. 75. Abbe officially headed the meteorological division of the US Signal Services from 1870 (Bartky, pp. 34–35).

53. When scientists collected data on the explosion of the island Krakatoa near Java and transmitted it to their colleagues throughout the world by telegraph in 1883, it was clear that the earth is one world and that space and time had collapsed, at least in scientific circles (George James Symons, ed., *The Eruption of Krakatoa* . . . [London: Trubner & Co., 1888]). Simultaneous news transmission still amazed people at the beginning of the twentieth century. The American Railway Guild's 1905 banquet in Washington, D.C., concluded with a visit to a display map of the world with bulbs marking the receivers of a midnight telegraph signal. As the signal sped out, lamps marking receivers in the United States, Europe, Africa, and the Philippines lit up within seconds, to the acclaim of the spectators (*Engineering News,* 11 May 1905, p. 489).

54. John F. Stover, "One Gauge: How Hundreds of Incompatible Railroads Became a National System," *American Heritage of Invention and Technology,* vol. 8, no. 3, Winter 1993.

55. Like the British mail coaches before them, trains presumably adjusted their clocks to local time as they passed. Bartky, pp. 27–28.

56. It was only officially adopted in 1880 (Bartky, p. 30, footnote 16). New England adopted railway time in 1849 (ibid, p. 28).

57. Charles F. Dowd proposed hourly zones, apparently unaware that the idea was already in use in Europe (Bartky, p. 32). For a detailed discussion of the adoption of standard time in the United States, see also Carlene Stephens, "'The Most Reliable Time': William Bond, the New England Railroads, and Time Awareness in 19th-Century America," *Technology and Culture,* vol. 30, 1989, pp. 1–24, and Comment and Response to "The Most Reliable Time," *Technology and Culture,* vol. 32, 1991, pp. 185–186.

58. *Min. Proc. ICE,* vol. 4, 1845, pp. 63–77.

59. Bartky, p. 26.

60. Henri Brézol in *La Science Illustrée,* vol. 2, no. 45, 6 October 1888, p. 292. The original reads:

> L'administration des télégraphes, et les compagnies de chemins de fer, faisant abstraction des heures locales, règlent les horloges de leurs stations et de leurs bureaux sur l'heure en temps moyen de l'Observatoire de Paris, que les bureaux télégraphiques reçoivent chaque matin. Les horloges extérieures des gares de chemins de fer indiquent cette heure exacte, mais les horloges intérieures qui règlent les mouvements des trains ont un retard de cinq minutes; l'heure des chemins de fer n'est donc pas absoluement l'heure de Paris. Quant aux horloges des édifices publics, elles marquent généralement l'heure locale. . . . Les télégraphes et les chemins de fer ont donc amené en France un commencement d'unification d'heure, que le colonel Laussedat, directeur du Conservatoire des Arts et Métiers, propose de compléter. Il demande, en effet, qu'à partir du 1er mai 1889, date de l'ouverture de l'Exposition, toutes les horloges des édifices publics et des gares de chemins de fer adoptent l'heure de Paris, qui deviendrait ainsi l'heure nationale. . . .

61. Bartky, p. 35, footnote 35.

62. East-west–oriented countries, like Bavaria and the extended Austro-Hungarian Empire, first stuck to a combination of sun time and political time by adopting two zones. Bavaria used Munich and Ludwigshafen (Pfalz), Austria-Hungary used Prague and Pesth. Sweden and Japan, both north-south–oriented countries, opted for meridians 15° and 135° east of Greenwich. Italy decreed Roman time the standard for the national railway system and used the twenty-four-hour clock it had pioneered in 1850. Russia, which was to begin building the trans-Siberian railway in 1891, organized its immense expanse into eight time zones.

63. The American delegate to the congress, railway engineer William F. Allen, perceived advantages for American commerce too, and he successfully lobbied other industrialized nations to adopt the system.

64. The meter was proposed as the unit of length in 1790 and legally adopted in France in 1793. But popular acceptance was slow. The government published "mesures transitoires" in 1812 and finally abolished alternate systems in 1837.

65. Heated cesium oscillates 9,192,631,770 times in 1/299,792,458 sec.

66. This development is related to Bishop George Berkeley's thinking on existence and causality, and it has an older, even more profound tradition in the Advaita Vedanta school of Hindu philosophy.

67. The travel distance from London to Hong Kong would be reduced by 32 percent from 27,000 to 18,500 kilometers, to Calcutta by 35 percent from 23,000 to 15,000 kilometers, to Karachi by 43 percent from 21,000 to 12,000 kilometers, and to Bombay by 45 percent from 21,000 to 11,500 kilometers.

68. The travel distance from London, Bristol, Southampton, or the Clyde to Tokyo would be reduced by 42 percent from 11,520 to 6,720 kilometers; from Marseilles, Calais, Dieppe, or Bordeaux to Valparaiso by 32 percent from 7,040 to 4,800 kilometers; from France and Britain to San Francisco by 51 percent from 10,400 to 5,120 kilometers; from New York to San Francisco by 67 percent from 8,560 to 2,800 kilometers (A. Faure, in *Mém. et Compte-Rendu,* 1859, p. 65; also Emory R. Johnson in *Transactions,* vol. 1, pp. 31–65).

69. Zenker, p. 41.

70. This was the period in which Sir Edward James Reed was putting the finishing touches on his basic manual, *Shipbuilding in Iron and Steel* (London: Murray, 1869), which laid the foundation for modern iron ship construction.

71. Flachat, "Mémoire sur les travaux," p. 484.

72. The British Hydrographic Office published sea charts for the merchant marine in 1795. Throughout the course of the nineteenth century it coordinated its efforts with other countries'. Matthew Fontaine Maury, Superintendent of Charts and Instruments of the United States Navy, improved the charts with his standard work on winds and currents in 1855 (*Sailing Directions from Sea to Sandy Hook* [Philadelphia: Biddle, 1855]). Maury's work helped sharpen the competition between steam and sail shipping and draw it out over many more years.

73. The first tea transport on the clipper *Orient* entered London in 1850 after a trip of only ninety-seven days from Hong Kong. The botanist Robert Fortune made several trips to China during the Taiping rebellion of the mid-1840s, where he examined cotton, tea, and silk plantations and discovered new plants. His 1847 report (*Three Year's Wanderings in the Northern Provinces of China* . . . [London: J. Murray, 1847]) was translated into French (1853) and German (1854). He reported on tea to the British government in 1851 and to the British East India Company, which had commissioned him to smuggle tea plants out of the country (*Report upon the Tea Plantations in the North-Western Provinces* . . . [London: Foreign Office, 1851]; *A Journey to the Tea Countries of China* . . . [London: J. Murray, 1852]). China guarded its monopoly on the tea industry, and laws forbade the export of tea plants on pain of death. The other tea-producing nation, Japan, was still isolated and exported nothing. Fortune succeeded in bringing plants and detailed knowledge of the varieties, their cultivation, and the manufacture of tea to the East India Company's plantations in Assam in the Himalayan foothills. The adventure excited the fantasy of Europe, although in fact the tea industry had already existed in India on a modest scale. With a high-quality tea industry now securely in British colonial hands, financial pressure was increased to get the product to London quickly (D. W. H. Townsend, "Before the Tea Bag," *Country Life,* London, 02 October 1975, pp. 876–877).

74. He did this in 1840 by pitting two differently equipped but otherwise identical ships against each other in a tug-of-war (Rennie, pp. 97–103).

75. Landes, *Unbound Prometheus,* p. 153.

76. R. Stephenson, "Presidential Address," p. 150.

77. Ibid., p. 151.

78. Smiles, *Lives of the Engineers,* vol. 3, pp. xxviii-xxix. Thomas Brassey, *On Work and Wages,* p. 60, documents the rise in wages through railway construction.

79. Almost two decades of searching have not yielded an account of the building process, not even in that ultimate purveyor of anecdote, the *Illustrated London News.*

80. Zenker thought the canal would create a new balance in which the European northwest would trade more with North America and the south more with the Orient. Landlocked Central Europe would play a mediating role between the two. However, railway tariffs were ten times higher in the German Tariff Union, the Zollverein, than the cost of the longer sea route, while Italian and Austrian railway costs were double the German. Planners hoped that the Swiss Gotthard Tunnel would put an end to the Austrian Brenner and Semmering monopoly and lead to lower tariffs (Zenker, pp. 60–61, 64).

81. Petitti, introductory chapter, pp. 11–40.

82. Ibid, pp. 20–33 and map.

83. The Crimean War (1854–1856) was relatively early and peripheral to European trade routes. Italy's unification (1859–1870) affected commerce positively, since it did away with many borders and tariffs. Poland rose against Russia in 1863, Germany and Austria attacked Denmark in 1864, and Germany and Italy then turned on Austria in 1866, while Spain revolted against its monarchy in 1868 and 1869. Germany and France fought in 1870 and 1871. Colonial wars had an influence too. In the East there were continual wars in China between 1850 and 1864 and then again in 1870, which involved British, French, and US troops. The British had a mutiny in India in 1857, the French a war in Indochina in 1862, the Spanish a revolt in Cuba in 1868, and there were other conflicts in Latin America and Africa.

84. Petitti, introductory chapter, pp. 11–40.

85. Many projects are documented by Louis Figuier in *L'Année scientifique et industrielle,* 1856–1914.

86. There were exceptions like the highly rationalized French and Venetian armament industries, and improved steam engines gradually did speed up the manufacturing process, but qualitative improvements through rationalization were few and far between (Barry Russell, p. 33, citing Lewis Mumford's *The Pentagon of Power;* and Claude S. George Jr., *The History of Management Thought* [Englewood Cliffs, NJ: Prentice-Hall, 1968], pp. 33–39, citing F. C. Lane; *Venetian Ships and Shipbuilders of the Renaissance*).

87. Zenker, p. 53.

88. The same is now hoped from the reorganization of Eastern Europe and the former Soviet Union and a possible opening of China through Hong Kong in 1997.

89. The idea of "progress" seems to be akin to the Renaissance concept of "new" as discussed by George Basalla in *The Evolution of Technology* (Cambridge: Cambridge University Press, 1988), p. 131. Basalla, in fact, suggests that the concept of "new" lies at

the origin of the idea of progress, but he stops short of examining the development of its meaning. In *The Idea of Progress* (1920, rpt. New York: Dover, 1987), pp. 326–327, John Bagnell Bury traced the origins of the concept to the Enlightenment. He focused on philosophical and social reformatory theory and neglected the idea's influence on technology, as was usual at the time.

90. In *Mechanization Takes Command* Sigfried Giedion discussed how it changed meaning (pp. 714–723). The background for his concern was the conflict between mechanization and progress that appeared so menacing after World War II. L. T. C. Rolt documented how the thinking of Alfred Lord Tennyson and H. G. Wells changed (*Victorian Engineering*, 1974 ed., p. 166).

91. Turgot, in Pierre-Samuel Dupont de Nemours, *Oeuvres de Mr. Turgot, Ministre d'État . . . ,* vol. 2 (Paris: Delana, 1808), p. 212, "Plan des Discours sur l'histoire universelle. Idée de l'Introduction": "le genre-humain toujours le même dans ces bouleversemens, comme l'eau de la mer dans les tempêtes, et marchant toujours à sa perfection." Quoted, with minor changes, in Giedion, *Mechanization*, p. 716.

92. Gibbon proposed that "All that is human must retrograde if it do not advance" (Edward Gibbon, *The History of the Decline and Fall of the Roman Empire* [London: Strahan & Cadell, 1776], vol. 6, chapter 71, p. 622); Browning declared, "For all these things tend upward—progress is / The law of life; man is not man as yet" (Robert Browning, *Paracelsus* [London: Wilson, 1835], act 5, p. 192); von Ranke wrote, "Der Fortschritt ist wie ein Strom, der sich auf seine eigene Weise den Weg bahnt."

93. Bury, *Idea of Progress,* chapter 13.

94. Condorcet, as quoted on the title page of *Mechanics' Magazine,* vol. 8, 1828.

95. Bury, *Idea of Progress,* p. 228; see also footnote for Robert Wallace's prior observations in 1756.

96. The American abolitionist Wendell Phillips in "Freedom for Women," speech at the convention held at Worcester MA, October 15–16, 1851. *Women's rights tracts* no. 2, p. 3.

97. Heinrich Heine, *Reisebilder* (Hamburg: Hoffmann und Campe (2nd. ed.), 1830), chapter 30: "Aber ach! jeder Zoll, den die Menschheit weiter rückt, kostet Ströme Blutes"; Proudhon, "Philosophie du Progrès" (Brussels: Lebègue, 1853). The British historian Henry Thomas Buckle was perhaps the least emotional about it. He downplayed the role of the forces of nature and exalted human character as the true motor of progress: "The only progress which is really effective depends not on the bounty of nature, but upon the energy of man" (*History of Civilization in England* [London: Parker, 1857–1861], vol. 1, chapter 2, paragraph 8).

98. For Tennyson see Rolt, *Victorian Engineering;* for Browning see note 92 above, and this 1864 poem: "Finds progress, man's distinctive mark alone, / Not God's, and not the beasts': God is, they are: / Man partly is, and wholly hopes to be" ("A Death in the Desert," in *Dramatis Personae* [Boston: Houghton Mifflin, 1886], p. 115).

99. Original: "Es kann ein heilbringender Fortschritt nur gedacht werden, wenn man nach besonnener und ruhiger Prüfung der Zeitlage die wirklichen Bedürfnisse zu befriedigen und die lebensfähigen Elemente in den bestehenden Einrichtungen zu benutzen weiss."

100. Edouard-René Lefèbvre de Laboulaye, *Discours populaire* (Paris: Charpentier, 1869) p. 36. Quoted in Trachtenberg, p. 32.

101. For the genesis of weekly journals in Britain, see Morison, *The English Newspaper,* pp. 81–118.

102. As in this statement: "whatever barriers Nature opposed, Science has entirely surmounted." Robert Stephenson, "Presidential Address," p. 32. Quoted in Bradshaw, "Stephenson, De Lesseps, and the Suez Canal," p. 241.

103. Darwin, *On the Origin of Species by Means of Natural Selection* (London: Murray, 1859) chapter 14, pp. 489–490. See also Collins, *Changing Ideals,* p. 149, which traces evolutionary thought back to Buffon's *Histoire Naturelle* of 1749.

104. William Edward Hartpole Lecky, *History of European Morals from Augustus to Charlemagne* (London: Longmans, Green, 1869), vol. 1.

105. Discussed by Dreicer (see above, preface, note 3).

106. For example: Rennie, p. 81; M. E. Perrot, *Des chemins de fer belges,* quoted in Petitti, pp. 34–35, footnote 2.

107. *Min. Proc. ICE,* vol. 5, 1846, pp. 121–122.

108. Thomas Huxley, essay 1888: "The Struggle for Existence in Human Society."

109. *The Oxford English Dictionary* documents the first use of the term in 1923 in conjunction with a radio circuit (1971 ed., supplement, p. 3963).

110. "Der Weg zu Vollkommenheit und zu jedem Fortschritt ist fortwährende Selbstkritik."

111. The French engineer and social philosopher Georges Sorel expressed his suspicions in *Illusions du Progrès* (Paris: Rivière, 1900). See also his 1908 *Réflexions sur la violence,* cited in Giedion, *Mechanization,* p. 715.

112. Hermann Alexander Keyserling, *Das Reisebuch eines Philosophen* (Munich: Duncker & Humblot, 1919), chap. 8: Original text: "Die Welt wird mit jedem Tage ärger: Dass dies der eigentliche Sinn des Fortschritts ist, illustriert mit erschreckender Deutlichkeit Amerika, weil hier der Weisse am stärksten im Sinne des Zweckmenschen typisiert erscheint."

113. See chapter 6.

114. G. K. Chesterton wrote, "The fatal metaphor of progress, which means leaving things behind us, has utterly obscured the real idea of growth, which means leaving

things inside us" "The Romance of Rhyme," in *Fancies versus Fads* [London: Methuen, 1923], p. 3. Chesterton was wrong when he suggested that "growth" had heretofore been the main concern of progress. It had been "development," and he reformed the meaning so as to make it a new, quantitatively measurable concept.

115. Hanns Henny Jahn is credited with the statement that "Der Fortschritt ist alles in allem ein Fortschreiten hin zur Kollektivisierung, zum Konformismus, zum Auslöschen des Individuums gleichermassen in den Reichen des Ostens und des Westens."

116. See Fritz Lang's 1926 film *Metropolis* or Aldous Huxley's *Brave New World* (London: Chatto & Windus, 1932).

117. This attitude permeates José Ortega y Gassett's *La Rebelión de las Masas* (Madrid: Reviste de Occidente, 1929). See also Norbert Wiener, *The Human Use of Human Beings: Cybernetics and Society,* 2nd ed. (Boston: Houghton Mifflin, 1954), p. 2: "Progress imposes not only new possibilities for the future but new restrictions." See also the whole of his chapter "Progress and Entropy."

2   Structural Materials, Methods, and Systems: The Prerequisites of Change

1. Transportation made the price a little higher in Chicago—$64 a ton in 1892 and $30 in 1894—but the tendency to drop was clear everywhere (Purdy, p. 49); see also *Engineering News Record,* fiftieth anniversary number, 17 April 1924, plate 4 (following p. 686), for the development of material prices between 1874 and 1924, which shows more or less stable steel prices without the inclusion of transportation costs until 1914, when the war increased all prices dramatically.

2. Not considering inflation. Figuier, *L'Année scientifique,* vol. 9, pp. 466–469.

3. The James and Skinner theory of combined labor scarcity and raw material abundance is borne out in the building industry (John A. James and Jonathan S. Skinner: "The Resolution of the Labor-Scarcity Paradox," *Jnl. of Economic History,* vol. no. 3, September 1985, p. 534, footnote 42, and pp. 513–514).

4. Jacques-Germain Soufflot and his successor Maximilien Brébion covered a staircase in the Louvre with a wrought-iron roof in 1779–1781. Victor Louis built a similar roof over the Théâtre Royal in 1790, and an iron curtain was installed as fire protection in a theater in 1820 (Bannister, pp. 233–234).

5. Braidwood 1849, p. 142, citing the *Seventh Report of the British Association,* vol. 6, 1837, p. 409. Fairbairn further discussed the problem in his article in *Min. Proc. ICE,* vol. 6, 1847, although some of the discussion by others confused the two issues of incombustibility and fireproofing. Hodgkinson, 1846, p. 378, art. 85, cited by himself in *Min. Proc. ICE,* vol. 8, 1849, footnote p. 151. Iron is incombustible under normal conditions and does not melt at temperatures normally encountered in a conflagration. But it loses its loadbearing capacity rapidly at temperatures of only a few hundred degrees above normal unless it is protected by insulation. It "goes soft," analogously to spaghetti when it becomes wet.

6. Session of 26 September 1778. *Phil. Trans. Roy. Soc.* 1778, p. 884, cited by Piper in *Min. Proc. ICE,* vol. 8, 1849, p. 151; Aubrey Newman, *The Stanhopes of Chevening* London: Macmillan St. Martin's Press, 1969), pp. 171–172.

7. Thomas Le Seur, François Jacquier, Ruggiero Giuseppe Boscovich, *Parere de tre mattematici sopra i danni che si sono trovati nella Cupola di S. Pietro sul fine dell'Anno 1742: dato per ordine di nostro signore Papa Benedetto XIV* (Rome, 1743); Giovanni Poleni, *Memorie istoriche della gran cupola del Tempio Vaticano, e de danni di essa, e de ristoramenti loro: divise in libri cinque.* (Padua, 1748); Euler, "Sur la force des colonnes," *Mémoires de l'Académie royale des sciences et Belles lettres* (Berlin, 1757), vol. 13, p. 252; Coulomb, "Essai sur une application des règles de maximis & minimis à quelques problèmes de statique, relatifs à l'architecture," *Mémoires de Mathématique & de Physique, présentés à l'Académie Royale des Sciences par divers Savans, & lues dans ses Assemblées* (Paris, 1776), vol. 7, 1773, pp. 343–382.

8. *Min. Proc. ICE,* vol. 8, 1849, p. 157.

9. Ibid., pp. 147, 159–160. May also mentioned brick cladding in his discussion of Barrett's paper in *Min. Proc. ICE,* vol. 12, 1853, pp. 266–267.

10. Braidwood, referring to safes built by Chubb, Marr, and Milner in *Min. Proc. ICE,* vol. 8, 1849, p. 147; also John Chubb's letter on pp. 154–155 citing American examples using gypsum.

11. Albert Einstein popularized the idea of thought experiments *(Gedankenexperimente)* in physics. They are a preparatory phase for model simulation or other forms of experimentation and have become part of the accepted repertory of scientific method. They could easily be applied to design and construction.

12. *Min. Proc. ICE,* vol. 8, 1849, p. 143.

13. Sheahan and Upton, pp. 120–121.

14. *Min. Proc. ICE,* vol. 5, 1846, pp. 56–57; Jennifer Tann has looked at some facets of the issue, while most concentrate solely on the structural frame.

15. The earliest known sprinkler system was installed in a mill at Oldham (Bateman in *Min. Proc. ICE,* vol. 8, 1849, p. 159; Fairbairn, *Life,* pp. 186–187). Engineers proposed many fire-protective ideas that were only implemented much later, like reinforced concrete floors; brick-clad, water-filled iron columns that cooled and could be used as conduits for fire-fighting, or brick fire walls with draft-tight, iron fire doors (Edington in the discussion of Barrett's paper in *Min. Proc. ICE,* vol. 12, 1853, p. 269).

16. Books have been written on the evolution of the iron industry and the development of iron structure, but no one has discussed what the new material changed conceptually in building methods and processes. Bannister, Giedion (*Bauen in Frankreich*), Shand, and Johnson and Skempton are the most prominent. Elliott gives a good abstract of the development (pp. 68–108).

17. Such forms were not skiamorphs or remnants of former structural meaning in the sense in which archaeologists use the term. Skiamorphs imitate detail forms, especially connections in a new material, but with alienated function. In iron construction, both the forms and their function were adopted from timber construction.

18. There were several prior, unsuccessful attempts to build cast-iron bridges in France and Britain, but wrought-iron suspension bridges had been in use in the Chinese sphere of influence since the first century A.D., and at least one in northern England (Peters, *Transitions,* pp. 16–27).

19. Collins, *Changing Ideals,* p. 155.

20. Based on Thomas Paine's design; see John G. James in *Newcomen Transactions,* vols. 50, 1978–79, pp. 55–72, and 59, 1987–88, pp. 189–221.

21. Some of Roussel's work, including good details of the structure of the Halle aux Blés, is to be found in the *Allgemeine Bauzeitung* of Vienna, 1837 (vol. 2), and 1838 (vol. 3). It is not clear whether this was Simon Roussel or another.

22. Charles Taylor, pp. 885–886 and pls. 17–18.

23. Railway rails were rolled in the 1760s. By 1820 the Bedlington Iron Works near Durham were rolling fifteen-foot lengths (John Birkenshaw, GB patent 4503, 23.10.1820; Elton, *Railways,* no. 88). They were used as deck beams in the ship *Aaron Manby* built by the Horsley Iron Works at Tipton in 1821 (*Concise history of rolled beams,* in Jewett; Singer, vol. 4; Tipton mentioned in Smiles, *Industrial Biography,* p. 322). Deck beams had small, bulbous top flanges and enlarged bottom ones like rails or the many forms of cast-iron beams whose bottom flanges compensated for the low tensile strength of that material.

24. See later under concrete for Fox and Barrett's system.

25. Turner 1850, p. 205, citing *London Journal,* vol. 30, 1847, footnote p. 428. The first rolled I-joists may have been manufactured for a floor in Paris in 1845, although most sources state 1846–1849 (Steiner, chap. 4, footnote 29, citing *Le Propagateur des travaux en fer,* vol. 1, 1867, p. 79; Diestelkamp, p. 14 and footnote 74). Rolled I-beams, H-columns, and built-up forms came to be used on wrought-iron lattice bridges all over Europe. The I-beam was introduced into the US around 1855 (*The Architectural Record,* vol. 25, no. 5, May 1909, p. 375). Rolled members were used everywhere, e.g.: Britannia and Conway bridges by Fairbairn and Robert Stephenson, 1846–1850, E. Gouin et Cie.'s bridge at Clichy on the Paris-Saint-Germain railway in 1852, and as stiffening ribs in the construction of the compressed-air caissons at Kehl in 1857 (*Mém. et Compte-Rendu,* 1861, p. 406). The contractors of the Clichy Bridge, Borel Lavalley et Cie. later built the Suez Canal (Mathieu and Lavalley, pp. 137, 153). Lavalley presented the second part of the paper on 18 June 1852 (discussion on p. 382); see also Forey. For years the Institution of Civil Engineers held exhaustive discussions of the relative roles of flange and web in loadbearing and their implications for beam form in bridge design and construction (Fairbairn in *Min. Proc. ICE,* vol. 9, 1850, pp. 233–287; and especially James Barton in *Min. Proc. ICE,* vol. 14, 1855, pp. 443–490).

26. See chapter 6 for Turner's structures. The beams he used were patented by James Kennedy and Thomas Vernon in Liverpool, GB patent 10143, 15.04.1844 (cit. in Diestelkamp, p. 13).

27. *Useful Information for Engineers,* 2nd. series, 1860, p. 225, cit. in Smiles, 1876, pp. 396–397; *Min. Proc. ICE,* vol. 2, 1843, pp. 125–126; John Farey's comments to Braidwood in *Min. Proc. ICE,* vol. 8, 1849, p. 150; Fairbairn, *Life,* pp. 123–129 (Johann Caspar Escher erroneously referred to as "G. Escher"), 168–176, 184–188.

28. Braithwaite, 1854, p. 466; ref. on p. 467 to Rankine's article "On the Causes of the Unexpected Breakage of the Journals of Railway Axles" in *Min. Proc. ICE,* vol. 2, 1843, p. 105, and Fairbairn's comment, p. 469.

29. Fairbairn suggested increasing the standard safety factor of three to six (*Min. Proc. ICE,* vol. 13, 1854, p. 470).

30. Koerte, pp. 12–16. The Tay collapse directly influenced the design of the 1890 Forth Bridge, the world's first large all-steel bridge, by Sir John Fowler and Sir Benjamin Baker.

31. Cit. in Rosenberg, *The American System,* p. 343, quoted in James and Skinner, "The Resolution of the Labor-Scarcity Paradox," p. 524; see also Rosenberg in Hindle, pp. 49–51. Whitworth must have visited New York twice, once in 1852 (cf. *Transactions of ICE,* 1851–1852, p. 384) and again in 1854.

32. Mansfield, in *Proceedings of Wood Symposium,* pp. 70, 71, 75, 76.

33. See the discussion of reinforced concrete, below. Dreicer is currently examining Town's development and its ramifications in cross-cultural engineering development.

34. Peters, "An American Culture."

35. The principle is analogous to the iterative way a computer works. Computers originated in Europe. The Colossus was the first computer in Britain. It was used for code cracking in 1932. Konrad Zuse's machines in wartime Germany are also very early computers, but the concept and the use of computers proliferated first in the United States, probably for precisely these cultural reasons.

36. Rendel, p. 185.

37. See chapter 6, section "Hybrid Types: The American Light-Wood Frame."

38. Herbert, pp. 4–5, 8, 23.

39. Peters, *Transitions in Engineering,* pp. 50–54; Peters, "An American Culture of Construction."

40. In 1831 Jean-Robert Bréant and A. Payne invented a pneumatic method for impregnating wood. They placed lumber in closed metal containers, evacuated the air to empty the capillaries, and injected fluids under pressure. The method, known as "Paynizing," came to be the basis for later developments like "Kyanizing" (John Howard Kyan: GB patents 6253, 31.03.1832; 6309, 22.09,1832; 7001, 11.02,1836), Joshua John Lloyd Margary's patent (GB patent 7511, 19.12.1837), or "Bethellizing," now known as creosoting (John Bethell: GB patent 7731, 11.07.1838). (Burt, pp. 206–243, also commented on by Goschler and Schweitzer in 1852; Molinos in 1853.)

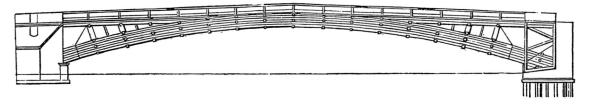

166.
Karl Friedrich von Wiebeking built the Regnitz Bridge at Bamberg using laminated soft-wood arches in 1809. He placed the wood too close to the waterline and the bridge rotted quickly, but others copied his system with more success. (Cresy, 1847, p. 1381.)

41. Later Parisian examples were the roofs of the Halle aux Blés by Jean-B. Legrand and Jacques Molinos (1780), the Halle aux Draps (1810), and the dome of the Petites-Ecuries in Versailles (Vallot, in *Annales des Ponts et Chaussées,* vol. 1, 1831, p. 407). In 1809 Ritter Karl Friedrich von Wiebeking used a similar method to build his short-lived Regnitz bridge in Bamberg, and a French engineer named de Saint-Far proposed it for an arch over the Rhine at Mainz in 1811. Saint-Far's flat-arch design used long boards bolted between radial pairs of struts. The Mainz building authorities thought the idea too risky, and the model was placed in the halls of the École des Ponts et Chaussées in Paris, where students passed it daily. Armand-Rose Emy, a graduate of the school, built two halls using an almost identical system in 1825 and 1826 in Marac (near Bayonne) and Livorno (Armand-Rose Emy, *Traité de l'art de la charpenterie,* 2 vols. and atlas [Paris: Carilian-Goeury, 1837]). A Prussian example had a single thick beam, sawn partway into layers, bent and clamped, avoiding the need to drill bolt holes (R. T. Nelson, in *Papers on Subjects Connected with the Duties of the Corps of Royal Engineers*); also L. G. Booth, "The Development of Laminated Timber Arch Structures in Bavaria, France and England in the Nineteenth Century," *Jnl. of the Inst. of Wood Science,* vol. 7, 1971, pp. 3–16.

42. A shipwright named John Cumberland patented it for marine construction in Britain in 1720 (GB patent 427, 14.04.1720), while John Vidler in England (GB patent 2020, 05.11.1794) and an Austrian wheelwright named Melchior Fink independently developed it (1810 with an Austrian patent in 1821) for making wheel rims.

43. Fourteen as opposed to forty-four cords for a small brig (*Annales des Ponts et Chaussées,* vol. 1, 1831).

44. François-Joual Eustache, *Annales des Ponts et Chaussées,* vol. 1, 1831, pp. 400ff.

45. *Min. Proc. ICE,* vol. 8, 1849, pp. 282–286.

46. Albrecht Bangert *Thonet-Möbel. Die Geschichte einer grossen Erfindung . . .* (Munich: Heyne Verlag, 1979), pp. 43, 48–51. Bangert states that Thonet patented his process in England, Belgium, and France. Woodcroft does not list either Thonet or his partner Van Meerten.

47. John K. Mayo's 1865 and 1868 US patents showed sewing machine and furniture makers how to use a combination of plywood and bentwood techniques (Perry, in *Proceedings of Wood Symposium,* pp. 57–58).

48. Gehri, p. 808, citing L. G. Booth, "Laminated Timber Arch Railway Bridges in England and Scotland," *Transactions of the Newcomen Society,* vol. 44, 1971, pp. 1–23; and Culmann, "Bau der hölzernen Brücken." The first successful structural glue lamination was patented by the German engineer Otto Hetzer in 1906 (DR patent 197773

22.06.1906); Kühne, pp. 2–3; also L. G. Booth, "Henry Fuller's Glued Laminated Timber Roof for Rusholme Road Congregational Sunday School and Other Early Timber Roofs," *Construction History,* vol. 10, 1994, pp. 29–45.

49. GB patents 1038, 26.11.1791; 1951, 23.04.1793; and 2035, 24.01.1795. For Bentham's popularity and influence, see Nicholson, vol. 2, p. 303; Tomlinson, vol. 2, p. 423. The 1791 machine was a slow, reciprocating plane. Most early planes were like Bentham's first, a modest-quality reciprocating machine, but one by Leonard Hatton milled boards and fluted columns earlier (GB patent 1125, 21.05.1776).

50. GB patent 2652, 30.10.1802. Bentham was then inspector general of naval works.

51. Tomlinson, vol. 2, p. 423, mentions 28 blades per disk, whereas the *Buch der Erfindungen,* vol. 6, p. 234, states that there were 32 and two lateral ones. James Bevans improved the Bramah patent: GB patent 2742, 19.11.1803 (Nicholson, vol. 2, p. 304). This was a reciprocating plane, but it had a better blade arrangement for cutting molding; Tomlinson, vol. 2, p. 424. There were others: William Hickling Burnett (GB patents 7926, 08.01.1839, and 8551, 24.06.1840). Roguin had built a milling plane for flooring in Paris in 1817. Once the mechanical principles of milling were established and the complexities solved, detail improvements followed in rapid succession, enhancing precision and reliability and reducing wear. In Paris, Marechal and Godeau used a corkscrew-shaped cutter similar to that of the contemporary lawnmower which gave a more even wear on the machine and the blades (Darmstaedter). Self-sharpening cutters improved productivity, and speeds of up to 1,000 rpm improved precision.

52. See chapter 6 for Marc Brunel's assembly lines.

53. Bentham's first plane had a jiglike arrangement that stopped the plane at a desired board thickness, and it could also plane wedge-shaped pieces. Jigs guide machines precisely through complex, three-dimensional trajectories. See Tomlinson on the origin of the jig, quoting Robert Willis, probably from *Principles of Mechanism,* 1841.

54. 1820: Battison, in Post, p. 49, but he provides no detailed sources of information; K. R. Gilbert, in Singer, vol. 4, p. 435; Rosenberg, in Hindle, pp. 48–49.

55. They only began to import British machines with fixed cutting heads around 1850.

56. Laboulaye, vol. 2, "Raboter, machine à."

57. Based on his four patents: GB patents 6850, 11.06.1835; 7332, 28.03.1837; 7441, 05.10.1837; and 8188, 07.08.1839.

58. In spite of Whitworth's machine there were no good English metalworking planes or mortising machines. So machinery had to be imported from American manufacturers to the Canada Works in London for making parts for the Victoria Bridge over the St. Lawrence River in Montreal on the Grand Trunk Railway (Helps, p. 191; Brassey, pp. 135–136). See also Ferguson, *Early Eng. Reminiscences,* p. 116.

59. *Das neue Buch der Erfindungen,* vol. 6, p. 29. Not in Darmstaedter or van Dyck. Murray and Fox, both 1814, and Roberts, 1817, in Smiles, *Industrial Biography,* pp. 314–320. By 1853 iron planes were common in the United States and of much better quality than in Britain (Brassey, pp. 135–136). Still, woodworking machinery was generally better in the US and ironworking machinery in Britain (Brassey, p. 139).

60. His original system was based on previous work by Walter Taylor, of Fox and Taylor, blockmakers to the navy in Southampton (Clements, pp. 25, 34).

61. *Crystal Palace and Its Contents,* pp. 81–82; *Official Descriptive and Illustrated Catalogue,* vol. 2, pp. 774–775.

62. GB patents 9962, 25.11.1843; 10517, 10.02.1845; and 12073, 23.02.1848.

63. *Min. Proc. ICE,* vol. 4, 1845, pp. 250–251; GB patent 10538, 03.03.1845.

64. GB patent 10523, 17.02.1845, followed by an improved version, patent 11564, 08.02.1847; *Report of the Juries,* p. 551, for an "oak screen, &c, carved by machinery."

65. By 1867, Jordan-type machines were produced in France and Spain (Tresca, in *Mém. et Compte-Rendu,* 1867, pp. 454–455).

66. See also Cox's machine in ibid., p. 454.

67. Wornum, pp. xi***, and xvi***, in *The Art Journal Illustrated Catalogue* (London: George Virtue, 1851).

68. In both *Seven Lamps* and *Stones;* also his "The OPENING of the CRYSTAL PALACE, considered in some of its Relations to the Prospects of Art," advertised at the end of *Seven Lamps.*

69. The eighth-century B.C. Shang dynasty city wall and several buildings in the central Chinese city of Zhangzhou are made of loess tamped in forms (information from Dr. Puay-Peng Ho, Chinese University of Hong Kong). Later versions of the material contained pebbles or seashells. The method was expanded and refined in the twelfth to seventeenth centuries for fortified Hakka villages of Quandong (Canton) and Fujien Provinces with their massive perimeter walls cast in clay tamped in layers with ground sea shells or rice paste added (information from Frank Chi-Hsien Sun, Chinese University of Hong Kong). Needham mentions a material containing lime that was used in foundations (vol. 4.3, pp. 38–40). He was only able to identify nonhydraulic materials but presumed (without substantiation as yet) that hydraulic concrete too was known in China (vol. 1, p. 83). Chinese builders used other concreting methods unknown in Western construction, such as a "living" mortar method, in which oysters were planted on submerged, drywalled bridge piers where their lime-rich excreta effectively cemented the masonry (Huan-Cheng Tang, *Ancient Chinese Bridges* [Beijing, 1958; 2nd ed. 1987, expanded with abridged Engl. text], p. 263). Analogously, Reid mentions coral as a model for cement makers in the West (p. 30).

70. He found the material in Carthaginian watchtowers in Spain and North Africa and called it *formaceus paries.* Pliny credited two Athenian brothers, Eurialus and Hyperbius, with its invention (Caius Plinius Secundus, *Naturalis historia sive historia mundi, libri 37* [London: Heinemann, 1952], book 35, chap. 48, Rakham's translation, p.

385; and Cody, footnote p. 13). Bosc quotes from book 35, chap. 14; also book 7, chap. 57. Vitruvius (*Vitruvius: The Ten Books on Architecture,* trans. M. H. Morgan [Cambridge: Harvard University Press, 1914]) called the conglomerate *signinum* (book 8, chap. 7; see Michaelis, p. 283), and he called it by the Greek term *emplekton* when it was used as fill behind walls (book 2, chap. 8, p. 52). Our *cement* derives from a mistranslation of Pliny's use of *caementum* by Loriot in 1774 (Michaelis, footnote 2 p. 60).

71. Vitruvius described the material in book 2, chap. 6. Michaelis went to great lengths to analyze the various Vitruvian cements and their components, footnote pp. 3–8 and p. 11.

72. According to Vicat, Roman builders used local variants of pozzolana (1840, footnote p. 90, cit. in Michaelis, footnote 1 p. 21). Cresy claimed to have found remains of artificial Roman "water cement" in Britain (p. 273). But since pozzolana, trass, and slaked lime mortar all occasionally contain carbonized organic traces, he may have been mistaken (Michaelis, p. 15). Trass was exported through Dutch ports in the seventeenth century and competed with pozzolana in price in northern Europe until the end of the eighteenth century. Some sources state that it was rediscovered by a Dutch miller named van Santen who built a trass mill in 1682 (Michaelis, pp. 12–13; Möll in *Caementum,* vol. 1, pp. 32–33; Darmstaedter gives 1684). Santorini earth, the third commercially popular natural hydraulic cement, was only discovered in the nineteenth century on the Greek island Santorini, ancient Thera.

73. The cathedral foundations at Salisbury and the foundation of one of the Strasbourg towers are hydraulic concrete (the latter discovered by the contractor Ed. Züblin & Cie. in 1916). Part of Kendall Castle in Britain is concrete, as are other castles in Germany, the gates of the Alhambra, the watchtower above the Generaliffe Gardens, and the fortifications of Carmona (Engel, p. 3, and my own observation in Spain).

74. Aside from Pliny and Vitruvius, the Persian Rashid al-Din Fadlullah (al-Hamadani) described it in Jami al-Taqwarikh 1307 (Needham, vol. 4.3, p. 38); the sixteenth-century *Priegnitzer Chronik* mentioned concrete (Engel 1856, addendum, footnote p. 2); and Alberti, Scamozzi, and Delorme mentioned pozzolana mortar.

75. Rondelet knew Cointereaux's publications but gave him no credit, although each apparently privately recognized the contributions of the other.

76. C. H. Rydin, a Swedish contractor from Borås (a town between Göteborg and Jönköping), patented the Amalfi method between 1828 and 1834, by which stone was placed in a formwork and mortar poured in to fill the voids. After Higgins and Smeaton, J. T. Smith's translation of Vicat appeared in English in 1837, Pasley in 1838, Joseph Gilbert Totten's compilation in 1842 (the first in the US), Quincy Adams Gillmore in 1863, and Henry Reid in 1869. In Germany, F. Krause and Friedrich Engel both published in 1851. The latter included a translation of Rydin's Swedish publication of 1834.

77. Christopher Wren (1675–1747), *Parentalia, or, Memoirs of the family of the Wrens* . . . (London: T. Osborn and R. Dodsley, 1750; also 1970 reprint). This is Christopher Wren the younger's account of his family and his uncle's works. A monk named

Coudret is said to have published on cements around 1651 (Bosc, whose dates are sometimes questionable; his source, *Dissertations sur l'histoire générale de la Franche-Comté,* is untraceable, but it is unlikely that Smeaton knew it).

78. Documented by Norman Smith and others, in Skempton, pp. 35–57.

79. The inductive method that Western science would later use was first formulated by Roger Bacon, followed by Galileo and Francis Bacon. Descartes and the Encyclopedists gave it its present prominence.

80. Among the better known were Marchese Giovanni Poleni, Thomas Le Suer, François Jacquier, and Ruggiero Giuseppe Boscovich in Italy, Ritter Franz Joseph von Gerstner in Austria-Hungary, Jacob Bernoulli and Charles Augustin Coulomb in France, Leonhard Euler in Prussia and Russia, and Smeaton and George Atwood in Britain.

81. Smeaton, *Edystone Lighthouse,* chap. 4, pp. 102–123: "Containing experiments to ascertain a compleat composition for water-cements with their results." Smeaton used two types of artificial hydraulic cement in the construction of his lighthouse that had less than half the silica (thirteen percent instead of twenty-five percent) than was later usual, and this made it a very slow-curing material (*Reports,* 1812, vol. 3, p. 414: "Directions for preparing, making and using Pozzolana Mortar"). Smeaton cast a monolithic canal lock using a gravel aggregate in 1760, possibly the Wear lock described in *Reports,* vol. 1, pp. 18–20. Telford is said to have used a Smeaton mortar for the piers of the 1826 Menai suspension bridge. Other researchers were Barthélemy Faujas de Saint-Fond, who published in France in 1778, and Bryan Higgins in England in 1780, on his cement: GB patent 1207, 18.01.1779. By 1785–1786 the chemist Chaptal and several Swedish researchers had also analyzed hydraulic cement (Michaelis, pp. 19–20). Other early treatises were published by Antoine-Joseph Loriot, Fleury, and Polycarpe de la Faye.

82. The Vicat method was patented by Maurice de Saint-Léger (GB patent 4262, 19.05.1818; Michaelis erroneously writes November) and produced in Meudon near Paris in 1822. Vicat used the mortar for the masonry arch of his Souillac Bridge over the Dordogne (1811–1822; Guy Grattesat, *Ponts de France* [Paris: ENPC, 1982]; p. 103 says 1812–1824) and as concrete in the piers of Marc Seguin's Tain-Tournon suspension bridge over the Rhône (1825).

83. Vicat (1840 and 1853) attempted to develop more economical manufacturing methods, while the German chemists Johann Friedrich John (1819) and Johann Nepomuk von Fuchs (1833) analyzed curing and hardness.

84. Schafhäutl, p. 285.

85. John Grant, *Experiments on the strength of cement, chiefly in reference to the Portland cement used in the southern main drainage works* (London: Spon, 1875); see also Elliott, p. 157.

86. James Parker of Northfleet, Kent, GB patent 2120, 28.06.1796, and his preparatory patent 1806, 17.05.1791; Elliott, p. 152; Bosc, p. 451; Vicat, *Résumé des Connaissances positives actuelles,* 1828, pp. vi, ix; James Frost, GB patent, 4679, 11.06.1822; 4710, 27.09.1822; and 4772, 03.04.1823. Lesage found one in France in 1802

(Bosc, p. 451). A few years later, the material had been found all over France (Vicat, *Résumé*, 1828, pp. vi, ix). Canvass White prospected for and discovered a natural cement in the United States in 1820 while working on the Erie Canal. For Scott's cement, see *Encyc. Brit.,* 11th ed., "Brickwork," vol. 2, p. 223; for Troughton's, see GB patent 6303, 08.09.1832. See also Michaelis and Bosc. Several dozen proprietary cements were exhibited in the Crystal Palace. Several of them used sintered furnace slag, which had known hydraulic properties: John Vernon, GB patent 3705, 31.05.1813; Abraham Henry Chambers, GB patent 4527, 15.01.1821.

87. Cresy, p. 721. A cement with a minimum of ten to twelve percent clay sets in twenty days underwater. Above thirty percent, quality decreases. Most nineteenth-century mortars and cements took months to harden and almost a year to cure fully.

88. For example, the Southampton Docks and the foundations of Sir Charles Barry's Houses of Parliament (1839–1852).

89. Lime production was a labor-intensive cottage industry. Countries with the lowest labor costs generally had the best lime mortar, and labor costs were continuing to rise in the industrializing nations. Quality control was much simpler in an industrialized environment. Lime's usefulness depended on careful roasting in the kiln, and lime mortar depended on the length of time the mixture was turned and beaten before use (Peter Nicholson, vol. 1, p. 133).

90. Joseph Aspdin, Master Mason in Leeds, GB patent 5022, 21.10.1824. Twenty-six years later, when our modern product of the same name was developed, the seventy-two-year-old Aspdin was still producing it in his original factory across from Wakefield station and at another at Gateshead (Schafhäutl, p. 203).

91. Elliott, p. 153. William had previously set up the first Portland Cement firm in Germany.

92. White bought out James Frost in 1833 and also produced Parker's Roman Cement in license. He was possibly the John White of GB patent 3269, 29.09.1809; see also Elliott, p. 153.

93. G. F. White, pp. 481–482.

94. Elliott, p. 155, caption 6.3. Johnson developed a chamber kiln in 1872 and died a centenarian in 1911, having seen his discovery develop into a worldwide industry.

95. The first modern Portland Cement factory opened in France in 1850, and the first German one (William Aspdin's) about five years later (Shand, p. 176). Much of the cement imported into America came from the German firm Dyckerhoff & Widmann, presently Diwidag. In 1879, 40,000 tons entered New York harbor alone (Henry Reid, p. 78). Ernest Leslie Ransome began producing cement in New Jersey in 1866 to free the industry from having to import the raw material, and by 1876 Gillmore reported on the crushing strength of three American and one Canadian artificial Portland Cement to the Exhibition jury in Philadelphia (Shand, p. 174).

96. Brighton had concrete seawalls, and Ranger cast Pasley's experimental vaults at Woolwich and warehouse foundations at Chatham Dockyard (*Papers on Subjects connected with . . . ,* vol. 1, pp. 23–28, 32–37). Vicat used concrete in France, and in 1830

the architect François-Martin Lebrun built himself a three-story, unreinforced concrete house near Albi with vaulted floors (*Papers on Subjects connected with . . .*, vol. 1, p. 286, cit. in *Caementum,* vol. 1, p. 20; Lebrun 1835 and 1843, cit. in Cody; and Gourlier in *Bulletin de la Société d'Encouragement,* 1832, p. 99, cit. in Cody). Lebrun's house continued traditional pisé techniques as explained by Cointeraux and Rondelet. By 1835 he had built two bridges and another house in Marssac, and in 1837, the same year J. B. White built himself a house of concrete block in England and G. A. Ward one on Staten Island in New York, Lebrun erected a vaulted church in concrete (Collins, *Concrete,* p. 26). By the 1850s, large-scale fortifications were being cast in Denmark (Michaelis, p. 287).

97. Shand, p. 176; see Schafhäutl for John Kent, GB patent 3357, 03.07.1810.

98. GB patents 6341, 04.12.1832, and 6729, 04.12.1834. By 1837, G. A. Ward was also using blocks in New York (Collins, *Concrete,* p. 56).

99. Schafhäutl, p. 284, and *Papers on Subjects connected with . . .*, vol. 2, pp. 261–264. Artificial stone was evidently difficult to manufacture properly, and it tended to degenerate in an English climate, although in India and in other warm climates it was more successful (Henry Reid, pp. 26–27).

100. Michaelis states 1833, Elton gives 1838 (*Timber,* no. 240, p. 105). The principle was not new; Vitruvius described it (book 5, chap. 12), and Pliny described the expansion of Ostia harbor under Trajan (letter 6: Michaelis, p. 297). Other successful block patents came later. Frederick Ransome based his successful block on a preparatory GB patent 10360, 22.10.1844. His important patents were GB patents 11282, 06.07.1846, and 11596, 24.02.1847. A rotating kiln he patented in 1845 facilitated the bulk production of Portland cement. He also made the first known reinforcing cages for concrete beams in 1865. Figuier considered it so remarkable that he described its development and James Nasmyth's comments on it at length (*L'Année Scientifique et Industrielle,* vol. 2, 1857, pp. 402–404). Ransome's son, Ernest Leslie Ransome, introduced the block to the United States and produced it between 1874 and 1886. The Ransome block became the forerunner of many successful American concrete block systems. A lime cement brick was proposed by A. Bernardi in Germany in 1852, but it received its present form through the work of Wilhelm Michaelis in 1880, who developed the autoclave which cured it in hours instead of weeks or months.

101. Toulon, Cette, Cherbourg, La Ciotat, Port Vendre, and Marseilles (G. F. White, pp. 486–488); Germany's Baltic harbors; Holyhead in Wales; Plymouth Bay, Massachusetts, and Cape Henelopen, Maryland, in the US (Michaelis, p. 297). The system was used at Port Said in 1868.

102. They also used it to build the *vespassiennes* on the Paris quays in 1863.

103.

> Les inventeurs forment avec leur pierre factice des panneaux creux, ornementés et mobiles, à l'aide desquels on peut établir des maisons. Les panneaux creux sont garnis intérieurement, soit des châssis en fer ou tôle,

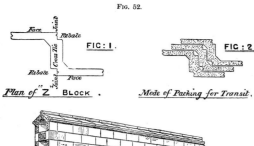

F<small>IG</small>. 52.

FIC : 1 .
Face   Joint
        Rebate
Cross Tie
Rebate
Joint   Face

Plan of "Z" B<small>LOCK</small> .

FIC : 2 .

Mode of Packing for Transit.

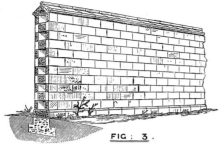

FIC : 3 .

Wall built of "Z" B<small>LOCK and</small> S<small>LABS</small>."

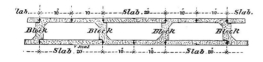

Slab. | 10 | 10 | Slab. | 20 | 10 | 10 | Slab.
Block | Block | Block | Block
Slab. | 20 | 10 | 10 | Slab. | 20

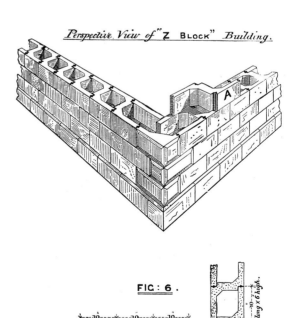

Perspective View of "Z" B<small>LOCK</small> *Building.*

FIC : 6 .

167.
Concrete blocks were popular in the United States even before Ernest Ransome imported his father's system from England in the 1880s. An inventor named Lish used interlocking "Z-blocks." (Henry Reid, 1879, pp. 291, 292.)

soit de briques ou poteries creuses, ces différentes combinaisons intérieures prévues dans le but de produire le légèrté en même temps que la solidité. Les panneaux sont établis avec rainure, et comportent intérieurement des dispositions qui en rendent le montage et le scellement faciles. Ces maisons, étant mobiles, peuvent par conséquent s'exporter au loin.

Les premières constructions en similipierre et similimarbre qui furent faites pour l'exportation sont dues à l'initiative d'un riche négociant des Indes, M. J. Henriquez Moron, consul général du Brésil à Saint-Thomas. Elles ont été, pour la première fois, établies et exportés par M. Alfred Bing jeune; cet habile exportateur à nolisé à cet effet, en avril 1860, le navire français *Élisabeth,* qui a ainsi portée dans des contrées éloignées les *premières* maisons *mobiles* complètement faites en France.

Depuis, pleusieurs maisons en similipierre et similiemarbre ont été expediées dans d'autres colonies. (Château, vol. 1, pp. 301–302)

Château mentions three Paris addresses of houses built by the firm. One was rebuilt conventionally in 1910, one street could not be found since it had changed its name, and the third lies in an inaccessible suburb.

Component prefabrication had a future, while large-scale prefabrication went awry. Fifteen years later William Henry Lascelles's reinforced, component system for housing won a gold medal at the Paris exhibition of 1878, and Lascelles himself was inducted into the Légion d'Honneur (Lascelles, *Improved method of the construction of buildings,* 1875). The prize-winning buildings were designed by the British architects Ernest Newton and Richard Norman Shaw. For Newton, see William Duck antiquarian book cata. 70, no. 101; Henry Reid, pp. 267–268; see also Shaw.

Thomas Edison and Ernest Ransome's 1907 system, on the other hand, which cast whole houses on reusable shuttering, was doomed to failure. The Edison-Ransome system was based on Thaddeus Hyatt's work and on the New York architect A. C. Pauli's 1906 Monocast studies. Edison's assistants Small and Harms emigrated to Holland, where they worked on a prototype designed by the architect Hendrik Berlage (Collins, *Concrete,* p. 90). The Edison-Ransome system's extreme inflexibility condemned it, much like the room-sized French and Russian systems half a century later.

104. See Vitruvius, book 7, chap. 1.

105. See Stephen Tobriner's two articles, and Haas, who cites analogous research by C. Strickler on embedded timber frames (*Anker aus Holz,* p. 123). A primitive form of timber stiffening is also known in Spanish colonial adobe structures in the southwestern United States.

106. Haas, *Hölzerne und eiserne Anker,* p. 151; see also Elliott, p. 68, citing various sources. Churches like the Ste.-Chapelle in Paris have such iron reinforcement.

107. Thanks to mason Egidio Andreola of the Valtellina for this information.

108. Beamish, p. 284; see also chapter 4.

109. See chapters 4 and 6.

110. Beamish, pp. 286–287. He used straw, hemp, wood fibers, reeds, birch or fir lath, and hoop iron. As late as 1850–1855 George Totten was embedding wooden sticks in concrete telegraph poles on the Panama railway (Otis, p. 75).

168.
Richard Norman Shaw and William Lascelles exhibited a prefabricated, concrete panel house on the "rue des nations" at the Paris Exhibition of 1878. It won a gold medal and Lascelles became "Chevalier de la Légion d'honneur." (Henry Reid, 1879, p. 263.)

111. Schafhäutl, pp. 192–193; the adhesion was reported in *Min. Proc. ICE,* vol. 1, 1837, p. 16.

112. 3.2 meters (10.5 feet) high and 3.05 meters (10 feet) deep, and 18.29 meters (60 feet) and 11.28 meters (37 feet) long, with a 25.5-tonne (28-ton) counterweight. Clements, p. 201; Beamish, pp. 284–285. The experiment was first reported in *Min. Proc. ICE,* vol. 1, 1837, pp. 16–20. Charles Larkin Francis.

113. *The Rudiments of Civil Engineering,* part 2, chap. 4, pp. 134–135.

114. 1.45 meters (4.75 feet) high and 7.42 meters (24.3 feet) long. It failed at 22.95 tonnes (G. F. White, pp. 492–493); Pasley, *Observations,* 2nd ed. 1847, part 1, p. 164; Brunel in *Min. Proc. ICE,* vol. 1, 1838, p. 16; also given as 50,652 lb. (G. F. White, p. 495).

115. Skempton and Chrimes, p. 210.

116. Rennie, p. 35.

117. These beams were two bricks wide and four high and spanned 3.05 meters (10 feet) (G. F. White, p. 480).

118. White's beam was 1.35 meters (4.5 feet) high: G. F. White, footnote p. 493 and pp. 492–495; Pasley, *Observations,* 2nd ed. 1847, part 1, p. 164; Brunel in *Min. Proc. ICE,* vol. 1, 1838, p. 16.

119. 28.5 tonnes (G. F. White, p. 481). George Frederick White deduced from the results that Portland cement was more than twice as strong as Roman cement. All things being equal, he estimated that the Crystal Palace beam should have withstood a load of 48.8 tonnes (=107,787 lb.: G. F. White, p. 495). G. F. White may have been J. B. White's son.

120. Navier's work was based on Edmé Mariotte's (*Traité du mouvement des eaux et des autres fluides* [Paris: Michallet, 1686]), who defined the concept of a neutral axis separating the zones of tension and compression in the seventeenth century (Szabo, pp. 360–362), and work done by Jacob Bernoulli in the eighteenth.

121. Navier, *Rapport sur le projet pont suspendu.* Fritz Stüssi erroneously read an "invention" of the concept of reinforced concrete into this traditional use of tension members in masonry. See Peters, *Transitions,* p. 180, footnote 41.

122. Vicat, "Ponts suspendus en fil de fer sur le Rhône," 1831, p. 119, and footnote 12.

123. Peters, *Transitions,* pp. 153–154, 170–171, citing Dupuit, pp. 407–408. The Swiss engineer Guillaume-Henri Dufour puddled the wrought-iron anchor bars of the world's first permanent wire cable bridge, the Pont St.-Antoine in Geneva, in hydraulic mortar in 1823. Berg reported it in 1824 (p. 35) and considered it a faulty detail.

124. *Min. Proc. ICE,* vol. 1, 1839, p. 37.

125. Official recognition came through the examination of one of François Coignet's concrete houses in Saint-Denis, and in Germany through Johann Bauschinger's observations of 1892 (Mörsch, 2nd ed., p. 2).

126. Schafhäutl, pp. 192–193; the adhesion was reported in *Min. Proc. ICE,* vol. 1, 1837, p. 16.

127. The same anecdote was attributed in the same year to G. A. Ward in New York.

128. Elliott, pp. 171–172.

129. *The Times,* 20 February 1851, cit. in *Min. Proc. ICE,* vol. 12, 1853, footnote p. 259.

130. The Tain-Tournon suspension bridge, 1825 (Cotte, p. 128 and fig. E).

131. Dobbs, GB patent 3376, 02.08.1810 (*Caementum,* vol. 1, Teil A, p. 42). Dodd, GB patent 3141, 03.06.1808, and Frost, GB patent 4710, 1822 (Bracher, p. 39). Loudon, *Encyclopaedia of Cottage, Farm and Villa Architecture,* 1833, article 1792 (Collins, *Concrete,* p. 29; Shand, p. 177).

132. Barrett in *Min. Proc. ICE,* vol. 8, 1849, p. 162, and vol. 12, 1853, p. 253; also Fox and Barrett, 1849, and Humber, 1857, pp. 103–104.

133. GB patent 10047, 10.02.1844; *Min. Proc. ICE,* vol. 12, 1853, p. 267.

134. *Min. Proc. ICE,* vol. 12, 1853, pp. 253, 259 (footnote), 261, 262, 271.

135. *Architectural Record,* vol. 25, no. 5, May 1909, "Fireproof House Number," p. 23.

136. *Min. Proc. ICE,* vol. 8, 1849, pp. 162–163, and vol. 12, 1853, pp. 244–272.

137. Built around 1853 (ibid., vol. 12, pp. 257, 269).

138. Ibid., footnote p. 253, citing "The Ninth Report of the Directors of the Metropolitan Association for improving the Dwellings of the Industrious Classes," and p. 269, Edington's comment.

139. William Fairbairn used a similar system for a factory floor in 1845. The fact that he did not patent it suggests that it may have been someone else's. Giedion, *Space, Time and Architecture,* p. 194; Fairbairn, *On the Application of Cast and Wrought Iron,* 4th ed., pp. 180–181.

140. *Min. Proc. ICE,* vol. 12, 1853, p. 252.

141. GB patent 2293, cit. in Collins, *Concrete,* p. 38.

142. See Damstaedter and Hoppe. Industrially produced wire ropes were patented by Wilhelm August Julius Albert in 1834 in Germany, from where they spread to Britain and other mining areas. Robert Stirling Newall, GB patent 8594, 07.08.1840. By the mid-1850s wire ropes began to replace leather belts in factory transmissions, and discarded ones were readily available. See Gustave Adolphe Hirn's work in Figuier, *L'Année scientifique,* 1857, vol. 2, pp. 418–419; 1859, vol. 3, pt. 2, pp. 214–221.

143. Elliott, p. 168.

144. William Littell Tizard reinforced concrete blocks with wire netting in 1853 for walls and ceilings. Joseph-Louis Lambot is said to have built reinforced concrete planters since 1845. He suggested columns and beams and built boats in reinforced mortar which he called *ferriciment,* patenting and exhibiting one in Paris at the exhibition of 1855. The potential of Lambot's material as a membrane or shell structure went unnoticed, and Lambot himself praised only its fireproof qualities. Mesh-reinforced mortar had to be reinvented again and again (Donath, in *Baukunde des Architekten,* vol. 1, p. 153). It reappeared in François Coignet's conduits in the 1860s, and again in the 1880s as lightweight wall construction in Berlin, in the "expanded metal" system patented in the United States in 1884 (J. F. Golding, US patent 297382), in the concrete ship built by Christiani and Nielsen in 1920 (Ostenfeld, *Christiani and Nielsen,* pp. 144–146), and again in Robert Maillart's "Gunite" hall in Zurich at the Swiss National Exhibition of 1939. Pier Luigi Nervi reinvented it as *ferrocimento* in 1942–1943 and used it for the permanent shuttering of his coffered roof structures and the covered stadia for the 1960 Olympic Games in Rome.

145. He began by building himself a three-story house in Saint-Denis in 1853 with concrete walls and floors reinforced with T-beams spaced a meter apart, connected by joists on the Fox and Barrett system. A smaller three-story house with a barrel-vaulted roof of eight meters' span followed in 1857 (*Mém. et Compte-Rendu,* 4 April 1862, pp. 142–145). Collins (*Concrete,* p. 29) documents the development of Coignet's patents in detail: F patents 29.03.1855, 11.12.1855, GB patent 26.11.1855, referring to tension rods (like Wilkinson the year before), followed by F patent 24.06.1856.

146. *Mém. et Compte-Rendu,* 7 September 1855, 1 February and 17 October 1856, 20 February and 6 March 1857, 20 May 1859, 20 January and 3 February 1860, and 4 April 1862, p. 145.

147. *Mém. et Compte-Rendu,* 4 April 1862, pp. 143, 144, 146. The bridge he built around 1861 may have been unreinforced.

148. Marrey, pp. 35–36; Collins, *Concrete,* pp. 33–35.

149. Beginning in 1855 Hyatt tested reinforced beams, and he registered over thirty patents between 1871 and 1881, including his collective system patent of 1878: US patent 206112, 16.07.1878.

150. Hyatt's 1874 patent for columns with spiral and longitudinal reinforcement pre-dated Considère's in 1902: DR patent 149944, 10.05.1902, presented by Considère to the Académie des Sciences, 25 August and 8 September 1902, and discussed in *Beton und Eisen,* 1902 no. 5 and 1903 nos. 1 and 2 (Wayss and Freytag, p. 7). Following Frederick Ransome's reinforcing cage for concrete beams of 1865, Hyatt invented a reinforcing hoop otherwise attributed to Hennebique in 1884, and Hyatt is now also credited with the concept of the T-beam, the monolithic combination of slab and beam, also hitherto attributed to Hennebique.

151. F patent 77165, 16.07.1867 for planters; 1875 for bridges; November 1877 for beams and columns; 1878 for railway ties, slabs, conduits, and staircases; protected in Germany by DR patent 14763, 04.08.1881.

152. Collins, *Concrete,* p. 60; for Matthew Allen, see Raafat, p. 19.

153. Collins, *Concrete,* pp. 50–61.

154. *Zentralblatt der Bauverwaltung.* There is some confusion about this article; see bibliography under Koenen.

155. Mörsch expanded the book, which came to be called *Der Eisenbetonbau,* in five multivolume editions up to 1923.

156. One of the earliest concrete theaters in Germany was the Leipzig Kristallpalast, a combined circus and panorama building finished in 1887. Arwed Rossbach was the architect and Wayss the contractor. They knew that the structure was monolithic, but its fireproof qualities were more important to them (Moser, p. 42).

157. Robert Maillart and Gustav Gull's Stauffacher Bridge in Zurich (1899) is an example, as were the many concrete structures by Hennebique and others at the 1900 Paris Exhibition.

158. The best known were Porccheddu in Turin, Samuel de Molins in western Switzerland, Züblin in Naples, Alsace, eastern Switzerland, southern Germany, and Russia, and Mouchel in Britain.

159. Wayss & Freytag and Dyckerhoff & Widmann in the German-speaking countries, Hennebique and later the Danish firm Christiani & Nielsen all over the world. Hennebique's erstwhile licensee Eduard Züblin built throughout Europe, while Ernest L. Ransome and the Kahn brothers, Albert and Julius, built in the United States. For a good list of the many smaller systems available by the end of the century, see Marsh and Dunn.

160. See A. Geiser, Wilhelm Ritter, and Franz Schüle, *Expertenbericht betreffend den Gebäude-Einsturz in der Aeschenvorstadt Basel am 28. August 1901* (Zurich: Zürcher & Furrer, 1901). The first German and temporary Swiss codes appeared the following year.

161. Only a few of the names are generally known, and more needs to be done on the work of the engineers Robert Maillart, Alexandre and Robert Sarassin, Eugène Freyssinet, Pier Luigi Nervi, Eduardo Torroja, and Heinz Isler. Some architects concentrated on structural form too, and their names are better known to architectural historians: Toni Garnier, Auguste Perret, Félix Candela, and Angelo Mangiarotti. There were also many architects of the early modern movement and expressionism who attempted to develop forms expressing monolithic structure. Some of them were only partly successful, since many experiments were carried out in other materials and were clearly an experimentation with form and not structure. Erich Mendelsohn's Einstein Tower (1919–1920) was built in brick and stucco, Ludwig Mies van der Rohe's house in the Weissenhofsiedlung (1926–1927) with steel framing and brick and stucco infill, and municipal engineer Emil Klöti's extravagantly cantilevered streetcar shelters at the Bellevueplatz in Zurich were steel rendered with stucco. What had begun as an experiment in structure and method sometimes regressed into formal play.

162. Especially US patents 314398, 24.03.1885; 349058, 14.09.1886; 515015, 20.02.1894; 651019, 05.06.1900; and 652733, 26.06.1900, which led to 694580, 04.03.1902, the same date as his patents 694575, 694576, 694577, 694578, and 694579. His cold-twisted reinforcing bar could take higher stresses than mild steel, although the reason for twisting his steel was stated in the patent as "to form a continuous bond" with the concrete: US patent 305226, 16.09.1884, expanded in 516113, 06.03.1894.

163. Coignet's and Monier's systems. Joseph Melan's Austrian system was introduced into the United States by the engineer and contractor Fritz von Emperger in 1893.

164. Six of them, including the Turner Construction Company, were not controlled by Ransome (1904 Ransome Brochure, caption under frontispiece).

165. Cincinnati architects Alfred Oscar Elzner and George Anderson built the sixteen-story Ingalls Building that became known as the first skyscraper to have a reinforced concrete frame. Like many other Ohio architects who worked in reinforced concrete, the older partner Elzner had graduated from the first American academic architecture program (MIT, 1869), and had worked for Henry Hobson Richardson.

In 1887 he joined Anderson, who had returned to Cincinnati from Columbia University and the École des Beaux-Arts where he may have known teachers who were to influence Auguste Perret in the following decade. Those were also the years in which Hennebique erected his first factory buildings. Parisian architecture students may well have known of them. Gustave W. Drach was another Cincinnati architect from MIT. By 1904 he and a partner had built eight eight-to-ten-story reinforced concrete framed buildings. Thanks to Chris H. Luebkeman for the information on the Cincinnati development. Even earlier (1875–1877), William L. Ward, who had studied the work of Coignet in France, built a house in Port Chester, New York, but it remained a unique example (*Architectural Record,* vol. 25, no. 5, May 1909, "Fireproof House Number," pp. 359–363).

3   The Human Element: Manual Work, Mechanization, Progress, and Technological Thought

1. Giedion related the rise of mechanization to the ideology of progress in *Mechanization Takes Command* (pp. 714–717 in both eds.), and Paulinyi, "Die Entwicklung," suggested that material-forming technology contributed. Others assigned a leading role to energy production.

2. See for instance Andrew Li (Chinese University of Hong Kong), "Why Do Chinese Buildings Have Curved Roofs? A First Look at Intellectual Bias in the Study of Chinese Architecture," paper presented at the "Architecture (Post)Modernity and Difference" conference in Singapore, 14–17 April 1993 (publication forthcoming).

3. *Scientific American* began publication in 1845 with a new series starting in 1859, and *Popular Mechanics* in 1912.

4. Cook, pp. 60–61.

5. Ruskin had risen to Turner's defense after the latter had been abandoned by the academic arbiters of taste, and used him as the basis for his treatise *Modern Painters.*

6. Kenneth Clark, p. 256 (1976 ed.).

7. GB patents 2599, 24.03.1802; the crucial 3922, 06.06.1815; 6082, 21.02.1831; and 6308, 22.09.1832, registered the year before his death.

8. Today, our ideal machine has no moving parts; it minimizes wear and produces no pollution. The eighteenth century produced the walking beam and the mine pump, the nineteenth the locomotive, and the twentieth the computer. Our nostalgia is different from Ruskin's. We look back to his era and express nostalgia through our fascination for railroad memorabilia and the bizarre, mobile sculpture of a Jean Tinguely or a Bernard Luginbühl.

9. The most highly industrialized countries in the nineteenth century had many building sites that relied on manual labor. Even in our own century, many large sites in the Orient used only muscle power. Gandhi founded his resistance to mechanization in India on the apparent paradox that labor-intensive work would raise the level of Indian technology quicker than capital-intensive mechanization. Many agreed with him and

others disagreed, among them India's foremost industrialists. Both routes helped India develop. The ideas that led Gandhi to create the *khadi,* or cottage-industry movement, are basically different from William Morris's anti-industrial arts-and-crafts movement at the end of the last century. Morris tried to solve the problem of artistic quality and industrialization, and he looked backward to medieval guild systems. Gandhi tried to develop a strategy to build an independent economic strength using abundant resources and conserving scarce ones.

10. Beamish, p. 105.

11. The first official union was founded in Britain in 1824, and collective bargaining was legalized the following year but resisted for a long time by industrialists and society at large. In the United States, the issue was social and political, not primarily one of mechanization, and the development followed along somewhat different lines. Philadelphia shoemakers formed a temporary, first union in 1792, but several courageous organizations, such as the New York Typographical Society of 1794, survived, and by 1837 there were several trade unions in all large east coast cities.

12. See Karl Marx, "Der 18. Brumaire des Louis Bonaparte," in *Die Revolution* (newspaper), New York, 1852; rpt. Insel, Germany: n.p., 1965. Britain was slow to accept change, and the first effective European union was the Swiss printers' union in 1858, followed by a German one in 1863. By that time the movement was well established in the United States.

13. Kay's GB patent 542, 26.05.1733. Kay continued to perfect weaving machines in patents 555, 1730; 566, 1738; and 612, 1745. See Smiles, *George and Robert Stephenson,* p. 50, quoting Curr.

14. Papin had wanted to sail from Kassel to London and use the ship as self-advertisement in applying for a position at the British court (Figuier, *Les Merveilles de la Science,* vol. 1, pp. 58–59). Beamish, footnote p. 103.

15. Coleman, p. 47, citing Klingender, p. 166, citing John Bourne, p. 20.

16. Hyde, pp. 400, 402; Rolt, *Victorian Engineering,* p. 248 (1974 ed.); and Frederick McDermot, quoted in Coleman, p. 55. The Albert Docks were built between 1875 and 1880 (Rolt, *Victorian Engineering,* p. 248).

17. Coleman, pp. 53–55.

18. Geoffrey Turnbull's use of the degree of mechanization as an indicator of the organization and capitalization of an enterprise does not apply here (*A History of the Calico Printing Industry of Great Britain,* ed. John G. Turnbull [Altringham: John Sherratt and Son, 1951], pp. 52–54).

19. Hyde, p. 399.

20. Rennie, p. 56.

21. Helps, pp. 195–196, 220.

22. Coleman (p. 54) is in error here; the term "steam navvy" was only common in Britain.

23. Other European engineers were equally admiring. The Austrian journal *Allgemeine Bauzeitung* reported with enthusiasm on moving masonry houses in New York in 1836.

24. Helps, pp. 206–207.

25. Henry Howe in 1841 (p. 392), possibly quoting from earlier British sources. This ceased to be true after World War II in the United States.

26. Rennie, pp. 50–51; Lavalley, 1867, pp. 425–426 (reprint, pp. 3–4); Haskin, pp. 77–78. These issues will be discussed in chapters 5, 6, and 7.

27. Rolt, *Victorian Engineering,* p. 25.

28. Purdon was site engineer under Charles Vignoles and Joseph Locke, and later Isambard Brunel's representative and chief engineer on the East Bengal Railway (Buchanan, p. 151).

29. Purdon, cit. in Coleman, p. 119 (1972 ed.).

30. Electric detonators and safety caps were first used in Britain by Pasley in 1839 to blow up the wreck of the *Royal George.* Between then and 1843, when William Cubitt used them at Round Down Cliff on the South Eastern Railway between Dover and Folkestone, they became common (Rennie, pp. 104–105). Even earlier than that, engineers were concerned about careful blasting techniques (*Min. Proc. ICE,* vol. 1, 1837, pp. 37–38, on blasting techniques used in India).

31. Purdon's testimony before Select Commons Committee, cit. in Coleman, p. 125.

32. As social conditions improved, workmen's safety became an increasingly important issue. Eiffel set up a site canteen on the first level of his tower in 1887. The workmen had to use it on their lunch break if they didn't want to climb down to the ground and up again on their own time. They did so willingly as it was convenient and comfortable in inclement weather. At the same time, Eiffel could rigorously enforce a ban on alcoholic beverages and preserve the workers' reaction speed and precision on the job, which benefited both him and them. This safety measure contributed to the result that not a single death was reported for the entire process, with one exception that occurred when the site was closed for the night (when a young worker walked a beam high above the ground to impress his girlfriend and fell to his death). Eiffel acted responsibly to protect his laborers' lives. His almost perfect safety record stands unique in the annals of large-scale construction and is still cited as a model for the profession.

33. See chapter 5.

34. See chapter 6.

35. They represented a movement that eventually led to the foundation of the Wharton School of Management at the University of Pennsylvania in 1881 (Claude S. George, Jr., *The History of Management Thought* [Englewood Cliffs, NJ: Prentice-Hall, 1968], pp. 71–85). Theoreticians had attempted to quantify manual work even earlier, beginning with Philippe La Hire's paper on levers and Guillaume Amontons's on work that he presented to the French Académie in 1699 (Ferguson, *The Measurement*, p. 96). Daniel Bernoulli and Charles-Augustin Coulomb also contributed theoretically, while William Cubitt introduced man-powered treadmills in English prisons in 1818 and Lammot Dupont in Wilmington, Delaware, in 1872.

36. Christo Casacof, *La technique de l'organisation scientifique du travail . . .* (Paris, 1948), p. 17. Fayol's book appeared in 1918 as a reprint of an article in *Bulletin de la Société de l'industrie minérale* from 1916 or 1917. Jane Morley is currently finishing a dissertation at the University of Pennsylvania titled "Motion Is Money: Frank Bunker Gilbreth, Inventor, Building Contractor and Consulting Engineer."

37. *A Piece Rate System: Being a Step toward Partial Solution of the Labor Problem* (n.p.: n.p., 1895), reprint from the *Transactions of the ASME,* vol. 16.

38. Information from Morley.

39. Paraphrasing Franklin's credo, Gilbreth began a letter to his wife in the early 1920s with the words, "TIME IS MOTION" (information from Morley).

40. Marey photographed bird flight between 1873 and 1890 in France (*La machine animale; locomotion terrestre et aérienne* [Paris: Ballière, 1873]; *La méthode graphique dans les sciences expérimentales . . .* [Paris: Masson, 1878]; *Le vol des oiseaux. Physiologie du mouvement* [Paris: Masson, 1890]). The *Scientific American* reported his work (information from Morley). Muybridge's 1882 studies of animal and human movement were widely publicized.

41. George, *History of Management Thought,* p. 106. Like Marey's and Muybridge's images, Gilbreth's models were also regarded as art. For Marey see Felix Rosenthal, *Flight,* L'Art Ancien S.A. Catalog 70 (Zurich, 1980); for Muybridge, see Jacob Stillman, *The Horse in Motion as Shown by Instantaneous Photography, with a Study on Animal Mechanics . . .* Boston: J. R. Osgood, 1882).

42. They used the term "scientific" in its earlier definition of "quantitative," in contrast to its definition as "pure science" or examination by applying scientific method, which first appeared toward the end of the nineteenth century. The term "one best way" was a Gilbreth slogan that appeared in many of his writings.

43. Lillian Gilbreth, pp. 20–21.

44. The towns of Woodland and Sprague's Falls, Maine, Piercefield, New York, for the Pierce Arrow Automobile Company, and Canton, North Carolina, were all built by his firm in months. Spriegel and Myers, p. 4.

45. Gilbreth was in good company here. By the end of the last century the Swede Alfred Nobel had built an international concern based on explosives, and the Frenchman

François Hennebique an international engineering consulting practice. The Swiss Eduard Züblin had created an international contracting firm, while the Englishman Sir Samuel Marcus had gone a step further to organize one of the first successful multinational corporations, Shell Oil.

46. As far as we know, Gilbreth was the first to use photography on a large scale to document building processes. It had previously been used for public relations purposes to document unusual sites like the Eiffel Tower (1887–1889) or the Firth of Forth Bridge (1883–1890). (A short series was published in Eiffel, *La Tour de 300 Mètres,* 1900, and some of the Forth photographs were published in part in *Engineering,* 29 February 1890, and then in the final report later that year. Such series continued an old tradition of monumentally illustrated building reports like Domenico Fontana's on moving the Vatican obelisk, 1584, Jean-Rodolphe Perronet's on the Neuilly Bridge, 1772, or Edwin Clark's on the Britannia and Conway bridges, 1850.) Gilbreth used his photographs as advertising material, too, but he went further than that and used them as part of the building process itself. They were progress reports and could be analyzed or produced as documents in litigation.

47. Anyone who wished to advance in the organization filed a monthly report containing suggestions for improved rationalization, productivity, client service, and contract acquisition. Successful suggestions were rewarded with money and with organization-wide publicity, which proved even more effective. Good workers received periodical evaluations as incentives and recommendation. Gilbreth's management psychology used both the carrot and the stick shrewdly. He concentrated on spurring incentive while downplaying and carefully curbing behavior detrimental to productivity.

48. Gilbreth recognized that difficulties with bulk production could cause bottlenecks in the critical path. François Cointeraux had attributed his success to the invention of an efficient concrete mixer over forty years earlier, and a German mixer based on the Archimedes screw in 1861 had reached an output of a hundred cubic meters in a ten-hour work shift (*Engineer and Architects' Journal,* vol. 24, 1861, p. 346). Gilbreth patented his ladder gravity mixer in 1899, three years before Ransome's rotating cube (US patent 694,575, 04.03.1902; for Gilbreth's mixer, see Morley). There is some doubt about how original Gilbreth's invention was, however. The *Annales des ponts et chaussées* reported what looked like a very similar if not identical mixer in 1857 used in the building of the Sarthe Viaduct near Le Mans (*Annales des ponts et chaussées,* vols. 9/10, 1857, and *Zeitschrift für Bauwesen,* 1858, p. 494).

49. Gilbreth, *Bricklaying System,* p. 4, §§18, 21.

4 Worlds Apart: From the Thames to the Mont Cenis Tunnel

1. The Euphrates tunnel of 2180–2160 B.C., reported in Diodorus Siculus, required the diversion of the river during construction. Epaulinos's tunnel on Samos was surveyed by an undeciphered method (West, p. 21, has 535–522 B.C.; *Encyc. Brit.* has 687 B.C.). The Roman catacombs and aqueducts, the tunnel under Marseilles harbor, the Pausilippo road tunnel of 36 B.C. by Lucius Cocceius Auctus (West, p. 22), the tunnel that drained Lake Fucino under Monte Salvino, or the eighth-century water system in Jerusalem are equally amazing constructions.

2. Ivan the Terrible had passages cut under Moscow in 1565, and the first alpine tunnel was briefly begun in 1450 under the Col di Tende in the Alpes Maritimes between Nice and Genoa, reopened in 1782 and carried about 2,500 meters into the rock before being abandoned for good in 1794.

3. Financed by Pierre-Paul Riquet de Bonrepos, described in Melvin Kranzberg and Carroll Purcell, *Technology in Western Civilization* (New York: Oxford University Press, 1967). pp. 204–205. Also called the Canal du Midi. See Darmstaedter (1666 Andréossy). Gunpowder is said to have been introduced in mining as early as 1613.

4. Harecastle Hill Tunnel, built 1766–1777.

5. Telford, *Life,* p. 155, cit. in Gibb, p. 185.

6. Rennie, pp. 36, 108.

7. Clements gives ferry prices for the 1820s (p. 81).

8. Cit. in Clements, p. 90 (without attribution); Pudney, p. 12.

9. The Duke of Wellington alluded to funds needed for this purpose when he argued for a renewed subscription in 1828 (Clements, p. 179).

10. Cit. without attribution in Clements, p. 191.

11. 823 meters long and 4.9 by 3.7 meters in cross section (West states 4.9 by 4.9).

12. *Min. Proc. ICE,* vol. 1, 1837, p. 32.

13. West, p. 107.

14. Clements, p. 83; Monthly Supplement of *The Penny Magazine,* 1–29 September 1832, vol. 1, p. 257.

15. Gravel, according to Clements, p. 84.

16. West, p. 106.

17. Ibid.

18. The method resurfaced in the late nineteenth century. Water mains and sewers were built by this method in Sydney, Australia, in 1885 and in Boston, Massachusetts, in 1893–1894. But its use on the scale Trevithick had envisioned had to wait for the construction of the Detroit River Tunnel on the Michigan Central Railway (1904–1910) between Windsor, Ontario and Detroit, Michigan (Black, pp. 165–171; West, pp. 209–213).

19. Clements, p. 86, has 49; West, p. 204, and others mention 54.

20. West, pp. 203–209. See also L. Franchot and Tessié du Motay's proposal for a cast-iron version in *Revue de l'architecture et des travaux publics,* vol. 6, 1845, pp. 192, 290–298, pl. 28 (thanks to Gregory Dreicer for this information).

21. Rolt, *Brunel* (1972 ed.), p. 41.

22. Until the mid-1850s, when iron began to replace wood in shipbuilding, the Institution of Civil Engineers repeatedly discussed treatments or wood types that could avoid the damage these animals caused.

23. GB patent 4204 20.01.1818; details in Clements, p. 89.

24. Rolt, *Brunel,* p. 42, names I. W. Tate, while the *Penny Magazine* supplement, p. 258, names J. Wyatt. Clements is undecided (p. 95).

25. Clements gives the details of the beginning fund drive, in which George Wollaston was prominent.

26. *The Thames Tunnel* . . . ; Skempton and Chrimes, p. 200.

27. Law, then a very young apprentice engineer on the site, quoted by Harding in Pugsley, p. 26. For a complete discussion of the process and the ensuing problems, see Skempton and Chrimes.

28. Clements, p. 100.

29. Forty-three years later, in 1866, the firm of Charles De Bergue & Co. took corings for the piers of the three-kilometer-long Tay Bridge. The results were later found to be inaccurate, which led to the redesign of the piers. And these half-baked changes ultimately contributed to the collapse of 1879 (Koerte, pp. 28, 35–36).

30. Skempton and Chrimes, pp. 202–204.

31. Ibid., pp. 206, 208.

32. Clements, p. 96.

33. Brunel had mechanized bootmaking and provided the army with a superior, machine-made product between 1810 and 1814. Wellington recognized the contribution the boots had made to his victory at Waterloo and showed his gratitude in many instances, especially in his unwavering support of the tunnel project (Clements, pp. 52–54, 72).

34. However, Donkin was to build a machine as innovative as the shield itself—the world's largest-diameter waterwheel—which he installed in an Italian textile mill in 1843 (Ferguson, *Early Eng. Reminiscences,* p. 116).

35. *The Thames Tunnel* . . .

36. Maigne, p. 346.

37. *The Thames Tunnel* . . . ; Clements, p. 112; Skempton and Chrimes, p. 204.

38. *The Thames Tunnel.* . . . Horizontal excavation started on 1 January 1826, at a depth of 19.2 meters.

39. See Chrimes et al. for all traceable editions of these informative ephemera.

40. Buchanan, pp. 166–167, for Gordon, and Atkinson, p. 30, for Page. Beamish was assistant engineer 1826–1828 under Isambard Brunel as resident engineer, and resident engineer himself 1835–1836; Page was assistant engineer 1835–1836 and resident engineer 1836–1843; and Gordon was assistant engineer 1835–1836 (Skempton and Chrimes, p. 194).

41. See chapter 6.

42. Comparable in its way to Rennequin of Liège's 1682 gargantuan waterworks at Marly; see Figuier, *Les Merveilles de l'Industrie,* vol. 3, pp. 360–368.

43. *Min. Proc. ICE,* vol. 1, 1837, p. 34.

44. Tubbing appears to have been first used for lining a vertical shaft by John Buddle, Sr., at Percy Pit Mine in 1796–1799: West, p. 161 (Atkinson, p. 171, states 1779).

45. The Thames shield model that was later exhibited in the Crystal Palace of 1851 was apparently neither Maudslay's nor Rennie's but that of their unsuccessful rival Donkin (*Official and Descriptive Catalogue,* vol. 1, p. 314: Civil Engineering, Architecture, and Building Contrivances. Section II, class 7, no. 46, "Donkin, Bryan & Co., Bermondsey"). A gradual development followed. Samuel Dunn patented a monolithic shield in 1849 (GB patent 12632, 05.06.1849), and R. Morton installed hydraulic jacks in 1866 and used the word "shield" for the first time (Hewett and Johannesson, p. 29; J. Vipond Davies, p. 678). But the first shields to follow the Brunel patent of 1818 closely were one for the second Thames tunnel in London and another in New York. The "Tower Subway" in London was a small, pedestrian tunnel. Peter William Barlow built it and James Henry Greathead was site engineer. They used a cylindrical shield that Greathead designed and Barlow patented in 1864 and 1868. It was small and monolithic, and it had a bulkhead to prevent flooding through the face. The Tower Subway was lined with cast-iron tubbing and grouted with lime mortar. Greathead refined the system on further sections of the London "Tube" 1884–1890, and it has remained essentially unchanged since (Black, pp. 31–32). The same year, Alfred Ely Beach, inventor and editor of the *Scientific American,* built a small-bore test section of an intended pneumatic subway under Broadway in New York between Warren and Murray streets (Hewett and Johannesson, p. 37; Black, pp. 32–33; *Scientific American,* 5 March 1870, pp. 154–156). Vogel (p. 238) suggests that Beach may have known of the Barlow-Greathead shield. His was lined partly with cast iron and partly with brick, and the cylindrical shield was pushed forward by hydraulic jacks like those Brunel had originally proposed but abandoned on Maudslay's advice. Beach shields were used in the following years in Cincinnati and Cleveland, the latter of which was abandoned when the shield was submerged. Several years later, 1874–1879, Hildevert Hersent used compressed air without a shield to build the rectangular Kattendyk Tunnel in Antwerp, and in 1886 Greathead used both together on a small shield on the City and South London Railway, followed by the contractor S. Pearson & Son in 1889 (Hewett and Johannesson, pp. 30–32, 37; Black, pp. 95–106). Dewitt Clinton Haskin patented Hersent's technique for the far larger Hudson River railway tunnel in New York, begun in 1874. The Hudson tunnel went through many engineering and financial troubles before it finally opened in 1905. Many experts, including Sir John Fowler, Sir Benjamin Baker, Greathead, and William Sooy Smith, consulted on it at

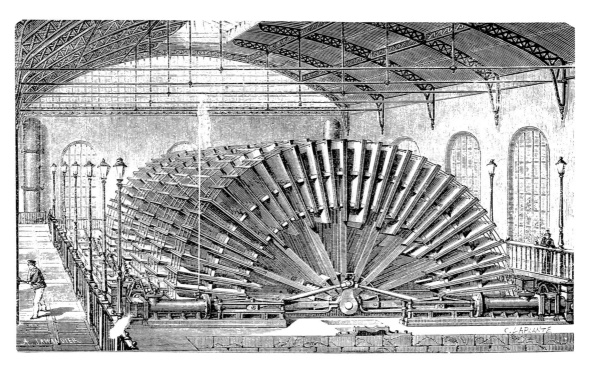

169.
Exterior of the Marly pumping station in 1725 and interior around 1870. The wheels were about the same size as the 1675 originals. Fourteen waterwheels and 221 pumps raised water 155 meters from the Seine to an aqueduct that fed the royal gardens at Marly and Versailles. (Marzy, 1871, pp. 265, 273.)

various times. The first shield to reach the dimensions of Brunel's was built by Joseph Hobson for the St. Clair River tunnel built in 1888–1891 between Sarnia, Ontario, and Port Huron, Michigan. Hobson combined the shield with compressed air, and mounted his cast-iron tubbing using an erector arm. The St. Clair shields had radii of 6.58 meters and weighed 80 tons. Later techniques stabilized silt by baking it, injected grout into the surrounding earth, or froze it, like the Milchbuck Tunnel built in Zurich in 1978–1980. Automated shields, or "moles," were proposed by Thomas Russell Crampton for the Channel Tunnel in 1882, albeit without any visible form of lateral protection. They were preceded by two simpler tunneling machines on the French and the English sides during the first attempt (c. 1875) by John Dickson Brunton (*Mém. et Compte-Rendu,* 1882, pp. 528–540, pl. 46), and Thomas English with Frederick Beaumont (West).

46. The tunnel must leak a little, since the railway planned to have the tunnel sheathed with Shotcrete in 1995. The attempt was postponed by the initiative of Julia Elton, who organized a protest to preserve the historical engineering monument intact.

47. Clements, p. 91. The argument is illogical, since round tubes would have been equally, or perhaps even less high.

48. Skempton and Chrimes, p. 208.

49. *Mechanics' Magazine,* no. 204, 21 July 1827, p. 7, and no. 216, 13 October 1827, p. 202. Each tarpaulin was made of four layers of canvas, and the largest measured 595 square meters or 24.4 by 24.4 meters (Black, pp. 32–33).

50. *Mechanics' Magazine,* no. 216, 13 October 1827, p. 202.

51. Technology translation between fields was common and gave the term "Industrial Revolution" its vibrant validity. Astronomers like James Nasmyth built steam hammers. Mechanical engineers built structures. The success of the Britannia Bridge depended on the contributions of an engineering theoretician, Eaton Hodgkinson, and a ship and locomotive builder, William Fairbairn. Other examples abound.

52. *Mechanics' Magazine,* no. 216, 13 October 1827, p. 203. The difference in cost was £6.19 per cubic yard versus £16.50 (*Penny Magazine,* no. 42, 30 November 1832, p. 342). According to Brunel his price was forty-eight percent of Trevithick's: £16.3 for the original Archway Company and £7.75 for his own (Memo of 9 March 1828, cit. in Clements, p. 173).

53. *Mechanics' Magazine,* no. 216, 13 October 1827, p. 203.

54. Ibid.

55. Ibid.

56. Clements, pp. 102, 122; Rennie, p. 35.

57. Investors had been badly burned in the South Sea Bubble in 1771. The lesson hadn't been forgotten half a century later. When a visionary entrepreneur, Junius

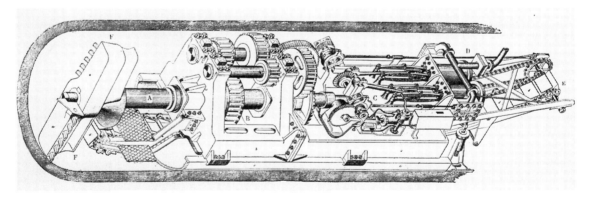

170.
Beaumont developed his
soft-rock "mole" for the English Channel project in
1875. It was a smaller but
more sophisticated machine
than Brunel's. (Figuier,
*Nouvelles Conquêtes de la Sci-
ence*, 1883–1885, vol. 2,
pp. 465, 468.)

171.
Brunton's automated 1875
"mole." (Figuier, *Nouvelles
Conquêtes de la Science,*
1883–1885, vol. 2, p. 469.)

172.
Beach dug a tunnel in New
York for a pneumatic railway. It used a full Brunel
shield fitted with a bulkhead to prevent flooding
through the face. (Figuier,
*Nouvelles Conquêtes de la Sci-
ence,* 1883–1885, vol. 3,
p. 285.)

Smith, attempted to raise £100,000 in 1835 to fund a steamship line between Liverpool and New York, he found no takers. He persevered and eventually succeeded in chartering the *Sirius* to compete with Isambard Brunel's *Great Western,* resulting in the famed 1838 race between the two ships (Wohleber, pp. 23–24).

58. See, e.g., *Times,* 7 November 1827, cit. in Clements, p. 159.

59. Clements, p. 163.

60. See Chrimes et al.'s exhaustive bibliography.

61. Letter from M. Brunel to Bentham, 27 April 1827, communicated by Felix Rosenthal, L'Art Ancien S.A., Zurich, c. 1975.

62. Colladon is mentioned in Perdonnet, vol. 1, p. 550, cit. in Figuier, *L'Année Scientifique,* vol. 15, p. 96. Both erroneously date the first blow to 1826; see Black, p. 28. The Franco-Genevan banker Delessert mentioned in Colladon, p. 92.

63. GB patent 6018, 20.10.1830. West, pp. 130–136.

64. Oiled leather valves were used in the pump that fed John Rennie's diving bell with which Brunel examined the bed of the Thames after the blow of 1828.

65. Rolt, *Brunel,* 3rd ed., pp. 47–48; Clements, p. 154.

66. *Mechanics' Magazine,* no. 231, 26 January 1828, pp. 442–444.

67. Ibid., p. 442.

68. The earliest known was a twelfth-century shareholding company that ran a French flour mill (Gimpel, Engl. ed., pp. 12–13, citing Sicard *Aux origines des Sociétés anonymes,* 1953).

69. Charles Manby, permanent secretary of the Institution of Civil Engineers, suggested a subscription for building the Crystal Palace as late as 1850, but only as a deficit guarantee (*Mém. et Compte-Rendu,* 1885, 1.sem., p. 251).

70. Clements, p. 177.

71. *Mechanics' Magazine,* no. 231, 26 January 1828, p. 443.

72. Ibid., pp. 444–445.

73. *Min. Proc. ICE,* vol. 1, 1840, p. 86.

74. *Min. Proc. ICE,* vol. 1, 1837, p. 35.

75. The Bletchingly, Saltwood, Tavistock Canal, Manchester-Bolton Railway, Primrose Hill, Kilsby, Mosely, and the younger Brunel's own Box Hill tunnels were those discussed by the Institution of Civil Engineers in 1842 and 1843 at meetings that both Brunels attended.

76. *The Builder,* vol. 1, 1844, p. 443, citing Knight's "London." The Wapping shaft was sunk with a monolithic caisson, similar to that at Rotherhithe except that it was tapered to making the sinking easier (Skempton and Chrimes, p. 214).

77. Pudney, p. 21.

78. Clements, p. 251.

79. Ibid., p. 223.

80. Beamish recorded many of the facts later reported by others. He was, however, a former assistant and admirer of Brunel's, and his evaluation of events must be taken as subjective. Clement's view is more broadly founded, but is still almost exclusively laudatory. His characterization of Brunel's detractors is still biased as their arguments are not clearly explained.

81. Only the professions were socially acceptable in Britain, especially the traditional ones in the church and military, which had long absorbed noble second sons excluded from aristocratic inheritance by the British legal custom of entailment.

82. Northampton's obituary in *Min. Proc. ICE,* vol. 11, 1851–1852, pp. 93–95, discusses social acceptability; Colladon, p. 228, intimates Lovelace's support.

83. Smiles, *George and Robert Stephenson,* counts 620 (footnote p. 408); Elton, *Railways,* no. 112, has 594.

84. *The Cambridge Economic History of Europe,* 1965 ed., vol. 6, p. 72, table 10, quoting L. I. Dublin, A. J. Lotka, and M. Spiegelman, *Length of Life,* p. 39.

85. *Min. Proc. ICE,* vols. 10–12. In 1849–1850, nine active members of the Institution over forty for whom information was available had died. Their average age was 61.8 years. In 1851, it was seven with an average age of 61.6; and in 1852, it was twelve with an average age of 62.3. For the four years 1849–1852, therefore, twenty-eight had died, at an average 61.9 years of age. And if we include the four engineers in 1850, the three in 1851, and the one in 1852 who had died before reaching forty, we have mean ages of 52.3, 53.1, and 60.1. And for all three years, the mean age of death was 55.3 years.

86. Vignoles, p. 281.

87. Ibid., footnote p. 142, quoting from letter of 4 December 1829.

88. Simmons, p. 23.

89. The earliest railway tunnel was the 1826 Terrenoire Tunnel near St.-Etienne on the Roanne-Andrieux horse-drawn railway. It was dug just two years after the Thames Tunnel began (Black, pp. 20–21). Railway tunnels soon appeared in the United States and then in Britain. Although tunneling began relatively late in America with the Auburn canal tunnel in 1818–1821, the first American railway tunnel, the Allegheny Portage Tunnel of 1831–1833 at Staple Bend near Johnstown, Pennsylvania, was still earlier than any in Britain. But by the early 1840s both Britain and the United States

had several, while longer tunnels, like the Mont Cenis and the 7.6-kilometer Hoosac Tunnel near North Adams, Massachusetts, on the Troy-Boston line, only became feasible with the maturation of a new pneumatic energy source and drilling method.

90. Capt. Goodwyn of the Bengal Engineers used them before they were introduced to Britain in 1740–1747 by Charles Labelaye for Westminster Bridge (Rennie, pp. 63–65), to France by Jean-Rodolphe Perronet and others, and to the United States by William Weston for Timothy Palmer's "Permanent Bridge" over the Schuylkill at Philadelphia in 1805 (Upton, p. 66).

91. An iron one was built for the pier at Milton-on-Thames in 1835 (Maigne, p. 347), while Sir Proby Cautley began using concrete caissons in India in the 1850s (Buchanan, p. 152).

92. Bernard Marrey, *Les Ponts Modernes: 18e–19e siècles* (Paris: Picard 1990), calls him Charles Jean; Guy Grattesat, *Ponts de France* (Paris: ENPC, 1982) calls him simply Charles; Elton refers to him as Jacques.

93. *Comptes Rendus de l'Académie des Sciences,* quoted in *Min. Proc. ICE,* vol. 10, 1851, pp. 361–362. Details in *Min. Proc. ICE,* 1837, vol. 1, p. 34; Hewett and Johannesson, p. 31. The sources Triger may have known were Denis Papin's 1691 *Manière de conserver la flamme sous l'eau,* John Smeaton's 1778 pump for the diving bell at Ramsgate harbor (C. E. Fowler, 3rd ed., pp. 14–18), and Colladon's 1827 proposal.

94. Triger, in Maigne, p. 349; Mougel, in Nepveu, p. 192; Cavé, in Robert Stephenson, *Min. Proc. ICE,* vol. 10, 1851, pp. 368–369.

95. Oiled leather was used even though rubber tubes were first made in 1768. George Medhurst's compressed-air-driven engine was designed in 1799 (GB patent 2299, 28.02.1799). Medhurst apparently used his engine to power an automobile (GB patent 2431, 02.08.1800), and he became known for his patent to turn rotary into reciprocating motion: GB patent 2467, 27.01.1801.

96. Fairbairn, *Life,* p. 169.

97. *Report from the Select Committee on Atmospheric Railways,* 1845; Elton, *Railways,* nos. 165, 166.

98. Vulcanization was invented by Charles Goodyear. See *Min. Proc. ICE,* vol. 4, 1845, pp. 58–59, for early use of vulcanized rubber. By 1845 vulcanized rubber was readily available and Robert William Thomson had patented the first inflatable rubber tire: GB patent 10990, 10.12.1845. The Institution of Civil Engineers discussed the use of vulcanized rubber for shock absorbers in 1845 and the results of its long-term behavior in water meter valves in 1854. It proved excellent for valves (*Min. Proc. ICE,* vol. 4, 1845, pp. 58–59; Hovine, 1854; also Bateman, pp. 432–435). Gutta-percha lasted underground or in water and was useful for buried or submerged telegraph wires, but it became brittle when exposed to air (*Min. Proc. ICE,* vol. 4, 1845, pp. 58–59; vol. 12, 1853, pp. 456–459 [E. A. Cowper on pump valves]; vol. 13, 1854, pp. 432–435).

99. GB patent 9975, 05.12.1843. This was based on his previous patent 9642 of 21.02.1843.

100. The piles were 11–75 centimeters in diameter (*Mém. et Compte-Rendu,* 1848, pp. 77–78).

101. Nepveu, pp. 189–190; Clegg, p. 319; *Mém. et Compte-Rendu,* 1848, pp. 77–78. John Hughes used the "vacuum cleaner" method on the Great Northern Railway for William Cubitt's Nene Bridge at Peterborough, and Fox and Henderson used it again for Isambard Brunel's Wye Bridge at Chepstow in 1850 (Clegg, pp. 319, 366; Humber, p. 168; Hughes, pp. 356–357; Nepveu, p. 192).

102. Nepveu, pp. 192, 193, 196. It was in this context that Hughes first used the term "air lock" (Hewett and Johannesson, p. 31).

103. Nepveu, pp. 191, 195–199, footnote p. 195 for a Saône bridge; Emile Fortin-Hermann, *Mémoire sur les procédés,* pp. 253–258, for Eiffel, citing reports by Regnauld of 31 August 1859 and 7 April 1860; Emile Fortin-Hermann, in *Mém. et Compte-Rendu,* 7 September 1860, p. 263, for bridges in Spain.

104. The pneumatic caisson method replaced Alexander Mitchell's screw pile foundation that had been widely used in iron lighthouse and pier construction since 1838 (GB patent 6446, 04.07.1833, improved in patent 11777 of 04.07.1847; see also Hague and Christie, pp. 133, 136–137, 207, 221, 225, for information on Alexander Mitchell). The many European examples included two by Castor and Hersent in St.-Gilles (1865) and Arles (1866). While the new Argenteuil Bridge used "ordinary" tubular piling (*Mém. et Compte-Rendu,* 1861, p. 406), Knippels Bridge between the islands of Amager and Sjelland in Copenhagen used the pneumatic caisson method (*Illustrerede Tidende,* 1868; the contractor Burmester & Wain still exists as part of the German M.A.N. concern), and so did a bridge over the Po in Italy in the mid-1880s (*Mém. et Compte-Rendu,* 1886, p. 12). The technique was introduced to the US in 1852 by L. J. Fleming in Georgia (Daniel E. Moran, p. 671), or for the Pee Dee and Santee River bridges in South Carolina (Jacoby and Davis, 3rd ed., p. 319). About 1865 William Sooy Smith used it for the foundations of a small lighthouse at Waugaschance (Daniel E. Moran, p. 671), and in 1868–1869 for the piers of the 1872 Omaha Bridge over the Missouri River (C. E. Fowler, 3rd ed., p. 21; Daniel E. Moran, p. 671); James Eads used it for the 1874 Mississippi Bridge at St. Louis and John Roebling for the 1883 Brooklyn Bridge in New York.

105. See Vugnier and Fleur Saint-Denis.

106. Vugnier, in *Mém. et Compte-Rendu,* 1858, p. 49; Castor received a prize from the Institut de France for his work in 1863 (Figuier, *L'Année Scientifique,* vol. 7, 1863, p. 488). Castor's system remained virtually unchanged until the pneumatic caisson was abandoned in favor of modern piling techniques in the 1950s.

107. *Mém. et Compte-Rendu,* 1861, pp. 406–407. A swinging span had to be built at either end of the bridge so that rail traffic could be interrupted by either nation in case of hostilities. Louis Figuier, the widely read French science popularizer, reported in detail on the development of the method and its history in several annual volumes of his periodical *L'Année Scientifique et Industrielle:* vol. 4, 1860, pp. 179–192; vol. 6, 1862, pp. 158–165.

173.
Pneumatic caissons replaced
Alexander Mitchell's 1840
screw-piling technique for
lighthouse and pier con-
struction. Screw piles were
made of brittle cast iron
and were limited to individual foundations in soft, homogeneous subsoils.
(Tomlinson, 1852, vol. 2,
p. 177.)

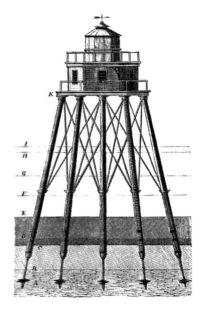

108. Medical publications on the probable causes and treatment began to appear from 1857 in Germany and France (Jacoby and Davis, pp. 331–333). Variant hypotheses about the causes persisted until the twentieth century, especially in the United States.

109. Flachat, "Mémoire no. VII," pp. 357–358, 392–396. The Mont Cenis Road was built by Fabroni.

110. Benedikt Laroche of Basel had debated the feasibility of building one across the Gotthard Pass with Eugène Flachat (Flachat, "Mémoire no. VII," p. 314).

111. The 1707 Urner Loch on the Gotthard Road was the first alpine road tunnel; the second appears to have been in Austria. Semmering, *Upton,* p. 117.

112. The Hoosac Tunnel in Massachusetts (1855–1876) was similarly utopian when it was planned in 1825. But as influential as it was from the point of view of innovation, that project is less easy to analyze because of major design alterations, changes in contractors, and severe accidents that delayed the process until modern tunneling means were available.

113. Figuier, *L'Année Scientifique,* vol. 21, 1877, pp. 211–227; vol. 25, 1881, pp. 214–217; vol. 26, 1882, pp. 218–219; vol. 27, 1883, pp. 187–189; vol. 28, 1884, pp. 225–231; vol. 30, 1886, pp. 237–239. The French war ministry showed interest in a project suggested by Georges Lavigne in 1869, and had the area surveyed (*Revue Moderne,* cit. in *Mém. et Compte-Rendu,* 1883, 2nd sem., p. 111). A report of 1877 suggested creating a lake of 8,200 square kilometers, about 14–15 times the size of Lake

Geneva. Its chief proponent, François-Élie Roudaire, died in 1885, and it was last mentioned in 1886, by which time artesian wells were being drilled in the area (see also *Mém. et Compte-Rendu,* 1883, 2nd sem., pp. 32, 110–119, 482, 484–515, 595–624). Charles Laurent drilled the famed artesian well at Passy in Paris 1855 and had begun looking at the Sahara in 1856 (Laurent, 1856 and 1859).

114. In May 1840 (Petitti, p. 561).

115. Médail's plan was worked out by June 1841 (ibid., document 12, pp. 558–567).

116. To five kilometers (ibid., p. 560).

117. *Annales des Ponts et Chaussées,* 1843.

118. In preliminary reports of 1845 and 1848 (Petitti, p. 568).

119. Fontenay, p. 193.

120. A prototype was built by Thémar in Turin and tested in the Val d'Oc.

121. Possibly inspired by Maus's design, two French engineers developed a rotating cast-iron plate drill that cut slits in the face that were easy to break out manually (Figuier, *L'Année Scientifique,* vol. 5, 1860, p. 106).

122. Energy transmission using drive chains had been unsuccessfully attempted as early as 1724 (Butterworth, p. 51; not in Darmstaedter). The Liège ropes are mentioned in Colladon, p. 342. Maus surely knew of and may even have influenced the replacement of hemp by wire ropes about 1845 on the inclined plane between Fenchurch Street and Minorities on the London-Blackwall Railway (Rennie, p. 79).

123. Maus calculated the cost to be equivalent to 150–200 laborers' wages.

124. Ducuing, vol. 1, pp. 338–339, ills. pp. 337, 168–169. Hirn's transmissions were soon widely used and influenced the spatial organization and grouping of factory buildings all over Europe.

125. The other members of the committee were Mosca, Carbonazzi, Cavalli and Meano, two engineers Federico Luigi Menabrea and Giulio, and the geologist Angelo de Sismonda; see also Figuier, *L'Année Scientifique,* vol. 3, 1859, pt. 1, p. 307; Figuier, *Nouvelles Conquêtes,* vol. 2, pp. 71–72.

126. Two further proposals, one using vacuum as motor force, were equally unsuccessful.

127. Fontenay, p. 192.

128. Colladon may have heard of Papin's 1687 idea of transporting energy over distance using an air compressor, of Triger's 1845 proposal to drive a machine in a mine at Chalonnes using pneumatic force 230 meters away from the source (Pernolet, pp. 1, 9, 12), or August Leopold Crelle's article on the subject published in Berlin in 1846. He may also have heard of Stouvenel's report to the Académie des Sciences,

Mémoire sur la Transmission à grande distance de la puissance hydraulique au moyen de l'air comprimé, or of the pneumatic motor installed in a Scottish mine near Glasgow in 1849 (Stouvenel, cit. in Pernolet, pp. 9–10).

129. This brought him to the attention of scientists like Jean-Baptiste Dumas of the Académie des Sciences and engineers like Baron Armand Séguier. It made him part of mainstream research.

130. Fairbairn, *Life,* p. 169.

131. Colladon was surely aware of the book on compressed air written by Andraud in 1840. He submitted his report to the Ministry of Finance and the engineers Cavour, Menabrea, and Giulio, and applied for a patent on 30 December 1852 in Turin.

132. Menabrea, in *Gazette officielle de Savoie,* Chambéry, 19 January 1853, cit. in Figuier, *L'Année Scientifique,* vol. 15, pp. 100, 101: "Il a perfectionné la machine de M. Maus, ou pour mieux dire, inventé un nouveau mécanisme et proposé de nouveaux et puissants moyens qui sont de matière à abréger considérablement l'opération et la rendre beaucoup moins coûteuse. . . . La commission reconnaît surtout de quelle importance peuvent être les inventions de M. Colladon pour hâter la construction des chemins de fer destinés à franchir les Alpes."

133. Colladon, pp. 341–342.

134. The contractor for the line between Chambéry and Culoz was Brassey Jackson and Henfrey. The Bartlett drill may have profited from the 1844 experiments of C. Brunton in England, who had tried to use compressed air, and it may also have been influenced by Waterhouse's pneumatic hammer. (Darmstaedter calls the inventor Bruxton, West calls him C. Brunton; there is no patent registered, although William Brunton did have mining patents). Bartlett's drill seems to have been independent of the American J. J. Crouch's of Philadelphia, who patented the first steam-driven, mechanical percussion rock drill on 29 March 1849, or his assistant Joseph W. Fowle's drill patented 11 March 1851 (Crouch shown in Butterworth, pl. 70; also West, pp. 40–41).

135. Probably as a result of the success of these tests, Aimé Thomé de Gamond suggested a steam drill and no explosives for his Channel tunnel proposal in 1856.

136. Several mechanical drills were also under development at the time. The Société des Ingénieurs Civils reported at their meeting of 15 March 1858 on two, an unspecified American one that may have been Fowle's and one built by a Mr. Booman, reported in the journal *L'Invention.* (*Mém. et Compte-Rendu,* 1858, pp. 296–297).

137. It was possibly based on de Caligny's 1837 patent (Colladon asserts the influence, p. 344).

138. Cavour, cit. in Figuier, *L'Année Scientifique,* vol. 14, 1869, p. 291.

139. It grossed 45,981 francs per kilometer while British lines grossed 40,417 francs, German 30,288 francs, and Italian 22,070 francs (Figuier, *L'Année Scientifique,* vol. 9, 1865, p. 467).

140. Flachat, "Mémoire no. VII," p. 317.

141. Designed by Michel, Karl Pestalozzi, and Kaspar Wetli (Flachat, *De la traversée des Alpes,* p. 376).

142. Flachat, "Mémoire no. VII," pp. 313–314.

143. Ibid., p. 317.

144. Flachat, "Compte Rendu," pp. 222–223.

145. 50 francs per ton, including transportation over the pass at 0.12 francs per kilometer; others calculated even less (Flachat, "De la traversée des Alpes," pp. 311, 313).

146. Ibid., p. 318. The final project featured a tunnel 12,700 meters long with conservative gradients of 2.0 and 2.3 percent and curves of 350-meter radius. The French portal at Modane lay 1,324 meters above sea level and the Italian at Bardonecchia at 1,190. The line climbed 3.5 percent on the French side and 3.0 percent to the south (ibid., footnote p. 324).

147. West, p. 47, speaks of a drill patent of December 1858.

148. Figuier, *L'Année Scientifique,* vol. 15, 1870–1871, p. 103. The average cost of a meter of tunnel proved to be 4,000 francs and the engineers were paid 4,617 francs.

149. Fines had been used to control building processes as far back as ancient Greece, but the bonus incentive may have been an innovation (Alison Burford, *The Greek Temple Builders of Epidauros: A Social and Economic Study of Building in the Asklepian Sanctuary, during the Fourth and Early Third Centuries B.C.* [Toronto: University of Toronto Press, 1969], pp. 92–93, citing J. Bundgaard, 1946, *Class. et Med.,* vols. 2, 7, 8).

150. The drills needed only 667 cubic meters at six atmospheres, while the lion's share of the total of 14,320 cubic meters was needed for ventilation and cooling. The engineers expected temperatures as high as 59°C at the workface.

151. Figuier, *Nouvelles Conquêtes,* vol. 2, p. 154: "Un nuage noir et épais se répand dans la galerie, par suite de l'inflammation de la poudre. Mais bientôt ce nuage de fumée oscille, se déchire peu à peu, et s'evanuit comme un décor de théâtre, pour laisser voir l'extrémité du tunnel."

152. Alfred Nobel began producing his safer dynamite from 1867 on, but it only came into use after Cenis opened and was first used on the Gotthard, the Musconetong, and the Hoosac tunnels (J. Vipond Davies, p. 675).

153. F. Ducuing in "L'Opinion nationale," cit. in: Figuier, *L'Année Scientifique,* vol. 7, 1863, pp. 175–176:

> J'ai pris en main . . . la lampe fumeuse du mineur, et . . . nous nous sommes avancés dans le tunnel sombre, par les trottoirs qui bordent la double voie de fer déjà établie.

Des wagons chargés de déblais passaient devant nous. A mesure que nous avancions, la lumière des lampes apparaissait plus vague et, pour ainsi dire, plus éstompée au milieu d'une fumée plus dense. Du fond du tunnel nous arrivaient comme des grondements de tonnerre; c'était tantôt un trou de mine auquel on venait de mettre le feu, tantôt d'injecteur d'air comprimé qui s'ouvrait pour renouveler l'atmosphère.

Nous étions parvenus au fond de tunnel, au milieu des mineurs qui paraient la voie, taillaient la voûte et ouvraient de nouveaux trous de mine devant eux, à coups de marteau et à la lueur des lampes projetant plus de fumée que de lumière. Les yeux, les oreilles et les poumons finissent par s'habituer pourtant à cette obscurité pesante, à cette sonorité intense, et jusqu'à cet air qui se raréfie et se charge des vapeurs. La sensation la plus pénible qu'on éprouve est la chaleur dans cet atmosphère privée d'air ambiant.

Mais, tout à coup, l'injecteur s'ouvre, répandant dans tout le tunnel ses effluves d'air comprimé. Dans cet atmosphère instantanément rafraîchi et purifié, nous respirons tout à fait à l'aise, et un bien-être très-sensible se fait en nous. Nous étions à 870 mètres dans le coeur de la montagne, et isolés de tout air extérieur.

154. Fontenay, p. 194; Flachat, "Compte Rendu," footnote p. 231.

155. Figuier, *L'Année Scientifique,* vol. 6, 1862, pp. 99–100. Pneumatic drills were used in the Altenberg mines in Prussia (1863), Sars-Longchamp in Belgium (1864), Saarbrücken (1866), the Loire region (1867), Marihaye near Liège and Anzin (1868), and Ronchamp (1870). In 1866 a drill Charles Burleigh patented after examining Sommeiller's was tested with success in the Hoosac Tunnel (West, p. 42). By 1876 pneumatic technology was used in ten French mines, five Belgian, twenty-two Prussian, and eight Austrian (Pernolet, p. 11).

156. The principle of rotation had been proposed by Charles-Pierre Combes in 1844 based on the theoretical work of Belgian Major Coquilhat (Darmstaedter).

157. West, p. 52.

158. Flachat, "Mémoire no. VII," pp. 388–389.

159. Cazin, in *Revue des Cours Scientifiques,* 1869, cit. in Figuier, *L'Année Scientifique,* vol. 14, 1869, pp. 283–292. These conduits had specially designed expansion sleeves and were probably the longest yet built in cast iron.

160. Fontenay, p. 194; Flachat, "Compte Rendu," footnote p. 231.

161. Cazin, in Figuier, *L'Année Scientifique,* vol. 14, 1869, p. 286.

162. It is curious that the first description of the proposed drilling technique in the *Mémoires et Compte-Rendu* made no mention of the Society's own member Colladon in 1859, naming only nonmembers Bartlett and Sommeiller. The reason was that Flachat apparently based his information solely on what was contained in the Sardinian government report. Colladon was probably not present at the meeting and did not contribute to the discussion. But he surely received the proceedings, even though

Switzerland and France had recently disputed their claims to Savoy and the Swiss government had blocked French funds invested in Swiss transalpine projects (Flachat, "Compte Rendu," p. 222). Figuier, who used several sources, certainly recognized Colladon's seminal work (Figuier, *L'Année Scientifique,* vol. 7, 1863, p. 165; vol. 15, 1870, pp. 100–103; Noblemaire, *Mémoires de la Société des ingénieurs civils,* 1861, p. 103). After everything was over, the Italian government finally did indirectly acknowledge Colladon's contribution in 1871 by awarding him the order of Cavaliere di SS. Maurizio e Lazzaro, but with no remuneration for the use of his patents (Colladon, in *Mém. et Compte-Rendu,* 1872, pp. 110–111; Colladon, p. ix, has his honorary rank as "Commendatore").

163. Fontenay, p. 194; Figuier, *L'Année Scientifique,* vol. 13, 1868, p. 152.

164. Cazin, in *Revue des Cours Scientifiques 1869,* cit. in Figuier, *L'Année Scientifique,* vol. 14, 1869, pp. 283 ff.

165. At the end, work progressed rapidly on the railway link from Bardonecchia to Buscalino to the south, and more slowly in France between Saint-Michel and the tunnel mouth with a two-kilometer-long tunnel at Sordette.

166. Gottschalk to Flachat in *Mém. et Compte-Rendu,* 1871, p. 377.

167. Flachat, "Mémoire no. VII," p. 326.

168. Ibid., pp. 360–364, and Flachat, "Compte Rendu," p. 224, and footnote 2. The Simplon proposal is described in Flachat, "De la traversée des Alpes," There were exotic proposals too, like Antonio Gabrini's for a double-hung, reciprocating railway in a pneumatic tube that would shelter the whole line from snow (Politecnico, Milan, mentioned in Figuier, *L'Année Scientifique,* vol. 6, 1862, pp. 90–91).

169. Charles Ellet, Jr.'s, 5.6 percent temporary Mountain Top Track over a 575-meter pass in Virginia in 1854 (ibid., pp. 392–396), and a 5.56 percent temporary track on Benjamin Henry Latrobe's Baltimore and Ohio (pp. 365–366, citing *The Engineer,* vol. 3, p. 73).

170. Flachat, "Compte Rendu," p. 225.

171. Flachat "Mémoire no. VII," p. 339. Petiet's idea was later adopted by William Hood on the Southern Pacific Railroad in the Great Tehachapi Loop in California in 1876 (*The Builders* [Washington, D.C.: National Geographic Press, 1992], pp. 82–83), and on several alpine railways: the Gotthard in 1873–1882, the Albula in 1904, and the steepest of all traction railways, the Bernina in 1908.

172. Conybeare, lecture at Chatham, cited in Flachat, "Mémoire no. VII," footnote p. 340 and p. 365, condensed from Douglas Galton's report in *Mém. et Compte-Rendu,* 1858, pp. 59–80. James Berkley was using the switchback system on the Western Ghat segment of the Great Indian Peninsular Railway at that time.

173. Flachat, "Mémoire no. VII," pp. 355–356: "D'accord avec nous que les passages des Alpes ne doivent pas être abandonées aux lenteurs d'exécution et aux éventualités des projets en voie d'exécution, qu'il faut une solution immédiate, fût-elle provisoire,

et qu'en conséquence il ne faut pas hésiter à passer les cols à ciel ouvert, il ne croit pas indispensible d'accumuler, comme nous l'avons fait, tant de conditions nouvelles pour la solution du problème; il lui semble que l'on peut atteindre le but par les moyens que l'art consacre aujourd'hui."

174. Figuier, *L'Année Scientifique,* vol. 13, 1868, p. 149.

175. Tyler, pp. 451–452.

176. The system was based on studies by Nicholas Wood (*A Practical Treatise on Railroads . . .* [London: Knight and Lacey, 1825]), François Marie Guyonneau, Comte de Pambour (*Traité théorique et pratique des machines locomotives . . .* [Paris: Bachelier, 1835]; "De la résistance des machines locomotives en usage sur les chemins de fer," *Mém. et Compte-Rendu,* vol. 5 [1837], vol. 6 [1838]; "Expériences concernant le frottement des waggons et le résistance de l'air contre les trains . . . ," *Mém. et Compte-Rendu,* vol. 9 [1839] or vol. 17 [1843]), and Arthur Morin (*Nouvelles expériences sur le frottement, faites à Metz en 1831* [Paris: Bachelier, 1832–1833]) on the friction of iron wheels on rails, as well as on Koller's report on the Gotthard Railway, and Benjamin Henry Latrobe's thoughts on the Baltimore and Ohio. Flachat, "Mémoire no. VII," pp. 337–338, for the Gotthard; ibid., pp. 372–384, citing E. Morris in the *Journal of the Franklin Institute* with additional comments by Flachat, for the Baltimore and Ohio; Séguier presented his proposal to the Académie des Sciences in December 1843. Several systems for steep inclines appeared in those years. John Brunton's 1815 cogwheel system was revived in the United States by Sylvester Marsh for a thirty percent gradient, and by Niklaus Riggenbach for the Rigi-Viznau Railway in Switzerland. Another system developed by Wetli claimed to use twenty to forty percent less energy, but it must have had other disadvantages, since it did not survive.

177. Desbrière in *Mém. et Compte-Rendu,* 1864, pp. 75, 77, and 1865, pp. 408, 412.

178. Tyler, p. 444; Desbrière in *Mém. et Compte-Rendu,* 1865, p. 426. The French permit followed by imperial decree on 4 November 1865 (Tyler, p. 446).

179. 104,000 francs per kilometer or a total of 8 million francs (Figuier, *L'Année Scientifique,* vol. 13, 1868, p. 149). Similar lines were subsequently built at Cantagallo in Brazil in 1869 (*Mém. et Compte-Rendu,* 1872, pp. 448–452) and between Wellington and Featherston in New Zealand (ibid., 1881, pp. 656–660).

180. Figuier, *Nouvelles Conquêtes,* vol. 2, pp. 5–6.

181. *Mém. et Compte-Rendu,* 1872, p. 610.

5   The Transition and the Catalyst: The Conway and Britannia Bridges and the Suez Canal

1. Fairbairn, working with Vignoles, built two in 1846 and Cubitt one. In 1849 Fairbairn built another two (Dempsey, pp. 24–25, 27–29; Fairbairn, "On Tubular Girder Bridges," p. 237; *Mém. et Compte-Rendu,* 1848, pp. 74–75). Neither form could be said to have been "invented" for this project as there were many approaches to them before, but this was their first appearance as conscious types on a large scale.

2. Turner, p. 207; Fairbairn, "On Tubular Girder Bridges," p. 241; *Mém. et Compte-Rendu,* 1848, pp. 74–75; Dempsey, pp. 22, 30–32, 42, 45; Braidwood, p. 149 (Cottam's discussion of Braidwood's paper).

3. Fairbairn, *Life,* preface by Mousson in 1970 ed., p. x; Fairbairn, *An Experimental Enquiry.*

4. Sir Alexander Gibb, *The Story of Telford: The Rise of Civil Engineering* . . . (London, 1935), p. 171.

5. Vignoles, pp. 225–226.

6. 24 May 1847 (*Builder,* May/June 1847, p. 316, on railroad accidents and their prevention; *Report of the Commissioners,* 1849).

7. Braithwaite, p. 474. Koerte has discussed the significance of bridge collapses on the development of British engineering and the transition from cast to wrought iron (pp. 12–16). In France, too, bridge collapses influenced structural development, especially ones where many lives were lost. The failure of Joseph Chaley and Bordillon's Basse-Chaîne Bridge at Angers in 1850 led to the abandonment of wire cable suspension bridge building for twenty years in France and to the loss of French preeminence in that field (Peters, *Transitions,* pp. 169–171).

8. For Stephenson's role, see Fairbairn, *An Account,* p. vii. Georg von Reichenbach built the first tubular arch bridge over the Oker in Braunschweig (1824). Tubes had subsequently been used for the top chords of several small bowstring trusses and arches in Hungary, for the large arches of Antoine Rémy Polonceau's Pont du Carrousel in Paris (1836), and for several small girder bridges in Britain.

9. GB patent 11401, 08.10.1846; Fairbairn, *Life,* p. 213.

10. See Peters, "Architectural and Engineering Design," for a full discussion of technological thought.

11. Rosenberg and Vincenti, pp. 85–86 note 38, pp. 87–89 note 47.

12. Fairbairn's bridges included the Trent Bridge at Torksey in 1851. Stephenson's bridges were two on the Alexandria-Suez railway over the Nile near Damietta with their tracks running on the tube, not through it. One of them near Benha had eight spans, including two swing spans. The third was the twenty-five-span Victoria Bridge over the St. Lawrence River in Montreal (1854–1859), designed with Alexander Ross, the Grand Trunk Railway's engineer. It was built by James Hodges of Peto Brassey and Betts (Ivan Flachat, in *Mém. et Compte-Rendu,* 6 December 1861, pp. 408–409; Helps, pp. 199–213). Stephenson imported the iron from his cousin George Robert Stephenson's Canada Works at Birkenhead in England. That firm with its 600 employees (Brassey, p. 156) went on to manufacture the parts for Rendel's great Jumna Bridge at Allahabad in India. Others built plate girders too. George Totten built a remarkable 190.5-meter, six-span one over the Chagres River at Barbacoas on the Panama railway in 1850–1855 (Otis, pp. 41, 108).

13. Clark, vol. 2, p. 483.

14. Dreicer is currently studying this phenomenon.

15. Fairbairn, *An Account,* p. 170, citing Stephenson's recommendation in this regard in Minutes of the Board, p. 80.

16. The gradual development of the tubular, cellular, plate girder form precludes its "invention" out of whole cloth, simplisticly implied by Stephenson and repeated by historians since (Rosenberg and Vincenti, p. 6, citing Clark, vol. 1, p. 9).

17. Fairbairn, *An Account,* p. 42.

18. Clark, vol. 1, p. 25.

19. Rosenberg and Vincenti, pp. 12, 87 note 47.

20. John S. Scott, *Penguin Dictionary of Civil Engineering,* 1980 ed., p. 39.

21. Clark, vol. 1, p. 35.

22. Fairbairn, *An Account,* pp. 53–54.

23. Fairbairn, *An Account,* p. 88.

24. Ibid., p. 63.

25. Ibid., footnote p. 23.

26. He had replaced the usual hand ram with a steam hammer on the pile foundations of his Tyne Bridge between Newcastle and Gateshead in 1846 and succeeded in driving ten-meter piles in four minutes (Straub, 1st German ed., p. 235; English ed. 1960, p. 216).

27. Robert Smith, GB patent 7302, 16.02.1837. Fairbairn used the machine for years in his factory and it was later exhibited to an interested public at the Crystal Palace in 1851. He claimed to have paid for the patent and given the rights to his assistant Smith (Fairbairn, *Life,* pp. 163–164). However, Smith held GB patent 7126, 22.06.1836, with the identical title. In spite of Fairbairn's claim to authorship, Smith had obviously already worked on the idea.

28. Fairbairn, *An Account,* pp. 90–91. Clark claimed to have had the idea first, as he noted on his copy of Fairbairn's book in the archives of the ICE: "This planned floating and raising was entirely Mr. Clark's suggestion, he explained his views to Mr. Fairbairn, before he had an opportunity of seeing Mr. Stephenson & in the presence of Mr. Blair. Mr. Fairbairn immediately adopted these views and approved them and wrote the above ungenerous letter as though they were his own views . . ." (manuscript note at the bottom of p. 90 in Clark's copy).

29. Clark, vol. 1, pp. 30–31.

30. Fairbairn, *An Account,* pp. 166–167.

31. Ibid., pp. 172–173.

32. Ibid., p. 35 (Stephenson's report to the directors of 9 February 1846); Smiles, *George and Robert Stephenson,* p. 448.

33. Billington, *The Tower and the Bridge,* pp. 120–121, 48–49, 55, 59.

34. David Billington's thesis that there is an "engineering art" distinct from architecture is a provocative idea, but it needs more radical implementation than it receives in *The Tower and the Bridge* where he treats it as another form of aesthetics of product.

35. Glynn, pp. 370–371.

36. Figuier, *Nouvelles Conquêtes,* vol. 4, p. 11.

37. According to *Encyc. Brit.* this was Charles Lepère, apparently J.-M.'s brother.

38. Glynn, p. 370.

39. Captain Chesney did the 1830 survey (ibid., p. 374). Chesney later surveyed the Euphrates Railway in 1857 as major-general.

40. Landes, *Bankers,* p. 81, citing L. Wiener, *L'Egypte et ses chemins de fer,* pp. 54–57.

41. Abbas followed the one-month rule of his uncle Ibrahim.

42. Alexis Barrault in *Mém. et Compte-Rendu,* 1858, p. 277.

43. In 1857 Eugène Flachat and Léon Molinos mentioned differences of 40–103 centimeters depending on tides and the weather (p. 34). Brüll observed only 18 centimeters in 1864 (*Mém. et Compte-Rendu,* 1864, p. 413).

44. Glynn, p. 378; Negrelli, pp. 278–279.

45. Stephenson cited by Barrault in *Mém. et Compte-Rendu,* 1858, p. 282.

46. Ibid., pp. 282–283; *Min. Proc. ICE,* vol. 10, pp. 10–13; Glynn, pp. 376–377.

47. K. Bell, p. 122.

48. Flachat and Molinos, pp. 27–29.

49. *Revue des Deux Mondes,* 1 January 1856, cit. in Figuier, *Nouvelles Conquêtes,* vol. 4, p. 36; Flachat and Molinos, pp. 29–32; Barrault in *Mém. et Compte-Rendu,* 1858.

50. Smiles, *George and Robert Stephenson,* p. 484. A radical parliamentary group tried to change British opposition to the canal, but met with no success (D. Bradshaw, p. 240).

51. Barrault in *Mém. et Compte-Rendu,* 1858.

52. Bradshaw, pp. 240–241.

53. Glynn, footnote p. 375, and pp. 375–376; Figuier, *Nouvelles Conquêtes,* vol. 4, p. 52.

54. Flachat and Molinos, pp. 32–33.

55. Ibid., p. 35–40.

56. Figuier, *Nouvelles Conquêtes,* vol. 4, pp. 47–50.

57. The khedive held 176,000 shares; the average for those 188 French shareholders was 170 shares (K. Bell, p. 122; Landes, *Bankers,* pp. 176–177, p. 183 footnote 1).

58. Landes, *Bankers,* p. 176; Landes *Unbound Prometheus,* pp. 206–207, for the broadening of the investing public. Subscription, lottery, limited and private sale of shares, or patronage had financed earlier large-scale projects.

59. Lesseps, *Percemat: Conférences populaires,* pp. 27–28: "Lorsque le fils de Mehmet-Ali m'appela auprès de lui et me donna le concession du canal, la science de l'ingénieur et le principe nouveau de l'association des petits capitaux permettaient d'exécuter l'entreprise, quelque difficile et quelque coûteuse qu'elle pût être. Aujourd'hui vous savez où nous sommes arrivés, grâce au concours de la France, grâce au concours, je ne dirai pas des petites gens, comme a dit lord Palmerston, car il n'y pas de petites gens aujourd'hui en France, où tout le monde appartient à la démocratie, mais des petites bourses."

60. *Mém. et Compte-Rendu,* 1864, pp. 419, 444.

61. Landes, *Bankers,* pp. 177–178.

62. There was precedent for this method of raising money for public works, especially in Britain. The first was organized under Elizabeth I for the repair of the Cinque Ports; and Virginia was settled and the London aqueducts and Westminster Bridge built by the proceeds of lotteries.

63. Landes, *Bankers and Pashas,* pp. 83, 181, and footnote 1; Lavalley "Travaux d'exécution," p. 525 (reprint p. 3).

64. The tank was built by Charles Lasseron. It delivered drinking water along what would later be the north branch of the freshwater canal (*Mém. et Compte-rendu,* 1864, p. 414).

65. Serf labor was traditional in Egypt, and had been common in much of Europe until the French Revolution: the infrastructure of France was built using the same *corvée* system.

66. K. Bell, p. 123.

67. Palmerston to Delane, cit. in K. Bourne, p. 345.

68. Landes, *Bankers,* pp. 71–77, for a comparison between Egyptian and Indian cotton production.

69. K. Bourne, p. 90.

70. Flachat in *Mém. et Compte-Rendu,* 1864, p. 418; Otis, pp. 31–32, 35–36, only hints at the high mortality rate on the Panama railway site.

71. Figuier, *Nouvelles Conquêtes,* vol. 4, p. 167.

72. Landes, *Bankers,* p. 180, footnote 1.

73. Cotton became the basis of Egyptian prosperity from the doubling of prices at the beginning of the Union blockade until they collapsed in 1866 (Landes, *Bankers,* pp. 88, 125, 181).

74. The Egyptian government built the first segment of ninety kilometers to Ras-el-Wadi. The company dug the next fifty-six kilometers to Lake Timsah by February 1861 and to Suez, thirty-two kilometers further south, in December 1863. The northern branch to Ismailia and El Qantara was only finished in 1869.

75. Aiton's dredges were built by Gouin. *Mém. et Compte-Rendu,* 1864, p. 416, states that he was to dig 28,800,000 cubic meters; see also Flachat in ibid., p. 468.

76. Flachat in Lavalley, *Communication faite par . . . ,* p. 1: "que jusqu'à l'époque des dernières communications faites à la Société sur les travaux du percement de l'Isthme de Suez, l'organisation de ces travaux avait reposé presque entièrement sur la main-d'œuvre des fellahs; que l'influence de l'Angleterre ayant amené une révolution dans les conditions techniques d'exécution de l'entreprise, en faisant enlever soudainement à la Compagnie la ressource du travail manuel, le travail mécanique devenait seul possible."

77. Flachat in *Mém. et Compte-Rendu,* 1864, p. 422.

78. *Mém. et Compte-Rendu,* 1864, pp. 416–417, 422–426.

79. Flachat and Molinos, p. 46.

80. The ladder dredge had been known at least from 1845: *Allgemeine Bauzeitung,* 1846, vol. 11, pl. 12; Weale, *Ensamples;* Malézieux 1873. For discussion of the steam shovel, see Sciama in *Mém. et Compte-Rendu,* 1864, pp. 427–428.

81. Lavalley, "Travaux d'exécution," p. 525 (reprint p. 3). Mechanical dredging was developed in the eighteenth century but had not changed much since (Flachat in Lavalley, "Travaux d'exécution," p. 430, reprint p. 25). A sixteenth-century dredge is shown by Roland Savery, illustrated in H. Arthur Klein, p. 137. Most dredges were manually or animal powered, although some steam dredges did exist in Italy from about 1845 on (Cialdi).

82. *Mém. et Compte-Rendu,* 1864, p. 426.

83. Lavalley, "Travaux d'exécution," p. 431 (reprint, p. 27).

84. Report by Sciama, in *Mém. et Compte-Rendu,* 1864, p. 428.

85. Ibid., p. 427; Lavalley, "Travaux d'exécution," p. 527 (reprint p. 6).

86. Lavalley, "Travaux d'exécution," p. 527 (reprint p. 5).

87. Badois in *Mém. et Compte-Rendu,* 1864, p. 446; Lavalley, "Travaux d'exécution," pp. 527–528 (reprint p. 6).

88. Lavalley, "Travaux d'exécution," pp. 528, 532 (reprint pp. 6–7, 11).

89. See chapter 7, subsection titled "The French project."

90. Flachat in *Mém. et Compte-Rendu,* 1864, p. 487.

91. Badois, "Étude," pp. 488–505.

92. Lavalley, *Communication faite par . . . ,* p. 9: "La transformation était difficile et longue. La recherche, le préparation du matériel devait prendre bien du temps. Il a fallu, en outre, transformer les premières rigoles, suffisantes pour l'alimentation des chantiers à bras, en une profonde et large voie capable de porter un gros matériel. Il a fallu construire, de distance en distance, de véritables villes dont les maisons en maçonnerie offrent maintenant des logements convenables à nos ingénieurs, nos employés et nos ouvriers européens, et où s'élèvent des chapelles, des hôpitaux, des magasins."

93. Lavalley, "Travaux d'exécution," p. 527 (reprint pp. 5–6).

94. Ibid., pp. 525–526 (reprint pp. 3–4).

95. Ibid., pp. 529–530 (reprint pp. 8–9). The gypsum dredged from Lake Ballah was inappropriate for forming banks.

96. Ibid., p. 531 (reprint p. 10).

97. Ibid., p. 523 (reprint p. 1).

98. Lavalley, *Communication faite par . . . ,* p. 22.

99. Lavalley, "Travaux d'exécution," p. 534 (reprint p. 14).

100. Lavalley, *Communication faite par . . . ,* p. 43: "Nous avions bien songé à remplacer les mulets par des treuils à vapeur qui, au bas et au haut du plan incliné, feraient le mouvement des wagons au moyen d'un câble et de poulies de retour facilement attachées aux traverses des voies. Le temps nous a manqué pour exécuter ce complément d'installations dont l'étude nous a montré la complète possibilité."

101. Zenker, *Der Suez-Canal,* p. 21; Figuier, *Nouvelles Conquêtes,* vol. 4, p. 156.

102. Bunau-Varilla, p. 45.

103. Lavalley, "Travaux d'exécution," pp. 535–536 (reprint pp. 15–16).

104. Ibid., p. 536 (reprint pp. 16–17).

105. Ibid., p. 533 (reprint p. 13); Zenker, *Der Suez-Canal,* p. 21.

106. Flachat and Molinos erroneously say from the south (p. 32); see Lavalley, "Travaux d'exécution," pp. 427, 532.

107. Zenker, *Der Suez-Canal,* pp. 30–31.

108. Lavalley, *Communication faite par . . . ,* p. 22.

109. See note 122 below.

110. Lavalley, *Communication faite par . . . ,* p. 48: "La Compagnie, alors en possession d'un énorme matériel déjà amorti, n'aurait à payer que le fonctionnement des dragues, et le travail ne lui coûterait pas plus cher que les terrassements à sec fait même par les fellahs aux termes des anciennes conventions."

111. Lavalley, "Travaux d'exécution," p. 433 (reprint p. 30).

112. Lavalley, *Communication faite par . . . ,* p. 20. After the demonstration in Paris in 1844, Moritz Hermann von Jacobi and Acherau had unsuccessfully attempted to light the Admiralty in St. Petersburg electrically in 1849 and the lower house of the Belgian parliament in 1852. According to Thomas Brassey, British navvies had worked night shifts as early as 1846 on the Trent Valley railway, but he makes no mention of how the site was lit (Brassey, p. 195). The first known use of electric arc lighting in building was for the reconstruction of the Pont de Notre-Dame in Paris in 1853. The construction of the bleachers for the closing ceremony at the exhibition building in Paris in 1855 was electrically lit on a large scale (Figuier, *L'Art de l'Eclairage,* pp. 231–232). Night work followed on the Louvre and the North Docks, also in Paris, as well as the port of Le Havre (Figuier, *Nouvelles Conquêtes,* vol. 1, p. 232) and the rigs and machinery for sinking the caissons for the Kehl-Strasbourg Bridge in 1857–1859 (Figuier, *L'Année Scientifique,* vol. 4, 1860, p. 190). Electric arc lighting was also used for underwater work in Dunkerque Harbor and on a shipwreck in Cherbourg Harbor in 1864. It was later to be used in Corsica in 1875 (Figuier, *Nouvelles Conquêtes,* vol. 1, p. 281), and on Sir Thomas Bouch's Tay Bridge in 1876 (Koerte, p. 41).

113. Lavalley, *Communication faite par . . . ,* pp. 58–59.

114. Figuier, L'Année *Scientifique,* vol. 6, 1862, pp 161–162: "C'était un spectacle magnifique que ces immenses ateliers suspendus au-dessus du fleuve. Les marteaux-pilons, qui ont joué un si grand rôle pour l'enfoncement des pieux des pilotis; les machines soufflantes, qui comprimaient l'air à l'intérieur des caissons; les scieries à vapeur; les chariots, qui glissaient sur les rails disposés tout le long des chantiers; les machines drageuses, qui rejetaient en dehors les débris enlevés au fond du fleuve: tout marchait à la fois, remplissant l'air des cris aigus, de grincements, de bruits sourds et

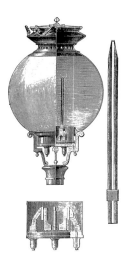

174.
In December 1844 Deleuil and Léon Foucault organized the first public demonstration of night lighting by electricity on the Place de la Concorde in Paris. They used an early carbon arc system. (Figuier, *Nouvelles Conquêtes de la Science,* 1883–1885, vol. 4, pp. 13, 43.)

175.
Carbon arc lamps also illuminated the building site for the bleachers for the 1855 Paris Exhibition's closing ceremony. Even underwater harbor work was electrically lit in the 1860s and 1870s. (Figuier, *Nouvelles Conquêtes de la Science,* 1883–1885, vol. 1, p. 283, and vol. 4, p. 217.)

répétés. L'arrivée de la nuit n'interrompait pas le travail; la lumière électrique remplaçait alors la clarté du jour et illuminait de reflets fantastiques cette immense fourmillière de travailleurs attachés à l'une des plus belles entreprises que l'industrie humaine ait conçues et réalisées."

115. Detailed descriptions in *Allgemeine Bauzeitung,* 1840; Michaelis, pp. 297–315; Zenker, *Der Suez-Canal,* p. 9; Lesseps, *Percement: Conférences populaires,* pp. 33–35.

116. *Mém. et Compte-Rendu,* 1864, p. 416; Lavalley, "Travaux d'exécution," p. 426 (reprint p. 20); 25 tonnes = 20 tons. In 1856 their cost had been estimated at 12.5 percent of the total cost, or 18 million francs (Flachat and Molinos, p. 41).

117. Coleman, p. 59; Zenker, *Der Suez-Canal,* p. 28.

118. From 58 to 100 meters.

119. Borel, in Lavalley, *Communication faite par . . . ,* p. 59: "Un avantage du genre de travail que nous avons à faire est dans son extrême homogénéité. Les mètres cubes se succèdent toujours les mêmes. Il n'en est pas de même dans l'exécution des chemins de fer qui exigent les travaux de terrassements les plus divers, de maçonnerie de toute espèce, de la charpente, des poses de voies, etc. Tout se réduit pour nous à une question d'installation."

120. Lavalley, *Communication faite par . . . ,* p. 60: "Chacune de nos dragues doit faire, pendant la durée de l'entreprise, un certain nombre de milliers de mètres cubes, et ce certain nombre de milliers de mètres cubes se trouve sur une certaine longueur du canal, sur 2, 3, ou 4 kilomètres suivant la hauteur du terrain naturel. A chaque drague nous donnons une de ces longueurs de canal à faire et elle y demeurera jusqu'à la fin de l'entreprise, de sorte que les hommes qui la montent resteront jusqu'à la fin dans les mêmes conditions de nature de terrain, de profondeur à creuser, etc. Faisant sans cesse la même chose, ils la feront de mieux en mieux, c'est-à-dire de plus en plus vite."

121. Lavalley, "Travaux d'exécution," p. 429 (reprint p. 24); Lavalley, *Communication faite par . . . ,* p. 49.

122. Ibid., p. 60: "Nous sommes dans d'autres conditions: les ouvriers qui sont sur nos dragues, nous ne pouvons pas les congédier et les reprendre. Nous n'avons qu'un temps très-limité pour faire le travail. Chaque jour est grevé de frais considérables d'amortissement des appareils; il faut donc à tout prix que nos dragues ne chôment pas."

123. Bell, p. 137. The khedive's interest was valued at $20 million and had potentially been on the market since 1868 (Landes, *Bankers,* pp. 128, 310–311, 313, 317; Haskin, p. 337).

124. Haskin, pp. 335, 338. The canal was 8 meters deep and the maximum allowable draft was 7.5 meters.

125. Ibid., pp. 336–337. In 1882 Britain threatened to invade Egypt and take control of the canal. Lesseps, who headed the French Panama project by then, used his international prestige to convince the European powers to force Britain to abandon its

intentions and recognize the canal's international status and neutrality. The international agreement held for almost a century and ultimately provided the diplomatic rationale for the Franco-British invasion when Egypt's President Gamal Abdel Nasser nationalized the canal in 1956 (shortly before the ninety-nine-year concession was anyway due to expire).

6   Patterns of Technological Thought: Buildings from the Sayn Foundry to the Galerie des Machines

1. Depping, p. 6.

2. *Min. Proc. ICE,* 1851–1852, vol. 11, p. 88.

3. European iron structures traced their ancestry to the Ironbridge of 1779, but there were other antecedents, too. In 1779 Jacques-Germain Soufflot designed a wrought-iron roof for a staircase in the Louvre, the Théâtre Royal in Paris was roofed in iron in 1790, and English mill construction used iron structure from 1792 on.

4. Ruskin, *The Stones of Venice,* vol. 1, appendix 17, "Answer to Mr. Garbett," pp. 386–394.

5. Edward Lacy Garbett, *Rudimentary treatise on the principles of design in architecture as deductible from nature and exemplified in the works of the Greek and Gothic architects* (London: John Weale, 1850) (Weale's rudimentary treatises, vol. 18).

6. Originally invented by John Claudius Loudon around 1817, the ridge-and-furrow roof became intimately associated with Paxton's name (Hix, 1981 ed., pp. 20–21).

7. Augustus Welby Northmore Pugin, *The True Principles of Pointed or Christian Architecture: set forth in two lectures delivered at St. Marie's, Oscott* (London: John Weale, 1841), p. 1. In Pugin's view, decoration is an overlay. It is only readable if we know the cultural meaning of a form. Ornament is an integrated visual enhancement. It is readable across cultures and time.

8. P. G. Custodis discovered the building, recognized its unusual characteristics, and restored and published it.

9. Althans added four bays and the swiveling cranes in 1844–1845 (Custodis, p. 4; the swiveling cranes in 1845 according to Franz Reuleaux, cit. in Darmstaedter, 1845 S).

10. Werner, p. 257.

11. Ball bearings were patented by Courtois, Tihay, and Defrance (F patent 1857). See Darmstaedter for their use from 1869 for bicycles in France as well. The fishbelly truss was the inversion of the bowstring truss that railway engineers used around 1840. Fox and Henderson published a book on the bowstring type in 1849. George Stephenson used the more common lenticular version with curved upper and lower chords for the Gaunless Bridge on the Stockton and Darlington Railway (1822). Laves used it for a wooden bridge in Hannover (1835) and for several iron ones, notably Hannover-Herrenhausen (1839–1840) and a project for St. Petersburg (1838). The engineer Friedrich August von Pauli and contractor Ludwig Werder popularized the form in the Isar bridge near Grosshesselohe, Bavaria, in 1857.

12. Custodis, p. 9. Schinkel was a high official in the Baudepartement from 1815 and became its head in 1830.

13. Charles Taylor, pp. 886–887 and pl. 20.

14. Herbert, p. 150; Ullrich.

15. Diestelkamp, pp. 2–9.

16. See Diestelkamp for the history of the design process

17. The designer was Rodolphe Maehly, the engineer of the Jardin d'Hiver in Paris. A foundry in Charleville was to cast it (*Illustration,* vol. 16, 1850, p. 160).

18. British workshops exported thousands of them between the end of the eighteenth and the mid-nineteenth century. The earliest on record was apparently sent to Bermuda in 1805 (information from Ted Cavanagh, Halifax). The Darby foundry in Coalbrookdale shipped its first cast-iron bridge to Jamaica in 1807 (Herbert, p. 30, citing Raistrick), and two of Marc Brunel's suspension bridges went to the Îles Réunion in 1823 (Navier, *Rapport à Monsieur Becquey . . .*). Larger buildings followed, like a timber-framed "palace" with cast-iron panels built for King Eyambo of Calabar on the Guinea River in 1843, a house for two ladies on St. Lucia, and another sent to Nova Scotia (*The Builder,* 1843, p. 170). Prefabricated iron churches became popular export items, and complex buildings, like Isambard Brunel's hospital at Renkioi in Turkey or Paxton's prefabricated housing, were shipped out during the Crimean War (B. Russell, p. 53, citing Hughes, *Seaport: Architecture and Townscape in Liverpool,* 1964). Herbert catalogues hundreds of examples. A kiosk for India, possibly from the 1840s, is illustrated and described in Walmisley, 2nd ed. 1888, p. 30, fig. 50; see also Buchanan, p. 152, citing John Brunton.

19. Barry Russell, p. 33, citing Lewis Mumford, *The Pentagon of Power;* Claude S. George, Jr., *The History of Management Thought* (Englewood Cliffs, N.J.: Prentice-Hall, 1968), pp. 33–39, citing F. C. Lane, *Venetian Ships and Shipbuilders of the Renaissance.*

20. *Manchester as It Is,* London: Love and Boston 1839 pp. 210–211, cit. by Musson in preface to Fairbairn, *Life,* 1970 ed., p. xv; compare also Gilbreth.

21. Cecil Smith, p. 660, footnote 8, citing Howard Rosen; Claude S. George, *History of Management Thought* (Englewood Cliffs, NJ: Prentice-Hall, 1968), pp. 61–62, quoting W. F. Durfee in *Jnl. Franklin Inst.,* vol. 137, no. 2, February 1894. Jefferson letter to John Jay, 30 May 1785.

22. Rennie, pp. 50–51. See chapter 2 for Bramah's machine.

23. Unlikely according to the account given by Clements.

24. This is Taylor of Fox and Taylor, Southampton.

25. See Rees's *Cyclopaedia* for a detailed description of the production line. For the block machine, see GB patent 2478, 10.02.1801; for Brunel's saws, GB patent 2844,

07.05.1805; for the veneer saw, GB patent 2896, 23.09.1806; and for his famed circular saw, patent 3116, 14.03.1808. The whole sawmill system was patented in GB patents 3529, 28.01.1812, and 3643, 26.01.1813. Clements, pp. 25, 34, 56, 80; Tomlinson, vol. 1, p. cxli.

26. Clements, p. 33.

27. Marc Brunel to Sir Evan Nepean, Secretary to the Admiralty, February 1802, cit. in Beamish, pp. 59–60.

28. Surprisingly, the use of interchangeable parts spread more slowly in Britain than in the United States, where a lack of craftsmen drove the development of precision manufacture. British industrialists were astonished forty-five years later when they visited the American exhibit in the Crystal Palace. They saw a Springfield rifle made entirely of industrially produced, interchangeable parts, which made it simple to repair weapons in the field. The British ordnance corps immediately imported the technology in its entirety to produce the Enfield rifle.

29. Sir Samual Bentham to Sir Evan Nepean, 30 April 1803, in Beamish, pp. 69–70.

30. Clements, p. 38.

31. Beamish, pp. 112–116. Beamish claimed (p. 125) that the Chatham sawmill began "a new era in the economical management of timber."

32. Giedion, *Mechanization,* pp. 88–90, for the Deptford Biscuit Manufactory of 1833, leading to William Bruce's GB patent 6661, 14.08.1834. Brassey, p. 112, for the English locomotive works. The Cincinnati meat-processing plants were first described by Giedion in *Mechanization,* citing Peter Barlow, *A Treatise on the Manufacture.* See also Gordon's sources and his documentation of the overhead rail in Cincinnati, p. 65, fig. capt. 13.

33. Navier supposed people packed as tightly as possible into a square meter, which he calculated at three persons weighing about 60 kilograms each, or 180–200 kilograms per square meter, and on the load of a wheeled vehicle, which came to the same amount when spread over its footprint.

34. Dufour, "Observations sur le rapport de M. Navier," Travaux E 16, Archives d'état, Geneva, pp. 1–2: "Quant à la force, je sais fort bien qu'au maximum on doit compter sur 200 Kilog de surcharge par mètre carré, mais cette évaluation ne me semble nécessaire que pour les petits ponts qui peuvent facilement se couvrir du monde et pour les grands ponts de Capitales très peuplées comme Paris, Londres &c. Partout ailleurs il faut se régler d'après les probabilitiés pr. ne pas se jeter dans des dépenses exagerées; or il m'a semblé que sur un pont à péage et dans une de nos villes de Suisse on ne pouvait pas raisonnablement supposer qu'il y eut plus de mille personnes à la fois sur chaque moitié du pont car deux mille personnes réunis sur un pont font une véritable foule, et l'on ne pourrait y en faire entrer trois par mètre carré qu'en les rangeant espacés côté à côté en colonne serée, ce qui ne peut être admis. En outre les réglemens de police peuvent toujours empécher de grandes foules sur les ponts." (Cit. in Peters, *Transitions,* pp. 111–112).

35. Peters, *Transitions.*

36. Pickett, p. 28.

37. Ibid., p. 70.

38. Collins, *Concrete,* p. 114, citing *Révue générale d'architecture,* vol. 8, 1849–50, col. 30.

39. They had experience in specialized construction as well, like the foundations of the Rochester Bridge in 1844 and George Willoughby Hemans's 1850 Althone Bridge over the Shannon in Ireland. See also Humber, p. 229.

40. Matthew Digby Wyatt, in *Min. Proc. ICE,* 1850, pp. 136, 157; Charles Fowler, Jr., p. 186.

41. Paxton later "rectified" the quick design in the Sydenham Crystal Palace in 1854, where he reused the system and put most of the design effort into diversifying the overall form.

42. *Art Journal Illustrated Catalogue,* preface, pp. xvii-xviii.

43. Charles Fox held six patents, among which was one for building machinery: GB patent 11381, 24.09.1849, "machinery for shearing, cutting, and punching metals." So his "machine-building" was a natural extension of the building process.

44. Charles Fowler, Jr., p. 47.

45. Demountable buildings are older than iron construction. According to traditional Germanic law, wooden houses were considered movable rather than real estate, the principle being "Was das Feuer verzehrt ist Fahrniß" ("what fire consumes is chattel.") The upper classes, therefore, built in stone, while the lower had to make do with wood. In the Swiss canton of Appenzell, the bishop granted the medieval peasantry the right to take their building lumber from church forests free of charge. In the sixteenth century, clever businessmen among them built a lucrative trade by erecting houses on their own land to satisfy the letter of the law, and then disassembling them for export. An agreement between the church and an Appenzell municipality in 1596 put an end to this misuse by granting the church the right of first refusal on all wooden buildings, but the influence this practice had on the construction and detailing of the Appenzell farmhouse can be seen to this day. (Tom F. Peters: "Das Appenzeller Bauernhaus," in *Wohnbau in Europa. Seminarbericht. ETH Zurich Architekturabteilung,* (Zurich: Verlag der Fachvereine und der ETH, 1972), pp. 82–83.)

46. *Art Journal Illustrated Catalogue,* pp. xix–xx.

47. Matthew Digby Wyatt, in *Min. Proc. ICE,* 1850, pp. 171, 179–180. Airy was right in this instance, but later, in his equally unscientific opinion of the strength of lateral wind forces in the Firth of Tay, his misjudgment contributed to one of the most notorious disasters in British construction history, the Tay Bridge collapse of 1879.

48. Mallet, in *The Record of the International Exhibition 1862,* p. 60.

49. Thomas Zieman analyzed the original structure in 1985. James Linsley, Jr., discovered the cross bracing in the nave roof and included it in 1992. Zieman's model failed at a wind load of just over 8 pounds per square inch and Linsley's at about 21 pounds per square inch. The two manuscript reports are in the author's possession.

50. The two sets differ in details. Charles Fowler, Jr.'s, was published in the *Allgemeine Bauzeitung* in 1850. The other by Charles Downes was published in 1852 after the building was demolished. The second set was annotated by Charles Cowper (like Edward Cowper, Charles may have been an employee of Fox and Henderson). Presumably this set shows the structure as built and incorporates the contractors' reactions to the critique of 1850. It may also show what ideally should have been built. The only known originals perished in the fire of 1936.

51. Zieman manuscript. Turner criticized the lack of connection between the base plates and the foundation. Apparently the original idea had been to use Alexander Mitchell's screw piles (Matthew Digby Wyatt, in *Min. Proc. ICE,* 1850, p. 168).

52. The basic module was the same, the detail forms were recognizable, but the contractors added a cellar and made many other structural changes. The highest part was seven stories; it had three vaulted transepts and a vaulted nave, high loggias, and two long, three-story exedra, one of which might well have been the collapsed wing Mallet mentioned.

53. Mallet, in *The Record of the International Exhibition 1862,* p. 59.

54. Buchanan, p. 126; Record, p. 60.

55. Matthew Digby Wyatt, in *Min. Proc. ICE,* 1850, p. 151.

56. The problem of "keying" or wedging railway rails to the "chairs" attached to the sleepers using cast iron or oak had been discussed at length in a meeting of the Institution of Civil Engineers five years before (W. H. Barlow). The problems must have been solved differently when the Crystal Palace was reerected on a much larger scale in Sydenham in 1854, since the building stood without obvious damage until it burned down on 30 November 1936.

57. Charles Taylor, p. 885.

58. Ivan Flachat, in *Mém. et Compte-Rendu,* 6 December 1861, pp. 410–411. It must have worked somehow, probably by the spontaneous formation of plastic joints in the iron floors. The much shorter Britannia Bridge worked without expansion joints too, but it moved ten centimeters at either end.

59. Mallet, in *The Record of the International Exhibition 1862,* p. 59.

60. Furthermore, the London building was to house the future South Kensington Museum. In spite of everything, stone was still considered the appropriate representational material for "works of architecture." Robert Mallet criticized the London building. He was scandalized that none of Britain's more experienced builders had been

involved in the project (Record, p. 585). However, Fowke had built the Edinburgh Museum of Science and Art and the Dublin National Gallery extension (Elliott, p. 58).

61. Charles Fowler, Jr., p. 80.

62. Ibid., p. 81. It is not clear whether Mallet knew this when he estimated the columns to be two inches out of plumb. If he didn't, and took the floor to be horizontal, it is a coincidence that his observation corresponded precisely to the thermal deflection calculated for that place and height by Zieman.

63. Charles Fowler, Jr., pp. 81, 186.

64. See Peters, *Transitions,* for iron suspension bridges.

65. Elliott, p. 132.

66. The panes measured 124.5 by 25.5 centimeters (Charles Fowler, Jr., p. 48). The statistics are from 1852, but they were of the same order of magnitude in 1850.

67. Beamish, pp. 60–61.

68. David Henderson held two patents relevant to the building's construction: GB patents 10713, 10.06.1845, "cranes"; and 12537, 26.03.1849, "manufacture of metal castings." The crane was developed from the one built by Francis Watt for Bell Rock Lighthouse in 1808 (Gale, pp. 287, 333, pl. 45, ills. 341–345), and that in turn was based on Bramah's which Peter Kier improved for him at Ramsgate Harbor (Charles Taylor, p. 840 and pl. 19). (Thanks to Robert Thorne and John James's notes kindly supplied by Mike Chrimes of ICE for clarification of the relationship between David and John Henderson).

69. Matthew Digby Wyatt, in *Min. Proc. ICE,* 1850, p. 153. There is some confusion as to whether this was Edward or Charles Cowper.

70. Paxton's experience lay in greenhouse construction, in which most of the prefabricated parts were wood. He was influenced by the writings of John Claudius Loudon, who advocated cast iron to permit maximum solar gain. Paxton preferred heavier wooden members because they reduced heat loss. He had begun making wooden components mechanically for the forcing beds at Chatsworth in 1828 and perfected his machinery on the "Great Stove" (1837–1839).

71. Herbert, p. 172; Matthew Digby Wyatt, in *Min. Proc. ICE,* 1850, p. 159; Charles Fowler, Jr., pp. 48, 64, 112–114.

72. Charles Fowler, Jr., pp. 114, 130–131, 186.

73. Ibid., pp. 113, 215.

74. Ibid., p. 112.

75. Matthew Digby Wyatt, in *Min. Proc. ICE,* 1850, p. 139.

76. Elliott, p. 132 caption, citing the *Illustrated London News,* 7 December 1850.

77. The idea of roving assembly teams was reinvented by Volvo in automobile assembly 120 years later.

78. Fox's name lives on in the second firm Sir Charles founded after the collapse of the first in 1856: Freeman Fox and Partners, known today for its long-span suspension bridges.

79. Hütsch, p. 69.

80. Report of a committee charged with examining its safety in 1914, cit. in Hütsch, p. 48.

81. For sources on Roussel see chapter 2, note 21.

82. Mechanized sawing was known in Roman times, and sawmills were in operation at Augsburg in 1322 and in Norway about 1530, where they were called the "new art of manufacturing timber" (Beamish, p. 103, footnote citing Johann Beckmann). They appeared again sporadically in other parts of seventeenth-century Europe based on Cornelis Corneliszoon's wind-driven sawmill of 1593. But until the middle of the nineteenth century, saw blades were so thick and the control of their cut so approximate, usually about 9.5 millimeters, that up to thirty percent of the timber ended up on the skids as sawdust. Only locations with seemingly unlimited supplies of timber could tolerate such wastage. It was what Rosenberg calls a "resource-intensive" technology (Rosenberg, in Hindle, p. 54). The resistance of skilled workmen to labor-saving devices that threatened their livelihood also inhibited the spread of mechanized sawing in seventeenth- and eighteenth-century Europe (Beamish, footnote p. 103). Millers and engineers were interested in mechanical sawing nevertheless, because it was faster than manual pit sawing, which produced at most sixty meters a day (Mansfield, in *Proceedings of Wood Symposium,* p. 72). By the mid-nineteenth century, in contrast, mills with sash saws cut twenty-five times as much. This is why the first large-scale lumber mills were built in labor-scarce and raw-material-rich North America, and one of the chief reasons why American light-wood framing systems, which use many members of small cross section, developed so differently from wood construction elsewhere. The first machine patent taken for an invention in North America was for a sawmill, Joshua Jenks of Massachusetts in 1646 (Rosenberg, in Hindle, p. 42), although the Dutch had built sawmills on Manhattan and the Germans in Virginia before that. Circular saws began to appear in 1777 and Marc Brunel developed them between 1805 and 1808 (Samuel Miller, GB patent 1152, 11.04.1777; Brunel, GB patents 2844, 07.05.1805; 2968, 23.09.1806; 3116, 14.03.1808; 3529, 28.01.1812; and 3643, 26.01.1813). American firms began importing them in 1814 (Mansfield, in *Proceedings of Wood Symposium,* p. 72). Circular saws are economical because they cut a smaller kerf. But their size is limited and they work slower than sash or gang saws, cutting at most three hundred meters a day (Elliott, p. 10). So they were primarily used for cutting veneers until after 1850, when band saws became even more precise and high-quality steel reduced blade fracture (William Newberry, GB patent 3105, 30.01.1808; see Rosenberg, in Hindle, p. 27). Band saws first appeared in Britain and the United States. The first American band saw mill is said to have opened in 1869 (Mansfield, in *Proceedings of Wood Symposium,* p. 74).

83. Nail machines were invented in the latter half of the eighteenth century, flaunting the British ban on mechanized production in the colonies. Jacob Perkins's nail machine of 1795 was the best known of the early ones and possibly the most successful. US patent 16.01.1795; Rosenberg, in Hindle, p. 43.

84. See Peters, "An American Culture of Construction," for a full discussion of the consequences.

85. See Bogardus, pl. 2. A number of studies have been done on the relationship between this form of flexibility and American living, especially in various Levittowns. See for instance Saim Nalkaya, "The Personalization of a Housing Environment: A Study of Levittown, Pennsylvania," dissertation, University of Pennsylvania, 1982; Barbara Kelly, "The Politics of House and Home: Implications in the Built Environment of Levittown, Long Island," dissertation, SUNY Stony Brook, 1989; and Kelly's *Expanding the American Dream: Building and Rebuilding Levittown* (Albany: SUNY Press, 1993).

86. However, American pragmatic framing did influence twentieth-century European architects. Translating American empiricism into European concept, Hennebique developed the concrete frame, Le Corbusier expressed independence from the site by raising buildings on stilts, Walter Segal examined interior and exterior flexibility in prefabricated houses, and Archigram explored physical mobility in utopian designs. During the Second World War some architects exported their theoretical interpretations back to the United States. Some of these exports flourished, like Ludwig Mies van der Rohe's ideas, while others failed, like Walter Gropius and Konrad Wachsmann's manufactured housing.

87. The oldest identified example of the fully developed balloon frame dates from around 1850. The balloon frame cannot reliably be traced to a single event, although popular myth claims that it was invented in Chicago in 1833. But there are many transitional forms, ranging from plank framing (which seems to more closely resemble the 1833 Chicago version) to the Chesapeake frame. Numerous intermediate stages are yet unrecognized. Boorstin (vol. 2, p. 193), following Condit (vol. 1, p. 22, giving no source), claimed that St. Mary's Church in Chicago was the first building of the new type. The church was single-storied, while the balloon frame typically has two; it was built in 1833 by Augustine Deodat Taylor, a Hartford, Connecticut, carpenter. This account is supported by Walker Field. Giedion had previously claimed that George Washington Snow, a New England Quaker, was the builder and inventor (*Space, Time and Architecture,* 5th ed., pp. 352–354). No doubt the two did have something to do with the development and proliferation of light-wood framing. The light frame survives in a stackable, one-story form: the Western platform frame, which today forms about eighty percent of America's construction volume.

88. In 1850 a New York firm shipped the hundred-room Astor House Hotel to San Francisco, complete with a fifty-five meter frontage and ten stores. The same firm exported over five thousand prefabricated houses to California (Boorstin, vol. 2, p. 196).

89. The most current research considers this building to have been a one-story, plank frame.

90. *Allgemeine Bauzeitung,* vol. 9, 1844, see plate 626.

91. Broadside illustrated in Dibner, p. 42.

92. It led to the mobile home, a prefabricated house theoretically attached temporarily to its site. In reality, once it is placed, it is generally only moved when sold. The mobile home is considered a vehicle, much as the wooden house of ancient Germanic culture was considered a chattel according to the ancient Germanic law (see note 45 above). It is not considered elegant to live in, but it is amortized much quicker than a house and is taxed at a lower rate than real estate. For these reasons, it constitutes about ten percent of American housing (see the cultural study of Allan D. Wallis, *Wheel Estate: The Rise and Decline of Mobile Homes* [New York: Oxford University Press, 1991]). The recreational vehicle is related to the mobile home. This house on wheels ranges from the simply modified pickup truck to the elaborate Airstream trailer. Its background is in George Pullman's popular drawing room–cum–sleeping railway cars with their transformable and stowable furniture (Pullman patented the folding upper berth with Ben Field in 1864 and the lower a year later, and began manufacturing his cars on a large scale when the Pullman Palace Car Company was established in 1867).

93. The terrace house had its roots in the rural and early industrial croft, the workman's attached row of cottages, but upper-class acceptance of complete standardization and the consequent urban regimentation was peculiar to Britain. Apartment living was never as popular in Britain as in other European cultures. For military and political reasons continental cities needed to be protected by walls until well into the nineteenth century and so had to build upward. Britain's population was more or less safe after the Renaissance, so burgeoning urban populations built outward. By 1911, only three percent of English and Welsh dwellings were apartments (Stefan Muthesius, *The English Terraced House* [New Haven: Yale University Press, 1982], p. 1, who speculates on socioeconomic reasons). The dislike of apartment living was so strong in Britain that even the population displacement 1840–1880 did not radically change it. Pierre Le Muet's 1623 book on middle-class housing (Pierre Le Muet, *Manière de bastir. Pour toutes sortes de personnes* [Paris: Melchior Tavernier, 1623]) had an impact on English and Dutch townhouse construction (cit. in Paul Breman, Ltd., London, antiquarian book catalog 157, 1991) a century before John Wood and John Nash built their elegant row houses in Bath and speculators like Nicholas Barbon built standardized, cheap housing (Summerson).

176.
George Pullman's railway cars were carriages by day and sleeping cars by night. Flexible, multifunctional spaces and furniture are part of American culture. (Malézieux, 1873, plate 27.)

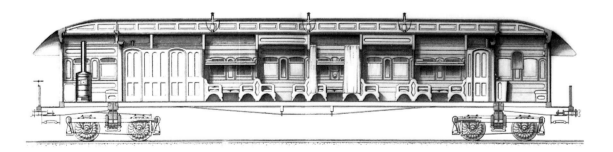

94. Most of the lumber was imported in bulk from North America (Vignoles, in *Min. Proc. ICE,* 1844, vol. 3, p. 256). Speculators imported sleepers in 1848, anticipating increasing railway construction. In 1849 imports increased to 86,680 cubic feet. Exotic woods were frequently exhibited at the Institution of Civil Engineers (Burt, in *Min. Proc. ICE,* 1853, vol. 12, pp. 212, 214, 228, 233).

95. Brick production was increased by Friedrich Hoffmann and Licht's continuous-firing, German ring kiln in 1862 (Prussian patent 25.07.1858; Michaelis pp. 128–130). It received a prize at the Paris exhibition of 1867 and spread to all brick-producing nations except the United States, where it only appeared after 1890 (Elliott, p. 43, citing W. Johnson, "Brickmaking in America," *American Architect and Building News* 28, 7 June 1890, p. 147, reprinted from *Architect*).

96. See note 85 above.

97. Terrace houses were usually sold as ninety-nine-year leaseholds, after which the ground reverted to the original owner and the buildings were considered amortized. Such a system only made sense where social stability was taken for granted. The lessee was responsible for upkeep, so the landowner, unlike the apartment-house owner on the continent, had no incentive to demand or pay for quality.

98. Young was possibly the same who had built the central building of the Dublin Botanical Garden in 1853 (Hix, p. 121).

99. *The Builder,* London, 24 January 1857, p. 46.

100. The competition for the Paris building had been won by the architect Jean-Marie Victor Viel, who designed the masonry parts in the final building. Barrault was responsible for the iron halls, and most of the final design and execution of that part was his.

101. For example, many Fox and Henderson roofs, like slip no. 4 in Woolwich Dockyard, Tythebarn Street Station in Liverpool, and New Street Station in Birmingham; also Turner's 24.4-meter Galway Station, the largest roof in Ireland in 1850. While condensation was not a problem in railway sheds, galvanized iron deteriorated when sulfur oxides from engine smoke reacted with atmospheric moisture to form sulfuric acid.

102. *The Engineer,* London, 2 May 1856, p. 245.

103. *The Builder,* 24 January, 19 April, and 10 May 1857, pp. 46, 213, 262.

104. Ibid., pp. 46, 213.

105. The painter Eastlake was president of the Royal Academy and Barry had been knighted in 1852.

106. A few more corrugated-iron-clad buildings were built, like the Shearness Boat Store (1858–1860) by Godfrey Thomas Greene, but none for representative structures.

107. *The Builder,* London, 24 January 1857, p. 46.

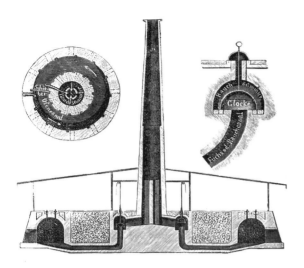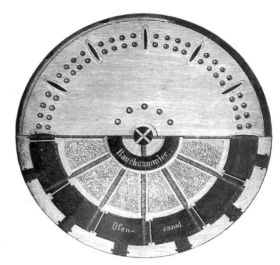

177.
Hoffmann and Licht's ring kiln fired continuously and at controllable temperatures. It produced bricks quicker and with less energy. Cannisters of coal dust burned downward into the chambers through holes in the kiln roof. Adjustable bulkheads were lowered in a rotating cycle to block all flues but one, forcing the heat and smoke to circle the entire kiln before venting through the central chimney. As the heat source and bulkheads advanced around the ring, the chamber segments were alternately preheated, fired, and cooled from the same source. (Michaelis, 1869, pp. 128, 130.)

108. Herbert, p. 87.

109. *The Builder,* vol. 10, 1852, p. 281; *Scientific American,* vol. 30, 1874, pp. 47–48, 50. Clarke Reeves and Co. owned the Phoenix Ironworks in Phoenixville, Pennsylvania. They later became the Phoenix Bridge Company.

110. The guy ropes were more organized than the ones John Roebling had used in 1855 to hold the Niagara Suspension Bridge in place, and they outwardly resembled the filigree netlike radio towers Valdimir Shuchov would build half a century later in Russia (Graefe et al.). Shuchov was twenty-two when the project was published in *Scientific American* in 1874, and he may well have seen it.

111. Designed by Joseph Phillips (Elliott, p. 86).

112. Phillips, in *Min. Proc. ICE,* vol. 14, 1855, pp. 251–272.

113. Monod, vol. 1, p. 181.

114. Eiffel's role in the development of modern steel construction is also recognized, although how his skeleton for the Statue of Liberty in New York influenced American high-rise framers has not been studied.

115. Eiffel was unusually generous in crediting those whom he worked with and who worked for him, making it relatively easy to trace influences on his work. Eiffel, *La Tour de 300 Mètres,* p. 3; and Steiner, chapter 5, footnotes 28 and 29. Dreicer is currently writing on Nördling's role in the development of iron truss bridge construction.

116. Steiner, pp. 94–95, 115–116.

117. The system was first historically discussed by Svante Lindquist at a meeting of the Society for the History of Technology, in Madison, Wisconsin, in 1991.

118. That record then belonged to the 486-meter Brooklyn Bridge, but it was soon to be surpassed by the 521-meter spans across the Firth of Forth. Eiffel's 1884 Garabit Bridge near Clermont-Ferrand, Théophile Seyrig's 1877 Douro Bridge in Portugal, and James Eads's 1874 Mississippi Bridge at St. Louis were all larger than the Galerie des Machines.

119. The Galerie des Machines of 1889 was a three-hinged arch of the type C. Köpke and Johann Schwedler had developed to avoid the difficulty of calculating indeterminate structures in 1861. Schwedler built a three-hinged frame in 1865, and a thirty-eight-meter arch over Berlin's Ostbahnhof Station in 1866. (Georg Mehrtens documented two earlier three-hinged bridge arches that may not have been influenced by Schwedler; see Mehrtens, *Vorlesungen über Ingenieur-Wissenschaften* [Leipzig: W. Englemann, 1908], part 2, vol. 1.) However, after Emil Winkler published a method to calculate statically indeterminate arches under temperature change in 1868, the only reason to build a three-hinged frame was foundation instability ("Vortrag über die Berechnung der Bogenbrücken," in *Mitteilungen des Architekten- und Ingenieurvereins Böhmen,* 1868, pp. 6–12, and 1869, pp. 5–7; information from Karl-Eugen Kurrer, writing to the author in 1982).

120. Monod, vol. 1, p. 232.

121. Shand, repeated by Giedion, *Time,* 1941 ed., p. 270, footnote p. 327; Straub, 1949 ed.; Pevsner, 1949 ed. Dutert's obituary in *L'Architecte,* p. 41 (cit. in Collins, *Concrete,* p. 113) does credit it to him. Dutert won the Prix de Rome in 1869. His first projects do seem to indicate an interest in the formal expression of structure (Steiner, p. 99, and Stamper, p. 335), and he displayed the same formal interest in structure in his later Galerie de Paléontologie (Marrey, pp. 65–66, 88). Contamin delegated the calculation and dimensioning to his assistant, J. Chardon (*L'Exposition de Paris 1889,* vol. 1, p. 98).

122. This Galerie de Trente Mètres had an interesting fate at the exhibition of 1900. The flexible frame was to be raised on tracks and moved to another position. Its "softness" made the operation more difficult than moving masonry and wooden buildings in the United States or transporting heavy, brittle Egyptian obelisks. The maneuver failed because the engineers underestimated the problem and neglected to stabilize the frame. Moving individual American buildings was first reported in the *Allgemeine Bauzeitung* in 1844. In 1855–1859 George Pullman raised the whole city of Chicago house by house out of the swamp on which it was built. The Romans moved several obelisks to Rome, Beneventum, and Constantinople. Pope Sixtus V had Domenico Fontana move one in Rome in 1584, and more were moved to Paris, Arles, Vincennes, Fontainebleau, London, and the last to New York in 1881.

123. See the distinction between ornament and decoration in note 7 above. There was a great deal of colored glass, mosaic, and colored brick, but it was all secondary to the grand frame and didn't swaddle it (Stamper, p. 337).

124. Monod, vol. 1, pp. 255–256. Siegfried Bing's firm L'Art Nouveau, which gave its name to the movement, was to open its doors in 1895.

178.
The "Galerie de Trente Mètres" connected the Galerie
des Machines and the Palais
des Industries Diverses in
1889. The organizers of the
1900 exhibition mounted it
on a track to move it to another part of the site. It collapsed on 9 December
1898. (Monod, 1890, vol.
1, 205; *Exposition de Paris
1900*, vol. 1, pp. 105, 106,
129.)

125. They had interesting structural aspects, as Steiner documented (p. 100), but these were hidden.

126. The "arts and crafts" group surrounding William Morris supported the rational use of materials too, but they fought mechanization and were for a return to the guild tradition.

127. Monod, vol. 1, p. 256.

7 The Result in Small and Large: The Langwies Viaduct and the Panama Canal

1. See Buchanan for Dutch contributions. For Switzerland, see Landes, "Von den Vorzügen," who does not discuss the building industry and its special criteria in any of his writings.

2. Ibid., and personal communication to the author by Hans Locher, CEO of Zellweger Uster AG, in 1981.

3. Züblin was the son of a Swiss industrialist in southern Italy and was related to the German-Swiss industrialist Escher and Sulzer families.

4. Favre, in *Schweizerische Bauzeitung,* 1893.

5. The firm spread internationally until World War I broke out: to Basel in 1908, to Milan and Duisburg in 1910, to Stuttgart in 1911, to Zurich in 1912, to Riga, Paris, Luxembourg, and Vienna in 1914. Züblin died in 1916, and new laws limited international corporations after 1918. Züblin's son-in-law and successor Hermann Schürch moved the corporate headquarters to Basel, with two firms in Zurich and Stuttgart that became independent after 1945.

6. He built the cantilevered balconies of the Men's Choir Hall in Strasbourg (1901) virtually simultaneously with Samuel de Molins's in the Casino Theater, Morges (1899), and the Stadttheater, Bern (1900). Among Züblin's Swiss structures were the coal bunkers of the Zurich gasworks at Schieren (1904) (participation strongly indicated but not entirely confirmed), the artillery stables in Thun (1908), the Basel Life Insurance building in Basel (1911–1912), pile foundations of the central post office in St. Gallen, and the Swiss Reinsurance Company's administration building in Zurich (1912).

7. Züblin designed the Pérolles Railway Viaduct for the canton of Fribourg as a record-setting 150-meter double span. It was built after his death as a series of five sixty-meter arches. The firm lost its daring with its founder.

8. The Risorgimento Bridge was the world's first 104-meter span in reinforced concrete.

9. Brandenberger, p. 307.

10. Mörsch had been one of the consultants; Nater, p. 3; Brandenberger, p. 305.

11. Nater, p. 5.

12. The federal specifications were revised in 1913.

13. From 9,900 to 924,200 Swiss francs (Gustav Bener, cit. in Schürch, p. 1).

14. Schürch, p. 5.

15. Railways preferred structural stone to concrete wherever it was available. The Albula, Bernina, and lower Inn Valley lines have the last large group of solid stone bridges built in the Western world. The slender, engineered structures are comparable in daring to the frames of medieval cathedrals. Among them are the curved 1902 Landwasser Viaduct and the 1903 Solis Bridge on the Albula line, the spiraling 1908 Brusio Viaduct on the Bernina line, and the 1908 Wiesen Viaduct. All of them are now tourist attractions.

16. The German firm Wayss & Freytag built a twenty-one-meter, channel-shaped bridge on lands belonging to the Wildegg Cement Factory in Aargau 1890. In 1894 a Hennebique licensee, probably Samuel de Molins, cast the earliest known flat-plate bridge with a 2.4-meter span at Wiggen station near Lucerne.

17. Schürch, pp. 8–9.

18. For the distinction between ornament and decoration, see chapter 6, note 7.

19. See Giedion, *Space, Time and Architecture*; Max Bill, *Robert Maillart — Bridges and Constructions* (Erlenbach ZH, 1949; rev. eds. 1955, 1969); and David Billington, *Robert Maillart's Bridges: The Art of Engineering* (Princeton: Princeton University Press, 1979). None of them have looked into the work of other pioneers of monolithic construction.

20. Schürch, p. 18: "Es bringt die Übereinstimmung von Baustoff und Bauform zum Ausdruck und mag in diesem Sinne als technisches Kunstwerk gelten und unser ästhetisches Empfinden befriedigen, wenn auch das Auge mangels von Vorbildern sich erst an die rein statischen Verhältnissen entsprechenden Formen des Eisenbetons, als einem neuen Baustoff, dem biegungsfesten Stein, gewöhnen muss."

21. Ibid., p. 9: "Obwohl eine Lösung mit kleineren Oeffnungen . . . wegen der Stellung der Zwischenpfeiler im Gerölldelta und des mangelnden Characters des ganzen Bauwerks unerwünscht war, wurde doch eine solche studiert, da es sich vor allem darum handelte, die wirtschaftlichste Lösung zu finden."

22. Ibid., p. 16: "Die Einführung von Doppelpfeilern war aber nicht nur durch konstruktive, sondern auch durch ästhetische Gesichtspunkte begründet, da sich dadurch auch in der Ansicht ein deutlicher Abschluß zwischen den drei verschiedenen Teilen des Hauptbauwerks ergab. . . . Mit der vorher geplanten normalen Lösung . . . , welche einen einzigen Pfeiler mit breiter, massiver Vorderfläche und Pendelwände, wie bei der Gmündertobelbrücke . . . vorsah, war aber diese Wirkung, trotz der bedeutenden Massenverschwendung nicht befriedigend zu erreichen gewesen."

23. Ibid., p. 15.

24. The Ironbridge possibly also used a cable crane in 1779; see John Smith, "A conjectural account of the erection of the Iron Bridge," paper presented under the auspices of the Institution of Structural Engineers History Study Group (London: North East London Polytechnic, Department of Civil Engineering, Engineering History Section, 1979), 19 pp.

25. It was invented by the English political economist William Playfair (Edward Tufte, *The Visual Display of Quantitative Information* [Cheshire, CT: Graphics Press, 1983], p. 33). The process was coordinated by Schürch, seconded by K. Arnstein for the design and Gustav Bener for the organization. Site supervision was the responsibility of A. Zwygart and J. Fleury under J. Müller, who made the diagrams and kept them current. Richard Coray and his team built the centering.

26. Schürch, p. 38.

27. There was nothing new in carefully examining the subsoil, in spite of the fact that it had been poorly done in both the Thames Tunnel and the Tay Bridge. Pierre Simon Girard, Peter Barlow, Duleau, and others had introduced regular and controlled material testing in shipbuilding, iron construction, and the steam boiler industry at the beginning of the nineteenth century (Peters, *Transitions,* pp. 54–57). Robert Stephenson, burned as he had been by the collapse of the Dee Bridge in 1846, carefully check all structural aspects in the construction of the Britannia and Conway bridges.

28. Coray worked from 1897 to 1940. See Conzett.

29. E. R. Johnson's report, cited in *Transactions,* vol. 1, pp. 51, 33–34.

30. Goethals, in *Transactions,* vol. 1, p. 2.

31. Sir Francis Drake and Sir Henry Morgan destroyed the city of Panamá in 1671 (ibid., pp. 2–3).

32. Haskin, p. 197; Goethals, in *Transactions,* vol. 1, p. 10.

33. The team, consisting of the Englishman John Augustus Lloyd and the Swede Falmarc recommended a canal on the Caribbean side and a railroad on the other (Bennett, p. 86; Haskin, pp. 196–197).

34. Goethals, in *Transactions,* vol. 1, p. 8.

35. Wyse, *Le Canal de Panama,* pp. 347–360; Haskin, p. 94.

36. They were first hired as contractors, but the California gold rush made it hard to find laborers. So the company took on the construction work itself and rehired them as engineers.

37. Trautwine left to survey a Darien route, and Totten finished the line in 1855 at great cost to human life (Bennett, pp. 88–90; *Biogr. Dict. of Am. Eng.; Min. Proc. ICE,* 1856, pp. 384–385).

38. For details, see Bennett, p. 91; Haskin, p. 93.

39. Wyse, *Le Canal de Panama,* pp. 363–368.

40. Félix Belly and Aimé Thomé de Gamond's first report, *Mém. et Compte-Rendu,* 4 February 1859, pp. 50–67, and 4 March 1859, pp. 82–83.

41. Bennett, p. 103; Wyse, *Le Canal de Panama,* p. 3 and *table synoptique* following p. 176.

42. Bishop, pp. 109–110.

43. *Mém. et Compte-Rendu,* 1879, pp. 571–572. Two other tunneled routes were even more expensive. One penetrated the San Blas Range to the south and the other lay farther south yet, starting from the Gulf of Darien and following the Atrato and Napipi rivers through the Choco Range to Cupica Bay on the Pacific coast. They are not shown in Wyse, *Le Canal de Panama,* but are mentioned in *Min. Proc. ICE,* 1856, pp. 383–385. Any tunneled version had to take the seismic instability of the area into account. The San Blas and Panama variants had the added disadvantage that the company would have to negotiate permission both with the government of Colombia and with the Panama Railway in whose contractual zone they lay.

44. Bunau-Varilla, pp. 29–30.

45. Ibid., p. 25.

46. Ibid., p. 29.

47. Ibid., pp. 29–31.

48. Haskin, p. 213.

49. *Mém. et Compte-Rendu,* 1879, pp. 577–578. This truth was confirmed when the Suez Canal had to be widened eight times between 1869 and 1956.

50. Bunau-Varilla, p. 24 and footnote 1, p. 10.

51. Haskin, pp. 94, 214. Lesseps soon fell out with Wyse (Wyse, *Le Canal de Panama,* p. 303).

52. *Mém. et Compte-Rendu,* 1882, p. 639. The group suffered an annual mortality rate of seven percent. It was high but comparable to French expectations in Algeria and American experience on the Panama Railway (*Mém. et Compte-Rendu,* 1882, p. 640). Bunau-Varilla cites a mortality rate of eleven percent (p. 44).

53. The Corinth Canal averaged 99 meters deep and was 6,300 meters long. This project was organized by Türr.

54. *Mém. et Compte-Rendu,* 1882, p. 643.

55. Ibid., p. 642.

56. The tide fluctuates 60 centimeters on the other side (Haskin, p. 280).

57. Wyse, *Le Canal de Panama,* p. 304.

58. *Mém. et Compte-Rendu,* 1882, p. 646; Wyse, *Le Canal de Panama,* p. 307.

59. *Mém. et Compte-Rendu,* 1882, p. 645.

60. Bunau-Varilla, pp. 32–33; Wyse, *Le Canal de Panama,* p. 304.

61. Bunau-Varilla, pp. 48, 57–58.

62. Wyse, *Le Canal de Panama,* p. 304.

63. *Mém. et Compte-Rendu,* 1882, list on p. 647.

64. Wyse, *Le Canal de Panama,* p. 311.

65. Ibid., pp. 311–312.

66. Comber, in *Transactions,* vol. 1, pp. 461, 463, 471; Bunau-Varilla, p. 8. All of the materiel rehabilitated after twenty years in the jungle and swamps was reconditioned at less than ten percent of its original cost (Haskin, p. 218).

67. Comber, in *Transactions,* vol. 1, p. 462.

68. Typical of many subcontractors, a firm called the Anglo-Dutch Company had begun digging the 1.6-kilometer-long Culebra saddle in 1884 and failed two years later (Bunau-Varilla, p. 38).

69. Ibid., p. 73; see also McCollough, p. 288, for the probable financial reason Bunau-Varilla involved his brother.

70. Bunau-Varilla in various parts of the text, for example, pp. 130–131; Wyse, *Le Canal de Panama,* p. 307.

71. Wyse, p. 307.

72. Haskin, pp. 84–85.

73. Ibid., pp. 81–82.

74. *Compagnie Nouvelle,* p. 13.

75. Bunau-Varilla, p. 83.

76. The French *fossoyeur* also carries the secondary connotation of "ditch digger."

77. In spite of that, Eiffel never received another construction contract. Still, he was the only one of the five principal defendants to recover professionally. He sold his firm at the age of sixty-seven and concentrated on aerodynamic studies for the final quarter-century of his life, becoming one of the pioneers in the field. He built the first wind tunnel in France, wrote a seminal work on air resistance, and developed the strutless, cantilevered airplane wing.

78. Bennett, pp. 103–104.

79. Bunau-Varilla, pp. 6–7.

80. Ibid., p. 35.

81. It was severely undercapitalized at thirteen million dollars (Haskin, p. 218; *Nouvelle Compagnie*, title page states sixty-five million francs; Bunau-Varilla, p. 141, gives twelve million dollars).

82. *Nouvelle Compagnie*, p. 21.

83. Ibid., for example p. 27.

84. Ibid., pp. 9, 19.

85. Ibid., pl. 2.

86. Bunau-Varilla, p. 156.

87. Haskin, p. 196.

88. It was to have been 215 kilometers long, climbing 213 meters and carrying 7,000-ton ships on dry dock cradles running on multiple sets of tracks. Eads's death in 1887 put an end to the idea.

89. Illinois and Chicago agreed to give the 54.75 kilometer drainage canal to the federal government if the Mississippi were rendered completely navigable.

90. Goethals, in *Transactions,* vol. 1, p. 15.

91. *Min. Proc. ICE,* 1856, pp. 378–380.

92. The members were Admiral John G. Walker, former chairman of the Nicaragua Canal Commission, and the engineers Lewis M. Haupt, Alfred Noble, and Peter C. Hains, all former members; three other engineers, George S. Morison, William H. Burr, and Oswald H. Ernst; an economist, Emory R. Johnson; and a lawyer and ex-senator, Samuel Pasco.

93. Bunau-Varilla, p. 206.

94. The American preference for Nicaragua and the French for Panama reflected the empirical American penchant for detouring around problems and the continental European preference for conceptual approaches to problem-solving by attacking rather than avoiding them (Peters, "An American Culture of Construction"; Bunau-Varilla, p. 20). The United States has never abandoned its interest in Nicaragua. In 1914, the year the Panama Canal opened, the United States government signed the Bryan-Chamorro Treaty by which for $3,000,000 Nicaragua gave the United States a concession for a canal and naval bases on the Gulf of Fonseca on the Pacific coast and on the Islas del Maís (Corn Islands) in the Caribbean. No use has been made of the treaty, but it throws light on American concern for the political situation in Nicaragua under

President Ronald Reagan and its possible connection to the abandonment of American sovereignty over the Panama Canal Zone by President Jimmy Carter in 1979.

95. Haskin, p. 230; Bunau-Varilla, p. 178.

96. Haskin, p. 238, who states that Cromwell was the railroad's representative. The railroad belonged to the French canal company at that time (Bennett, p.468).

97. Bunau-Varilla, p. 310.

98. Ibid., pp. 310–333.

99. Ibid., p. 94.

100. Ibid., pp. 100–101.

101. Ibid., pp. 96–98.

102. Goethals, in *Transactions,* vol. 1, p. 20. The others were Henry L. Abbot, William H. Burr, George W. Davis, Alfred Noble, William B. Parsons, Frederick P. Stearns, and Joseph Ripley, who later became assistant chief engineer to Goethals. Burr and Noble were members of the Isthmian Canal Commission.

103. The French had proposed an upper and a lower reservoir, revised from the original single dam at Gamboa. It would have retained only a third of the maximum Chagres discharge and would have overflowed if two floods occurred in rapid succession (*Nouvelle Compagnie,* p. 13; Haskin, p. 280).

104. Haskin, p. 82.

105. Haskin, p. 277; D. F. Mac Donald, in *Transactions,* vol. 1, pp. 67–83; Goethals, in *Transactions,* vol. 1, p. 18.

106. Goethals, in *Transactions,* vol. 1, p. 27. The excavators at Culebra and the concreting teams later worked up to twelve-hour shifts.

107. Wyse, *Le Canal de Panama,* pp. 363–368; Haskin, p. 292. Officially the canal was to be neutral like the Suez Canal (Convention of Constantinople, 1888). Britain never challenged the fortification of the canal under the 1850 Clayton-Bulwer or the 1910 Hay-Pauncefort treaties.

108. Under the pressure of public criticism, the president and the navy negotiated the width of the locks, an executive order widened the bottom of the canal, the slope of the Gatun Dam was flattened to allow hydraulic filling to be more effective, and the breakwaters and channel line at the harbors changed, while foundation difficulties led to compromises in siting the various flights of locks.

109. The separation between press and government theoretically controls government license. In some societies public debate is constitutionally anchored in the political process itself. For example, Switzerland controls the process through the complex

practice of *Vernehmlassung* (prelegislative consultation with interested groups) and referendum, and major public expenditure or change in project cost must be submitted by law to plebiscite. In other societies, like France, the process is exclusively governmental and the public can only react through the postfactum medium of elections.

110. Haskin, p. 135.

111. Ibid., p. 27.

112. Boggs, in *Transactions,* vol. 1, p. 207.

113. Ibid., p. 208.

114. Ibid., p. 210.

115. Haskin, p. 119; Bishop, pp. 62–65, 88.

116. Bishop, p. 143.

117. Ibid., pp. 152–152.

118. Haskin, p. 30, for the large amounts of money and provisions consumed on the project. As a measure of its organizational success, the canal transported traffic a year ahead of the original completion date of January 1, 1915 (ibid., pp. 26–27). Neither the Crystal Palace nor the Eiffel Tower had been quite that successful. Most of the tower elevators were only finished after the exhibition had opened.

119. All the early civil engineering programs developed out of military schools, and this strongly influenced the professional bias of civil engineers toward the procedural aspects of building.

120. Haskin, p. 29.

121. Mason, in *Transactions,* vol. 1, p. 86.

122. Ibid., p. 87. The percentages are vague because the number of laborers who survived and stayed more than a single year is unknown.

123. Ibid., pp. 88–89.

124. Formerly known as *Stegomyia fasciata.* The mosquito lives twelve days and becomes a carrier by ingesting the bacterium in the brief, three-day window of the human infectious period. Then it must inject it into a nonimmune person to spread the disease.

125. Mason, in *Transactions,* vol. 1, p. 92.

126. Ibid., pp. 95–96.

127. Ibid., p. 98. Apparently these procedures only partly worked.

128. Ibid., p. 105.

129. Durham, in *Transactions,* vol. 1, p. 117; Gorgas, in *Jnl. of the American Medical Association,* 30 March 1912, p. 907, cit. by Mason in *Transactions,* vol. 1, p. 114.

130. R. E. Wood, in *Transactions,* vol. 1, p. 190; Goethals, in *Transactions,* vol. 1, p. 335.

131. R. E. Wood, in *Transactions,* vol. 1, p. 194.

132. Haskin, pp. 159–160. Separation was not along racial lines, since the "silver" group was mixed, but the "gold" force was exclusively professional, American, and white. The post office and the commissaries had "gold" and "silver" entrances, and the railroad made a similar distinction by virtue of first and second class tickets.

133. R. E. Wood, in *Transactions,* vol. 1, p. 190.

134. Ibid., p. 193.

135. Ibid., pp. 200–201.

136. Sibert, in *Transactions,* vol. 1, pp. 408–409.

137. The first subsidence mass was softer than the consolidated fill and compacted up to 4.5 meters (ibid., p. 417).

138. Bishop, pp. 202–203.

139. Sibert, in *Transactions,* vol. 1, p. 392.

140. Ibid., p. 394.

141. Ibid., p. 396.

142. Ibid., pp. 398–399.

143. Boggs, in *Transactions,* vol. 1, p. 214. Atlas's contribution was 4.5 million barrels according to an advertisement at the end of the 1909 edition of Taylor and Thompson, p. xxxix. Much of the remainder came from the Alpha Portland Cement Company of Easton, Pennsylvania (Bennett, p. 374).

144. The railway ran 90 meters per minute and was automated except for starting and stopping the carts, which was controlled by a dispatcher (Sibert, in *Transactions,* vol. 1, p. 402).

145. Bishop, pp. 65–69.

146. Williamson, in *Transactions,* vol. 1, pp. 430–431.

147. Ibid., p. 439.

148. Ibid., p. 434.

149. Ibid., p. 431.

150. Haskin, p. 57.

151. The French accomplished 14,256,000 cubic meters (Goethals, in *Transactions,* vol. 1, p. 336; Haskin, p. 71; Bunau-Varilla, p. 31).

152. The total was 78–83.4 million cubic meters (Goethals, in *Transactions,* vol. 1, p. 362, gives the higher figure).

153. 550 meters (Haskin, p. 71).

154. $15 million per mile (Haskin, p. 80).

155. Bunau-Varilla, for example, p. 155.

156. A little was dredged at Gamboa, and slides were also later dredged from the finished canal (Comber, in *Transactions,* vol. 1, p. 479).

157. Goethals, in *Transactions,* vol. 1, pp. 379–380.

158. Ibid., pp. 349–350.

159. Ibid., p. 351.

160. Haskin, p. 150.

161. Goethals, in *Transactions,* vol. 1, pp. 353–354, 357.

162. Haskin, pp. 149–150; see also F. B. Gilbreth, *Field System.*

163. Goethals, in *Transactions,* vol. 1, p. 354.

164. Haskin, pp. 37–38.

165. Haskin, pp. 59–61.

166. Goethals, in *Transactions,* vol. 1, pp. 343–344.

167. Ibid., p. 345.

168. Ibid., p. 352.

169. Ibid., pp. 352–353.

170. Ibid., p. 353.

171. Ibid., p. 363.

172. Ibid., p. 355.

173. These figures are derived from the estimated total of 81 million cubic meters of earth moved, minus the 14.256 million cubic meters the French had dug, divided by the 290.5 cubic meters each train carried, divided by eight years (1905–1913) and by 300 working days a year. This improbable number may have been even higher since neither 1905 nor 1913 were full working years.

174. Haskin, p. 76.

175. Goethals, in *Transactions,* vol. 1, p. 366.

176. Ibid., p. 368.

177. Ibid., p. 364.

178. Ibid., pp. 364–365; Haskin, pp. 77–78; Bennett, pp. 348–355.

179. D. F. Mac Donald, in *Transactions,* vol. 1, p. 78.

180. 25.32 percent (Goethals, in *Transactions,* vol. 1, p. 378).

181. D. F. Mac Donald, in *Transactions,* vol. 1, p. 79.

182. Ibid., p. 78.

183. Ibid., p. 79. Today, tubes can be drilled obliquely into unstable slopes, reinforced with cables, and grouted to form irregular, bulb-shaped anchors of earth-concrete at their ends. There was no such system available at the time.

184. Goethals, in *Transactions,* vol. 1, pp. 374–375.

185. Haskin, pp. 78–79.

186. D. F. Mac Donald, in *Transactions,* vol. 1, pp. 79–80.

187. Ibid., p. 83.

188. Goethals, in *Transactions,* vol. 1, pp. 346–347.

189. Haskin, p. 74.

190. Peters, *Transitions,* pp. 50–54, esp. p. 52.

191. The cost of excavation and spoil removal fell 53 percent, from $1.35 to $0.72 per cubic meter (from $1.03 to $0.55 per cubic yard) between 1908 and 1912 (Haskin, p. 74).

192. Haskin, pp. 72–73.

193. Ibid., p. 92.

194. Ibid., p. 90.

195. Goethals, in *Transactions,* vol. 1, p. 352; Haskin p. 71.

196. Comber, in *Transactions,* vol. 1, p. 474; Goethals, in *Transactions,* vol. 1, p. 381; Sibert, in *Transactions,* vol. 1, p. 389.

Conclusion: The Building Process and Technological Thinking

1. I have based the distinction between "vertical" logic and "lateral," associative thinking on Edward de Bono.

2. See preface, note 1.

3. The desire to create stiff frame corners in iron frames was another area that led to monolithic structure.

4. For example in Galileo Galilei, *Discorsi e dimostrazioni matematiche, intorno a due nuove scienze . . .* (Leyden: Elsevier 1638), p. 129, where he compares the bone of a giant and a normal human.

5. Even this distinction is now under attack in the so-called smart buildings and transportation systems.

6. Charles Garnier, *Le nouvel Opéra de Paris* (Paris: Ducher, 1876–1881), 6 parts in 8 vols.

7. Horatio Greenough's comparison between ships and buildings made the connection; see Collins, *Changing Ideals,* p. 160.

8. This was not, of course, a one-way street. The general technological world influenced military engineering too; see Barton C. Hacker, "Engineering a New Order: Military Institutions, Technical Education, and the Rise of the Industrial State," *Technology and Culture,* vol. 34, no. 1, January 1993, especially p. 12, footnote 40. President Eisenhower's "military-industrial complex," a term he coined shortly before leaving office in 1961, indicates that the conflation of the two areas continued into the mid-twentieth century.

9. César Daly used the anthropomorphical metaphor to describe the mechanical installations in Sir Charles Barry's 1840 Reform Club in London (cit. in Collins, *Changing Ideals,* p. 99, quoted in Elliott, p. 199).

10. Collins, *Changing Ideals,* p. 155; de Zurko, p. 4, for the connection between functionalism and the biological metaphor.

11. Collins, *Changing Ideals,* p. 157. Contextualism runs the whole gamut from the naive "fitting a structure into the landscape," through climatological and material correspondence, to the subtleties of political, sociological, and cultural concordance.

Bibliography

This selection contains pertinent monographs, periodicals, articles, ephemera, and manuscripts of general interest to the field. It gives the full data on those references that are abbreviated in the notes and captions.

Abbot, Willis John. *Panama and the Canal in picture and prose. A complete story of Panama, as well as the history, purpose and promise of its world-famous canal — the most gigantic engineering undertaking since the dawn of time. Approved by the leading officials connected with the great enterprise. Profusely illustrated by over 600 unique and attractive photographs taken expressly for this book by our special staff.* London: Syndicate Publishing Company, 1914. (2), 414, (2) p., ills.

Adley, Charles Coles. "The Electric Telegraph; its History, Theory, and Practical Applications." *Min. Proc. ICE* 11 (1851–1852): 299–329.

Allgemeine Bauzeitung mit Abbildungen für Architekten, Ingenieurs, Dekorateurs, Bauprofessionisten, Oekonomen, Bauunternehmer und Alle, die an den Fortschritten und Leistungen der neuesten Zeit in der Baukunst und den dahin einschlagenden Fächern Antheil nehmen. Herausgegeben und Redigiert von Christ. Friedr. Ludwig Förster, Architeken. Vienna: Verlag von L. Försters artistischer Anstalt, 1836–1916. Text and illustrations in two volumes per year until 1872, thereafter in 1 volume. The "Wiener Allgemeine Bauzeitung" or "Förster" was the earliest German-language journal devoted to building. (See also Culmann; Downes.)

Andraud, M. Antoine. *De l'air comprimé et dilaté, employé comme moteur, ou des forces de la nature recueillies sans dépenses et mises en réserve.* 2nd ed. Paris: Guillaumin, 1840. Augmentée d'une partie experimentale en collaboration avec M. Tessie du Motay. Variant title in next edition: *De l'air comprimé et dilaté comme moteur, ou, Des forces naturelles receuillies gratuitement et mises en réserve.* 3rd ed. Paris: Guillaumin, 1841. (4), 144 p., 1 pl., ills.

Annales des Ponts et Chaussées. Mémoires et documents relatifs à l'art des constructions et au service de l'ingénieur; lois, ordonnances et autres actes concernant l'administration des Ponts et Chaussées. Paris. 1er partie: Mémoires et documents, 1 (1831)–104 (1934); 2ème partie: Lois, décrets, arrêts, 1 (1831)–104 (1934); Annales des Ponts et Chaussées, 105 (1935)–149 (1971); Nouvelle série 1977 ff. The *Annales* were one of the first and the most influential of all engineering journals in nineteenth-century Europe. They were preceded by several collections of articles by Pierre Charles Lesage and others, published as *Receuil de divers mémoirs, éxtraits de la Bibliothèque (Impériale) des Ponts et Chaussées . . .* between 1808 and 1810. The *Annales* took over and expanded the role previously played by the "Bibliothèque Universelle" of Geneva in the spread of civil engineering information in the French-speaking world.

Arms, Richard G. "From Disassembly to Assembly: Cincinnati, The Birthplace of Mass Production." *Bulletin of the Historical and Philosophical Society of Ohio* 17 (July 1959): 195.

Art Journal Illustrated Catalogue of the industry of all nations. London: George Virtue., 1851. xxvi, 328, xvi, viii, viii, viii, xxii p., ills. 2nd ed. (reduced facsimile) New York: Dover Publications, 1970. Variant title: *The Crystal Palace Exhibition Illustrated Catalogue London 1851 An unabridged republication of the Art-Journal special issue with a new introduction by John Gloag, F.S.A.* xiii, (3), xxvi, 328, xvi, viii, viii, viii, xxii, 14 (Dover adverts) p., ills. The best and most comprehensively illustrated catalog of the contents of the Crystal Palace of 1851, supplemented by articles that provide an overview of contemporary intellectual reactions to the exhibited material, including the notorious prize-winning essay "The Exhibition as a Lesson in Taste" by Ralph Nicholson Wornum. (See also Illustrated Exhibitor.)

Atkinson, Robert Thomas. "On the Sinking and Tubbing, or Coffering of Pits, as practised in the Coal Districts of the North of England." *Min. Proc. ICE* 2 (1842–1843): 170ff.

Babbage, Charles. *On the Economy of Machinery and Manufactures.* London: Charles Knight, 1832. 2nd ed. 1832. 3rd ed. 1833 enlarged. xxiv, 392 p., front. U.S. ed. Philadelphia: Carey & Lea, 1832. xix, 15–282 p. Also serialized (1833 ff.) in *Mechanics' Magazine,* New York. One of the first attempts to assess the effects of the Industrial Revolution on the production of goods, and a forerunner of "operations research" (Isaac Asimov. *Isaac Asimov's Biographical Encyclopedia of Science and Technology. The lives and achievements of 1195 great scientists from ancient times to the present. New revised edition.* New York: Avon, 1976. # 404). The substance of a considerable portion of the work appeared among the preliminary chapters of the mechanical part of the *Encyclopedia Metropolitana* (preface). Babbage attacked the publishing industry for manipulation of information and was boycotted by all publishers and booksellers. (See also Barlow, Peter, *A treatise on the manufactures.*)

Badois, Edmond. "Description de l'excavateur ou drague à pivot pour terrassements à sec applicable aux travaux de l'isthme de Suez, construite par MM. Frey et A. Sayn." *Mémoires et Compte-Rendu des travaux de la Société des Ingénieurs Civils* (1864): 444–450; 506–510, pl. 42.

Badois, Edmond. "Étude sur les moyens mécaniques à employer aux travaux du canal maritime de Suez, dans la traversée des lacs Menzaleh et Ballah." *Mémoires et Compte-Rendu des travaux de la Société des Ingénieurs Civils* (1864): 488–505.

Banham, Reyner. *A Concrete Atlantis. U.S. Industrial Building and European Modern Architecture 1900–1925.* Cambridge, MA: MIT Press, 1986. ix, (1), 266, (4) p., ills.

Banham, Reyner. *Theory and design in the first machine age.* New York: Praeger, 1960. 338 p., ills. 2nd ed. 1967

Bannister, Turpin C. "The First Iron-Framed Buildings." *Architectural Review* (London, April 1950): 230–245, ills.

Barlow, Peter. *Essay on the Strength and Stress of Timber, founded upon experiments performed at the Royal Military Academy, on specimens selected from the Royal Arsenal, and His Majesty's dock-yard, Woolwich. Preceeded by an historical review of former theories and experiments, with numerous tables and plates. Also an appendix, on the strength of iron, and other materials.* London: J. Taylor, 1817. 2nd ed. 1826, 3rd ed. 1826 which included tests on iron wire carried out by Thomas Telford. Revised edition with variant title: *A treatise on the strength of timber, cast iron, malleable iron, and other materials; with rules for application in architecture, construction of suspension bridges, railways, etc.; with an appendix on the power of locomotive engines, and the effect of inclined planes and gradients, With seven plates.* London: J. Weale, 1837. xii, 492 p., 7 pls., ills., diagrs. New edition with variant title: *A treatise on the strength of timber, cast and malleable iron, and other materials . . . A new edition, revised and corrected by I. F. Heather . . . to which is added an essay on the effects produced by causing weights to travel over elastic bars.* By the Rev. Robert Willis. London: Weale, 1851. xii, 516 p., 16 pls. New edition with variant title: *. . . railways, etc. A new edition, revised by his sons, P. W. Barlow and W. H. Barlow, to which are added a summary of experiments by Eaton Hodgkinson, William Fairbairn, and David Kirkaldy; an essay by the Rev. Robert Willis, and formulae for calculating girders, etc. The whole arranged and edited by William Humber.* London: Lockwood, 1867. xii, 396, 12, 12 p. 32 p. publ. cata. 19 pls. (I–X; I–IX) ills. 1st. French edition: *Essai sur la résistance des bois de construction, avec un appendice sur la résistance du fer et d'autres matériaux, résumé de l'ouvrage anglais de P. Barlow, membre de l'Académie Royale Militaire; avec des notes par A. Fourier.* Paris: Arthus Bertrand, 1828. (iv), 94, (2) p., 1 pl.

Barlow, Peter. *A treatise on the manufactures and machinery of Great Britain by P. B. To which is prefixed, An introductory view of the principles of manufactures by Charles Babbage.* London: Baldwin & Craddock, 1836. viii, 834 p., 87 pls., ills. (See also Babbage.)

Barlow, William Henry. "Remarks on the different methods of fastening Railway Bars in their chairs; and a description of a new hollow wrought iron key." *Min. Proc. ICE* 4 (1845): 49–58, paper 684, 14 January 1845.

Barrault, Alexis. On the Suez Canal. "Résumé des Procès-Verbaux des Séances, seance du ler octobre 1858." *Mémoires et Compte-Rendu des travaux de la Société des Ingénieurs Civils* (1858): 277–293. (See also Negrelli, Stephenson, *Response.*)

Barrett, James. "On the Construction of Fire-proof Buildings." *Min. Proc. ICE* 12 (1852–1853): 244–272. paper # 883.

Bartky, Ian R. "The Adoption of Standard Time," *Technology and Culture* 30 (1989): 25–56.

Bartky, Ian R. Comment and response to "The Most Reliable Time." *Technology and Culture* 32, no. 1 (January 1991): 183–185.

Barton, James. "On the Economic Distribution of Material in the Sides, or Vertical Portion, of Wrought-Iron Beams." *Min. Proc. ICE* 14 (1854–1855): 443–491. paper no. 907 (24 April 1855).

Bateman, J. F., and Brockedon et al. Discussion of vulcanized rubber. *Min. Proc. ICE* 13 (1853–1854): 432–435.

Baukunde des Architekten. Unter Mitwirkung von Fachmännern der verschiedenen Einzelgebiete, bearbeitet von den Herausgebern der Deutschen Bauzeitung und des Deutschen Baukalenders. Mit 1759 Abbildungen und 12 Tafeln im Text. 2 vols. Berlin: Kommissionsverlag von Ernst Toesche, 1884–1890. 1: 594 p.; 2: 1123 p., ills. Second, independant part of the "Deutsche Bauhandbuch." In the words of the subtitle, "Eine systematische Zusammenstellung der Resultate der Bauwissenschaften mit allen Hülfswissenschaften in ihrer Anwendung auf das Entwerfen und die Ausführung der Bauten." The title promises a rather dull text but the book is a useful source of plans, dates, names, and details of vanished German buildings.

Beamish, Richard. *Memoir of the Life of Sir Marc Isambard Brunel.* London: Longman, Green, Longman, and Roberts, 1862. xvi, (2), 359 p., frontis., port., ills. 2nd ed. revised and corrected, 1862. (8), ix–xviii, (2), 357, (1), (2 adverts.) p., frontis., ills.

Becker, Carl M. "Evolution of the Disassembly Line: The Horizontal Wheel and the Overhead Railway Loop." *Bulletin of the Historical and Philosophical Society of Ohio* 26 (July 1968): 276.

Beckmann, Johann. *Beytrage zur Geschichte der Erfindungen.* Leipzig: Verlag Paul Gotthelf Kummer, 1782–1805. 5 vols. New editions Hildesheim: G. Olms Verlagsbuchhandlung, 1965, 1972, 1981. English edition translated by William Johnston. *A history of inventions and discoveries.* London: J. Bell, 1797. 3 vols. Other editions: 1814, 1817, 1846, 1872, 1973, 1974, 1976, 1978, 1980.

Bélidor, Bernard Forrest (or Forest) de. *Architecture hydraulique, ou l'art de conduire, d'élever, et de ménager les eaux pour les différens besoins de la vie.* 2 parts in 4 vols. Paris: Charles-Antoine Jombert, 1737–1753. 1: xii, 312 p., 44 pls., frontis.; 2: 424, xxvi p., 55 pls.; 3: xvi, 412, 16 p., 60 pls., frontis.; 4: viii, 480, 19 p., frontis. German ed. in 2 vols. 1764–1771.

Bell, K. "British policy towards the construction of the Suez Canal." *Trans. Roy. Hist. Soc.,* 5th ser., 15 (1965): 121–143.

Bell, S. P. *A Biographical Index of British Engineers in the 19th Century.* New York: Garland Publishing, 1975. x, 246 p.

Belly, Félix. *Percement de l'isthme de Panama par le canal de Nicaragua. Exposé de la question.* Paris: Aux bureaux de la direction du canal, 1858. 177, (1), 3 fold. maps. Further editions: 1859, 1869. German edition 1859.

Belly, Félix. *A travers l'Amerique Centrale. Le Nicaragua et le canal interocéanique.* 2 vols. Paris: Librairie de la Suisse romande, 1867. Further editions: 1870, 1968.

Belly, Félix, and Charles Potvin. *L'isthme americain. Notes d'un premier voyage, 1858. Precédé d'une biographie de l'auteur.* Bruxelles: P. Weissenbruch, 1889. xlii, (1), 161 p., ills., map.

Bennett, Ira Elbert. *History of the Panama Canal its construction and builders.* Washington, D.C.: Historical Publishing Company, 1915. (6), vii–xi, (1), 5–543 p., ills.

Berg, C. F. W. *Der Bau der Hängebrücken aus Eisendrath: nach Stevenson* [sic], *Séguin, Dufour, Navier u.a.* Leipzig: Im Industrie-Comptoir, 1824. xii, 161, 1 p., 7 pls. The first German book on wire cable suspension bridges.

Beton und Eisen. Berlin, 1905–1942. Preceded by *Neuere Bauweisen und Bauwerke aus Beton & Eisen,* followed by *Beton- und Stahlbetonbau.*

Billington, David Peter. *The Tower and the Bridge. The New Art of Structural Engineering.* New York: Basic Books, 1983. xx, 306 p., ills.

Bishop, Joseph Bucklin, and Farnham Bishop. *Goethals Genius of the Panama Canal.* New York/London: Harper Brothers, 1930. xvi, 493 p., ills.

Black, Archibald. *The Story of Tunnels.* New York: McGraw-Hill, 1937. xv, (1), 245 p., ills., frontis. (incl. in pag.).

Bogardus, James, and John W. Thomson. *Cast Iron Buildings: Their Construction and Advantages. By J. B., C. E. architect in iron, iron building, corner of Centre and Duane Sts.* New York: J. W. Harrison, 1856. 4–16 p., 3 pls. Although the title mentions Bogardus as the author, Bogardus himself, in his preface "to the reader," states that his friend John W. Thomson, A.M., wrote it.

Bono, Edward de. *The Use of Lateral thinking.* London: Cape, 1967. 2nd ed. Harmondsworth: Penguin, 1990. 141 p., ills.

Boorstin, Daniel Joseph. *The Americans. I: The Colonial Experience. 2: The National Experience. 3: The Democratic Experience.* vol. 1: New York: Random House, 1958. 434 p.; vol. 2: New York: Random House, 1965. 517 p. 2 vols. Harmondsworth: Penguin Books, 1969. 1: 487 p.; 2: 649 p. vol. 3: New York: Random House, 1973. xiv, 717 p.

Bosc, Ernest. *Dictionnaire raisonné d'architecture et des sciences et arts qui s'y rattachent.* 4 vols. Paris: Librairie de Firmin-Didot et Cie, 1877–1880. 1: 1877: Abacule-Cymaise. xi, (1), 551, (1) p. ills.; 2: 1878: dais-ivoire. (4), 570 p., ills.; 3: 1879: jabloir-pont (4), 575, (1) p., ills.; 4: 1880: pontceau-zotheca. (6), 519, (1) p., ills.

Bourne, John Claudius. *Drawings of the London and Birmingham Railway by J.C.B. with an historical and descriptive Account by John Britton FSA.* London: Bourne and Ackerman and Co., 1839. 26 p., 31 pl., ills.

Bourne, Kenneth. *Foreign Policy of Victorian England 1830–1902.* Oxford: Clarendon Press, 1970. xii, 531 p.

Bracher, Kurt. *Entwicklung der Deckenkonstruktion im Spiegel der Patentliteratur. Dissertation an der Technischen Hochschule Wien.* Typescript, 1949. 84 p., ills. Still the only overview of the evolution of floor construction patents in the 19th century.

Bradshaw, Dan F. "Stephenson, De Lesseps, and the Suez Canal. An Englishman's Blindspot." *Journal of Transport History* 4 (1978): 239–243.

Braidwood, James. "On Fire-proof Buildings." *Min. Proc. ICE* 8 (1849): 141–163. paper no. 767 (27 February 1849).

Braithwaite, Frederick. "On the Fatigue and consequent Fracture of Metals." *Min. Proc. ICE* 13 (1854): 463–475 (16 May 1854).

Brandenberger, G. "Bogenbrücke in armiertem Beton über die Rhone bei Chippis im Kanton Wallis." *Schweizerische Bauzeitung* 49, nos. 25 & 26 (1907): 306–311/ 319–321.

Brassey, Thomas. *On Work and Wages.* 3rd ed. London: Bell and Daldy, 1872. xvi, 296 p.

Brockedon. "Vulcanized India Rubber." *Min. Proc. ICE* 4 (1845): 58–59.

Brüll, A. On the Suez Canal. *Mémoire et Compte-Rendu des travaux de la Société des Ingénieurs Civils* (1864): 411–417.

Brunel, Sir Marc Isambard. "An Account of the actual State of the Works at the Thames Tunnel (June 23, 1840)." *Min. Proc. ICE* 1 (1837–1841): 85–86.

Brunel, Sir Marc Isambard. Accounts of the Thames Tunnel. *Min. Proc. ICE* 1 (1837–1841): 23; 33–35; 41; 44; 46. 2 (1842–1843): 80–82. 11 and 18 April 1837, 15 and 29 May 1838, 1839.

Brunel, Sir Marc Isambard. Comment on cement and iron hooping in the brick beam at Nine Elms, 1837. *Min. Proc. ICE* 1 (1837–1841): 20.

Brunton, John. *John Brunton's book; being the memories of John Brunton, engineer, from a manuscript in his own hand written for his grandchildren and now first printed.* Cambridge: the University Press, 1939. viii, 163 p., ills. introduction by Sir John Harold Clapham.

Buchanan, Robert Angus. *The Engineers. A History of the Engineering Profession in Britain 1750–1914.* London: Jessica Kingsley, 1989. 240 p.

Buel, Albert Wells, and Charles Shattuck Hill. *Reinforced Concrete.* New York: The Engineering News Publishing Co., 1904. x, 434 p., ills. 2nd ed. 1906. xii, 499 p., ills. Apparently the first English-language theoretical text on reinforced concrete. (See also Christophe; Morel; Mörsch; Taylor and Thompson.)

The Builder. An illustrated weekly magazine for the architect, engineer, archaeologist, constructor, sanitary-reformer and art-lover. London 31 December 1842–25 February 1966. No issues between 7 January and 11 February 1843. Absorbed into *Architecture. British Architect; a journal of architecture and its accessory arts* in 1966. Continued as *Building.*

Bunau-Varilla, Philippe. *Panama. The creation, destruction, and resurrection.* New York: Robert M. McBride, 1920. (4) v–xx, 568 p., ills. pls.

Burton, Anthony. *The Railway Empire, a synopsis of the achievements of British Railway Engineers and Contractors around the world.* London: John Murray, 1994. 264 p., ills.

Butterworth, Benjamin. *The Growth of Industrial Art. Arranged and compiled under the supervision of the Hon. B.B., Commissioner of Patents and Representative of the Department of the Interior on . . . Reproduced and printed in pursuance of Act of Congress March 3, 1886, and Acts supplementary thereto.* Washington, D.C.: Government Printing Office, 1892. Facsimile edition with foreword by Mark Kramer. New York: Alfred A. Knopf, 1972.

C.C. *1789–1939 Ransome's "Royal" Records. A Century and a Half in the Service of Agriculture.* Ipswich: Ransome, n.d. (1939). 79 p., ills.

Charlton, T. M. *A history of theory of structures in the nineteenth century.* Cambridge: University Press, 1982. viii, 194 p., ills.

Chateau, Théodore. *Technologie du Bâtiment ou étude complète des matériaux de toute espèce employés dans l'art de bâtir . . .* 2 vols. Paris: Bance, 1863–1866. 1: 517 p., 1 map; 2: 851 p. 2nd ed., 1880–1882. 1: (6), (i), ii–ix, (x), 819 p., 1 map; 2: (4), 756 p. Dry, but it contains unknown building details and technological surprises.

Cialdi, Alessandro. *Delle Barche a Vapore e di alquanti proposizioni per rendere più sicura e più agevole la navigazione del Tevere e delle sua face in fiumicino ragionamento del Commend. . . .* Roma: Tipografia delle Belle Arte, 1845. (6), 416 p. frontis, 5 pls. cit in. Palinauris, cata. 28, #157. variant: 3, 1, 416 p., diagrs., plans.

Chrimes, Michael M., Julia Elton, et al. *The Triumphant Bore. A celebration of Marc Brunel's Thames Tunnel.* London: Institution of Civil Engineers, 1994. 96 p., ills. Catalog of an exhibition at the ICE.

Christophe, Paul. *Le béton armé et ses applications.* Paris: Béranger, 1899. iv, xix, (1), 755, (1) p., ills. 2nd ed. 1902. (See also Buel and Hill; Morel; Mörsch; Taylor and Thompson.)

Clark, Edwin. *The Britannia and Conway tubular bridges. With general inquiries on beams and on the properties of materials used in construction. By E. C., resident engineer. Published with the sanction, and under the supervision, of Robert Stephenson.* 2 vols. and atlas. London: for the author by Day & Son and John Weale, 1850. 1: xii, 466 p.; 2: viii, 467–821, iv p., ills., atlas with variant title: . . . *With the sanction and under the immediate supervision of Robert Stephenson.* London: for the author by John Weale, 1850. 46 pls. numbered: 1–12, 12*, 13–19, 19*, 20–29, 40/41, 42–45. The "official" history of the famed structure and a reaction to William Fairbairn's account of 1849. (See also Fairbairn, *An Account,* Dempsey.)

Clark, Kenneth McKenzie. *The Romantic Rebellion. Romantic versus Classic Art.* London: John Murray and Sotheby Parke Bernet, 1973. 2nd ed. An Omega Book. London: Futura, 1976. 366 p., 24 pls., 278 ills., U.S. edition New York: Harper and Row, 1973. 366 p., 24 pls., ills.

Clarke, Charles. *Observations on the Intended Tunnel beneath the River Thames; Shewing the Many Defects in the Present State of that Projection.* London: Robinson/J. Taylor; Gravesend: R. Pocock, 1799. 28 p. (misnumbered as 25). (See also Dodd.)

Clausewitz, Carl von. *Hinterlassene Werke des Generals Carl von Clausewitz uber Krieg und Kriegfuhrung.* 10 volumes. 1–3. *Vom Kriege.* Berlin: F. Dummler, 1832. maps, tabs. English edition 1873.

Clegg, Samuel Jr. "On Foundations, Natural and Artificial." *Min. Proc. ICE* 10 (1850–1851): 317–320. paper no. 850 (22 April 1851).

Clements, Paul. *Marc Isambard Brunel.* London: Longmans, Green, 1970. xv, (1), 270 p., ills.

Cody, Jeffrey William. *Earthen Wall Construction in the Eastern United States. A Thesis Presented to the Faculty of the Graduate School of Cornell University. . . .* Typescript 1985. (2), xv, 460 p., ills.

Cointeraux, François. *De la Distribution des Batimens de Pisé.* Paris: chez Vezard et le Normand, 1793.

Cointeraux, François. *L'Ecole d'Architecture Rurale ou Leçons par Lesquelles on Apprendra Soi-Même à Bâtir Solidement les Maisons de Plusieurs Etages Avec la Terre Seule.* 4 cahiers. Paris: chez l'auteur, 1791.1: *Premier cahier, dans lequel on apprendra soi-même à batir solidement les maisons de plusieurs étages avec la terre seule.* 32 p., 14 pls., ills.; 2: *Second cahier, dans lequel on traite: 1° de l'art du pisé ou de la massivation, 2°. des qualités des terres propres au pisé, 3° des details de la main d'oeuvre, 4° du prix de la toise, 5° des enduits, 6° des peintures. . . .* (4), 76 p., 4 pls./ills.; 3: *Troisième cahier. . . .* 4: *Quatrième cahier, dans lequel on traite du nouveau pisé inventé par l'auteur; de la construction de ses outils, &c. . . .* 68 p., 4 pls., ills. 2nd ed. 1796. (For the German translation see Seebass.)

Coleman, Terry. *The Railway Navvies. A history of the men who made the railways.* London: Hutchinson, 1965. 2nd ed. London: Pelican, 1968, reprinted 1969, 1970, 1972. 265 p., ills.

Colladon, Jean-Daniel. *Souvenirs et mémoires. Autobiographie.* Geneva: Auber-Schuchardt, 1893. 10, 636 p., portrait.

Collingwood, William Gersham. *The Life and Works of John Ruskin.* 2 vols. London: Methuen, 1893. 1: 243 p. portrait; 2: 285 p., ills.

Collins, Peter. *Concrete. The Vision of a New Architecture. A Study of Auguste Perret and his precursors.* London: Faber and Faber, 1959. 307 p., ills. Still a good study of the history of reinforced concrete. It concentrates on systems, buildings and personalities, while *Vom Caementum* concentrates on machines and methods. Together they give a fairly good, but now dated overview.

Collins, Peter. *Changing Ideals in Modern Architecture, 1750–1950.* London: Faber and Faber, 1965. 308 p., ills.

Condit, Carl W. *American Building Art.* 2 vols. New York: Oxford University Press, 1960. 1: The Nineteenth Century. xvii, (1), 371 p., ills.; 2: The Twentieth Century. xviii, 427 p., ills.

Condit, Carl W. "The Wind Bracing of Buildings." *Scientific American* (February 1974): 92–105. A lay overview of the subject, since improved upon by the scholarly work of Elwin Robison on the genesis of the stiff steel frame.

Conzett, Jürg. "Richard Coray (1869–1946)." *Fünf Schweizer Brückenbauer.* Schweizer Pioniere der Wirtschaft und Technik. Zurich: Verein für wirtschaftshistorische Studien 41 (1985): 32–57.

Cook, Sir Edward Tyas. *Studies in Ruskin: Some Aspects of the Work and Teachings of John Ruskin. With reproductions of drawings by Mr. Ruskin in the Ruskin Drawing School, Oxford.* Orpington & London: George Allen, 1890. xvi, 334 p., 13 pls., ills. 2nd ed. 1891.

Cooke, Thomas Fothergill. *Authorship of the Practical Electric Telegraph of Great Britain; Or, the Brunel Award Vindicated; in VII Letters, Containing Extracts from the Arbitration Evidence of 1841, Edited in Assertion of His Brother's Rights.* Bath: R. E. Peach, 1868. i–xvi, (i)–(ii), xxv–xxxii, 131, (1) p., 5 pls.

Cotte, Michel. "Le système technique des Seguins en 1824–25." *History and Technology* 7; no. 2 (1990): 119–147.

Cowper, Edward Alfred. *Trans. ICE* 12 (1853): 456–459; 13 (1854): 432–435.

Crelle, August Leopold. *Mémoire sur les différentes manières de se servir de l'élasticité de l'air atmosphérique comme force motrice sur les chemins de fer. Une de ces manières constitue les chemins de fer atmosphériques proprements dits.* Berlin: G. Reimer, 1846. vi, 199 p., 6 pls.

Cresy, Edward. *An Encyclopaedia of Civil Engineering, Historical, Theoretical, and Practical by E. C. Architect and Civil Engineer. Illustrated by upwards of three thousand engravings in wood by R. Branston.* London: Longman, Brown, Green and Longmans, 1847. xii, 1665, 32 p., ills. 2nd ed. 1856. 1752 p., ills. Further editions 1861, 1865, 1872, 1880. Together with Ure, who concentrated more on mining, John Nicholson, and Tomlinson, one of the important early technological encyclopedias in English.

Cross, Hardy. *Analysis of continuous frames by distributing fixed-end movements.* New York: ASCE, 1932. 156 p., ills. Paper no. 1793.

The Crystal Palace, and Its Contents; being an illustrated cyclopaedia of the Great Exhibition of the Industry of All Nations. 1851. Embellished with upwards of five hundred engravings. With a copious analytical index. London: W. M. Clark, 1852. viii, 424 p., ills.

Culmann, Karl (later Carl). "Der Bau der eisernen Brücken in England und Amerika." *Allgemeine Bauzeitung* (1852):163–222 and plates 478–487.

Culmann, Karl (later Carl). "Der Bau der hölzernen Brücken in den Vereinigten Staaten von Nordamerika. Ergebnisse einer im Auftrage der Königl. bayerischen Regierung in den Jahren 1849 und 1850 unternommenen Reise durch die Vereinigten Staaten." *Allgemeine Bauzeitung* . . . (1851): 69–129 and pls. 387–397. The first comprehensive and insightful article on North American building innovation in German. Its influence was more pervasive than for instance, the information on timber building published in the same journal in 1837 or Karl von Ghega's 1845 monograph. Culmann's study was the first of a projected three part "Darstellung der neuesten Fortschritten in Brücken-, Eisenbahn- und Flussdampfschiffsbau, so wie in der Errichtung elektromagnetischer Telegraphenlinien in den Vereinigten Staaten von Nordamerika und England. . . ." However, only a second part appeared: the previous item on iron bridges. No manuscript of the third part seems to have been prepared, and the only surviving material on the rest of Culmann's observations is contained in the diary preserved in the archives of the ETH Zurich.

Curr, John. *Railway Locomotion and Steam Navigation; their Principles and Practice.* London: J. Williams and Co., 1847. 2, 1, 181, (1) p., ills.

Custodis, Paul-Georg. *Die Sayner Hütte in Bendorf.* Cologne: reprint from *Rheinische Kunststätten.* (1980), no. 241. 15 p., ills.

Darmstaedter, Ludwig. *Handbuch zur Geschichte der Naturwissenschaften und der Technik. In chronologischer Darstellung. Zweite umgearbeitete und vermehrter Auflage. Unter Mitwirkung von Professor R. du Bois-Reymond und Oberst z. D. C. Schaefer.* 2nd. ed. Berlin: Julius Springer, 1908. x, 1262, 1 p. The first edition was merely a brief version of few pages. Darmstaedter is surprisingly complete and free of errors, at least where I have been able to check it. With Poggendorff the most comprehensive source for the verification of dates and the evolution of invention in the history of technology extant.

Davies, J. Vipond. "Progress in the Art of Tunneling." *Engineering News Record. Fiftieth Anniversary Number* (17 April 1924): 674–679.

Debonnefoy, E. "Note sur le caoutchouc vulcanisé et sur son emploi comparé à celui de l'acier fondu pour les ressorts des voitures et wagons dans les chemins de fer." *Mémoires et Compte-Rendu des travaux de la Société des Ingénieurs Civils* (1854): 86–95.

De la Beche, Sir Henry, and Thomas Cubitt. *Report on the Fall of the Cotton Mill, at Oldham, and part of the Prison at Northleach.* London: Clowes and Sons, 1845.

Dempsey, George Drysdale. *Tubular and other Iron Girder Bridges, particularly describing the Britannia and Conway Bridges; with a sketch of Iron Bridges, and Illustrations of the application of malleable iron to the art of bridge-building. With Wood Engravings. Rudimentary Treatise.* London: John Weale, 1850. viii, 132 p., ills. (frontis. incl. in pagination). 2nd ed. 1851.

Depping, Guillaume. "La Première Exposition à Paris en 1798." *L'Exposition de Paris de 1889* 6, no. 1 (15 Oct. 1888).

Desbrière. Article on J. B. Fell's railway system. *Mémoires et Compte-Rendu des travaux de la Société des Ingénieurs Civils* (1864): 75–80; (1865): 408–414, 426.

Desbrière. "Études sur la locomotion au moyen du rail central contenant la relation des Expériences entreprises par MM. Brassey, Fell et Cie. pour la traversée du Mont-Cenis." *Mémoires et Compte-Rendu des travaux de la Société des Ingénieurs Civils* (1865): 457–503 and plate 54.

Description de l'Égypte: ou Receuil des observations et des recherches qui ont été faites en Égypte pendant l'expédition de l'armée française. Commission des sciences et arts d'Égypte. 21 vols. Paris: Imprimerie impériale, 1809–1828. 2 vols. Antiquités: Descriptions, 1809–1818; 2 vols. Mémoires, 1809–1818; 5 vols. (in 6) Planches, 1809–1822; 2 vols. (in 3) État moderne 1809–1822; 2 vols. (in 3) Planches, 1809–1817?; 2 vols. Histoire naturelle, 1809–1812; 2 vols. (in 3) Planches, 1809–c.1826; 1 vol. Carte topograph-ique, 1828; 1 vol. Préface et explication des planches, 1828. 2nd. ed. of parts already issued. Paris: C. L. F. Panckoucke, 1821. 24 vols. in 26.

De Zurko, Edward Robert. *Origins of functionalist theory.* New York: Columbia Univer-sity Press, 1957. xiv, 265 p., ills.

Dibner, Bern. *The Atlantic Cable.* Norwalk, CT: Burndy Library, 1959. 96 p. ills.

Dickinson, Henry W. "A Study of Galvanized and Corrugated Sheet Metal." *Transac-tions of the Newcomen Society* 24 (1943): 27–36.

Diestelkamp, Edward J. "Richard Turner and the Palm House at Kew Gardens." *Trans-actions of the Newcomen Society for the study of the history of engineering and technology* 54 (1982–1983).

Dinglers Polytechnisches Journal. Stuttgart 1820–1931. *Polytechnisches Journal.* 1 (1820)–221 (1873). *Dinglers Polytechnisches Journal* 212 (1874)–346 (1931). Belongs with the *Allgemeine Bauzeitung* to the first and most influential technological journals in Ger-man. (See also Fuchs; Pettenkofer; Schafhäutl.)

Dodd, Ralph. *Reports, with Plans, Sections, &c of the Proposed Dry Tunnel, or Passage from Gravesend, in Kent to Tilbury, in Essex: Demonstrating its Practicability, and Great Impor-tance to the two Counties, and to the Nation at Large: also on a Canal from Near Gravesend to Stroud, With Some Miscellaneous and Practical Observations by R. D. . . .* London: printed for J. Taylor at the Architectural Library, 1798. viii, (2), 28, (2) p., 3 pls., map, ills. (See also Clarke.)

Doorman, Gerard. *Octrooien voor uitvindingen in de Nederlanden uit de 16'–18' ceuw mit bespreking von enkele anderwepen uit de geschiedenid der techniek.* s-Gravenhage: M. Nij-hoff, 1940. 3, 1, 5–348 p. German ed. 1941. Engl. eds. 1942, 1980.

Downes, Charles. *The Building erected in Hyde Park for the Great Exhibition of the Works of all Nations 1851. Illustrated by 28 large plates, embracing plans, elevations, sections, and de-tails, laid down to a large scale from the working drawings of the Contractors, Messrs. Fox, Hen-derson, and Co. by C.D., Architect, with scientific description by Charles Cowper, Assoc. Inst. C.E.* London: John Weale, 1852. Reprint London: Victoria and Albert Museum, 1971. (6), iv, 45 p., 28 pls. (1–20, 20a, 21–27).

Drinker, Henry S. *Tunneling, Explosive Compounds, and Rock Drills. Giving the Details of Practical Tunnel Work; the Constituents and Properties of Modern Explosive Compounds; the Principles of Blasting; the History of the Rise of Machine Rock-Drilling; and Detailed Descrip-tions of the Various Rock-Drills and Air-Compressors in Use. Also, Descriptions of the European and American Systems of Timbering and Arching, and Tables Giving the Dimensions and Cost of over Seventeen Hundred Tunnels, from Notes Furnished by Engineers and Railroad Companies in Europe, North and South America, and New Zealand, with a History of Tunnel-ing from the Reign of Rameses II to the Present Time. Illustrated with about One Thousand Cuts Set in the Text, and Several Large Folding Plates, Comprising Geological and Working Profiles of the Nesquehoning, the Musconetcong, and the Hoosac Tunnels, Etc, Etc.* New York: John Wiley and Sons, 1878. i–iv, 1–2, v–viii, 1031, (1), iii–xliv p., 19 pls., ills.

Ducuing, Fr., ed. *Exposition universelle de 1867 illustrée. Publication internationale au-thorisée par la Commission impériale.* 2 vols. Paris: Administration (de l'exposition), (1867). 1: (8), 480 p., ills.; 2: (2), 480, (6) p., ills. Originally issued as sixty brochures.

Dufour, Guillaume-Henri. *Calculs et Details sur le nouveau projet de pont à établir de la Fusterie aux Bergues.* Manuscript. Geneva: State Archives. Travaux B 10 (22 Dec. 1832). Regarding the construction of the Pont des Bergues in Geneva 1833.

Dufour, Guillaume-Henri. *Description du Pont suspendu en fil de fer, construit à Genève.* Paris: Paschoud, 1824. 93 p., 3 pls. This book documents the transition from the "art" to the "science" of engineering at the beginning of the nineteenth century and the appearance of technological thought. (See also Peters, *Transitions in Engineering.*)

Dufour, Guillaume-Henri. *Observations sur le rapport de M. Navier. Projet de Pont Sus-pendu pour Frybourg.* Manuscript State Archives: Geneva Travaux E 16 (Nov. 1825). 13 p. + sketches + report by Navier. *Rapport sur le projet de pont suspendu à construire sur la Sarine à Fribourg* (20 May 1825). 17 p. w. sketches + Dufour's answer. *Observa-tions sur le Rapport de M. Navier.* 4 p.

Dupuit, Arsène Emile Juvénal. "Rapport de la commission d'enquête nommée par ar-rête de M. le Préfet de Marne-et-Loire, en date de 20 avril 1850, pour rechercher les causes et les circonstances qui ont amené la chute du pont suspendu de la Basse-Chaîne." *Annales des Ponts et Chaussées.* 2e. sém. (1850): 394–411.

Durupt, J. "Maisons demontables en tôles ondulées ganvanisées. Matiêrtes isolantes et bois." *Mémoires et Compte-Rendu des travaux de la Société des ingéneurs Civils.* 2e. sem. (1889): 369–375, with discussion: 25–28.

Dyck, Walther van. *Georg von Reichenbach. Deutsches Museum Lebensbeschreibungen und Urkunden.* Munich: Selbstverlag des Deutschen Museums, 1912. frontis, (4), 140 p., 8 pl., 74 ills.

Eiffel, (Alexandre) Gustave. *Notice sur le Viaduc de Garabit (près Saint-Flour) Ligne de Marvejols à Neussarques.* . . . Paris: Imprimerie Administrative & des Chemins de Fer de Paul Dupont, 1888. 26 p., 5 pls.

Eiffel, (Alexandre) Gustave. *La Tour de 300 Mètres.* 2 vols. Paris: Imprimeries Lemer-cier for the author, 1900. 1: text: 368, 13 p. ills.; 2: atlas: 53 pls., 11 photogravures, 2 p. photographs, 1 map. This is one of the most complete and lavish technical reports on a structure ever produced. It was issued in five hundred numbered copies and dis-tributed by the author to professional institutions. It contains the plans of the Eiffel Tower from the first sketches to the minutest details, a series of large photographs of the building process and two of the very early photographs to be made with a tele-photo lens. The text explains the design, calculation, and the construction process as well as the changes made for the Paris Exhibition of 1900 and many of the scientific experiments carried out using the tower (however, not including Eiffel's own experi-ments on wind resistance; which were separately published shortly thereafter). The text volume also contains the *raison d'être* for the elaborate publication, a passionate defense of Eiffel's role in the Panama Canal scandal.

Elliott, Cecil D. *Technics and Architecture. The Development of Materials and Systems for Buildings.* Cambridge, MA: MIT Press, 1992. x, 467 p., ills.

Elton, Julia. *Railways. Including a section on the atmospheric railway and a selection of prints & drawings.* Antiquarian book catalog number 7. London: Elton Engineering Books, 1992. 96 p., ills.

Elton, Julia. *Timber & Masonry, Iron & Steel, Cement & Concrete. The science and development of materials and their application to building and civil engineering.* Antiquarian book catalog number 6. London: Elton Engineering Books, 1991. 158, (2) p, ills.

Elton, Julia. See also Chrimes, Michael M., et al.

Engel, Friedrich. *Der Kalk-Sand-Pisébau. Anleitung zur Kunst: Gebäude von gestampftem Mörtel aufzuführen, nach eigenen, sowie mit Benützung der besten bisher gemachten Erfahrungen, besonders für die Bedürfnisse des landwirtschaftlichen Publikums bearbeitet von F. E. Bevorwortet von A. P. Thaer. Zweite, mit einem Nachtrage versehene Auflage mit 8 Tafeln Abbildingen und Holzschnitte.* 2nd ed. Wriezen a.O.: Verlag von E. Roeder, 1856. 2, 88, 21 p., 7 pls. 1st. ed. 1851. 3rd ed. . . . *verb. u. verm. m. 46 Holzschnitten und 10 lithogr. Tafeln.* Berlin: Wiegandt, Hempel & Parey, 1856. vi, 1, 118 p., ills., 10 pls. 4th ed. 1877. With Sebass's translation of Cointereaux and Krause the first popular study on concrete construction in German.

Engels, Friedrich. *Die Lage der Arbeitenden Klasse in England. Nach eigener Anschauung und authentischen Quellen.* Leipzig: O. Wiegand, 1845. 358 p., 1 pl., 1 plan. 2nd ed. . . . *Zweite, durchgesehene Auflage.* Leipzig: O. Wiegand, 1845. 358 p., 1 pl., 1 plan.

Engineering News. Chicago. *Engineering News and American Contract Journal* 1 (1874)–18 (1887) *Engineering News and American Railway Journal* 19 (1888)–48 (1902) *Engineering News. A Journal of civil engineering and construction* 49 (1903)–77 (1917). *Engineering News Record* 78 (1917) ff.

Erdmanns Journal für technische und ökonomische Chemie. See *Journal für technische und ökonomische Chemie.*

Evill, William. "Description of the Iron Shed at the London Terminus of the Eastern Counties Railway." *Min. Proc. ICE* 3 (1844): 288–290. Paper no. 683.

Exhibition of the Works of Industry of All Nations 1851. Reports of the Juries on the Subjects in the Thirty Classes into which the Exhibition was Divided. London: William Clowes & Sons, printed for the Royal Commission, 1851. (6), cxx, 867, (1), 16 p., ills. Printed uniformly with the 3-, and later 4-volume *Official Descriptive and Illustrated Catalogue.* A large type edition was issued in 2 volumes.

L'Exposition de Paris (1889), publiée avec la collaboration d'écrivains spéciaux. Edition enrichie de vues, de scènes, de reproductions d'objets d'art, de machines, de dessins et gravures par les meilleurs artistes. 80 nos. (although only 40 were advertised on the title) 4 vols. (in 2). Paris: La Librairie Illustrée, 1888–1980. 1: 324 p.; 2: 324 p. w. supplements and ills. The most detailed popular account of the 1889 Paris exhibition. It appeared (as did many others), as a journal during the duration of the exhibition. (See also Depping.)

L'Exposition de Paris (1900) publiée avec la collaboration d'écrivains spéciaux et de meilleurs artistes. Encyclopédie du Siècle. 3 vols. Paris: Librairie Illustrée. Montgredien et Cie. Éd., 1900. 1, 2, 3: (4), 324 p., ills.

Exposition universelle de 1867. See Ducuing.

L'Exposition universelle de 1889. See Monod.

Eytelwein, Johann Albert. *Handbuch der Mechanik fester Körper und der Hydraulik: mit vorzüglicher Rücksicht auf ihre Anwendung in der Architektur aufgesetzt von J.A.E.* Berlin: bei F. T. Lagarde, 1801. xxiv, 498 p., 5 pls., ills.

Fairbairn, Sir William. *An Account of the Construction of the Britannia and Conway Tubular Bridges, with a complete History of their Progress, from the Conception of the Original Idea, to the Conclusion of the Elaborate Experiments which Determined the Exact Form and Mode of Construction ultimately Adopted.* London: John Weale and Longman, Green and Longmans, 1849. xii, 291 p., 22 pls., frontis., ills. London: J. Weale, 1900. xii, 291 p. 20 pls., ills. Fairbairn's justification of his part in the development of the construction of Robert Stephenson's bridges. It contains a comprehensive description of the development of the construction and the building process with drawings, tables, calculations, and correspondence. Eaton Hodgkinson's annotated copy is now in Stanford University; Edwin Clark's annotated copy in the Institution of Civil Engineers' archive. Together with Clark, Fairbairn's account forms one of the most detailed building process reports of the nineteenth century. (See also Dempsey.)

Fairbairn, Sir William. *An Experimental Enquiry into the Strength and other Properties of Cast Iron, from Various Parts of the United Kingdom.* Manchester Memoirs, vol. 6, New Series. Manchester: Printed by Francis Looney, 1838. 105 p., 1 tab., tabs. in text. Subsequently also in *Trans. Phil. Soc. of Manchester* 7 (1842).

Fairbairn, Sir William. *The Life of Sir William Fairbairn, Bart., partly written by himself. Edited and completed by William Pole.* London: Longmans, Green and Co., 1877. xvi, 507 p., ills. 2nd ed. Newton Abbot: David & Charles, 1970. xxii, xvi, 507 p., portrait, frontis.

Fairbairn, Sir William. "On some defects in the Principle and Construction of Fireproof Buildings." *Min. Proc. ICE* 6 (1847) 213–224. Paper no. 758 (20 Apr. 1847).

Fairbairn, Sir William. *On the Application of Cast and Wrought Iron to Building Purposes.* London: John Weale, 1854. vii, 183, (1) p., ills. 2nd ed. . . . . *To which is added a short treatise on wrought iron bridges.* London: John Weale, 1857–1858. xii, 292 p., 4 pls., 1 tb., ills. 4th ed. London: Longmans, 1870.

Fairbairn, Sir William. "On Tubular Girder Bridges." *Min. Proc. ICE* 9 (1849–1850): 233–287. Paper no. 826 (12 Mar. 1850).

Fairbairn, Sir William. A report on iron buildings in Turkey. *Min. Proc. ICE* 2 (1842–1843): 125–126.

Fairbairn, Sir William. *Treatise on Mills and Millwork.* 3rd ed. London: Longman etc., 1871.

Faujas de Saint-Fond, Barthélemy. *Recherches sur la Pouzzolane sur la Théorie de la Chaux et sur la cause de la dureté du Mortier, avec la Composition de différens Cimens . . .* Grenoble/Paris: J. Cuchet, 1778.

Faye, Polycarpe de la. *Mémoire pour servir de suite aux recherches sur la préparation que les Romains donnoient à la Chaux. Dont ils se servoient pour leurs constructions & sur la composition & l'emploi de leurs mortiers.* Paris: Imprimerie royale, 1778. viii, 110, xviii, (ii) p.

Faye, Polycarpe de la. *Recherches sur la préparation que les Romains donnoient à la chaux dont ils ser servoient pour leurs constructions, & sur la composition & l'emploi de leurs mortiers.* Paris: Imprimerie royale, 1777. vi, 83, (1), xi, (i) p.

Ferguson, Eugene S., ed. *Early Engineering Reminiscences (1815–40) of George Escol Sellers.* Washington, D.C.: Smithsonian Institution, Museum of History and Technology, 1965. xix, (1), 203 p., ills.

Ferguson, Eugene S. "The Measurement of the 'Man-Day.'" *Scientific American* (October 1971): 96–103.

Festschrift zur Feier des fünfzigjährigen Bestehns des Eidg. Polytechnikums. 2 vols. Zurich: for the ETH (1905). 1: *Geschichte der Gründung des Eidgenössischen Polytechnikums mit einer Übersicht seiner Entwicklung 1855–1905 von Wilhelm Oechsli.* xvi, 406 p., portraits; 2: *Zweiter Teil: die bauliche Entwicklung Zürichs in Einzeldarstellungen von Mitgliedern des Zürcher Ingenieur- und Architektenvereins.* 480, viii p. ills.

Field, Henry Martyn. *History of the Atlantic Telegraph.* New York: Charles Scribner & Co., 1866. viii, 8–364, (3), (5 ads.) p., frontis., ills.

Field, Henry Martyn. *The Story of the Atlantic Telegraph.* New York: Charles Scribner's Sons, 1892. ix, (3), 415 p., frontis., ills. 2nd ed. New York: Arno Press, 1972.

Field, Walker. "A Reexamination into the Invention of the Balloon Frame." *Jnl. Am. Soc. Arch. Hist.* 2, no. 4 (Oct. 1942): 3–29.

Figuier, (Guillaume) Louis. *L'Année scientifique et industrielle, ou exposé annuel des travaux scientifiques, des inventions et des principales applications de la science à l'industrie et aux arts, qui ont attiré l'attention publique en France et à l'étranger.* 57 + 2 index vols. In vols. 9 & 10 (1865 and 1866), the title included: *accompagné d'une nécrologie scientifique et d'un Index bibliographique des ouvrages de science parus dans le courant de l'année.* From vol. 11 on solely: *accompagné d'une nécrologie scientifique.* From 1895 on, the title was: *L'Année scientifique et industrielle fondée par Louis Figuier.* Paris: Hachette, 1857–1915 (For the years 1856–1914). 1 vol per year, 2 vols for the third year and 1 vol. for the 15th–16th (war) years 1870–1871. Vol. 38 (1894), was completed by Daniel Bellet. Thereafter, the series was continued by Emile Gautier. The first year two printings of 3,000 were made. By the third year, 8,000 copies were printed. In 1866 the edition had grown to 15,000 where it remained until at least 1877 (information from the prefaces to the index vols.). Index 1: *Tables décennales de l'Année scientifique et industrielle par Louis Figuier 1856–1865.* Paris: Librairie de L. Hachette et Cie., 1866. (4), 200 p.; 2: *L'Année scientifique et industrielle par Louis Figuier Tables des vingt premiers volumes*

1857–1877. Paris: Librairie Hachette et Cie, 1877. (4), 295, (1) p. Louis Figuier, originally a physician by training, was far and away the most interesting scientific popularizer of the nineteenth century. His complete works run to at least 75 titles and over 150 volumes. (A checklist of all known titles and editions by Tom F. Peters. Bethlehem, PA: Lehigh University Libraries, 1996). Figuier was no chauvinist. His work represents a global cornucopia of projects, inventions, developments, dead ends and forgotten plans valuable for the history of nineteenth-century technology, (and in part science too). It appeared in an unbroken series covering half a century. Building projects can be followed year by year from inception to success or abandonment. Projects that have a history predating the series are briefly introduced, commonly with names, dates, statistics and sources. The series is supplemented by three multi-volume historical works on the evolution of science and technology: *Les Merveilles de l'Industrie, Les Merveilles de la Science,* and *Les Nouvelles Conquêtes de la Science.* The technological evolution of the western world is minutely documented in these works as in no other encyclopedia. Figuier was primarily interested in education. A true child of his age, he adopted a developmental model in technology and in science, which explains his value to the modern historian of technology.

Figuier, (Guillaume) Louis. *L'Art de l'Eclairage, ouvrage illustré de 114 gravures sur bois.* Bibliothèque Instructive. Paris: Librairie Jouvet et Cie., 1882. 284 p., ills. An evolutionary explanation written in connection with the 1881 Paris exhibition.

Figuier, (Guillaume) Louis. *Les Grandes Inventions Modernes dans les sciences, l'industrie et les arts. Ouvrage à l'usage de la jeunesse. Neuvième édition, revue, augmentée, et illustrée de 424 gravures sur bois.* 9th ed. Paris: Hachette, 1886. xii, 616 p., ills.

Figuier, (Guillaume) Louis. *Les Merveilles de la Science ou Description populaire des inventions modernes.* 4 vols. Paris: Furne, Jouvet et Cie, 1868–1870. Later editions identical but without dates. 1: 734 p.; 2: 703 p.; 3: 752 p.; 4: 744 p., all with many illustrations. Two supplemental vols. appeared in 1891 and 1892. 5: 740 p.; 6: 674 p. In 1911 the six-volume work was reissued by Max de Nansouty with a foreword by Alfred Picard. Paris: Bovin et Cie., 1911. 1: 728 p.; 2: 748 p.; 3: 748 p.; 4: 759 p.; 5: 392, 396 p.; 6: 362, 368 p.

Figuier, (Guillaume) Louis. *Les Nouvelles Conquêtes de la Science.* 4 vols. Paris: Librairie Illustrée et Marpon & Flammarion (1883–1885). 1: *l'Electricité.* iii, 644 p.; 2: *Grands Tunnels et Railways Metropolitains.* 644 p.; 3: *Les Voies Ferrées dans les deux Mondes.* 644 p.; 4: *Isthmes et Canaux.* 630 p., all with copious illustrations. A continuation of the earlier, four-volume *Merveilles de la Science.*

Figuier, (Guillaume) Louis (1819–1894). See also *La Science Illustrée.*

Flachat, Eugène. "Compte Rendu et Observations sur le projet de M. Toni Fontenay . . . sur la construction des grands tunnels." *Mémoires et Compte-Rendu des travaux de la Société des Ingénieurs Civils* (1863): 221–235. See also Fontenay, "Construction."

Flachat, Eugène. "De la traversée des Alpes par un chemin de fer. Analyse par MM. H(enri) Mathieu et E. Deligny." *Mémoires et Compte-Rendu des travaux de la Société des Ingénieurs Civils* (1861): 309–367.

Flachat, Eugène. "Mémoire no. VII sur la traversée des Alpes par un chemin de fer." *Mémoires et Compte-Rendu des travaux de la Société des Ingénieurs Civils* (1859): 313–396.

Flachat, Eugène. "Mémoire sur les travaux de l'isthme de Suez." *Mémoire et Compte-Rendu des travaux de la Société des Ingénieurs Civils* (1864): 417–429; 468–487.

Flachat, Eugène, and Léon Molinos. "Note sur le rapport de la Commission internationale pour le percement de l'isthme de Suez." *Mémoires et Compte-Rendu des travaux de la Société des Ingénieurs Civils* (1857): 25–47.

Fleuret, M. *L'art de composer des pierres factices aussi dures qui le caillou, et recherches sur la manière de bâtir des anciens, sur la ses de durcissement de leurs mortiers.* 2 vols. Pont-à-Mousson: for the author, 1807. 1: (ii), 298 p.; 2: 32 pls.

Fontana, Domenico. *Della Trasportazione del'Obelisco Vaticano et delle Fabbriche de Nostro Signore Papa Sisto V [1521–1590] fatte dal Cavalier D.F. architetto de Sua Santità.* Rome: Domenico Basa, 1590. 108, (4) p., 38 pl., 1 portrait. (title page date: 1589).

Fontenay, Toni. "Construction des grands tunnels." *Mémoires et Compte-Rendu des travaux de la Société des Ingénieurs Civils* (1863): 192–220 and plates 27, 28. See also Flachat, "Compte Rendu."

Forey. "Note sur le pont en tôle construit en 1855 sur le Cher pour le passage du chemin de fer de Commentry à Montluçon, et sur le rétablissement de ce pont, affouillé dans le inondations de 1856." *Mémoires et Compte-Rendu des travaux de la Société des Ingénieurs Civils* (1857): 96–102 and plate 68.

Försters Allgemeine Bauzeitung. See *Allgemeine Bauzeitung.*

Fortin-Hermann Frères (Emile Fortin-Hermann). "Mémorie sur les procédés et appareils de fondations tubulaires de . . ." *Mémoires et Compte-Rendu des travaux de la Société des Ingénieurs Civils* (1862): 218–258 and plates 24, 25.

Fowler, Charles, Jr. "The Crystal Palace Building." *The Illustrated Exhibitor.* London: Spicer Bros., 1851. nine parts: pp. 44–48, 63–66, 79–82, 95–98, 112–114, 130–131, 185–187, 215–217, 243–245, ills. (See also *Illustrated Exhibitor.*) One of the most comprehensive descriptions of the building process of the Crystal Palace of 1851. Charles Fowler, Jr., understood building and was probably an engineer like his father, who built the iron pavillion in the Hungerford Fish Market in 1835.

Fowler, Charles Evan. *The Coffer-Dam Process for Piers.* New York: John Wiley & Sons, 1898. xv, 159 p., ills. 2nd ed. revised and enlarged. New York: John Wiley & Sons, 1906, variant title: *Ordinary Foundations. Including the Coffer-Dam Process for Piers. With numerous practical examples from actual work.* xxvi, 314 p., 19 p. ads. ills., frontis. incl. 3rd ed. New York/London: John Wiley & Sons, 1914. xliv, 814 p., frontis., pls., ills., variant title: *A Practical Treatise on Sub-Aqueous Foundations including The Coffer-Dam Process for Piers and Dredges and Dredging with numerous practical examples from actual work.*

Fox, Henry Hawes, and James Barrett. *On the construction of public buildings, and private dwelling houses, on a fire-proof principle, without increase of cost.* London: Mudie, 1849. (11), 11, (1), frontis., 1 plate. (Mentioned in Elton, catalog 5.)

Francis, Charles L., and Heymans. "On the Brick Beam at Nine Elms." *Min. Proc. ICE* 1 (1837–1841): 16.

Fuchs, Johann Nepomuk. "Über die Eigenschaften, Bestandtheile und chemischen Verbindungen der hydraulischen Mörtel," German translation from the Dutch. *Dinglers Polytechnisches Journal* 49 (1833): 271 ff. This article, based on work done between 1828 and 1832, received a prize from the Maatschappi der Wetensch. te Haarlem in 1832 and first appeared in their *Natuurkund. Verhandl.* 20 (1832).

Fuchs, Johann Nepomuk. "Über Kalk und Mörtel." *Journal für technische und ökonomische Chemie.* 6 (1829): 1 ff, 132 ff.

Gale, William. "Remarks of the utility and defects of the Movable Jib Crane, according to the construction now generally used in Glasgow, with proposed Improvements to obviate its Defects." *Min. Proc. ICE* 4 (1845): 333–348. Paper no. 703.

Gallatin, Albert Abraham Alphonse. *Report of the Secretary of the Treasury on the subject of Public Roads and Canals; made in pursuance of the resolution of Senate, of March 2, 1807.* Washington, D.C.: R. C. Weightman, 1808. 123 p.

Gehri, Ernst. "Entwicklung des ingenieurmässigen Holzbaus seit Grubenmann. Teil II: 20. Jahrhundert und künftige Möglichkeiten." *Schweizerischer Ingineur und Architekt* 33/34 (1983): 808–815.

Gerstner, Franz Joseph von. *Handbuch der Mechanik.* 3 vols and atlas. Vols. 1 and 2 Prague: Johann Spurny, 1831–1832. Vol. 3 and atlas: Vienna: J. P. Sollinger, 1831/1834. 1: 1831. viii, (8), 633, (1) p.; 2: 1832. xii, 547, 1 p.; 3: 1834 portrait, vii, 570 p.; Atlas: pls 1–40 Prague, 1831; pls 41–68 Prague, 1832; pls 69–109 Vienna, 1834. The work was edited and published by the author's son Franz Anton von Gerstner. 2nd. ed. of vol. 1, 1833 with portrait added. English edition Vienna, 1834 apparently in one volume only.

Gerstner, Franz Joseph von. *Zwey Abhandlungen über Frachtwägen und Strassen und über die Frage, ob, und in welchen Fällen der Bau schiffbarer Kanäle, Eisenwege, oder gemachten Strassen vorzuziehen sey. Nach einer Untersuchung, ob die Moldau mit der Donau durch einen Schiffahrtkanal zu vereinigen sey, aufgesetzt von . . . Für die Abhandungen der k. böhm. gelehrt. Gesellschaft.* Prague: gedruckt bey Gottlieb Haase, 1813. (6), 146 p., 2 pls.

Giedion, Sigfried. *Bauen in Frankreich, Eisen, Eisenbeton.* Leipzig: Klinkhardt & Biermann, 1926. 127 p., ills. 2nd ed. 1938. One of Giedion's most original and fascinating books. Engl. edition 1995.

Giedion, Sigfried. *Mechanization Takes Command, a Contribution to Anonymous History.* New York: Oxford University Press, 1948. xiv, 743 p., ills. Reprinted 1955. 2nd ed. London: W. H. Norton & Co., 1969. French edition Paris: Centre Georges Pompidou, 1980. Title: *La mechanisation au pouvoir: contribution à l'histoire anonyme.* 591 p., ills.; 2nd. abbreviated edition 1983. One of the early studies in the history of technology, especially interesting for building construction, furniture, household machinery, and food processing in the United States. Giedion wrote a collage in the history of invention, and, although it displays all the shortcomings associated with both that form and content, it is as inspiring as only an associative collage can be.

Giedion, Sigfried. *Space, Time and Architecture, the growth of a new tradition*. Cambridge, MA: Harvard University Press/H. Milford: Oxford University Press, 1941. xvi, 601 p., ills. Reprinted 1943. Further eds. of increasing scope 1944, 1949, 1954, 1956, 1962, 1963, 1965, 1967, 1973, 1974, 1980, 1982. German edition *Raum, Zeit und Architektur*. Munich: Artemis, 1976. 536 p., ills. 2nd ed. 1978. Although this book is more renowned than "Mechanization Takes Command," it is more speculative, prejudiced and contains more errors of fact. Although it neglects to quote sources, it is still inspiring in its collage technique.

Gilbert, K. R. *Henry Maudslay. Machine builder. A Science Museum Booklet*. London: Her Majesty's Stationery Office, 1971. (1), 2–31 p., ills.

Gilbreth, Frank Bunker. *Bricklaying System*. New York: Myron, Clark & Co., 1909. xi, 321, 3 p., ills. 2nd. ed. Easton, PA: Hive Publishing Co., 1974. xi, 321 p., ills. Hive management series 31. Gilbreth began his motion studies at about the same time and independently of the better-known Frederick Winslow Taylor's time studies. Gilbreth concentrated on building in his work and was the one who introduced Taylor to the field. He is best known from the film *Cheaper by the Dozen* made from his autobiography.

Gilbreth, Frank Bunker. *Concrete system*. New York: The Engineering News Publishing Company, 1908. 2nd. ed. Easton, PA: Hive Publishing Co., 1974. 182 p., 10 pls., ills. Hive management history series 70. Reprinted 1981.

Gilbreth, Frank Bunker. *Field system of Frank B. Gilbreth*. New York: Bruce & Banning, 1906. 105 p.: ills. This was a private edition only loaned to contractors. 2nd. ed. New York: M. C. Clark Publishing Co., 1908. Variant title *Field system*. 194 p. ills.

Gilbreth, Frank Bunker. *Process of construction of the Augusutus Lowell Laboratory of Electrical Engineering for the Massachusetts Institute of Technology*. Boston: np., 1902. [16] p. ills.

Gilbreth, Frank Bunker. See also Spriegel.

Gilbreth, Lillian Evelyn Moller. *The Quest of the One Best Way. A Sketch of the Life of Frank Bunker Gilbreth*. New York: Society of Women Engineers (1925). 64 p., portrait. Further eds. 1926, 1930, 1952, 1973, 1990.

Gilette, Halbert Powers, and Charles Shattuck Hill. *Concrete construction, methods and cost*. New York: The M. C. Clark Publishing Co., 1908. viii, 690 p., ills.

Gillmore, Charles Stewart. *Coulomb and the evolution of physics and engineering in eighteenth century France*. Princeton: University Press, 1971. xviii, 328 p., ills.

Gillmore, Quincy Adams. *Practical treatise on limes, hydraulic cements, and mortars. Containing reports of numerous experiments conducted in New York City, during the years 1858 to 1861, inclusive*. New York: Van Nostrand, 1863. 333, (1) p., ills. 3rd ed. New York: Van Nostrand, 1870. 333, (1) p., ills. 4th ed. New York: Van Nostrand, 1871. 334 p., ills. 11th ed. 1896.

Gimpel, Jean. *La révolution industrielle du Moyen Age.* Paris: Editions du Seuil, 1975. 244 p., ills. English edition New York: Holt, Rinehart and Winston, 1976. Title: *The Medieval Machine. The Industrial Revolution of the Middle Ages.* xi, (3), 274 p., ills. Further eds. 1977, 1979, 1986, 1988. Portuguese ed. 1976, German ed. 1980, Spanish ed. 1982.

Girard, Pierre-Simon. *Traité analytique de la résistance des solides, et des solides d'égale résistance, auquelle on a joint une suite de nouvelles Expériences sur la force, et l'elasticité spécifiques des Bois de Chêne et de Sapin.* Paris: Firmin Didot/Du Pont, 1798 (an VI). lv, (1), 238, 23 p., 48 p. tables, 10 p. publ. cata., 9 pls.

Glaser, Hermann. "Zur 500 jährigen Kulturgeschichte der Post. Vom 'reitenden Bott' zur Telematik." *Neue Zürcher Zeitung.* Wochenendbeilage, no. 155 (7–8. July 1990): 75–77.

Glynn, Joseph. "On the Isthmus of Suez and the Canals of Egypt." *Min. Proc. ICE* 10 (1850–1851): 369–380. Paper no. 859 (20 May 1851).

Goodspeed, E. J. *History of the Great Fires in Chicago and the West. A proud career arrested by sudden and awful calamity; towns and counties laid waste by the devastating element. Scenes and incidents, losses and sufferings, benevolence of the nations, Etc., Etc. with a History of the Rise and Progress of Chicago, the "Young giant."* New York: H. S. Goodspeed and Co., 1871. xvi, 17–676 p., ills.

Goodwyn. "On the mode pracised in India for obtaining solid Foundations for Bridges, &c., in sand soils, by means of Wells." *Min. Proc. ICE* 2 (1842–1843): 63–64.

Gordon, Steve C. "From Slaughterhouse to Soap-Boiler: Cincinnati's Meat Packing Industry, Changing Technologies, and the Rise of Mass Production 1825–1870." *I.A. Jnl. of the Soc. for Industrial Archaeology* 16, no. 1 (1990): 55–67.

Goschler, Ch. "Note sur la pénétration des bois par les sels métalliques (extrait des annales de la Société des Ingénieurs autrichiens)." *Mémoire et Compte-Rendu des travaux de la Société des Ingénieurs Civils* (1852): 91–101.

Gould, Marcus (reporter). *Trial of Twenty-Four Journeymen Tailors Charged with Conspiracy Before the Mayor's Court in the City of Philadelphia* . . . Philadelphia: George Bausch (The Society of Journeymen Tailors), 1827. (2), iii–iv, (2), 7–167, (1) p. Taken from Palinaurus Antiquarian Books, catalog 27, 1991, no. 111 with history and explanation by John G. Hellebrand.

Graefe, Reiner. "Projektbereich Architektur: Geschichte des Konstruierens. Hängedächer des 19. Jahrhunderts." *Arcus,* no. 2 (1985): 7–81, 94.

Graefe, Reiner, et al., eds. *V. G. Suchov 1853–1939. Kunst der Konstruktion.* Stuttgart: Institut für Auslandsbeziehungen, 1990. (5), 6–195 p., ills.

Grenier, Achille. "Note sur les chemins de fer aux Etats-Unis d'Amérique." *Mémoires et Compte-Rendu des travaux de la Société des Ingénieurs Civils* (1856): 109–142.

Haas, Walter. "Anker aus Holz und aus Eisen in mittelalterlichen Bauwerken." *Il Brunelleschi. Quaderni dell'Instituto di Storia dell'Architettura e di Ristauro.* Facoltà di Architettura dell' Università degli Studi di Firenze, no. 1 (October 1982): 118–132.

Haas, Walter. "Eisen in der Architektur vor dem Aufkommen der Eisenarchitektur." *Die Rolle des Eisens in der historischen Architektur der ersten Hälfte des 19. Jahrhunderts. International Council of Monuments and Sites ICOMOS-Deutsches Nationalkomitee. Internationales Colloquium vom 18. bis 22. September 1978 in Bad Ems.* Hannover: Curt R. Vincenz, 1979. pp. 1–6; 167–172, 3 pls.

Haas, Walter. "Hölzerne und eiserne Anker an mittelalterlichen Kirchenbauten." *architectura. Zeitschrift für Geschichte der Baukunst.* Munich: Deutscher Kunstverlag, 1983. pp. 136–151.

Hadley, Arthur Twining. *Railroad Transportation. Its History and Its Laws.* 15th ed. New York: G. P. Putnam's Sons, 1903. (2), iv, (2), 269, (3) p.

Hague, Douglas Byland, and Rosemary Christie. *Lighthouses: their architecture, history and archaeology.* Llandysul Dyfed (Wales): Gomer Press, 1975. xiv, (2), 307 p., ills., frontis.

Harlacher, A. R. *Wetlis' Eisenbahnsystem zur Ueberwindung starker Steigungen: sein absoluter und relativer Werth für den Locomotivbetrieb steiler Bahnen, und seine Verwendung für die schweizerischen Alpenbahnen. Separatabdruck aus dem Jahrbuch der Gesellschaft ehem. Studierender der Eidg. Polyt. Schule.* Zurich: Zürcher & Furrer (Meyer & Zeller, 1871. (2), 69, (1) p., 1 pl.

Harris, John R. "The Rise of Coal Technology." *Scientific American* (August 1974): 92–97.

Harriss, Joseph. *The Tallest Tower. Eiffel and the Belle Epoque.* Boston: Houghton Mifflin Co., 1975. xi, 257 p., ills.

Haskin, Frederic Jennings. *The Panama Canal. Illustrated from photographs taken by Ernest Hallen . . .* Garden City, N.Y.: Doubleday, Page & Co., 1914. x, 386, (2) p., ills.

Helps, Sir Arthur. *Life and Labours of Mr. Brassey 1805–1870.* London: Bell and Daldy, 1872. xiv, (2), 386 p., frontis, 7 ills. Boston: Roberts Brothers, 1874. Title addendum: *with a preface to the American edition, by the author.* xviii, 1, 386 p., ills.

Herbarth, Dieter. *Die Entwicklung der Optischen Telegrafie in Preussen. Landeskonservator Rheinland. Arbeitsheft 15.* Cologne: Rheinland-Verlag, 1978. 203 p., ills.

Herbert, Gilbert. *Pioneers of Prefabrication. The British Contribution in the Nineteenth-Century.* Baltimore/London: Johns Hopkins University Press, 1978. (10), xi–xii, 228 p., ills.

Hewett, B. H. M., and S. Johannesson. *Shield and Compressed-Air Tunneling.* New York: McGraw-Hill, 1922. x, 465 p., ills., pls.

Heyman, Jacques. *Coulomb's Memoir on Statics. An Essay in the History of Civil Engineering.* Cambridge, GB: Cambridge University Press, 1972. ix, 211 p., ills.

Higgins, Bryan. *Experiments and observations made with the view of improving the art of composing and applying calcareous cements, and of preparing quick-lime: theory of these arts; and specification of the author's cheap and durable cement for building, incrustation, or stuccoing, and artificial stone.* London: T. Cadell, 1780. viii, 232 p. For evaluation see: Elton, catalogue 6 (variants: 1, 1, v–xi, 232 p./1, 1, x–xi, 233 p.).

Hilgard, Karl Emil. *Über Geschichte und Bau des Panamakanales mir 9 graphischen Beilagen und 40 Text-Abbildingen nach offiziellen Photographhien.* Zurich: Art. Inst. Orell Füssli (1915?).

Hindle, Brooke, ed. *America's Wooden Age: Aspects of its Early Technology.* Tarrytown, NY: Sleepy Hollow, 1975. vii, 2–218 p., ills.

Hix, John. The Glass House. Cambridge, MA: MIT Press, 1974. London: Phaidon Press, 1981 ed., 208 p., ills.

Hodges, James. *Construction of the Great Victoria Bridge in Canada, by H. J., engineer to Messrs. Peto, Brassey, and Betts, Contractors.* 2 vols. London: J. Weale, 1860.1: text: (8), 104 pp., ills.; 2: atlas: frontis, (4), 81 pls.

Hodgkinson, Eaton. *Experimental Researches on the strength and other properties of cast iron. Forming a second part to the fourth edition of Tredgold's Practical Essay . . .* London: John Weale, 1846. vii, 13, 308–504 p., 5 pls. (See also Tredgold for the first part of this work.)

Hodgkinson, Eaton. "On the transverse strain, and the strength of materials." *Memoirs of the Literary and Philosophical Society of Manchester.* 2nd series 4 (1824): 25.

Hodgkinson, Eaton. "Theoretical and experimental researches to ascertain the strength and the best forms of iron beams." *Memoirs of the Literary and Philosophical Society of Manchester.* 2nd series 5 (1831): 407.

Hodgkinson, Eaton. See also Barlow, Peter, *Essay.*

Hoppe, Oskar. *Das Drahtseil.* Essen: G. D. Baedecker, 1907. 48 p., fourth part of *Beiträge zur Geschichte der Erfindung.* The only reliable secondary source on the German history of wire rope I have yet found.

Hosking, William. *A guide to the proper regulation of Buildings in Towns as a means of promoting and securing the health, comfort and safety of the inhabitants.* London: J. Murray, W. Clowes, 1848. 295 p.

Hovine. "Note sur l'emploi des rondelles en caoutchouc vulcanisé comme ressort de choc et de traction." *Mémoires et Compte-Rendu des travaux de la Société des Ingénieurs Civils . . .* (1854): 80–85.

Howe, Henry. *Memoirs of the most eminent American mechanics: also, lives of distinguished European mechanics; together with a collection of anecdotes, descriptions, &c. &c. relating to the mechanic arts. illustrated by fifty engravings.* New York: Alexander V. Blake, 1841. 482 p., ills. Further eds. 1844, 1900. This work seems to have been the first book containing engineering biography. It predates Smiles by 18 years.

Huard, C.-L. *Livre d'Or de l'Exposition (1889)*. 2 vols. Paris: ed. L. Boulanger, (1889–1890). 1: (2), 404 p.; 2: (2), 401–796 p., both with ills. The reason for the discrepancy of the numbering in the second vol. is that the last 4 pp., in vol. 1 are an index.

Hughes, John. "On the Pneumatic Method adopted in Constructing the Foundations of the New Bridge across the Medway, at Rochester." *Min. Proc. ICE* 10 (1850–1851): 353–369 and plate 8. Paper 858 (13 May 1851).

Humber, William. *A complete treatise on cast and wrought iron bridge construction including iron foundations. In three parts: theoretical, practical and descriptive*. 2 vols. London: E. & F. N. Spon, 1861. 1: (7), x–xii, (2), 238 p., front., ills., pls.; 2: (2) p., front., 79 pls. Further editions. London: Lockwood, 1864, 1870.

Humber, William. *A Practical Treatise of Cast and Wrought Iron Bridges and Girders, as applied to Railway Structures, and to buildings generally, with numerous examples, drawn to a large scale, selected from the public works of the most eminent engineers*. London: E. & F. N. Spon, 1857. (5), vi–x, (4), 106 p., ills., frontis. (incl. in pag.), 57 pls. Reprinted 1987.

Hütsch, Volker. *Der Münchner Glaspalast 1854–1931. Geschichte und Bedeutung*. Munich: Münchner Stadt Museum, 1981. 199 p., ills.

Hyatt, Thaddeus. *An account of some experiments with Portland Cement-Concrete combined with iron as a building material, with reference to economy of metal in construction, and for security against fire in the making of roofs, floors and walking surfaces*. London: private for the author by Chiswick Press, 1877. 28 p., front., ills., 16 pls., tables. The book is escessively rare. Only three copies known in the United States.

Hyde, Joshua Burrows. An adaptation of the American Exavator for Dredging. *Min. Proc. ICE* 4 (1845): 399–402.

The Illustrated Exhibitor, a tribute to the world's industrial jubilee; comprising sketches, by pen and pencil, of the principal objects in The Great Exhibition of the Industry of all Nations 1851. London: John Cassell, (1851). xlvi, 566 p., 10 pls., ills. (See also Fowler, Charles, Jr., *Art Journal*.)

Isherwood, R. F. See Weale.

Jacoby, Henry Sylvester, and Roland Parker Davis. *Foundations of Bridges and Buildings*. New York: McGraw-Hill, 1914. xvi, 535 p., ills. 2nd ed. 1925. xix, 665 p., ills. 3rd ed. 1941. xvi, 535 p., ills. 4th ed. 1953. xvi, 535 p., ills.

James, John G. "Thomas Paine's Iron Bridge Work 1785–1803." *Transactions of the Newcomen Society* 59 (1987–1988): 189–221.

James, John G. "Thomas Wilson's Cast-Iron Bridges 1800–1810." *Transactions of the Newcomen Society* 50 (1978–1979): 55–72.

Jewett, Robert A. "Structural Antecedents of the I-Beam." *Technology & Culture* 8 (1967): 346–362.; 9 (1968): 415–429, discussion by Harold Dorn and the author.

John, Johann Friedrich. "Über Kalke und Mörtel usw." Article awarded a prize by the Maatschapij der Wetensch. te Haarlem. 1819 Berlin.

Johnson, H. R., and Alec W. Skempton. "William Strutt's Cotton Mills 1793–1812." *Transactions of the Newcomen Society* 30 (1955–1957): 179–211.

Jones, Eliot. *Principles of Railway Transportation.* New York: Macmillan, 1925. xxv, (1), 607 p., map.

Journal für technische und ökonomische Chemie (Erdmanns) Lepizig: Barth, (1) 1827–(18) 1833, then joined with: *Journal für praktische Chemie.* Halle: Anton, and issued under that title (1) 1834–(108) 1869. New series Leipzig: Barth, (1=109) 1870–(162=270) 1943. Third series: (1=271) 1943–(2=272) 1945. The journal did not appear between 1946 and 1953, but was replaced by *Journal für makromolekulare Chemie.* fourth series under the title: *Journal für Chemie und Physik:* (1=273) 1954/55 ff.

Kelley, Frederick M. "On the Junction of the Atlantic and Pacific Oceans, and the Practicability of a Ship Canal, without Locks, by the Valley of the Atrato." *Min. Proc. ICE* 15 (1855–1856): 376–417 and plate 2. Paper no. 948 (22 April 1856).

Klein, H. Arthur. "Pieter Breugel the Elder as a Guide to 16th-Century Technology." *Scientific American* (March 1978): 134–140.

Klein, Maury. *Union Pacific. Birth of a Railroad 1862–1893.* New York: Doubleday, 1987. xiii, (5), 865 p. ills.

Klein, Maury. "What hath God wrought?" *American Heritage of Invention and Technology* 8, no. 4 (Spring 1993): 34–42.

Klingender, Francis Donald. *Art and the Industrial Revolution.* London: N. Carrington, 1947. xiii, 232 p., ills. 2nd ed. *edited and revised by Arthur Elton, further revised by Winifred Klingender.* London: Evelyn, Adams & Mackay/New York: A. M. Kelley, 1968. xvii, 222 p., ills. Further eds. 1968, 1970, 1972, 1975. German ed. Frankfurt A.M.: Syndikat, 1976. 268 p., ills. An attempt to make a connection between nineteenth century aesthetics and the evolution of the Industrial Revolution. Klingender died before the revision for the second edition was complete, and the book was finished and published by Sir Arthur Elton, the documentary filmer whose vast specialized collection of paintings, drawings and prints formed the basis for the study. Today, the major part of the Elton Collection forms the nucleus of the holdings of the Ironbridge Gorge Museum Trust.

Koenen, Matthias. "Berechnung der Stärke der Monierschen Cementplatten." *Centralblatt der Bauverwaltung* 6, no. 47 (1886): 462.

Koenen, Matthias. "Theorie einiger wichtiger Konstruktionen nach System Monier. Metallgerippe mit Cementumhüllung." *Centralblatt der Bauverwaltung 1886.* Republished as part of Wayss.

Koerte, Arnold. *Two Railway Bridges of an Era. Zwei Eisenbahnbrücken einer Epoche. Firth of Forth and Firth of Tay. Technical Progress, Disaster and New Beginning in Victorian Engineering. Technischer Fortschritt, Desaster und Neubeginn in der Viktorianischen Ingenieurbaukunst.* Basel: Birkhäuser Verlag, 1992. 224 p., ills.

Krause, P. *Anleitung zu Kalk-Sand-Baukunst oder zur Errichtung von Bauwerken aus gestampftem Mörtel mit verhältnißmaßig weit geringeren Kosten gegen die bisher üblich gewesene Bauart, unter Beifügung einiger Entwürfe und Kostenberechnungen von Schul- und Wirtschaftsgebäuden, um die durch diese neue Bauart zu erzielende Kostenersparnis speziell nachzuweisen.* Glogau, 1851. With Seebass and Engel, the earliest popularly available work on concrete construction in German.

Kühne, Helmut. "70 Jahre geleimte Holz-Tragwerke in der Schweiz" offprint from *Schweizer Ingenieur und Architekt,* no. 32–33 (1979): 17 p.

Kurrer, Karl-Eugen. "Zur Frühgeschichte des Stahlbetonbaus in Deutschland — 100 Jahre Monier-Brochüre." *Beton und Stahlbau* 83, no. 1 (1988): 6–12.

Laboulaye, Charles-Pierre Lefèbvre de. *Dictionnaire des arts et manufactures; description des procédés de l'industrie française et étrangère.* 2 vols. Paris: Librairie scientifique-industrielle de L. Mathias (Augustin), 1847. 2nd ed. Paris: Librairie de Lacroix-Comon, 1854–1855 (variant: 1853/1853–1854). Title: *Dictionnaire des Arts et Manufactures de l'Agriculture, des Mines, etc. Description des Procédés de l'Industrie française et étrangère.* 1: A-F, lxxvi, c.1400 unnumbered pp.; 2: G-Z, c.1600 unnumbered pp., both with ills. *Complément du dictionnaire . . . avec le concours de plusieurs savants et ingénieurs.* 2 vols. (in 1). Paris: Librarie Scientifique de E. Lacroix, 1861. 696, 256 p., ills. Complément . . . Paris: Librairie du dictionnaire des arts et manufactures. 3 vols., 1867. 3e ed. 1867, Complément. 1872, 4th ed. Paris: Librairie du Dictionnaire des arts et metiers, 1874. 3+1 vols. 1: A–D; 2: E–M; 3: N–Z; 4: Complément 1872. Another 4th ed. 3 vols. 1875. Reprinted 6th ed. 1886. 7th ed. 5 vols. 1891. Poggendorff calls Laboulaye a collaborator in this work, but he appears as its author, or at least, editor.

Landes, David S. *Bankers and Pashas. International Finance and Economic Imperialism in Egypt.* Cambridge, MA: Harvard University Press, 1958. (6), vii–xvi, 354 p., ills.

Landes, David S. *Revolution in Time. Clocks and the Making of the Modern World.* Cambridge, MA: The Belknap Press of Harvard University Press, 1983. xx, 482 p., ills.

Landes, David S. *The Unbound Prometheus. Technological change and industrial development in Western Europe from 1750 to the present.* Cambridge, GB: Cambridge University Press, 1969. xi, 566 p.

Landes, David S. "Von den Vorzügen des Kleinseins. Der Weg der Schweiz in die Industrialisierung." *Neue Zürcher Zeitung,* no. 71 (25 March 1992): 65–66.

Laurent, Charles. "Mémoire no. 46, sur le Sahara oriental au point de vue de l'établissement des puits artésiens dans l'Oued-Souf, l'Oued-R'ir et les Zibans." *Mémoire et Compte-Rendu des travaux de la Société des Ingénieurs Civils* (1856): 21–90.

Laurent, Charles. "Mémoire sur les sondages exécutés dans le Sahara oriental (Campagne 1857–1858). *Mémoire et Compte-Rendu des travaux de la Société des Ingénieurs Civils* (1859): 227–256.

Lavalley, Alexandre Théodore. *Communication faite par M. A.L. (Entreprise Borel-Lavalley et Cie.) sur les travaux d'exécution du canal maritime de l'Isthme de Suez. Extrait du*

Compte-Rendu des travaux de la Société des Ingénieurs Civils, Séances des 7 et 21 septembre 1866. Paris: offprint. P.-A. Bourdier, 1866. 62 p., 1 map, 4 pls. One of the prime sources for the study of this building process.

Lavalley, Alexandre Théodore. "Travaux d'exécution du canal maritime de l'isthme de Suez . . . deuxième communication." *Mémoires et Compte-Rendu des travaux de la Société des Ingénieurs Civils, 1867, pp. 523–536, with discussion on pp. 424–435, reprinted as: Deuxième communication faite par M. A.L. (Entreprise Borel-Lavalley et Cie.) sur les travaux d'exécution du canal maritime de Suez. Extrait du Compte-Rendu des Travaux de la Société des Ingénieurs Civils. Séance du 26 juillet 1867.* Paris: Imprimerie P. Bourdier, Capiomont et Cie., 1867. 32 p. The author received the gold medal of the society for this paper in 1869.

Law, Henry. *A memoir of the Thames Tunnel. Pt. 1, from the commencement of the works to their suspension in 1828.* London: John Weale, 1846. 112 p., 16 pls. appears to be reprinted from: *Weale's Quarterly Papers on Engineering,* 3 (1845–1846): 1–25; 5: 1–86. (From Vogel.)

Lepère (Le Père), Jacques Marie. *Sur la jonction des deux mers.* See *Description de l'Égypte.*

Lesseps, Ferdinand Marie de. *Lettres, journal et documents pour servir à l'histoire du canal de Suez.* 5 vols. Paris: Didier, 1875–1881.

Lesseps, Ferdinand Marie de. *Le Percement de l'Isthme de Suez. Conférences populaires faites à l'Asile Impériale de Vincennes sous le patronnage de S.M. l'Impératrice.* Paris: Librairie de L. Hachette et Cie., 1868. 50 p., 1 map. This is a little-known popular lecture given by de Lesseps shortly before the canal was finished and probably as part of his intensive public-relations efforts to achieve widespread national financial support for the canal.

Lesseps, Ferdinand Marie de. *Percement de l'Isthme de Suez. Exposé et Documents officiels.* Paris: Henri Plon, 1855. 280 p., 1 map. Written four years before work on the canal began, de Lesseps's study is counted among the most important of the nineteenth century.

Leupold, Jacob. *Theatrum pontificale, oder Schauplatz der Brücken und Brücken-Baues: das ist, eine deutlich Anweisung, wie man nicht nur auf mancherley Arth über Gräben, Bäche und Flüsse gelangen, auch so gar in Wassers-Noth mit gewissen Machinen und besonderen Habit sei leben retten kan . . .* Leipzig: Joh. Friedrich Gleditschens seel. Sohn, 1726. (16), 153, (5) p., ills., 60 pls., misnumbered as 57. This is volume 7 of 10 in the Theatrum machinarum 1824–1834.

Linsley, James E., Jr. *Analysis of the Crystal Palace in 1851.* unpag. unpubl. manuscript, Lehigh University.

Livre d'Or de l'Exposition (1889). See Huard.

London Gazette Great Exhibition Awards. London Gazette No. 21254, Friday, 17.10.1851, pp. 2587–2723. My copy contains ten handbills and two newspaper advertisements concerning the dismantling of the exhibition. Publication of the Great Exhibition Awards was provided for under article 6 of the "Programme of the Proceedings on the

Presentation of the Jurie's Reports and the Closing of the Exhibition on Wednesday, 15th October 1851": "Lord Canning, on behalf of the Juries will read a report of their proceedings, and present a List of the Names of those Exhibitors entitled to Rewards, together with the Reports of the Juries. The Names will be published in the London Gazette, on Friday, October 17 . . ."

Loriot, Antoine-Joseph. *Instruction dur la nouvelle méthode de préparer le mortier-Loriot.* Paris: Barbou, 1775. 13, 2 p., 1 pls.

Loriot, Antoine-Joseph. *Mémoire sur une découverte dans l'art de bâtir, faite par le Sr. Loriot, Mécanicien, Pensionnaire du Roi; Dans lequel l'on rend publique, par ordre de Sa Majesté, La méthode de composer un Ciment ou Mortier propre à une infinité d'ouvrages, tant pour la construction, que pour la décoration.* Paris: Michel Lambert, 1774. 53, 3 p. First English edition 1774.

Loudon, John Claudius. *Encyclopaedia of Cottage, Farm and Villa Architecture and Furniture; containing numerous designs for dwelling . . . each design accompanied by analytical and critical remarks . . .* London: Longman, Rees, Orme, Brown, Green, & Longman, 1833. xx, 1138 p., ills. *New ed. by Jane Webb Loudon.* 1853. 2 vols. ". . . containing numerous designs for dwellings . . . each design accompanied by analytical and critical remarks." xxiv, 1317 p., ills.

Lovelace. "On the Construction of a Collar Roof, with arched trusses of bent timber, at East Horsley Park." *Min. Proc. ICE* 8 (1849): 282–286 and plate no. 8. Paper no. 811 (12 Jun. 1849).

Maigne, M. *Histoire de l'Industrie et exposition sommaire des progrès réalisés dans les principales branches du travail industriel.* Paris: Librairie Classique d'Eugène Belin, 1873. (5), vi–vii, (1), 622 p., ills.

Malézieux, Emile. *Les Travaux publics des États-Unis d'Amérique en 1870. Rapport de mission, mar M.M . . . , ingénieur en chef. Publié par ordre de M. le ministre des travaux publics.* 2 vols. Paris: Dunod, 1873. 1: 572 p.; 2: 3 p., 61 pls. Facsimilie ed. Alburgh Harleston, GB: Archival Facsimilies, 1987. 67, ii, 175 p., 7 pls.

Marrey, Bernard, and Paul Chemtov. *Familèrement inconnues . . . Architectures Paris 1848–1914.* Exhibition catalog. Paris: published for the authors, 1976. 168 p., ills., 1 plan inserted.

Marsh, Charles Fleming, and William Dunn. *Reinforced concrete.* London: A. Constable / New York: D. Van Nostrand & Co., 1904. 4, 545, (1) p., ills., pls. Further eds. 1905, 1906 (twice), 1907 (twice).

Marzy, E. *L'Hydraulique. Ouvrage illustré de 59 gravures par A. Jahandier. Bibliothèque des Merveilles.* 2nd ed. Paris: Librairie Hachette et Cie., 1871. (4), 330 p., ills.

The Masterpieces of the Centennial International Exhibition Illustrated. 3 vols. Philadelphia: Gebbie & Barrie, 1876. 1: *Fine Art by Edward Strahan.* xii, 366 p. pls., ills.; 2: *Industrial Art by Prof. Walter Smith.* x, 521 p., ills.; 3: *History, Mechanics, Science by Joseph M. Wilson.* clxxxvi, 375 p., pls., ills.

Mathieu, Henri, and Alexandre Théodore Lavalley. "Sur la reconstruction du pont biais de Clichy, Chemin de fer de Saint-Germain." *Mémoire et Compte-Rendu des travaux de la Société des Ingénieurs Civils* (1852): 134–157.

Maus, (Jean-Marie) Henri Joseph, and Pietro Paleocapa. *Relazione del cavaliere Enrico Maus sugli studii da lui fatti della strada ferrata da Chambery a Torino e sulla macchina da lui proposta per il perforamento dell'Alpi fra Modane e Bardonneche, e Rapporto dell'Ispettore cavaliere Pietro Paleocapa fattone alla Commissione incaricata dell'esame, coi Processi verbali della commissione medesima.* Turin: Stamperia Reale, 1850. 56 p. 8 plates, fold. map. Simultaneous French ed.: *Rapport sur les etudes du chemin de fer de Chambery a Turin et de la machine proposée pour executer le tunnel des Alpes entre Modane et Bardonneche.* Turin: Imprimerie royale, 1850. 56 p. 5 fold. pl., fold. map, fold. plan.

McCollough, David. *The Path Between the Seas. The creation of the Panama Canal 1870–1914.* New York: Simon and Schuster, 1977. 698 p., ills.

Mechanics' Magazine, Museum, Register, Journal, and Gazette. London: Knight and Lacey, 1 (1823)–43 (1845).

Mémoire et Compte-Rendu des travaux de la Société des Ingénieurs Civils. Paris: Société, (1) March–May 1849–December 1893.

Michaelis, Wilhelm. *Die hydraulischen Mörtel insbesondere der Portland-Cement in chemisch-technischer Beziehung für Fabrikanten, Bautechniker, Ingeniure und Chemiker mit 62 Abbildingen im Text.* Leipzig: Quandt & Händel, 1869. xii, 315 p., tables, 64 ills. (not 62 as in the title: 1–3, 3a, 4–35a, 35b–62). One of the most valuable compendia for the study of the history of cement and unreinforced concrete.

Michel, Jean. "The geneaology of the 'Grandes Ecoles': Origins and development of the French system for the training of engineers." *European Journal of Engineering Education.* 5 (1981): 189–214. Amsterdam: Elsevier Scientific Publishing Company.

Minutes of the Proceedings of the Institution of Civil Engineers. London: ICE, (1) 1837/41–(240) 1934/35, then merged with Selected Papers from Journal of the Institution of Civil Engineers (1) 1935–(36) December 1951. (Abbreviated here as Min. Proc. ICE.)

Molinos Léon. "Note sur la conservation des bois." *Mémoires et Compte-Rendu des travaux de la Société des Ingénieurs Civils* [1853] 132–145.

Monod, Emile. *L'Exposition Universelle de 1889, grand ouvrage illustré, historique, encyclopédique, descriptif, publié sous le patronnage de M. le Ministre du commerce, de l'Industrie et des Colonies, Commissaire général de l'Exposition.* 3 vols. + album. Paris: E. Dentu, 1890. 1: xxxi, 666 p.; 2: 615 p.; 3:? all with ills.; album: 81 pls.

Moran, Daniel E. "Foundation Development During Fifty Years." *Engineering News Record, Fiftieth Anniversary Number.* (17 April 1924): 670–673.

Morel, M.-A. *Le Ciment armé et ses applications. Encyclopédie scientifique des aide-mémoire.* Paris: Gauthier-Villars/Masson & Cie., 1902. 158, 16, 16 p., ills. Apparently the second theoretical text on reinforced concrete in French after Christophe 1899. See also Buel and Hill; Mörsch; Taylor and Thompson.

Morley, Jane. "Frank Bunker Gilbreth's Concrete System." *Concrete International* 12, no. 11 (November 1990): 57–62.

Mörsch, Emil. *Wayss & Freytag AG: Der Betoneisenbau.* Stuttgart: Konrad Wittwer, 1902. 2nd ed. 1906. Title: *Der Eisenbetonbau, seine Theorie und Anwendung, 2., vermehrte und verbesserte Auflage mit 227 Textabbildungen und einem Anhang.* viii, 252 p., ills. Further eds. of increasing scope and size 1908, 1912, 1922, 1923. 1909. Engl. ed. Title: *Concrete-Steel Construction (Der Eisenbetonbau). Authorized translation from the 3rd. (1908) German ed. translated into English by E(rnest) P(ayson) Goodrich . . .* New York: The Engineering News Publishing Company, 1909. ix, 369 p., 2 tables, ills. (variant: ix, 368 p., ills). French ed. Title: *Le béton armé. Etude théorique et pratique. Avec essais et construction de la Maison Wayss et Freytag à Neustadt.* Paris: Béranger, 1909. (iv), vi, 358 p., 2 tables, ills. (variant: ii, 358, vi p., 2 pls., ills). Mörsch's book is one of the earliest theoretical examinations and attempts to create a theory of reinforced concrete. It went through many subsequent editions under its final title. All editions are of interest to the historian as they continued to expend and change under the influence of the most current practise and theory. Although Mörsch's book is currently known as the first attempt to create a coherent theory, this appears to have been only true for the German-speaking world. In Germany, Koenen had published a partial theory in 1886, while in France, Christophe's book appeared in 1899 and Morel's in 1902. In the United States, Buel and Hill published theirs in 1904, and Taylor and Thompson in 1905. No-one has yet clearly determined what each of these authors really contributed to the basis of current reinforced concrete theory.

Moser, Emil. *Der Erbauer des Leipziger Kristall-Palastes mit dem Circus und Diorama.* Leipzig: Frankenstein & Wagner, 1889. 56 p., portraits. A very early account of the design of a reinforced concrete structure in Germany.

Napier, David Dehane, and David Bell. *David Napier engineer 1790–1869. An Autobiographical Sketch with Notes.* Glasgow: James Macklehose and Sons, 1912. x, 136 p., 1 map, ills.

Nater, H. *Untersuchungen und Verstärkungen an der Eisenbetonbrücke über die Rhone bei Chippis.* n.d. (c. 1906), n.p. 16 p., ills.

Navier, (Claude-Marie Louis) Henri. *Rapport à M. Becquey . . . et Mémoire sur les ponts suspendus.* 1 vol. + atlas. Paris: Imprimerie Royale/Carilian-Goeury, 1823. 1: text. xxiv, 228 p.; 2: atlas. 13 pls. The book was first paraphrased in a German edition in Berlin in 1825: J. F. Dietlein: *"Auszug aus Naviers Abhandlung über die Hängebrücken"* and fully translated by J. G. Kutschera in Lemberg in 1829: *"Bericht an Herrn Becquey,"* but never was translated into English, although it seems to have been used by subsequent English writers on suspension bridges. 2nd ed. According to Ostenfeld, *Franske Broingeniøre* p. 54, published on 18 September 1830. It includes an addendum on Navier's own, partially built and subsequently demolished Pont des Invalides over the Seine in Paris. The text is the first modern theoretical, analytical treatise on engineering.

Navier, (Claude-Marie Louis) Henri. *Rapport sur le projet de pont suspendu à construire sur la Sarine à Fribourg. 20.05.1825.* 17 p., sketches. Part of a ms. by G.-H. Dufour. *Projet de Pont Suspendu pour Frybourg. Novembre 1825.* State Archives, Geneva. Travaux E 16.

Navier, (Claude-Marie Louis) Henri. *Résumé des leçons données à l'Ecole royale des ponts et chaussées sur l'application de la mécanique à l'établissement des constructions et des machines.* Paris: Firmin Didot père et fils, 1826 part 1: *Leçons sur la résistance des matériaux, et sur l'établissement des constructions en terre, en maçonnerie et en charpente.* 27 1/2 feuilles (=440 p.), 5 pls. 2e. éd. *corrigée et augmentée.* 3 parts in 2 vols. Paris: Carilian-Goeury, 1833–1838. 1: xxiv, 448 p., 5 pls. part 1: same subtitle as before; 2: viii, 156, 157–422 p., 3, 6 pls., part 2: *Leçons sur le mouvement et la résistance des fluides, la conduite et la distribution des eaux.* part 3: *Leçons sur l'établissement des machines.* The title dropped the term "royale" following the revolution of 1830. The text includes a compilation of all previous work done by others such as Euler, Bernoulli and Coulomb. Navier's main contribution is a useful definition of mathematical models which permitted similar structures to be compared analytically and the major shift in engineering viewpoint which this entailed. 3rd ed. 2 vols. Paris: Dunor, 1864. with notes and appendices by Adhémar Jean Claude Barré de Saint-Venant. Saint-Venant seems to have done the same popularizing service for Navier as Wilhelm Ritter was later to do for Carl Culmann's *Graphische Statik,* and the popular use of Navier dates from this third edition. German ed. translated by G. Westphal. Title: *Mechanik der Baukunst (Ingenieur-Mechanik) oder Anwendung der Mechanik auf das Gleichgewicht von Bau-Konstruktionen.* Hannover: Helwing'sche Hof-Buchhandlung, 1851. xxvi, 402, xvii–xix, (1), 403–406, xxi, xxiv, (2) p., ills. 2nd German edition. Hannover: G. Westphal & August Foeppl eds., 1878. The work never seems to have been translated into English. According to Charlton (p. 17), Navier's influence on the development of English theory stems from Moseley 1843. The analytical phase of engineering based on mechanics really began with Navier's study on suspension bridges published in 1823.

Needham, Joseph. *Science and Civilization in China.* London: Cambridge University Press, 1954 ff, ongoing series. 4: *Physics and Physical Technology: Part III: Civil Engineering and Nautics. with Wang Ling and Lu Gwei-Djen.* 1971. lvii, 931 p., 1 map, ills.

Nef, John Ulrich. "An Early Energy Crisis and Its Consequences." *Scientific American* (November 1977): 140–151.

Negrelli, Alois von, Ritter von Moldelbe. Letter to the editor, published 18 June 1858 in the *Oesterreichische Gazette,* and cited in *Mémoires et Compte-Rendu des travaux de la Société des Ingénieurs Civils* (1858): 278–280. The letter is part of Barrault. (See also Stephenson.)

Nepveu, Charles. "Note sur les fondations en rivière." *Mémoires et Compte-Rendu des travaux de la Société des Ingénieurs Civils* (1855): 173–232 and plates 55–58.

Das Neue Buch der Erfindungen, Gewerbe und Industrien: Rundschau auf allen Gebieten der Gewerblichen Arbeit. Sechste, umgearbeitete und verbesserte Auflage (Prachtausgabe). 6th ed. 6 vols. Leipzig/Berlin: Otto Spamer, 1872–1874. 1: *Einführing in die Geschichte der Erfindungen.* viii, 520 p.; 2: *Die Kräfte der Natur und ihre Benutzung. Eine physikalische Technologie.* x, 510 p; 3: *Die Gewinnung der Rohstoffe aus dem Innern der Erde, von der Erdoberfläche sowie aus dem Wasser.* vi, 446 p.; 4: *Die chemische Behandlung der Rohstoffe. Eine chemische Technologie.* vii, 520 p; 5: *Die Chemie des täglichen Lebens.* vii, 448 p.; 6: *Die mechanische Bearbeitung der Rohstoffe.* vii, 540 p., all ills. A supplement volume was published in 1873. 2nd ed. Leipzig/Berlin: Otto Spamer. 1875. *Der Weltverkehr und seine Mittel. Rundschau Über Schiffahrt und Welthandel im Jahre 1873.* vii, 732 p., ills. Earlier editions of the encyclopedia have fewer volumes, and the 8th edition of 1884 ran to nine volumes.

Newman, John. *Notes on concrete and works in concrete. Especially written to assist those engaged upon public works.* London: E. & F. N. Spon, 1894. x, 240 p.

Nicholson, John. *The Operative Mechanic, and British Machinist; being a Practical Display of the Manufactories and Mechanical Arts of the United Kingdom.* 3 vols. London: printed for Knight and Lacey, 1825. 1: xvi, 416 p.; 2: 417–795, (1) p.; 3: 95 pls., 71 pls. 2nd ed. 1980. xvi, 795 p., 92 pls., ills. See also Charles Taylor's supplement.

Nicholson, Peter. *Nicholson's dictionary of the science and practice of architecture, building, carpentry, etc. from the earliest ages to the present time, with detailed estimates, quantities, prices, etc. edited by Edward Lomax and Thomas Gunyon.* 2 vols. + atlas issued in parts. London: The London Printing and Publishing Co., 1811–1819. 2nd ed. 2 vols. London/New York: The London Printing and Publishing Co. [after 1851]. Title: *Nicholson's Dictionary of the Science and Practice of Architecture, Building, Carpentry, etc, etc, from the earliest ages to the present time. Second edition Edward Lomax and Thomas Gunyon editors. Illustrated by upwards of 1600 working drawings.* 1: Aba–Hyp. iv, 6, 516 p., 101 pls.; 2: Ice–Zot. iv, 604 p., 116 pls. both w. ills. Innumerable intermediate and later editions. In Lives of the Engineers, vol. 2, p. 117, Samuel Smiles writes about the author: ". . . a man who had almost as great an influence on the development of mechanics and the art of engineering as did Rennie himself . . . author of innumerable works on carpentry and architecture that still belong to the best of their kind."

Niebelschütz, Wolf von. "Züblin-Bau 1898–1958." *75 Jahre Züblin-Bau 1898–1973.* Stuttgart: Karl Krämer Verlag, 1973: 11–49.

Nixon, Charles. "Description of the Tunnels, situated between Bristol and Bath, on the Great Western Railway, with the methods adopted for executing the works." *Min. Proc. ICE.* 2 (1842–1843): 138–141 (3 May 1842).

Nouvelle Compagnie du Canal de Panama, société anonyme, au capital de soixante-cinq millions de francs . . . Rapport Présenté au Conseil d'Administration par le Comité Technique constitué en vertu de l'article 31 des Statuts. Paris: Société Anonyme de Publications Périodiques, 1899. 74 p., 6 pl.

Official Descriptive and Illustrated Catalogue of the Great Exhibition of the Works of Industry of all Nations, 1851. By Authority of the Royal Commission, in three Volumes. 3 vols. London: Spicer Bros, 1851. 1: *Index and Introductory. Section 1: Raw Materials, classes 1–4, section 2: Machinery, classes 5–10.* cxcii, 478, 76 p., 1 map; 2: *Section 3: Manufactures, classes 11–29, section 4: Fine Arts, class 30.* pp. 479–1002; 3: *Foreign States.* pp. 1002–1469, all ills. A fourth, supplemental volume was issued the same year. (See also: *Exhibition of the Works of Industry* for the companion vol. of the Juries' reports.)

Ostenfeld, Christian. *Christiani & Nielsen. Jernbetonens danske pionerer.* Lyngby: Polyteknisk Forlag, 1976. (4), 5–246 p., ills.

Ostenfeld, Christian. *Franske Broingeniører og videnskabsmænd, deres historie, ingeniørskoler og bøger. Danmarks Tekniske Bibliotek. Publikation no. 34.* Lyngby: Polyteknisk Forlag, 1975. 153 p., ills.

Otis, Fessenden Nott. *Illustrated History of the Panama Railroad, together with a traveler's guide and business man's handbook for the Panama Railroad and its connections with Europe, the United States, the North and South Atlantic and Pacific coasts, China, Australia, and Japan, by sail and steam.* New York: Harper and Bros., 1861. xiv, 15–263, (5) p., ills. Further editions in 1862, 1867, 1971.

Panama and the Canal Zone. Panama: Vibert & Dixon, 1914. Unpaginated brochure of photographs.

Papers on Subjects connected with the Duties of the Corps of Royal Engineers. London: For the Corps, (1) 1837–(10) 1848. 2nd ed. (1) 1844–(10) 1848. New series (1) 1851–(23) 1851. Reissued 1876. These papers are a rarely used, but rich source for material on the history of building in Great Britain.

Pasley, Sir Charles William. *Observations deduced from experiments upon the natural water cements of England and on the artificial cements that may be used as substitutes for them.* Chatham: Burrill, 1830.

Pasley, Sir Charles William. *Observations on limes, calcareous cements, mortars, stucco and concrete, and on puzzolanas, natural and artificial.* London: John Weale, 1838. 37, 288, 124 p., ills. (Elton has (lxxiv), 288, 124, (2) p.). 2nd ed. of part 1. London: John Weale, 1847. xiv, 209 p., ills.

Paulinyi, Akos. "Die Entwicklung der Stofformungstechnik als Periodisierungskriterium der Technikgeschichte." *Technikgeschichte* 57; no. 4 (1990): 299–314.

Paulinyi, Akos. "Revolution and Technology." *Revolution in History.* 261–289. (ed. Roy Porter and Niklaus Teich. Cambridge, GB: University Press, 1986.

The Penny Magazine of the Society for the diffusion of useful knowledge. London: Knight, 1832 ff. The first weekly magazine for the general public, the Penny Magazine continued to appear until the beginning of the twentieth century. Like the Illustrated London News, the Penny Magazine contained tidbits of useful knowledge which other more serious journals failed to record.

Perdonnet, Auguste. *Traité élémentaire des chemins de fer.* 2 vols. Paris: Langlois et Leclercq, 1854. 2nd eds. 1858 and 1860. 3rd ed. 4 vols. Paris: Garnier Frères, 1865.

Pernolet, Arthur. *L'Air Comprimé et ses Applications; production-distribution et conditions d'emploi.* Paris: Dunod, 1876. xi, 598 p., 3 pls., 3 tables, ills.

Perronet, Jean-Rodolphe. *Description des projets et de la construction des ponts de Neuilly, de Mantes, d'Orléans & autres; du projet du canal de Burgogne, pour la communication des deux Mers par Dijon; et de celui de la conduite des eaux de l'Yvette et de Bièvre 'a Paris, en soixantesept planches . . .* 2 vols. Paris: A l'Imprimerie royale, 1782. atlas: front., 67 pls. 2nd ed. Variant title: *Description des projets et de la construction des ponts de Neuilly, de Mantes, d'Orléans, de Louis XVI, etc. On y ajoute le projet du canal de Burgogne, pour la communication des deux Mers par Dijon; et de celui de la conduite des eaux de l'Yvette et de Bièvre 'a Paris . . . Nouv. éd., augmentée des ponts de Château-Thierri, de Brunoi, de celui projété pour S. Petersbourg, etc., d'un mémoire sur les cintres, et d'un autre sur les eboulements des terres, etc. Pour servir de complément à la nouvelle Architecture hydraulique.* Paris: Chez Didot fils ainé, Jombert jeune, 1788. 1: 1, 1, viii, 696 p.; 2: atlas. 75 pls. 3rd ed. 2 vols. Paris: Didot, 1820. 1: vi, 634 p.; 2: atlas. 75 pls.

Peters, Tom Frank. "An American Culture of Construction." *Perspecta 25. The Yale Architectural Journal.* New York: Rizzoli, 1989: 142–161.

Peters, Tom Frank. "Architectural and Engineering Design, two forms of technological thought on the borderline between empiricism and science." *Bridging the Gap. Rethinking the Relationship of Architect and Engineer.* New York: Reinhold Van Nostrand, 1991: 23–35.

Peters, Tom Frank. *Die Entwicklung des Grossbrückenbaus-L'évolution du pont à grande portée-The evolution of long-span bridge building.* Zurich: Verlag der Fachvereine an der ETH, 1979. 188 p., ills., 2nd ed. 1979. 3rd ed. in English, 1981.

Peters, Tom Frank. *Transitions in Engineering. Guillaume-Henri Dufour and the Development of the wire cable suspension bridge in the early nineteenth century.* Basel: Birkhäuser Verlag, 1987. 244 p., ills.

Peterson, Charles E. "Early American Prefabrication." *Gazette des Beaux Arts.* 6th. series no. 33 (1948): 37–46.

Peterson, Charles E. "Iron in Early American Roofs." *The Smithsonian Journal of History,* no. 3 (Fall 1968): 41–76.

Peterson, Charles E. "Prefabs for the Prairies." *Journal of the Society for Architectural History,* no. 9 (1952): 28–29.

Peterson, Charles E. "Prefabs in the California Gold Rush 1849." *Journal of the Society for Architectural History* (December 1965): 318–324.

Petitti di Roreto, Carlo Ilarione. *Delle Strade Ferrate Italiane e del migliore ordinamento di esse. Cinque discorsi.* Capolago (Switzerland): Tipografia e Libreria Elvetica, 1845. 625 p., 1 map.

Pettenkofer, Max Joseph von. "Über die Unterschiede zwischen den englischen und deutschen hydraulischen Kalken." *Dingler's Polytechnisches Journal,* no. 113 (1849): 55 ff.

Pevsner, Sir Nikolaus. *Pioneers of the Modern Movement from William Morris to Walter Gropius.* New York: Museum of Modern Art/Simon and Schuster, 1949. 153 p., ills. Further eds. and reprints 1949, 1965, 1966, 1975, 1986. (See also Shand.)

Phillips, Joseph. "Description of the Iron Roof, in one span, over the Joint Railway Station, New Street, Birmingham." *Min. Proc. ICE* 14 (1854–1855): 251–272 and plate 3. Paper no. 925 (30 January 1855).

Phillips, Samuel. *Guide to the Crystal Palace and Park.* London: Crystal Palace Library, 1854. 175, 76 p., 1 plan, 1 map, ills.; further eds. 1854 (3 times), 1855, 1856. London: Crystal Palace Library, 1858. Variant title: *Guide to the Crystal Palace and its park and gardens. A newly arranged and entirely revised edition by F. K. J. Shenton. With new plans and illustrations and an index of principal objects.* xvi, 192 p., 4 pls. ills. Further eds. 1860, 1861. A guide to the Crystal Palace as it was rebuilt in Sydenham in 1854, including a brief account of the reconstruction and expansion of the original structure.

Pickett, William Vose. *New System of Architecture, founded on the forms of nature, and developing the properties of metals; by which a higher order of beauty, a larger amount of utility, and various advantages in economy, over the pre-existent architectures, may be practically attained: presenting also, the peculiar and important advantage of being commercial, its productions forming fitting objects for exportation.* London: Longman & Co., 1845. 144 p.

Poggendorff, Johann Christian. *Biographisches-Literarisches Handwörterbuch zur Geschichte der exakten Wissenschaften.* Leipzig. 1863 ff., presently 36 vols. New edition of the first two vols. Amsterdam: B. M. Israel, 1970. Together with Darmstaedter, the most reliable and complete compendium of inventions, persons, and dates in technology.

Poirel, Léopold-Victor. *Mémoire sur les travaux à la mer, comprenant l'historique des ouvrages exécutés au port d'Alger, et l'exposé complet et détaillé d'un système de fondation à la mer au moyen de blocs de béton.* 2 vols. Paris: Carilian-Goeury et Dalmont, 1841. 1: vii, (v), 152 p.; 2: 18 pls.

Poirel, Paul. *La France Industrielle ou Description des Industries Françaises . . . ouvrage contenant 422 gravures dessinées par Bonnafoux et Jahandier et gravées par Laplante.* 3rd. ed. Paris: Librairie Hachette et Cie., 1880. ix, 712 p., pls., ills.

Post, Robert C. *1876 A Centennial Exhibition.* Washington, D.C.: Smithsonian Institution, 1976. 223 p., ills.

Proceedings of Wood Symposium. One Hundred Years of Engineering Progress with Wood. The Centennial of Engineering Convocation. September 3–13, 1952, Chicago, Illinois. Washington, D.C.: Timber Engineering Company, 1952. (4), 111 p., ills.

Pudney, John. *Brunel and his World.* London: Thames and Hudson, 1975. 128 p., ills.

Pugsley, Sir Alfred Grenville, ed. *The Works of Isambard Kingdom Brunel: an engineering appreciation.* London: Institution of Civil Engineers/Bristol: University of Bristol, 1976. (10), 222 p., ills.

Purdy, Corydon Tyler. "The Steel Construction of Buildings. Lecture delivered before the students of the College of Mechanics and Engineering of the University of Wisconsin, March 2, 1894." *Bulletin of the University of Wisconsin, Engineering Series.* 1 no. 3 (Oct. 1894): 41–67. Madison: published by the university, 1896.

Raafat, Aly Ahmed. *Reinforced Concrete in Architecture.* New York: Reinhold, 1958. 240 p., ills.

Raistrick, Arthur. *Dynasty of Iron Founders: the Darbys and Coalbrookdale.* London: Longmans, Green, 1953. 308 p., ills. 2nd ed. 1981.

Ransome System Concrete-Steel Construction. New York: A. Mugford (printer), 1904. 75, (2) p., ills. Company brochure.

Rasmussen, Steen Eiler. *London The Unique City, with an introduction by James Bone.* New York: Macmillan, 1937. 404 p., ills. Further eds. 1948, 1960, 1964, 1982. Italian edition. Title: *Londra città unica.* Rome: Officina Edizioni, 1972. 320 p., ills. 40 pls. French Edition. Title: *Londres.* Paris: Picard, 1990. 367 p., ills.

The Record of the International Exhibition 1862. Glasgow: William Mackenzie, (1862). 592 p., 18 pls., ills.

Rees, Abraham. *The cyclopaedia, or universal dictionary of arts, sciences, and literature.* 39 vols. London: Longman, Hurst, Rees, Orme & Brown, 1803. 1st.US ed. 47 vols. . . . *revised, corrected, enlarged and adapted to this country by several literary and scientific characters.* Philadelphia: Samuel F. Bradford and Murray, Fairman and Co., 1805. Before producing his own, Rees collaborated on editions of Chambers Cyclopedia.

Reid, Homer Austin. *Concrete and reinforced concrete construction.* New York: The Myson C. Clark Publishing Co., 1907. xviii, 884 p., ills.

Reid, Henry. *A practical treatise on concrete and how to make it: with observations on the uses of cements, limes and mortars.* London: E. & F. N. Spon, 1869. xv, 108 p., 5 pls. New ed. 1879. Variant title: *A practical treatise on natural and artificial concrete: its varieties and constructive adaptations.* xxiv, 384 p., frontis., pls., ills. Reid had published a book on artificial mortars the year before. (Elton catalog 6, p. 109).

Rendel, James Meadows. "Presidential Address." *Min. Proc. ICE* 11 (1852).

Rennie, Sir John. "Address of Sir John Rennie, President to the Annual General Meeting, January 20, 1846." *Min. Proc. ICE* 5 (1846): 19–122.

Report from the Select Committee on Atmospheric Railways; together with the Minutes of Evidence, Appendix and Index. (Communicated by the Commons to the Lords). Ordered to be Printed 6th May 1845. London: HMSO, 1845. vii, 196, 33, (1) p.

Report of the Commissioners appointed to Inquire into the Application of Iron to Railway Structures. London: HMSO: Wm. Clowes and Sons, 1849. 439 p., ills., map.

Ritchie, T. "Plankwall Framing, a Modern Wall Construction with an Ancient History." *Journal of the Society for Architectural History* 30 (March 1971): 66–70.

Rolt, Lionel Thomas Casawall. *Isambard Kingdom Brunel. A Biography.* London: Longmans, Green, 1957. 345 p., ills. Reprint 1957, 1958. Further eds. 1959, 1961, 1970, 1980, 1985.

Rolt, Lionel Thomas Casawall. *Victorian Engineering.* London: Allen Lane/The Penguin Press, 1970. 300 p., 48 pls., ills. Further eds. 1974, 1987.

Rondelet, Jean-Baptiste. *Traité théorique et pratique de l'art de bâtir.* 5 vols. (in 7). Paris: chez l'auteur, 1802. At least sixteen further editions were published between 1810 and 1881.

Rosenberg, Nathan, ed. *The American System of Manufactures: the report of the Committee on the Machinery of the United States 1855, and the special reports of George Wallis and Joseph Whitworth 1854.* Edinburgh: University Press, 1969. (8), 440 p.

Rosenberg, Nathan, and Walter G. Vincenti. *The Britannia Bridge: The Generation and Diffusion of Technological Knowledge.* Cambridge, MA: MIT Press, 1978. x, 107 p., ills., map.

Routledge, Robert. *Discoveries and Inventions of the Nineteenth Century.* 14th ed. London: George Routledge and Sons, 1901. xvi, 820 p., ills., frontis.

The Rudiments of Civil Engineering for the use of beginners, and for those who are in practice: also applicable for the instruction of the working engineers of H. M.'s army and navy. In one complete volume, with plates and diagrams. New edition, with additions. Weale's Rudimentary Treatises, no. 13. London: John Weale, 1862. x, 102, 152, 126, 193 p., 12 p. adverts., pls., ills.

Ruskin, John. *The Crown of Wild Olive three lectures on work, traffic and war.* London: Smith, Elder, 1866. xxxiv, 219 p. 47–49th thousand. London: George Allen, 1904. 276 p. There were innumerable other editions.

Ruskin, John. *The Seven Lamps of Architecture. with illustrations, drawn and etched by the author.* London: Smith, Elder and Co., 1849. xii, 206, (2), 16 p. ads. ills. Since the advertisments are dated March 1854, there must have been later reissues of the first edition.

Ruskin, John. *The Stones of Venice (with illustrations drawn by the author).* 3 vols. London: Smith, Elder & Co., 1851–1853. 1: (1851) *The Foundations;* 2: (1853) *The Sea-Stories;* 3: (1853) *The Fall.* Vol. 1 reissued in 1858 followed by *Examples of the Architecture of Venice, Selected and Drawn to Measurement from the Edifices,* 3 parts, 1176 p., 15 pls., 1851.

Ruskin, John. See also Collingwood; Cook.

Russell, Barry. *Building Systems, Industrialization, and Architecture.* London: John Wiley & Sons., 1981 (6), vii–xii, 758 p., ills.

Russell, Sir William Howard. *The Atlantic Telegraph by W. H. R. LLD. Illustrated by Robert Dudley. Dedicated by Special Permission to His Royal Highness Albert Edward, Prince of Wales.* London: Day & Son Limited [1866?]. vi, 117 (1),(4 adverts.) p., frontis., 25 pls.

Sabin, Louis Carleton. *Cement and Concrete.* New York: McGraw, 1905. x, 507 p., diagrs.

Samuda, Jacob. "The Atmospheric Railway." *Min. Proc. ICE* 3 (1844): 256–283 and pl. Paper no. 681 (14 May 1844).

Schaeffer, Robert K. "The Standardization of Time and Space." *Ascent and Decline in the World-System,* Edward Friedman, ed. Beverly Hills: Sage Publication, (1982?): 69–90.

Schafhäutl, Karl Emil (pseudonym Pellisov). "Das Portland- und Roman-Cement. Ein Beitrag zur Geschichte der Cemente oder hydraulischen Mörtel in England, nebst einem Anhange über die Theorie der Erstarrung der Mörtel und über den glänzenden Stucco der Alten." *Dinglers Polytechnischem Journal* 3 no. 122 (1851): 186–209, 267–293 and 1 pl.

Schürch, Hermann. *Der Bau des Talüberganges bei Langwies an der elektrischen Bahn Chur-Arosa.* Berlin: Jul. Springer, 1916. 4, 82 p., ills. Offprint from: *Armierter Beton.* nos. 7–12 (1915) and nos. 1–2 (1916).

La Science Illustrée. Journal hébdomadaire publiée sous la direction de Louis Figuier. 2 vols. per year. Paris: La Librairie Illustrée, 1887 ff. Adolphe Bitard was editor from 1887 until 21 April 1888, only then did Figuier edit the journal. He had, however, been a regular contributor from the beginning.

Seebaß (Sebass), Christian Ludwig. *Die Pisé-Baukunst, in ihrem ganzen Umfang, oder vollständige und faßliche Beschreibung des Verfahrens, aus blosser gestampfter Erde, ohne weitere Zuthat, Gebäude und Mauerwerk von aller Art wohlfeil, dauerhaft, feuerfest, und sicher gegen Einbruch aufzuführen. Aus dem französischen Original des Herrn Cointereaux, bearbeitet und mit Zusäzen versehen von C.L.S.* . . . 2 vols. Leipzig: in der Baumgärtnerischen Buchhandlung, (1803). 1: iv, 132 p., 12 pl.; 2: iv, 187 p., 12 pl. (See also Engel and Krause.) First German edition of Cointeraux.

Shand, Morton P. "Steel and Concrete. A Historical Survey." *Architectural Review* 72 (November 1932): 169–179. Shand's article served both Giedion and Pevsner as basis for their writings.

Shaw, Richard Norman. *Sketches for Cottages and other Buildings: Designed to be Constructed in the Patent Cement Slab System of W. H. Lascelles, 121 Bunhill Row, Finsbury, London E.C. From Sketches and Notes by R. Norman Shaw, R.A. Drawn by Maurice B. Adams, A.R.I.B.A.* London: W. H. Lascelles, 1878. (10) p., 28 pls.

Sheahan, James W., and George P. Upton. *The Great Conflagration. Chicago: its past, present and future. Embracing a detailed narrative of the great conflagration in the North, South and West Divisions: Origin, Progress and Results of the Fire. Prominent buildings burned, character of buildings, losses and insurance, graphic description of the flames, scenes and incidents, loss of life, the flight of the people. Also, a condensed history of Chicago, its population, growth and great public works. And a statement of all the great fires of the world . . . with numerous illustrations.* Chicago: Union Publishing Co., 1871. (2), 3–458 p., ills., 2 frontis.

Simmons, Jack, ed. *The Birth of the Great Western Railway. Extracts from the Diary and Correspondance of George Henry Gibbs.* Bath: Adams & Dart, 1971. (5), vi–viii, 96 p., portrait.

Singer, Charles Joseph, et al.: *A History of Technology.* 8 vols. London: Clarendon Press, 1954–1958 and 1984. 1: *From early times to the fall of ancient empires;* 2: *The Mediterranean civilizations and the Middle Ages c. 700 B.C. to c. 150 A.D.;* 3: *From the Renaissance to the industrial revolution c. 1500 to c. 1750;* 4: *The industrial revolution c. 1750 to c. 1850;* 5: *The late nineteenth century c. 1850 to c. 1900;* 5 and 6 edited by T. I. Williams: *The twentieth century c. 1900 to c. 1950;* 8 (1984): *Consolidated indexes edited by Richard Raper.*

Skempton, Alec W., ed. *John Smeaton, FRS.* London: Thomas Telford Ltd., 1981. (8), 291 p., ills.

Skempton, Alex W., and Michael M. Chrimes. "Thames Tunnel: geology, site investigation and geotechnical problems." *Géotechnique* 44 no. 2 (1994): 191–216.

Sketches for the Works for the Tunnel under the Thames from Rotherhithe to Wapping. London: Messrs. Harvey and Darton, 1828. 21 p., 15 pls. (2 polychrome). (See Chrimes et al. for all other editions. This one is no. 61.)

Smeaton, John. *An experimental enquiry concerning the natural powers of water and wind to turn mills.* London, 1760. 77 p., 3 pls.

Smeaton, John. *A Narrative of the building and a description of the construction of the Edystone* [sic] *Lighthouse with stone: to which is subjoined an appendix, giving some account of the lighthouse on the Spurn Point, built upon a sand.* London: for the author by H. Hughes, 1791. xiv, 198 p., 23 pls. 2nd ed. London: G. Nicol, 1793. xiv, 198 p., 23 pls., 1 title vignette. Further eds. 1796, 1813. This report contains the first publication on a scientific examination of hydraulic mortar. All successful attempts to make artificial hydraulic mortars derive from the publication of this work.

Smeaton, John. *Reports of the late John Smeaton F.R.S. made on various occasions, in the course of his employment of* [sic] *an engineer.* London: for a select committee . . . sold by Faden, 1797. 2nd ed. 3 vols. London: Longman, Hurst, Rees, Orme, and Brown, 1812 . . . *as a civil engineer. In three volumes.* 1: xxx, xxv–xxxii, 412 p., 33 pls., 1 portrait; 2: xi, 440 p., 23 pls.; 3: vii, 420 p., 16 pls. Supplement volume. London: Longman, Hurst, Rees, Orme, and Brown, 1814. viii, 208 p. 14 pls. Further eds. 1837, 1900.

Smiles, Samuel. *Industrial Biography: Iron-Workers and Tool-Makers.* London: J. Murray, 1863. xiv, 342 p. Further eds. 1864, 1876.

Smiles, Samuel. *Lives of the Engineers, with an account of their principal works; comprising also a history of inland communications in Britain with portraits and numerous illustrations.* 2 vols. London: John Murray, 1861. 1: xvi, 1, 484, 12 p.; 2: xiv, 502 p., both with ills. 3rd vol. 1864. *The Life of George Stephenson and of his son Robert Stephenson: comprising also a history of the invention and introduction of the railway locomotive with portraits and numerous illustrations.* This volume, with several variant titles and repeated publications in the first year, was developed out of his previous book, *The Life of George Stephenson, railway engineer* (1859), after the death of Robert. Volume 3 went through several subsequent editions on its own (the pirate edition, New York: Harper, 1868, was used here). The whole work was revised several times and grew finally to six vols. Smiles wrote with a social agenda: he was interested in promoting self-education and the betterment of the working classes. His most popular book was called *Self-Help* (1859). Smiles chose an area of industry that was hitherto neglected by contemporary writers (although he had been preceded by Henry Howe in the U.S.), and collected much oral material from people who had known the pioneers he described. The continuing value of his work lies in this anecdotal material. Otherwise, since Smiles idealized his heroes and neglected many other contributors to the field, both his balance and objectivity must be subjected to careful analysis.

Smiles, Samuel. *Self-Help; with illustrations of character and conduct.* London: John Murray, 1859. 343 p. Numerous further editions with various publishers in many places and languages between 1860 and 1986.

Smith, Cecil O., Jr. "The Longest Run: Public Engineers and Planning in France." *American Historical Review* 95 no. 3 (Jun. 1990): 657–692.

Smith, J. Bucknall. *A Treatise upon Wire, its manufacture and uses, embracing comprehensive descriptions of the constructions and applications of wire ropes.* London: Office of "Engineering"/New York: John Wiley and Sons, 1891. 223 p.

Smith, J. T. *A practical and scientific treatise on calcareous mortars and cements, artificial and natural; containing, directions for ascertaining the qualities of the different ingredients, for preparing them for use, and for combining them together in the most advantageous manner; with a theoretical investigation of their properties and modes of action. The whole founded upon an extensive series of original experiments, with examples of their practical application on the large scale. By L. J. Vicat . . . translated, with the addition of explanatory notes, embracing remarks upon the results of various new experiments, by Captain J.T.S.* . . . London: John Weale, Architectural Library, 1837. xii, xiv, iv, 302 p., 3 pls., tables. Includes Vicat's memoir of 1828 as well as that of 1818, and Smith's observations and explanations.

Spearman, Frank H. *The Strategy of Great Railroads. with maps.* New York: Charles Scribner's Sons, 1905. (8), 287 (3) p., maps. A popular account which contains a curious version of the Golden Spike Transmission on the Union Pacific Railroad.

Spriegel, William Robert, and Clark E. Myers, eds. *The Writings of the Gilbreths.* Homewood, IL: Richard D. Irwin, 1953. xi, 513 p., ills.

Stamper, John W. "The Galerie des Machines of the 1889 Paris World's Fair." *Technology and Culture* 30 no. 2 (April 1989): 330–353.

Steiner, Frances H. *French Iron Architecture.* Studies in the Fine Arts: Architecture, No. 3. Ann Arbor, MI: UMI Press, 1984. xiv, 240 p., ills.

Stephenson, Robert. Article on the Suez Canal. *Min. Proc. ICE* 10 (1851): 10–13, 20.

Stephenson, Robert. "Iron Bridges." *Encyclopaedia Britannica.* 8th ed. Boston: Little Brown & Co., 1856.

Stephenson, Robert. "Presidential Address." *Min. Proc. ICE* 15 (1855–1856): ?–154.

Stephenson, Robert. Response to Negrelli's letter of 18 June 1858 in the *Oesterreichische Gazette. Mémoires et Compte-Rendu des travaux de la Société des Ingénieurs Civils* (1858): 281–287. Part of Barrault.

Stevenson, David. *Sketch of the Civil Engineering of North America comprising remarks on the harbours, river and lake navigation, lighthouses, steam-navigation, waterworks, canals, roads, railways, bridges, and other works in that country.* London: John Weale, Architectural library, 1838. xvi, 17–320, 8 ads., frontis (map), 1 tab. 2nd ed. London: John Weale, 1859. Part of Weale's Rudimentary Series.

Straub, Hans. *Die Geschichte der Bauingenieurkunst. Ein Überblick von der Antike bis in die Neuzeit.* Wissenschaft und Kultur Band 4. Basel: Verlag Birkhäuser, 1949. xii, 285 p., 79 figs. Further eds. 1964, 1975. English edition. Title: *A History of Civil Engineering. An outline from ancient to modern times. English translation by E[rwin] Rockwell.* London: Leonard Hill Ltd., 1952. 258 p., ills. 2nd ed. 1960. Straub was the first to attempt a general history of civil engineering in German. He based his writing on his personal collection of old engineering reports and studied them as an amateur historian, but professional civil engineer during World War II when work was lacking in Pier Luigi Nervi's office in Rome. Thus what he writes is usually correct, but much is missing and therefore often misjudged in context.

Stüssi, Fritz. "Ein unbekanntes Gutachten L. Navier's." *Abhandlungen der Internationalen Vereinigung für Brücken- und Hochbau IVBH.* 7 (1943/1944) Zurich: 1–13. Stüssi discovered Navier's report while examining the papers of G. H. Dufour in the State Archives in Geneva. See also Dufour, *Observations.*

Summerson, Sir John Newenham. *Georgian London. with forty-eight plates and thirty-seven text figures.* London: Pleiades Books, 1945. xi, 315 p., ills. Further eds. 1962–1978.

Szabó, István. *Geschichte der mechanischen Prinzipien und ihrer wichtigsten Anwendungen.* Basel: Birkhäuser, 1976. xxiv, (32), 491 p., ills. pls.

Tann, Jennifer. *Gloucestershire woollen mills: industrial archaeology.* Newton Abbot: David & Charles / New York: A. M. Kelley, 1967. 254 p. ills.

Tarbé de Saint Hardouin, François-Pierre H. *Notices Biographiques sur les ingénieurs des Ponts et Chaussées Depuis la création du Corps, en 1716, jusqu'à nos jours.* Encyclopédie des Travaux Publics. fondée en 1884 par M(arc) C(lément) Lechales . . . Paris: Librarie polytechnique, Baudry & Cie., 1884. 276 p.

Taylor, Charles. *A Supplement to Nicholson's Operative Mechanic, and British Machinist; consisting of a series of Descriptions, elucidated by Engravings of Plans, Elevations, Sections, and Details of the most remarkable Public Works and National Improvements of the British Empire. translated and arranged from Baron Charles Dupin, "On the Commercial Power of Great Britain," etc. by C.T.* London: printed for Robert Thurston, 1829. (2), 785–792, xi–xxviii, 20 pls. (pl. 1 as frontis.), 793–902 (8 title pages for all vols.) p. (See also John Nicholson, *Operative Mechanic.*)

Taylor, Frederick Winslow, and Sanford Eleazar Thompson. *A Treatise on Concrete, plain and reinforced. Materials, construction, and design of concrete and reinforced concrete with chapters by R. Feret, William B. Fuller, Frank B. McKibben and Spencer W. Newberry.* New York: John Wiley / London: Chapman & Hall, 1905. xviii, 585 p., frontis., ills. diagrs. 2nd ed. 1909 (1), (2), frontis., xviii, 1–2, 2a–2d, 3–807, (1), xix–xl p. (incl. adverts. from p. xxi–xl). (See also Christophe; Buel and Hill; Morel; Mörsch.)

Telford, Thomas. *Life of Thomas Telford, civil engineer. Written by himself; containing a descriptive narrative of his professional labours: with a folio atlas of copper plates. Edited by John Rickman, one of his executors; with a preface, supplement, annotations, and index.* 2 vols. London: James and Luke G. Hansard and Sons, 1838. 1: xxiv, 719 p., 1 pl., ills.; 2: *"sold by Payne & Moss."* portrait, title (2 contents) p., 82 pls. (numbered 1–83, but 28 not called for), several pls. double or folding. 2nd ed. London. Text only.

The Thames Tunnel, is open to the public every day (except Sunday) from Nine in the Morning, until dark. Teape Broadsheet: Company's Office, Walbrook Buildings, Walbrook, February, 1840. (This version not in Chrimes et al. This issue lies between his nos. 95 and 96 on p. 64. See pp. 61–64 for other editions of this broadsheet.)

Thomé de Gamond, Aimé. *Carte d'étude pour le tracé et le profil du Canal de Nicaragua par T.d.G.* Paris: Dalmont et Dunod, 1858. 90 p., map.

Thomson, John W. See Bogardus and Thomson.

Tobriner, Stephen. "Earthquakes and planning in the 17th and 18th centuries." *Journal of Architectural Education*. Washington, D.C. no. 33 (1980): 11–15.

Tobriner, Stephen. "A History of Reinforced Masonry Construction Designed to Resist Earthquakes: 1755–1907." *Earthquake Spectra* 1 (November 1984): 125–149.

Tomes, John. "Tomes' machine for dental carving." *Min. Proc. ICE* 4 (1845): 250–251.

Tomlinson, Charles. *Cyclopaedia of Useful Arts, Mechanical and Chemical, Manufactures, Mining, and Engineering. The whole illustrated by forty steel engravings and two thousand four hundred and seventy-seven wood engravings.* 2 vols. in 9 parts. London: G. Virtue, 1852. 1: xvi, clx, 832 p., 19 pls.; 2: 1052, (8) p., 25 pls., ills. 2nd ed. 2 vols. (1854). 1: *Abatoir to Hair-Pencils. With an introductory essay on the Great Exhibition of the Works of Industry of all Nations, 1851.* clx, 832 p.; 2: *Hammer to Zirconium.* iv, 1052 p., both with ills. Further edition in 3 vols. 1866. Together with Ure, Spon, and Cresy, one of the most useful of early technological encyclopedia in English.

Totten, Joseph Gilbert. *Essays on hydraulic and common mortars and on limeburning. Translated from the French of Gen. Treussart, M. Petot* [Jean Constant], *and M.* [C.] *Courtois. With brief observations on common mortars, hydraulic mortars, and concretes, and an account of some experiments made therewith at Fort Adams* . . . New York: Wiley & Putnam, 1842. 256 p., pls., ills. Reprint in book form of a paper published in the Journal of the Franklin Institute, 1837–1838.

Trachtenberg, Marvin. *The Statue of Liberty.* New York: Viking Press, 1976. 224 p., ills.

Transactions of the International Engineering Congress, 1915. The Panama Canal. 2 vols. San Francisco: Press of the Neal Publishing Company, 1916. 1: *General Papers and Construction in Three Divisions of Canal. Sessions held under the auspices of: American Society of Civil Engineers, American Institute of Mining Engineers, The Americal Society of Mechanical Engineers, American Institute of Electrical Engineers, The Society of Naval Architects and Marine Engineers. San Francisco, California, September 20–25, 1915.* (6), 527 p., ills., pls. 2: *Design and Erection of Structures.* Vol. 1 contains 13 papers, vol. 2 contains 12.

Tredgold, Thomas. *Practical Essay on the Strength of Cast Iron, intended for the assistance of engineers, iron masters, architects, millwrights, founders, smiths, and others engaged in the construction of machines, buildings &c. Containing practical rules, tables, and examples; also an account of some new experiments, with an extensive table of the properties of materials. Illustrated by four engravings.* London: J. Taylor, 1822. xvi, 175 p., 4 pls. 2nd ed., 1824. *Practical essay on the strength of cast iron and other metals; . . . containing practical rules, tables, and examples; founded on a series of new experiments, with an extensive table of the properties of materials.* xx, 306 p., ills., 4 pls. (variant pagination gives xix, 306 p.) substantially revised, enlarging particularly the section devoted to cast iron which was largely founded on the work of Thomas Young (according to Elton). Tredgold also added a new section of experiments on wrought iron. 3rd ed. corrected reprint, 1831. 4th ed., 1842. *Practical Essay on the Strength of cast iron and other metals; containing practical rules, tables and examples, founded on a series of experiments; with an extensive table of the properties of materials.* xxviii, 303, 1 p., 4 pls. This issue was edited by Eaton Hodgkinson who added copious notes to the original text. 5th ed. 2 vols. London: John

Weale, 1846. xxviii, 303, 1 p., 4 pls. Eaton Hodgkinson, who had written seminal papers on the subject from 1828 on, expanded the work as *Experimental researches on the strength and other properties of cast iron. Forming a second part to the fourth edition of Tredgold's Practical Essay* . . . (See also Hodgkinson.) 5th ed., 1860–1861. ix, 223 p., ills., tables, pls. Variant pagination: x, 224, iii–viii, 225–384 p., 32 + 9 engr., ills. 1825 French ed./1826 German ed.

Tresca, Henri-Edouard. Article, on machinery. *Mémoire et Compte-Rendu des travaux de la Société des Ingénieurs Civils* (1867): 453 ff.

Treussart, Clément-Louis. *Mémoire sur les mortiers hydrauliques et ordinaires.* Paris: Carilian-Goeury, 1829. iii, 236 p., ills. Engl. trans. Title: *Essays on hydraulic and common mortars and on limeburning. Reprinted from the Journal of the Franklin Inst. 1837–1838.* Philadelphia: (Franklin Inst.), 1838. 2, 1, 256 p., 2 pls., tables. Further edition. Title: *Essays on hydraulic and common mortars and on limeburning. Translated from the French of Gen. Treussart, M. Petot* [Jean Constant], *and M.* [C] *Courtois. With brief observations on common mortars, hydraulic mortars, and concretes* . . . New York: Wiley and Putnam, 1842. 256 p., 2 pls., tables. See also Totten.

Turner, Richard. "Description of the Iron Roof over the Railway Station, Lime-street, Liverpool." *Min. Proc. ICE* 9 (1849–1850): 204–214. Paper no. 824 (19 February 1850).

Tyler, [Sir Henry Whatley?]. "Rapport du capitaine Tyler (du corps royal du génie) au Board of Trade, sur le chemin de fer proposé par MM. Brassey et cie. pour la traversée du Mont Cenis." *Mémoire et Compte-Rendu des travaux de la Société des Ingénieurs Civils* (1865): 441–456.

Ullrich, Ruth-Maria. *Glas-Eisen Architektur. Pflanzenhäuser des 19. Jahrhunderts.* Grüne Reihe Quellen und Forschungen zur Gartenkunst, Band 12. Worms: Wernersche Verlagsgesellschaft, 1989. 440 p., ills.

Upton, Niel. *An Illustrated History of Civil Engineering.* London: Heineman, 1975. 192 p., ills. New York: Crane Russak, 1976. 191 p., ills.

Vicat, Louis-Joseph. "Ponts suspendus en fil de fer sur le Rhône." *Annales des Ponts et Chaussées* 1 (Paris 1831): 93–145 and pl. 3. The single most influential article in the French dispute on the relative merits of chain versus wire cable suspension bridges and the publication of Vicat's experiments on the rust-reducing properties of hydraulic cement.

Vicat, Louis-Joseph. *Recherches expérimentales sur les chaux de construction, les bétons et les mortiers ordinaires.* Paris: Goujon, 1818. (ii), 97, xii, (7) p., 25 tables., 3 pls. A theoretical study on artificial hydraulic mortars and the most influential after Smeaton's study of 1791. Up until his death in 1862, Vicat periodically produced many addenda to his original study, including the following:

Vicat, Louis-Joseph. *Recherches sur les propriétés diverses que peuvent acquérir les pierres à ciments et à chaux hydrauliques par l'effet d'une incomplète cuisson; précédées d'observations sur les chaux anomales qui forment le passage des chaux éminemment hydrauliques aux ciments.* Paris: Carilian-Goeury et Vve. Dalmont, éds., 1840. (4), 34 p., 4 pl. Republished together with the following item (2) p. added mentioning the date 1846.

Vicat, Louis-Joseph. *Résumé des Connaissances positives actuelles sur les qualités, le choix et la convenance réciproque des matériaux propres à la fabrication des mortiers et ciments calcaires; suivi de notes et tableaux d'expériences justificatives.* Paris: Firmin Didot, 1828. xii, 149 p., 16 tables (I–XV/III*), 4 pls. In 1846 republished together with the preceding item. Italian edition 1836. English edition 1837 (see Smith, J. T.).

Vicat, Joseph-Louis. "Sur l'oxidation des fers dans les constructions, sur l'inefficacité des enduits ou vernis et sur la puissance préservatrice de la chaux et des mortiers." *Annales des Ponts et Chaussées* 1er. sem. (1853): 335–342.

Vicat, Louis-Joseph. See also Smith, J. T.

Vignoles, Olinthus. *Life of Charles Blacker Vignoles [1793–1875] F.R.S., F.R.A.S., M.R.I.A., &c. soldier and civil engineer, formerly lieutenant in H.M. 1st. Royals, past President of Institution of Civil Engineers. A reminiscence of early railway history. By his son.* London: Longmans, Green & Co., 1889. xx, 407, 24 p., ills.

Vinchent. "Mémorie sur les lignes télégraphiques du royaume de Belgique, leur matériel et leurs rapports avec l'exploitation des chemins de fer." *Mémoires et Compte-Rendu des travaux de la Société des Ingénieurs Civils* (1864): 255–294.

Vogel, Robert M. "Tunnel Engineering. A museum treatment." *United States National Museum Bulletin 240: Contributions from the Museum of History and Technology.* Washington, D.C.: Smithsonian Institution, 1964. (2), 203–239, (1) p., ills. Paper 41, pp. 201–240.

Vom Caementum zum Spannbeton. Beiträge zur Geschichte des Betons. 3 vols. Wiesbaden: Bauverlag, 1964–1965. 1: 72, 198, 57 p.; 2: 164 p.; 3: 126 p. ills. There have been several theses and articles on individual machines and methods used in manufacturing concrete structures since this compendium appeared, and there is now more information available, but it is not easily accessible and this is therefore still the best general study of the development of concrete construction methods and machinery. Together with Collins, *Vom Caementum* forms a fairly comprehensive overview of the field. But the whole history of concrete is now urgently in need of revision.

Vugnier, Emile, and Edouard Fleur Saint-Denis. *Le Pont sur le Rhin à Kehl. Détails pratiques sur les dispositions générales et d'exécution de cet ouvrage d'art.* 2 vols. Paris: Dunod éditeur, 1861. 1: text. xxiii, (1), 156, (2) p. 2: plates. 7, (1) p., 22 pls.

Vulliamy, Benjamin Lewis. "On the Construction and Regulation of Clocks for Railway Stations." *Min. Proc. ICE* 4 (1845): 63–77. Paper no. 708 (4 February 1845).

Walmisley, Arthur T. *Iron roofs, examples of design.* London: Spon, 1884. 36, 64 p. pls. 2nd ed. 1888. Addendum to title: *description, illustrated with working drawings.* 91 p., 70 pls.

Wayss, Georg A., and Matthias Koenen. *Das System Monier (Eisengerippe mit Cementumhüllung) in seiner Anwendung auf das gesammte Bauwesen. Unter Mitwirkung namhafter Architekten und Ingenieure herausgegeben von G. A. W. Ingenieur Inhaber des Patentes "Monier" Wien, I. Bez., Elisabeth-Strasse 3.* Vienna: n. p., 1887. vii, (1), 128 p., ills. Printed simultaneously in Berlin, identically — as far as can be ascertained. 10,000 copies printed and distributed by the authors (see Kurrer.)

Wayss & Freytag. *Umschnürter Beton (Beton fretté) Seine Theorie und Anwendung im Bauwesen. Herausgegeben von W & F A.G.* Stuttgart: Verlag von Konrad Wittwer, 1910. 55 p., ills.

Weale, John. *Ensamples of Railway Making . . . with R. F. Isherwood: scientific description of the mechanical works on the Ithaca and Syracuse railroad, and Edward Dobson: historical, statistical, and scientific account of the railways of Belgium.* London: John Weale, 1843. viii, xlii, 54, xvi, 101, (1) p., frontis., 2 maps, 24 pls., 2 tables.

Weale, John. *Theory, Practice, and Architecture of Bridges of Stone, Iron, Timber, and Wire; with examples on the principle of suspension: illustrated by One Hundred and Thirty-eight Engravings and ninety-two woodcuts.* 4 vols. London: John Weale, 1839–1843. 1: xvi, 88, 72, 140, lxiv p. ills.; 2: viii, 248, ccxxiv p., pl. 69a, ills.; 3: ; 4: tp., pls. 65–122.

Webb, Walter Loring, and W. Herbert Gibson. *Masonry and reinforced concrete; a working manual of approved American practice in the selection, testing and structural use of building stone, brick, cement and other masonry materials, with complete instruction in the various modern structural applications of concrete and concrete steel.* Chicago: American School of Correspondence, 1909. 444 p., ills.

Werner, Ernst. "Die Giesshalle der Sayner Hütte." *Zentralblatt für Industriebau* (June 1973): 254–260.

West, Graham. *Innovation and the Rise of the Tunneling Industry.* London: Cambridge University Press, 1988. 355 p., ills.

Wheatstone, Sir Charles. "A pair of electro-magnetic signal telegraphs, constructed for the Aix-la-Chapelle railway . . ." *Min. Proc. ICE* 2 (1843–1843): 181–183. Paper no. 663.

White, George Frederick. "Observations on Artificial Hydraulic, or Portland Cement; with an account of the testing of the Brick Beam erected at the Great Exhibition, Hyde Park." *Min. Proc. ICE* 11 (1851–1852): 478–510 and plate 5. Paper no. 870 (18 May 1852).

Wiener Allgemeine Bauzeitung. See *Allgemeine Bauzeitung.*

Willis, Robert. *Principles of mechanism, designed for the use of students in the universities and for engineering students generally.* London: J. E. Parker, J. & J. J. Deighton, 1841. xxxi, 446 p., ills.

Window, Frederick Richard. "On the Electric Telegraph, and the principal improvements in its Construction." *Min. Proc. ICE* 11 (1851–1852): 329–388.

Winkler, Emil. "Vortrag über die Berechnung von Bogenbrücken." *Mitteilungen des Architekten- und Ingenieurvereins Böhmen* (1868): 6–12, (1869): 5–7 (information from Karl-Eugen Kurrer).

Witteck, Karl H. *Die Entwicklung des Stahlhochbaus.* Düsseldorf, 1964.

Wohleber, Curt. "The Annihilation of Time and Space." *American History of Invention and Technology* 7 no. 1 (Spring/Summer 1991): 20–26.

Woodcroft, Bennett. *Alphabetical Index of Patentees of Inventions from March 2nd. 1617 (14 James I)–October 1st 1852 (16 Victoria). Printed and published by Order of the Honourable the Commissioners of Patents, under the Act of 15 & 16 Victoria, Cap. 83, sec. XXXII by B. W.* London: Queen's Printing Office, 1854. 645 p. Reprint. London: Evelyn, Adams & Mackay, 1969.

Woodcroft, Bennett. *British Patent Office. Subject Matter Index (made from titles only) of Patents of Invention from March 2nd 1617 (14 James I)–October 1st 1852 (16 Victoria). Printed and published by Order of the Honourable the Commissioners of Patents, under the Act of 15 & 16 Victoria, Cap. 83, sec. XXXII by B.W.* 2 vols. 2nd ed. London: Queen's Printing Office, 1854. 1: A-M. lix, 508 p.; 2: N-W. pp. 509–970.

Woodcroft, Bennett. *Reference Index of Patents of Invention, from March 2nd. 1617 (14 James I)–October 1st 1852 (16 Victoria). Printed and published by Order of the Honourable the Commissioners of Patents, under the Act of 15 & 16 Victoria, Cap. 83, sec. XXXII by B.W. pointing out the Office in which each enrolled Specification of a Patent may be consulted, and the Books containing Notices of specifications; also Law Proceedings, and other Subjects connected with Inventions.* 2nd ed. London: Queen's Printing Office, 1862. vii, 710 p.

Woodcroft, Bennett. *Titles of Patents of Inventions, chronologically arranged from March 2nd. 1617 (14 James I)–October 1st 1852 (16 Victoria). Printed and published by Order of the Honourable the Commissioners of Patents, under the Act of 15 & 16 Victoria, Cap. 83, sec. XXXII by B.W.* 2 vols. London: Queen's Printing Office, 1854. 1: 8,784 p.; 2: pp. 785–1554. These four items are very useful compendia for the study of inventions patented in Britain up until the middle of the nineteenth century, until the exhibition of 1851, when Britain was the most prolific and inventive nation.

Wyse, Lucien-Napoléon Bonaparte. *Le Canal de Panama. L'Isthme Américain. Explorations; Comparaison des traces étudiés, négotiations; état des travaux par . . . ouvrage contenant une grande carte de l'Isthme Colombien, un plan panoramique du Canal de Panama supposé achevé, un tableau synoptique des divers projets dressés spécialement par Lucien N. B. Wyse et 90 gravures sur bois.* Paris: Librairie Hachette et Cie., 1866. (6), 401 p., 3 pls., 90 ills.

Wyse, Lucien-Napoléon Bonaparte. *Félix Belly et le Percement de l'Isthme de Panama. Extrait de la Revue de Belgique.* Bruxelles: P. Weissenbruch, 1893. 23 p.

Zeitschrift für Bauwesen. Berlin, (1) May 1851–(81.3) March 1931.

Zeitschrift für Beton- und Eisenbau. Mitteilungen über Zement, Beton- und Eisenbetonbau sowie über die gesamte Ton-, Ziegelei- und Kunststeinindustrie. Bern: Wagner'sche Verlangsanstalt, 1 (1903)–11 (1913).

Zenker, Wilhelm. *Der Suez-Canal und seine commercielle Bedeutung, besonders für Deutschland.* Offprint from *Weser-Zeitung.* Bremen: Schünemann, 1869.

Zieman, Thomas. Unpublished manuscript analysis of the structure of the Crystal Palace, 1985, Cornell University, author's collection.

Index

Concepts and General Subject Matter

navvy. *See* labor: manual
night work. *See* organizational method

organizational method. *See also* construction; labor; prefabrication
  assembly versus construction, 42, 351
  bar graph, 291–*292*
  closed system, 38–45, 211–221, 258–261
  critical path (*see* technological thought)
  dialectic design method (*see* technological thought)
  electric illumination of sites (*see* organizational method: night work)
  military, 314–315
  modular design, 40, 228–230, 249–250 (*see also* construction)
  night work, 197–198, 334, 417 n.112, *418–419*
  open system, 40, 49, 209–210, 221, 226–258, 264–266, 350–351
  teamwork, 161–165
  telephone, 289–291
organizing versus composing. *See* architectural theory
ornament. *See* aesthetics

perpetuum mobile. *See* technological thought
photography, 392 n.46
piling. *See* foundation
pneumatic caisson. *See* foundation
pneumatic drill. *See* machinery: drill
pneumatics, 119
  communication and transportation, 409 n.168
  energy (*see* power)
  foundation (*see* foundation: caisson)
  ventilation, 127, 145–146, 149
post-tensioning, 108–110, 218–*219, 294*
power
  electric, 289, 323, 326, 334, 344
  hydraulic, 174
  pneumatic, 119, 126–127, 139–147, 150–*153,* 195–198, 334, 401–402 n.89, 402 n.95, 405–406 n.128, 406 nn.131,134, 407 n.155
  steam, 140, 406 nn.134,135
  vacuum, 405 n.126
  water, 136, 140–141, 150–153, 187

wire rope, belt, and chain transmission, 136–138, 228, 385 n.142, 405 nn.122,124
prefabrication, 40, 49, 64, 90, 224, 239–247, 255, 258, 266, 380–381 n.103, *383,* 422 n.18, 423 n.28, 428 nn.87,88, 429 n.92. *See also* assembly; manufacturing process; organizational method; wood
printing press. *See* machinery
process, xii–xiii
  concept, 31–33
  empirical, 102–104
  linear, 250–253
  partly mechanized, 194–195
  planned, 105, 201, 285–295, 323–328
  quantitative versus qualitative improvement, 25–26, 45, 47–49, 90–97, 373 n.35
  repetitive, 201
progress. *See* technological thought
Pullman railway car. *See* mobile structures

railway timetable. *See* technological thought
rationalization. *See* labor
record size, 262–266
redundancy. *See* engineering theory
reinforcement. *See* concrete
ridge and furrow. *See* construction
riveting machine. *See* machinery
roads, 7–8, 133, 360 n.13
  Brenner Pass Road (1772), 7, 133
  Cumberland Road (National Pike, 1811–1838, Maryland-Illinois), 8
  Gotthard Pass Road (1832), 133, 404 n.111
  Great Northern Road (London-Edinburgh), 8, 360 n.13
  Holyhead Road (London-Liverpool-Anglesea), 360 n.13
  Markham-Newark Road (1768), 360 n.13
  Mont Cenis Pass Road (1803–1810), 7, 133, 404 n.109
  Philadelphia-Lancaster Turnpike (1794), 8
  Simplon Pass Road (1806–1812), 7, 133
  Travers-Pontarlier Road (1854), 8
rubber and gutta percha, 127, 402 n.98

safety. *See* health, deadline pressure, and safety

scaffolding and formwork, *247,* 250–*251,* 264, 269, 272, 276–*277,* 289–295, 323

scale. *See* technological thought: scale issues

scientific method, xi–xii, 61–63, 162, 166, 348, 378 n.79, 391 n.42
goals, xi
thought mode, xi–xii, 60, 347–348

shipbuilding, 19–20, 252–254

shipping. *See* transportation

shipwreck, 171, *176,* 390 n.30

slipform method. *See* construction

soil stabilization. *See* foundation

stability. *See* engineering theory

steam. *See* power

stiffening systems. *See* engineering theory

structure. *See also* arch; beam; construction; foundation; truss
monolithic, 61–75, 286–289, 349–350, 386 nn.156,157, 445 n.3

system. *See* organizational method

teamwork. *See* organizational method

technological thought, xi–xii, 14–19, 26–33, 81–83
aesthetics of process (*see* aesthetics)
border-crossing, 105–106, 282, 347–348
building and machine, 217–218, 228, 275–278, 357–*355*
building method and war, 351–354
building process and life, 351, 354–356
composition and organization, 281, 354–356
critical path, 161, 178, 347, 350, 392 n.48
cultural influences, 47, 311, 349 n.94
dialectic between analysis and synthesis in design, 218–220, 348
empirical and pragmatic, xi, 61–63, 138–139, 163, 311
hybrid of empirical and scientific thinking, xi, 37, 60–61, 347
language, xii, 164
loading and scale, 225–226
logic, 225–226
mathematics and physics, 225

matrix thinking (associative, lateral), xi, 40, 106, 347–348, 359 n.1, 445 n.1
military thinking, 314–315, 345, 351, 445 n.8
opposition, 81–83
perpetuum mobile, xii, 138
procedural thinking, 161, 347
progress, concept of, 26–33
quantity versus quality, 25–26, 45, 47–49, 90–97, 373 n.35
scale issues, 38, 70–71, 348–349
separation and reconstitution of problems, 177–178, 218–220, 266, 350
soft technology, xi
space, time, and awareness, 14–19, 363–364 n.48, 364 n.53
system, concept of, xi–xii, 40–42, 225–226, 264–266, 349–350
three-dimensional thinking, 249–253
time-and-motion studies, 93–*97,* 272
timetables, 168, 291–292, 364 n.49
transformation, 106, 217, 347
translation, 37–38, 106, 347–348, 397 n.51

telegraphy, 11–15, 16–17, 20, 362 nn.33,35,40, 363 n.44
Belgian lines, 13, 362 n.40
Chappe semaphore system, *11*
Cooke-Wheatstone telegraph (1836 ff), 11–13
Indian Ocean cable, 20
Mediterranean Sea cable, 20
optical telegraph, *11*
Pacific Ocean cable, 362 n.33
Prussian semaphore, 362 n.35
Sömmering telegraph (1809), 11–*12*
Transatlantic cable (1858–1867), 14, 16–*17,* 20, 257
underground lines, 363 n.44

telephone. *See* organizational method

terrace house. *See* housing

testing. *See* experimentation and testing

time, relativity of. *See* technological thought: space, time, and awareness

time-and-motion studies. *See* technological thought

time zones, 15–19

trade union. *See* labor

transportation, 5–10, 20–21, 23–26, 323, 336–341

Bridges

Canals and Hydraulic Structures

Railways and Related Structures